LANDLORDING

Dedication

This book is dedicated to the scrupulous landlady in my life. Ivy, that's you.

Acknowledgements

I would like to acknowledge the following good people for their help in one way or another: Robert Armentrout, Denise Berger, Bob Bochemuehl, Maynard Briggs, Bob Bruss, Nelly Bunn, Norma D'Andrea, Wallace Darling, James Doherty, Bud Ekstrom, Ron English, Dan Faller, Fred Felder, Robert France, Herb Frank, Ruth Furey, Dave Glubetich, Al Good, Vernon Graves, David Halbrook, Scotty Herd, Larry Hughes, Tom Javorina, Robert Jones, John Koczan, Carl Lindh, Marion Mahnken, Charles Manning, Robin Maydeck, Oliver McClory, Margaret Miglia, Rita Moore, Connie Nakano, David Patton, Carol Pladsen, Richard Randolph, Jack Reed, Daniel Robinson, Dario Robinson, Nancy Robinson, Corinne Schultz, Ira Serkes, Jo Stender, Suzanne Stevenson, Jeffrey Taylor, Joel Vuylsteke, Paul Warren, Suzanne Wehausen, David Williams, Nancy Williams, Jay Wilson, Jim Woollen, and the hundreds of landlords and landladies who've endured my landlording classes with many suggestions and few complaints.

Without their help, this book wouldn't be in the shape it's in.

The Usual Caveat

This publication is designed to provide accurate and authoritative information in regard to the subject matter covered. It is sold with the understanding that the publisher is not engaged in rendering legal or accounting service. If legal advice or other expert assistance is required, the services of a competent professional person should be sought.

— From a declaration of principles jointly adopted by a committee of the American Bar Association and a committee of publishers and associations.

LANDLORDING

A Handymanual for Scrupulous Landlords and Landladies Who Do It Themselves

written by
LEIGH ROBINSON

illustrated by
DAVID PATTON, NANCY ROBINSON, and JAN BROWN

published by

P.O. BOX 1639
EL CERRITO, CA 94530-4639
landlording.com

FIRST EDITION   September, 1975
SECOND EDITION   May, 1976
         Revised   February, 1977
         Revised   March, 1978
         Reprinted September, 1978
         Reprinted November, 1978
         Revised   June, 1979
THIRD EDITION   March, 1980
         Revised   October, 1980
         Revised   October, 1981
         Revised   February, 1983
         Reprinted January, 1984
         Reprinted August, 1984
         Reprinted January, 1985
         Reprinted May, 1985
FOURTH EDITION   January, 1986
         Revised   July, 1986
         Revised   April, 1987
         Revised   February, 1988
FIFTH EDITION   October, 1988
         Revised   April, 1989
         Revised   February, 1990
         Revised   February, 1991
SIXTH EDITION   February, 1992
         Revised   November, 1992
         Revised   October, 1993
SEVENTH EDITION   July, 1994
         Revised   February, 1995
         Revised   February, 1996
EIGHTH EDITION   December, 1997
         Revised   January, 1999
         Reprinted September, 2000
NINTH EDITION   September, 2001

COPYRIGHT ©1975, 1976, 1977, 1978, 1979, 1980, 1981, 1983, 1986, 1987, 1988, 1989, 1990, 1991, 1992, 1993, 1994, 1995, 1996, 1997, 1999, 2001 by Leigh Robinson

LIBRARY OF CONGRESS CONTROL NUMBER: 2001095607

INTERNATIONAL STANDARD BOOK NUMBER: 0-932956-25-4

COVER DESIGN by David Patton

COMPOSED ON A MACINTOSH® USING ADOBE PAGEMAKER®

PRINTED IN THE U.S.A.

The LANDLORDING SERIES™, of which this is BOOK ONE, and the LAND-LORDING CHARACTER™, who appears on the front cover and elsewhere in this book, are trademarks of ExPress and Leigh Robinson.

Prefaces

Preface to the First Edition (1975)

After I bought my first rental property, I soon learned how little practical information there was to help landlords and landladies through the many tribulations they face day after day after day. So, I took "Landlording" at Hard Knocks College. The tuition was dear, but I learned what I needed to survive.

This book was written to be the text for the course at good old HKC. If you study it carefully, you should be able to make a good grade.

As a landlord who does in fact teach school and who also does all of the bookkeeping chores, some of the maintenance, some of the repairs, and some of the managing of thirty-five rental units, I have indeed spent many years at HKC, but I have had little uninterrupted time to write. These pages bear the marks of many interruptions to fix cold heaters, broken windows, leaky faucets, leaky roofs, dead electrical outlets, wet-bottom water heaters, and so on and so on. Sympathize, if you will, dear landlord or landlady. No one else will.

Preface to the Third Edition (1980)

Since *Landlording* first appeared in 1975, I have learned much more about the residential income property management business from my tenants, my students at dozens of University of California Extension seminars, and from readers of the first two editions who have kindly taken the time to write.

This new edition incorporates those suggestions made so generously, as well as some new ideas which have occurred to me spontaneously over the past four years. In addition, that information in the earlier editions which was specific to California has been deleted, so that barring certain local laws and regulations, this edition may be used anywhere in the U.S.

The old evictions chapter has been replaced by a new one on getting rid of problem tenants, both because the old one contained information useful only in California and because there are other good ways to "evict" people which you should know about and which you should try as your first resort, good ways landlords and landladies can use anywhere. That old evictions chapter, by the way, is still available, but in a new guise. It has been expanded and now appears separately under the title, *The Eviction Book for California*.

There are other changes in this edition which are equally important. Some, such as the discussion of whether or not you should do a task yourself, have resulted from an increase in the size of my own landlording business. Those 35 rental units my wife and I used to have in 1975 have become 244. With that many tenants to look after, there's no way we can handle everything ourselves. We have had, therefore, to learn more about hiring people to work for us—managers, painters, bookkeepers, gardeners, maintenance helpers, and others. In the process, we learned, surprisingly enough, that some work in this business, no matter how few or how many units you may have, is not worth doing yourself. In fact, doing it yourself may be costing you money rather than making or saving you money.

Other changes in this edition, such as the much expanded chapter on getting good tenants and the new chapter on keeping good tenants, have resulted from a continuing search for methods which work successfully for many people under varying conditions.

One change suggested by a female reader, re-titling the book *Landladying*, I have politely rejected. Someone else will have to write that book.

Incidentally, you will notice that various product brand names and suppliers' addresses appear in this book, and you may wonder whether these companies pay for the plugs. The answer is no. Having had first-hand experience with each of these products and companies and having been thoroughly satisfied, I am pleased to recommend them to you along with their names and addresses so you won't have to waste the time hunting for them that I did. If you choose to use any product or company mentioned here and you are dissatisfied for any reason, please write me in care of ExPress stating the nature of your complaint, and I will investigate. Likewise, if you know of any outstanding company or product related to this business which would be of use to other landlords and landladies throughout the U.S., please let me know, and I will consider including it in a later edition.

I hope you find this new edition of *Landlording* useful.

Preface to the Fourth Edition (1986)

A little more than five years ago I last revised and updated *Landlording* from cover to cover. Since then, I've acquired more properties, dealt with more tenants, encountered more problems, made more mistakes, met more people in the business, listened to more battle stories, given more seminars, attended more seminars, heard from more readers, and read more books and articles on the subject. As a result, I have learned still more about how to survive and succeed at landlording.

Much has happened during that time in the world at large to change how we ought to go about this business, too. New laws and new interpretations of old laws have compelled us to make certain changes. Microcomputers have entered our lives in force and abundance. And a wealth of new ideas and materials have appeared on the scene.

With so much having happened all 'round since the third edition appeared, I have felt obliged to produce a completely new edition of *Landlording*.

In this "new and improved" fourth edition, I have retained the best of the rest of the earlier three editions, generally in an expanded form. I have split two old chapters into four, added six new chapters, and dropped two old ones.

Dropped were the two chapters with maintenance and tool information, including information on subjects such as repairing sheetrock holes, locksmithing, using a ceiling access plate, and exterminating abominable pests. One of these days, all of that and much more will appear in a new book.

Added were six chapters on subjects which I hope you'll find of interest: managing the rental house, coping with legal matters, participating in the Section 8 subsidized housing program, fattening the bottom line, counting your assets, and using a computer.

Split were the two old chapters, "Taking Over & Keeping Good Tenants" and "Insurance & Security." Each of these subjects cried out for separate treatment and more space, so I gave it to them.

Although I have been experimenting with singing eviction notices, I haven't quite succeeded in perfecting them yet. I am still trying, but I've been having some problems setting them to the right music, finding the right key, getting them to stand up in court, hogtying tenants so they'll hear the entire message out, and subduing bystanders' laughter. If you think of any ways to solve these persistent problems, please let me know.

Singing eviction notices may not appear here, but a dozen new graphic rent reminders do. I have no conclusive, scientific proof that they work 76.893% of the time. All I can say for sure is that they work pretty well most of the time and that they aren't carcinogenic. I'm as unbiased as a pathologist working on cancer research for a tobacco company when I make that statement, of course. Give them a try sometime and see whether you agree that they can be effective.

Besides the graphic rent reminders, there are lots of other new illustrations here. I hope you enjoy them and this new edition and that you go about landlording with a broad smile on your face. It's the only way!

Preface to the Fifth Edition (1988)

This edition marks a milestone in the happy life of *Landlording*. Born in 1975, it's a teenager now, and I am pleased to report that it has reached this important stage in its life without bursting out in pimples or tripping over its own gawky prose.

Still, I have wanted to make some changes before sending it out into the world again, and this fifth edition has afforded me the perfect opportunity to dress it up, add a chapter, redesign all of the old forms, create several new ones, and fiddle more with the text. I think that it's a better book than it was, and I hope that you will agree.

Preface to the Sixth Edition (1992)

We're in the nineties now, and we cannot manage rental property as if we were landlords in the seventies, or even the eighties.

The business of landlording keeps changing, and so must this book change if it is to be of any use to the troops in the trenches. Some of these changes in our business have resulted from legislation and lawsuits. Some of them have resulted from the availability of new products and technology. Some are for the better. Some are for the worse.

We cannot ignore what's happening around us because we are, after all, businesspeople. We are subject to more scrutiny than ordinary citizens, and we are subject to more laws. Ignore what's happening, and sooner or later we will come to grief.

This sixth edition of *Landlording* is no more of a lawbook than previous editions. It does not purport to take into consideration every landlord-tenant law enacted around the country. Nor is it particularly exhaustive. It remains the words of one person who tries to keep abreast of what's happening in the business, who tries to gather together the ideas and suggestions of many knowledgeable people, and who tries to make some sense of it all.

This is a bigger book than ever. It has more forms, more drawings, and more good ideas. I hope that it will help you become a more successful landlord, a landlord of the nineties.

Preface to the Seventh Edition (1994)

While reviewing the sixth edition of this book prior to reprinting it, I decided that too much had happened in the world of landlording over the past two years for me not to do a new edition. Just think, two years ago Sears was still the king of the catalog merchandisers, and I was still saying in SOURCES & RESOURCES that you had to be a time traveler or a refugee from the second or third world if you hadn't heard of the Sears Catalog. As you know, the unthinkable happened. Sears stopped publishing the big catalog.

Of course, that change alone wouldn't have been sufficient justification for a new edition. It's merely an illustration of the changes going on in our world, changes which seem to be accelerating year after year.

Today, because of all these changes, being a scrupulous landlord requires more than an attitude of fairness. It requires information, hard work, and vigilance. This new edition should give you some of the information you need to be a scrupulous landlord at the end of the 20th century. You will have to work hard and be vigilant on your own.

Long may you prosper!

Preface to the Eighth Edition (1997)

What has happened over the past three years to warrant another edition of *Landlording*? Plenty!

When the last edition of *Landlording* came out three years ago, few people had heard of the Internet, and fewer still were using it. Nowadays "everybody" has heard of it, and many are using it. You might be able to use the Internet yourself in landlording. You'll find some practical suggestions for doing so in this new edition.

You'll also find some new topics scattered here and there throughout the book's twenty-one chapters. One I'd like to draw your attention to is "itemizing rents." I've become a believer in itemizing rents because it has helped me pass along certain of my increased expenses much sooner than I otherwise could have. Maybe you will become a believer, too, after reading something about this timely and important topic.

As always, *Landlording* contains lots of forms designed to lessen the burden of being a landlord. Among them are four new ones, one of which can save you much time and grief because it serves to weed out unqualified applicants before they ever submit their applications to you. It's called "Rental Application Instructions." It intimidates applicants who have something to hide. It informs applicants who have nothing to hide. Take a good look at it and try it the next time you have a vacancy.

Besides having more information and more forms, this new edition has a whole new look. It's the book's first real design overhaul in years, and it's supposed to make everything more readable. I hope that you find this new edition of *Landlording* both readable and useful.

Preface to the Ninth Edition (2001)

This ninth edition of *Landlording*, the first of the new century, is the first to use a two-column format. It's more readable than the single-column format used in earlier editions, even more readable than the narrowed single-column format used in the eighth edition.

Readers familiar with the eighth edition may have noticed that this edition has fewer pages. These fewer pages resulted from having less white space on a page and slightly smaller type, not from having fewer illustrations, fewer forms, or less text. There are no fewer nor any more illustrations in this edition, but there are more forms and more text than in any previous edition. I want you to get your money's worth.

Table of Contents

Introduction

Of all the people in the world, who's more detested than the landlord? After all, he puffs big cigars, sneers, wears a black cape, drives an ostentatious Cadillac car, dallies with divorcees, runs down little kids, raises rents whenever he pleases, drives unfortunates from their homes, ignores all tenant complaints, keeps at least one family of roaches in every unit, loves the fresh air which broken windows provide, and welcomes rodents of all kinds to make their home in his rentals.

And if that landlord happens to be a landlady—well, then, everybody knows what she's like! She's got a nose longer than Pinocchio's, larger than Durante's, and she puts it into every tenant's business. Her ears rival Dumbo's, and they are ever on the alert to pick up the latest gossip. She's got Big Brother's omniscience, and she blabs every bit of it. She's devised ways to pinch her pennies that Jack Benny never dreamed of, and while there may not be snakes growing in her hair, big pink rollers sure do.

You're a landlord or landlady, aren't you? Don't these descriptions sound just like you? They don't?

Aha! Then you must be a scrupulous landlord or landlady. Wonderful! Thank heavens we found each other! You're pretty difficult to recognize, you know. You're not at all like the characters described above, those weird legendary creatures. You look and act reasonably normal. Well, that's just great because this book was written with you in mind!

Being quite normal yourself, you have probably wondered how the landlords of this world ever got such terrible reputations in the first place and why they get so little sympathy from most people today, no matter what the situation, no matter who's at fault.

They got such bad reputations deservedly years ago because they were largely unfettered by laws (what laws there were, were of their own making) and could easily take advantage of their tenants, and so some did, arbitrarily controlling their tenants' lives like petty dictators. They were feared for the power they wielded and naturally they were hated, becoming folklore villains who were always portrayed as being insensitive, cruel, thoughtless, heartless, and greedy to an extreme.

Although they have been stripped of most of their power, landlords are hardly liked even today because they provide an essential service (who likes the telephone company or the utility companies?), and they continue in ill repute (tarts are in ill repute, too, of course, but at least they're frequently portrayed as having hearts of gold) because they make such good news stories when they try creative remedies to extricate themselves from seemingly impossible situations.

What kind of a story do you think the news media made out of the landlord who chopped down the outside stairway to his deadbeat tenant's second-story duplex apartment or the landlady who poisoned her tenant's mongrel pooch which she and the tenant had been feuding over for months? Nobody cared that this landlord and landlady were really good people at heart who had been driven temporarily crazy when they committed these foolish acts. They committed the acts and thus they unwittingly succeeded in perpetuating the old folklore-villain stereotypes.

Don't be suckered into believing these old stereotypes. They're wrong, terribly wrong. Most landlords today are just like you, decent human beings who happen to own some rental property which they'd rather rent out than leave vacant. It is true that they're more skeptical, more practical, more resourceful, more imaginative, more circumspect, and more intelligent than the average Tom, Dick, and Harriet, but it's not true that they're any greedier, uglier, smellier, or stingier.

What happens when Dick and Harriet sell their house for whatever the market will bear and get twice what they paid for it? Are they considered greedy? Are they called price gougers? Heck no! They're considered smart.

All right, then, what happens when Lester Landlord rents out his apartment for whatever the market will bear? He's not called smart. He's called greedy. He's an "A-Number- One Rent Gouger," a scourge of society! Try sorting that one out! The "greed" charge is a bum rap, and don't you forget it!

You cannot charge more for anything than someone is willing to pay for it. That's how "the market" works. And it applies to rents just the same as it applies to anything else which is bought and sold, from rice to garlic, from flashlights to computers, from gasoline to automobiles, from stocks to bonds.

If you don't believe me, go ahead and try some industrial-strength rent gouging. Raise your rents 100% and see what happens. At first you'll be vilified, that's for sure. Then your tenants will look around for somewhere else better and cheaper to live. If they find it, they'll move and you'll be left with vacancies. Then you'll have to adjust your rents to market levels or despair of ever getting anybody else to rent from you. If they can't find a cheaper place, they'll grumble and stay.

Market forces determine what your rents are. You don't. You can be way under the market, but you can't be way over. You can be a rent slouch, but you can't be a rent gouger, that is, not unless you want to have lots of vacancies.

I have met many a rent slouch in my day. They're the landlords who never have any vacancies. They have "waiting lists," and they brag about how long their waiting lists are. Now, think for a moment about why they have those waiting lists of people who can't wait to move in.

Rent slouches have waiting lists because their rent is too low. Tenants-in-waiting know that the rent is a deal. That's why they're on the list. They could tell the rent slouch a thing or two, but why should they? They want to take advantage of the deal themselves.

As for rent gougers, I have to admit that I have yet to encounter one. I keep looking, though, and I know exactly what I'm looking for, but there must not be many of 'em around. I have to assume that they exist because I read about them in the newspaper now and then. I read about one who surfaced after the big fire in the Oakland hills. He had wanted something like $1,600 per month for his rental before the fire and then he raised the rent to $2,500 after the fire. The columnist who wrote about this rent gouger wanted all the world to know that such terrible landlords exist. Tsk, tsk, tsk! What the columnist failed to mention was that this landlord still had a vacancy three months after the fire. He may have tried to be a rent gouger, but he wasn't being very successful at it. The market taught him a lesson. He couldn't charge more in rent than the market would bear. He still wound up with a vacancy, a vacancy which lasted and lasted, even during a tight rental market, because his rent was too high. Rent gougers, wherever they are, are not successful landlords. They don't understand the nature of the business they're in. They think they can do whatever they please. They can't. Bigger forces hold sway.

Okay, you know the landlording stereotypes. Who doesn't? What should you do about them?

Don't overreact to them. That's what. Don't say to yourself that you're going to be different from your money-grubbing counterparts, that you're going to win your tenants' hearts by becoming friends with them and giving them cheap rent. You won't succeed, I can assure you. They won't think you're kind. They'll think you're daft. They'll think you have an I.Q. equal to the outside temperature on a cool day. What's more, you'll be costing yourself more money than you think.

Don't go out and buy yourself a hairshirt because you want to atone for the sins of being a landlord. There aren't any.

Don't be ashamed to admit that you're a landlord when people ask you the second question they have on their minds upon meeting you socially. Be proud of yourself for doing something so smart and for doing it so well.

Don't be apologetic about this role you're playing in our society. It's not merely important, it's absolutely essential. Be pleased with yourself that you're providing an essential service. You have people depending on you for a roof over their heads. You're giving them that roof. You're keeping them warm and dry. You may be the butt of jokes and you may get worse press than serial murderers, but so what? Regardless of what some people may say or think, nobody provides rental housing better than does the private-enterprising landlord like yourself. Nobody but nobody out there does it better.

Ask yourself what the state of housing in general would be like in this country if you and others like you weren't around to provide rental housing. There'd be a whole lot more people living with outdoor plumbing than there are now; that's for sure. People would be living in tents, lean-to's, mud huts, caves, cars, and cardboard shanty towns on a permanent basis. Anybody lucky enough to obtain conventional housing would jam two, three, and four generations into it. Each room would become a multiple-family dwelling in itself. Families would be sleeping in shifts. People would be waiting years to get even remotely habitable accommodations.

Take a look at those *National Geographic* photographs showing what life is like in the Third World. Well, that's how people would be living in this country except for you.

Americans wouldn't be happy living that way, you say? Perhaps you're right. Perhaps they would be out there clamoring to that solver of all society's problems, government, to do something about the country's wretched housing conditions. Perhaps government would try to provide residential rental housing for one and all. So how do you think the government would fare as the country's landlord?

Well, we happen to have some way of knowing because the President's Private Sector Survey on Cost Control, otherwise known as the Grace Commission, reported some time ago that the federal government as landlord employs seventeen times the people and spends almost fourteen times as much money on total management costs as a private company. Can you imagine spending that much more on management costs than you already do? I can't either. The government can do it. The government can find all kinds of ways to be inefficient. It wrote the book on inefficiency.

What kind of shape would rental housing be in if the federal government were the sole provider? That's some question to consider! First of all, you know that there wouldn't be enough housing to go around. Young couples would have to live with their parents for a few years until a vacancy became available somewhere, maybe a hundred miles from where they worked. Yet, with all this demand, when somebody moved or died, the unit would remain vacant for six months until it could be made ready for new occupants, any of the hundreds of people on the waiting list. Of course, nobody would be allowed to have two rental dwellings in two different cities where they do business, nobody except high government officials, that is. Nobody would be allowed to live alone either.

The federal government would probably have a full-time manager for every fourplex, and those managers would probably be so busy doing their paperwork that they wouldn't have time to fix a faucet themselves. No, I forgot. That wouldn't be the main reason. It would be their 616-page job description which would keep them from repairing a faucet. Management people don't do "maintenance" work, not even minor repairs. So they'd call an $80-an-hour approved plumber who'd either replace the leaky faucet with an approved $350 model or fix the old one with $55 worth of approved parts. Where would the money come from to pay for seventeen times the people and fourteen times the management? Oh, from the usual sources, a billion from here and a billion from there. Borrow more, tax more, print more. That's how it's done. And that's how it would be done without you.

Do you know how much the federal government spent on its White House "rental" complex during the eight years of the Reagan administration? $44,600,000! $9,472,100 of that went just to renovate the presidential guest house. The work was undertaken after a gas leak developed at the house and a chandelier fell to the floor in the bedroom reserved for heads of state. Sounds as if the place had a little deferred maintenance, wouldn't you say?

How about state governments? What kind of a job are they doing? The State of California did a great job looking after the governor's mansion. They kept it in perfect shape. The only trouble was that in a decade it never had a tenant. What was the problem? After the place was built, the governor then in office didn't want to live there. So what happened to it? Did they rent it out to somebody else? Are you kidding? It was vacant for more than ten years before it was put up for sale. They didn't have to worry about loan payments and property taxes, so why should they worry about generating rental income? What a luxury that would be! Owning rental property and not having to rent it out, not having to deal with tenants! Boy, oh boy! But that's not really landlording, is it? That's not providing anyone with housing.

How about local governments? How do they fare? Well, the City of San Francisco with its 7,000 units is by far the biggest residential landlord in San Francisco. Are the city-owned rental dwellings kept up? Are the tenants happy? Are the costs kept under control? No, no, and no! Resounding noes!

A federal audit revealed that the San Francisco Housing Authority was failing to collect $42,504 in damage charges and $239,000 in rent every year. Its total *monthly* deficit was around $180,000, and "nobody" on the scene seemed to be aware of it. Can you imagine that? Losing $180,000 every month and nobody knowing a thing about it? I can imagine how that much negative cash flow might be possible for a time in some privately operated housing projects with 10% loans to service and high vacancy factors during fill-up periods, but these places had no loans to service and no vacancy factors to worry about.

This deficit was no temporary matter either because the housing authority owed millions of dollars in overdue utility bills to the Pacific Gas & Electric Company alone. How many private landlords could get away with that? The housing authority was receiving almost half of its $24 million annual operating budget from the U.S. Department of Housing and Urban Development (HUD), and yet it was still $5 million in the hole!

What's more astonishing, though, is that the city's public housing projects weren't even being properly maintained. According to HUD's regional administrator, the San Francisco Housing Authority was "failing to adequately maintain its housing units in a decent, safe and sanitary condition." The enormous monthly deficits were resulting in housing which was actually going downhill!

Finally, the housing authority hired a new director to straighten up the mess. The last thing I heard he was being praised for reducing the turnover time from 125 days to 21! That's a considerable improvement, to be sure, but can you imagine taking an average of three weeks to redecorate every time you have a vacancy? Me neither.

Remember that famous photograph showing a huge St. Louis public housing building being blown to smithereens when it was structurally sound and still had lots of good years left in it? Something similar occurred in my own home town, except that the building there was only twenty-four units and it was only five years old. Private-enterprising landlords had nothing to do with these projects. Perhaps they should have.

Oh, and here's one for the books. When residents who were living in Oakland's public housing projects began raising their voices in unison to complain about the poor maintenance there, the housing administrators hired a *consultant*. Consultants don't do maintenance, do they? Have you ever hired a consultant to take care of your maintenance problems? No, neither have I. We take care of our rental properties' maintenance problems ourselves, or we hire maintenance people to take care of them for us. Who needs a consultant for this kind of work? Apparently, public housing administrators do.

So much for the government as landlord. Are we mom-and-pop operations any better at landlording than these faceless, feckless, wasteful government operations? How can we not be? We are so much closer to the problems. We act quickly. We show understanding. We keep our costs in check. We provide our customers with what they want in a place to live for a price they're willing to pay. We are truly free enterprise at work.

Not only are we free enterprise at work, we are, for the most part, true mom-and-pop businesses. Landlording is not the oil business. The sky doesn't darken with Lear jets around the country when politicians discuss rental housing legislation in Washington or Tallahassee, Sacramento or Austin, Albany or Springfield. No, all in all, we're strictly coach-class in our political activities.

People go about lamenting the passing of the corner grocery store and the family farm, but they don't seem to realize that the landlords in this country are in the same category. We're small-time operators, too, and we're being driven out of business as well. What's driving us out of business, however, is not big-time operators coming in and taking over. It's excessive legislation spawned by do-gooders who still believe in those old stereotypes. They still believe that tenants are noble, that landlords are greedy. They still believe that government could do a better job of housing people. They still believe in the fairy godmother, Robin Hood, deficit spending, and the resolution of any kind of problem in time for the 11 o'clock news, too. They don't understand that tinkering with the rental housing business makes it less competitive and that less competition creates poorer housing at a higher price to society.

What they do understand is a sobbing welfare mother and her half dozen waifs being evicted in front of a TV camera on Christmas Eve. That news item and others like it provide them with further verification of our terrible reputation.

That's what we landlords are supposed to be doing on Christmas Eve, isn't it? Sure, we've got a past. Sure, we've got a reputation. The fact that few of us live up to that reputation doesn't matter much, though.

Part of the problem is that most people know full well what it's like to be a tenant, but they have never experienced the problems and frustrations of being a landlord. Never have they been cursed or threatened or cheated or robbed by an unscrupulous tenant. They cannot know the mental anguish and anxiety of waiting out an eviction week after week while some devil-may-care tenant who's being evicted for nonpayment of rent uses free legal aid to contest the eviction, hammers holes in the walls, puts out cigarettes on the carpets, burns the linoleum, plays music late and loud, and hurls insults at all the neighbors. Most people cannot possibly know what it's like to deal with that unscrupulous tenant and to feel so helpless, so wronged.

Another part of the problem is that people love to have someone to hate. We're one of those "someones." We're it.

Don't get too upset about being hated. Don't bother starting a local chapter of the Landlord Anti-Defamation League (LADL). Just expect to be hissed and booed now and then, and retaliate by thinking bad thoughts about the unscrupulous people who make the landlording business tougher than it ought to be.

If only the unscrupulous tenants would get together with the unscrupulous landlords of the world to do business with each other, rent to each other and rent from each other! That would solve most of the problems the rest of us poor folk have in this business. Unfortunately, since that's about as likely to happen as our ever again being able to buy gasoline for thirty cents a gallon, gold for thirty-five dollars an ounce, or rooms for six bucks at Motel 6, we have little choice but to seek help.

To help the scrupulous tenant deal with unscrupulous landlords, there are pamphlets, books, hot lines, tenant action groups, government-provided legal aid, and publicly funded housing organizations. The scrupulous tenant is hardly alone. Helping hands abound.

We scrupulous landlords, on the other hand, seem to be so totally alone as we deal with an unscrupulous tenant. Nothing is free to us. We are expected to have unlimited funds available for legal counsel, management, repairs, and services. We shouldn't need any other help.

Well, we do. You know it and I know it. This book is intended for scrupulous landlords who want to do well by themselves and by their tenants but need some help to do so. I hope it provides you with the help you're looking for.

1
Do-It-Yourself Landlording

When Sad Sack Landlord decided to sell his fourplex and learned what it was worth, he was not pleased. "$152,000? Holy buckets!" he exclaimed. "That's almost eight thousand dollars less than what I paid for the place seven years ago!"

"It may be, but you've had some mighty rough tenants in here. You've got vacancy problems that won't quit. And there's so much deferred maintenance now that you just can't get any more for it."

Sound familiar? I hope not. "Deferred maintenance" is a euphemism for gross neglect in real estate jargon. Those dilatory property owners who ignore their tenants, neglect maintenance, and do slipshod repairs on their property suffer more losses than they realize. They can't get good tenants, they can't get good rents, and they can't get a good price when they sell. Their buildings are depreciating not only on paper at tax time, they're depreciating in terms of real money every month.

Anyone who neglects a business, any business, deserves to lose money at it, and people do lose money at landlording, for it's nothing if it's not a business, a business involving some very serious money.

Ah, but you don't have to lose money in this business so long as you take some time to learn the ropes. Here's a look at some of those ropes, together with something of an overview of this very funny business.

Understanding the Business

Landlording is a funny business, to be sure. It requires one to know at least the rudiments of the skills of an accountant, appliance repairer, arbitrator, architect, attorney, banker, bill collector, bookkeeper, buyer, carpenter, carpet layer, color consultant, contractor, counselor, custodian, diplomat, drapery hanger, electrician, financial analyst, garbage collector, gardener, glazier, insurance agent, interior decorator, landscape architect, lobbyist, locksmith, painter, pest controller, plumber, psychologist, real estate agent, roofer, salesperson, secretary, sleuth, social worker, trucker, vinyl tile layer, and wallpaper hanger.

In addition, the landlord must have some business savvy, some common sense, and equanimity by the semitrailerload. A sense of humor, though not absolutely required, sure helps.

Breathes there a person with all these skills and all these attributes?

Hardly! The only people I know of who have every bit as much equanimity as this landlording business requires have body temperatures considerably below 98.6° Fahrenheit (37° C.), and equanimity is their only attribute. They have none of the other attributes nor any of the skills. The only people I know of who have all the skills and common sense this business requires are purely fictional. Even if they did exist, these James Bonds and Wonder Women, they wouldn't have any time for a pursuit so mundane as landlording. They'd be out of town a lot, spending most of their time saving the world from villainy.

Where does this leave us real-world landlords who are very much alive and bent on providing decent housing to decent people at decent prices in anticipation of making a decent profit? It leaves us with lots to learn and lots to do.

No wonder so many people neglect their rental properties and fail at landlording! They're overwhelmed by what's required of them in terms of skills, attributes, and time. Make no mistake. Landlording is not simply an investment opportunity as it is often regarded by the uninitiated, one you sink your money into and forget all about. It's a business, a tough business. You have to work at it. You have to know so much. You have to be so self-sufficient, and you have to understand people so well, too.

You even have to understand that you are an imperfect landlord dealing with imperfect tenants and that you will make mistakes, mistakes which hopefully will not sour you on the business forever. "We should be careful to get out of an experience only the wisdom that is in it and stop there lest we be like the cat that sits down on a hot stove lid. It will never sit down on a hot stove lid again, and that is well. But it will never sit down on a cold one either," wrote Mark Twain. You will sit on more than one hot seat in this business. Don't abandon the business altogether because of them.

We have to be like those old inflatable clown toys. Remember them. About four feet tall with sand in their shoes and air in their bodies, they always bounce back whenever somebody knocks 'em flat. One moment they're down, the next moment they're back for more punishment.

We have to bounce back when we're flattened, too, that is, when we fail to check out an applicant thoroughly or fail to mollify an irate tenant or fail to raise the rent on a "friend" or fail to repair a roof properly or fail to confront a tenant about a mysteriously appearing bulldog. All of us fail at landlording a little bit in one way or another. We can't help it, but we shouldn't let it worry us so long as we learn from our failures and keep them from overwhelming us. After we have failed, we just have to get up off the floor, dust ourselves off, remind ourselves for the thousandth time that landlording is a business which must be operated like any other business, and then we must doggedly continue, resolving not to make the same mistake again.

Do-it-yourself landlording is surely more mistake-prone than the ordinary homeowner variety of do-it-yourselfing, and it differs also because

you as the landlord must repair and maintain your property promptly and professionally. You have contracted with your tenants to provide them with habitable accommodations. That's what the business is all about. You cannot leave messy, unfinished, or neglected jobs if you wish to continue landlording successfully. That might work all right at home, but tenants won't stand for it, nor should they. After all, if they are paying full price for habitable shelter, they have every right to expect full service for their money.

On the other hand, being businesslike when you are handling the maintenance and repairs on your property yourself requires that you do the work as quickly and as well as you can and then leave. Tenants have a knack for finding just one more little job for you to do if you linger around, and you can waste precious time fixing the little things they should be fixing themselves. If you don't have any business there, stay away. Otherwise you tend to develop personal relationships which will hinder your making wise business decisions. Being there too much and getting too involved with your tenants is almost as bad for your business as neglecting the place entirely.

Being businesslike doesn't mean that you should be austere and avaricious either. Let your common sense guide you. Be flexible when a situation calls for flexibility.

If a tenant gives you a six-day notice that he's moving after having been there only two months, and he asks you whether he can get any of his deposits back in spite of his agreement to give you thirty days' notice, tell him "sure" so long as he leaves the place clean. Agree to give him back a generous portion of his deposits, even though you may be legally entitled to keep every dollar, and if he does leave the place clean, pay up. Otherwise, what incentive does he have to leave everything in good shape? He might take out his frustrations on your rental property's windows, doors, and walls over your angrily refusing to return any of his deposits. You know that you don't want a mess on your hands because you know how much messes cost to clean up. By returning more of his deposit than you have to, you will ensure that he doesn't leave you with a mess and you will be creating the good will that you need to succeed. He will want to rent from you again if the need arises, and he will tell others that they should rent from you, too, because you treated him fairly.

Yes, landlording is a funny business, but through many trials, many errors, much tribulation, and much work, you can make it into a good business, one which will be very good for you and to you.

Joining with Others in the Business

It's good business to ally yourself with other landlords through membership in a rental housing association. Such groups offer a wide range of services and benefits to the small-timer as well as to the big-timer.

Besides distributing a publication, holding periodic meetings, sponsoring seminars, supplying readily available and current landlording information over the phone, providing access to credit bureau information on rental applicants, and in some cases maintaining websites with listings of available rentals, these associations advise their members of pending legislation and support lobbying efforts so that not every new landlord-tenant law will favor the tenant.

If all this doesn't seem to you to be worth the basic membership fee of around $100 (the fee varies according to the number of units you have), then consider the advantage of meeting people who can keep you current on rents and vacancy factors in your area, people who will listen sympathetically to your woeful tales of landlording despair because the same thing happened to them only last week, people who can understand the lack of balance in media stories about landlords, and people who know what choice rental properties are coming on the market even before they're listed. A hundred dollars a year is a small price to pay for all that.

If you can't locate a rental housing association in your area, contact the National Apartment Association (naahq.org). They will provide you with the information you need to contact a nearby association if there is one. If there isn't one, why not think about starting one? The National Apartment Association can help.

Mr. Landlord (mrlandlord.com) and Rental Housing On Line (rhol.org) are other sources helpful in locating local rental housing associations (see SOURCES & RESOURCES).

Don't assume that because you own only one rental house or one fourplex you'd be out of place in such an association. You won't be. You'll find people just like you at their meetings.

Finding Discounts

As a landlord do-it-yourselfer, you use more supplies than the average homeowner do-it-yourselfer does, and suppliers know it.

Your local hardware store may give you charge-account privileges and a ten-percent discount to boot. Ask. Even if you can't qualify for a volume-buyer's discount yet, open a charge account anyway because it will simplify your bookkeeping chores to pay a bill only once a month and make only one bookkeeping entry for most of your hardware needs. Many hardware store owners will special-order for you those items which they don't stock regularly, items such as glass-fronted fire extinguisher boxes, apartment house mailboxes, and locksmithing supplies. (My local hardware store owner even found me a portable, hand-cranked Keil key-cutting machine which has proven to be a big timesaver, cutting my umbilical cord to the local locksmith; unfortunately, these handy little machines are no longer in production, so don't expect to find one readily.)

Other firms are anxious to do business with you, too, if you let them know who you are and what your requirements are. Sears has a commercial sales department which offers rental property owners special discounts on certain merchandise, like coin-operated laundry machines and other appliances. Home Depot, the nationwide chain of big box stores selling hardware and lumber, offers commercial accounts to landlords.

Check the advertisements in your rental housing association's publication for those firms which specifically solicit business from landlords. They should understand the nature of your business and give you the service and discounts you deserve as a volume buyer.

Don't forget the catalog companies which cater to commercial customers, companies such as Maintenance Warehouse and Grainger. They have catalogs, but they also have websites and, in some cases, even stores, although the stores may not be convenient for you to visit. You'll find some of these catalog companies listed in SOURCES & RESOURCES.

Cultivating Business Contacts

There are certain business people in your community who are in a position to help you run a successful landlording business, and you should strive to cultivate personal contacts with them whenever you can. You may have to shop around awhile before you find trustworthy people in these relevant business pursuits, people who suit you and who know their businesses well, but once you find good contacts and you come to know each of them personally, you will find that they will go out of their way to assist you with service, advice, equipment, and supplies. Remember that your relationship should be mutually beneficial. You are in a position to help your contacts by recommending their services to the other landlords you know, and you should.

At one level, you should seek out and nurture business contacts with an accountant, an attorney, a banker, an insurance agent, a loan broker, a real estate agent, and a social worker, each of whom has some special expertise directly related to your making or losing substantial sums of money in landlording. These people can help you with specific and knowledgeable answers to your many questions in their fields.

At another level, you should seek out an appliance repairer, a carpet layer, a hardware store owner, a painter, a plumber, and a roofer. While these contacts may save you money with their advice, they benefit you chiefly by coming to your aid with their labor, materials, and supplies when you need immediate solutions to your pressing problems.

How well should you know these people?

You should know them at least well enough so that you could reach them on the telephone and be greeted familiarly, and then you could pose a question involving their field of expertise, expecting them to give you a direct answer, perhaps free of charge, perhaps not.

Be good to these people. Take them out to lunch now and then and, of course, patronize them.

If you elect to expand your business at all, you will come to rely on these people more and more, and they will become a kind of advisory board for you, absolutely essential to your success.

In addition, and surely as important as any of the business people whose acquaintanceship you should be cultivating, is that contact you should make with another landlord who either owns as much rental property as you do or has owned rental property longer than you have and is willing to compare notes about matters of local concern to landlords.

You are in a position to help each other psychologically and physically more than you may ever imagine at first. Consider just the benefit you'd get out of knowing someone you could call upon to look after your properties when you're sick or out of town. The two of you could form your own "rental-property-sitting co-op" so you'd know your properties would be well looked after when you're unable to look after them yourself. That alone is reason enough to cultivate a relationship with another landlord, isn't it?

Handling the Bucks

It's good business to have a separate checking account for your landlording transactions. Some landlords even open a separate account for every building they own (if their rentals are single-family dwellings, they have one account for all) and then use that account as their only "bookkeeping system," channeling all of the building's income and expenses through the account, a simple but workable approach. Whatever you do, open at least one checking account specifically for your rental properties, and itemize your deposits and checks carefully so your bookkeeping chores will be easier later.

Before you visit the bank, though, select the name you want to use for your property account. This name has nothing to do with how you hold title to your property, how you write rental agreements, what name the property bears on the sign out front, who is authorized to write checks, or what street the building is on. It is only the name which your tenants will use as the payee for their checks and money orders.

Presumably to prevent someone else in the area

from using the same name you have selected, banks require that everyone opening an account under a business name, which does not include the owner's real name, must file a fictitious name statement, a process involving a filing fee and legal advertising.

Whereas your business name would be a valuable asset to you if you were operating the "Playtime Tavern" or the "Capri Motel," it's hardly important in the rental property business, except for large, heavily advertised complexes. Even then, no one else would want to confuse people in the area with a second "Sun Garden Apartments" if you were using that name already, and it would not likely be used except through an oversight.

Since your business name itself is really not important, you might as well circumvent the folderol of filing a fictitious name statement by opening your account under your own name and having your checks imprinted in bold letters with your surname followed by the word "PROPERTIES." If your name were Lester Landlord, for example, then your tenants could make their checks and money orders payable to "LANDLORD PROPERTIES," and you could distinguish between accounts for different buildings, if you wanted to, by simply calling them "LANDLORD PROPERTIES ONE," "LANDLORD PROPERTIES TWO," and so on sequentially.

If you want to open an account under a fictitious name like "Sun Garden Apartments," expect to encounter a banker who will insist that you file a fictitious name statement. If you do not wish to go to all the trouble of filing, however, and you want to use the name "Sun Garden Apartments" as payee, merely open the account under the name "Lester Landlord's (use your own name here, of course) Sun Garden Apartments," and you may accept checks made out simply to "Sun Garden Apartments." That's really all you care about anyway, isn't it? You want to get the rent checks deposited into an account that you can write checks on, an account which is easily distinguishable from your personal account and carries a name easy enough for your tenants to remember when they're preparing their rent checks or money orders every month.

Don't become so involved with picking a name for your landlording bank account that you fail to familiarize yourself with the bewildering array of checking and savings accounts available nowa-

days. Don't expect your financial institution to open an account for you which will necessarily be the best for your situation, either. Financial institutions make their profit by obtaining your money at the lowest possible rate (they like it free if they can get it; did you know that when Swiss banks are overwhelmed with deposits, they not only stop paying interest, they actually *charge* interest on new deposits?) and lending it out at the highest possible rate. Ask about the options available. Look out for yourself.

Your checking account should bear maximum interest with the minimum of minimum balances (you should make yourself keenly aware of this minimum balance so you don't start incurring the dreaded fees assessed accounts which fall below the minimum). It should allow you to write without charge as many checks as you'll reasonably need each month. It should provide printed checks at a minimum charge. It should not hold the deposits you make to your account until your tenants' checks have cleared their accounts. It should charge reasonable fees for stop-payments, and it should have some kind of overdraft protection so your own checks don't start bouncing after you have deposited several tenants' checks which do bounce.

In addition to keeping at least one separate checking account for your landlording funds to flow through, you may want to open a savings account as your "escrow account" for refundable deposits only. These monies are not taxable when you receive them and should be distinguished as separate from your other landlording income, all of which is taxable. These deposits still belong to your tenants, not to you, and separating them will make them readily available when you need them to use or return. Separating them will also help to remind you to pay interest periodically if you are compelled to do so by law in your area or if you are inclined to do so as a good-faith gesture.

Sums designated as last month's rent belong to you, not to your tenants. They are taxable as soon as you receive them, and they should not be kept in the same savings account as your tenants' refundable deposits. All rents paid in advance, whether they be first month's or last month's or any month in-between, are designated as rent and nothing else and should be deposited into your regular property checking account for operations use.

Circulating Business Cards

After you have opened the bank accounts you need for your rental property, order yourself some business cards. "Business cards for landlords you say? Ridiculous! What a waste of money!"

Although you might scoff at the idea initially, consider some of the many uses for business cards in your do-it-yourself landlording business before you reject the idea completely—

✔ Use them as your "open sesame" for access to many "Wholesale Only" suppliers of appliance parts, plumbing wares, and the like. These suppliers may refuse to sell to the general public, but they will sell to you if they think that you have a legitimate business, and yours, landlord, is a legitimate business.

✔ Pass cards out to your tenants for handy reference when they need to contact you (designating yourself as owner, manager, or partner on your business cards lends credibility to your adopted landlording role; see "Should You Own Up to Being the Owner?" in chapter 12).

✔ At rental housing association meetings, pass your cards out to other owners. You never can tell what might come of the contacts. They might call you when they need to consult with somebody about rents, or they might give you a call when they're thinking about selling their buildings directly to another landlord.

✔ When those good business contacts you're cultivating hand you their business cards, hand them each one of yours in return. Then they'll understand that you do know one of the first things about running a business.

Besides being useful, business cards are one of the least expensive landlording purchases you will ever make. Local printers will print you up an adequate supply for around $40 (even though you're tempted by the small incremental cost of a greater number, order the minimum; telephone area code changes and changes in other relevant data occur just often enough to make cards obsolete rather quickly). Office-supply stores, mail-order firms, and printers with websites (enter "business card printing" to search for them) will print up a sufficient supply for a pittance as well. Peachtree, which supplies property management products and is listed in SOURCES & RESOURCES under "Catalogs from Various Suppliers," offers business cards.

You may even print your own business cards using your computer, a word processing program, your printer, and the business card blanks designed for this purpose and carried by office-supply stores. Each sheet yields ten cards.

While ordering or printing cards for yourself, print some for your manager, too, if you have one. Personalized business cards show managers that you have confidence in their professionalism and their permanence and are always much appreciated.

Here are some samples of what your business cards might look like—

---

123 Neat Street
Littletown, CA 91111
(510) 123-4567

LANDLORD PROPERTIES

LESTER LANDLORD
Partner

DANDY PROPERTIES

LESLIE LANDLADY
Manager

453 Sweet Street
Littletown, CA 91111   *(510) 123-6789*

Mastering the Telephone

Much of your landlording business involves communicating with people either face to face, by letter, or by telephone. Of course, there are times when you ought to make a personal visit to talk with someone, and there are times when you ought to write a letter, but there are also many times when you really ought to pick up a telephone and call.

In most cases, telephoning is cheaper all 'round. According to "bean counters" who study such things, business letters now cost companies more than $10 apiece because there's so much labor involved. Each business letter you write might not cost you quite that much, but it does cost you something even if you don't have an office staff to compensate.

Each trip you make to your property as an absentee owner costs you something for fuel or shoe leather, too, don't forget, no matter how close that property is to your home or workplace. Besides, you simply cannot afford the time to go traipsing all over the country looking for hard-to-find parts, wayward tenants, special services, best buys, and so on. For many of these tasks, you can communicate just as well by telephone, while using considerably less of your money and precious time.

Now I know that there are some people who seem perfectly normal in other ways, but they have an irrational fear of the telephone. They have no fear of flying, public speaking, darkness, high places, or their mother-in-law's raw-fish dinners, but they will not initiate a telephone call for any reason. You, landlord, cannot afford such a phobia. The telephone is one of the tools you must learn to use well in order to succeed in landlording. It's as necessary to your business as a garlic press is to an Italian chef.

Think rationally about the telephone. Think of it as a freedom machine enabling you to get a whole lot more work accomplished in a whole lot less time. Thumb through the Yellow Pages and imagine how many different kinds of business people you can contact just by punching a few buttons. That's freedom! That's power! That's convenience!

Master your telephone and use it!

Here are some hints which might help you use your telephone more efficiently for both outgoing and incoming calls—

✔ Keep all your tenants' telephone numbers handy. Because many tenants nowadays have unlisted numbers which no operator or directory could possibly provide you with, having the numbers handy will save you from having to make a personal visit to inform tenants of minor, but necessary, matters, such as an anticipated utility shutdown the next day. Make up a directory using the Tenant Record form in the FORMS section of this book, or better still, create a tenant database on your computer to keep track of tenant telephone numbers and other relevant tenant information. (Pushbutton Landlording [see SOURCES & RESOURCES] includes just such a database of tenant information which may be printed out in different ways.)

✔ Tenants seem to change their telephone numbers more frequently than the rest of us do. Therefore, we need to update their numbers constantly. Whenever you happen to be on a maintenance call inside a tenant's dwelling, check the number on the tenant's phone and write it down. Compare it with the one in your records, and update your records if necessary. Do the same whenever you're looking at tenants' rent checks. If all else fails and you find that you can't reach tenants by phone, ask them what their phone number is the next time you see them.

✔ Keep a categorized list of telephone numbers for all of your landlording business contacts or keep their business cards handy in a small file. Personal data assistants like the Palm Pilot were designed for keeping this data organized and handy. Consider buying one.

✔ When you use the Yellow Pages to shop locally for product availability and prices, make relevant notes right in the book next to the listings of those firms you've called so you'll have some clues to follow next time.

✔ If your rental property is located in an area served by a telephone directory different from the one you use at your home or workplace, secure a copy of that directory from the telephone company so you can shop conveniently from the Yellow Pages for that area. Usually there's no charge for a reasonable number of additional directories. The phone company wants to provide greater exposure for its Yellow Pages advertisers.

✔ Get a directory of toll-free numbers from AT&T by calling 800.562.2255 and ordering one. They have a business version, which lists all kinds of businesses likely to be of interest to other businesses, and a consumer version, which lists businesses likely to be of interest to consumers. There is a charge for these directories, but they can save you quite a bit in toll costs if you use them.

✔ Get a copy of your telephone company's regional directory of businesses. They're called Business-to-Business directories, and they cover a very large area. They can save you from having to consult, say, twenty directories to find credit reporting agencies or eviction services or suppliers of traffic safety devices.

✔ When you want to contact people or businesses outside your area-code region and you don't have their numbers, find them quickly by using the telephone company's long-distance information number, 555.1212, preceded by the area code of the region you wish to call. Since the breakup of the American Telephone & Telegraph Company and the availability of alternative long-distance telephone services, access to this long-distance information is no longer "free." The charges are nominal, however, so don't be deterred from using this service when you need it. Make a note of the numbers you inquire about so you won't incur the charge a second time for any one number. Call 800.555.1212 for information on toll-free numbers.

✔ If you have access to the Internet, you may go to any of a number of websites to find telephone numbers. Try "switchboard.com" and "superpages. com" for starters. If they don't have what you're looking for, go to one of the search engines, such as Yahoo or Google, and indicate that you're looking for "directories." You'll find what you're looking for, and you may find a whole lot more.

✔ Buy an answering machine with remote access so you can call your machine when you're away and find out who's left a message. Use it to screen those calls you don't want to take right when they come in, and use it to provide an unattended message announcement for the benefit of those people who are responding to your advertisement of a vacancy. Combined with a second telephone line, an answering machine will allow you to conduct landlording and personal business simultaneously.

✔ Consider installing a second telephone line for your landlording calls, but don't have it installed as a "business phone" unless you crave a listing in the Yellow Pages for some reason or other and unless you also understand that you

will be paying the higher fees charged to business users. They pay a charge for every outgoing call, even local ones. Have it installed as a second personal line instead; you know, like an extra phone for the teenager in the family. This landlording line will help keep your private affairs separate from your business affairs (answering it, "XXX Properties," you'll sound more professional, too) and simplify your business-call recordkeeping as well because it will save you from having to prorate your bills and from having to keep track of each business call you make on your one personal line. If you make all of your outgoing business calls on the landlording line, you can expense the entire bill without having to spend time poring over it.

A separate landlording line also enables you to install an answering machine separate from your personal answering machine so you can screen your landlording calls when necessary and leave a special recorded message during those times when you have a vacancy and want to provide callers with timely information about the vacant dwelling, as well as provide any specific information about your upcoming open houses.

✔ Take advantage of the cheapest rates available for long-distance calls by buying a prepaid phone card. You prepay for your calls and then use it when you call from any phone, residential, business, or pay. There's a small surcharge for using one from a payphone.

✔ Get a telephone credit card from your local or long-distance phone company and use it when your prepaid phone card runs out of time. Telephone credit cards never run out of time. They're a real convenience. They enable you to call from any phone and have the call billed to your home or business phone, and the phone company will give you a tally of the charges so you won't forget to expense your business calls. To avoid unauthorized use, memorize your card's PIN and keep it a closely guarded secret.

✔ Get a cellular phone which you can take with you wherever you go. They're much cheaper than they were only a few years ago, much clearer, and much smaller. They work over a greater area, and they come with so many choices of calling plans that you'll surely find one to fit your circumstances. Because the calling plans and rates keep changing all the time, review yours as a matter of course at the end of your first commitment period and regularly thereafter. The cellular phone company won't automatically give you the best current rates which they advertise to attract new customers. Once they have you as a customer, they think you won't care so much how much you're paying for their service and that you won't compare rates. Besides being convenient and useful, cellular phones are good security devices. See "Taking Personal Safety Precautions" in chapter 17.

✔ Check into call forwarding. It's an inexpensive telephone company service, and it's useful if you divide your time between two locations and want to make sure you don't miss a call. It's especially useful for forwarding calls to your cellular phone when you don't want to miss an important call and you don't want to wait around your regular phone for the call to come in.

✔ Buy a cordless telephone for yourself and/or for your manager. They're especially handy when you're preparing an empty rental for occupancy, and you have to be near a phone to take calls from prospective tenants. If you were dissatisfied with the performance of the early cordless models, give them another chance. You will likely be satisfied with the performance of the latest ones. They're smaller, they have better security, and they have a greater range.

✔ Get a toll-free number and use it together with your regular number whenever you advertise a vacancy. Nobody balks at calling a toll-free number, whereas they frequently do balk when they have to make a toll call.

Once upon a time, I bought a fourplex owned by a fellow who had moved twelve miles away from his rental property, out of the local calling area. Only one of the units was occupied when I bought it. Three tenants happened to move out at the same time, and the poor fellow was trying desperately to rent the three units without success. He advertised them in the paper and put a sign outside, but he just couldn't get people to call his new number. It was a toll call. He practically begged me to buy the building and then he practically gave it to me when I did buy it because he couldn't fill it.

All I had to do was put my local phone number on the for-rent sign, and I had plenty of prospects calling for information. I filled the place within ten days. I figure that not having a toll-free number for people to call cost that seller a quarter of the value of the property! Toll-free numbers are inexpensive nowadays. $5 per month and 10¢ a minute is common. Compare AT&T, MCI, and Sprint. They all offer toll-free numbers.

By the way, if you were to order a toll-free number today, you wouldn't get an 800 number; they're all gone. The only way to get one is to find somebody who isn't using theirs and will give it to you (selling toll-free numbers is illegal). Instead of an 800 number, you'd get another number in the toll-free series, 888, 877, or 866. Because many people don't know that these numbers are toll-free, you should put "toll-free" in front of your toll-free phone number on whatever signage or advertising you use.

Whenever you face a landlording task which involves communication, ask yourself first whether Ma Bell can help before you crank up the Ford or get out the old Smith-Corona.

Using the Internet

Dot-com companies may come and go, and the stocks of the survivors may be more of a crapshoot than a real crapshoot in Vegas, but the Internet is here to stay. It's a boon in many ways to many people in many walks of life. It's definitely a boon to landlords. No, it's many "boons."

It's a boon for advertising vacancies and reaching prospects far beyond the reach of your local newspaper.

It's a boon for enabling prospects to see what a rental dwelling looks like without your having to show it to them personally.

It's a boon for checking market rents.

It's a boon for checking applicants' credit histories and eviction records quickly and conveniently at any time of the day or night.

It's a boon for tracking the whereabouts of

tenants who skip out owing you money.

It's a boon for finding the latest landlord-tenant laws for your city, county, and state.

It's a boon for learning the latest about federal housing laws and federal housing programs.

It's a boon for communicating with tenants, managers, and other landlords at everybody's convenience.

It's a boon for researching the best products to do a job.

It's a boon for locating and ordering tools, equipment, parts, and supplies, including those which would otherwise be hard to find.

Use it for these tasks, and you will be saving yourself time and money. You'll know that you're charging the right rent because you checked the rents for other dwellings similar to yours. You'll know that you're buying the right low-flow toilet because you checked plumbers' comments about the various brands and models. You'll know that you rented to the right applicants because you checked them out thoroughly. You'll know that you have a better handle on your business than ever before because you are using the Internet to help you with your business.

Organizing Everything

There are many sources of discouragement in this do-it-yourself landlording business, many of which you can do absolutely nothing about, but there is one source of discouragement which you can do something about, and that is disorganization.

Disorganized landlords make the job much more difficult than it already is, and consequently, they become needlessly discouraged time and time again because they cannot find what they're looking for in the chaos of their stacks and piles.

There are tenant records to keep organized as well as receipts, insurance policies, building records, checks, keys, supplies, tools, and spare parts, and you cannot have a memory sufficient to locate all of them when you need them. You have to get them organized or you will fail miserably in this business.

You will find a number of hints and forms in this book to help you get organized. Use them, adapt them to fit your needs, and you will succeed in making your job easier and surely far less discouraging.

Don't make this business any harder than it already is. Get organized. Stay organized.

Continuing Your Education

If you own no rental property at all right now, you are wise ("Wise people learn by others' mistakes; fools, by their own."–says an old proverb), not because you own no rental property, but because you are taking the time to educate yourself about landlording before you actually become involved. Few first-time landlords ever have the street smarts or the training necessary to cope with the multitude of problems they will encounter in this business. Some cope well and thrive. Some give up after the first setback and sell. Some capitulate and commit hari-kari. Most of us just manage to muddle through.

There's no reason for you to repeat all the same mistakes that others have made so many times before and to pay a high price for making those mistakes again because now there's an abundance of good information available in books, on tapes, in periodicals, in classes, over the Internet, and in seminars, some of which are referred to in the SOURCES & RESOURCES section in the back of this book.

Learn all you can from these sources, but especially take the time to attend classes and seminars. Hard Knocks College no longer has a monopoly on rental property management education. Thank heavens! Adult schools, community colleges, university extensions, rental housing associations, educational exchanges, and proprietary schools all offer sessions for those landlords who want to know more about this business they find themselves in.

If such sessions are not available where you live, ask for them. The people who schedule these sessions try to accommodate local needs, but sometimes they overlook the need for rental property management courses entirely because they have no familiarity with the business themselves. If nobody requests these courses, there won't be any.

New owners obviously profit from attending these sessions, but experienced owners profit from continuing their education, too. Remember, whether you are experienced or inexperienced, you are dealing with large sums of money in this business and you cannot afford to be complacent or uninformed. Times change and laws change, and you need to reassess your business operations all the time, picking up one good idea here and another there, and you can do that best by continuing your landlording education both formally and informally. Continuing education offers you the opportunity to spend a little and save a lot.

Maintaining Your Image

As a landlord, you are always in the crosshairs, targeted by some ignorant ninny or other as one of the banes of society. Be on your guard. What you do, what you say, and how you look, all of these things affect the way your tenants see you and react to you.

If you really must have a Cadillac SUV or a Mercedes roadster or a Jaguar sedan, don't drive it anywhere near your rental properties. Your tenants know for a fact that you paid for it in cash with their rent money. You didn't earn the money to pay for it. No way!

No matter how warranted any rent increase is, if your tenants think of you as a wealthy and uncaring owner, they will resent the increase and resent you, too. Give them little cause to resent you.

Don't tell your tenants about your country club activities or your tours around the world. Don't show them your gold Rolex watch, your two-carat diamond solitaire ring, or your jet helicopter. Sure, you've worked hard for these trappings of success, but you ought to save the display for the gatherings with your in-laws.

Keep a low profile around your tenants. Drive your oldest car or pickup truck around to your rental properties. Make your tenants think that you need this month's rent money to pay this month's mortgage payment and the property's various other expenses, whether you do or you don't.

The image you maintain around your tenants should be as neutral as possible. It shouldn't call attention to you as a miserable miser or as a high roller. It should be the image of the average Jill or Joe struggling to make ends meet. It should be one suitably matched to your tenants.

Wearing Proper Attire

Not every rental property has them—busybodies who thrive on buttonholing the manager or owner and babbling on interminably. If you do have such tenants, however, you know they can be more of a nuisance than hemorrhoidal tissues. They're usually model tenants otherwise and you hate to offend them, but you also hate to waste your precious time lending them your ears for very long.

Take courage. You can avoid these gossipmongers by wearing overalls that are all speckled with paint whenever you set foot on your rental property. You may have just showered or awakened from your afternoon nap, but they won't think so. Those overalls clothe you with a certain busy-worker mystique and give you license to do what you came to do and then leave without having to make or listen to small talk.

Prioritizing Your Work and Keeping Sane

Don't expect spontaneous remission to remedy many of your tenants' complaints for repairs, but do give it a try sometime by prescribing the tardy treatment for certain piddlin' problems. Since no one has yet found a way to fix a leaky roof over the telephone, you must make a visit for that kind of thing and you should make it soon after you're notified, but if the problem's of a lesser magnitude, you should reassure the tenant with a gentle voice that everything will be taken care of in due time and then jot down the job on your list of priorities. Don't rush over to your properties for every little thing. You'll soon need a new spouse and an expensive shrink if you do. Accumulate the little repair jobs until they warrant a fixit visit themselves or until you need to go there for some other reason. You'll be surprised how often the little problems will have taken care of themselves in the interim.

Just because you don't leap up immediately to respond to every tenant's complaint doesn't mean that you should discourage your tenants from reporting the little maintenance problems they notice. On the contrary, you should be encouraging them to report these problems to you because you will pay dearly for postponing repairs on your rental property too long.

Linoleum which is just beginning to pull loose at a seam is so much easier and cheaper to repair correctly right then than it is when a piece has torn away and been lost. A water leak under a kitchen sink will eventually cause wood decay in the cabinetry if it's neglected, decay which the termite inspector's piercing eyes won't overlook when he comes to inspect the place for a buyer.

Use your good common sense to determine when you should make a visit to your property and when you should stay away.

Equating Your Own Time with Money

Remember that all of your landlording expenses are tax-deductible as business expenses and that there will be times when you'll have to pay more than you think you should for something you need in a hurry. There will be times when you'll have to call for professional help because you lack the expertise or the tools to do a job, because you're fed up and shouldn't do it, or because you simply don't have the time to do it. Call for the help and think of the bill as a business expense. That's what it is. Don't get frustrated because you couldn't do it yourself and save the money. You can't always do everything yourself.

Sometimes it pays you to do something yourself and sometimes it pays you not to (see "Should You Do It Yourself" in chapter 12). You're not the ordinary do-it-yourselfer, remember, and you don't have their kind of time to case creation for what you want to buy at the price you want to pay. Let ordinary do-it-yourselfers boast about how they spent long hours scrounging for something and then got it for little or nothing. You

have no time for that. You have a business to tend to, a business in which time translates directly into money, your money.

Monitoring Your Turnover Rate and Equating Your Dwelling's Downtime with Money

On average, 45% of all rental dwellings in the U.S. turn over every year, and the downtime for turnover averages eighteen days. These averages include professionally managed properties as well as owner-managed properties. As a do-it-yourself landlord managing your own rental properties, you should keep these averages in mind and use them as benchmarks for your own operations.

Keep in mind that this average turnover rate of 45% translates into tenancies which last a little more than two years, 2.2 years or 811 days to be more exact (365 days per year divided by .45). In contrast, a turnover rate of 100% translates into tenancies which last exactly one year.

Keep in mind that a downtime of eighteen days translates into a loss of rent equal to 2.22%, based upon one turnover per dwelling every 811 days. That's the equivalent of losing one day of rent for every forty-five days of occupancy.

Another way to calculate the cost of eighteen days of downtime for every turnover is to divide one month's rent by thirty (yields the daily rent) and multiply that times eighteen. If the rent is $750 per month, a downtime of eighteen days reduces your rental income by $450 every 811 days. That's for one dwelling only. For four dwellings, a downtime of eighteen days reduces your rental income by $1,800 every 811 days!

Of course, we're assuming here that the turnover rate is 45%. If it were 100% and the downtime were still eighteen days, then the reduction in rental income would be $450 every 365 days. That's equivalent to losing one day of rent for every twenty days of occupancy.

Any way you look at equating a dwelling's downtime with money, you can see that there's serious money involved here, your money.

There's no doubt as to whether a shorter downtime is better than a longer one. It is. A longer downtime reduces your income. A shorter downtime increases your income.

You can shorten your downtime between tenants by being quick about everything required to prepare the dwelling for occupancy and by being quick about getting good tenants. Using the suggestions in this book for being quick, you should be able to beat the average. Concentrate on shortening your downtime every time you have a vacancy. Be nimble, be quick, and you'll beat the eighteen-day average. After all, that average includes properties managed by people who don't own them. You as a do-it-yourself landlord, you who care about your property more than anyone else, you who will work 24/7 when you have to, you will beat the average.

Beating the downtime average of eighteen days is one thing; beating the turnover average of 45% is quite another. There is some doubt as to what is the optimum turnover rate. Is a turnover rate of 20%, which means the tenants stay five years, better than a turnover rate of 45%? How about a turnover rate of 100%, which means they stay a year, or one of 200%, which means they stay six months? Are they any better than 45%? There is no simple answer to these questions, not if your objective is to maximize your landlording income.

There is a simple answer if your objective is to minimize your landlording troubles, that is, if you want to put your landlording business on automatic pilot as much as possible and distance yourself from it so you can spend more time on other things. That simple answer is this—Strive for a lower turnover rate if you want to minimize your landlording troubles. If you have a turnover rate approaching zero, if your tenants move only from your rentals to the cemetery, then you're seldom troubled with turnovers and all the associated work involved, but you're also charging too little in rent, for you need do nothing else to reduce your turnover rate other than keep your rents low.

On the other hand, if you want to maximize your landlording income, you will experience a higher turnover rate, somewhere between 45% and 100%. In other words, your tenants will average tenancies lasting from one to two years. Some might stay longer than two years, and some might stay shorter than one year. If one tenant stays four years and another stays four months, the turnover rate for those two tenancies averages out to 45%.

A turnover rate in the 45%-to-100% range indicates that you are charging market or near-market rents, that you are providing your tenants with the services they want, and that you are maximizing your income.

Remember, these figures are only benchmarks, nothing more. Use them to get a better idea about how you're performing as a do-it-yourself landlord compared to everybody else in the business.

Ignoring Tenant "Chaff Clouds"

Landlording do-it-yourselfers tend to be more patient, understanding, helpful, and credulous than their professional counterparts who work for the corporate owners of large apartment complexes. Landlording do-it-yourselfers know their tenants and are known by them. They develop a personal relationship with their tenants. They will give their tenants one chance, two chances, even three or four chances to shape up before they begin eviction proceedings, and when they do, they feel as if they themselves have failed somehow, not their tenants.

There's no reason you have to lose your humanity when you become a landlord. You should be patient, understanding, and helpful, but you should not be credulous, especially not when you are dealing with applicants or new tenants. You don't know them, and you don't know what they're capable of.

When a fighter pilot is trying to confuse an enemy missile headed straight for him, he releases a chaff cloud from the rear of his aircraft to make the missile veer away or detonate out of harm's way.

Some tenants know this technique well and know how to use it to their benefit. They release their chaff clouds whenever they feel the need to confuse a landlord. Their chaff consists of half truths and whole lies which work only too well to make credulous landlords veer away from the target.

Don't you be credulous. Be on the lookout for these tenant chaff clouds both before and during any tenancy. Try to recognize them for what they are, and try your best to ignore them and head straight for your target.

In every case, you can best ignore tenant chaff clouds by following your standard operating procedure, whether it's for getting good tenants, for collecting all the move-in monies, for collecting rents promptly, or for enforcing the rental agreement.

Let's say that some well-dressed, well-mannered applicants want you to rent to them right away before you have a chance to check out their application. They show you a stack of greenbacks which equal more than the amount you require for them to move in. They tell you that they're new to the area and need a place to rent for the long term. They need it right now, today. What do you do?

Take your eyes off that stack of greenbacks for starters, and remain calm. Tell these people that you do not rent to anybody without checking them out. That's your standard operating procedure, and you can't deviate from it. Tell them that you will check them out and give them an answer within hours, whatever number of hours allows you enough time, 6, 12, or 24. If they say they'll have to find some other landlord who will let them move in immediately without checking them out, tell them to go ahead. Tell them that a landlord who doesn't check applications is a landlord who has tenant problems or will have tenant problems, and those tenant problems will affect them as good tenants. If they want to rent from such a landlord, that's their business. Be firm.

Let's say that some applicants tell you after you have approved them to move in that they don't have all the money required because their son was in a car accident out of state and they had to wire him some money. They ask you whether you'll allow them to move in if they pay you the first month's rent now and promise to pay the deposits over the next three months. What do you do?

Tell them you're sorry that their son was in a car accident, especially now when their own lives are in turmoil during the process of finding a new place to live and moving into it. Tell them you're also sorry that you cannot allow them to move in without paying all of their move-in monies. That's your standard operating procedure, and you can't deviate from it. Tell them that you will hold the dwelling for them if they give you the money to hold it but that you cannot let them move in until they have paid everything required to move in, both rent and deposits. Be firm.

Let's say that some other applicants whom you have approved to move in now want to move in a few things so they can save the upcoming charge on their self-storage unit. They're still living elsewhere for another two weeks while you're completing some remodeling. They have paid you nothing other than the small sum they gave you to check out their application. What do you do?

Tell them that you can appreciate their wanting to save money on their storage unit. Tell them that you would be happy to let them move their things from the storage unit to the rental dwelling's storage area or garage, provided that they pay everything required to take possession, even though their rent won't start until the move-in date you have agreed upon. That's your standard operating procedure, and you can't deviate from it. Be firm.

Let's say that some tenants who moved in a little more than a month ago are a week behind on their rent and they have made no effort to contact you about it. You contact them, and they say that they are really stressed out. The husband just lost his job. The wife broke her arm. The son was thrown out of school for smoking pot on campus, and the thirteen-year-old daughter ran off with her twenty-one-year-old boyfriend. They say that they'll pay you their rent as soon as they can.

Tell them you know that "bad things happen to good people" and you know that they are good people, but something even worse is going to happen to them if they don't pay you their rent money now. They're going to be evicted for non-payment of rent, and they're going to have an eviction on their tenancy history and on their credit report for a long time to come. Give them the notice to pay rent or quit which you brought along with you already filled out. Tell them that giving them the notice is part of your standard operating procedure when people haven't paid their rent on time and you can't deviate from it. Be firm.

Let's say that some tenants who just moved in are keeping two dogs in their dwelling when they have an agreement to keep only one. A neighboring tenant informs you about the two dogs because barking duets have been interfering with her afternoon naps. You approach the tenants and they admit that they have a second dog, but they say that it's not theirs. It's there only temporarily. They're looking after it for a friend who has gone abroad. As soon as the friend returns, they say, the second dog will go. When you ask them about the friend's return, they become elusive and can't give you an exact date.

Tell them that they have an agreement for one dog and one dog only. The second dog will have to go within seven days or else they will have to go themselves along with both dogs. Tell them that you must give them a written notice about this breach of their contract and that it will remain in their tenant file. Tell them that giving them the notice is part of your standard operating procedure. Be firm.

Enough of these stories! You get the picture, don't you? In each story, the applicants or tenants release chaff clouds to convince you that you ought to veer away from your target, that you ought to let them take possession before you've checked them out thoroughly or collected all the move-in monies normally required, that you ought to let them pay their rent whenever they can, and that you ought to let them break their rental agreement for an indefinite period.

You know the consequences of renting to someone whose credit and tenancy history you haven't checked, especially if they're trying to entice you to rent to them by flashing a stack of greenbacks.

You know the consequences of letting new tenants move in just a few of their things or everything they own without paying all of the move-in monies you normally require.

You know the consequences of letting tenants get behind on their rent, no matter how compelling their story, no matter how sincere their promises.

You know the consequences of letting tenants break their rental agreement and keep an extra pet, no matter whose pet it is, no matter how well behaved they say it is, no matter how soon they say it will go.

You know these consequences instinctively. You don't want to know them intimately. Listen to your instincts. Don't be confused by tenant chaff clouds. Don't be credulous. Stick with your standard operating procedures. Be firm.

Learn to ignore tenant chaff clouds and you will go a long way in the landlording business.

Noting Store Hours

That portion of your spare time given over to maintaining your rental properties hardly coincides with normal business hours. Most likely you work at your properties in the evening, at night, in the morning, and on weekends.

Because these times are on the fringes of most stores' normal hours, you have undoubtedly experienced the frustration of scurrying off to the paint store at 6:15 on a Sunday evening to buy that last can of paint you need to complete redecorating a dwelling which a new tenant wants to move into the very next day, and when you

arrive, you find that the paint store closed at six. What's all the more frustrating is that you could have been there before six had you known that it closed at six.

How can you avoid a repetition of this frustrating situation? The next time you go on one of your buying errands, write down the hours for each store you visit. Keep these times in that wallet, purse, or glove compartment which usually accompanies you on your landlording tours of duty. One quick glance at this information will tell you which store is still open at 9:12 on a Tuesday night when you need to buy the parts to replace a useless toilet valve that came apart in your hands.

You will spare yourself more spare time for plotting rent raises and smoking noxious cigars if you aren't waiting around for stores to open in the morning, if you aren't driving wildly about town looking for any supplier who's open late at night.

Doing It Your Way

Some people prefer their toilet paper to roll off the front of the roll, some prefer it to roll off the back, some prefer it to roll off sideways, and I'm sure there are those who prefer no roll at all. They like their toilet paper in separate sheets. No one way is "right." Likewise, there is no right or wrong way to do every little thing in landlording. You have to decide what's right for you, what you're comfortable with, and then continue in that direction. There are many ways to collect rents promptly, for example, and though I do give more than one way in the chapter on rents, I don't give them all. In truth, I'm sure that I don't know them all.

Use what you read in this book as starting points for developing your own ways of doing things. Don't suppose that there are no other ways to do them. There are. Be creative. Find your own way. You'll enjoy landlording much more when you do.

Taking Your Front-Row Seat at a Long-Running Comedy

Do-it-yourself landlording isn't all cleaning up other people's messes, coaxing heaters to work on Christmas Eve, painting wall after wall the same ivory white, chasing deadbeats for their rent, taking nuisance calls in the middle of the night, doing battle with uncooperative tenants, and studying the latest landlord-tenant laws.

No, it's not.

It's a front-row seat at a long-running human comedy. There are humorous things happening all around you, landlord. Take the time to recognize and enjoy them.

Chuckle to yourself when your tenant tells you that he couldn't pay his rent because he had to pay his girlfriend's rent or she was going to be evicted. Chuckle to yourself when you're looking into the eyes of a tenant who, with a straight face, is making up some pretty imaginative reasons why there just happens to be a St. Bernard in his no-pets apartment when you come by unannounced to check on the smoke detectors. Chuckle to yourself when your very worst tenant, the one who has told you where to go more than once, tells you to get rid of his neighbor right away because the neighbor has been smoking pot.

Don't work all the time with your head hanging down, muttering to yourself, "Woe is me! Nobody ever appreciates what I do for them. Everybody tries to take advantage of me. I work such long hours while everybody else seems to be having all the fun."

Look for the humor that there is in this business. It's there, and it will provide you with the comic relief you sometimes need as you plug away doing the nasty work which comes with the territory, landlording territory.

Some Last Words

Some of the things you have to do in landlording may be tough to do. No scrupulous landlord ever said this business was easy, but if you practice sound business methods, use your common sense, keep a level head, learn enough skills to do some things yourself, and know enough to call for help when you need it, you won't find your property declining in value. It will actually be increasing in value, making money for you while you sleep. Indeed it will!

Haven't you always wanted to make money while you sleep? Haven't you always wanted to buy the mixed nuts without the peanuts and not give the purchase a second thought? Landlord, you can! Just keep minding your landlording business, and in time it will pay better dividends than you ever expected.

2
Taking Over
As the New Owner

Let's eavesdrop on some new owners as they're sharing their initial landlording experiences and impressions with anyone who will listen.

"Here I am paying for the privilege of being those people's landlord. The rent they pay me doesn't nearly cover all of my expenses, and still they expect me to hotfoot it over there day or night to unplug the toilet which they stopped up. Hear what I'm saying? Their kids stop up the toilet with a full roll of toilet paper, and I'm supposed to come running, unplug the thing, and clean up the stinkin' mess which is all over the floor. What kind of a business is this anyway?"

"I felt like maybe I'd died and gone to hell! My phone never stops ringing. There's always somebody calling me up with their problems. They're unhappy about this. They're unhappy about that, and they want me to do something right now to make them happy. Trouble is, I can't make them happy, no matter what I do. I've tried. My, how I've tried!"

"My landlording bloopers that first week were enough to start a whole new TV series."

"I felt as lonely as a flatulent sheep dog."

"I could almost feel my hair turning gray when I had to serve eviction papers on this muscle-man doper guy. I think he's the real reason the previous owner sold me the building so cheap. Until he and his motorcycle gang are out of there, I'm keeping a low profile and keeping protection handy."

"Never before had anybody called me up at 3 o'clock in the morning demanding that I come right over and kill a monster roach which was darting about their kitchen."

"I never realized before just how many tenants are street lawyers. Why, they know the chapter and verse of every landlord-tenant law there is and every court decision, too! What is it with these people? Don't they have anything else to do with their lives?"

Yep, becoming a landlord, taking over as the new owner of a rental property, can be pretty traumatic for some people. At the very least, it's an eye-opener for all but the thickest skinned. You may find yourself wondering what ever possessed you to get involved in this odd business in the first place. Take heart; it's not all that bad, and there's a lot you can do to get things running smoothly right off the bat.

Let's say that you have just acquired some residential income property and you are anxious to get started fulfilling your role as the new owner. You have already bought a copy of *Landlording*, a most commendable beginning. You have joined your local rental housing association and have bombarded all the people there with your questions. You have secured a copy of the applicable housing codes from the powers that be and have familiarized yourself with the basic services and amenities which you must provide by law. You have notified the appropriate utility companies about the property's change in ownership so that the bills will be sent directly to you. You have decided already how you're going to be doing the banking and bill-paying for the property. You have decided to handle the off-site management yourself and are looking over the existing tenants for somebody to assume certain on-site management responsibilities. You have thought about the building and about what needs to be done there, having made several inspections before you ever bought the place, and you have lined up some workers to help you take care of the property's obvious deficiencies.

You're certainly on the right track, but because the former owner kept such abominable records, you have no information whatsoever about the tenants you have inherited, and, what's more, they have none about you. They're now wondering

September 16, XXXX

Dear *Ms Melander*,

   You probably know already that the building where you live has changed hands. Because tenants usually feel some apprehension every time such a changeover occurs, we would like to take this opportunity to clear the air by letting you know just what you can expect in the future about a few things.

   DEPOSITS...One special concern you must have is your deposits. We are concerned, too, and we want to make absolutely certain that all of your deposits are credited to you. To avoid any misunderstandings about your deposits and other matters related to your living here, we would like you to answer the questions on the sheet attached. They are questions which you should be able to answer quickly from memory or by referring to information readily available to you. Please do so as soon as possible and return your answers to us in the envelope provided.

   PAYMENT BY CHECK OR MONEY ORDER...Since it is unwise for anyone to keep or carry cash around in quantities, we request that you pay your rent by check or money order (made payable to us exactly as underlined below). You will be protected and so will we.

   PROMPT PAYMENT...You are expected to pay your rent within three days after the due date. For example, rent due on the first must be paid by the fourth at the very latest. If you anticipate being late beyond that for any reason whatsoever, please let us know beforehand. If you don't, we will assume that you are deliberately avoiding payment, and we will immediately serve you with the notice which starts eviction proceedings.

   MAINTENANCE...We expect you to pay your rent promptly, and you can expect us to respond promptly to maintenance problems. Sometime within the next week, we will visit you to inspect for any building maintenance work that should be taken care of. You can help by starting now to make a list of such work which you notice around the house.

   RENTAL AGREEMENT...We will also stop by soon to explain to you the standard rental agreement we use, and we will leave you with a copy of your own.

   We are reasonable people and we will try anything within reason to make living here enjoyable for you, but naturally we need your cooperation. If we have it, we will get along well together and we can all take pride in this place that you call home.

                    Sincerely,

                    Margaret Miglia, Manager
                    DANDY PROPERTIES (123-4567)
                    400 Busy Ave., Goodloc, CA 09777

what to do with their rent monies, whom to call about their roaches, when the rent's going up, what's happened to their deposits, and how soon they're going to get the new carpets which were promised to them last Christmas by the previous owner's property manager.

Making Contact—The Letter

The very next thing you should do is communicate with them, for communication is the lifeblood of this business. Send them a letter or, better still, for establishing good rapport with them all the more quickly, take a letter around to each one of them and meet these people who are now your tenants. They want to put a face on you, landlord. They want to know what they're up against. Are you an ogre? Are you a pushover? How big are your horns? Do you smile? How do you dress? What do you drive? What kind of a creature are you? They want to know. Consider this an opportunity to let them have a good look at you and judge for themselves.

Advise them in the letter that the building has indeed changed hands, just as they suspected, and that you are now looking after it as the owner or one of the owners or the manager (determine now whether you intend to stop the buck or pass it—see chapter 12). Give them your name, address, phone number, and e-mail address so they will know how they can contact you when necessary. Allay their fears about their deposits, inform them about your rent collection procedure, tell them you do want to hear about their maintenance problems, and mention that you expect to come calling soon with a rental agreement.

The letter given here includes all of these elements and more, and like the other forms shown in the text, you will find a full-size copy ready for your use in the FORMS section in the back of the book. You may photocopy this letter as is, or you may enter the text into your word processor and adapt it to fit your own circumstances. If you do plan to use the letter as is, make sure you intend to follow through with all that you are promising to do in it, visiting your new tenants within a week or two to check for maintenance problems, and so forth. Don't say you're going to do anything unless you can do it and will do it, especially not now, not when people you've never done business with before are looking at you with a "show-me" eye. Prove yourself to be a person of your word and not a flim-flammer.

Gathering Tenant Information

Besides telling your new tenants about their building's new management, you need to gather some information on them as well, so along with your first letter to them, provide them with a Tenant Information form and include a stamped, self-addressed envelope for its return. This information is intended to take the place of most of what you would already have in your files on those tenants you select yourself, information normally available on the Rental Application and the Condition & Inventory Checksheet forms. Neither the application nor the checksheet is really appropriate to use when you have inherited new tenants whom you know nothing about, however, for then you are trying merely to establish some basic facts about them and their tenancy. The Tenant Information form is specifically designed for gathering the information needed in this particular situation.

Give your new tenants two weeks to return the information to you. Then, whether they have returned it or not, arrange to meet with each of them face to face to discuss your policies and go over the written rental agreement you intend to use. Or, if you prefer, combine your visit to do a maintenance check with your visit to gather tenant information and review the rental agreement. There's no good reason to separate them.

Some tenants are inclined to be stubborn and secretive when asked to reveal anything at all about themselves which they consider to be none of your business. Like some primitive people who are afraid to be photographed lest their inner spirit be robbed of them, they imagine that you are snooping into their private lives so you can lay them bare to some big-brother intelligence gathering agency.

To counteract this paranoia, try to be as delicate and inoffensive as possible if they don't volunteer to provide you with the information themselves. Be neither offensive nor defensive about gathering it. After all, there are sound, logical reasons why you need every bit of it, so you may want to stress that their own best interests are being served by their divulging the information to you.

If you have to, explain why you are asking for each item on the Tenant Information form. You need to know their home and work telephone numbers in case there's an emergency and you need to get in touch with them in a big hurry.

Tenant Information:

Your Name _Nelly Bunn_

Your Address _452 Summit, Apt. 206_ Soc. Sec. No. _577-40-6532_

Your Home Phone Number _555-0912_ Work Phone _555-5000_

Who lives with you? (Include ages of children, please) _Nobody_

_____

What pet(s) do you have? _3 small dogs_

Do you have a waterbed? _no_

What vehicle(s) do you have? Make(s) _Toyota_ License(s) _442A701_

Where do you work? (Company name) _Sears_

Where does your co-tenant work? (Company name) _N/A_

When did you move in? _March 1, xxxx_

What is your current rent per month? _$650-_

What date is your rent paid up to right now? _September 30, xxxx_

When is your rent due each month? _1st_

What refundable deposits have you paid? Keys $_5-_ Security $_1,250-_

   Cleaning $_150-_ Other (please explain) $_∅_

When you moved in, you paid your first month's rent. Did you also then

   pay your last month's rent? _no_ If so, how much was it? $_____

Which of the following furnishings in your dwelling belong to the owners
of the building? (Please give room locations where appropriate.)

   Carpets _Living room, hall and bedroom_ Drapes_____

   Shades _Kitchen and bath_ Blinds_____

   Stove _Kitchen_ Refrigerator _Kitchen_

   Other appliances? (Please list)_____

   Other furniture? (Please list)_____

Do you have a rental agreement or lease in writing? _Yes_

   If so, what is the date of the latest one? _March 1, xxxx_

In case of an emergency, what friend or relative should we contact?

   Name _Martha Washington_ Telephone Number _555-0011_

   Date _9/18/xx_ Your Signature _Nelly Bunn_

Let's say that a neighbor notices somebody prowling about their dwelling and calls you about it or else their smoke alarm starts wailing and nobody seems to be home. Your having their telephone numbers available at those times may save much grief later. If they say they have an unlisted number and prefer not to give it out, tell them that you will take every reasonable precaution to keep their number from falling into anyone else's hands.

You need their Social Security numbers so you can verify information for credit reporting agencies which sometimes call you as the landlord when tenants are applying for credit somewhere.

You need to know who lives with them so you will be able to help keep unauthorized people from entering their dwelling. For example, you want to know what you ought to do if a complete stranger asks you to let her in, someone who says she lives there and forgot her key. Does she really live there? Should you let her in?

Emphasize especially the concern you have for determining precise sums and dates, both of which you need to establish now in order to prevent misunderstandings later. You need to know exactly how much they paid in deposits to the previous owner so you will know exactly how much to set aside for them when they move out. You also need to know whether they paid anything as last month's rent and if so, how much.

Tell them that the previous owner provided you with a set of figures before you bought the property but that you want to verify them against the tenants' own figures.

If they just won't cooperate with you in providing the information, there's nothing you can do to force them, and you shouldn't bother getting upset about the matter yourself or making them upset by saying unkind words or threatening them. Retreat. Let them be. Consider them to be ignorant, foolish, mentally unbalanced, generally uncooperative, or any combination of these possibilities. Then rely on others to supply the information. Use the deposit figures provided by the previous owner, and ask him what else he knows about that tenant. Uncovering the few facts needed to complete the Tenant Information form from other sources shouldn't be too difficult.

Remember that part of your effort to communicate with your new tenants involves proving yourself to be a reasonable human being. Don't allow yourself to be drawn into an argument. Don't talk about other tenants. Don't talk about yourself unless you're asked, and then be brief. Find out what's on these new tenants' minds, what's troubling them. Let them talk if they want to, and listen carefully to what they have to say. Look them in the eye, be concerned, be polite, and be more ready to smile than a Miss America contestant at a press conference.

Coming to Terms Using Your Rental Agreement

Before you ever bought the property, you should have found out what kind of rental agreements or leases were being used there, but if you didn't, during this visit you will want to establish how your relationship with these new tenants is governed. You should ask to see a copy of the tenants' rental agreement, if any. You may be flabbergasted when they actually produce one whereas the previous owner couldn't. So do ask.

Look it over carefully, understanding full well that you as the new owner are bound by it. If you don't have a copy and you want one, give them a dollar and ask them to make you a copy. Don't ask them to give you their copy to take to a copy shop because they may become suspicious that you won't return it. Don't give them cause to be suspicious. By giving them a dollar for a copy, surely more than it will cost them to copy the agreement at a copy shop, you will have them thinking that you're trustworthy rather than suspect, generous rather than parsimonious, someone who will be a much better landlord than the "scoundrel" who was their previous landlord.

When you inherit tenants, your business relationship with them is governed by whatever agreement they had with the previous owner, be it a current lease, an expired lease which has become a month-to-month agreement, a written month-to-month agreement, a written agreement for some period less than a month, or a verbal agreement.

No matter which one of these five possibilities governs your relationship, you are governed by it for a period of time. Generally the contract period coincides with the rent payment schedule, so if the tenants pay their rent on a weekly basis, they're probably on a weekly contract. If they pay their rent on a fortnightly basis, they're probably on a bi-weekly contract. If they pay their rent on a monthly basis, they're probably on a monthly contract or on a lease. If there is a lease involved, you're bound by its terms, whatever they happen to be, and for whatever period it covers, six months, one year, or even more, like it or not. Do take a look at the lease to see what it says, if anything, about the sale of the dwelling. It may enable you as the new owner to take possession upon notice of thirty, sixty, or ninety days. In any case, you may not shove a new agreement at anybody and tell them they have to sign it right away and abide by it from that day forward. You have to give them a certain amount of notice. That is their due.

You may give them your Rental Agreement any time you want to, of course, but you may not enforce it until they have signed it and have had some period of time to get accustomed to it. How much time must you give them? Barring any especially restrictive local ordinances, before you can change the terms of their existing periodic-term (month-to-month, week-to-week) contract you have to give them the same amount of time as the term of their existing contract. When tenants have an existing contract covering periods shorter than a month, you ought to give them thirty days' notice of a change anyway. That's only fair. When they have only a verbal

agreement and nothing in writing, give them thirty days, too. In fact, to be fair to everyone, you ought to give thirty days to everyone except those who are on leases. Give them a contract at least thirty days before the lease expires so it will take effect the very day the lease actually does expire.

You have every right to expect tenants who are on leases to sign a new lease agreement when their old one expires. If they want to continue their tenancy and don't want to sign a new lease, then they have no lease at all. They become month-to-month tenants if you accept rent from them, and you may treat them the same way you'd treat any other month-to-month tenants.

Spend some time with each inherited tenant and explain the various terms of your Rental Agreement just as you explained the Tenant Information form to them. Listen to their objections and make adjustments if warranted.

What do you do if they are contrary and refuse to sign? Can you have an enforceable written contract signed by only one of the two parties involved?

In most cases involving contract conditions, when the tenant already occupies the premises, you certainly can change the contract conditions yourself without their signature. If they won't sign, explain to them that you will then simply go ahead and prepare a Notice of Change in Terms of Tenancy and attach it to a copy of the Rental Agreement you intend to use. This notice is very much like the one you use to increase rents. Their signature is not required for a notice of this sort to take effect in thirty days. It takes effect regardless. By refusing to sign, they gain absolutely nothing. They label themselves uncooperative. That's all. Tell them that you would like to have their cooperation in your mutual business dealings but that you will go ahead and manage the property your way, which you feel is quite a reasonable way, whether you get their cooperation or not.

The conditions in your new agreement must be legal, of course, and they ought to be sensible as well. You can't make your inherited tenants tolerate elephants upstairs or rats underfoot any more than you can make any other tenant tolerate such things. You can set quiet hours, require them to pay their rent by a certain day of the month, stipulate that they pay their rent by check or money order, limit the premises to personal use only, make them responsible for drain stoppages which they themselves cause, designate acceptable parking areas for residents and guests, restrict motor vehicle repairs, and make other similar conditions.

If your new conditions are much different from the ones under which your inherited tenants have been living, especially if you try to initiate a no-pets policy when the tenants already have a pet, understand that you will have a fight on your hands, a fight you cannot win because it will be aggravating to you and to the tenants, and it may wind up costing you more than you ever thought it would. People simply will not give up a pet without a fight.

Rather than trying to get existing tenants to give up their pets, you might be wise to adopt a no-pets policy for all new tenants and a policy of no-new-pets for existing tenants. After all, the old pets have probably already done as much damage as they're going to do both in and around the building. Be reasonable. Try to think through the consequences of your new conditions. Ask yourself how you would react if you were the tenant and your new landlord were imposing these conditions upon you.

Consider asking a tenant whom you have come to know better than any of the others since taking over the property to give you his reactions to the agreement you want to use. Listen to him. Question him. Discuss his ideas with him and with your "partner." Thank him for his input with a little gift, a plant or a pound of candy.

Once you determine that your agreement is reasonable for this particular property, be resolute about imposing it upon your new tenants. This may be your first test as the new owner. Be firm. Stand up to your tenants now, and they will be easier to deal with later. They will respect you.

Handling Tenants' Deposits

The only time I've ever been hauled into court for failing to return a tenant's deposit was when I acquired a small property and hadn't received any of the deposits from the previous owner. He claimed that he didn't have any deposits. That owner always collected $50 up-front as a cleaning deposit and never returned any of it to his departing tenants. Though he called it a "deposit," he really thought of the money as a cleaning "fee." He assumed that none of his tenants would leave their places clean enough to get a deposit back anyway, so he gave his manager the money as compensation for cleaning the apartments before the tenants moved in. The tenant who was suing me had assumed in the absence of a written agreement that the $50 was a cleaning deposit, not a fee. He left his apartment clean and, as far as I was concerned, he did deserve to get the money back, but because I had never received it from him or from the previous owner, I didn't think that I was the one to return it.

Don't get caught in a squeeze like this. If possible, get all the tenants' deposits sorted out and credited to you at closing. In order to do it the right way, you should know precisely what the seller *and* the tenants believe those deposits to be before you ever take over. Then you'll be able to take care of any discrepancies while you still owe the seller money. You won't have to take him to court later to collect.

Besides worrying about whether they're actually receiving the correct deposit amounts, new owners frequently worry about whether the deposits they do receive are going to be enough to compensate them for future difficulties. Worry about it if you want to; just don't do anything about it. Don't even consider raising your ten-

Notice of Change
in Terms of Tenancy

TO   <u>Suzanne Stevenson</u>, Tenant in Possession
<u>12 Apollo Avenue</u>
<u>Big City, CA 09501</u>

YOU ARE HEREBY NOTIFIED that the terms of tenancy under which you occupy the above-described premises are to be changed.

Effective <u>May 3</u>, <u>XXXX</u>, there will be the following changes:

<u>the terms of the RENTAL AGREEMENT attached, which you</u>
<u>have refused to sign, shall take precedence over any</u>
<u>written or verbal agreement which you may have</u>
<u>had with a previous owner.</u>

Dated this <u>1st</u> day of <u>April</u>, <u>XXXX</u>.

<u>Julius Caesar</u>
Owner/Manager

This Notice was served by the Owner/Manager in the following manner (check those which apply):

(X) by personal delivery to the tenant,
( ) by leaving a copy with someone on the premises other than the tenant,
( ) by mailing,
( ) by posting.

ants' inadequate deposits at this time or at any other time unless you want to precipitate a mass revolt. Most tenants will simply refuse to give you more deposit money. Then what do you do? Evict them? Take them to small claims court? Yell and scream at them? Threaten to raise their rents to unconscionable levels? Forget it. You'll look toothless and inept trying to collect higher deposits, and you'll spend too much energy trying. Don't undermine your position as a no-nonsense landlord by attempting to accomplish that which none but a Mafia capo with hired guns at his side could accomplish.

Raising the Rent

You'll find a few words about the "right" and "wrong" times to raise rents in chapter 6. Read those words when you have the opportunity. All you need to know now is that one of the right times to raise rents is when you acquire a new property, not necessarily the very day you acquire a new property, mind you, but certainly within a month.

I recommend that you do not raise the rent immediately upon assuming possession. You have enough else to do. If you feel that a raise is definitely warranted when you take over, wait several weeks until you have begun to establish yourself and have become better acquainted with the situation you've acquired or until you are ready with your new rental agreements, whichever comes first. That's the right time to raise the rents when you acquire a new property.

If the former owner raised the rents to realistic levels within the previous twelve months, and the rents now are only slightly below market, make your rent raise coincide with the anniversary date of that last rent raise. Under normal conditions, raising rents any more frequently than

once a year causes tenants too many anxieties.

If you know that the rents are too low, though, regardless of when they were last raised, don't wait any longer than a month to raise them. Not only will you be losing income by delaying, but your tenants will come to think of you as so soft in the financial head that you would probably "pay interest on borrowed time." Don't miss this perfect opportunity to increase the property's income.

What's the right amount to raise the rent when you acquire a new property? That all depends upon the market. There is no rule of thumb. How much you raise it should not be limited to percentages or to amounts.

I can tell you this much. I once raised a tenant's rent by a whopping 50% when I bought a property. I gave him sixty days advance notice of the increase, and he neither screamed, "Rent gouging, rent gouging!" nor did he move. He knew he had been enjoying a good deal from the previous landlord and that I was well justified in raising his rent by 50%. After that, I gave him rent increases every year to keep pace with the market, and he stayed there for years.

Sorting Out the Keys

At the same time you're sorting out all the paperwork for your newly acquired rental property, you ought to take the time to sort out the keys for the property as well. A handful of keys given to you by the previous owner may be so mixed up that they're virtually useless when you're trying to find a particular key to open a particular lock, especially if you're in a hurry.

Almost anything may have happened to mix them up. Tenants may have changed their own locks and neglected to give the previous owners

Notice of Intention to Enter

TO _Mayme Frank_____, Tenant in Possession
_730 Delta St., Apt.3_____
_Dumps, CA   09007_____

YOU ARE HEREBY NOTIFIED that at or about _10:00_ (a.m.) (~~p.m.~~)
on _____May 17_____, _xxxx_, the Owner, Manager, Owner's
agent, or Owner's employees intend to enter the premises
identified above which you hold and occupy. They should need to
stay approximately _ONE_ hour(s).

The purpose for entry is as follows:
_TO REPLACE ELECTRIC OVEN ELEMENT_____
_____

You are not required to be on the premises to provide access.
Whoever comes to enter will first knock and after determining that
no one is available to answer, will enter using a passkey.

If the lock has been changed without proper notice and you
have not given management a duplicate key, a locksmith will be
called upon to open the door and rekey the locks. Your account
will be charged for these services, and you will be provided with
a new key.

This is intended to be a reasonable notice of at least twenty-
four (24) hours.

This Notice was personally served by the Owner/Manager at the
following time: _6:15_ (~~a.m.~~) (p.m.) and date: _May 15, xxxx_ .

_Pauline Felder_____
Owner/Manager

a duplicate copy of the key. A maintenance person may have mislabeled some keys. A set of locks that were installed on one place may now be installed on another, but the installer neglected to change the labels on the landlord's keys. Some may have been misplaced. Others may have been lost for good.

Take all the keys you have for the property with you when you make your maintenance rounds and try to match up each unit with the right key. If you can't make a proper match, ask to borrow the tenant's key for a time so you can have a copy made, and then try the copy when you get back to make sure it works.

Because some tenants insist on being the only ones with keys to their rental dwellings, you may have to approach the matter of obtaining copies with strong resolution. If they are insistent, tell them that they have no right to withhold keys from you, that you, in fact, have every right to have copies of all the keys for all the locks restricting entry to the premises, no matter who installed them. Tell them that you recognize they have a right to privacy and that you have no intention of violating that right. Tell them that you will use the passkey only when you are legally entitled to do so, that is, in four situations—

1) In case of an emergency;
2) In order to make repairs after giving appropriate advance notice;
3) In order to make repairs after obtaining the tenant's consent; or
4) In order to show the property to prospective tenants or buyers after giving appropriate advance notice.

Show them a copy of the Notice of Intention to Enter form if you plan to use it to advise tenants when and why you intend to enter their dwelling. Tell them that you want to be reasonable and cooperative and that you expect them to be the same.

After all this, most people realize that you're being reasonable and they will cooperate. If they flatly refuse, stay calm and leave. Don't fight them. Don't take it upon yourself to change their locks in retaliation. Merely treat them coolly from then on.

Handling the Last Month's Rent

For the various reasons given in chapter 6, I recommend that you do not collect a last month's rent when tenants move in, but you may acquire a property where the previous owners have followed a policy of collecting it all along from every new tenant. Their having collected it may present a problem for you now, and then again it may not.

So long as the last month's rent as turned over to you by the previous owners is the equivalent of the current rent, there is no problem, but a problem arises should you inherit a tenant whose last month's rent has never been increased to the current level. Why? Tenants generally assume that the last month's rent which they originally paid when they moved in ought to suffice as the last month's rent when they actually move out. They're wrong, of course.

Let's say that when they moved in they paid $600 for their first month's rent and another $600 for their last month's rent. Let's say that they stay six years, and during that time their monthly rent has increased to $925. When they give notice that they're going to move, they may think that their last month's rent has been paid in full with the $600 which they paid as "last month's rent" when they moved in. Wrong, wrong, wrong! They actually owe you an extra $325, and you should take the time to explain the facts to them when they give you notice.

If they are adamant about not paying you the extra amount they owe, you're going to be out the money yourself unless you can determine their new address and you want to go to the trouble of taking them to small claims court. There's no time to pursue any other remedy.

You never would have had to consider a remedy like small claims court had the former owners been more aware of what they were doing. With each rent raise, they should have increased the amount earmarked for use as the tenant's last month's rent to the amount of the current rent. Then there would have been no confusion over whether the full last month's rent had been paid or not.

Whenever you take over as a new owner and encounter this situation, you might want to give your new tenants a choice so as to avoid needless conflict. Tell them that they may increase their last month's rent to the equivalent of the current rent or they may convert their last month's rent into a deposit, augmenting the other sums already designated as such. The first choice would require them to part with some funds right away; the second would not. Either choice would eliminate the confusion which is certain to arise later unless the situation is dealt with now.

No matter what you decide to do, no matter what choice your tenants make, be sure that you spell out in writing everything that you've decided. Don't wait until the tenants are ready to move before trying to sort everything out. Anticipate the problem and deal with it now.

Some Last Words

Make the transition of ownership as smooth as possible by showing your human side, while at the same time you are giving every indication that you are businesslike and reasonable and that you sincerely want to improve the operation of the property.

3 Advertising

You don't know them yet and they don't know you yet, but out there somewhere are some very nice people searching for a suitable place to live and a nice landlord like you. They may have placed an ad in the "Rentals Wanted" column of your local newspaper (look there). They may have posted notices in public places (look around). They may be pumping their friends for information (keep your ears open). They may even be out pounding on doors in the neighborhood where they would like to live (open up).

Of course, they may not be doing any of these things because they may not be so enterprising. They also may be able to find vacancies aplenty without having to take any such initiatives. Since you cannot count on every good prospective tenant to find you so easily, you may have to take the initiative yourself when you have a rental dwelling available or coming available. You may have to spread the word out there to reach those nice people you want as your new tenants. In other words, you may have to advertise your rental property.

There are lots of ways to advertise a rental property. You might put the word out to your tenants, friends, and acquaintances that you have a place available for rent. You might let people know with a card on a community bulletin board, a card on a bulletin board at a local business, a card on a bulletin board at a nearby church, an item in the employee newsletter where you work, a handbill in local circulation, a sign on the premises, an ad in a newspaper, or a listing in a rental guide. You might list your rental with a housing office or a real estate agent. You might even try the newest method for attracting prospective tenants, the Internet, often referred to as the World Wide Web, also known as "WWW" or "the web," for short.

You might try any one or any combination of these methods, but first, whatever you do, stop and take a good look at the exterior appearance of your building. Here's why. No matter how skillful, how costly, or how comprehensive is your advertising campaign, you will never get your place rented to those desirable tenants who are out there looking for you if they are repelled by the exterior of your rental property. Any rental dwelling's foremost "advertisement" is a well-kept, neatly painted exterior which looks so inviting to good prospective tenants that they will take the time to inspect the inside. That's a lesson I had to learn from experience. It's a lesson I will never forget.

Once, shortly after my wife and I had purchased a fixer-upper sixplex with two vacancies, we prepared one of the apartments for rent, advertised it in the local daily newspaper, and found that we couldn't get a single good prospect to stop by and inspect the interior of the apartment itself, even after the people had called and promised to show up at an appointed hour. We would notice cars slowing down and necks craning, and then off they'd go, roaring down the street before we could begin to get out there and convince them to stop and take a look at the inside. What a disappointment! We had redecorated this one apartment beautifully, and we were already working on the second, but because the exterior of the building looked so shabby and because everyone who responded to our newspaper ad saw that exterior first, no one except the truly undiscriminating would venture further.

Faced with the dismal prospect of renting only to leather-faced transients chugging through the neighborhood in their battered Ford station wagons, which appeared to levitate on clouds of exhaust smoke and which were towing utility trailers piled high with distressed furniture and even more distressed kids, we reacted in a hurry. We fixed up the exterior. We hadn't planned to do anything to the outside quite so soon, but as soon as we did the make-over, the quality of our prospects improved dramatically.

People do judge a rental dwelling by its exterior. Why not? They intend to live there and invite their friends to visit them there, and they want themselves to be identified with a building which projects the kind of image they have of themselves.

A building with a well-kept exterior advertises to one and all that the living is better there than it could possibly be in a dilapidated building. It shows that the managers have carefully selected good tenants and that everyone living there takes pride in the property.

Remember, whenever you have a vacancy and you're trying to interest prospective tenants in the place by using any of numerous advertising methods to spread the word, you will no doubt attract all kinds of prospective tenants through your advertising, but you won't ever attract good tenants unless you give your building what real estate people call "curb appeal," that is, an attractive appearance on the outside which creates a good first impression.

Got that? Good! Now let's consider what you should be doing to stay out of trouble when you're advertising.

Advertising for Trouble

You're hoping that your rental advertising will attract the attention of people who are looking for a place to rent and that you will find good tenants as a result. Unfortunately, people who are looking for a place to rent aren't the only ones likely to be attracted by your advertising. People who want to determine whether you're practicing any kind of illegal discrimination in your advertising or in your selection process are likely to be attracted as well.

These people have no intention of renting from you. They do have every intention of making you suffer dearly if they can prove that you are practicing illegal discrimination in "thought, word, or deed." They may work for some fair housing agency, or they may work for themselves and earn their living by bringing discrimination claims against landlords. In either case, they are looking for telltale signs that you are discriminating against children or American Indians or Jehovah's Witnesses or the handicapped or any other protected group. They are also looking for telltale signs that you favor certain protected groups over others.

If they conclude that you are discriminating illegally, they will file a claim against you with HUD or with some other government agency and demand that you pay them some money to settle it. If you refuse to pay and they refuse to drop their claim, they will get all the free investigative and legal assistance they need to help them prove their case. You will have to hire assistance and pay for it out of your own pocket, and if the claimants can prove that you were indeed discriminating, you will have to pay the claim and the penalties out of your own pocket as well. Your insurance company won't help you at all unless you have purchased a special policy to protect yourself from such claims.

Because your advertising is the first indicator of your rental policies and because it is the first thing to attract the "discrimination police" or the "discrimination opportunists," be very careful what you say when you advertise and be very careful how you say it.

A statement in your advertising like this—"adult nonsmoker preferred"—would be advertising for trouble. The word "adult" would be taken as evidence that you are discriminating against children. The word "nonsmoker" is all right to use in your advertising because smokers are not in a protected category.

Stating that your rental dwelling is—"close to the Jewish synagogue"—would be advertising for trouble regardless of whether you meant merely to help people determine the dwelling's location with the synagogue reference. Some people would say that your use of the words "Jewish synagogue" in your advertising shows that you prefer Jews over Roman Catholics, Moslems, Buddhists, and fundamentalist Christians.

Be careful in your advertising, and do not suppose that you will be able to fend off any discrimination-in-advertising claim brought against you because you made some innocent mistake and didn't know any better. Government agencies charged with the responsibility of enforcing fair housing laws presume that you know what you're doing and that what you're doing is by design. As far as they're concerned, that's a given. They are deadly serious in their efforts to root out illegal discrimination in housing, and they will not absolve you of any wrongdoing merely because you say that you were confused or uninformed or careless and that you would never think of discriminating illegally and that you will never again do what you did unknowingly to get yourself into trouble. Forget the pleading on bended knee. It won't do you any good. If your advertising signaled some kind of illegal discrimination on your part and you were accused of discriminating illegally, you will have to pay the consequences.

You can avoid trouble in your advertising by concentrating on the dwelling itself. Describe it and trumpet its amenities when you advertise. Make no reference whatsoever to the type of tenant you're looking for. You're looking for good tenants. You're looking for tenants who are clean, who have regard for their neighbors, who have a good track record as tenants, and who pay their rent on time. That's all. Make no mention of your preference for tenants of a certain age. Make no mention of the dwelling's restrictions for the handicapped which might be construed as an ill-concealed effort to discriminate against people who have that handicap. Make no mention of its proximity to a certain landmark which might be construed as your preference toward tenants who have a special interest in that landmark.

Play your advertising straight, and you'll stay out of trouble.

With this stern caution out of the way, let's go on to what people normally think of nowadays when they think of advertising vacant rental properties.

Advertising Methods

Here are the nine advertising methods most commonly used today by do-it-yourself landlords, together with some of the advantages and disadvantages of each, and a listing of the various factors affecting the decision to choose one method over another, all of which may assist you first in selecting the best advertising methods for your rental property and then in making them work well for you.

■ **Word of Mouth**—Existing tenants in your multiple-family dwellings have as much of an interest in whom you select to be their new neighbors as you do, perhaps more. That rental building of yours may be your business, but, after all, it's their home twenty-four hours a day, and you can't blame them for wanting to have compatible neighbors.

No matter who they are, what they do for a living, or where they live, above all, your tenants want to feel safe and secure where they live, and they hope that you will select new neighbors for them who will assure their safety and security, not jeopardize it. They might even hope that their new neighbors would be pleasant, accommodating people with a cup of milk or a bottle of brew handy when they run out, if that's not too much to ask.

Because of this common interest in securing good new tenants that you and your existing tenants share (neighbors around a rented single-family dwelling share this same common interest and should be included in any word-of-mouth advertising you do, too), you are wise to advise them of any impending vacancy as soon as you know about it, and, if warranted, even to offer them a finder's fee of, say, fifty or a hundred dollars for their efforts in helping to find the new tenants.

You should include all of your tenants in your word-of-mouth advertising campaign so that none of them can accuse you of favoritism or discrimination. Much as you might want to exclude your marginal tenants, remember that they are precisely the ones who will try to find some reason to sue you. Don't give them cause. Besides, they seldom respond to these offers anyway, so you have more to lose by excluding them than you do by including them

If you do elect to offer a finder's fee, forestall any misunderstandings over your obligation to pay by insisting that the finders accompany those whom they have interested in the place on the first visit or, at the very least, that they call you and give you the person's name before the first visit. You don't want a tenant claiming a finder's fee unless that tenant was directly responsible for the prospect.

Besides approaching those who, because of where they live, will be most affected by the selection of the new tenants, approach others who meet and talk with the public in the course of doing business in the area, people such as Avon ladies, barbers, beauticians, clergy, corner grocers, insurance agents, mail carriers, neighborhood pharmacists, service station managers, motel desk clerks, and apartment house managers. They are certainly in positions to pass the word along.

Whenever you enlist anyone in your word-of-mouth advertising campaign, apprise them of at least these relevant facts about your vacancy—amount of rent, size of building, size of unit, location, and availability, and then give them your business card so they'll know how to get in touch with you when they do find someone. There should be no confusion in these matters.

You may want to consider preparing an informal information sheet to augment what you're telling people about the vacancy. They might have occasion to pass it along to somebody who's interested. It needn't be anything fancy. Something on a half sheet of paper in your neatest handwriting would do fine. In fact, I have found that something which looks informal works better than something formal because people tend to think that the place hasn't been exposed much and that they could be the first person to see it.

No matter who the referral is, even if it's a relative of someone you know well, don't be swayed by the source of the referral. Judge applicants on their own merits, and, by all means, complete the full procedure outlined in the next chapter, "Getting Good Tenants." Sometimes the friends and relatives of finders are not up to your standards for tenants at that particular property, and you may be the only one discriminating enough to understand why you shouldn't rent to them. Make that decision the same way you would make it concerning anyone else who applies to rent from you.

Now what are the advantages and disadvantages of this kind of advertising?

Advantages—inexpensive, targeted, usable anywhere for any kind of rental.

Disadvantages—uncertain, inclined to be slow, time-consuming, awkward if you have to refuse unqualified prospects.

■ **Bulletin Boards**—Just as general stores used to provide community forums around their pickle and cracker barrels years ago, many supermarkets and some other stores provide community bulletin boards as a service to their customers, but the exposure, and hence the efficacy, of bulletin board advertising varies widely. Some boards are prominently located within busy stores where customers can't miss them, while others are almost hidden from view by stacks of merchandise and rarely ever discovered. Some boards are well organized and well maintained by the management, and others are just a jumble of flyers, business cards, 3"x5" announcements, posters, and small lost-and-found items. For best results, select the busiest boards which are within the trading area surrounding your rental. Ask your tenants where these boards are if you don't shop much in the area yourself.

To make your bulletin board rental ad most effective on any bulletin board, whether it be a community board or a more specialized board such as one where you work or where others work (schools, fire departments, bus "barns," county offices, and the like generally have their own bulletin boards for employees and will gladly post your ad if you mail or take it to them) or where people worship in the vicinity of the rental dwelling, take the time to prepare it carefully. Use a 3"x5" card with a large "FOR RENT" at the top; list all the particulars as you would in a newspaper ad; add color or a simple eye-catching design to make it stand out; and date it. Because you are advertising something perishable, a vacancy, the date is important to anyone who is out looking for a rental and happens to see your ad. Therefore, you should try to replace the card every week with one bearing a more current date.

One danger with this kind of advertising is that without your knowing it, your ad card may simply disappear into the hands of someone who is interested in responding but has forgotten to bring paper and pencil. To accommodate these people, you might make a few cuts into the card at the side and put your telephone number on each removable tab so the entire card won't be removed, just bits of it.

Advantages—inexpensive, localized.

Disadvantages—time-consuming to prepare and post, limited in exposure.

■ **Handbills**—Handbills are a time-honored advertising method for a variety of things, and today with transfer lettering, computers, photocopying, and "instant" printing all readily available, you can prepare professional-looking handbills faster and cheaper than ever before, but preparing them isn't everything. You have to distribute them as well. Aye, there's the rub! You have to make certain that they reach the kind of people you're looking for.

When you do put them before the public, you have to make certain that your handbill distribution doesn't cheapen the image of your rental, either. To keep from cheapening your rental, avoid plastering handbills "everywhere." Avoid stapling them to telephone poles and fences, for example, both of which should be left to political messages and lost-pet handbills. And avoid hiring kids to pass them out on street corners. Instead, use handbills primarily to extend and reinforce your word-of-mouth advertising campaign within the community. Give some to the local businesspeople you patronize and ask them to display the handbills by their cash registers or in their store windows. Give some away as reminders to people you know who appear interested

either for themselves or others. And post some on those bulletin boards which allow handbills. You'll be reaching the public you want to reach in ways which won't turn them off.

When you distribute any handbills, keep a list of their locations so that when you do rent your dwelling, you will know exactly where to go to retrieve them. If you leave them hanging about for more than a few weeks, people will begin to wonder what's wrong with this rental that won't rent.

Advantages—relatively inexpensive, localized.

Disadvantages—time-consuming to prepare, distribute, and retrieve; suitable primarily for less expensive rentals; dependent upon your personality and contacts.

■ **The Sign**—You might be surprised by how many people there are who will pick an area where they want to live and then scout that area for vacancies. Believe it or not, more than half of all tenants do it this way, and some of them don't even wait for signs to appear before knocking on doors. When they see any indication that someone is moving, they begin making inquiries about the dwelling's availability. These super-sleuths aren't always around hunting U-Hauls, though. Most people who are looking through a neighborhood for places to rent look for a "For Rent" sign.

The "For Rent" sign you use reveals to the public something about the kind of business you're running and should be consistent with the exterior image of your rental building. A crude, cheap-looking sign indicates a penny-pinching operation run by amateurs, and whereas such a sign will do all the advertising you'll ever need during periods of high occupancy, when everyone becomes a super-sleuth, it's just not good enough during periods when you're competing with everyone else for good tenants.

There's no reason to skimp on a sign purchase anyway, no matter what the vacancy factor in your area happens to be, because, unlike the classified ad, which costs you a few bucks every time it appears, the sign is a onetime expense, and that onetime expense is actually quite reasonable, especially now that sign makers no longer have to be skilled painters to make good-looking signs. Anybody who has a computer with a sign-making program and a computer-controlled vinyl cutter can make a sign today both quickly and cheaply.

A professionally produced sign cost me the same as two newspaper ad insertions and has lasted for years. It's a two-sided 20"x30" sign in three colors on a tan-painted 5/8" exterior-plywood "blank," and it's designed to hang at any of my buildings from a yardarm positioned at right angles to the street so that people passing in either direction can see it readily (the hardware used to attach the sign consists of eye bolts, clevis hooks, and harness snaps). The "1" in the "1 BDR APT" is on the board itself because some of my apartments happen to be one-bedroom units, but this number may be covered over with another number on sheet metal which bolts right to the board. If necessary, a similar provision for changing "unfurnished" to "furnished" could be added. The telephone number on the sign is my own rental properties number, of course, so prospects may call me directly if the manager is unavailable at the site.

Create your own sign design to look as good as your rental units and say whatever you require, and then hire someone to make it for you. You'll like the image this combination projects and so will your discriminating tenants.

Because a sign maker may require a day or two to make a custom sign, order yours before you need it so it'll be ready for use when a vacancy arises and you really need it.

Whereas a sign makes good sense for advertising multi-family dwellings, it may or may not make any sense at all for single-family dwellings. Kids will sometimes mess with the sign. Squatters and vandals will sometimes have their way with the vacant house. Interested parties will sometimes bother the occupants. Moreover, the sign itself will sometimes attract not a single interested party.

To minimize these problems, use a sign on the premises of a rental house only while the soon-to-be-vacant house is still occupied. Locate it out near the street where it's easily visible. Make it similar to a "property for sale" sign in size, appearance, mounting, and height. Include the wording, "Do not disturb occupants," at the bottom of the sign. Used together, even if only on a trial basis, these measures will help make the sign work to attract interest without jeopardizing the condition of the house or the departing tenants' peace and quiet.

Advantages—inexpensive, orthodox, immediate.

Disadvantages—dependent on traffic exposure, inviting to troublemakers when used at vacant single-family dwellings.

■ **Classified Ads**—For some people, classified ads in daily newspapers are their first resort for information when they're looking around for a rental dwelling, and because tenants are so conditioned to consulting the classifieds, no one would begin to question this kind of advertising's effectiveness. Many landlords would question their cost, however, and since they can be expensive, you should make the dollars that you spend on classified ads pay off.

Here's how.

Be certain, first of all, that the people you want to reach are among the paper's readers. There's no reason for you to be paying the higher classified advertising rates charged by a widely circulated daily newspaper when a smaller readership daily will do just as well, assuming that you do have a choice. Look also at special-interest newspapers and periodicals which carry classifieds. They're especially useful for advertising vacation rentals.

Don't overlook the local weekly newspapers or those free shoppers which carry classifieds. Because they are so localized, they frequently draw more responses than dailies, and you'll find that their advertising rates are more reasonable than mass-circulation dailies. If you do plan to advertise in a weekly, though, be certain you know when the deadline for ad copy is, and if you miss it, by all means, don't keep your available rental off the market for a whole week while waiting for the next issue's deadline. Advertise it somewhere else.

Because many people prefer to rent from small-time landlords, avoid the appearance of a big-time operation in your classified advertising. Restrict each ad to a maximum of two vacancies with different addresses or descriptions. One vacancy per ad is preferable, of course. That way you can avoid classification complications if the two properties would normally appear under different headings. You can emphasize the features of each rental, and you also have greater flexibility for canceling the ads when each property is rented.

To write effective ads for rental properties, you don't have to think like a Madison Avenue copywriter. You're not trying to sell ten million sticks of still another underarm deodorant. Those people who are looking for you have a definite need for housing. All you have to do is direct their attention your way so that they will read the ad and respond.

Word your ad succinctly, but make sure it's descriptive and appealing as well. Take a look at these two ads—

> **3-BEDROOM APARTMENT** in Boyle Heights. Wall-to-wall carpets, stove, refrigerator, drapes. Close to transportation and shopping. $550 per month. Deposit required. Available now. For more information, call 123-4567.

> **CLOSE-IN 3-BEDROOM.** Carpets, stove, refrigerator, drapes. $550. 123-4567.

Just look at all the wasted words in the first ad! The second ad conveys in three lines the same message that the first one does in seven.

Because classified ads are arranged under distinct headings, which already tell the readers a few things about the ads appearing there, you do not need to duplicate the same information in words you are paying good money for. The ads above were printed in the "Unfurnished Apartments—Boyle Heights" section of a city paper, and they need not specify any of this information again in the body of the ad. Many of the other wasted words in the first ad express ideas which the reader takes for granted anyway. "Deposit required," "Available now," "For more information." Such expressions are completely unnecessary when you're trying to say as much as you can in as few words as possible and still attract attention.

Besides avoiding unnecessary verbiage, consider carefully the first word or two you plan to use. Think of your ad as a billboard which must catch the reader's eye immediately or be missed completely, and you'll understand the importance of your ad's initial words. Since you can't include a picture of the place in your ad, the descriptive words you use must conjure up the most appealing picture possible. Words like "sparkling," "just painted," "quiet," "superclean," "cozy," "superbig," and "quaint" all create positive, pleasant pictures in readers' minds. They'll want to take a closer look. If your newspaper arranges its ads alphabetically under its various classifications, you may want to make sure that your first word begins with one of the first letters in the alphabet. How about "A-1" or "beautiful"? If you have trouble selecting alluring words appropriate for your own rental, scan the ads in several daily newspapers and you'll find enough good words to last for years. You're not trying to win some prize for creativity in advertising. You're merely trying to fill your vacancies. Don't be afraid to appropriate other people's good ideas and incorporate them into your own ads.

Include in your ad just enough information so you or your manager won't be bothered with lots of calls inquiring where the place is, how much it rents for, and the like. Here are the kinds of things you might want to include if they apply: number of bedrooms, carpets, drapes, laundry hookups, garage, carport, fireplace, dining room, utilities, stove, refrigerator, child OK, adults, pet OK, yard, storage, and pool. Include the size of the building only if it is favorable, that is, if it is relatively small, below five units (some people prefer the community feeling of smaller buildings over the institutional feeling of larger ones). These other items to include are marginal, depending upon the rental area: water, garbage, air conditioning, hardwood floors, and steam heat. Include price, for sure, along with the exact address and your on-site manager's telephone number, if any, followed by your own. An ad with these elements will create a favorable impression and tell readers what they need to know before they call.

Keep your ad readable by using only those abbreviations which are commonly understood in your area. Spell out "bedroom" rather than "BR"; use "kitchen," not "kit"; "dishwasher," not "D/W." Abbreviations commonly understood are A/C, St., Ave., and OK. Aren't they?

Study the way your newspaper charges for its ads. You might find that an ad running only Saturday and Sunday will bring enough responses all during the week while costing you just half as much as an ad running every day, or you might find that an ad running only one day, no matter what day it is, will do the same. Experiment. Your newspaper's classified rate schedule may be such, however, that your ad could run the whole week for slightly more than the cost of shorter insertions. If so, take advantage of these discounted rates, and cancel the ad only when you are certain you have the place rented. Watch also the minimum number of lines, the abbreviations allowed, the size of type used for the first word or first line, and the number of spaces per line. You can always dictate your ad to the ad taker, ask for a quote on that number of lines, and then add or subtract words to suit yourself and your pocketbook.

Here's an ad for placement in an expensive metropolitan daily which has a one-line minimum and allows any and all abbreviations—

> **6 RMS RIV VU**. 123-4567.

This kind of ad is all right for a tight rental market and for those readers who are savvy about all the arcane abbreviations used in rental advertising in big-city newspapers, but just think of all the questions such an ad raises! Why, you could write a play about them!

Here's an attractive ad designed for placement in a community daily with a four-line minimum and a prohibition against abbreviations—

> **QUAINT 2-BEDROOM** in fourplex. Carpets, drapes, stove, refrigerator, carport. By bus. 858 Sweet St. $485. 123-4567; 800-123-4567. www.ourprops.com

For greater advertising "punch" when you have several units for rent at one time and you want to attract all the attention you can get, you may want to increase your advertising budget (think of the increase in terms of its cost per vacant unit rather than as a lump sum; that way you can compare it to your advertising cost when you have only one unit for rent) and devise an ad which will stand out from the rest, one which will draw readers' attention with its cleverness or graphics or both. Large apartment complexes hire advertising agencies to design their ads. You needn't go that far. Look at their ads and come

up with your own ideas. Here are several such ads with punch—

Once you have devised a well-worded ad that suits you and yields a good response, make a copy and keep it on file so you can use it over and over again or at least have a model to follow, and you won't have to waste time making up a new one from scratch each time you advertise.

When your ad first appears in the newspaper, check it out yourself to verify that it's in the proper classification and that it's worded exactly the way you want it to be. Ad takers do make mistakes, you know, and you might find that you're waiting around for calls that never come because your ad was misclassified or had an incorrect telephone number.

After you've verified that the ad is correct and you're still not getting any calls, reassess the ad's other factors and consider making some adjustments.

Advantages—well-exposed, simple, timesaving, orthodox.

Disadvantages—relatively expensive.

■ **Rental Guides**—Rental guides, if available in your area, provide yet another medium for reaching tenants who are searching for new accommodations. These guides, which are nothing more than mimeographed, photocopied, or quick-printed lists of places for rent, tend to flourish mostly in areas with low vacancy factors, where finding just the right place to live is such a tiring, time-consuming task that some weary searchers will pay around $50 for the convenient and detailed listings of rentals which may not otherwise be advertised as available.

The guides may be useful to you, landlord, because they cost you absolutely nothing and because you can be expansive in your praise and specific in your details about your rental. Consequently, you may save time by not having to answer call after call from those who are merely seeking more information. The guides are good for tenants, too, because they are more current and more detailed than newspaper ads tend to be. Before pounding the pavement or telephoning, tenants have a pretty good idea what each listing is like and whether it's still available.

Below you see the kind and extent of information likely to be included in a rental guide listing.

A newspaper ad running every day with all that information would cost half a month's rent!

Remember, though, that rental guide firms earn their only income by selling their listings to tenants. To attract paying customers to their service, they will sometimes place misleading ads in the regular classifieds, offering swanky penthouses at basement rents. To find out where these bargains are, tenants have to buy the guide, and when

---

RENTAL GUIDE
Listing Information Categories

listing date	blinds	cat only
date available	hook-up for laundry	dog only
rental location	machines	caged bird only
cross streets	laundry room	other pets OK/
no. bedrooms	den	negotiable
no. baths	family room	amount of pet deposit
home	fireplace	other restrictions
cottage	wood-burning stove	utilities included:
flat	dining room	water, garbage, gas,
studio	breakfast area	electricity, heat, hot
apartment	basement	water
size of bldg.	pool	rent per month
lower/upper unit	sauna	length of lease
furnished	spa	required/negotiable
unfurnished	garage	first/last month's
gas stove	carport	rent required/
electric stove	off-street parking	negotiable
refrigerator	fenced yard	security deposit
garbage disposer	patio	cleaning deposit
dishwasher	balcony	other deposits/fees
carpets	deck	agent fee
hardwood floors	view	person to contact
drapes	other features	phone number
shades	number of occupants	best time to call

they do, they all too frequently learn that these come-ons have "already been rented." Such flim-flam may have alienated those who learn of your available rental through a guide, and they may be chagrined at having been duped, but there is a way you can give them some preferential treatment. Because this advertising is free to you anyway, even over a long period of time, use a rental guide to advertise an upcoming vacancy several weeks before it's actually available, thereby giving the rental guide customer an exclusive, a genuine advantage over everyone else. That way, everyone profits. Then, if you haven't rented your place as the vacancy date approaches, continue using the rental guide, by all means, but begin supplementing that listing with other advertising as well.

To find out whether rental guides exist in your area, contact your rental housing association, check the Yellow Pages under "Real Estate Rental Service," or scan the classified ads in your local daily newspaper, looking for numerous ads that list bargain rentals all without addresses and all with the same telephone number.

> *Advantages*—inexpensive, timesaving, fully descriptive.
>
> *Disadvantages*—limited in exposure to those willing to pay for the service.

■ **Housing Offices**—Many college campuses and military installations, as well as large public and private employers, maintain their own housing offices to assist their students and staff in finding local housing. These offices are subsidized and hence charge neither the renter nor the landlords who use the service.

Once you have established which of these local housing offices you wish to use, you may use them repeatedly for only the cost of a telephone call, but do remember to call and cancel your listing as soon as you come to terms with a new tenant, so the housing office can keep its records up to date.

> *Advantages*—inexpensive, targeted, simple to use.
>
> *Disadvantages*—slow and inefficient at times.

■ **Real Estate Agents**—Not every real estate agent will help you find a renter, but those who will, generally list themselves in the Yellow Pages under the same classification as rental guides, "Real Estate Rental Service." The range of services they provide in this context varies widely

from simply advertising your vacancy in their window free of charge to advertising it actively in newspapers to fully managing the property, including advertising the vacancy, showing it, and screening the prospective tenants.

Seldom do real estate agents make any money by providing these services. Mostly they are just trying to build a dedicated and obligated clientele who will bring them more lucrative business later when old properties are disposed of and new properties are acquired.

Agree in advance on the exact services your agent will provide, including the kinds of advertising to be used, and agree upon the charges for those services as well. You should have to pay only if your agent secures a renter and only if that renter stays at least six months. Shorter tenancies should entitle you to more services without additional charge. Get the arrangement down on paper.

> *Advantages*—based on commission (no results, no payment), helpful to owners living out of the area.
>
> *Disadvantages*—obligating, expensive in comparison to other kinds of rental advertising.

■ **World Wide Web (Internet)**—With more and more people using the web to search the whole wide world for information, goods, services, people, properties, and pleasure, its potential as an advertising medium is fast becoming realized. As you may have noticed, print and television advertisers have really taken notice of this potential. Many of them are including their website addresses in their advertising, hoping that their customers will visit their websites to learn more about them and what they have to offer.

One major advantage of the web is that anybody can create a web presence for very little time and money. Another is that you can include an almost endless amount of information on your site. You can store it somewhere accessible to everyone for little or nothing, whether you have your own virtual domain or not (all service providers provide web-accessible space as a service for "members"), and you can update the information easily whenever you wish. That updated information is then available immediately to anyone, anywhere in the world, that is, to anyone who has access to the web. The potential of this technological marvel boggles the mind.

You may use the web to advertise a vacancy in

a number of ways today, and surely there will be other ways to advertise vacancies in the future as the web evolves. Here are three possibilities you should know something about: 1) Listing your vacancy on one of the sites set up to expose classified advertising of all kinds (run a search on "classifieds" to find the sites); 2) Listing your vacancy on one of the sites focused primarily on rental housing listings (run a search on "rental housing listings" to find the sites); 3) Creating your own site and putting it up on your Internet service provider's computer.

Let's look at each of these in turn.

1) Unlike your local newspaper's classified ads, web classifieds are completely free. That's right. They're FREE. They're supported by banner advertising. Not only are they free to the person who has something to advertise, they're free to the person who is looking to acquire something, and they're readily accessible to everyone who uses the web.

There are sites devoted exclusively to classified advertising, and there are sites which offer classified advertising as a sideline. Yahoo, the well-known search engine, offers classified advertising as a sideline, but because it's one of the most visited sites on the web, it's one of the best sites of any for classified advertising. Use it.

To get to their rental housing classifieds, go to Yahoo's home page (yahoo.com) and click on the word "Classifieds." Go next to the "Rentals and Roommates" ads for your particular area, and browse through them to see how everything works when a tenant is looking for a place to rent.

Then register with Yahoo (registration is free) and place your ad. It's good for a minimum of thirty days, and you may change it if you wish during that time. You may also submit it again after it expires. You may list many particulars about your vacancy in your Yahoo classified ad. You may even include a photograph of the property and a link to your website, where you may have many more things to show and say about the property.

Listing your vacancy with a Yahoo classified ad does not list it on other classified advertising sites as well. You must go to each site where you want to list your vacancy and enter the appropriate information there to generate another ad.

What other sites should you try? Try "classifieds2000.com," and then try a site which is specific to your area.

Note also that some newspapers, wary of losing a major source of advertising revenue, have developed their own classified advertising websites where they list the ads currently running in their newspapers.

2) Four sites focused on rental housing listings primarily are "apartments.com," "rentals.com," "vacancylist.net" (a service for Rental Housing On Line members), and "vacancy-net.com." Pay them and others a visit to see how they work and see whether you might benefit from using them yourself. Each of them works differently and charges differently.

Once you understand how they work and how they charge, check to see how many listings they have in your area for your type of property. Avoid those which have no listings and those which fail to suggest listings in nearby communities.

3) Creating a website of your own to advertise a vacant rental house may seem like a waste of time at first, but when you consider all that you can say about a house or apartment on your own site and how you can show a floor plan and photographs and provide a map pinpointing its location, you begin to see the possibilities.

Besides, creating a website is not nearly as hard as it used to be when you had to know how to use cryptic HTML codes to do anything at all. Now, if you know how to use a word processor, you can create web pages using a web authoring program like FrontPage, HomePage, PageMill, or WebEasy.

Take a look at the website I created myself using PageMill (Adobe) for a vacation rental my wife and I used to own in San Francisco. After selling this townhouse, I left the website up as an example of what an amateur can do with a web authoring program. The web address is "landlording.com/townhouse." You can do the same for a rental house and then direct prospects to the site for more complete information.

Another example of a site I created myself using WebEasy (ixla) as the web authoring program is "cloud9inns.com" (motels which I have an interest in).

Both of these sites are simple and informative rather than elaborate and flashy. They provide relevant information, including prices, color photos, and maps. The townhouse site even includes a floor plan.

Just because you have a site on the web, though, doesn't mean that millions of people will flock to see it or even that the one tenant you're looking for will see it. You could spend all kinds of time building a beautiful site with your rental property's floor plan, photos, map location, description, and availability information and still never attract anybody to it. Nobody would know it's there.

Don't worry. Your site doesn't have to attract people on its own. It might attract some people, of course, if you index it properly with the web search engines (check out the indexing capabilities of "submit-it.com"), but it doesn't have to be both a billboard on the "information superhighway" and a repository of information to supplement the listing of its availability elsewhere. It ought to be a repository of information primarily, a site which all the rest of your advertising could point to with just a reference to the web address, so that anybody who is interested could find more information, enough to help them determine whether they should arrange to see the dwelling themselves.

In addition to advertising a vacancy, your website can help prospects prequalify themselves because it can include your prequalification questions and even a copy of your rental application, so that by the time the prospects first contact you, they are already well informed and you don't have to waste time on people who need more information before they can determine whether your vacancy fills their needs.

Try one or all of these possibilities to see which one works best for you, and keep looking for other good advertising possibilities on the web as well.

> *Advantages*—available to people anywhere, inexpensive.
> *Disadvantages*—available only to people who have access to the web, somewhat time-consuming initially to set up.

Advertising Factors

Now that you know something about the advertising methods commonly used by landlords and something about the various advantages and disadvantages of each, you might wonder how to select the best methods for advertising your $950-per-month rental house. Should you break with tradition and advertise it with a 30-second TV spot on the six o'clock news? The answer to that question is an obvious "no" because your rental doesn't need that much exposure and because you'd have to sell, or at least mortgage, the property to pay for the ad, but the answer isn't so obvious if you're considering which of the nine methods you should use to advertise your rental house next door. All kinds of factors affect that advertising decision. Here are fourteen of them:

■ **Number of Units**—Is the rental dwelling a house, a fourplex, or a twenty-five unit complex? Use on-site signs at multiple-family dwellings for maximum exposure, but avoid using them at single-family dwellings unless the old tenants are still in possession and agree to cooperate or unless you live nearby and can keep an eye on the place. As a rental house owner, you do not want people trampling the petunias to get a peek in the windows, and you definitely do not want vandals or squatters to suspect that the house may be empty.

■ **Location**—Is it in a high-, medium-, or low-traffic location, that is, Main Street, Middle Road, or Boondocks Lane? Rely upon on-site signs more at high- and medium-traffic locations. If enough people pass by your rental property, a sign might be all the advertising you'll ever need.

■ **Amount of Rent**—Does it rent for a song or an aria, $395 or $3,950? Pull out all the stops to advertise the expensive rental because you stand to lose so much more every day the place is vacant and because it has a much smaller number of potential renters to reach than the $395-a-month rental dwelling has.

■ **Rental's Availability**—Is the rental vacant and available now or have your tenants just informed you at Christmas time that they're moving by Easter? Before your rental becomes vacant, try the less expensive methods.

■ **Areawide Vacancy Factor**—Are vacant rental dwellings scarce or in ample supply? The appearance of outward-bound furniture will suffice for advertising during scarcities, while searchlights and sideshows may be insufficient during high-vacancy periods. Prepare to spend more on advertising and be more creative when the areawide vacancy factor increases. If a major employer leaves the area and tumbleweeds begin to litter the streets, you may need to change more than your advertising. A changeover to allowing pets and encouraging nudists might save you. Then again, you might want to consider advertising in motorcyclists' and pet owners' periodicals. You won't find many other landlords advertising there.

■ **Distance from Management**—Are you managing a rental property seventy miles from where you live or do you live in the building? Find a local contact, perhaps another tenant, a real estate agent, or a next-door neighbor, to take phone calls and show your rental if you live some distance from the property. Few people will dial a number with an unfamiliar prefix unless they have to. Consider getting your own toll-free number.

■ **Effort**—How much effort do you or your manager wish to devote to your advertising campaign? Very little or whatever it takes? Remember that advertising through newspaper classified ads, Web classifieds, rental guides, signs, real estate agents, and housing offices all take less effort than full-scale word-of-mouth, bulletin-board, handbill, and Web site advertising campaigns.

■ **Time of Year**—Is there a seasonal nature to rental accommodations in the area? Vacation and student rentals have obvious seasons, but, surprisingly enough, so do other rental properties. The most active periods for permanent rentals precede the beginning and ending of summer as identified by the Memorial Day and Labor Day holidays. People like to be settled in by then. Advertise during these periods with the less expensive kinds of advertising and add the more expensive kinds only in the final week before Memorial Day or Labor Day.

■ **Targeted Clientele**—Are you looking for little old ladies with Harleys, students with Moog synthesizers, newlyweds with round waterbeds, municipal bus drivers with tabbies, Mother Hubbards with umpteen urchins, or nerds with Internet access? To appeal to a particular clientele, select certain people as contacts, certain housing offices, certain bulletin boards, certain newspapers, or certain Web sites. Colleges and other institutions of higher learning have housing offices which should attract students aplenty in late August and early September. Some senior centers, businesses, churches, and union halls have bulletin boards and news organs which should appeal to the precise type of renter you seek.

■ **Exposure**—Should your advertising reach 1 or 100,000 people? Naturally each of your rental dwellings can accommodate only one living group at a time and you need to find only that one, but you may have to expose your rental to many people in the general population to find that one, especially if it's an expensive rental. Do not pay extra for exposure to people obviously too distant to be interested. Renters, even those who don't live in the area where they plan to locate, consult local sources after deciding where they plan to relocate.

■ **Advertising Availability**—Are rental guides, housing offices, bulletin boards, and real estate agents who list rentals all available in your rental's area? Make some effort to discover all the locally available advertising sources and use those which suit your needs.

■ **Advertising Cost**—How much are you willing to spend? Nothing or whatever it takes? Take full advantage of all the inexpensive advertising available to you: word-of-mouth, bulletin boards, handbills, signs, rental guides, Web classifieds, and housing offices, but weigh the cost of eschewing more expensive advertising with the loss of rent you are sustaining so long as your rental remains unoccupied.

■ **Previous Experience**—Have you had previous good experience with a local newspaper shopper, a particular bulletin board, a certain rental guide, or a cooperative real estate agent? Conduct your own advertising survey by asking those who come to look at your rental how they learned about it, and then continue using whatever works for you. Whenever you notice that the effectiveness of your old reliable methods is diminishing, try others.

■ **Orthodoxy**—Are rental housing seekers accustomed to responding to this particular advertising method? Advertise in ways and places that rental seekers expect you to use so they'll be looking for you there. Whereas skywriting, TV spots, searchlights, and helium air bags will undoubtedly yield some results, the nine methods mentioned in this chapter are more orthodox and will yield more results per dollar than unorthodox methods ever will.

There's nothing wrong with using unorthodox methods, of course, so long as they pay off. One landlady who caters to pets and pet owners advertises her vacancies in the "Pets for Sale" classifieds of all places. She begins her ads with the words "Pets and Pet Owners Wanted." That's not a very orthodox way to advertise, but she claims it works because pet owners read those ads, and it costs no more than placing an ad in the usual "For Rent" classification.

An Application of the Fourteen Factors

Applying the fourteen factors to your own particular vacancy, you might construct a scenario like this.

If your available rental is a three-bedroom house located on Boondocks Lane, if it rents for $950 and is one among several similar houses for rent in the area, if you are willing to spend between $50 and $100 on advertising, if it's around the middle of July, if you live next door to this rental house, if the house is now ready for occupancy, if you have little time yourself to spend on spreading the word, if you know your way around the Internet, then you would be wise to take a three-method approach to advertising the vacancy, place a "For Rent" sign on the property, put a classified ad in your local daily newspaper for one week, and list it in Yahoo's classifieds. If there are no nibbles at all, reconsider very carefully the rent that you are advertising and reword the ad to expand on the best features of the house, but be prepared to have a vacancy for a few weeks until the market becomes especially active again around Labor Day.

Some Last Words

Whichever method of advertising you prefer, whichever you use, be sure you keep word about the availability of your rental dwelling before the public, for if nobody knows it's vacant, it can't possibly get rented. It might as well be off the market altogether. You're not collecting any rent while those fixed expenses of yours continue unabated. Hustle the place. Lace up your black patent leather shoes, wax your mustache, slick down your hair, practice your business card tricks, shell out a few bucks, and get the place rented.

Remember—somewhere out there are some very nice people searching for a suitable place to live and a nice landlord like you. Go all out to help them find you.

4 Getting Good Tenants

Vacancy times are times which try landlords. They're working times, loss-of-revenue times, doubtful times, and if you're a small-time landlord whose every vacancy represents a high percentage of all your rentals, you are likely to be especially anxious to get that vacant rental filled.

Be anxious, but don't be hasty. You want a smooth operation, one which won't continue to be trying when there's no vacancy at all.

The most important factor of all in the smooth operation of rental properties is getting good tenants. If you become adept at this, all your landlording troubles will be little ones, and you may skip the whole of chapter 9, "Dealing With Problem Tenants." How lucky you are, getting to skip a whole chapter! How shrewd you are, knowing enough to "evict" bad applicants in the first place, before they ever have a chance to become your problem tenants! You practice prevention when you should. Good for you! A few minutes of prevention now are worth many hours of cure later.

No matter what procedure you follow for selecting tenants, so long as it's legally nondiscriminatory and it's working well for you, keep at it. No one can argue with success. But if you have reason to doubt your tenant selection procedure, consider making some modifications until you hit upon a successful combination which does work well for you. This chapter may give you some ideas.

The Ten Steps

Just as anyone can pick a horse to bet on in a race, anyone can pick a tenant, but picking winners ain't easy. It requires lots of diligence and patience, as well as a little luck and some good intuition. Fortunately, though, the odds are better for picking good tenants than they are for picking winning horses, and the odds improve geometrically if you follow these ten steps which are arranged here more or less chronologically—

1) Prepare the dwelling for occupancy.
2) Prequalify the prospects.
3) Show the dwelling.
4) Accept and scrutinize applications.
5) Check references and qualify the applicants.
6) Visit applicants' current home.
7) Review your rules, requirements, and policies, and satisfy the federal lead-based paint regulations.
8) Fill out and sign the rental agreement.
9) Request all monies or a hefty deposit.
10) Create a written and photographic record of the dwelling's condition, contents, and tenants.

You may skip every one of these steps except the seventh (the part having to do with lead-based paint) and the ninth if you're remiss about your business, and you might actually get good tenants. Who knows, you just might get lucky! You just might beat the odds. But you might as well be buying a used car from Slick Tawker down at Kurt's Kar Korner without so much as starting the engine or kicking the tires. Sooner or later you'll get a lemon for a tenant, and then you'll learn the hardest way possible that getting rid of a lemon tenant is considerably more difficult than getting rid of a lemon automobile. You can always donate the car to a charity, find some sucker to take it off your hands, sell it to a junkyard for parts, park it where it's sure to be stolen, bury it somewhere, shove it off a cliff, give it to an art school so they can transform it into a work of "art," or charge a buck to let people take a mighty sledgehammer swing at it. The list is endless, and after your lemon car is gone, you can forget all about your car troubles.

Ah, but you cannot dispose of lemon tenants so easily. You can't even get some cheap satisfaction out of pummeling them or, at the very least, depriving them of electricity and running water, much as you'd like to. Once you get lemon tenants, you're stuck with them for some time to come, and when you finally do succeed in getting rid of them, they'll likely leave a few remembrances just so you won't forget them.

Cull out the lemons from among your applicants. Follow the ten steps religiously, steps which any landlord can follow, including you, and you'll never rent to them. Leave the lemon tenants for those unscrupulous landlords you hear and read about. They deserve each other.

These ten steps are hardly what one might call difficult, but they do require time and attention, some of them more than others. Take the time and give them the attention they require, for when you consider the dreadful alternatives to getting good tenants, the time and the attention are well spent indeed.

After any of the seven initial steps, you might choose to reject the prospective tenants, and you shouldn't be afraid to do so. You *are not* obligated to rent an available rental dwelling to the first person who expresses an interest in renting it. You *are* obligated to rent an available rental to the first person who expresses an interest

in renting it *and* also qualifies according to your legally nondiscriminatory standards. There's a big difference. Read on.

You're looking for a good tenant, right? Right! So keep on looking until you are satisfied that you have found an applicant who will be a good tenant for your building. Maybe the first person who wants to rent from you and has the means to rent from you will be a good tenant, and then again maybe not. You never know straightaway. You have to dig through the information available to you to make that determination. Just remember that nobody can force you to rent to a particular person, not the government, not the

applicant's mother, not the mayor of your town, and not the applicant's motorcycle gang. You get to make the selection yourself, and in doing so, you must be very, very discriminating, legally discriminating, of course.

Exercising Discrimination

Be as discriminating as you can possibly be in making your selection, but by all means, do not be discriminating about race, color, religion, sex, handicap, familial status (includes individuals or families with children under 18 years of age and pregnant women), and national origin. Such discrimination is illegal throughout the U.S. That's federal law.

To find answers to your questions about federal discrimination laws, call the local office of the U.S. Department of Housing and Urban Development (HUD). You'll find their number listed in the blue pages of your telephone directory. To order HUD documents, call them at 800.767.7468. You may also keep up to date by checking HUD's website (hud.gov), where you may search through their fair housing documents.

In addition to the federal discrimination criteria we all must follow, some locales have specific laws prohibiting discrimination regarding marital status, sexual orientation, source of income (occupation), personal appearance, political affiliation, place of residence, place of business, matriculation (student status), and family responsibilities. Other regions have less specific but more encompassing antidiscrimination laws which prohibit discrimination in rental housing unless it is based on legitimate business grounds. To find answers to your questions about your state's discrimination laws, call the office of consumer protection or the department of fair employment and housing.

What is left that you may be discriminating about? Quite a bit, believe it or not. You may still be discriminating about the tenant's ability to pay, willingness to pay, past record as a tenant, pets, waterbeds, number of vehicles, type of vehicles (motorcyclists you may not be allowed to discriminate against, but noisy motorcycles are another matter), recommendations, number of cotenants (even though you may not discriminate against children, you may still limit the number of people you will allow to occupy the premises), honesty, attitude (use care with this one; I measure their attitude by whether they laugh, or at least smile, at my stupid jokes), smoking or drinking habits, permanence, noisiness, cleanliness, and the like. In other words, you may be discriminating about any number of things which will affect your business relationship with your tenants.

Although in the areas with the strictest antidiscrimination laws, you may not refuse to rent a two-bedroom apartment to an applicant on the grounds that she is a lesbian who collects welfare, wears black leather hotpants and frizzy pink wigs, solicits tricks at the local tavern, lives with her seven-year-old bastard son and a succession of painted ladyloves, and is an anarchistic student twenty-one years old, you may refuse to rent to her if she smokes cigars, and you rent only to nonsmokers. That's the equivalent of the government's pursuing an underworld character for tax evasion when they don't have enough evidence to nail him on any other charge even though they know he's running illegal gambling, prostitution, toxic-waste-disposal, and drug operations. Refusing to rent to someone who's undesirable on many counts only because she smokes cigars is perfectly legal, and it's perfectly just. There is a legitimate business reason for doing so. Furthermore, you'd have to be totally indifferent to the matter if you couldn't find some reason to refuse to rent to her.

Don't despair about antidiscrimination laws. They mean well. A great many people have been unfairly discriminated against in finding housing only because they were old or HIV-positive or Mormon or black or female or Irish or Jewish or divorced. The laws merely declare that those are no longer valid reasons by themselves to refuse to rent to someone. You may not discriminate arbitrarily. That's all. You should always be able to find a valid legal reason not to rent to those people who are objectionable. Set your own stan-

dards well within the law, and then set about getting good tenants you can work with.

Your standards for a particular two-bedroom rental might look like these—

> *Gross income*—four times rent
> *Income stability*—at least six months with same source of income
> *Assets*—five times rent (bank account and automobile equity)
> *Credit*—established, nothing negative; FICO score of 620 or better
> *Credit cards*—one major card
> *Checking account*—established
> *Rent punctuality*—prompt, never late
> *Pets*—none
> *Waterbed*—one queen-size OK
> *Vehicles*—one auto, no motorcycles louder than an auto
> *Former landlords' recommendations*—good
> *Personal recommendations*—one available (preferably local)
> *Number of tenants*—maximum of four
> *Attitude*—cooperative
> *Smoking*—no
> *Drinking*—moderation (maximum of two drinks daily)
> *Illegal drug usage*—no
> *Permanence*—at least six months in each of last two residences
> *Cleanliness*—average
> *Interest in the dwelling*—average to high (willing to pay more in rent than asked)

Whatever your standards are, put them in writing so that you can prove to anybody that you do not discriminate illegally. You do discriminate legally according to your own well-conceived and equally applied standards. You treat everybody the same way.

Naturally some of the standards you use are relative to a given dwelling, some are relative to you, some are relative to a particular state or county or municipality, and some are relative to commonly accepted rules of thumb. Be reasonable in determining your standards because if they are overly restrictive, you may well find that no one who wants to live in your rental can possibly qualify. For most standards, you will have to determine yourself what is reasonable and what is overly restrictive (see chapter 12 for ideas about accepting pets and waterbeds), but there are some rules of thumb you might want to follow. One of them covers gross income.

For gross income, the commonly accepted rule of thumb is *four times rent*, though some landlords have seen fit to reduce that to three. If an applicant's gross income is less, then you must reject him outright unless you have adopted a policy which you apply to every applicant equally that you will accept applicants whose gross income is less than your standard so long as they come with sterling recommendations from two previous landlords or they come up with a larger deposit, say, an additional $200 (be careful when asking for a larger deposit because you must not exceed the maximum deposit permitted under your state's laws governing deposits; for unfurnished units, it's likely to be two times the monthly rent; for furnished units, three times).

You may also adopt a gross-income policy requiring that *every* adult occupant have a gross income equal to three or four times the rent. After all, tenants' living arrangements, whether sanctified by marriage vows or not, may break up, and you, dear landlord, may get stuck with the one tenant who has no income and can't pay the rent. (You don't have to be this restrictive if you don't wish to be, but you may be this restrictive if you do wish to be.)

Note that if you choose to separate the income of two adults who volunteer the information that they're unmarried, then you must separate the income of couples who volunteer the information that they're married. Likewise, if you combine the income of married couples, you must combine the income of unmarried couples. Apply your standards to one and all alike. That's what antidiscrimination laws require you to do.

Regarding occupancy standards, there used to be a rule of thumb. It was *one fewer than the number of rooms.* A studio or efficiency dwelling (two

rooms) would accommodate one occupant; one bedroom (three rooms), two occupants; two bedrooms (four rooms), three to four occupants; and three bedrooms (five rooms), four to five occupants. Were you to apply that rule of thumb to rentals in most states today, you could be accused of illegal discrimination for your two- and three-bedroom units.

Today there are federal, and in some cases, more restrictive state standards, and you must comply with them. You have no choice. Federal occupancy standards say that you must allow up to two people per bedroom in your rentals. This translates as follows—studio or efficiency dwelling (no bedrooms), one occupant; one bedroom, two occupants; two bedrooms, four occupants; three bedrooms, six occupants; and four bedrooms, eight occupants.

In other words, you must not discriminate against applicants on the basis of the number of people in their living group so long as they do not exceed two people per bedroom. You may rent to a family of three who want to rent a two-bedroom house if you want to, but everything being equal otherwise, you must not give them any preference over a family of four who also want to rent the house. You must treat them exactly the same.

Some states modify the federal occupancy standards somewhat by increasing them slightly. They say that you must allow two people per bedroom plus an additional one. This translates as follows—studio or efficiency dwelling (no bedrooms), one occupant; one bedroom, three occupants; two bedrooms, five occupants; three bedrooms, seven occupants; and four bedrooms, nine occupants

Some landlords fudge on the numbers by decreasing them. Don't, at least not arbitrarily. Decrease them only if you have good reason, say, because your three-bedroom rental house's septic system is sized for only four people and you can prove that additional people would severely strain the system, or because the rooms are small and the fire codes dictate that only three people can safely occupy the house on a square-footage basis. Those are good reasons for decreasing the numbers.

What does all this hullabaloo about discrimination mean to you? It means simply that you cannot be discriminating in certain prejudice-oriented ways when you're selecting tenants, but you can be, and you should be, discriminating in a great many other ways, business-oriented ways, if you wish to protect your property and make it a good investment.

The truth is that you have to be discriminating when you're selecting tenants because you will find that some people are completely incapable of selecting their own living accommodations prudently themselves. They think that a family of five, soon to be six, one dog, one cat, and a pet crocodile will fit comfortably into one of your one-bedroom apartments. You have to instruct them in the folly of their thinking.

The Ten Steps Amplified

Now let's take a closer look at how you can be discriminating in selecting tenants. Let's examine individually each of the ten steps for getting good tenants.

1) Prepare the dwelling for occupancy.

This first step in getting good tenants would appear to be totally unrelated to the overall task, but it is, in fact, just as important to getting good tenants as their payment of rent is to their staying on as tenants.

Your job at this point is to fix up, paint up, clean up, and dress up your rental dwelling to make it attractive enough so that a good prospect will want to rent it from you for the rent you want to charge. You will always attract the best tenants and get the most rent from that dwelling which shows well and smells good. (Give vacating tenants an incentive to clean well and hope that they do, but don't bank on it.)

Even so, don't become overly concerned about sanitation or perfection when you are preparing a dwelling for occupancy. Remember that you are appealing primarily to the senses of sight and smell. In this context, clean the appliances, stove hood, and cabinets (under the sink, too) both inside and out. Remove all nonadhesive shelf paper. Clean the showers, tubs, toilets, sinks, mirrors, and medicine cabinets (inside as well). Dust the ceilings (for cobwebs), the baseboards, window sills, miniblinds, and closet shelving. Wash the kitchen and bathroom walls, and spot-clean the walls in other rooms. Dry-clean the draperies. Wash the light fixtures and windows inside and out. Vacuum and deep-clean the carpets. Scrub and wax the floors. Sweep the entry, patio, storage enclosure, and garage. Remove all personal belongings of the previous tenants (including clothes hangers and cleaning supplies). Finally, dispose of all trash.

One landlady I know who takes this business very seriously took her preparation cues from hotels and motels. She asked herself how they manage to make their rooms appear clean every day when they can't possibly clean every square inch of those rooms every day. She noticed that motels spend extra effort in the bathroom, wrapping the glasses, supplying new bars of soap, sanitizing the toilet bowl, wrapping a paper band around the seat, folding the next sheet on the toilet paper roll carefully, and sometimes providing shower caps and shampoo. Now she prepares her rentals in somewhat the same fashion. She bought a supply of those paper bands, and she wraps one around each toilet seat after it's been thoroughly cleaned. She leaves a new dispenser of liquid soap at the sink, and she puts an unwrapped roll of toilet paper in the paper holder. Needless to say, the people who look at her vacancies are impressed. Then, on the day her new tenants move in, she leaves a small box of chocolate-covered mints on the kitchen counter with a welcome note.

Do a good job of cleaning overall, but do not do such a good job that you get callouses on your knees from crawling all over the floors scrubbing them laboriously and polishing them to a mirrorlike finish. Do not work your fingers to the bone by scrubbing the tile grout with a toothbrush. That's wasted effort.

Remember this one very important truism about each of your rentals—

You, landlord, are not going to live there.

Remind yourself. Remind your partner. Say it out loud now and then while you're cleaning, "I am not going to live here." Do not give way to excessive cleaning. Clean your rentals well, but don't try to clean them any better than a housekeeper would clean a room in a motel which is part of a nationwide chain.

Your new tenants may be as fastidious about housekeeping as Felix Unger is in *The Odd Couple*, and if they are, they will probably clean everything again themselves anyway. Your thorough housecleaning efforts are a waste of time and energy in that case, and they're definitely a waste if your new tenant is an Oscar Madison.

In addition to preparing the place for occupancy by cleaning, perfume it as well. No, not with Chanel No. 5. That's for people, not dwellings. Perfume the place by cleaning the kitchen and bathroom with a lemon or pine-oil scented cleaner. Or use a commercial air freshener to make the place smell of honeysuckle, limes, or new-mown hay. Or make it smell of grandma's fresh-baked delights by heating two tablespoons of imitation vanilla extract on the stove. Or allow the new paint odor to dominate the air. Any *one* of these smelly procedures is sufficient to make the place smell clean and fresh. Be careful about mixing them.

The sense of smell is very important. Those who study such things say that smell revives memories more than any of our other senses. Remember the wonderful aroma of homemade cookies and all the pleasant memories that go along with them? Who doesn't! Well, those boutique cookie shops which have become successful in shopping malls around the country are trading on those very memories and, of course, on your weakened sales resistance once your salivary glands start reacting to the fresh-baked-cookie aromas. That's how they snag you as a customer. Good odors conjure up pleasant memories and help to sell products.

Likewise, they can help to rent residences. If prospective tenants are charmed by agreeable odors of one kind or another, they become more willing to pay good rent for a place. You know what new cars smell like, don't you? Can you imagine someone ordering a new car to be delivered without that new car smell? Give your vacant rental dwelling a fresh, clean, pleasing odor, too.

2) Prequalify the prospects.

Begin learning whether prospects are qualified to rent from you when you make your first contact with them. You simply cannot assume that everybody who inquires about your vacancy is qualified, and you don't want to waste their time or yours if they aren't.

You begin learning whether they're qualified in this second step. Based upon your tenant standards, whatever they happen to be, it consists of certain determinations which you can make rather quickly, even over the telephone. It will save you untold time, gasoline, shoe leather, and grief. This step serves to eliminate those people who are interested in renting from you but fail to qualify. Here you are prequalifying them before you ever take the time to show them the rental or have them fill out an application, so you won't be exasperated to learn late in the process that they really didn't qualify to rent from you in the first place.

You can't very well determine at this stage whether someone will qualify according to all of your tenant standards. That questioning would be much too tedious to go into right now, and besides, it wouldn't yield useful information anyway (certain things you must observe in people, not ask about; can you imagine asking callers straightaway about their cleanliness?), but you can certainly select a few important items and prequalify callers with them, devising questions suitable for getting truthful answers.

To avoid wasted time, wasted effort, and possible embarrassment later on, then, you might prequalify prospects when you first speak with them by making these eight determinations about them and their circumstances—

1) When they are ready to move in;
2) Whether they have enough money to move in;
3) Whether they have good credit;
4) Whether they have ever been evicted or asked to move out;
5) Whether the number of people who intend to live there falls within your limits;
6) Whether they smoke;
7) Whether they have pets; and
8) Whether they have a waterbed.

If the prospects are not ready to move in yet and your dwelling is ready for immediate occupancy, look for someone else. If you require $735 to move in and they have only $400 to commit right now, why talk to them; look further. If they admit to having bad credit, tell them they'll have to rent elsewhere. If they admit to having been evicted before, thank them for being honest and tell them you aren't in the business of rehabilitating problem tenants. If they are a family of four, and you're looking for a maximum of three people, tell them so. If they smoke, and you don't want smoke to permeate the place, tell them you don't rent to smokers. If they have a cat and a canary, and you don't take pets, say the magic words, "Sorry, no pets!" If they have a huge heart-shaped waterbed for themselves and a twin-sized waterbed for their four-year old, and you have decided against allowing any liquid-filled furniture in this house you inherited from your favorite uncle, well, then, that's that.

Unless you have a lie detector handy, though, establishing the truth regarding these particulars may take some doing. Certain people will tell you exactly what they think you want to hear. They will move in whenever you want; they have $2,000 in cash to cover move-in costs, wonderful credit, no evictions on their record, nobody else who lives with them other than a spouse, no smoking habits, no pets, and no waterbed, and besides, they will tell you with a smile in their voice, "We're nice religious people. We live by the Golden Rule." That's what they may say, but where does the truth lie? Who knows?

How do you get at the truth? At this stage, without being omniscient, all you can do is phrase your questions whenever possible in such a way that you give few clues to the answers you're looking for.

Because people seldom dissemble in answering questions about their readiness to move, their ability to pay the move-in costs, and their credit, you can be pretty direct about the first three questions. State whether the place is available now or will be in two weeks, and ask whether the prospects' moving plans might coincide with that time frame. State flatly what sum you require to be paid before they move in so much as a bag of groceries or a kitchen chair, and ask them whether this is within their means right now. Tell them you run a credit check on every applicant, and ask them whether theirs is good.

The next four questions are the ones which generally involve the most deceit—tenant history, people, smoking, and pets. These are the ones to be most wary about.

To learn something approaching the truth about their tenant history, simply ask the prospects disarmingly what kind of recommendations their current and previous landlords will give them when you call.

Then ask them how many people will be living with them. Do not say, "We allow only three people to live in this rental. How many people will be living with you?" That approach will surely elicit this response, "There are only three of us."

After establishing that the prospects fall within your definition of acceptable numbers, ask them point blank, "Does anyone in your household smoke?"

Likewise, ask them, "How many pets do you have?" Don't reveal your policies on smoking and pets before asking the questions, of course, or you will likely be able to predict their answers. Reveal your policies only after you hear their answers.

Finally, now that you have prequalified the prospects on seven counts, and they pass, ask whether they plan to keep a waterbed in the place they are seeking to rent. Again, reveal your policy only after you hear their answer.

With all of these matters settled to your mutual satisfaction, invite them to take a look at the place. They're prequalified.

3) Show the dwelling.

This step requires no special talent or skills, but you might wisely employ a number of ideas to make showing the dwelling less time-consuming, less troublesome, and more productive.

✔ After you have prequalified those who phone and express an interest in renting your available dwelling, answer whatever questions they may have while they're still on the phone, and explain exactly where the rental is located so they aren't astounded by the neighborhood if it's not quite what they'd expected. Also, give them clearly understandable directions so they won't lose their way trying to get there.

✔ If you're one of those much maligned absentee landlords who rents out a house or an apartment complex which is located at some distance from where you live or work, you'll want to refrain from making repeated trips there. Do so by encouraging people to drive by the building first and then call back for an appointment to see the inside, or do so by holding an "open house" for showing your vacancy at designated hours (should be one to two hours long) which are convenient for most people. Tell those whom you have prequalified just when you intend to hold this open house and then make certain that someone is there to show the place. You will save yourself

Rental Application for (address) 456 Sweet Street

Name Richard Renter Home Phone 555-1975 Work Phone 555-1996

Social Sec. No. 432-10-6789 Drivers License No. A0987677 Date of Birth 4/13/XX

Present Address 1510 Morton Ave

How long at this address? 10 mo. Rent $640 Reason for moving want to be closer to work

Owner/Manager Muretta Norby   Phone 555-3210

Previous Address 1 Bunn Circle, Apt. 105

How long at this address? 2yrs. Rent $480 Reason for moving got married, apt. too small

Owner/Manager Betty Hardison, owner   Phone 555-1001

Name and relationship of every person to live with you, even if only temporarily (include ages of minors): Rose Renter, wife

Any pets? NO Describe —   Waterbed? YES

Present Occupation operator Employer Bi-Lift   Phone 123-4440

How long with this employer? 2½ yrs. Supervisor George Judge Phone 123-4444

Previous Occupation operator Employer Upstate Lifts Phone (200) 111-2160

How long with this employer? 6 yrs. Supervisor Herb Frank Phone (200) 111-2160

Current Gross Income Per Month (before deductions) $ 2150

List sources and amounts of other income NONE

Amount of alimony and/or child support you receive $ NONE or pay $ NONE

Savings Account: Bank Safe Savings Branch Downtown Account Number 111-11-0011

Checking Account: Bank Big Bank Branch MAIN Account Number 43-09586-3

Major Credit Card NONE Account Number — Average Balance — Expires —

Credit Reference A-Z Furniture Account Number R-1345 Balance Owed 650 Monthly Payment 85

Credit Reference — Account Number — Balance Owed — Monthly Payment —

HAVE YOU ever filed bankruptcy? NO ever been evicted? NO ever been convicted of a felony? NO

Vehicle(s) Make(s) VW Model(s) Golf Year(s) 1995 License(s) ZZZ0013

Personal Reference Delwyn Levno Address 101 Beaver, Littletown Phone 555-1933

Contact in Emergency Glenda Renter Address 400-15 ST., Honest, CA 09666 Phone (200) 185-3061

I declare that the statements above are true and correct. I authorize verification of my references and credit as they relate to my tenancy and to future rent collections.

Date 1/6/XX Signed Richard Renter

Verified: SSN ✓ DL/ID ✓ CurTenancy ✓ Prev ✓ Credit ✓ Inc ✓ PersRefs ✓ By db many wasted trips and hours of waiting around for a specific caller who may or may not even bother to show up.

✔ While holding an open house may be a real convenience to the absentee landlord, it has another advantage which even the landlord or manager who lives on the premises should bear in mind. It tends to stimulate greater interest. When several people show up and express an interest in renting a particular place, each one feels all the more interested just because someone else wants it. The open house creates a kind of "auction atmosphere" which stirs the bidders' blood and puts you, the "auctioneer," in command. You needn't negotiate rent and conditions, as some crafty tenants would have you do. You are in a position to dictate rent and conditions. You are in a position to be courted. You may even have somebody tell you they like the place so much that they'll pay more for it than what you're asking.

✔ If you do make appointments to show the dwelling to specific callers, get their names and telephone numbers. They then will feel a little more responsible about showing up, and you will be able to call them back in case something happens and you can't keep the appointments yourself.

✔ Never rent out a dwelling sight unseen. Some prospective tenants will tell you over the phone that they want to rent your place without even looking at it. If they're that eager, don't insist that they see it, but don't rent it to them either. Something's sure to be suspect if they're that undiscriminating.

✔ Never rent to any person sight unseen. Be wary of the prospective tenant who does not appear in person but is being represented by somebody else, say, a social worker, parent, friend, or minister. The prospective tenant could be a soon-to-be-released felon or a mental incompetent who might be a real danger to your other tenants and to you. Insist that the prospective tenant appear in person. After all, should this person become your tenant, you will have to deal with him in person then. That nice social worker or minister isn't going to be available all the time as a go-between to make sure that everything goes smoothly during the tenancy.

✔ If a dwelling which will soon be available is still occupied and you know it's in such poor condition that it won't show well, don't show it. Instead, show another one which is similar and is occupied by a clean, cooperative tenant. Before you do, however, be absolutely certain that the prospects are well qualified and very interested in renting from you. In other words, you should feel reasonably certain that the prospects are not really well dressed burglars casing the joint.

✔ If possible, accompany your prospects on their tour of the premises rather than handing them a key and telling them to look everything over by themselves. Consider the showing as something of an opportunity to talk with the prospects and size them up. If you can't accompany them on their tour, take precautions about getting the key back promptly. Look at the Property Viewing & Keys Agreement in chapter 10 and consider using it. It's designed specifically for the absentee landlord who allows prospects to take self-guided tours of vacant rental houses.

✔ Ask every prospect to produce a government-issued ID before you show a dwelling. Log the ID on a list and lock it and the ID up somewhere (in your office, if it's on the premises, or in your car) during the showing. Return it after you show the dwelling. This precaution assures you of the prospect's correct identity right from the start, and it serves as notice that the prospect must behave in order to get his license back. His anonymity will not protect him if he robs or assaults you.

✔ If you have any reason at all to suspect that a prospect is more interested in robbing or assaulting you than in seeing the vacancy you have available, do not show the dwelling alone. Wait until somebody is available to accompany you. At the very least, carry some sort of personal protection device such as a personal alarm or pepper spray, and be prepared to use it.

✔ Do not "steer" prospects to a particular dwelling when you have several available. You might think that the small family of four who answered your ad for a three-bedroom apartment ought not to see the two-bedroom you also have available because it shares a common wall with two quiet spinsters, but you ought to show it to them anyway. You can be accused of discriminating against families if you don't show it to them and you do show it to a childless couple who appear right after the family leaves.

RENTAL APPLICATION INSTRUCTIONS

We appreciate your interest in the rental dwelling we currently have available. Because we want to rent this dwelling to people who are considerate of their neighbors, clean in their living habits, capable of paying the rent, and prompt in paying their bills, we use a rental application to help us determine whether our applicants meet these qualifications.

In order for you to rent from us, you must complete a rental application. We want you to know how to complete the application we use, and we also want you to know what our company does with your application.

When filling out the application, put something in every blank, even if you have to put "None" or "N.A." in some blanks. Try to write so that your entries fit in the spaces provided. If they don't, continue them on the back side. Take your time and look up any information called for on the application which you're at all uncertain about. Don't guess.

Make sure that you read the declaration just above the signature line and agree to it before you sign your name to the application. It states that the information on your application is true and correct, and it authorizes us to verify your references and your credit as they relate to your tenancy now and to your paying rent in the future.

When you have completed your application, read it over carefully to make sure that it is accurate, complete, and legible. Look especially for misspellings and transposed numbers.

Once we receive your application, we verify as much of it as we can. If you look at the last line on the application itself, you will notice all of the things we verify. We verify your Social Security number (SSN), your driver's license (DL) or personal identification number (ID), your current tenancy (CurTenancy), your previous tenancy (Prev), your credit (Credit), your income (Inc), and your personal references (PersRefs). When we have verified each of these items, we put a check mark next to its abbreviation.

We verify this information in a variety of ways. We look at your Social Security card or some other evidence of your Social Security number. We look at your actual driver's license or some other official picture identification which you use whenever you cash a check. We call your current landlord or manager to ask whether the information you put on your application is correct about how long you've been at your current address, how much you've been paying in rent, and why you are moving. Then we call your previous landlord or manager and ask the same questions about your previous tenancy.

At the same time that we order a credit report, we also order an eviction report and a bad check report. The credit report tells us whether you pay your bills on time. The eviction report tells us whether you have ever been evicted and why. The bad check report tells us whether you write bad checks.

Next, we call whoever can verify your source of income to determine how much you generally receive from that source every month and how long you have been receiving it.

Finally, we call your personal references to verify that they know you and that we have their correct addresses and phone numbers so that we can contact them should anything happen to you.

That's the procedure we follow when we check applications.

Now, if you suspect we might discover a "skeleton in your closet" when we check your application and you want to tell us about it before we go to all the trouble of checking you out, please feel free to do so. We'd be glad to talk with you about it. Otherwise, we will expect no surprises when we're checking you out and hope that we will soon be doing business together as landlord and tenant.

✔ When you show prospects through any dwelling, you'll want to make a little sales pitch. Point out all the features of the place, including the special features of the building and the neighborhood. Be honest, though. Don't say it's quiet in the evening when, in fact, right next door there's a fundamentalist church which rattles and rolls to loud gospel music every Tuesday, Friday, and Sunday night. If you ignore the drawbacks, you may have to contend all over again with another vacancy very soon. The prospective tenants have a right to know what the place is really like at all hours, and you should tell them. Of course, you may want to speak of the drawbacks as if they were advantages: "One thing I really like about this place is the great gospel music they play next door three evenings a week. It's such a joyful sound, don't you think?"

✔ The first impressions you have of prospects when you're showing them around may tell you all you need to know to reject them outright, but there's no need to alienate them by telling them right now. Do what small claims court judges do when they don't want to anger a losing party in court, take the matter "under submission." This simply means that to avoid fistfights in the corridors, the judge will render his decision at a later time even though he may already have made the decision.

✔ Offer rental applications and instructions for completing the applications to all who look at the place, and tell them that you check the applications thoroughly. Applications are your best defense against discrimination lawsuits because they show that you are methodical rather than arbitrary in tenant selection.

4) Accept and scrutinize applications.

Your rental application should be simple to read, simple to follow, brief, and yet thorough. You don't need applicants' entire life histories to help you decide whether to rent to them. You might satisfy your idle curiosity by reading those life histories, but they likely wouldn't be any more useful to you in determining whether you ought to rent to somebody than would the information contained in a simple one-page application.

The application you use should have sections with information on the applicant's current and previous tenancies, current and previous jobs, fellow occupants, pets, financial status, vehicles, Social Security number, date of birth, and driver's license. If this information is complete, you will have plenty to consider and check in the next step.

Notice that among other things, the application included here asks for the name of a person to contact in an emergency. This information is of no real use now, when you're still trying to decide whether an applicant would make a good tenant. Yet, it may prove vital later when the applicant has become your tenant, and he disappears without a trace, as some are wont to do, fails to show up to pay rent, or dies on the property. Such things do happen, you know, and you ought to be prepared for them when they do.

Along with the rental application, you should give every applicant a sheet of instructions which tells them how to fill out the application and what you do with the information once you get it. The form I use for this purpose also includes a paragraph which puts the dishonest applicant on full alert that you check applications thoroughly and do not look kindly on any attempt to lie or cover up negative information. It asks applicants to reveal any negative information in advance of your checking out their application so that you may discuss whether it is important enough to disqualify them from renting the dwelling you have available.

Dishonest applicants are betting that you won't check out their applications at all, that you'll be so charmed by their broad smiles and winning ways when you first meet them that you will rent to them without bothering to check them out. They're betting that you're a fool, that you will take them at face value and rent to them simply because they seem like such nice people. You cannot afford to take that bet. It's too risky.

It's not the least bit risky for you to ask all of your applicants to be upfront with you about the skeletons in their closets. Ask them and see what happens. If they say nothing, you go ahead and check them out. If they say something and it's enough to disqualify them, you needn't bother checking them out. You've saved yourself time and money.

As mentioned before, because landlords may no longer refuse to rent to someone on the basis of familial status, you should ask every adult who expects to occupy your rental dwelling to fill out an application. Husbands and wives should fill out separate applications, and adult roommates, regardless of their relationship to one another,

Deposit Receipt & Agreement

RECEIVED FROM ___Richard Renter_____, Applicant,

the sum of _____Two hundred fifty dollars_____ $ _250‾_

for the purpose of verifying information submitted on the application and for holding the rental dwelling commonly known as

___456 Sweet Street_____

until _____January 10, XXXX_____ or such earlier time as the undersigned Owner/Manager is able to complete a verification of the information submitted on Applicant's rental application.

This dwelling will be rented to the Applicant provided that:

    1) The Applicant's rental application and credit history satisfy the Owner/Manager;

    2) Within 24 hours of being approved, the Applicant signs the rental agreement offered by the Owner/Manager, a copy of which the Applicant has received, read, and approved; and

    3) Within 24 hours of being approved, the Applicant pays all of the sums necessary to move in.

Should the Applicant be approved to rent this dwelling and meet all three conditions above, all monies received will be refunded except for the sum of $___30⁰⁰___, used to process Applicant's rental application, here itemized as follows:

    1) Cost to obtain credit report, eviction report, and/or other screening reports $___20⁰⁰___

    2) Cost to process and verify information (time and associated costs) $___10⁰⁰___

Should the Applicant be approved to rent this dwelling and not do so, none of the monies received will be refunded.

Should the Applicant not be approved to rent this dwelling, the Owner/Manager will refund all monies received except for the sum used to process Applicant's rental application (itemized above).

Date: ___January 7, XXXX___   ___Leslie Landlady___
Time: _____1 PM_____   Owner/Manager

                     ___Richard Renter___
                             Applicant

                             Applicant

should each fill out an application as well. Check out that live-in boyfriend or girlfriend, by all means, whenever one appears on the scene. You never know when the primary tenant might get itchy feet, move out, and leave you with somebody you know nothing about and wouldn't have rented to in the first place. You'll use a good many more applications this way, but you'll be well protected against accusations of unfair discrimination and you'll have plenty of good information for later reference.

Some landlords require applicants to submit deposits along with their rental applications. Some don't. In the old days, when I didn't have to prove to anybody how fair I was in selecting my tenants, I used to be among the latter. Now I'm among the former. I do require applicants to submit deposits along with their rental applications because deposits separate the shoppers and the testers from the serious applicants, and they help me prove that I treat everybody the same way.

You don't want to bother with anybody except those who are serious about renting from you, and there's only one way to tell the difference. Require them to put up a deposit with their application.

The deposit commitment between you and the applicant is temporary, to be sure, and it can be either exclusive or nonexclusive. Tell the applicants which it is. Before you accept a deposit, tell the applicants whether you will be accepting several deposits on the same vacant dwelling or only one. Be consistent with everybody who is interested in the dwelling. Let them know whether you're asking for their deposit because you're serious about them in particular or whether you're just trying to eliminate those applicants who aren't serious about the place so that you don't waste any time checking applications submitted by people who aren't all that interested.

Whenever you take deposits with applications, give the applicants a receipt which explains exactly what their deposit means. There are two deposit receipt forms given here. Use the one which best approximates your agreement with the applicant.

The amount of deposit you require with an application depends upon what you're trying to do. If you're trying to snag an applicant who has made a good first impression on you, ask for $100 or more to hold the place. If you're trying to eliminate frivolous applicants, ask for $30 or

thereabouts to pay for your costs in checking the application (your state may have a law stating a maximum amount you may keep for running a credit check, whether you rent to the applicant or not).

As for filling out the rental applications, you have the option of asking the applicants the questions verbally and writing the answers on their applications yourself, or you may let the applicants do it all by themselves. Both options have advantages. Asking the questions verbally gives you the opportunity to ask certain pertinent questions which don't appear on the application, open-ended questions which allow them to reveal something about themselves. On the other hand, letting them fill out the application saves you time and gives you some idea how neat and thorough they are.

When you get the completed applications, look them over quickly for legibility and completion. Look to see whether the information listed can be checked. You can't check out a Judy who lives on Lee Lane in Peach Creek if you don't have Judy's phone number or her last name or her exact address.

Make sure that the applications are signed, too. Applicants' signatures authorize you to conduct credit checks. Without those signatures, you're invading the applicants' right to privacy if you begin snooping into their affairs, and you may be fined for doing so. Remember that credit bureaus keep track of everyone who inquires about someone's credit. You will be found out if you make unauthorized inquiries. Do not make them.

Tell the applicants once more that you're going to be checking them out thoroughly. You're going to be calling their landlords and their employers, and you're going to be running a credit check, ordering an eviction report, and inquiring about their bad checks. Ask them again whether there's anything negative which might show up when you're checking them out because now would be the time for them to give you their side of the story. You'd be surprised how many negative things some people will volunteer to tell you about themselves which you never would have uncovered in your snooping. Make careful note of this information on the back of their application, and take it into consideration when you make your decisions. You may find from what they tell you about themselves that you don't need to check them out any further because they

Credit Check & Screening Receipt

RECEIVED FROM _____*Richard Renter*_____, Applicant,

the sum of _____*thirty dollars*_____ $__*30ºº*__

for the purpose of verifying the information submitted on the
application to rent that dwelling commonly known as

_____*456 Sweet Street*_____.

Sum received will be used as follows:
1) Cost to obtain credit report, eviction $__*20ºº*__
   report, and/or other screening reports

2) Cost to process and verify information $__*10ºº*__
   (time and associated costs)

It is understood that this sum received is in no way to be considered
a deposit to hold the dwelling. The Owner/Manager may take other
applications to rent the dwelling and indeed may already have done
so.

The sum received is refundable only if the owner/manager selects
another applicant to rent the dwelling BEFORE checking Applicant's
credit history. Otherwise, this sum is entirely non-refundable.

Date:__*January 6, xxxx*__   _____*Leslie Landlady*_____
Time:__*5 P.M.*__   Owner/Manager

                                              _____*Richard Renter*_____
                                                      Applicant

                                              _____
                                                      Applicant

have eliminated themselves from consideration.

Then ask to see their driver's licenses and credit cards for identification. Write down their date of birth as it appears on their driver's license. You will need it to run a credit check. Ask non-driving applicants for some other form of "official" identification with their picture on it, such as a passport, military ID, or other government agency ID card. Compare the pictures on the identification with the faces you see before you, and say something kind or droll about the likenesses if you can. Compare the numbers on the identification and credit cards with those given on the applications to verify the information as given. Then compare the address on the identification or license with the address on the application. Do likewise with the signatures. If these things don't match up, ask why they don't. You have no way of knowing otherwise whether the person whose name and references are listed on the application is the same person who wishes to rent from you.

While you have the driver's license or other identification available, make a photocopy and keep the photocopy together with the application. You may find that there's more information on the license which you need later and don't have available to you anymore.

Remember that whenever you rent out a dwelling, you are entrusting a valuable piece of property to a stranger. You must know whether that stranger is a proper stranger. You must know what that stranger's true identity is. Automobile rental agencies ask for identification before they will rent you a motorcar. Merchants even ask for identification before they will cash a five-dollar check. Yet your rental property is many times more valuable than an automobile or a check for a paltry sum. Shouldn't you at least check your applicant's

I.D.? You stand to lose plenty if you rent to an unscrupulous tenant, not to mention all the grief and aggravation you could suffer. Be cautious. Check the applicant's identification for certain.

If, for one reason or another, you fail to check an applicant's identification while you are looking the application over initially, don't despair. You can still check it when you visit the applicant's home. I prefer to check it at the first opportunity, however, so I don't waste any more time than I have to if an applicant proves to be impersonating someone else, such as a friend or relative who has impeccable credit and references.

Unless you already know more about the applicants than what's on their applications, look at each application as if you were trying to collect an eviction judgment. If applicants have no job, no automobile, and no bank accounts to attach, then how will you be able to get any money out of them if they stop paying their rent and you have to take them to court? Some applications may be rejected at this step without further checking. You can "evict" now at the lowest possible cost. (On the backs of all applications you reject, write the reasons for your decisions and then file away each application for at least three years as proof of your fairness in tenant selection.)

Not only is the information on applications essential to the selection process, but also because you have more information to base your selection on than just the obvious things such as sex, race, or color, the chances of your being considered culpable of illegal discrimination on the basis of these criteria are substantially reduced. Face it. You are less vulnerable to charges of illegal discrimination if you solicit applications than if you do not. Without applications, you have little information to base your decision on, and the deciding factors may more easily be construed as illegally discriminatory.

Once you have scrutinized the applications to check for internal inconsistencies and obvious disqualifying factors as measured by your tenant standards, you should act promptly. Other landlords are looking for good tenants, too, and your prospects may be filling out applications for more than one dwelling.

5) Check references and qualify the applicants.

Note the very last line on the Rental Application provided here. It's a checklist for you and whoever else may be checking applications for you. It's there so you will know what has been checked and what hasn't. Use it.

Some tenant applicants know that because many landlords fail to check the information given on rental applications, they can probably get away with a lie here and there. I know that it's a revelation to you that anyone would ever lie on a rental application. It isn't? Good, then you should be able to hold your own in this business.

You see, nobody has ever gone to jail for lying on a rental application. Nobody has ever had to pay a fine for lying on a rental application. It's not a capital offense. Why, it's not even a misdemeanor. So what do applicants have to lose by being "creative" when they fill out their rental applications? Nothing, absolutely nothing. Neither a jail term nor a fine awaits them if you discover they're lying. They don't even get a slap on the wrist. They just move on and try to dupe some other unsuspecting landlord.

The burden of discovery rests upon you. You have to separate the truth from the falsehoods, and you get no special reward for your efforts when you do make a discovery. You merely get to sigh in relief that you didn't rent to somebody who might have been a terrible tenant.

Be suspicious about the information given on *every* rental application submitted to you. Tenants who have had problems with their landlords in the past are not going to disclose those problems on their rental applications. They're not going to give an honest reason why they're moving from their present address. They're not going to admit that they have ever been evicted. They know full well that you won't rent to them if they tell you the truth about themselves. So, they fabricate. They lie. They dare you to prove them wrong. They force you to dig for the truth. Sometimes you need only scratch the surface, and you'll discover something which causes you to have second thoughts about them. One phone call might be enough. Sometimes you have to dig deep to get at anything which can help you make your decision. Ten phone calls might not be enough. Keep digging. You have too much to lose by renting to just anybody.

Start your checking with tenancy references. If they give you any serious doubts, you needn't bother checking further. No matter how good their employment and credit references are, if the applicants have defied their previous landlord and sneaked in a dog or refused to pay late fees when they were late with their rent, you don't want 'em.

■ **Tenancy References**—Call the current landlord to learn whatever you can about the applicants' tenancy, but be careful, very careful, about two things—whether you are speaking to the real landlord or an impersonator and whether the landlord is telling you the truth or telling you what he knows you want to hear in order to get rid of his bad tenants.

Since it is relatively easy for anyone to impersonate a landlord over the telephone, you might be talking to someone other than the applicants' real landlord, so you need to be a trifle cagey at first. Say something like this when you call to check the reference: "Hello, I'm Lester Landlord, a landlord in Littletown. Richard and Mary Renter have given you as a reference on an application they made to rent a house from me. Can you tell me how you came to know them?" Don't say, "Richard and Mary Renter have listed you as their landlord on their rental application, and I'm calling to find out what kind of tenants they've been for you." There's a big difference in the two approaches, a crucial difference.

You do not want the person answering the phone to know what his role is supposed to be. In the first approach, you give him no clues. You ask how he knows the applicants. That's all. The real landlord will say straightaway that he is the applicants' landlord. The phony won't know whether he's supposed to pretend to be a friend, a neighbor, a landlord, or an employer. If you give him a clue, then the phony landlord will know what role he's supposed to be playing.

Should you still have doubts about whether you're talking with the applicants' real landlord, tell the person who answers the phone and claims to be the landlord that the rent is substantially higher or lower than what's given on the rental application and ask for a verification. The real landlord will know right away what the correct rent is. A phony won't.

Once you feel reasonably confident that you are talking with Richard and Mary Renter's honest-to-goodness landlord, try to learn the answers to the following questions—

How long have they lived there?
How many people are there in the household?
Do they have any pets?
Do they bother the neighbors?
Are they quiet?
Are they clean?
Are they cooperative?
Are they demanding?
How much rent are they paying?
How many times have they been late with their rent?
Why are they moving?
Did they give proper notice that they would be moving?
Have there been any particular problems with them?

The final question, the key question, you should ask a landlord is whether he would rent to these tenants again if he were given the opportunity.

Honest answers to all of these questions will give you some good clues as to whether you want Richard and Mary Renter to be your tenants, but a yes-or-no answer to the key question will tell you everything.

Besides the pitfall of the phony landlord routine, one other pitfall you might encounter when asking an applicant's current landlord to say a few words about a departing tenant is that the current landlord may be so anxious for the tenants to move that they may be recommended to you even if they are being evicted. Be especially wary, therefore, of glowing recommendations made by the current landlord, and weigh them cautiously against whatever else you have learned about the applicants. Compare the reasons for moving given by the tenants on their applications with the reason given by the current landlord, and if there's even a hint of a discrepancy in their stories, check with their previous landlord.

More than likely, some time has elapsed since the applicants rented from their "previous landlord," and you might not be able to contact that person. He might have gone out of the business, moved away, kept poor records, forgotten all about his previous tenants, lost his memory, or died in the interim. But if you can contact the previous landlord, do. That person no longer has any interest in whether the tenants stay or move and would be the best one to give you an unbiased appraisal.

Approach the previous landlord warily, just as warily as you approached the present landlord, that is, until you feel certain that you are speaking with the indisputable previous landlord. With the information given on the Rental Application as a starter, find out whether it's correct. Then ask the same questions you asked the current landlord.

Sometimes you may not be able to contact the applicants' present or previous landlords at all by phone. You'll want to try contacting them somehow, perhaps by fax or mail. To get your responses most quickly, fax the "Fellow Landlord" form to the landlord, asking for a prompt response. As a last resort, send the form to the landlord by Priority Mail, and ask that it by faxed back or mailed back as soon as possible.

Fellow Landlord:

___Dennis Lee___ has applied to rent from us and has identified you as a current or former landlord or rental property manager having first-hand experience with him/her as a tenant.

We are trying to determine what this person was like when living at ___7 Leeway Lane, Horace___ as your tenant and would appreciate your answering the following questions about him/her:

How long was this person your tenant?
Less than six months [ ] Six months to a year [ ]
One to two years [ ] More than two years [X]

When did this tenant move out? ___7-31-XX___

How much was the rent when he/she moved out? $___630-___

How many other people were living with this tenant?
None [ ] One [X] Two [ ] Three [ ] Four [ ] Five [ ] Six [ ]

Did the tenant have any pets?
Yes [X] No [ ] If so, what kind? ___Dog___

How many times did the tenant fail to pay the rent on time?
Once [X] Twice [ ] Three times [ ] More than three times [ ]

Did you ever have to serve the tenant with a notice to pay rent or quit? Yes [ ] No [X]

Did you ever have to serve the tenant with any other notice?
Yes [ ] No [X] If so, what kind? _____

Was this tenant reasonably quiet? Yes [X] No [ ]

Was this tenant reasonably clean? Yes [X] No [ ]

Did the tenant give enough notice that he/she was moving?
Yes [X] No [ ]

Did the tenant leave the premises clean and undamaged?
Yes [X] No [ ]

If you withheld any of the tenant's cleaning/security deposit, why did you withhold it? ___N/A___

Did the tenant leave owing you any money?
Yes [ ] No [X] If so, how much? $_____

On a scale of one to ten, with ten being the most cooperative and zero being the least cooperative, how would you rate this tenant in terms of his/her cooperating with you?
(10) 9 8 7 6 5 4 3 2 1 (Circle only one number.)

If you had the opportunity, would you rent to this tenant again?
Yes [X] No [ ]

Thank you very much for answering these questions.

Sincerely,

Maya Ward

Sorry to say, because we landlords are so afraid of being sued, you may encounter some who are reluctant to talk about their tenants at all. In those cases, be as sweet as you can be, and tell them that you aren't asking for a good or a bad recommendation. You're not asking for opinions. You're merely asking for a verification of information of the "name, rank, and serial number" variety. The least they can do is verify the information which the tenants have supplied on their application. Even the most lawsuit-shy landlord should verify for you how much the tenants' rent is, how long they've lived there, and whether they gave proper notice. That's straightforward stuff which doesn't require any interpretation and shouldn't drag anybody into lawsuitland.

Still, you ought to try to drag an answer out of them for the key question, whether they would rent to these tenants again. It is a question of opinion, of course, but it's also a question which they can answer with a simple yes or no, and they may give you their answer without even thinking about what kind of a question it is. They know the answer.

■ **Employment References**—After checking into the applicants' current and previous tenancies and finding nothing negative, you will want to know something about their employment. You will want to know how much each applicant earns, how long he has been employed, whether the work is part-time or full-time, and whether it is temporary or permanent. This information will help you determine whether the applicants can afford the rent month after month.

First, try to obtain this information by making a phone call, being just as wary about some trickery as you were when calling the landlord. Check the telephone book for the employer's phone number and try calling that number rather than the one given on the application. The number on the application might ring at the employer's all right, but it might be a direct line to one of the applicant's friends who works there. It might be a complete phony, too. Be wary if the "employer" answers with a "hello" rather than with a business name.

When you get through to somebody at the employer who has the information you seek, you might say something like this, "Hello, my name is Lester Landlord. I'm a landlord in Littletown. Richard Renter, who says he works for you, has made an application to rent a house from me,

and I'd like very much to verify some information about him so I can qualify him and his wife to move in as soon as possible." In effect, you are saying that your inquiry will benefit the employee and that you are only trying to verify some information you already have. Smaller firms will agree to this reasonable request readily because they know their people individually and want to help their employees obtain housing. Larger firms may switch you around until you reach somebody with authority, and you may have to repeat your speech from the top, but they will generally verify the information you give them as well.

Continue by saying, "Richard Renter says he has been working there for a year and three months. Is that about right?" If they answer in the affirmative, say, "He has indicated that he earns a gross income of $1,855 per month. Is that about right?" Phrasing your questions in this way, so they may be answered either affirmatively or negatively, relieves employers of the anxiety they sometimes feel about divulging information they shouldn't.

Sometimes you may get nowhere with a large employer which has restrictive policies about divulging employee information over the phone. Go in another direction. Stop trying to search through the normal channels for personnel information. Try the applicant's immediate supervisor. Immediate supervisors likely have no policies about discussing personnel matters. They tend to be frank in talking about their staff so long as you approach them in the right way.

If you can't seem to get much information out of anyone over the telephone, ask the applicant to get a letter signed by his employer verifying the information you need, or send the company an Employment Verification form letter such as the one given here and request the information in writing. To be taken seriously and to ensure a prompt reply, send it with a self-addressed, stamped envelope.

To verify the income of applicants who are self-employed, you will want to see their personal income tax returns for the past two years. Examine them for authenticity first. Look at the second page and note who prepared the return. I tend to give a little more credence to those prepared by someone other than the taxpayer only because the taxpayer who does his own can easily prepare two returns, one to submit to the IRS and another to submit to lenders and others who want

Employment Verification

TO: EMPLOYER   <u>Bi - Lift</u>
                <u>100 Walter Avenue</u>
                <u>Littletown, Calif.</u>
RE: EMPLOYEE   <u>Richard Renter</u>

We are in the process of checking out a rental application submitted by the person named above as "EMPLOYEE."

This person claims to be working for you currently as a <u>operator</u> earning $<u>2,150</u> per <u>month</u>. This person also claims to have started working for you as of <u>2½ years ago</u>.

Because time is a factor in our approving this employee to rent from us, we would appreciate your PHONING us as soon as possible with a verification of this information. Our telephone number is <u>123-6789</u>, and we are generally available at the following times: <u>8 AM - 6 PM</u>.

If you cannot phone us, please complete the section below and mail this entire letter back to us at your earliest convenience.

Thank you.   Signed   <u>Leslie Landlady</u>
                Address <u>453 Sweet Street</u>
                         <u>Littletown, Ca. 09090</u>

- -

The above information is correct with the following exceptions:

_____ (if none, write "none.")

Is this employment part-time?   or full-time?

Is this employment temporary?   or permanent?

INFORMATION PROVIDED BY

Name_____ Title_____ Date_____

to verify income. Next, check the income section. Is at least some of it from dividends and interest, showing that the applicant has set aside some money for a rainy day. Is the income high enough to afford the rent?

In addition, you will want to see some bank statements of the self-employed person's operations account, not the personal account. Ask for statements covering the past six months or at the very least, the past three months. Look at the average balances and the deposits. How consistent are they? How high are they? Is there enough money available to pay the rent?

■ **Other Income**—Should the applicant derive income from sources other than ordinary employment, say, from Social Security, pension funds, welfare, alimony, child support, inheritance, investments, unemployment, disability, scholarships, school loans, or relatives, you will want to verify the source, the amount, and the continuity of the source as best you can. Ask to see whatever records the applicant has to support the amounts shown on the application.

■ **Credit References**—Regarding credit information, you have four choices:

1) Choice one is to make no inquiries at all, relying solely on the applicant's self-reporting of his credit history and on the tenancy, employment, and other income references already obtained to provide good clues about his ability and willingness to meet the financial obligations incurred in renting from you.

2) Choice two is to check directly with some or all of the credit references listed on the application. Finance companies and merchants with customer charge accounts will usually give you the information you need over the phone, but banks will rarely release any information unless authorized to do so by the customer, and even then, it may take a few days. To get this information, use the Request for Verification of Deposit form. It must be signed by the applicant-customer first, then by you. Fill in as much of the information as possible in items 6 and 7, especially the account numbers. Send or take it to the bank with a self-addressed, stamped envelope, and they will return it directly to you by mail unless the people at the tenants' bank know you and will hand it back to you in person. You may, of course, do a "quick-and-dirty" financial resources investigation by calling the bank and inquiring whether

a fictitious check for a certain sum of money would clear the applicant's checking account.

3) Choice three is to request a full credit report on the applicant. These reports generally take from several seconds to several hours to obtain, depending upon how they're secured, and can reveal information on bad debt collections that you wouldn't otherwise uncover. They're available with or without credit bureau risk scoring.

Credit bureau risk scoring originated as a scientific approach to interpreting credit data, virtually eliminating the personal bias which a human might apply while interpreting such data. The scoring system developed by Fair, Isaac, commonly known as FICO®, is by far the most popular credit scoring system.

A FICO score tells a creditor how likely someone is to pay bills on time. It weighs a combination of five factors to come up with a score. Those factors are payment history, amounts owed, length of credit history, new credit, and types of credit use. FICO scores range from a low of 300 to a high of 850. An "A" score ranges from 690 to 850; a "B" score, from 620-689; a "C" score, from 560-619; and a below-average score, from 300 to 559.

Credit unions want a score of 570 or better; banks and credit card companies want a score of 620 or better. As a landlord, you might decide that you want a score of 560 or better for your apartment house at a marginal location and a score of 650 or better for your rental house at an upscale location.

Examine the table below, and you'll notice that people with scores between 550 and 599 have a delinquency rate of 51%. They're just as likely to pay a debt as not. That's not exactly good credit, and if I were a lender, I'd be reluctant to lend them a dollar out of fear that they'd repay only 49 cents. You might be reluctant to rent to cer-

CREDIT BUREAU RISK SCORING		
Score	Percentage of Population	Delinquency Rate (%)
800-850	11	1
750-799	29	2
700-749	20	5
650-699	16	15
600-649	11	31
550-599	7	51
500-549	5	71
300-499	1	87

Request for Verification of Deposit

Instructions: Landlord—Complete items 1 through 7. Have applicant(s) complete item 8. Forward directly to depository named in item 1.
Depository—Please complete items 9 through 15 and return DIRECTLY to landlord named in item 2.

Part I—Request

1. To (Name and Address of Depository)

Big Bank
501 Main St.
Littletown, CA 09090

2. From (Name and Address of Landlord)

Leslie Landlady
453 Sweet St.
Littletown, CA 09090

3. Signature of Landlord/Manager	4. Title	5. Date
Leslie Landlady	landlady	1/07/xx

6. INFORMATION TO BE VERIFIED

Type of Account	Account in Name of	Account Number	Balance
Checking	Richard Renter	V04309586	$ 2,285⁰⁰/xx

To Depository: I/We have applied to rent a dwelling and stated in the rental application that the balance on deposit with you is as shown above. You are authorized to verify this information and to supply the landlord identified above with the information requested in items 9 through 12. Your response is solely a matter of courtesy for which no responsibility is attached to your institution or any of your officers.

7. Name and Address of Applicant(s)

Richard Renter
1510 Zebra St.
Littletown, CA 09090

8. Signature of Applicant(s)

Richard Renter

To Be Completed by Depository

Part II–Verification of Depository

9. Deposit Accounts of Applicant(s)

Type of Account	Account Number	Current Balance	Average Balance for Previous Two Months	Date Opened
		$	$	
		$	$	
		$	$	
		$	$	

10. Bank Card Accounts of Applicant(s)

Type of Bank Card	Account Number	Current Balance	Average Monthly Payment	Expiration Date
		$	$	
		$	$	

11. Loans Outstanding to Applicant(s)

Loan Number	Date of Loan	Original Amount	Current Balance	Installments		Secured by	No. Late Pmts.
		$	$	$	per		
		$	$	$	per		

12. Please include any additional information which may be of assistance in determination of credit worthiness. (Please include information on loans paid-in-full in item 11 above.)

13. Signature of Depository	14. Title	15. Date

The confidentiality of the information you have furnished will be preserved except where disclosure of this information is required by applicable law. The form is to be transmitted directly to the landlord and is not to be transmitted through the applicant(s) or any other party.

tain people in this category, too, until you discover that they are never delinquent in their rent. Through inquiry, you discover that they always pay their rent on time before they pay any of their other bills. Their FICO score would be low, but that needn't concern you if they have a good record of paying their rent on time.

FICO scores aren't everything for landlords. They are a point of departure, a good one. If the scores are high, you needn't worry about whether the applicants will pay. They have demonstrated that they will. If the scores are low, you need to find out why. You need to discover how important the applicants' payment of rent is to them. That's how you ought to use FICO scores.

FICO scores add approximately $3 to the cost of a credit report and enable you to be just as objective as a banker in analyzing credit data. Without scores, you need to spend more time analyzing the data and may be accused of being too subjective. Of course, you would be.

You may obtain credit reports through many different sources.

Rental housing association—Almost every association belongs to a credit reporting agency and provides its members with credit reports for a nominal charge. Your association may also provide eviction, bad check, and tenancy reports for an extra charge.

RHOL—Rental Housing On Line (RHOL.org) provides its members with credit reports, including credit scoring for $9.

Bank—You may be able to call upon your bank as a resource and get them to run a credit check for you for a small fee. Some will accommodate you if they value you as a customer; some won't, no matter what.

Credit reporting agency—The drawback in dealing directly with an agency yourself instead of indirectly, through your association or your bank, is the high cost of securing a single credit report every so often. Most agencies charge annual fees and then a fee for each inquiry. If you make only one inquiry a year, it could cost you $50 directly through an agency because you'll have to pay the annual fees plus the inquiry charge, while it might cost you only $5 to $15 through a rental housing association.

Other alternatives—Use an Internet search engine and search their files using "tenant screening" or "background verification" as key words. You will find all kinds of companies listed under those key words. Go to their websites, compare their services and prices one with another, and order a credit report from one of them.

4) Choice four is to ask the applicant to order a copy of his credit report himself and make it available to you. Any one of the big-three credit reporting agencies will provide the report of a person making an inquiry to that person for a fee ranging from $3 to $9, depending upon the state where the person lives. Here are the toll-free numbers they may call for a copy of their own report: Equifax, 800.685.1111; Experian (formerly TRW), 888.397.3742; and TransUnion, 800.888.4213. The report the applicant provides you should be as recent as possible, no more than two months old at most, and it should be the original. Do not accept a copy unless you can also see the original. The copy might have been doctored with correction fluid to eliminate the negative references.

How much credit information you should obtain on applicants depends on the amount of rent involved, the percentage of their income that will be paid out in rent, and the difference between the old and new rents. If the new rent is high or if it's equal to more than a third of the applicant's gross monthly income (rent, together with monthly credit obligations, should total around 40% of gross income) or if it represents a considerable increase over what they have been paying, you should check the credit thoroughly.

There's a lot of information available, but you have to spend money or time to obtain it, and only you can determine how much information would be helpful to you in making your decision whether to rent to someone. All the information available to you on applicants is merely a supplement to your good judgment. You alone must decide whether they will make good tenants based upon your standards.

By the way, if you ever reject applicants because of a negative credit report, you must provide them with the information they need to secure a copy of their report. They will probably want to see it for themselves to check it for accuracy. They're entitled to a free copy of whatever report caused them to be denied credit, so long as they apply for it within sixty days of their having been denied. You are denying them credit when you refuse to rent to them because of the information in their report. For this purpose, use the form shown at the end of this chapter.

FINANCIAL QUALIFIER
(all figures monthly)

APPLICANT NAME   Sanders
Number of Adults   2
Ages of Children   3, 6
Adults all work?   Y
Health plan through work?   Y
Child care?   Y
Pets?   cat

G R O S S   V E R I F I A B L E   I N C O M E

	(amounts)	(notes)
Wages	3266	
Wages	2038	
Wages		
Wages		
Social Security		
Pension		
Alimony		
Child Support		
Interest	12	
Dividends		
Other		
TOTAL INCOME	5316 (+)	

E X P E N S E S   &   D E D U C T I O N S

	(amounts)	(notes)
Income Taxes	1103	20% if state inc tax; 17% if none
Credit Card Payments	180	
Vehicle Payments	623	
Loan Payments	420	
Vehicle Expenses	100	$100/fin; $75/not; add $30 hi risk
Gas & Electricity	80	check local utility for sq ft avg
Telephone	25	ask re avg bill; otherwise $25
Cable TV	32	
Food	560	$140/person
Health Care	100	$85/person wo paid plan; $25 with
Alimony		
Child Care	650	$450/child full day; $200 partial
Child Support		
Pet Care	25	$35/dog; $25/cat
Other	600	$200/adult; $100/child

TOTAL EXPENSES & DEDUCTIONS   4498 (−)

SAVINGS ACCOUNT BALANCE   3600   add 5% bal to "available for rent"

AVAILABLE FOR RENT   818 (=) ADJUSTED   998
(total income minus total expenses & deductions)

■ **Analysis of Applicants' Finances**—Analyze carefully the finances of those applicants you are serious about before committing to rent to them, and you will have fewer collection problems later because you will know in advance whether they can afford to pay you the rent. You want tenants who are able to pay the rent comfortably month after month after month, tenants who have sufficient income and know something about handling money.

Some applicants never analyze their finances for themselves. Either they don't know how, they aren't interested, or they don't want to know. They know little more about their finances than how much cash they have in their wallets and purses. You ought to do it for them and for yourself. Appearances can be deceiving. How much they earn and how much debt they have isn't everything. There's more to be concerned about in determining whether they can really afford to pay the rent on the dwelling they want to rent from you.

A young couple earning $4,850 per month gross and making a $750 car payment, a $180 MasterCard payment, a $200 boat payment, and a $220 medical bill payment, while they're both working and trying to raise two small children, cannot afford to rent a dwelling from you at $1,000 per month, even though they would appear to qualify easily based upon the rule-of-thumb multiplier for rent and gross income. The truth is that this family, for all its income, has one foot on a financial banana peel atop a house of cards and you'd be remiss in renting a dwelling to them for $1,000 per month when they can comfortably afford to pay only $678. If they make one little slip, their house of cards comes tumbling down, and you don't want to be in it with them when it does.

You can analyze your applicants' finances by spending a few minutes completing the Financial Qualifier form shown on the next page. Its end result is how much they have available every month to pay their rent. Here's what you do (all figures are monthly)—

✔ Itemize their total gross income from verifiable sources, including wages, Social Security, pension, alimony, child support, interest, dividends, and anything else they receive on a regular basis.

✔ Deduct 20% of their total gross income for state and federal taxes (if your state doesn't have income taxes, deduct 17%.

✔ Deduct the regular monthly payments they make on their credit card debts.

✔ Deduct the payments they make on their vehicles.

✔ Deduct whatever other payments they make to banks and finance companies (look at both their application and their credit report for information about these debts).

✔ Deduct vehicle expenses (insurance, repairs, maintenance, and fuel) equal to $100 per vehicle if currently financed or $75 if owned outright.

✔ Deduct a sum for gas and electricity which you have determined is an average in your area for this size dwelling (call your local utility company for figures if you have trouble; they'll help you; in Boston, it's going to be quite different from what it is in Los Angeles); add $25 for telephone service; and the basic rate for cable television service.

✔ Deduct $140 per person for food.

✔ Deduct $80 per person for health care if not covered by an employer; deduct $20 per person if covered by an employer.

✔ Deduct $450 per child for full-day child care; deduct $200 per child for after-school child care.

✔ Deduct $35 per dog, $25 per cat, for food and veterinary care.

✔ Deduct $200 per adult and $100 per child for miscellaneous expenses such as clothing, entertainment, etc.

✔ Credit them with 5% of their savings as being available to pay their monthly bills.

✔ Whatever is left over is what they can afford to pay you in rent.

Can the applicants afford to pay the rent? Let's hope so.

If the Financial Qualifier has raised any doubts in your mind, however, talk with the applicants. Show them your findings. Listen to what they have to say about how they spend their income. Don't try to suggest how they might spend less on such-and-such so they'd have more to spend on rent. You're not a financial counselor. You're a financial analyst. You are interested only in whether the figures you have come up with are reasonably accurate. If the applicants say that they don't subscribe to cable TV, remove that item. If they say they spend a minimal $12 per month for telephone service, change that item. If they say that a grandmother takes care of the two kids during the day free of charge, remove that item. You want their financial picture to be accurate. Sure, you might see how they could trim their expenses. Keep mum about it. These people's spending habits aren't going to change just because you have some good ideas for changing them. They have to want to change their spending habits.

■ **Eviction Search**—Computer databases being so easy and inexpensive to maintain and use nowadays once the data has been gathered and entered, more and more companies have come to specialize in providing landlords with information about tenants who have been evicted. They search through court records for this information on a daily basis so it is current, and they report evictions which have been filed and evictions which have been concluded. Some such companies combine this information with a more extensive tenant history solicited from landlords in the area. It can be very, very useful information indeed.

Avail yourself of this information if you possibly can. You may find that your local rental housing association has already contracted with an eviction search service and that they can order you an eviction search at the same time they order you a credit report. Tell them to order up both for you, by all means.

If you need to find a good eviction search service on your own, try the Internet. Go to one of the search engines and enter the key words "tenant screening." You'll get a lengthy list to select from. Choose the most promising of the listings and go to their websites, looking for one which operates in your area, offers speedy service, delivers its findings in a convenient form, and charges reasonable fees. When you find one which meets your criteria, contact them and ask whether they will do a trial search for you before you pay them their account setup fee. Run a check on a tenant you know who should set off all the warning whistles, and see what kind of information they come up with. If you're satisfied with the results, sign up for the service and use it every time you check the backgrounds of your applicants.

■ **Evaluation of Applicants' Qualifications**—By now you know more about the applicants than most of their close friends do. You have tenancy information, employment and income information, asset information, credit information, eviction information, and personal information. You need to evaluate this information you have gathered and determine whether these particular applicants would make good tenants for this particular rental property, whether they would be round pegs in a square hole or round pegs in a round hole. What do you look for? You look for *wincers*, items which cause you to wince and wonder whether you ought to accept these applicants as your tenants.

Remember, nobody this side of heaven is perfect. You're not looking for just one wincer, unless it alone is egregious enough to disqualify the applicants, you're looking for a number of them. You're creating a profile.

Here are the wincers you should look for—

Personal information (from application, conversation, and personal observation)
  Incomplete application
  Sloppy application
  No telephone
  No driver's license or other "official" identification
  Poor hygiene and grooming
  Expectations of a big lawsuit payoff
  Excessive anxiety about moving in right away
  Careless handling of a cigarette

Tenancy information
  Current housing–relatives or friends
  Current housing–motel or van
  Little or no information about previous landlords
  Repeated moves
  History of late payments
  No notice of intent to vacate
  Attempt to apply security deposit to last month's rent

Employment/Income information
  New job
  Frequent job changes
  Insufficient income
  No income documentation

Asset information
> No savings account
> No checking account
> Bad checks
> Insufficient move-in monies
> No car
> Car dented, broken down, or abused

Credit information
> No credit history
> Low credit score
> No credit cards
> Credit cards with high balances
> Bill collections
> Retail accounts with high balances
> Numerous inquiries into their credit history
> History of late payments
> Recent bankruptcy or foreclosure
> Car loan arrearages
> Car repossession
> Home foreclosure

Eviction information
> Move demanded by previous landlord
> Defendant in an eviction
> Eviction judgment on record

Has nothing you know about these applicants so far started you wincing? Good, good! Maybe, just maybe, they're the good tenants you're looking for.

■ **An Aside**—The screwups, bad actors, deadbeats, and scofflaws of this world who make terrible tenants and who account for fewer than 6% of all tenants, have reveled in playing their "Dupe the Landlord" game for years. They would find some landlord somewhere to rent to them without checking their references, and then they would proceed to make that landlord's life miserable, paying their rent in promises all the while they were destroying the property and staying put until the very last moment when an officer of the law arrived on their doorstep to remove them from the premises.

Only recently has the game's playing field been cleared and leveled. The bulldozer responsible for making this change in the playing field is the enormous database of personal information which agencies gather daily and make readily and cheaply available to those making decisions about granting credit to borrowers and entrusting rental property to tenants.

No longer can terrible tenants hide their wicked ways so easily as they once did. They leave crumbs every time they fail to pay a bill, every time they pass a bad check, every time they declare bankruptcy, every time they get arrested, every time they change jobs, and every time they become evicted. Put together, those crumbs take shape and tell you what you need to know when you're deciding whether to entrust your property to them.

As a landlord with a signed rental application, you have legitimate access to that information, and you should use it when checking out applicants unless you have a very good reason not to.

More and more landlords are using the bulldozer on the playing field and are winning at "Dupe the Landlord." A bulldozer may seem to be a heavy-handed approach to weeding out terrible tenants and winning the game. It isn't. It's only fair play. Besides, it works. I know it works. Self-storage managers have told me that the obviously recognizable terrible tenants of rental dwellings are leaving their worldly goods in storage longer and longer.

■ **Handling a Special Situation**—Your rental applicants may have good credit, poor credit, or no credit established at all. You'll want to eliminate those with poor credit, of course, but you may want to consider renting to those who have never established credit before.

Let's say that your applicant is a twenty-one-year-old registered nurse who's always lived at home before and has just taken a new job in the area. She hasn't had the time or the opportunity to build a tenancy, employment, or credit record yet. Should you refuse to rent to her for lack of credit references? You may, certainly, but you may be wise to consider renting to her if everything else checks out satisfactorily, and you feel inclined to give her a chance to prove herself. For your own peace of mind, however, you could request that she secure a co-signer, someone who already has an established credit rating which you could check by having the co-signer fill out a separate rental application.

Be as careful in checking the co-signer's credit as you were with the applicant's. If everything checks out satisfactorily, ask the co-signer to sign a Co-Signer Agreement in your presence when you complete the tenant's rental agreement. Completing both agreements either simultaneously or nearly simultaneously will avoid legal hassles later, but if you cannot complete the Co-

Co-Signer Agreement   Dated ___June 19, XXXX___

(Addendum to Rental Agreement)

This agreement is attached to and forms a part of the Rental Agreement dated ___6/19/XX___ between ___Vernon Graves___,
Owners, and ___Dana Levno_____, Tenants.
My name is ___Ellen Levno_____.

I have completed a Rental Application for the express purpose of enabling the Owners to check my credit. I have no intention of occupying the dwelling referred to in the Rental Agreement above.

I have read the Rental Agreement, and I promise to guarantee the Tenants' compliance with the financial obligations of this Agreement.

I understand that I may be required to pay for rent, cleaning charges, or damage assessments in such amounts as are incurred by the Tenants under the terms of this Agreement if, and only if, the Tenants themselves fail to pay.

I also understand that this Co-Signer Agreement will remain in force throughout the entire term of the Tenants' tenancy, even if their tenancy is extended and/or changed in its terms.

I am paying the sum of ten dollars ($10) as a consideration of acceptance of this Co-Signer Agreement by all parties concerned.

___Ellen Levno_____
                    Co-Signer

___Leslie Landlady_____
            Accepted by Owner/Manager

Page___6___ of _4_

Signer Agreement and have it signed along with the rental agreement, have it completed before. It should not follow the rental agreement because the rental agreement is dependent upon it.

Try to get a co-signer who lives in the area rather than one who lives elsewhere. You may have to contact that person at some time. You may even have to sue that person at some time. You don't need the aggravation you'd have to endure in trying to collect money from someone who lives out of the area.

With this additional agreement in hand, you reduce the risk involved in renting to someone who lacks established credit. If the tenant turns out to be a deadbeat, you have someone of substance to pursue.

■ **Handling Another Special Situation**—Every so often you will want to check the references of applicants who look outstanding both on paper and in person, but because it's a holiday weekend at the end of the month and you can't get a credit check or verify either their tenancy or employment, you're stymied. The information you need to make your decision is simply unavailable for a few days. What might you do? Here are three possibilities—

1) The first is to tell the applicants to wait until you can check all their references as you normally do. Apologize that you're unable to check their references immediately, but assure them that you will check everything as soon as the holiday weekend is over. The advantage of this option is that you run little risk of renting to someone who may be a professional deadbeat. You will know with some certainty when you check them out whether they are what they appear to be. The disadvantage of this option is that you risk losing good tenants who will likely continue looking around until they find another suitable place

which they can rent without having to wait for clearance. Take that risk rather than risk renting to somebody you wouldn't have rented to had you known more about them.

2) The second possibility should also protect you from deadbeats, but it does have its price. Tell the applicants to find accommodations for the weekend if necessary and tell them you will deduct, say, $50 from their first month's rent for every night they have to sleep at a motel, provided, of course, that their references do check out and that you do rent to them. If you have to pay for two or three nights' lodging in order to secure good tenants, the expense is money well spent compared to the loss you would sustain if you had to evict problem tenants.

3) The third possibility is a little more creative and requires some special shrewdness to carry off, but it is almost as cautious as the other two, and it usually settles the matter quite sufficiently. Ask the applicants to show you their latest rent receipts and their latest payroll stubs. If current, a rent receipt will verify an applicant's tenancy, and a payroll stub will verify both employment and wages.

Since few people carry these two items around with them and since the rent receipt could be forged pretty easily if the applicants were to leave your sight after you made the request, refrain from requesting the rent receipt unless you are visiting the applicants at their current residence in the next step. A payroll stub, on the other hand, is more difficult to forge, so have no qualms about asking to see one when you first decide to try this option. If the applicants claim to have stubs at home, tell them you'll meet them there shortly.

When you arrive, ask to see both their payroll stubs and rent receipts. With the latest rent receipt in hand, check whether the rent is current,

Disclosure of Information on Lead-Based Paint and/or Lead-Based Paint Hazards

Lead Warning Statement

Housing built before 1978 may contain lead-based paint. Lead from paint, paint chips, and dust can pose health hazards if not managed properly. Lead exposure is especially harmful to young children and pregnant women. Before renting pre-1978 housing, lessors must disclose the presence of known lead-based paint and/or lead-based paint hazards in the dwelling. Lessees must also receive a federally approved pamphlet on lead poisoning prevention.

Lessor's Disclosure

(a) Presence of lead-based paint and/or lead-based paint hazards (check (i) or (ii) below):

    (i) _____ Known lead-based paint and/or lead-based paint hazards are present in the housing (explain).

    _____

    (ii) _X_ Lessor has no knowledge of lead-based paint and/or lead-based paint hazards in the housing.

(b) Records and reports available to the lessor (check (i) or (ii) below):

    (i) _____ Lessor has provided the lessee with all available records and reports pertaining to lead-based paint and/or lead-based paint hazards in the housing (list documents below).

    _____

    (ii) _X_ Lessor has no reports or records pertaining to lead-based paint and/or lead-based paint hazards in the housing.

Lessee's Acknowledgment (initial)

(c) _____ Lessee has received copies of all information listed above.

(d) *ᏝᏝ ᏝᏝ* Lessee has received the pamphlet *Protect Your Family from Lead in Your Home.*

Agent's Acknowledgment (initial)

(e) _____ Agent has informed the lessor of the lessor's obligations under 42 U.S.C. 4852(d) and is aware of his/her responsibility to ensure compliance.

Certification of Accuracy

The following parties have reviewed the information above and certify, to the best of their knowledge, that the information they have provided is true and accurate.

Lester Landlord 7/25/xx
_____
Lessor   Date

Harold Link 7/25/xx   Lessor *Bella Link* 7/25/xx
_____   _____
Lessee   Date   Lessee   Date

_____   _____
Agent   Date   Agent   Date

whether the address for the rental property is the same as the address shown on their application, and whether the manager who signed the receipt has the same name as the one given on their application. Check the Social Security number shown on the payroll stub and verify that it's the same one given on the application.

Also, check the year-to-date total wages to determine how much the applicant has been making. Year-to-date wages yield a more complete picture of their employment history than the amount paid for any given pay period. Seasonal workers might be making large sums a few months during the year and nothing at other times. Calculate how much they are making per month, and determine from that whether they can afford to pay the monthly rent. You want to insure that there is a steady income stream, for rent comes due month after month. You know that. They may not be thinking about it.

6) Visit applicants' current home.

If everything about the applicants checks out satisfactorily so far, call them on the phone and arrange to visit them shortly at the place where they are currently living. Much as you might like to show up without letting them know you're coming, you'll find that calling them first will insure that they're home and save you a wasted trip. You are not trying to catch them completely off guard, only slightly off guard. You might want to invent an appropriate pretext for the visit, perhaps that you need to review their application with them or that you need more information about the credit and personal references given on their application, but the main reason for this visit is to see how the applicants live and to meet all those who would become your tenants.

Taking a look at where the applicants live now is like looking at the parents of a person you're planning to marry. The mother is a preview of what the daughter will look like in twenty-five years. The father is a preview of what the son will look like in twenty-five years. The place where the applicants live now is a preview of what your rental will look like in six months. You don't need a crystal ball to look into the future. All you need to do is visit the applicants' current home, and you'll see the future of your rental property with these applicants as its tenants.

If the applicants presently live too far away for you to make a visit, you may have to skip this step, but do so reluctantly.

On your arrival, say a few pleasantries and then begin asking questions such as these: "I see here that you work at Dario's Pizza Parlor. What are your hours there? Do you receive any commissions in addition to your regular salary? How long have you been banking at Midtown Bank? Is Cash Kramer still the manager there? Did you attend school in this area? How long have you lived around here? What keeps you living in this area?" and so on.

While you're conversing, strain your peripheral vision so hard that you'll need peripheral-vision glasses on your temples some day. Look around for various indications of how well these prospective tenants care for this place where they currently live. Is there a half-assembled motorcycle in the living room? How many holes are there in the walls and doors? Are there burns in the carpets? What shape is their furniture in? How's the housekeeping? How closely does this place resemble the dwelling they wish to rent from you? The closer the resemblance, the better they will be as your tenants.

Also, look and listen for pets and people likely to make the move with the household. You might expect that the springer spaniel asleep on the sofa will make the move. If he doesn't appear on the application, ask why he doesn't. If they say they're planning to get rid of old Rufus, make a note of their answer and judge for yourself whether they're telling the truth. If you hear two kids raising Cain somewhere out of sight and it appears to be the kind of dispute that siblings usually have, you can assume that these offspring will both probably be accompanying their parents in the move. If only one kid appears on the application, inquire into the matter. If the parents say they're trying to get rid of one of the kids, try to contain yourself and make a note of their answer. Who knows, maybe they have sold one already and the purchasers just haven't taken delivery yet. If you can, ask the kids why they're moving and compare their answer with the one their parents gave on the application.

At some time during your visit, if you haven't done so before, say that you'd like to see the applicants' driver's licenses, or another form of identification bearing their photographs, and some major credit cards so you can verify the numbers. When you have them in hand, check to see whether the numbers and the signatures match those shown on the applications, note the full

Rental Agreement

Dated **January 15, XXXX**

(Month-to-Month)

Agreement between **Lester Landlord**_____, Owners,
and **RICHARD and ROSE L. RENTER**, Tenants, for a dwelling
located at **456 Sweet Street, LITTLETOWN, CALIFORNIA**_____.
Tenants agree to rent this dwelling on a month-to-month basis for $**778** per
month, payable in advance on the **1ST** day of every calendar month to Owners
or their Agent*, **X X X X X X**_____, whose address is
453 Sweet Street, Littletown, CA 09090_____.
When rent is paid on or before the **4th** day of the calendar month, Owners
will give Tenants a (discount) (rebate) of $**20**.

The first month's rent for this dwelling is $**880**.

The security/cleaning deposit on this dwelling is $**1,000**. It is
refundable if Tenants leave the dwelling reasonably clean and undamaged.

Tenants will give **15** days' notice in writing before they move and will
be responsible for paying rent through the end of this notice period or until
another tenant approved by the Owners has moved in, whichever comes first.

Owners will refund all deposits due within **7** days after Tenants have
moved out completely and returned their keys.

Only the following **2** persons and **∅** pets are to live in this dwelling:
RICHARD and ROSE RENTER_____.
Without Owners' prior written permission, no other persons may live there,
and no other pets may stay there, even temporarily, nor may the dwelling be
sublet or used for business purposes.

Use of the following is included in the rent: **CARPETS, DRAPES, SHADES
and STOVE. REFRIGERATOR on TEMPORARY LOAN.**

Remarks: **WATER and GARBAGE PAID BY OWNERS. TENANTS PAY
ALL OTHER UTILITIES. PARKING IN SPACE #2. OCCUPANCY CONTINGENT**
TENANTS AGREE TO THE FOLLOWING: **UPON EXISTING TENANTS VACATING THE PREMISES.**

1) to accept the dwelling "as is," having already inspected it.
2) to keep yards and garbage areas clean.
3) to keep from making loud or bothersome noises and disturbances and to
   play music and broadcast programs at all times so as not to disturb other
   people's peace and quiet.
4) not to paint or alter the dwelling without first getting Owners' written
   permission.
5) to park their motor vehicle in assigned space and to keep that space
   clean of oil drippings and grease.
6) not to repair their motor vehicle on the premises (unless it is in an
   enclosed garage) if such repairs will take longer than a single day.
7) to allow Owners to inspect the dwelling, work on it, or show it to
   prospective tenants at any and all reasonable times.
8) ~~not to keep any liquid-filled furniture in this dwelling.~~ *RR LL*
9) to pay rent by check or money order made out to Owners. (Checks must be
   good when paid or applicable late-payment consequences will apply.)
10) to pay for repairs of all damage, including drain stoppages, they or
    their guests have caused.
11) to pay for any windows broken in their dwelling while they live there.

Violation of any part of this Agreement or nonpayment of rent when due
shall be cause for eviction under applicable code sections. The prevailing
party (shall) (~~shall not~~) recover reasonable legal services fees involved.

Tenants hereby acknowledge that they have read this Agreement, understand
it, agree to it, and have been given a copy.

Owner **Lester Landlord**, Tenant **Richard Renter**

*By_____   Tenant **Rose Renter**
*Person authorized to accept legal service on Owners' behalf

Pg 1 of 3

names (including middle names), and verify the birth dates.

If you have any doubts about the applicants after this interview, say only that you want to check the applications further and leave, but if everything meets with your approval, proceed at once with the next three steps.

7) Review your rules, requirements, and policies, and satisfy the federal lead-based paint regulations.

Before you finally commit yourself to accept any applicants as your tenants, review your rules, requirements, and policies with them in order to avoid possible ambiguities and prevent later misunderstandings (your rules ought to be in writing; see chapter 21 for suggestions). Remember that at this time, while you are talking with the tenants before they move in, you can get them to agree more readily to strict terms than you can at any later time.

Discuss your rules, requirements, and policies regarding the following: deposits, rent collections, rent payment, first month's rent, last month's rent, guests, parties, quiet hours, parking, utilities, garbage, pets, waterbeds, hanging things on the walls, changing locks, painting, maintenance, emergencies, window breakage, drain stoppages, lockouts, and renters' insurance. Add to this list any other special considerations which may apply to your situation such as pool hours and whether the pool is heated. Be candid. You want your new tenants to have realistic expectations about living there.

Indicate that you are especially concerned that they keep the dwelling clean, that they be relatively quiet, and that they pay their rent promptly. Tell them that you are quick to evict tenants who do not abide by the rules and ask them whether they think they can live there in your rental under those circumstances. If they agree, and you believe them, then commit yourself to rent the place to them.

Before you go any further in renting to these tenants, however, you must satisfy the mandatory federal lead-based paint regulations which apply to dwellings built prior to 1978.

To satisfy these regulations, you must disclose whatever you know about lead-based paint in the dwelling, you must give the tenants a sixteen-page EPA (Environmental Protection Agency) pamphlet entitled "Protect Your Family from Lead in Your Home," and both you and the ten-

ants must sign a statement entitled "Disclosure of Information on Lead-Based Paint and/or Lead-Based Paint Hazards."

You may obtain a copy of the pamphlet from many sources, including the Forms section of this book, the EPA, and the EPA's website. Along with the pamphlet, you must provide a copy of the disclosure statement shown here. You will find more information about the regulations in chapter 17. Become familiar with them.

8) Fill out and sign the rental agreement.

Now put in writing most of what you have already agreed upon verbally. Use a simply worded rental agreement (see chapter 5 for a more comprehensive agreement than the one shown here), one which most tenants can easily understand. In fact, you should use agreements written not only so they can be understood, but also so they cannot be misunderstood.

Explain every bit of your agreement to your new tenants, word for word. Give them blank copies and read everything to them as you are filling in the blanks. Many adults cannot read, and many others won't read anything thrust at them for their signatures. Because the rental agreement is so important to your future relationship with these people, read it to them now in order to avoid misunderstandings later.

If you decide to give tenants a discount or a rebate for paying on time instead of adding a late charge when they're late, explain that the monthly rental figure used in the agreement is higher than what you advertised because this gross rent includes an amount, usually between $10 and $20, which is granted as a discount or rebate when the rent is paid on or before the late date. Tell them you advertise the net rent because that's what most people pay. Make sure they understand this rent policy before you continue (see discussion in chapter 6).

If you know that the laws and courts in your area will permit you to charge new tenants something, anything, to cover some of your costs in servicing new tenants, then consider charging a higher first month's rent. Now is the time to discuss the matter with the new tenants. Explain that the first month's rent is higher than the usual rent because it is supposed to cover some of the many costs connected with a new tenancy, costs such as cleaning the carpets and drapes (tell them they won't have to clean the carpets or drapes or wax the floors when they move out; tell them

Lease

Dated APRIL 6, XXXX

Agreement between __Leslie Landlady__, Owners,
and __Dorthy Mae Mahoney__, Tenants, for a dwelling
located at __350 Boondocks Lane, Littletown, California__.
Tenants agree to lease this dwelling for a term of __one YEAR__, beginning
__MAY 1, XXXX__ and ending __April 30, XXXX__ for $__570__ per month, payable
in advance on the __1st__ day of every calendar month to Owners or their Agent*,
__X X X X__, whose address is __453 Sweet St., Littletown, CA__
When rent is paid on or before the __4th__ day of the calendar month, Owners
will give Tenants a (discount) (~~rebate~~) of $__20__.   (see PeT Agreement)
     The first month's rent is $__660__.
     The security/cleaning deposit on this dwelling is $__815__. It is
refundable if Tenants leave the dwelling reasonably clean and undamaged.
     Upon expiration, this Agreement shall become a month-to-month agreement
AUTOMATICALLY, UNLESS either Tenants or Owners notify the other party in
writing at least thirty days prior to expiration that they do not wish this
Agreement to continue on any basis.
     Should Tenants move before this Agreement expires, they will be
responsible for paying rent through the end of the term or until another
tenant approved by the Owners has moved in, whichever comes first.
     Owners will refund all deposits due within __10__ days after Tenants have
moved out completely and returned their keys.
     Only the following __ONE__ persons and __ONE__ pets are to live in this dwelling:
__DORTHY MAE MAHONEY and pet, FANG a Lhasa Apso.__
Without Owners' prior written permission, no other persons may live there,
and no other pets may stay there, even temporarily, nor may the dwelling be
sublet or used for business purposes.
     Use of the following is included in the rent: __Carpets, drapery rods, built-in stove and refigerator.__
     Remarks: __owner pays water and garbage. Tenant responsible for all other utilities.__
TENANTS AGREE TO THE FOLLOWING:
1) to accept the dwelling "as is," having already inspected it.
2) to keep yards and garbage areas clean.
3) to keep from making loud or bothersome noises and disturbances and to
   play music and broadcast programs at all times so as not to disturb other
   people's peace and quiet.
4) not to paint or alter the dwelling without first getting Owners' written
   permission.
5) to park their motor vehicle in assigned space and to keep that space
   clean of oil drippings and grease.
6) not to repair their motor vehicle on the premises (unless it is in an
   enclosed garage) if such repairs will take longer than a single day.
7) to allow Owners to inspect the dwelling, work on it, or show it to
   prospective tenants at any and all reasonable times.
8) not to keep any liquid-filled furniture in this dwelling.
9) to pay rent by check or money order made out to Owners. (Checks must be
   good when paid or applicable late-payment consequences will apply.)
10) to pay for repairs of all damage, including drain stoppages, they or
    their guests have caused.
11) to pay for any windows broken in their dwelling while they live there.
     Violation of any part of this Agreement or nonpayment of rent when due
shall be cause for eviction under applicable code sections. The prevailing
party (shall) (~~shall not~~) recover reasonable legal services fees involved.
     Tenants hereby acknowledge that they have read this Agreement, understand
it, agree to it, and have been given a copy.
Owner __Leslie Landlady__   Tenant __Dorthy Mae Mahoney__
*By_____   Tenant_____
*Person authorized to accept legal service on Owners' behalf
     PG. 1 of 4

that move-in costs are borne by those who cause them, new tenants; otherwise the rents would have to be higher for everyone), advertising, showing the dwelling, checking credit, and changing locks. Tell them that the difference between the first month's rent and the rent for succeeding months is in no way to be considered a deposit. It is not a deposit. It represents an all-inclusive charge to new tenants only for the services which they alone require.

I should mention here as an aside that landlords and tenants have done battle for years over move-in costs. Landlords have always maintained that new tenants should pay for the extra costs involved in a change of tenancy, and tenants have always maintained that these costs are nothing more than the ordinary costs of doing business, and as such, they should be absorbed into their regular rent. Personally, I feel that tenants who stay put should not be subsidizing those who don't. Tenants who come and go are more expensive to deal with, and consequently, they should pay something more. In times past, some landlords have collected this "something more" in devious ways, most notably by withholding deposits, and tenants have screamed loudly enough so that laws to curb these devious ways are now on the books.

The best way I have found to charge new tenants something more to offset move-in costs is to charge a higher first month's rent, just as tool rental yards charge one hourly rate for the first four hours and another hourly rate for the balance of a twenty-four-hour period. If you explain your reasons to your tenants at the outset of their tenancy, there won't be any confusion about refundability later. It won't be an issue.

You should know, however, that some California tenants have challenged the legality of charging a higher first month's rent, arguing through some pretty tortuous reasoning that the extra rent is in reality a deposit and therefore refundable. Rather than come under legal attack as a landlord doing business in California, a state with laws and courts which favor tenants in too many ways, I decided reluctantly to stop charging a higher first month's rent. You will have to decide for yourself whether you can use it in the area where you do business. Either put a higher sum in the rental agreement's blank for first month's rent and explain why you're doing it, or put the regular month's rent in the blank. The

decision is yours.

Next, explain what your policy is regarding deposits, that you lump all deposits together so that any of the money might be used for damages, extraordinary cleaning costs, unpaid rent, or other accrued and unpaid charges. Tell them that you make no distinction as to what is a cleaning deposit, what is a security deposit, and what is a key deposit. Tell them that you will give them their deposits back after they move out so long as they leave the place reasonably clean and undamaged and give proper notice and furthermore, that you *want* to give them their money back because you'd rather do that than have to clean up after them and have to chase after them for their rent. Tell them that you're fair about returning deposits, and if appropriate, tell them to check with the departing tenants if they don't believe you. Also tell them whether you will be paying them interest on their deposits and if so, when. In some areas it's mandatory; in others, it's voluntary.

Tell them how much notice they should give you before they plan to vacate. Thirty days is most common, but I use fifteen because that's all the time I really need to prepare for a vacancy, and fifteen days is much more realistic for tenants. It has another important side benefit for you as well, one which is explained in step nine.

Ask for the names of all persons and pets who will be living in the dwelling, and write them into the agreement by name. Explain that nobody else may live there without your written permission, even temporarily. Tell them that their "guests" become tenants after two weeks (in some areas, laws may set the guest limit for a longer period, up to one month, and may allow any one person to be a guest twice in one year; check the applicable law for your area) and will have to be approved and added to the agreement at a slight increase in rent. Tell them what your pet policy is (see "Should You Accept Pets?" in chapter 12). If it's a no-pets policy, tell them exactly what you mean by "no pets." Point out the words "even temporarily" in the contract. Tell them that those words mean what they say. You do not allow pet-sitting for even five minutes.

List briefly the appliances and furnishings which are included in the rent and indicate whether any of them are on "loan" (see "Should You Furnish the Major Kitchen Appliances?" in chapter 12). Explain that you and they together

Availability of Information Regarding Registered Sex Offenders

(Addendum to Rental Agreement)

    This disclosure is attached to and forms a part of the Rental Agreement dated ___9-26-XX___ between ___Vernon Graves___, Owners, and ___Richard Renter___, Tenants.

The following text applies in California only:
    Notice: The California Department of Justice, sheriff's departments, police departments serving jurisdictions of 200,000 or more and many other local law enforcement authorities maintain for public access a data base of the locations of persons required to register pursuant to paragraph (1) of subdivision (a) of Section 290.4 of the Penal Code. The data base is updated on a quarterly basis and a source of information about the presence of these individuals in any neighborhood. The Department of Justice also maintains a Sex Offender Identification Line through which inquiries about individuals may be made. This is a "900" telephone service. Callers must have specific information about individuals they are checking. Information regarding neighborhoods is not available through the "900" telephone service.

The following text applies in states other than California:
    Notice: The state justice department, sheriff's departments, police departments serving jurisdictions of 200,000 or more and many other local law enforcement authorities maintain for public access a data base of the locations of persons required to register pursuant to "Megan's Law" or a similar statute. The data base is updated on a regular basis and is a source of information about the presence of these individuals in any neighborhood. Contact the state justice department to determine whether it also maintains a telephone service through which inquiries about individuals may be made.

The following acknowledge that the Owner or Owner's Agent whose signature appears below has provided a copy of this Rental Agreement Addendum to the Tenant(s) whose signature(s) appear(s) below.

Date___9/26/XX___ Tenant ___Richard Renter___

Date_____ Tenant _____

Date___9-26-XX___ Owner or Agent ___Leslie Landlady___

PAGE 4 OF 4

will make a complete on-site survey of the dwelling using the Condition & Inventory Checksheet as a record.

Explain which utilities you pay for and which parking space or garage the tenants may use, and indicate this information under "Remarks."

Also, if the rental is still being occupied, stipulate here that the agreement is contingent upon the other tenants vacating the premises (see "Two Tenants—One Rental Dwelling" in chapter 21).

Review once more the other requirements in the agreement just as you did in step seven. Remind them that they are responsible for any drain or sewer blockages which they themselves cause. Tell them that you don't use their drains and you aren't going to unclog the drains or pay to have them unclogged unless the tenants can prove to your satisfaction that the *building* was at

fault. Remind them that they are responsible for any windows broken in their rental dwelling regardless of who breaks them. And remind them that they shouldn't expect you to provide lockout service 24 hours a day free of charge. Explain that the regulations will be strictly enforced and that after fair warning, you will evict them for any violations.

Read in chapter 5 about the pros and cons of asking for legal services (attorney) fees, and decide whether to put the word "not" in the blank to indicate that you do not want the prevailing party to recover reasonable fees or whether to put a horizontal line in the blank to indicate the opposite.

If applicable, complete roommate, pet, cosigner, and waterbed agreements, and an addendum disclosing the availability, per Megan's Law, of information regarding registered sex offenders.

Finally, sign the Rental Agreement yourself and have the tenants sign. Give them a copy and keep one for your records.

9) Request all monies or a hefty deposit.

Think back for a moment to step two, "Prequalify the Prospects," and remember two of the questions you asked then to determine the following—when the prospects would be ready to move in and whether they would have the money necessary to move in. These two considerations become very important now that you are preparing to conclude this initial phase of your rental relationship.

At this point you have a signed agreement in hand and you have taken the dwelling off the market. So as far as you are concerned, the place is now rented and the rent should begin today or tomorrow, but if the tenants cannot move in for a week or so, you might consider splitting the rent with them for this short period as a goodwill gesture. For example, if you come to terms with them on Monday, March 10th, and they can't move in until Wednesday, March 19th, you might begin their rent from March 14th. Whatever you do, though, don't split rents for more than two weeks, don't do it if the tenants are going to be moving in immediately, and don't do it at all around the first of the month. Above all, don't come to terms with prospective tenants, tie up the place for a week or two while they are preparing to move, and then begin the rent from the day they actually move in. That's not a goodwill gesture at all; that's a foolish gesture, for you suffer the full loss of rents due to circumstances which are beyond your control. It's their problem that they can't move in, not yours. You're ready for them to move in now. Share the loss, if you're inclined to, but don't assume it all yourself.

Agreement to Hold Dwelling Off the Market

RECEIVED FROM *Marion MahnKen* , Approved Applicant,

the sum of *nine hundred dollars* ————— $ *900* .

$ *300* of this sum is <u>nonrefundable</u>. It shall be used for the purpose of holding off the market the rental dwelling commonly known as

1100 Staples Ave., Apt. 716

for the period from *8/26/xx* through *9/05/xx* only.

$ *600* of this sum is <u>refundable</u> if approved applicant does not move in. If applicant moves in, it shall be applied to move-in monies.

The applicant whose name appears above has been approved to rent the dwelling identified above but for one reason or another cannot take possession now.

The applicant has read and approved the rental agreement but has not paid all of the sums required to move in. The applicant has no right to receive keys or take possession of the dwelling until all of the sums required to take possession have been paid in full.

The owner/manager retains possession of the dwelling under this agreement and is obligated to safeguard it and maintain its condition so that it does not deteriorate during the term of this agreement. If it is materially damaged, applicant shall receive a refund of all monies paid.

At least twenty-four hours prior to the termination of this agreement, the applicant must notify the owner/manager of his/her intentions to take possession or not take possession of the dwelling. Notice must be made in writing and delivered to the owner/manager during normal business hours (9am-5pm) at the owner/manager's address shown below.

Should the applicant fail to notify the owner/manager of his/her intentions to take possession as outlined above, owner/manager will put the dwelling back on the market upon the termination of this agreement.

Should the applicant take possession of the dwelling prior to the termination of this agreement, the applicant will be credited as having paid rent through the termination date of this agreement, and this agreement will then be superseded by the rental agreement.

Should the applicant not take possession of the dwelling prior to or upon the expiration of this agreement, the owner/manager will keep the entire nonrefundable sum paid as consideration for having held the rental dwelling off the market for the time period specified above and will refund the applicant's refundable sum within forty-eight hours.

8/26/xx 10:30 A.M.
Date/Time

Marion Mahnken
Approved Applicant--Name / Signature

657-11th St., #108   *555-1937*
Address / Phone

8/26/xx 10:30 Am
Date/Time

Suzie Que – Manager
Owner/Manager--Name / Signature

1100 Staples Ave., #201   *555-1109*
Address / Phone

If you and the Richard Renters agree that their rent should begin March 14th, then their rental period for that first month is March 14th through April 13th. Since you probably want their rent to be due on the first (see chapter 6 about the advisability of having rents due on the first) of the month, prorate their rent the second month, not the first. Request the full month's rent when they move in as a full commitment from them and a kind of insurance for you. On April 1st, collect rent to cover the period April 14th through April 30th. Make a point of telling them that the prorated rent for the balance of April is due on the first of April, not on the fourteenth, the same as it would be if they owed rent for the entire month. Keep them a full month ahead during this crucial early period of tenancy when you are just getting to know them and you don't know yet how dependable they are.

Be careful when you prorate rent. You can cheat yourself quite easily doing proration calculations. Consider the period of April 14th through April 30th, for example; is it 16 days or is it 17? It may appear to be 16 because the difference between 30 and 14 is 16, as every sixth grader knows, but it's not. It's not because this period includes both the 14th *and* the 30th, as well as the days in between. To calculate the number of days correctly, you have to subtract 14 from 30 and add one. If that doesn't make much sense to you, count the days on your fingers and toes, and you'll see that 17 is correct. Once you know the correct number, divide the monthly rent by the total number of days in the month and multiply that figure, which is the rent per day, by the number of days the tenants are going to be occupying the premises. Tell them what this amount is even before they move in so they will know how much to set aside to pay you on the first of the following month.

As for advance money, you should request as much as you can get from new tenants. How much is enough? Whatever the market will bear and the laws will allow. Some local laws restrict advance money for unfurnished dwellings to the equivalent of three months' rent and for furnished dwellings to four months' rent. That should be sufficient. All told, that would work out to the first month's rent and combined deposits for security, cleaning, pets, waterbed, and keys equal to two months' rent.

Unless the laws in your area specify exactly what you are allowed to collect in the categories of first month's rent, last month's rent, and combined deposits, do not require any last month's rent at all. Instead, add that amount to the deposits. Make the deposits larger because you can use them to offset repairs, cleaning, or rent, whereas whatever sum is designated as last month's rent must be used for last month's rent and nothing else. Last month's rent also must be reported immediately as income, whereas deposits are not considered income until they are used. They're limbo monies.

There is, of course, always the problem of tenants who want to use all or part of their deposits for last month's rent, and there's not much you can do about it except to require high deposits in the beginning and stress that these deposits are *not* to be considered last month's rent. So long as you hold a deposit significantly higher than their last month's rent, you won't have too much cause for concern if tenants do want to apply their deposits to the last month's rent.

Another solution to this problem is to require less than thirty days' notice to vacate. If you require only a fifteen-day notice, the tenants' rental period and the notice period do not coincide, and tenants are less likely to think about using their deposits for rent. In most cases, when they do decide to give notice, they will already have paid their last month's rent two weeks before and won't be tempted to use their deposits for rent.

Much as you'd like to get the equivalent of three months' rent before tenants move in, you can't always get it, so you should have a minimum, too. The minimum amount to request before letting tenants move in under a month-to-month agreement, no matter which day of the month they do so, is the sum of the first month's rent, a security/cleaning deposit equal to one month's rent minus $25, and a two-dollar deposit for each key. Consider that the minimum.

In bygone days when anybody could buy a new tract house for no money down, I used to request less than this minimum in order to be competitive, but I wound up losing too much to unscrupulous tenants. That's Lesson Number 2116 at Hard Knocks College—*Require plenty of upfront money.* For some strange reason, the greater the deposit, the more tenants will do to get it back. Hmm! Imagine that!

Of course, the more advance money you require, the better you're protected, but the harder

Condition & Inventory Checksheet

Tenants: RICHARD and ROSE RENTER   Dated: JAN. 15, XXXX

Address: 456 Sweet St., Littletown

Date Moved In: 1/15/XX   Notice Given: _____   Moved Out: _____

Abbreviations:

Air Cond, AC	Clean, Cl	Drape, Drp	Hood, Hd	OK, OK	Table, Tbl
Bed, Bd	Cracked, Cr	Dryer, Dry	Just Painted, JP	Poor, P	Tile, Tl
Broken, Brk	Curtain, Ctn	Fair, F	Lamp, Lmp	Refrigerator, Rf	Venet'n Blind, VB
Carpet, Cpt	Dinette, Din	Good, G	Lightbulb, LtB	Shade, Sh	Washer, Wsh
Chair, Ch	Dishwasher, Dsh	Heater, Htr	Linoleum, Lino	Sofa, Sfa	Waxed, Wxd
Chest, Chst	Disposer, Dsp	Hole, H	Nightstand, Ntst	Stove, Stv	Wood, Wd

Circle rooms; enter abbreviations	Walls, Doors cond.	chgs.	Floors cond.	chgs.	Windows cond.	chgs.	Lt. Fixtures cond.	chgs.	Inventory: Appliances, Furniture Item	cond.	chgs.
(Living Rm)	OK		CL. CPt.		wind-cr scrn-ok Drp-ok		⊘		⊖		
Dining Rm											
(Kitchen)	OK				scrn-ok sh-G		L+B OK		STV, Hd Ref (on loan)	Cl. Cl.	
(Bath 1)	JP				scrn-ok sh-G		Lt B OK				
Bath 2											
(Bedroom 1)	OK				Scrn-ok Drp-cl		L+B OK		⊖		
Bedroom 2											
Bedroom 3											
Other											
Itemized Charges											

TOTAL ITEMIZED CHARGES _____

Other Charges Not Itemized (Dirty garage, etc. Explained on Backside) _____

Deduction for Improper Notice _____

Deduction for Missing Keys _____

TOTAL DEDUCTIONS _____

TOTAL DEPOSITS $850

minus (-) TOTAL DEDUCTIONS _____

equals (=) DEPOSIT REFUND or (Amount Owed) _____

[X] Tenants acknowledge that the smoke detector was tested in their presence and found to be in working order and that its operation was explained to them. Tenants agree to test the detector at least every other week and to report any problems to Owners in writing. If the detector is battery operated, Tenants agree to replace the battery as necessary with a new ALKALINE battery (unless applicable laws require otherwise).

Tenants hereby acknowledge that they have read this Checksheet, agree that the condition and contents of the above-mentioned rental dwelling are without exception as represented herein, understand that they are liable for any damage done to this dwelling as outlined in their Lease or Rental Agreement, and have received a copy of this Checksheet.

Lester, Landlord
Owner

Richard Renter
Tenant

Rose Renter
Tenant

BY Person authorized to represent Owners

pg 2 of 3

becomes the search for new tenants who have a large advance sum.

To help you decide how much to require, inquire into the prevailing practice in your rental area and then follow suit.

No matter how much or how little you require, you will find that some people won't have on hand all the money they need to move in.

If they cannot pay you all the rent and deposits immediately, accept a minimum of half a month's rent, and use a form like the Agreement to Hold Dwelling Off the Market to establish without a doubt what your relationship is at this point and how their monies are to be used.

Make no mistakes here. Mistakes here can be very costly and very regrettable. People who have been approved to rent from you and have given you only a portion of their move-in monies are not your tenants yet until you give them possession, and you should not give them possession until they have paid all of their move-in monies. Just by giving them the keys, you are giving them possession and the rights of tenancy. Do not give them the keys until they have paid all of their move-in monies.

If you do give them possession before they pay all of their move-in monies and if things go awry at the very beginning of your landlord-tenant relationship, you will have to evict them, and you will be poorer by hundreds, if not thousands, of dollars. An eviction is a painful procedure, and you want to avoid it whenever possible, especially at this juncture when it's so easily avoidable.

The Agreement to Hold Dwelling Off the Market form refers to these people who don't have all of their move-in monies as "approved applicants," and that's what they are. They are not tenants. It states exactly how long a time they have to come up with the balance of their move-in monies. It states exactly what you will do with the monies if they do come up with the balance. It states exactly what you will do with the monies if they don't come up with the balance. It states exactly when and how they need to notify you of their intention to take possession. It states exactly what you will do if they do not notify you of their intention to take possession.

Use this agreement to avoid confusion whenever you accept monies from approved applicants to hold a rental dwelling off the market. Confusion occurs because tenants tend to think that their monies are a deposit, a refundable deposit.

If they do not come up with the balance or if they change their mind and decide not to rent from you, they want you to return their deposit, not just some of it, all of it. Likewise, if they do come up with the balance of the move-in monies and do take possession, they want you to apply all that they paid you initially to their rent and deposits beginning with the very day when they take possession. They don't expect to compensate you for the days you held the dwelling off the market for them and them alone.

Don't be bamboozled! Don't cheat yourself!

Monies which approved applicants give you to hold a rental dwelling off the market are not rent, and they are not a deposit. Neither are they refundable. Those monies compensate you for the rent you would have received had a paying customer been occupying the dwelling. When you're holding a rental dwelling off the market, you cannot rent it, even for a day, to someone else, and you should not lose income because the approved applicants cannot take possession. That's their problem, and you shouldn't be losing income because of a problem of theirs. You should be charging them for every day you hold the dwelling off the market. The Agreement to Hold Dwelling Off the Market form will help explain the charges before they become an issue of dispute.

When accepting monies to hold a dwelling off the market, go ahead and accept a personal or business check so long as you have enough time to verify that the check has cleared the bank before the approved applicants pay the balance of the money and receive possession.

When accepting move-in monies in full, *never* accept a personal or business check unless you withhold possession until the check actually clears. The check must be at least as good as the greenbacks the government prints before you issue keys.

Otherwise, insist that move-in monies be in the form of greenbacks, gold coins, silver bars, money orders, or cashier's checks.

Under no circumstances should you issue keys so they can move in a "few things." Every last cent of the move-in monies you have agreed upon must be paid first.

Too many landlords get burned by allowing tenants to move in some belongings without their having paid the full amount owed. Once they're in, the tenants pay not a cent more and have to

Date: _10/21/XX_

To: _Bourne A. Luzer_

We appreciate your applying to rent a dwelling from us. We regret to inform you that you will need to continue looking for a place to live somewhere else for the following reasons:

CIRCUMSTANCES

[ ] Dwelling rented to previously approved applicant

[ ] Unsigned application   [ ] Incomplete application

[ ] Discrepancies on application

CREDIT REPORT (If items here are checked, see attachment.)

[ ] Credit not verifiable   [ ] Bankruptcy filed

[ ] Judgments, garnishments, liens   [X] Slow pay

[ ] Account(s) sent for collection   [ ] Low credit score

INCOME/ASSETS

[ ] Income not verifiable   [ ] Insufficient income

[ ] Assets not verifiable   [ ] Insufficient assets

EMPLOYMENT HISTORY

[ ] Employment not verifiable   [X] Unsteady employment

[ ] Temporary employment

TENANCY HISTORY

[ ] Tenancy not verifiable   [ ] Eviction on record

[X] Late payments   [ ] Insufficient funds checks

[ ] Agreement violation(s)   [ ] Lack of cooperation

PERSONAL REFERENCES

[X] References not verifiable   [ ] Negative reference

OTHER REASONS

_____

Your application will remain in our files for a minimum of two years. If you would like to discuss it or our reasons above, please contact us for an appointment.

We wish you good luck in finding an even better place to live.

Sincerely,

Padre D. Clark

be evicted. Don't get burned with this little ruse.

Be sure to issue a receipt for whatever money they pay. If you don't have a receipt book with you, use the back of the Rental Agreement to write up an itemized receipt, making at least an original and one copy.

10) Create a written and photographic record of the dwelling's condition, contents, and tenants.

"The palest ink is better than the most retentive memory," states an old Chinese proverb. Because you and your nice new tenants will surely differ in your recollections of the rental dwelling as it was when they moved in compared with its condition when they finally do move out, you should have a record of its condition and contents to protect both yourself and them. That record ought to be written, to be sure. It also ought to be photographic, perhaps even videographic.

To make a good photographic record, take at least three inside shots of the areas which tend to show the most damage, and *include the new tenants somewhere in these shots.*

There are three reasons why you should include the new tenants in these shots. First, you should have a photo of them somewhere in your files so you will know how to identify them to a process server should you ever have to take them to court. Second, you should have a photo of them to discourage gang activity. Gang members do not want any photographic record linking them to the place where they live. They do not want to be so easily identified to the police. Third, you should have some proof that the photographs of the dwelling were taken right before the tenants moved in. Nothing else you can do will fix these photographs as firmly in time as including the tenants themselves in the photographs. Nobody can dispute later exactly when the photographs were taken. They were taken *before* the tenants moved in and showed the fine condition of the dwelling at that time. If you have a digital camera, use it for these shots so you know right away whether the photographs "came out." If you don't have a digital camera, use any camera and trust that your photographic talents and the camera itself will deliver adequate results.

To make a good videographic record, turn your camera on and start out by saying into the microphone, "Here we are on such-and-such date

doing a walk-through at such-and-such address. This rental dwelling will soon be occupied by the so-and-so's whom you can see over there." Pan *slowly* across every bit of the dwelling from room to room while talking into the microphone yourself about what you're looking at and remarking about the condition of the place. You might even ask the new tenants to make some comments about the condition of the place. Their own words will go far to prove to any judge or jury what the place really looked like before the tenants move in, should the matter ever come into dispute.

To make a good written record, complete the Condition & Inventory Checksheet. To fill it out properly, show the tenants the smoke alarm paragraph, take them to where the smoke alarm is located, demonstrate how it works, and get them to initial the paragraph to indicate that they know how to look after it. Then go through each room of the dwelling with the tenants, circle the applicable rooms, and fill in the "condition" and "item" columns with the appropriate abbreviations. Do not put anything in the "charges" columns. They're for you to fill in after the tenants have moved out. Now add up the security/cleaning, pet, waterbed, and key deposits and write down that sum as the total deposits. Date the checksheet, sign it yourself, and have the tenants sign it as well. Keep the original and a copy and give them a copy.

Later, when the tenants have moved out and are demanding their deposits back, take the original and your copy and make a comparison inspection of the dwelling, marking the charges for broken shades, dirty carpets, etc. (see chapter 8).

Now that you and your new tenants have signed the Rental Agreement, filled out the Condition & Inventory Checksheet, and settled all of your accounts, you should issue keys and change the mailbox label. Both of you are completely committed to one another, having created that special landlord-tenant relationship.

Even after you have completed all ten steps with Richard Renter and have created that special relationship, you and he will still be conjuring up strange mental images of one another, but you will have done all you can do to assure yourself of getting a good tenant. Give him a chance to prove that he is what he seems to be, at the same time you're proving to him that you are what you seem to be.

Date: _8/29/xx_

To: _Danni De Faltz_

Your application to rent from us has been rejected either partly or solely because of information provided by the following sources:

CREDIT REPORT

[X] Equifax Credit Information Service, P. O. Box 740241, Atlanta, GA 30374-2041; 800.685.1111

[ ] Experian Consumer Assistance, P. O. Box 949, Allen, TX 75002; 800.682.7654

[ ] Trans Union Consumer Relations, P. O. Box 1000, 2 Baldwin Place, Chester, PA 19022; 800.888.4213

[ ] _____

COURT RECORDS REPORT

[ ] American Tenant Screen, 131 N. Narberth Ave., Narberth, PA 19072; 610.664.2323

[ ] _____

BAD CHECK REPORT

[ ] Telecheck Services, P.O. Box 4513, Houston, TX 77210-4513; 800.366.2425

[ ] _____

The federal Fair Credit Reporting Act requires us to reveal the source of whatever credit reports figured in the decision to reject you as an applicant. Please note that the agencies checked above only provided information about you. They did not make the decision, nor can they explain the decision.

Under federal law, you have the right to obtain a free copy of your credit report within sixty days from the date when we inquired about your credit. That was _8_ / _28_ / _XX_ .

To secure the report, you must provide the following: your full name, your complete mailing address, your residential address if different from your mailing address, your daytime phone number, your employer's name, your Social Security number, your driver's license number and the state where issued (bad checks only), and the name of the company which rejected you. Our company name is _Madre and Padre Rentals_ .

If you believe your report is inaccurate or incomplete, you may contact the agency to dispute its accuracy and insert a 100-word consumer statement of explanation. Assistance is available at the credit reporting agency to help you with the statement.

You may have additional rights under the credit reporting or consumer protection laws of your state. To find out what they are, you may contact your state or local consumer protection agency or the office of your state attorney general. See the government listings in the white pages of your telephone book.

Sincerely,

Padre D. Clark

Rejecting Applicants

Rejecting those applicants whom you believe would be poor tenants for one reason or another is a corollary to this whole process of getting good tenants. Rejection is hard for some people to take, and it is still harder for others to give. Some landlords rent to the first person who expresses an interest in renting their place because they just can't say "no." That kind of timidity you can ill afford. You have to get used to saying "no" in this business every so often, and one of the most important times you'll ever say it is when you refuse to rent to an applicant.

The trick is to say "no" in a kindly way. If you have more than one applicant for a vacancy and the first among them qualified according to all of your standards and also decided to take the place, saying "no" to the others is relatively easy, for you are merely informing the unsuccessful applicants that you have rented the place to somebody else.

In that case, you might call them one by one and say something like this, "Hello, Gulley Jimson, I just wanted to let you know that somebody else rented the house on Sixth Street that you were interested in. We had four applications for it, and I sure do wish we'd had four places to rent because all four applicants would have made fine tenants, but unfortunately we had only the one vacancy and we could accommodate only one tenant. We'll certainly keep your application on file in case something else comes up, and we'd like to wish you good luck in finding something else even more suited to your needs. How do you want us to return the deposit you gave us with your application?" This kind of rejection sounds sympathetic enough to be acceptable to practically anybody. It's inoffensive and it's entirely plausible. It works well.

"Dear Mr. Burns:
    I've got some good news and some bad news for you. The bad news is that you didn't get the apartment you wanted to rent from us on Elm Street, so we're returning your deposit. The good news is that you won yourself $25 for submitting 'The Most Unbelievable Application of the Month'...."

If your dwelling has not been rented, however, such a rejection would be both foolish and risky. Never say a place has been rented unless it actually has been. Never say it has been rented in order to dissuade a persistent inquirer or anyone else, for that matter. Such a simpleminded ploy will only cause you trouble. Even when you are not actually discriminating against someone illegally, this falsehood, if discovered, could be construed to be a sign of blatant discrimination, and it could be all the evidence needed by those who thrive on suing unsuspecting landlords for discrimination.

Be more cautious than that. Even when you have yet to find a suitable tenant and you are being pestered for acceptance by undesirable applicants, don't ever resort to saying the place has been rented just to get them off your back. Stall if need be. Say that you turned the applications over to a tenant-checking service and that they are a little slow at times in notifying you of the results. It's not the best approach, but it will suffice for a few days while you pray for good acceptable applicants to come along so you can rent to them and then use the kindly rejection approach on the others.

Sometimes the best approach is one which is honest, direct, and timely. It may not appear to be kindly on the surface, but it is, because it deflates the applicants' high hopes for your rental early on so they can realistically assess their prospects and won't waste any more time waiting to hear from you.

Tell the applicants by phone, if possible, that you're sorry they just don't fit your tenant guidelines and that they should begin looking further for housing. They may take the news well, ask you a question or two about other places for rent, say thanks, and say goodbye. If they don't, be as polite as you can be while they argue their case, recount their sad story, bang the receiver in your ear, or string together a few profanities. Don't budge from your decision, no matter what they do or say. You know you don't want them to be your tenants because they don't fit your standards. Let them rent from someone else who has different standards.

Another good direct approach is rejection by letter with the reason or reasons clearly identified. For that, there's a form you may use consisting of seven sections and any number of reasons with checkboxes next to them. As soon as you know that you won't be renting to a particular applicant, complete the form, include whatever deposit monies you must return, make a copy for your records, and send everything off to the applicant.

No matter how you inform the applicants about their having been rejected, you must comply with the federal Fair Credit Reporting Act if one of the reasons for rejecting them was a negative credit report. You should not give or show them the report itself, and you should not show or discuss it with anyone else, either. You should give the applicants the name of the credit reporting agency you used and give them information about how to contact the agency, so they can obtain a complimentary copy of the report within the next sixty days. For that, there's another form. It tells them something about their rights, whom to contact and when, and how they can go about adding their own one-hundred-word statement of explanation to their credit report.

Rejecting applicants who want to rent from you is no pleasant task, but it's a very necessary task, one you cannot ignore. Grit your teeth and get it over with. Endure the few unpleasantries right now that your rejection of them might cause, and you won't have to cope with them later as unsuitable tenants.

Some Last Words

This whole process of getting good tenants without rubbing somebody the wrong way, without running afoul of some law or other, without getting sued, without getting cheated, and without getting stuck with the wrong tenants is challenging, even daunting.

It's minefield territory.

Some people would rather put up their hands and surrender than face this minefield and the dire consequences which can result from a single misstep. They're not landlord material. They surrender too easily.

You can traverse this minefield and get good tenants. The more you do it, the better you'll become.

Even so, you cannot become complacent about getting good tenants. The minefield is always dangerous. Step through it cautiously.

5
Searching
For the Right
Rental Agreement

Some poor souls keep searching for the Fountain of Youth as long as they live. You'll be searching for the "right" rental agreement as long as you're in this business. Laws change, practices change, locales change, times change, the business climate changes, your property mix changes, and your tenant mix changes. You have to adapt your business practices to these changes or suffer the consequences, whatever they may be.

The rental agreement you use is at the very core of your business. You must feel comfortable with it. You must feel that it covers everything you want it to cover, and you must feel sure that it's as legal as it can be in the very community where you do business.

The Kitchen Sink Agreement

The single-page rental agreement introduced in chapter 4 does not include the proverbial kitchen sink. Nope, it is simple and understandable, and it includes only the essentials needed to formalize a landlord-tenant relationship involving a residence. It is much better than a verbal agreement, that's for sure, but it is not nearly as good as a comprehensive umpteen-page agreement drafted for your particular rental property by an attorney familiar with all the pertinent laws and practices in the locale where the property happens to be. Naturally, such an agreement would include the kitchen sink and maybe a bathroom sink and tub as well.

The trouble with most lengthy agreements, however, be they custom-made or "standard" forms, is that they tend to be repetitive and incomprehensible. They're so full of legal jargon that they don't make much sense to the parties they're supposed to make sense to, and they're so lengthy that you can't possibly review them word for word with new tenants unless you spend half a day pouring over them. Try reading over a multi-page, small-print agreement with a new tenant sometime, and you'll barely be able to keep from stifling yawns and rolling your eyes as you read all the "wherefores," "whereases," and "hereinafters."

Long agreements aren't necessarily bad, especially not when they're well thought out and well organized. Incomprehensible agreements, on the other hand, are bad. Don't use any agreement, long or short, unless you are able to explain it to your tenants as you read it over with them. Anything else, especially if it has lots of fine print, may appear to them to be sneaky, whether it is or not. (One landlady I know goes to all the trouble of writing her rental agreements out by hand. She claims that her tenants trust handwritten documents more than those which are typed or printed, and she feels that her tenants' trust is more important than anything else.)

A rental agreement must communicate the particulars of what you and your tenants have agreed upon, and it must be legally enforceable. That's all. It needn't repeat every last detail of the applicable landlord-tenant law as some agreements do, and it needn't be written so that only someone with a law degree is able to interpret it.

If you feel somehow vulnerable unless you use a rental agreement lengthy enough to cover almost everything in your landlord-tenant relationships, that is, unless it includes the proverbial kitchen sink, get a long-form agreement from your local rental housing association, or if there is no association in your area, get one from your state rental housing association. You can be sure that that agreement has been reviewed by attorneys who are familiar with the applicable landlord-tenant laws and that it will include every essential element plus a whole lot more. But don't stop there. Read it over carefully. If it doesn't make perfect sense to you, translate it yourself into a more meaningful document so that you'll understand it well enough to be able to help your tenants understand it also.

Another good cover-all-bases agreement is

available from Professional Publishing, 122 Paul Drive, San Rafael, CA 94903, 800.288.2006 (profpub.com). Call them and order their *Loose Leaf Sample Book*, which consists of hundreds of pages of forms, including a rental agreement, a lease-option agreement, and a combined purchase agreement and deposit receipt. They sell this book to acquaint people with their many forms, and they sell the forms themselves in quantities as well.

No matter what agreement you use, keep checking it all the time for legality. Landlord-tenant laws do change.

One thing doesn't change and won't change in this country so long as democracy is alive. That one thing is people's rights. No matter what you write into a rental agreement, you cannot take people's rights away from them.

As you know, slavery is now against the law in this country. Were someone to agree voluntarily to become your slave and were you to draw up a slavery agreement which was then signed by your slave without any coercion whatsoever on your part, you could not enforce that agreement through any court in the land. When your "slave" wants out of those shackles, you'd better let him go. Don't try to argue that the shackles are foam padded. He has an inalienable right to liberty. That's a right he cannot sign away under any circumstances.

So, too, your tenants cannot sign away their rights even if they wanted to. Your agreement should not include any provision which deprives them of the rights guaranteed to them by the laws of the land, such as their right to privacy, their right to a habitable dwelling, their right to quiet enjoyment, their right to minimum notice periods, their right to have children living with them, their right to sue for injuries, and their right to the prompt return of their deposits. Such clauses would be unenforceable and would cause

a judge to look askance at your entire agreement.

Keep unenforceable clauses, needless repetition, and legal obfuscation out of your agreement entirely. Above all, keep your agreement reasonable enough so that you and your tenants can live with it throughout your relationship.

Here's My "Two-in-One" Kitchen Sink Agreement

Have you taken a good look at a new stepladder lately? Stepladders are plastered with as many stickers as a hippie van's bumper. They all warn ladder buyers to be careful. Here's a sample. "Do not stand on the top step or the bucket shelf." "Do not climb on the back section of the ladder." "Do not place the ladder in front of a door opening toward the ladder." "Maintain a firm hold on the ladder." "Lock the spreaders before use." "Keep metal ladders away from live electrical circuits." There are more of these stickers on the ladder I'm quoting from, but I'm not going to quote them all. I'm sure you get the picture.

You might ask yourself why all of these warnings have to spoil the appearance of your new ladder when they're so obvious. Doesn't every fool know that it's foolish to place a ladder in front of a door which might swing open and knock the ladder over? Doesn't every fool know enough not to stand on the bucket shelf? Doesn't every fool know that a metal ladder could shock the life out of him if it's touching an exposed live wire?

You know the reason for these superfluous warnings, don't you? Sure. Lawsuits. Lawsuits have forced the manufacturers to plaster warnings all over their ladders. Some fool *did* stand on the bucket shelf. After he fell and became a paraplegic, he sued, claiming that the ladder manufacturer should have warned him about standing on the bucket shelf. He settled for $7 million. That lawsuit and others like it added these various self-evident warnings to the ladders we buy today.

Now, you know that a ladder is pretty straightforward compared to a rental property, and I hope that the day never arrives when we landlords are forced to plaster the walls of our rental properties with warning stickers. "Do not touch light switch when in contact with water." "Keep stray fingers away from door jamb when closing door." "Keep head out of oven when gas is on and pilot light is off." "Enter and exit dwelling through doors only, not windows." "Keep hands out of garbage disposer at all times." "Sweep up and dispose of broken window glass to prevent accidental cuts." "Unscrew light bulbs from their sockets by turning them counterclockwise." "Cover ears when smoke alarm sounds to avoid loss of hearing." "Remove obstruction from toilet bowl when water overflows." "Close doors and windows to maintain inside temperature." Why, if ladder manufacturers can come up with twenty warnings, we should be able to come up with at least a thousand. Wouldn't you say?

True enough. Thank heavens we don't have to. Not yet anyway. But in these litigious times we may need to come up with a rental agreement which covers more than just the basics of the landlord-tenant relationship, an agreement which circumscribes as many potential problem areas as possible.

One apartment tenant sued his landlord because the landlord had moved the garbage dumpster from one part of the property to another, where the garbage truck could get to it more easily. The tenant sued claiming that the dumpster in its new location was obstructing his view and that he wouldn't have rented the apartment had he known that the dumpster might be moved. The judge looked at the rental agreement and let the landlord tell his side of the story, and then he ruled in favor of the tenant because the landlord had failed to include a paragraph in the rental agreement which specifically reserved him the right to place objects outside the building wherever he wanted to place them.

That landlord must have wished that he had paid more attention to his rental agreement. You can be sure that he does now. What a rental agreement says is important, you know. You'll know just how important it is when somebody hauls you into court on what you thought was some insignificant matter and clobbers you there because you were guilty of a minor oversight.

Although I still use the shorter agreement for many of my rentals, I finally gave in and drafted a longer agreement for those tenants who are more prone to "question authority" and sue when they feel wronged.

My agreement is short on the legalese and long on the vernacular. It's not a perfect agreement, by any means. It's a work in progress, and I'll be changing it as long as I'm in this landlording business. I call it my "two-in-one kitchen sink agreement." It's "two-in-one" because it can be used either as a month-to-month agreement or as a fixed-term agreement, and it's a "kitchen sinker" because it includes both practical considerations and boilerplate.

It may or may not be a good agreement for you to use. That's for you to decide. Some of it may be illegal where you do business. Some of it may be overly restrictive, as far as you are concerned. Some of it may not apply. Some of the things which are really important to you may have been overlooked. That's all right. If you want to make changes, make them. If you want to use this agreement as a source of material to help you draft your own agreement, go ahead. Just make sure that you know what's in any agreement you adopt as your own, regardless of the source, and try your best to be circumspect when you contemplate the consequences of including or not including a certain clause.

As written, this agreement will work for either fixed-term or month-to-month tenancies. It will work for single-family dwellings or multiple-family dwellings. It will work no matter how you handle late rent payments (see chapter 6 for a discussion of the various prompt-payment policies), no matter how you handle lockouts (see chapter 12 for a discussion of lockouts), no matter how you decide to handle the legal services fees question (that's coming later in this chapter).

This is a very versatile agreement, so versatile that you could overlook one of the opportunities it gives you to make choices. For example, if you were to decide to charge a set late fee of $20, you'd need to cross out the other alternatives in the late fees paragraph and cross out the discounts/rebates paragraph altogether. If you were to decide to use the rebate policy, you'd need to cross out the late fees paragraph altogether and cross out the word "discount" where it appears in the discounts/rebates paragraph.

Should any paragraph contradict your policy on guests, appliances, pets, liquid-filled furniture, or anything else, you could merely strike it out, initial it, and have the other parties do the same. If you felt compelled to include your own policy in these matters, whatever it might be, you could write it in wherever there's enough blank space.

The total number of pages the agreement contains is determined by the addition of other agreements, such as a Co-Signer Agreement or a Pet Agreement. The total number of all these pages goes in the blank at the top of each page of the Rental Agreement and at the bottom of the addendum agreements.

All in all, this agreement does not have as many teeth in it as some I've seen. It has only enough to nip wayward tenants and keep them in line. What's most important is that it shouldn't have any teeth in it which will bite back at you. Them's the worst kind.

Examine this "kitchen-sink" agreement and decide for yourself whether you could use all or any part of it.

Two Unresolved Questions

There are two questions which keep coming up whenever we landlords are searching for the right rental agreement. One is the hoary question of whether the agreement should be month-to-month or fixed-term. The other is a newer question, whether we ought to request that the loser in a lawsuit must pay the winner's legal services fees. The second question is not quite so pressing, perhaps, unless you happen to be affected. Then it can be more pressing than a bloated bladder before the intermission at a Wagnerian opera.

Here are some of the rationales used in formulating answers to these questions.

■ **Should you use month-to-month agreements or leases?**—You'll notice that there are only two choices given in the question above—month-to-month agreements and leases. In truth, there are four choices—oral month-to-month agreements, written month-to-month agreements, oral leases (leases for any period longer than a year must be written), and written leases, but oral month-to-month agreements and oral leases, while they may be binding, are seldom used anymore because people don't trust their memories or each other as much as they once did. Forget about making oral contracts yourself (after all, some people nowadays even put their nuptial agreements in writing to remind their spouses of certain obligations), and you'll avoid the many misunderstandings which can be caused by

people's foggy recollections of what was agreed upon initially. Consider only whether you should use a written month-to-month agreement or a written lease, and keep in mind the difference between the two.

Basically, the difference is a simple one, but it is an exceedingly important one. Month-to-month agreements cover time periods which are indefinite, whereas leases cover a definite and longer period of time (generally a year for residential property). Although they may be written to contain rent escalation and thirty-day termination clauses, in which cases they are essentially month-to-month agreements anyway, leases bind both parties to the terms of the agreement so that no changes may be made by either party until the lease expires or unless one party breaks it.

Lease breaking occurs every day and you don't have to think too much about the matter to figure out who usually breaks them. Tenants do. In theory, if tenants move before their lease expires and they do not have whatever your state or community defines as a good cause for breaking their lease legally ("good causes" might be entering active duty with the U.S. military or taking employment in another community or losing the main source of income used to pay rent), then they are responsible for paying the rent covering the entire lease period, so long as you have been unsuccessful in a reasonable effort to find new tenants at the best rent possible. In practice, however, even if you do make a reasonable effort to re-rent the place and find nobody to rent it, you would have a difficult time collecting all the rent owing on the lease unless the tenants had sufficient assets, and even then you'd probably have to sue them every month in separate small claims actions to recover.

Leases are like those treaties which the English so naively signed with Germany during the late '30s. They bound the English, just as leases bind landlords, while the Germans did exactly as they pleased, impudently enjoying the limitations they had placed upon their foolish adversaries. The Germans had nothing to lose, and neither do most tenants. The Germans were too powerful for any agreement to matter much. Most tenants are too poor.

Leases bind only those who have some assets and want to be bound. Tenants generally have little to lose by breaking a lease, but woe be unto you, landlord, if you should ever try to break a lease! That "Clark Kent of consumerism," Ralph Charell, in his book, *How I Turn Ordinary Com-*

Rental Agreement

Dated: *October 17, XXXX*

Agreement between Owners: *Delwin and Muretta Levno*

and Tenants: *James and Ann Phelan*

for a dwelling located at: *730 Beaver Avenue, Sunny, OR 08100*

[Initial ONE of the boxes below to indicate whether this Agreement is month-to-month or fixed term.]

Month-to-Month Agreement—Tenants agree to rent this dwelling on a month-to-month basis beginning *November 1, XXXX* .

Fixed-Term Agreement (Lease)—Tenants agree to lease this dwelling for a fixed term of _____, beginning _____ and ending _____.
Upon expiration, this Agreement shall become a month-to-month agreement AUTOMATICALLY, UNLESS either Tenants or Owners notify the other party in writing at least thirty days prior to expiration that they do not wish this Agreement to continue on any basis.

Rent—Tenants agree to rent this dwelling for $ *850* per *MONTH* , payable in advance. The first month's rent is $ *900* .

Rent Due/Late Consequences—Rent is due on the *1st* . It is late on the *5th* . Owners expect to RECEIVE the rent BEFORE the late date. Should exceptional circumstances prevent prompt payment, *Tenant will pay a late fee of $20* .

Returned Checks—If, FOR ANY REASON, a check used by Tenants to pay Owners is returned without having been paid, Tenants will pay a returned check charge of $ *15* AND take whatever other consequences there might be in making a late payment. After the second time that a Tenants' check is returned, Tenants must thereafter secure a cashier's check or money order for payment of rent.

Form of Payment—Tenants agree to pay rent in the form of a personal check, a cashier's check, or a money order made out to *LEVNO PROPERTIES* .

Rent Payment Procedure—Tenants agree to pay their rent in the following way: *in person to manager*

Deposits—Tenants agree to deposit with the Owners the sum of $ *1,100* , payable before they occupy the premises. Owners may withhold from these deposits only what is reasonably necessary to cover the following tenant defaults: 1) damages to the dwelling; 2) certain cleaning costs following Tenants' departure; and 3) unpaid rent and various other accrued and unpaid charges. Tenants may not apply any part of these deposits to their last month's rent.

Refund of Tenants' Deposits—Within *7* days after Tenants have moved out completely, Owners shall provide a written accounting of the disposition of the Tenants' deposits and shall at the same time return all deposits remaining.

Utilities/Services—Tenants agree to pay all utilities and services with the exception of the following which Owners agree to pay: *water and garbage*

Occupants—In addition to the Tenants mentioned above, only the following persons may live in this dwelling: X X X X X X X X
No one else may live there, even temporarily, without Owners' prior written permission.

Guests—Tenants may house any single guest for a maximum period of fourteen days every six months or for whatever other period of time the law allows. Provided that they maintain a separate residence, nurses or maids required to care for Tenants during an illness are excepted from this provision.

Subletting and Assignment—Tenants shall not sublet the entire premises or any part of the premises, nor shall they assign this Agreement to anyone else without first obtaining the Owners' written permission. Owners shall not withhold permission unreasonably.

Pets—Tenants have received permission to house the following pet(s) on the premises:
X X X X X X X X
Tenants may house no other pet of any kind on the premises, even temporarily, without first obtaining Owners' written permission. "Pets" includes, but is not limited to, both warm- and cold-blooded animals, such as dogs, cats, fish, hamsters, rats, birds, snakes, lizards, and insects. "Pets" does not include animals trained to serve the handicapped, such as seeing-eye dogs, hearing dogs, or service dogs. These animals may be housed on the premises so long as they are in the direct service of those they were trained to serve and so long as Owners are notified in advance in writing of the circumstances.

Liquid-filled Furniture—Tenants agree not to keep any liquid-filled furniture in this dwelling without first obtaining Owners' written permission.

Vehicles—Tenants agree to park their vehicles in assigned spaces and to keep those spaces clean of oil drippings. Tenants agree to keep no more than ___2___ vehicle(s) on the premises. Vehicle(s) must be both operable and currently licensed. Tenants agree to advise their visitors about parking and to take responsibility for where their visitors park. Only those motorcycles which have exhaust muffling comparable to that of a passenger car are allowed. Only those self-propelled recreational vehicles which are used for regular personal transportation are allowed. Tenants agree not to park boats, recreational trailers, utility trailers, and the like on the premises without first obtaining Owners' written permission. Tenants agree not to repair their vehicle(s) on the premises if such repairs will take longer than a single day unless the vehicle is kept in an enclosed garage.

Appliances—Although the following appliances are presently in the dwelling:
STOVE AND REFIGERATOR
the use of these appliances is not included in the rent. If Tenants wish to use these appliances, they agree to assume all responsibility for care and maintenance. If Tenants wish to use their own appliances, they may request that the owner's appliances be removed from the premises.

Tenant Inspection—Tenants have inspected the dwelling and its contents and agree that they are in satisfactory order, as are the electrical, plumbing, and heating systems.

Notification of Serious Building Problems—Tenants agree to notify the Owners immediately upon first discovering any signs of serious building problems such as a crack in the foundation, a tilting porch, a crack in the plaster or stucco, moisture in the ceiling, buckling sheetrock or siding, a leaky roof, a spongy floor, a leaky water heater, or termite activity.

Reasonable Time for Repairs—Upon being notified by Tenants that there is some building defect which is hazardous to life, health, or safety, Owners shall undertake repairs as soon as possible. Should there be a delay of more than seventy-two (72) hours in making the repairs, due to a difficulty in scheduling the work or obtaining parts or for any other reason beyond the Owners' control, Owners agree to keep Tenants informed about the progress of the work.

Windows—Except for those windows which are noted in writing as being cracked or broken when Tenants move in, Tenants agree to be responsible for any windows which become cracked or broken in their dwelling while they live there. Tenants may repair the windows themselves if they can do the work in a professional manner. Otherwise, they may hire a glazier or submit a maintenance request to Owners. If they submit a maintenance request, Owners will charge them no more for the work than the least expensive written bid for the work which Tenants can obtain.

Drain Stoppages—As of the date of this Agreement, Owners warrant that the dwelling's sewage drains are in good working order and that they will accept the normal household waste for which they were designed. They will not accept things such as paper diapers, sanitary napkins, tampons, children's toys, wads of toilet paper, balls of hair, grease, oil, table scraps, clothing, rags, sand, dirt, rocks, or newspapers. Tenants agree to pay for clearing the drains of any and all stoppages except those which the plumber who is called to clear the stoppage will attest in writing were caused by defective plumbing, tree roots, or acts of God.

Trash—Tenants agree to dispose of their ordinary household trash by placing it into a receptacle for periodic collection. They agree to dispose of their extraordinary household trash, such as Christmas trees, damaged furniture, broken appliances, and the like, by compacting it so that it will fit inside their trash receptacle or by hauling it to the dump themselves or by paying someone else to haul it away.

Outside Placement—Owners reserve the right to place trash receptacles, portable storage units, and the like wherever convenient on the premises. Owners further reserve the right to construct property improvements above or below the ground anywhere on the premises so long as they conform to all building codes.

Damage—Tenants agree to pay for repairs of all damage which they or their guests have caused.

Locks—Tenants agree that they will not change the locks on any door or mailbox without first obtaining Owners' written permission. Having obtained permission, they agree to pay for changing the locks themselves and to provide the Owners with one duplicate key per lock.

Lockouts—Should Tenants lock themselves out of their dwelling and be unable to gain access through their own resources, they may call upon a professional locksmith or the manager to let them in. In either case, they are responsible for payment of the charges and/or damages involved. Management charges a fee of $15 for providing this service between the hours of 8 a.m. and 6 p.m., Monday through Saturday, excepting holidays, and a fee of $25 at other times. This fee is due and payable when the service is provided.

Landscaping—[*This paragraph applies only if it is initialed by both parties.*] Tenants agree to maintain the existing landscaping by watering, weeding, fertilizing, mowing, and shaping it as necessary.

Alterations, Decorations, and Repairs—Except as provided by law, Tenants agree not to alter or decorate their dwelling without first obtaining Owners' written permission. Decorations include painting and wallpapering. Further, Tenants agree not to repair their dwelling or anything belonging to the Owners without first obtaining Owners' written permission unless such repairs cost less than one hundred dollars ($100), and Tenants agree to pay for them. Tenants shall hold Owners harmless for any mechanics liens or proceedings which Tenants cause. When approved by Owners, Tenants' plans for alterations and decorations shall bear a determination regarding ownership. If Tenants are able to convince Owners that Tenants can remove the alterations or decorations and restore that part of their dwelling to its original condition, then Owners may grant Tenants the right to remove them. Otherwise, any alterations or decorations made by Tenants become the property of Owners when Tenants vacate.

Painting—Owners reserve the right to determine when the dwelling will be painted unless there is any law to the contrary.

Access—Owners recognize that Tenants have a right to privacy and wish to observe that right scrupulously. At certain times, however, Owners, their employees, or agents may have to gain access to the Tenants' dwelling for purposes of showing it to prospective Tenants, purchasers, lenders, or others or for repairs, inspection, or maintenance. When seeking access under ordinary circumstances, Owners will schedule entry between the hours of 8 a.m. and 8 p.m., Monday through Saturday, excepting holidays, and Owners will provide Tenants reasonable notice of twenty-four hours, or less than twenty-four hours notice with Tenants' concurrence. In emergencies, there will be no notice.

Peace and Quiet—Tenants are entitled to the quiet enjoyment of their own dwelling, and their neighbors are entitled to the same. Tenants agree that they will refrain from making loud noises and disturbances, that they will keep down the volume of their music and broadcast programs at all times so as not to disturb other people's peace and quiet, and that they will not install wind chimes.

Telephone—If and when Tenants install a telephone in their dwelling, they will furnish Owners with the number within five calendar days. When divulging the number, Tenants shall advise Owners whether the number is listed or unlisted. If it is unlisted, Owners agree to take reasonable precautions to keep it from falling into the hands of third parties.

Rental Agreement—Page 3 of 5

Prolonged Absences—Tenants agree that they will notify Owners whenever they plan to be absent from their dwelling for more than ten days.

Business Use—Tenants agree to use this dwelling as their personal residence. They agree to conduct no business on the premises without first obtaining Owners' written permission.

Lawful Use—Tenants agree that they will not themselves engage in any illegal activities on the premises nor will they allow others to engage in any illegal activities on the premises insofar as they have the power to stop such activities.

Insurance—Owners have obtained insurance to cover fire damage to the building itself and liability insurance to cover certain personal injuries occurring as a result of property defects or owner negligence. Owners' insurance does not cover Tenants' possessions or Tenants' negligence. Tenants shall obtain a Tenants' insurance policy to cover damage to or loss of their own possessions, as well as losses resulting from their negligence. Tenants agree to show Owners evidence of such a policy within one month from the date of this Agreement.

Insurance Considerations—Tenants agree that they will do nothing to the premises nor keep anything on the premises which will result in an increase in the Owners' insurance policy or an endangering of the premises. Neither will they allow anyone else to do so.

Fire or Casualty Damage—During any time when the dwelling cannot be used because of fire or casualty damage, Tenants are not responsible for payment of rent. Should a portion of the dwelling become unusable due to fire or casualty damage, Tenants are not responsible for payment of rent on that portion. In either case, Owners reserve the right to decide whether the dwelling is usable and what portions are usable. Owners are not responsible for repairing or replacing any improvements made by Tenants if those improvements are damaged. Should the fire or casualty damage have been caused by Tenants' own action or neglect, they shall have not be relieved of the responsibility for payment of rent, and they shall also bear the full responsibility for repair of the damage.

Rules and Regulations—Owners' existing rules and regulations, if any, shall be signed by Tenants, attached to this Agreement, and incorporated into it. Owners may adopt other rules and regulations at a later time provided that they have a legitimate purpose, not modify Tenants' rights substantially, and not become effective without notice of at least two (2) weeks.

Service of Process—Every Tenant who signs this Agreement agrees to be the agent of the other Tenants and occupants of this dwelling and is both authorized and required to accept, on behalf of the other Tenants and occupants, service of summons and other notices relative to the tenancy.

Identity of Manager—The person who is responsible for managing this dwelling and is authorized to accept legal service on Owners' behalf is _BEVERLY HAVENS_ whose address is _728 BEAVER AVENUE, SUNNY, OR 08100, PHONE 123-4567_ .

Changes in Terms of Tenancy—[*This paragraph applies only when this Agreement is or has become a month-to-month agreement.*] Owners shall advise Tenants of any changes in terms of tenancy with advance notice of at least __30__ days. Changes may include notices of termination, rent adjustments, or other reasonable changes in the terms of this Agreement.

Notice of Intention to Vacate—[*This paragraph applies only when this Agreement is or has become a month-to-month agreement.*] When Tenants have decided to vacate the premises, they will give Owners written notice of their intentions at least __15__ days prior to their departure, and they will give an exact date when they expect to be moved out completely.

Holding Over—If Tenants remain on the premises following the date of their termination of tenancy, they are "holding over" and become liable for "rental damages" equaling one/thirtieth of the amount of their then current monthly rent for every day they hold over.

Possession—Owners shall endeavor to deliver possession to Tenants by the commencement date of this Agreement. Should Owners be unable to do so, they shall not be held liable for any damages Tenants suffer as a consequence, nor shall this Agreement be considered void unless Owners are unable to deliver possession within ten (10) days following the commencement date. Tenants' responsibility to pay rent shall begin when they receive possession.

Sale of the Dwelling—If Owners sell this dwelling or otherwise transfer its Ownership to another party, they shall have the right to terminate this Agreement by giving Tenants written notice of at least sixty days, notwithstanding any conflicting occupancy rights Tenants might have under a fixed-term agreement. Should Tenants have conflicting occupancy rights guaranteed them by law, however, those legal rights shall prevail.

Illegal Provisions Not Affecting Legal Provisions—Whatever item in this Agreement is found to be contrary to any local, state, or federal law shall be considered null and void, just as if it had never appeared in the Agreement, and it shall not affect the validity of any other item in the Agreement.

Non-Waiver—Should either Owners or Tenants waive their rights to enforce any breach of this Agreement, that waiver shall be considered temporary and not a continuing waiver of any later breach. Although Owners may know when accepting rent that Tenants are violating one or more of this Agreement's conditions, Owners in accepting the rent are in no way waiving their rights to enforce the breach. Neither Owners nor Tenants shall have waived their rights to enforce any breach unless they agree to a waiver in writing.

References in Wording—Plural references made to the parties involved in this Agreement may also be singular, and singular references may be plural. These references also apply to Owners' and Tenants' heirs, executors, administrators, or successors, as the case may be.

Application Part of Agreement—The rental application Tenants submitted to rent this dwelling forms a part of this Agreement. Falsified information on the application shall be considered a breach of this Agreement.

Entire Agreement—As written, this Agreement constitutes the entire agreement between the Tenants and Owners. They have made no further promises of any kind to one another, nor have they reached any other understandings, either verbal or written.

Consequences—Violation of any part of this Agreement or nonpayment of rent when due shall be cause for eviction under appropriate sections of the applicable code.

Trial by Judge—[*This paragraph applies only if it is initialed by both parties.*] Should any aspect of this Agreement or tenancy be litigated in civil court, Owners and Tenants agree to waive their rights to a trial by jury and have the matter tried by a judge.

Legal Service's Fees—If either party to this Agreement shall bring a cause of action against the other party for enforcement of the Agreement, the prevailing party [*cross out the alternative which does not apply and initial the beginning of this paragraph*] (shall) (~~shall not~~) recover reasonable legal service's fees involved.

Other—   NONE

Acknowledgment—Tenants hereby acknowledge that they have read this Agreement, understand it, agree to it, and have been given a copy.

_____   _____
Owner   Tenant

_____   _____
BY Person authorized to represent Owners   Tenant

plaints into Thousands of Dollars, boasts of collecting a $25,000 payoff from his landlords for dispossessing him before his lease was up, and his was a lease which new owners inherited.

Remember that any and all rental agreements, leases included, which are in effect at the time of a property transfer become the responsibility of the new owners to uphold, that is, unless there is a distinct provision to the contrary.

Covering extended periods of time as they do, leases can affect the transfer of property substantially if the new owner wants to assume possession of the dwelling or change the terms of the agreement. If you are renting out a house, for example, on a one-year lease which has four months to run, and you have found a buyer who wants to move in upon close of escrow, you may lose the sale entirely unless you can somehow convince your buyer to wait four months or you can convince your renters to move before their lease expires.

All of these considerations appear to reflect so negatively on leases that you may wonder why any landlord would ever use one. There are a few circumstances, precious few, where leases might prove favorable to the landlord, and even then they should be limited to periods of a year or less (except for commercial properties, which vary according to area and market conditions).

Those circumstances include student rentals (to assure year-round occupancy), luxury rentals (to encourage tenant improvements), established tenancies (to ease good, long-term tenants' fears), high vacancy areas (to offer security from rent increases as an incentive), Section 8 subsidized housing (to participate in the program at all), rental houses (to promote greater tenant commitment, but only if you feel certain that you won't be selling the house during the lease period), and commercial properties (to facilitate business cost projections and encourage stability and improvements).

Unless you can conceive of some obvious advantage to you for using leases, use written month-to-month rental agreements instead, and you'll stay out of some of the trouble leases can cause.

■ **Should you ask for any attorney's or legal services fees in your rental agreement?**—Before considering possible answers to this question, we should differentiate between "attorney's fees" and "legal services fees."

"Attorney's fees" is a narrowly defined term restricted to the fees charged by an attorney, and only an attorney, for services rendered, whereas "legal services fees" is a more broadly defined term which includes attorney's fees as well as the fees charged by anyone else who is rendering "legal" services, such as the secretarial service you might use to prepare your eviction paperwork. What's more, courts are interpreting "legal services fees" even more broadly and awarding landlords something for their time spent in representing themselves whenever they win a contractual dispute with their tenants. There's no way that you could possibly be awarded anything for your time if you were asking only for attorney's fees in your rental agreement.

If you are going to put anything in your rental agreements about such fees, don't limit them to the fees charged by attorneys. Go beyond attorney's fees. Use the term "legal services fees" instead.

Now let's consider whether you should ask for any of these fees at all.

As a matter of course, most rental agreements do include a provision which awards attorney's or legal services fees to the prevailing party in litigation between the landlord and tenant. Without such a provision, a landlord who wins a contractual claim cannot recoup these fees.

Not being able to recoup the fees sounds like an unpleasant prospect, doesn't it? But what happens if your tenant wins a long, drawn-out suit claiming that you failed to maintain his rental house adequately and that's why he hasn't been paying you any rent for six entire months?

Here's what would happen. You'd lose all or most of the rent for six months. You'd have to pay your own costs and legal services fees, and you'd have to pay the $3,000 or $4,000 for your tenant's costs and legal services fees as well. You'd be triply penalized for losing, and it wouldn't matter one whit that you knew full well the tenant was lying in court. His prevailing in court would entitle him to the fees because of that provision in your rental agreement.

You cannot know exactly how this provision or the lack of it is going to affect you at some time in the future. An attorney who's advising you on your rental agreement isn't going to know for sure either. Only in retrospect will you ever know whether you made the right decision.

You should certainly think about the matter, though, and here are some of the points you should consider.

Do not ask in your agreement that legal services fees be awarded to the prevailing party if—

- The kind of tenant you generally rent to is "judgment proof" anyway, that is, he wouldn't have the money to pay you if you did get a court judgment against him.
- Your tenants generally use legal-aid attorneys to represent them.
- The courts in your area tend to favor tenants in their decisions.

Do ask in your agreement that legal services fees be awarded to the prevailing party if—

- Your tenants tend to have enough money to pay a judgment.
- The courts in your area appear to be relatively impartial in landlord-tenant cases.
- You are confident that you will be the prevailing party forty-nine times out of fifty.

After thinking about these various points, review your rental agreement and see that it reflects your thinking on awarding legal services fees.

Some Last Words

As you search for *your* right rental agreement, keep your eyes and ears open wide for ideas wherever you are, whatever you're up to. Keep your Swiss Army scissors at the ready to cut out whatever pertinent newspaper articles you should chance upon. Unsheathe your Swiss Army pen to write down whatever ideas you should come across. Be prepared to make changes to your agreements as needs arise. Remember, you're dealing with people and a society in a constant state of flux. Recognize that you aren't going to find the right rental agreement for all time, so you might as well enjoy the search.

This much is certain. When one of those clauses that you were shrewd enough to include in your agreement helps you win a case in court, you'll feel the same immediate relief you feel when the full-grown St. Bernard you're petting decides to get off your foot.

6
Rents, Rents, Rents

Sometime, somewhere, two tenants were talking with one another, and the following conversation took place. I'd be willing to bet my biggest and best pipe wrench on it.

"What do you think our landlady does with all the rent money we pay her?"

"Oh, I suppose she buys designer clothes, makeup, expensive jewelry, and stuff, and she goes on trips every summer, 'love-boat' trips, I think someone told me. She must buy a new car every year or two as well. She just doesn't drive it around here. The rest of it she probably sews inside her mattress or puts in the bank. She's a rich lady to be owning this building. That's for sure!"

Many tenants believe that you pocket either their entire rent payment or a substantial portion of it. They cannot understand what else you might be doing with it. They are completely oblivious of loan payments, property tax bills, garbage bills, utility bills, gardening bills, maintenance bills, repair bills, advertising bills, insurance bills, legal bills, special assessments, vacancy losses, and replacement reserves, not to mention management costs.

They regard rent as a kind of legal extortion, an assessment levied upon the deserving poor by the idle rich, and thus, some of them feel completely justified in spearheading or joining efforts to enact rent control to deprive you of the freedom to charge whatever rent the market will bear or, if they can't stir up enough support for rent control, in trying various shenanigans to deprive you of their rent money.

Short of turning over the property completely to your tenants and letting them try to pay all the bills themselves out of what rent they are able to collect from one another, you may find that convincing them that their rent money pays bills directly related to their tenancy is just as hard as convincing them that their daily lottery ticket is a sucker's bet. Old, old notions about landlords and rents are deep-rooted indeed.

Try educating your tenants little by little whenever you have the opportunity, though. Sometime when you're collecting the rent, ask them what they think the rent money goes for, and be prepared for some very astonishing answers. Most tenants haven't a clue what you do with their rent money. Of course, you might not know yourself exactly what percentage of every rent check goes to pay utilities, what to insurance, and so on, and you should certainly calculate those percentages (use expenses for the previous tax year and include as an expense at least 5% of the income to represent your own time contribution for overall off-site property management) before you ever broach the subject to your tenants.

On an average, the percentages are as follows for multiple-family dwellings—insurance, maintenance, repairs, and utilities, 25%; taxes, 25%; interest, 35%; debt retirement, 2%; vacancy factor, 5%; overall property management, 5%; and cash flow, 3%.

Once you have calculated your own percentages, you may be astonished by how little of their rent money you do pocket (positive cash flow) or by how much you have to contribute (negative cash flow) to keep a roof over your tenants' heads. Like any teacher preparing a class lesson, you may learn more about rents while preparing to teach your tenants something on the subject than you ever knew before.

Don't be too hopeful that your students will learn their lessons, however, for you have some very reluctant learners. Neither these informal discussions nor formal disclosures with copious explanations will enlighten your tenants about their rent so thoroughly that they will volunteer to pay their "fair share" of the expenses. But through such attempts, you *might* find them a *little* more understanding about rent collection, rent raises, and rent control, all topics of this chapter.

Itemizing Rents

Before we proceed to the major rent topics, let's consider a minor one, although it is a topic which can have major consequences nowadays when a landlord's costs for certain essentials change unexpectedly overnight.

Let's say that you have just raised your rents $23. You're mighty pleased with yourself because you have weathered the usual tenant complaints about an increase in the rent, your rents are more than keeping pace with your costs, your vacancies are manageable, and you're showing some healthy positive cash flow at last. You're beginning to think that buying this rental property you bought several years ago was a stroke of genius. You're expecting most of the rent increase to add to your cash flow. Life is good. Landlording is wonderful. All is right with the world.

Then you read in the local paper that the sewer rate is going up $17 per dwelling within the next sixty days. There goes most of your rent increase, right down the drain. What should you do about the situation? Should you go back to your tenants and give them another rent increase, this time for $17? No, no, you should not. They wouldn't understand. They would blame you for everything wrong in their lives, everything wrong in the universe. They expect you to take the additional rent they're paying you as a result of the rent increase and use it to pay for all of the higher costs you'll be facing over the next year, no matter what those costs are and no matter how much they happen to be.

Your tenants will think that you don't know what you're doing if you raise their rent twice in quick succession. They would be saying to themselves and likely to you directly that you should have known the sewer fee was going up. That's your job as a landlord to keep track of your expenses and anticipate increases in certain of them. Why should they as tenants have to pay extra because you made a mistake and miscalculated your expenses?

Although for many years I resisted adopting the obvious solution to this problem, I have come to be a believer. It makes good sense. It works.

The solution I'm referring to here is itemizing rents. You determine a base rent and then you add your actual costs for certain basic items such as water, sewer, garbage, and special assessment districts (fire, ambulance, street lighting, storm drainage, libraries, and whatever else your local politicians decide to add onto your property tax bill to generate more revenue). When these costs go up, you pass the increase along to your tenants right away. When these costs go down, you pass the decrease along to your tenants right away as well.

I must admit that I resisted itemizing rents a long time because I had become completely conditioned to making my rents all-inclusive. I wanted to keep everything simple and keep my expenses as much a secret from my tenants as possible. Itemizing rents would only complicate my paperwork and confuse my tenants, I believed, and it would reveal to them what I was paying for certain expenses. I didn't want them to know what my expenses were because I didn't want them to be doing the arithmetic. They might think that I was making too much money and start questioning what I was charging them for rent.

How wrong I was!

Yep, itemizing rents does complicate the paperwork. You have to watch your basic expenses more carefully, and you have to give your tenants notice that their rent will be adjusted accordingly whenever there's a change. Then, you have to prepare a statement for them every month so they will know exactly how much they owe. That's the downside of itemizing rents.

The upside is that tenants don't seem to be any more interested in questioning their rent when it's itemized than they are in questioning it when it's not itemized. They seem to understand better why their rent is changing and to accept the changes as inevitable, even though the changes occur more frequently than otherwise. In addition, they seem to like the possibility that they will see a decrease in their rent if any of the itemized charges decrease.

Besides the primary advantage you realize in itemizing rents, being able to pass along increases in the fixed costs which you cannot control, you will also find that you can deflect your tenants' displeasure over the increases. They can't blame you for the increases. They can blame city hall, and they will. They can understand much better how increased fees affect them directly, and they will stand with you when you and other property owners challenge those increased costs in public forums.

To begin itemizing your rents, you should first calculate exactly how much the things you currently include in the rent, but want to itemize, are costing you per unit per month.

Let's say that you have a fourplex with rents of $675 per unit per month, and the rents include water, sewer, and garbage service. Your water bill has averaged $41 per month over the past year; your garbage bill is $47 per month; your sewer bill is $216 per quarter; and your street lighting assessment is $12.36 per quarter. These figures translate into per-unit figures of $10.25 for water, $11.75 for garbage, $13.50 for sewage, and $1.03 for street lighting. These are the figures you use for your initial setup. Add them all together and you get $48.89. Deduct them from your lump-sum rent and you get a base rent of $626.11.

Advise your tenants in a Notice of Change in Terms of Tenancy that their total monthly rent consists of a base rent of $626.11 plus so much for each of the itemized charges. Advise them that their base rent will change no more frequently than once every year but that the other charges may fluctuate at any time according to your actual costs. Advise them further that you will give them proper notice that their total rent is going up or down whenever one of the itemized charges changes.

Be sure you refer in your notice to the sum of the charges as being "the rent" or "the total rent" because you want to be able to mention that total figure as rent in any legal paperwork you may have to file to evict the tenants. You don't want to have to itemize it in your legal paperwork. That only confuses court clerks and judges.

You may have noticed that most of the itemized costs above are flat-rate charges, all except for water, which may or may not be a flat-rate charge if it's provided by a utility company (if it's well water which you are providing your tenants, don't itemize it). More than likely, water is the one item which fluctuates every month, and you may wonder how you can itemize it if the property is master metered, that is, unless you install a separate meter for every unit. All you're doing here is taking a twelve-month average as your initial cost for water, and you're going to change that figure only if the water *rate* changes. You would not change it according to the tenants'

usage. If the rate goes up, you'd take the percentage of the increase and add that to whatever sum you calculated as the initial cost for water. That's all.

If you do itemize your rents, do not play games with the figures when you're advertising the rent for a vacant dwelling. Advertise the total of what you are charging for everything, the base rent plus the various other basic items you're itemizing. Do not advertise the base rent alone and then tell applicants late in the game that they will be paying extra for basic items which they must have in order to live there. That approach, a kind of bait-and-switch, will cause them to question your way of doing business from the git-go. It's underhanded, and it's bad business.

Give this itemizing-rents procedure some thought. In certain circumstances, it can make a big difference in your income. At one of my larger properties, it bumped my income up by $1,400 per month when my costs increased that amount and I couldn't otherwise have passed along those costs in the form of an ordinary rent increase for eight months. Let's see now; eight times $1,400. That's $11,200! Why, that's real money!

I'm a believer, a true believer.

Collecting Rents

You may have your tenants trained to pay you their rent two weeks before it's due. If so, skip this section and the next. You don't need to know anything more about collecting rents. You should be giving lessons. Everyone else, read on.

Collecting rents on time requires persistence, consistency, and firmness. You can't expect tenants to pay their rent promptly if you aren't trying to collect it from them, or if they never know whether you will be coming on the first or the third of the month to collect, or if you give them the impression that you're an old softy.

Be persistent. You earn that rent money, and you shouldn't be the least bit timid about collecting it. Keep after those tenants who haven't paid up. Be aggressive. Hound them until they pay.

Be consistent. Rent collection is so important to landlording that you must learn to subordinate everything else when rents come due so you can pursue rent collection in the same way month after month, year after year.

Be firm. Convince your tenants that their rent money is your top priority and that you won't be swayed by their sob stories or tolerate their feeble excuses.

Remember that paying rent is just as unsatisfying to tenants as paying property taxes is to you. Neither rent nor taxes pay for anything that the payer didn't already have before, or so it would seem. Few would pay if they didn't believe that they would be penalized somehow for failing to pay. You have to establish yourself, therefore, from the very beginning as a threat, like the dreaded IRS, a landlord who expects the rent to be paid promptly, no matter what. When it isn't, you become menacing, a force to contend with. GRRRR!

All too frequently it is easier not to pay the landlord than it is not to pay the stock broker, the bookie, the dentist, the grocer, the utility company, the dress shop, the credit card company, the finance company, the barber, the gasoline company, the insurance company, or even the newspaper carrier. Who then gets paid last, if at all? You, that's who! Why? You're not firm enough when you should be. Be like the family dog that is faithful and loving except when someone tries to take away his food. Then he growls and bites. There's no reason why you can't be considerate to your tenants in all things except where rents are concerned. Then you have to be menacing. After all, you and your properties live on rent money just as dogs live on Alpo.

Make it more difficult for your tenants not to pay you than for them not to pay anyone else. Explain precisely what your policy is regarding rent collection. Tell them before you ever rent to them that their rent is due on the first, it is *late* on the fifth, and if it's not paid by the fourth, you'll be visiting them in person on the fifth to give them just three days to pack up and leave. Talk tough. Be tough when you collect rents. You won't be understood otherwise.

Besides persistence, consistency, and firmness, collecting rents on time requires a reasonable, lucid, and strict rent collection policy more than anything else, a policy which should include a mutually agreed upon collection procedure, a specified form of payment, statements when called for, written receipts, a set due date, a set late date, and either a definite penalty for late payment or an incentive to pay on time.

■ **Collection Procedures**—Which collection procedure you use will depend upon what kind of tenants you have, where you live in relation to the units, how many units you have, how much you want to be involved, and whether you have an on-site manager. Some landlords prefer to have the tenants visit them or the manager to pay the rent in person, some collect it by mail, some actually go themselves to their tenants' dwellings to collect rents, and some appoint a rent collector. There are merits to each procedure.

Having your tenants come to you or to your manager, if either of you lives or has an office close by, is surely the most common collection procedure. It's personalized and it's reasonably efficient, but it may make you feel confined to one place while you wait for tenants to come to you. To eliminate this feeling of confinement, consider installing a secure mail slot where they can put their rent checks when you're not available. Also, consider combining this procedure with one or more of the others.

Collecting the rent by mail is certainly the easiest and most efficient for you as a landlord. To make it easy for your tenants as well, you might consider sending them a self-addressed, stamped envelope on the 18th of each month and asking them to send you by return mail a check, postdated the first, to pay that next month's rent.

Then, when the first rolls around, you will already have their check in hand, and neither you nor your tenants need worry about whether it will reach you on time. What's more, you don't have to waste time going to the tenants' dwelling or waiting around for the tenant to come to you. You don't have to listen to the latest gossip about the neighbors, and you don't have to listen to the inevitable complaints. It's quick and it's easy, but it's also impersonal, and it separates you from your source of income to a point where you might lose touch.

If you keep in touch with your tenants at other times and in other ways, then by all means, have your tenants mail their rent to you, but if rent collection day is the only chance you have all month to see your property, then maybe you'd better collect the rent on the premises. You might see something that should be remedied soon, and you might see it while it still can be remedied easily, before it becomes an aggravating or expensive matter.

Despite some very real disadvantages to the third procedure, its inefficiency and its placement of the burden for the transaction on you, there are real advantages to collecting rents on the tenant's doorstep or inside the tenant's dwelling itself. It's as personalized as possible. It shows that you care enough to take the time to look after your property. It shows that rent collection is important to you. It lets you know straightaway whether a tenant is going to be late and, if so, what the tenant's excuse for late payment is. It also allows you more freedom of movement because you don't have to wait around for anybody to call on you. You're going to them.

There's one other rent collection procedure you might think about trying if you happen to be an absentee owner with no manager on the premises of a reasonably small multiple-family building. It involves selecting the most senior tenants you have in every building and giving them, say, $5 for every rent they collect, including their own. Seniors tend to like the responsibility involved. They like to feel useful, and they appreciate the opportunity to earn a little extra income. They're also more conscientious in their rounds than you would ever be. The other tenants are less likely to give the usual excuses for being late to one of their neighbors, especially when the neighbor is a senior and is almost like a parental figure who must be obeyed. You save yourself

from having to make repeated trips over to the property and having to spend time dealing with many people separately, too. At $5 per unit, the collection at a six-plex would cost you only $30 a month, money well spent.

Be certain that you have workers' compensation insurance if you use this procedure. A senior tenant who falls and breaks a hip or an arm while collecting rents for you would definitely qualify for compensation.

No matter which collection procedure you decide upon, you should be absolutely certain that your tenants understand how you expect to collect their rent. You don't want them to be waiting around for you to knock on their door to collect it when you're expecting them to mail you a check.

■ **Form of Payment**—You want to be absolutely certain that every cent of your rent money will reach your bank, don't you? Of course you do! You're not in this business for the fun of it, are you? All right, then; make sure that you get paid your rent and that what you get paid goes directly into your bank account as soon as possible.

Because cash money can disappear much too easily on its way to the bank, don't accept it. Stipulate in your rental agreement or in a special notice of change in terms of tenancy (use the special notice if you don't want to redraw rental agreements for existing tenants) that tenants are to make all their rent payments by check or money order, not in cash.

If your rental agreement says nothing about accepting cash for rent, you must then accept cash when it's offered because it is, after all, legal tender. Unless you state in your agreement that you do not accept cash, some of your tenants will pay you with wads of twenties that would choke a hippo. You could wind up looking like a dope dealer carrying an attache case full of cash around with you at rent collection time. You'd be worried sick that some low-life might snatch your rents for the month because everybody would know what was in your attache case. Don't accept cash. Insist upon checks and money orders and save yourself this worry.

Besides checks and money orders, there are several other "safe" forms of rent payment you might want to consider. One is payment through direct deposits. The other is payment by credit card.

To make arrangements for direct deposits, you

Landlady Properties
453 Sweet Street
Littletown, CA 09090
800-555-1212

STATEMENT

Date: August 21, XXXX

Mailing Address:

Dorothy Mae Mahoney
456 Sweet Street
Littletown, CA 09090

Unit Address:

456 Sweet Street
Littletown, CA 09090

Tenant: SS1DM   **Name:** Dorothy Mae Mahoney

Unit: SS1   **Property:** SS   Sweet Street

Our records show that your rent is current through August 31, XXXX.

Your next payment should amount to the following:

Stmt Date	ID	Category	Qty	Price	Amt Due
8/21/XXXX	4101	Rent		872.50	872.50
8/21/XXXX	4221	Garbage		16.00	16.00
			Total Balance Due		$888.50

Your rental payments are due on the 1st of every month. To avoid the consequences of paying late, please pay promptly.

Please make your payment payable to Landlady Properties.

Please report any leaky faucets or toilets. We'll fix them promptly!

ge⁺ ⌐ by the tenant
a⁻ s bank. The bank
⌐ to verify the au-
⌐ make the transfers,
⌐ant's bank will trans-
⌐ clockwork from the
⌐ur account according to
⌐ou and the tenant have

⌐ rents to the tenant's Visa or
⌐ a natural extension of our
⌐nt for charging everything now
⌐ it later.

⌐ drawbacks to this form of payment,
⌐u are concerned, are twofold—you
⌐blish yourself as a credit card "mer-
⌐nd you must pay a fee for accepting pay-
me⌐ ⌐y credit card.

You didn't think the Visa and MasterCard people offered their charge services for nothing, did you? They don't. They exact a percentage of every dollar charged. Out of $650 in rent charged to a tenant's card, they would take 2 or 3%, depending upon the volume of funds you run through your account. You would net $630 to $637.

You have to weigh those drawbacks against the advantage of accepting credit cards. The primary advantage for you in accepting credit cards is knowing that you could count on prompt and certain payment. The only circumstance which would keep you from getting paid would be where a tenant has exceeded the card's credit limit. You could find that out easily enough, of course, by calling the credit card company. They know and they will tell you immediately when you inquire as a merchant.

The primary advantages to tenants in paying by credit card is knowing that their rent would never be late and knowing that paying their rent this way would help them accumulate certain benefits, such as airline miles if they have an airline-affiliated card.

■ **Statements**—Many businesses send their charge account customers monthly statements. These statements serve two purposes—they inform the customer of the account balance and of the expected payment, and they remind the customer to pay promptly.

Except for some landlords who handle their rent collections by mail, landlords generally don't send statements to their tenants. "Why bother?"

the frugal landlord says, "Statements would just be too repetitious. My tenants pay the same amount month after month anyway. Why should I go to all the trouble of billing them?"

There's some logic to that point of view, to be sure. If your tenants do pay promptly and if they're paying the same amount of rent every month throughout the year, you needn't bill them, but if they don't and you think that sending them statements might remind them how much rent they owe and when they need to pay it, try sending them statements ten days before their rent due date. See what happens. Those statements may get them to pay more promptly.

At one of my properties which has an on-site manager who collects the rent in her office, we discovered that a third more of her tenants were paying their rent prior to the due date after she started sending them statements every month. Statements yielded good results in that case, and they do to this day.

On the opposite page is a sample of a statement created by Pushbutton Landlording. It creates statements quickly from the data in its files either on a tenant-by-tenant basis or on a property-by-property basis. You may do the same thing using a spreadsheet or word processing program and a template you create yourself, or you may do them the old-fashioned way, by hand.

■ **Receipts (Handwritten)**—Since you want to keep good rental income records which brook no argument, take the precaution of receipting all rents. The negligible expense and trouble involved in writing receipts for every rent collection, even for those paid by check or money order, have paid off for me more than once when I've had to come up with proof of something or other related to a tenant's payment.

Neither you nor your tenants should have to rely on your memories to remember dates, amounts paid, and rental periods. Put these things in writing. Write a receipt every time you collect rent. There is no substitute for a written receipt as proof of payment.

Of the two kinds of handwritten rent receipts readily available, receipt books and pegboard systems, receipt books will suffice for smaller operations, a few rental houses or a few small apartment houses which you handle on your own, but pegboard systems offer more features, and you should adopt one as soon as you find yourself hiring people to work for you, for then you will

Landlady Properties
453 Sweet Street
Littletown, CA 09090
800-555-1212

RECEIPT
RENT PAYMENT

Receipt Number: 5

Date: August 22, XXXX

Mailing Address:

Dorothy Mahoney
456 Sweet Street
Littletown, CA 09090

Unit Address:

456 Sweet Street
Littletown, CA 09090

Tenant ID: SS1DM   **Name:** Dorothy Mahoney

Unit: SS1   **Property:** SS   Sweet Street

Received From: Dorothy Mae Mahoney $888.50

Eight Hundred Eighty-Eight and 50/100 Dollars

Paid By Check: $888.50 **Check Number:** 5896

Cash: $0.00   **Money Order:** $0.00   **Other:** $0.00

ID	Category	Qty	Price	Owed	Amt Paid	Bal Due
4101	Rent		872.50	872.50	872.50	0.00
4221	Garbage		16.00	16.00	16.00	0.00
				TOTALS	$888.50	0.00

Date Rent Paid From: September 1, XXXX   **Through:** September 30, XXXX

Thank you for paying the full amount owed.

Please let us know if there is anything we can do for you!

Received by: *Leslie Landlady*
LL

be in need of a more thorough and foolproof recordkeeping system.

Pegboard systems, sometimes called "shingle systems" because the receipts resemble overlapping shingles, have three paper parts, receipts, receipt journals, and tenant ledgers, as well as a special board which has little pegs along its left side to help keep the journals and receipts aligned. When you write a receipt, you insert the tenant's ledger between the receipt itself and the journal. Then everything you write on the top line of the receipt will transfer via carbon through to both the tenant's ledger and the journal.

You'll have a receipt to give the tenant. You'll have a record of the tenant's payment on the tenant ledger, where all this tenant's other payments appear. You'll also have a record of the payment on the receipt journal, which lists chronologically all payments made by all tenants.

By sorting the tenant ledgers according to those tenants who have paid and those who haven't, you can tell at once who hasn't paid and take steps to remind them of their oversight. By glancing at the journals, you can tell

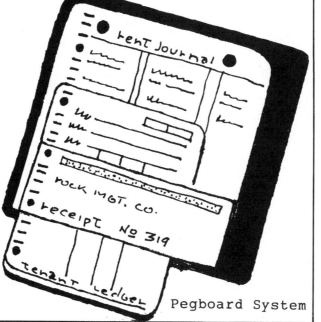

Pegboard System

how much has been collected over any given period, and you'll know how much you should have on hand to deposit as well as how much you should have deposited at other times.

Depending upon how many rents you receipt every month, you might want to use a new receipt journal for every bank deposit or for every month's receipts rather than filling each journal full of entries and then filing it. If someone other than you collects the rents, have the rent collector make two journals by putting a sheet of carbon paper between them. One is for himself and one is for the owner.

Should you elect to use a standard rent receipt book, receipt all rents in duplicate if you

collect the rents yourself or in triplicate if you have someone else collect them for you (one copy for the tenants, one for the person who collects the rent, and one for you).

Whichever type of receipt you use, make sure that each receipt is numbered sequentially. Unique numbers on the receipts help to keep everybody honest. Lax owners sometimes discover that their managers are keeping receipt books of their own which resemble the owners' receipt books, and they are writing receipts for monies paid by tenants but never turned over to the owners. Don't tempt your managers. Use a system which makes cheating difficult.

By the way, both Streamliners and Peachtree Business Products, which appear under "Catalogs from Various Suppliers" in the SOURCES & RESOURCES section of this book, list rent receipt pegboard systems in their catalogs. Many local stationery stores supply them as well, either from stock or by special order.

■ **Receipts (Computer-Generated)**—Computer programs designed specifically for rental property management will generate numbered rent receipts and print them out on blank paper, too. They do everything a pegboard rent receipt system does and more. They produce a variety of tenant, property, and delinquency reports using the data entered on the receipts, even in some cases producing delinquency letters and pay-or-quit notices based upon that same data.

On the opposite page is a sample of a receipt created by Pushbutton Landlording.

Be aware that these programs aren't for everybody or for every landlording situation, especially if using one of them would require the purchase of a computer which wouldn't do anything else except generate rent receipts for a dozen tenants every month. In that case, either of the handwritten methods of writing receipts would be less expensive and less troublesome to use.

■ **Due Date**—You may have noticed I mentioned before that rent ought to be due on the first. My rents all are, at least initially. Why the first? There are several good reasons.

Rents traditionally are due on the first. Tenants are in the habit of paying on the first. They associate the first of the month with bill paying and rent payments, and consequently they are more likely to remember to pay without having to be prompted. Busy as you are, you remember, too, when rents are due on the first. You can identify and handle the delinquencies more readily if the rents are all due at the same time instead of trying to remember which day of the month each tenant's rent comes due.

Once I bought a 41-unit residential income property which had rents due all throughout the month. This interminable series of rent due dates confused the tenants as much as it did the manager and me. So we changed all the due dates to the first. We were delighted by what happened. Collections immediately became easier, and delinquencies declined. The tenants remembered to pay, and we remembered to collect.

■ **Other Due Dates and Frequencies**—Sometimes tenants cannot pay you their rent on the first because the first doesn't coincide with their pay dates. Should you accommodate them? By all means, you should, but you might also want to charge them something extra for this privilege, so that it's worth your while to make the exception.

If they happen to be paid weekly or biweekly or semimonthly, you might even consider collecting their rent more frequently than once a month to insure that you get their rent money before they have a chance to spend it on something else, but in exchange for this accommodation, you should definitely charge them more. How much more? Anywhere from $5 to $50 per month.

Some landlords accommodate their tenants who get paid every other week by allowing them to pay the equivalent of half a month's rent every time they get paid. Do the math, and you'll discover that the tenants are actually paying an extra month's rent every year. That's an extra 8.3% they're paying for the convenience of paying their rent when they themselves get paid. It's not a

deal I would agree to if I were a tenant, but then I don't play the lottery either. I know the odds.

Should you encounter a tenant who wants to pay you half a month's rent every other week, instead of one month's rent every month, put the payment amounts and the payment frequency in writing as an addendum to the rental agreement or redraw the whole rental agreement to reflect this payment arrangement.

■ **Late Date**—Just as important as a realistic due date for rents is a realistic late date. This is the day when you first consider rents delinquent and start to assess penalties. I believe in giving my tenants several days of grace to get their rent to me, considering their rent late only if it hasn't been paid by the fourth. If it's paid on the fifth or thereafter, they're late, and they know they have to pay the penalty. Why? There are two good reasons, one somewhat legal and one very practical.

Some places around the country have a law which specifically requires that the rent due date be a banking day, that is, a weekday when the banks are open. According to the thinking behind the law, tenants must have had an opportunity to visit their bank to cash a check, buy a money order, or withdraw funds to pay the rent. If the rent due date falls on a Saturday, Sunday, or holiday, days when they cannot get to the bank in most places, you may not consider the rent late until the day following the next available banking day. If the rent due date falls on the Saturday of a three-day weekend, for example, the rent may be paid on the following Tuesday without penalty, and it is not considered late until Wednesday. Now if that Saturday were the first, and the first were your normal rent due date, that Tuesday would be the fourth of the month. Four days would be the longest possible legal period of time that tenants would ever have in which to pay their rent without incurring a penalty. In my opinion, there's some common sense behind this law. Tenants aren't known for their adherence to the Boy Scout motto, "Be prepared!" So in order to be entirely consistent, I use this same grace period throughout the year. There are no exceptions.

In practice, this grace period works well. You no longer have to listen to those hackneyed excuses tenants make up for not having paid their rent on or before the first. You know and they know that if the rent hasn't been paid by the fourth, there's either a serious excuse or there's a conscious attempt to avoid paying altogether. You save innumerable phone calls and trips on the second or third or fourth of the month to inquire after the rent, and you can feel entirely justified collecting more from a tenant who's missed the due date by at least four days.

While I was still requiring tenants to pay on or before the first of the month, I would feel guilty about charging a late paying tenant $20 more if that tenant were only a day or two late. Sometimes I'd just tell the tenant to forget it, or I'd allow some tenants to get away without paying the additional sum and say nothing about it because I knew that collecting it from them would be well nigh impossible anyway. Such inconsistency in my collections made the whole process too subjective, and it made me uneasy. On the one hand, I wanted to be reasonable when somebody's paycheck got held up, and on the other hand, I wanted to be tough and collect rents promptly when due. I couldn't be both reasonable and tough, not when I was trying to enforce a policy which forced me to make exceptions the rule. My first-of-the-month late date became as well enforced as a big city's panhandling ordinance.

Changing my definition of lateness and adopting a policy that the tenants and I could live with, a policy which brooks no exceptions, made all the difference. It works!

■ **Prompt-Payment Policies**—To encourage your tenants to pay you their rent on time, you need some sort of prompt-payment policy. There are four such policies that I'm aware of. Choose which one best fits your circumstances, and then write it into your rental agreement. That's all you have to do. Lacking some landlord bashing ordinance or another in the area where your rental property is located, you don't need to follow the dictates of a higher authority in selecting a policy, at least not yet. You get to decide which one to use yourself.

The first prompt-payment policy is the late fee policy. The second is the discounted rent policy. The third is the rebate policy. The fourth is the timely eviction policy. Let's take a look at each of them in turn.

The late fee policy has been around at least since some delinquent tenant first told his landlord, "Your check has been dispatched via pony express." Late fees penalize tenants for paying late. They're in the same no-nonsense category as library fines, parking tickets, income tax penalties, loan payment late charges, and property tax delinquency assessments, and they're hated just as much. They're downers. Nobody likes paying them, but everybody understands why they're necessary, so long as they apply to everybody else. They're for the other dingalings and scofflaws. Right?

Late fees carry negative connotations, and you should be sensitive to those connotations because you are always grappling with the stereotypical image of the landlord. In addition, you have to understand that tenants sometimes become so upset about being assessed late fees that they will seek vengeance, especially if they learn that you are enforcing your late fee policy selectively. They might punch another hole in the wall or sue you for discrimination or for charging excessive fees.

If you're writing a late fee into your rental agreement, make sure that it's a reasonable one. It should be coercive rather than punitive. It should serve to compel tenants to pay on time. It should not serve to generate additional revenue. Some judges have ruled that late fees must not exceed the damages you sustain when ten-

Notice to Pay Rent or Quit

TO: _CHESTER AND CATHY CAREFREE_

and all other tenants in possession of the premises described as:

460 SWEET STREET

LITTLETOWN, CA 09001

PLEASE TAKE NOTICE that the rent is now due and payable on the above-described premises which you currently hold and occupy.

Your rental account is delinquent in the amount itemized as follows:

Rental Period: _MARCH 1 to MARCH 31, XXXX_ Rent due $ _650.—_

Rental Period: _____ Rent due $ _____

Rental Period: _____ Rent due $ _____

TOTAL RENT DUE $ _650.—_

less partial payment of $ _____

equals TOTAL BALANCE DUE of $ _650.—_

YOU ARE HEREBY REQUIRED to pay said rent in full within _3_ days or to remove from and deliver up possession of the above-described premises, or legal proceedings will be instituted against you to recover possession of said premises, to declare the forfeiture of the Lease or Rental Agreement under which you occupy said premises and to recover rents and damages, together with court costs and attorney's fees, according to the terms of your Lease or Rental Agreement.

Dated: _3/5/xx_   _Leslie Landlady_
                                   Owner/Manager

PROOF OF SERVICE

I, the undersigned, being at least 18 years of age, declare under penalty of perjury that I served the above notice, of which this is a true copy, on the above-mentioned tenant(s) in possesssion in the manner(s) indicated below:

☒ On _3/5/xx_ , I handed the notice to the tenant(s).

☐ On _____, after attempting personal service, I handed the notice to a person of suitable age and discretion at the residence/business of the tenant(s).

☐ On _____, after attempting service in both manners indicated above, I posted the notice in a conspicuous place at the residence of the tenant(s).

☐ On _____, I deposited a true copy of the notice in the United States Mail, in a sealed envelope with postage fully prepaid, addressed to the tenant(s) at his/her/their place of residence.

☐ On _____, I sent by certified mail a true copy of the notice addressed to the tenant(s) at his/her/their place of residence.

Executed on _MARCH 5, XXXX_ , at the City of _LITTLETOWN_ ,

County of _SADLEBACK_ , State of _CALIFORNIA_ .

Served by _Leslie Landlady_

ants pay late, whatever those damages may be. You shouldn't get into trouble for charging excessive fees if you keep them in the $20 to $25 range, depending upon the amount of rent involved, or you might use a percentage, say 6%. After all, more than one of my real estate loans from institutional lenders has a late charge of 10% of the payment. Shouldn't 6% as a late rent penalty be considered reasonable?

A variation on the standard late fee imposed the very day rent becomes late is the imposition of an additional late fee which accumulates every day the rent is late. This daily fee, which ought to be a reasonable dollar or two per day, begins accumulating after the initial late fee is imposed and keeps accumulating until the tenants pay in full. I would advise you not to use this policy, however, because the "bookkeeping" becomes confusing, especially if the tenants make partial payments or are more than a month in arrears, and because judges tend to look upon it as somehow Shylockian and may treat you unsympathetically in court when you are otherwise reasonable in your policies and fair in administering them.

The second prompt-payment policy has been around at least since some clever merchant devised the idea of discounting, selling merchandise below its so-called "regular" price. Who wouldn't like to get a discount on rent, of all things, if one were offered? Yep, people love a bargain. They don't seem to care when you tell them that the advertised rent is what they pay if they pay on time and that it allows for the discount. The gross rent as written in their rental agreement is $20 higher. They hear only the word "discount," and they hear you say that if they pay their rent on time, you will give them a $20 discount off the gross rent. In other words, they pay the net advertised rent. Such a deal!

Is it legally defensible? That all depends on the judge. I know of nothing in landlord-tenant law specifically about a discounted rent policy, so its validation depends on whether the judge sees it as a ruse for collecting a late fee. Does it work? Of course!

It does have a drawback. It's self-administered, that is, tenants get to take the discount themselves. They will pay you whatever rent they feel they owe you, and that's the discounted rent, naturally. So you may have to remind them of the terms of your agreement whenever they're

late, and you may have to play tough to make sure they pay you that gross, non-discounted rent when they owe it to you.

The third policy has been around at least since the first rebate Plymouth rolled onto the showroom floor. Except for one important difference, the rebate policy for rent is just like the discount policy for rent. Instead of tenants determining for themselves whether they qualify to take their discount every month, you determine whether they qualify for their rebate. They send you the same amount of rent money every month, no matter what, and you send them a rebate check so long as they have complied with the terms of their rental agreement. As sole arbiter of whether they qualify, you get to exercise better control over the situation.

There's a price you pay for taking control, however. You have to take the time to make out and return those rebate checks every month. If that doesn't scare you off, you can be sure that your tenants will love you for giving them a rent rebate every month. They'll think you're a year-round Santa Claus.

A slight variation on this rebate policy involves your sending out a statement every month and including on that statement a credit for the rebate the tenants earned by paying their previous month's rent on time.

The fourth prompt-payment policy has been around at least since the tenants of the Garden of Eden left their first home under duress. Because Adam and Eve failed to comply with the terms of their rental agreement, their Landlord evicted them. He wasted no time. He accepted no excuses. He gave no written notice. He showed them the way out and shut the gate behind them.

You may not do the same. You must give your late tenants a notice first, and then you must follow the eviction procedure prescribed for the area where the rental property is located. What is most important about following this no-nonsense, zero-tolerance prompt-payment policy is that it be completed in a timely manner.

Timely evictions require careful attention, much persistence, and a working knowledge of the legal procedure followed in your area to force nonpaying tenants out. Show your tenants that you know how to evict them when they don't pay, and they'll get the message. Don't get discouraged. The message may take a while to get

Payment Pledge

Dear Landlord/Landlady:

On or before _OCTOBER 15, XXXX_ , I promise to pay you $_1,600—_ for rent and other charges now owing on the dwelling which I rent from you located at _1001 SWIFT ST., APT #4_ .

I expect to be receiving sufficient funds to pay you from the following sources:

Name	Address	Phone	Amount Expected
AID CREDIT UNION,	306 Willow Ave,	555-1337	$1,600—

Should you wish to, you have my authorization to verify these sources.

If I fail to honor this pledge, I understand that I will be evicted and that this pledge will be used against me as evidence of my bad faith in paying what I owe.

_X_ I acknowledge receipt of a Notice to Pay Rent or Quit as required by law to begin eviction proceedings. I understand that the Notice may show a balance owed which is different from that given above because a Notice to Pay Rent or Quit can demand only delinquent rent. I also understand that the period mentioned in this Notice is being extended to the date given above, at which time I promise to pay you what I owe. If I fail to pay on or before that date, you have the right to continue the legal eviction procedure against me without having to serve me another Notice to Pay Rent or Quit. I have already been served. I am being given the extra time to pay only as a courtesy and only this once.

Signed _John Hancock,_

Dated _OCTOBER 8, XXXX_

through.

Late fees and timely evictions are the "stick" approach to encouraging tenants to pay promptly as compared to the "carrot" approach of the other two policies. As any parent knows, some kids respond better to the stick and some respond better to the carrot or the candy bar. The trouble is that you don't know which policy is going to work best until you try it, and these policies, once set, aren't something you want to change every so often just to give them all a try with the same tenants. So, when choosing a policy, consider the circumstances carefully, and then try the one you think would work best. Don't change it for a particular set of tenants unless you feel you have to. Experiment with different properties and different tenants. Eventually you'll hit upon an effective policy which you and your tenants can live with.

Your prompt-payment policy is supposed to get your tenants to pay their rent promptly, but it won't work at all unless you make it work, unless you make your tenants understand that they have to pay their rent on time or face real consequences, one monetary, the other, bothersome. Not only are they going to have to pay more when they're late, they're going to be bothered. You are going to be after them to pay. You're going to be bothering them, and you're going to bother them in the extreme by turning them out on the streets if they don't pay.

■ **Late Rents**—Collecting rents requires an effective, pragmatic rental policy with teeth in it and someone to carry it out who is both firm and quick to act. You are in business and you should mean business when you are collecting rents.

Always treat late rents with gravity, but also treat late payers with understanding, depending upon your past experience with them as tenants. Sometimes the unexpected will cause even the most diligent of tenants to pay a few days late, and they will advise you voluntarily in advance just why they expect to be late and when they will have the money to pay. Such tenants deserve your patience while they cope with a calamity in their lives or a disruption in their income, and you would do well to accommodate them if you believe their explanation for the delay and if you believe the rent will be forthcoming in a couple of weeks.

If, however, by the third day after the rent due date, normally the fourth of the month, the tenants have neither paid you their rent nor have advised you that the rent will be delayed for some good reason or another, you should make plans to visit them the very next day to deliver a Notice to Pay Rent or Quit. Listen to their explanation sympathetically. If appropriate, talk with them about rental assistance programs available. Then have them make a definite commitment to pay on or before a certain date, not over two weeks hence for the best of tenants and within just a few days for those doubtful ones. Tell them that you will sue for eviction if they do not pay by the promised date. Have the notice already filled out so you can hand it to them before you leave and tell them, "We give everybody one of these notices if the rent isn't paid by the fourth, regardless of who it is. We treat everyone the same way."

In addition to serving the tenants with a Notice to Pay Rent or Quit, you might want to consider using another form, the Payment Pledge.

This form serves several important purposes. By asking the tenants to reveal the source of their anticipated funds and by committing them in writing to a particular payment date, it forces them to think twice about making you a hollow promise to pay at some vague time in the future. It also acts as a kind of receipt for the notice. With their signatures on the pledge, the tenants acknowledge that they have received their Notice to Pay Rent or Quit. They won't be able to appear in court and claim that they never received a notice that they were late with their rent, not when you have their signatures on the pledge.

Giving them the notice on the fifth strengthens your case should you have to go to court later because you would have waited a reasonable period before giving the notice and you would have waited longer than required by law before filing the court papers. You would not appear hasty to the court, but more importantly, you would already have begun your court case. If you fail to give the tenants a notice on the fifth, and they don't pay on the appointed day, you'll have to deliver the notice then, and you'll have to wait the required number of days following service of the notice before you can file your papers with the court. That wastes precious days; whereas, if you deliver the notice on the fifth and the tenants don't pay on the appointed day, you can go right ahead if you wish and file your court papers that very same day because you have already

served the notice and you should already have waited the required days.

What's that? Did I hear you say that you'd rather not give your delinquent tenants a Notice to Pay Rent or Quit the very first time you go after them about their late rent? Okay. That's somewhat understandable. Although a whack on the side of the head in the form of an "official" notice, along with the threat of a full-scale eviction, may be the only thing sufficient to motivate some tenants to pay, others may be motivated better through a tap on their funny bone in the form of a light-hearted rent reminder.

Displayed here are two of the twelve reminders in the FORMS section, all different, and all designed to remind tenants in a half-humorous, half-serious way that their rent hasn't been paid yet and that you are going to do something about it unless they do pay up.

Use these reminders sparingly, and vary them. Because each particular one loses its impact if used a second time, don't give the same one twice to the same tenants. Better tenants shouldn't need reminding that often anyway.

The dozen reminders should be enough to last a tenancy's lifetime.

Remember that these reminders do not take the place of a Notice to Pay Rent or Quit as far as legal eviction proceedings go. They're just a human-to-human approach intended to keep your relationship with your tenants from becoming too adversarial. They're a friendly nudge. That's all.

The reminders shown on these text pages are much reduced versions of those available in the back of the book. The full-scale versions are sized to accommodate copying on either half- or full-sized sheets of paper. Select the one you want, copy it, insert the appropriate names, deliver it, and expect to get your rent with a smile.

■ **Partial Rent**—Sometimes your tenants won't have all that they owe you, so they will offer to pay you part of the rent and promise to pay the balance before the month is out. If they do, hesitate a little just to be dramatic, and then take the money. Tell them you prefer not to accept part of the rent but that you will do it this time under the circumstances, provided they understand that they must pay the balance within a specified time frame. Much as I dislike the extra bother involved in collecting partial rent, I would rather get some of the rent money than risk getting none at all.

Whenever you accept partial rent, give the tenants a receipt which does not cover a specific rental period. Just identify it as "on account." The second receipt you write, the one for the balance, should include the rental period covered by both payments. Trying to calculate exactly how many days in a 31-day month are covered by 56% of the rent money is too confusing. Don't bother.

■ **Receipts for Past-Due Rents**—Writing receipts for past-due rents can be every bit as confusing as writing them for partial rents. Just remember that you should never write a receipt for a current rental period if the tenant is in arrears for an earlier period. All rent monies paid should apply to the earlier period first. Here's why.

Suppose some tenants are one month behind in their rent and you sue them for nonpayment. Suppose also that on July first they pay June's rent, but you give them a receipt covering the month of July. In court the tenants produce your receipt for the current month of July and tell the judge they lost the receipt for June. The judge has to assume that they are telling the truth because you can't prove conclusively that they didn't pay for June. Your not having a copy of their June rent receipt doesn't prove anything. It's only what you have with you that counts. How can you prove that you don't have something? How can you prove that their June rent receipt never existed? And your stating under oath that they didn't pay for June doesn't prove anything ei-

ther. It's your word against theirs. So the judge has to base his decision on the existence of their July rent receipt. It suddenly becomes important because it does prove that they paid for July, and if they paid for July, then they probably did pay for June. They win. You lose one month's rent.

Losing one month's rent can be very important, can't it? So I repeat—*Never write a rent receipt for a current rental period if the tenant is in arrears for an earlier period.*

■ **Ramifications of Late Payment**—When tenants do get behind on their rent, the chances are good that they're behind on their other bills as well, and they'll be shaping up a list of payment priorities mentally or on paper. See that yours is on top. Pressure them. Become a physical and psychological presence in their lives.

Credit experts rank most people's priorities for paying their bills in descending order as follows:

    1) Rent/Mortgage
    2) Utilities
    3) Telephone
    4) Car payments
    5) Insurance
    6) Taxes
    7) Heating fuel
    8) Cleaning/Laundry
    9) Schools
   10) Doctors
   11) Dentists
   12) Club dues

Surprising, isn't it? You're right up there on the top of most people's bill priority list. Even so, remember that landlords are fair game to some people. They think there's nothing wrong with trying to beat you out of your rent money. They think they can string you along with one promise after another and that you'll just be so beguiled by their ruses that you will neither collect rent from them nor evict them for a long time to come.

What do you wish to allow your tenants to get away with? It's up to you. I have seen a middle-aged schoolmarm, 4 feet 10 inches tall and all of 90 pounds, keep supposedly incorrigible, hyperactive high school boys under her complete control. Another teacher, marveling at the situation, asked one of the boys why he never misbehaved in Miss Cheever's class. The boy replied, "Oh, she doesn't allow it." You cannot allow your tenants to pay late. If you do, you'll be the one who "pays" in the long run. Don't allow it!

If tenants don't have one month's rent when it's due, they're surely not going to have two months' rent in thirty days. The longer they stay without paying, the harder it is for them to pay and the less desire they have to pay. Staying without paying becomes easier and easier. Why should they pay for time they have already spent under your roof? By allowing them to stay there rent free, you are only postponing the inevitable.

Don't think you're doing your tenants a favor by allowing them to stay there rent free, either. You aren't. You're spoiling them. You're leading them to believe that they don't have to be responsible for their debts.

Don't think your act of kindness in allowing them to stay there rent free is going to win you the tenants' undying love and sincere appreciation. It won't. They will think of you as a dupe and a weakling.

What's more, they see a big delinquent rent bill as your problem, not theirs. You caused them to owe you all that rent money.

Yes, you read right.

Tenants who owe their landlords months of rent don't blame themselves for their not having paid. They blame their landlords for allowing them not to pay. They blame their landlords for not trying to collect and for not evicting them in a timely manner. That's the reason they owe all the money they owe you. It's not their fault. You as the landlord should have known that they could never pay you months of rent in a lump sum. It's your fault that they owe so much money, you dummy. Now you must take the consequences.

Such thinking is much like that of the son who murdered his mother and father and asked the court for mercy because he was an orphan. Such thinking is ridiculous and self-serving, but it's the kind of twisted thinking you can expect from those tenants who do everything possible to avoid paying their rent until the very last minute, if then.

In all my experience as a landlord, I have never been pleased with myself when I have allowed any tenant to stay more than fifteen days beyond a missed rent due date. Dealing with these delinquencies has always cost me extra money, extra time, and extra aggravation. Even so-called good risks, teachers, preachers, police officers, apartment managers (yes, even them), and college student body presidents, have moved out owing me money when I have permitted them to get more than fifteen days behind. I have collected lots of promises and a sheaf of letters. In some cases I did manage to collect the past-due rent in full, but it always required more of my time, and I had to become a bill collector to do it.

Bill collectors generally charge 50% of whatever they are able to collect. They know how much time and effort such work requires. You aren't charging enough rent to include bill collecting among your many services, and you really do become a bill collector when you have to scurry around collecting late rents. Your rents should be paid promptly and voluntarily. Each collection shouldn't require more than ten minutes of your time per month. That's all. That's enough.

Remember, too, that tenants who aren't paying their rent are actually stealing from you. They might as well be picking your pocket or snatching your purse, but the law doesn't quite see it that way. The law gives you no immediate recourse. You can't call the cops for help. You have to rely upon your own self to get them to pay up or move out, and if you do something drastic, you're the one who'll be in trouble just like a homeowner who harms a burglar with a booby trap. Only after you have resorted to a legal eviction procedure can you get the law behind you to settle the matter.

Collecting your rents swiftly and doggedly on a scheduled basis will prevent evictions for nonpayment of rent more than anything else. Your tenants will know full well what to expect of you. They may test you once, but they won't do it again. It's too costly. If they have to, they will borrow the money from someone else to pay their rent rather than risk your wrath and risk being evicted.

Lowering Rents

"Are you crazy? Lowering rents is un-American! It's Communistic with a capital "C"! It's ludicrous! It's idiotic! Why, everybody knows that rents are supposed to go up, not down! Did the soft drink bottlers raise their prices when sugar skyrocketed? You bet your sweet closet auger they did. Did they lower their prices when sugar costs plummeted? Not on your paint-speckled spectacles they didn't. Well, I won't lower my rents either! I'd leave my places vacant before I'd ever lower my rents."

This subject tends to animate some landlords, those who think they have some sacred duty to society to raise rents whenever they can. Whether we like it or not, this is a competitive business. When somebody builds a new housing tract close to where your vacant rental house is, and investors snap them up and start renting them out for a hundred dollars less than what you have been renting your old house for, you've got a problem. Either you lower your rent accordingly, or you become accustomed to having a vacancy on your hands. The same holds true when the over-building of apartment houses or the departure of a big employer increases the vacancy factor in an area.

Some landlords cope with an area-wide high-vacancy situation by reducing the move-in costs, giving away premiums like television sets and microwave ovens, or offering a month's free rent, all with the express purpose of getting the occupancy rate up, as if occupancy is the name of the game. The one thing they'd never consider is lowering the rents. Too bad!

Let's stop to consider the costs and implications of these various incentives, though, and compare them with lower rents. Let's say that a standard 2-bedroom unfurnished apartment in our Sampletown is going for $500, and let's say, too, that each one of the three incentives being tried is reasonably successful in attracting tenants.

Reducing the move-in costs to, say, one month's rent, the first of our incentives, is certain to increase the potential number of customers who might want to rent our property. In particular, it will attract the kind of tenants who don't have any savings and can't afford to put up the normal deposit, but you have to imagine that such people are likely to be less responsible than tenants who do have savings. So what happens if you should rent to some of these irresponsible hand-to-mouth tenants. You collect one month's rent before they move in. That's well and good, but at the end of their first month's residency there, they have possession of your $50,000 apartment unit, and you have nothing of theirs, no prepaid rent, no security deposit, and no cleaning deposit, nothing to insure that they will live up to their obligations to you. If they choose to stay there until evicted and tear the place apart, which they might conceivably do, you're going to lose a bundle. You may even wind up buying them out with their original $500, and still you'd

have a devastated apartment on your hands. This incentive is too risky for me. It's strictly for high rollers. What can you possibly hope to gain by filling a building with tenants who haven't complied with the time-honored requirement made of tenants, that they put up a deposit in case there's a problem later? Not getting a deposit is an invitation to trouble, big trouble, for it puts you at the tenants' mercy. They can leave their rental in any condition they want to and at any time they want to, and there wouldn't be a thing you could do about it. The cost to you of this incentive is an unknown, too.

My advice is this—*Do not reduce your move-in costs in order to attract tenants.*

How about the second alternative which some owners seem to love, the free TV or microwave oven? This one may work, but it's going to cost you cash dollars up front, don't forget. Nobody who moves in to get a free television set is going to wait a day, let alone a year, for the payoff, and what do you do when the tenants give notice after three months that they're leaving? Ask for the merchandise back? What do you do when they decide to move out at the end of a year so they can get a new bedroom set offered as a move-in premium at another apartment complex?

My advice on offering premiums in order to attract tenants is this—*Don't.*

How about offering a month's free rent as an incentive? After all, everybody likes something for nothing. Free rent should attract tenants the way free love attracts shore-leave sailors. Yes indeedy, but the trouble is that neither the tenants nor the sailors tend to stay around very long. And good long-term tenants are the real name of the game in rental housing, aren't they? Then there's always the question about which month should be free. Should it be the first? the sixth? the twelfth? And again, what do you do when tenants move out immediately after they get their free month? Should those who stay longer than twelve months get an extra month's rent free? They'll want it, you know. Another problem with free rent is that it interferes with the smooth flow of your income. You could have some months with no income at all or at least much less than normal.

My advice on free rent is this—*Don't open the store every Monday and give away the product.*

All right, how about lowering the rent? Lowering your rent $25 below everybody else's will bring you all the tenants you can handle, and it will cost you $25 per month; that's $300 spread out evenly over a year's time, *but* it will likely gain you tenants who will still be around after a year, at which time you would be reassessing Sampletown's vacancy situation and resetting the rent.

My advice on lowering rents is this—*If you feel you have to do something in order to be competitive and keep your occupancy rate up, then, by all means, lower your rents. It can actually increase your income.*

If lowering rents makes sense as a marketing ploy, you have to wonder why there's so much resistance to it. The answer isn't hard to find. Owners are reluctant to lower their rents because they think that they're devaluing their property. Rents affect the value of a multiple-family rental property more directly than any other factor. If an owner were going to put the property up for sale, a buyer would want to know how much rent he could expect the property to produce. A seven-times-gross property would be worth $2,100 less if the rent on only one unit were reduced $25 per month (25x12x7). A ten-times-gross property would be worth $3,000 less (25x12x10). So most owners in high vacancy areas prefer to concede anything other than rent. They think of the cost of lowered rent in terms of property devaluation rather than annual rent loss. They'd much rather give away a $300 TV set or a month's rent to preserve the illusion that the property is worth thousands more. What they're really doing, though, is setting up an unsuspecting buyer for a sting. They're thinking in terms of bailing out of the investment for the most they can possibly get rather than holding onto it until the vacancy situation changes. Such people aren't going to take my advice on lowering rents. That I know. They're flim-flammers who're always chasing the fast buck, but their strategy doesn't make any sense for an investor who's content to wait out an adversity. If you're that kind of person, a tortoise of a landlord, you'll profit more from lowering your rents than you will from giveaways. Try it if you have to and see.

Setting Rents

Because rents used to be tied somewhat closely to property values, setting rents was simple. The rule of thumb for an unfurnished house or duplex was that the monthly rent should equal one percent of its fair market value. A $25,000 house, for example, would rent for $250 a month, and the tenant would pay for all the utilities and tend to the minor repairs.

For multiple-family dwellings larger than duplexes, the rule of thumb was that the monthly aggregate of rents would approximate 1.2% of the value of the property, a figure which is the reverse of the common yardstick that the value of multiple units should equal seven times their annual gross rents. Each apartment in a $40,000 fourplex, then, would normally have rented for $120 per month. Those old rules of thumb, when applied, pretty much guaranteed owners a decent cash flow return on the investment.

Today, they no longer apply as they once did, for property values have outstripped rents significantly in most areas. Today, a $100,000 house may rent for any sum of money, from $500 to $1,200, from one-half of one percent of the property value to 1.2%, and a multiple-family dwelling may rent for as little as one-half of one percent to as much as 1.4% of its value. Property values bear little relationship to the rents you can charge. Supply and demand set property values in the sales marketplace, and supply and demand set rents in the rental marketplace. They are two different marketplaces.

You cannot simply peg the rent to the value of the property, nor can you add up what you are paying for utilities, maintenance, financing, bookkeeping, taxes, and management, and then add a percentage for your profit and say that you're going to rent your property for that sum of money. That's not the way the business works. Nobody guarantees a landlord anything these days, least of all a profit. Rents no longer guarantee owners a cash flow return, and setting them is no longer a simple calculation using percentages and multipliers.

Since the residential real estate market, which is measured by property values, and the rental housing market, which is measured by rents, have diverged appreciably over the years so that they no longer are bound together by time-honored rules of thumb for setting rents, you must look to the rental housing market itself when you set rents today. In other words, with rents no longer contingent upon the value of your property or upon your costs for maintaining the property, you have to familiarize yourself with what people are willing to pay for a place to live like the one you have available for rent, and then charge accordingly.

You can't expect to get $1,000 a month for your $100,000 house if other owners are renting similar houses for $850, and some of those are going begging. You might have to ask $800 to get a good tenant. Then again, if houses like yours are renting for $1,200 a month and there are none available for rent when yours becomes available, you might find good tenants right away who are willing to pay $1,400 a month.

Whether we like it or not, the rental property business is no monopoly. It's private enterprise in action, and wherever there's private enterprise in action, there's a free marketplace. Some foolish landlords might think they have a monopoly. They might think they can set their rents as high as they want and then tell people, "Take it or leave it." They're wrong, and the marketplace will tell them they're wrong. People will "leave it" if they can rent the same thing for less elsewhere, and the foolish landlords are left with vacancies which produce zero revenue and profit them nothing until they come to their senses and set their rents at realistic levels according to the market.

People aren't complete fools with their rent money. They're price-sensitive. They try to figure out the market by looking at many available rental dwellings. They shop around.

People look for the best buys in rents just as consumers look for the best buys in automobiles, gasoline, corn flakes, orange juice, and bacon. What dictates the prices of these items? The market does, the market of supply and demand.

When Florida has a freeze and juice oranges suffer, the price of orange juice increases because the supply has decreased. The price increases until people stop paying it, until they say to themselves that they can do without orange juice at such high prices. They wait, maybe they substitute something else, until the price comes down. That's the free market at work.

When oil crews descend en masse upon a small Montana community to start drilling wells, the demand for rental housing outstrips the community's supply, and the rents increase until people balk and start living in their cars and motorhomes or until more housing becomes available. Maybe an enterprising farmer will level some acreage and build a trailer park. Maybe some contractors will throw together a few apartment houses. Finally, with everybody accommodated, rents stabilize. They fluctuate across a narrow range until the crews leave en masse several years later. When that happens, the demand plummets and the rents do, too, because the supply remains high while the demand has become low. That's the free market at work.

What you have to remember about this free market for rental dwellings is this—it's disorderly. It's disorderly just as the market for all real estate is disorderly. It has to be disorderly because every rental property is different, even those in the same building. Real estate in general and rental dwellings in particular do not have the sameness, the uniformity, of commodities like corn and crude oil and orange juice. Commodities and stocks have orderly markets because they are uniform. You can get a quote for a share of IBM or a bushel of corn delivered in Chicago just by placing a telephone call. One share of IBM is the same as any other share, and one bushel of corn delivered in Chicago is the same as any other bushel. Not so with rental dwellings. They're all different. Consequently, there's no one place you can call, no one place you can look, to get the market price for your rental dwelling. There's no orderly market.

Just because there's no orderly market for rental dwellings doesn't mean that there's no market at all. There is most definitely a market. It's just disorderly, that's all, and you have to do a little work to learn approximately what the market prices are, the same kind of work that those tenants are doing who are in the market for a rental dwelling themselves. They're out shopping.

Now comes another key element to this whole "disorderly rental dwelling market" discussion, something you should remember whenever you're setting your rents. The market in rental dwellings is not a market in *all* rental dwellings. It's a market in *vacant* rental dwellings. They alone are your competition. They alone are available for rent. They alone are *on* the market for people who are *in* the market to rent a dwelling. You needn't concern yourself with the rents being charged for occupied dwellings. Those places are no longer available to the public. They are currently off the market and can't be rented by applicants at any price. Only when they come back on the market do they become your competition. Then they become vacancies and they again become the "supply" in the supply-and-demand equation.

Whenever I think about how supply-and-demand affects rents, I think about the housewife who goes to the market to ask the butcher for a five-pound, cross-rib roast. He shows her a beautiful one, well-marbled and well-trimmed, and as he puts it on his scale, he says, "Let's see, at $3.39 a pound, that'll be $16.95." She looks at him wide-eyed and exclaims, "$3.39 a pound! Mr. Crump down the street sells me his cross-rib roasts, which are just as nice as this, for $2.49 a pound."

So the butcher asks, "Then why don't you go down the street and buy one from Mr. Crump?" "I'd like to, but he doesn't have any!"

To that, the butcher responds, "Well, if I didn't have any, I'd sell 'em for $2.49, too!"

The housewife couldn't buy the roast at $2.49 a pound because nobody had them available at that price. They were all sold out. She had to buy what was available or go without, and she chose to pay the $3.39 price.

Prospective tenants can compete with each other only for available rental dwellings. They might have some friends who are renting a two-bedroom house for $650, and they might think that they can get one similar for $650, but if all the two-bedroom houses now on the market are renting for around $725, that's what the prospective tenants are going to have to pay unless they can convince an anxious landlord, who currently has a vacancy and is worried about making his loan payment and paying his property taxes, to lower his rent. They might indeed be able to convince a landlord to lower his rent by pointing out how much rent their friends are paying unless the landlord understands that he shouldn't be trying to match the rent of occupied houses. The rent being paid for occupied houses may be way under the current market.

Don't set your rents according to those of occupied dwellings. They don't matter. Forget about what tenants are paying for occupied dwellings unless those dwellings were recently rented. Only then should you regard them as an indication of what market rents are now.

To set your own rents, you need to find out what your competition is asking in rent for vacant dwellings which are similar to yours in location, amenities, and upkeep. You need to do a market survey of sorts. Check newspaper adver-

tising, ask people at your rental housing association, ask other owners you know, ask the local housing authority which administers the Section 8 Housing Program (see chapter 14), and inspect other vacant properties yourself in the area. If you want to go further, check the classified ads for rental property similar to yours in a newspaper which is several weeks old. Call several of the advertisers and ask if their dwellings are still for rent. If they are, you know the rents are too high. If they have already been rented, the rents are either too low or about right.

When you have done your market survey, you will know what constitutes a competitive rent for your dwelling, and you won't have to wonder after it is rented whether you could have charged more.

Remember that when you set any rent, you are virtually fixing it at one level for a twelve-month period, so do treat this process seriously. It is serious business.

Remember also that setting the rent too low is the biggest mistake you can make in determining what rent to charge. Don't be afraid to set your rent high, because anyone who looks at the place will tell you if the rent really is too high, whereas they won't say a word if it's too low. If nobody offers an opinion and you're wondering what they think about the rent you've decided to charge, ask them. You can easily lower the rent any time you want, but you can't always raise it so easily.

By the way, there's another method you might want to try when setting the rent for a particular unit. It's not for the faint of heart because it's a little unorthodox and contains an element of risk. It also requires a little extra work.

The method is holding an auction. Auctions are as genuine a marketplace as there is, and so long as enough people who might be interested in the auction items know about the auction, the sales prices will be market prices.

Surely you've heard of the phenomenal success of the website known as eBay, where sellers come to auction off everything from soup bowls to nutcrackers, from yesterday's computers to today's software, from Japanese automobiles to Florida real estate. These auctions work because the website is well organized and because anyone anywhere with access to the Internet can participate. With so many people, dealers and end users alike, aware of the items for sale, sales prices reach levels higher than they would were the auctions held only for a limited audience, that is, for those able to attend in person.

Whereas you could try conducting an Internet auction for your vacant rental, it may not yield the best results. It may not yield the best results because the "merchandise" you're selling has two significant limitations. It's rooted in place, and it's rooted in time. You can't package it up and send it to Timbuktu, nor can you hold it off the market for the "buyer" who wants it six months from now. The buyer must have an immediate need for the unit and must want to live there in particular rather than anywhere else on the planet. An Internet auction would expose the unit to many people, that's true, but that's of no advantage when only a very small number of those people would be interested, and some people who would definitely be interested in renting it don't use the Internet and would never know about the auction. You want anybody and everybody who might be interested to know. You also want them all to see the unit before they bid on it. An Internet auction, eBay style, would limit the rental unit's exposure and unnecessarily complicate the renting process.

You could organize a live auction, just as Sotheby's and Christie's do when they organize formal auctions for collectibles, but such auctions would be impractical for rental dwellings. They take too much time to put together. By the time you could arrange a well-publicized auction to attract a gathering of potential renters, your property would have been vacant a month or more, and the prospects who were looking at rentals when you first had your vacancy would already have found a place. They wouldn't want to wait around for you to hold an auction and not know until then whether they were going to get the place. Time is too important in landlording to waste. Whereas you would know that your auction helped you determine the market rent for your rental dwelling, you'd have had to sacrifice too much to get it.

The best auction alternative for rental properties is a silent auction, one held during an open house or for some short (two days at most), specified period. You would start the bidding at the lowest price you're willing to take and invite those who have seen the place to submit a higher bid along with their applications. Before closing the bidding, you would contact all bidders, apprise

them of the highest current bid, and give them the opportunity to raise their b[...]
Then you would take the highe[...]
the highest bidder's application[...]
proval, rent to that person.

A silent auction leaves no d[...]
the market is for your rental, at [...]
you have advertised the place in th[...]
attract enough interest, but becaus[...]
extra time and involves some uncer[...]
bidders, you stand to lose good tena[...]
to conclude their search quickly and move in quickly. You also stand to lose good tenants who simply don't want to participate in something as unorthodox as a bidding process when they're in the market for a rental unit. In addition, you stand to lose face if nobody bids and you have to lower the lowest price you're willing to take, something which your current tenants will learn about soon enough and will create pressure on you to lower all your rents. Those are the risks you take in conducting a silent auction.

Try a silent auction if you're in a hot rental market, if tenants are beating down your doors to have a look at your vacancies. There's no better way to determine market-level rents at the very moment when you have a vacancy available.

Don't try a silent auction if you're in a cold rental market and cannot expect enough interest in your rental unit to attract more than a few applicants. Any auction under those circumstances would prove to be a futile exercise.

Raising Rents

If you are at all like most landlords, you dislike rent raises more than any other aspect of this business because of the tenant dissatisfaction and resentment they frequently cause. In spite of what you see in the media, statistics show that landlords have a real aversion to raising rents, for not only have rents failed to keep pace with percentage increases in property values over the years, they haven't even kept pace with the consumer price index. In other words, no matter what people in general think about rent levels, no matter how shrill their cries for rent control, landlords have actually been both lax and restrained in raising rents. Consequently, the profitability of rental property is shrinking perceptibly, and residential income property is becoming less attractive as an investment.

There's no good reason for you to stop dislik-

Notice of Change
in Terms of Tenancy
(Rent)

TO *Sam and Barbara Brooks*   , Tenant in Possession
3104 Dogwood Drive
Big Town, CA 09601

YOU ARE HEREBY NOTIFIED that the terms of tenancy under which you occupy the above-described premises are to be changed.

Effective _____*August*_____, *XXXX*, your rent will be increased by *$22* per month, from *$650* per month to *$672* * per month, payable in advance.

Dated this *2nd* day of _____*June*_____, *XXXX* .

Fred Felder, Manager
Owner/Manager

This Notice was served by the Owner/Manager in the following manner (check those which apply):

   (X) by personal delivery to the tenant,
   ( ) by leaving a copy with someone on the premises other than the tenant,
   ( ) by mailing,
   ( ) by posting.

* *When rent is paid on or before the third day following the rent due date, you may take a $20 discount.*

Sorry, Sam & Barbara! I hate doing this but our increased expenses are getting the better of us.

ing rent raises, but you should come to accept them as a necessary element in the conduct of your own landlording business, an element made absolutely necessary by the impact of inflation on your expenses. Since your very business survival depends upon your being able to meet these increased expenses with increased revenues, you have no choice but to raise rents or go out of business.

You must expect that any raise may expose you to charges of profiteering and may precipitate a whole host of tenant complaints, but you must learn to cope with these problems unless you have some perverse desire to subsidize your tenants, in effect, for the dubious privilege of serving them as their landlord, or unless you wish to invest your money and time in a business venture which only loses money. You are in this business to make a profit, aren't you? It certainly is not worth the worry, the risk, the trouble, the time, the sweat, or the investment otherwise.

To have the desired effect, raising rents requires a policy as carefully outlined as your rent collection policy, one which is calculated to minimize tenant dissatisfaction and resentment. Rent raises under this policy should occasion neither a mass revolt nor a mass exodus of your tenants because they should come to understand that your rent raises are fair, and therefore, acceptable.

This policy should involve six elements—careful preparation, proper timing, extended lead time, reasonable increments, amicable notices, and personal delivery.

■ **Careful Preparation**—Careful preparation for rent raises consists of much more than merely preparing the notices to change terms of tenancy. That's the most visible, most mandatory part of the preparation, but it's really the smallest part and the least time-consuming, too. Actually, careful preparation should continue year-round. As soon as you give one increase, you should already be preparing for the next one. Here's what you ought to be doing to prepare—

✔ Prepare by keeping up with your bookkeeping every month so you know how much your expenses are and how high you need to raise the rents to operate profitably and also so you can refer to your expenses knowledgeably whenever you must discuss with your tenants your reasons for raising the rent.

✔ Prepare by keeping track of market conditions in your area so you know what current rents are for other similar rentals.

✔ Prepare by beginning a rumor that the rent will increase to a level higher than what you anticipate, so the tenants are relieved when they learn later how small the increase was in comparison to what they had expected.

✔ Prepare by telling your tenants exactly when they can expect the rent to increase.

✔ Prepare by charging new tenants at the anticipated higher rents so that when the rents are raised for everyone else to those market levels, or close to them, you can indicate to your old tenants that new tenants have already been paying higher rents (because good, long-term tenants are hard to find and cost you far less in many ways than do short-termers, give them special consideration when you're raising rents; keep their rents a few dollars below market levels).

With such preparation, you should be able to forestall most charges tenants might make that your rent increase was unfair and irresponsible.

■ **Proper Timing**—The proper time to raise rents is always when tenants are expecting an increase. More than at any other time, they expect increases when there is a change in ownership, so give them an increase then if one is justifiable, but take a few weeks first to become acquainted with the property and determine whether an increase is, in fact, justifiable.

Once when I was new to the business of landlording and reluctant to raise rents at all, I waited twenty months after buying a building before making a well-warranted $20 increase, which amounted to 12% of the rent at that time. As soon as she received her notice, one irate tenant called to complain. She said that she had expected me to raise the rents when I bought the building almost two years before, but coming when it did, the increase was a complete surprise to her and therefore totally unfair. How do you argue with reasoning like that? You don't. Clearly, I had done things wrong even though I hadn't done her wrong. I had assumed that an impersonal increase notice and all that elapsed time since their last increase would be sufficient for the tenants to accept a new rent raise unquestioningly. Of course, that wasn't sufficient because the tenants simply were not expecting an increase right then.

I had failed to condition them. I hadn't timed the increase properly.

You should raise your rents when tenants expect increases, and you should condition them to expect increases like clockwork one year after the rents were last raised. Following this policy, you might want to stagger the increases throughout the year by scheduling them to coincide with the anniversary of each tenant's arrival. In doing so, you spread whatever repercussions there might be.

If possible, time your rent increases to coincide with some improvements you are making to the property so the tenants will believe they are getting something more for their money and will complain less at having to pay more.

Proper timing refers to the cycle of increases and to tenant conditioning, and it also refers to the actual moment when the official written rent increase notice will reach the tenants.

Now I have to admit that I haven't come to any conclusion yet as to what is the best time of the day to deliver rent increase notices. I'm still studying that one. But I do believe that I know the best time of the month to deliver them. The best time of the month to deliver rent increase notices is right after tenants have paid their rent, when they have put rent out of their minds for another month and it's no longer a matter of immediate concern.

■ **Extended Lead Time**—Normally, any changes in terms of tenancy, including rent increases, require a lead time equal to the rental period. Tenants who rent on a monthly basis are supposed to get thirty-day notices. Tenants who rent on a weekly basis are supposed to get seven-day notices.

This isn't enough lead time for rent increase notices. I recommend *doubling* the lead time for rent increase notices. Sound ridiculous? It isn't ridiculous in the least. It's a sound business strategy. Here's why.

Upon receiving a thirty-day notice that their rent is going up, some tenants have a knee-jerk reaction and immediately give notice that they're going to move. They know that they're supposed to give you thirty days notice (unless you follow my advice and stipulate in their rental agreement that they need give you only fifteen days notice), and they feel that they have to register a quick protest to your notice. Your notice is a threat to them, and they feel sure that they can find a better place to live for less. Even when they discover that they can't find a better place to live for less, they may feel too proud to approach you about canceling their notice of intention to move. As a consequence, you could wind up losing some good tenants by not giving them an extended lead time.

Your tenants will appreciate sixty days notice. They will feel far less threatened when you give them that much time to consider their alternatives. They will have a whole month to look around before they have to give notice that they intend to move if indeed they do decide to move. Such a strategy will lessen the tension and win as much of their cooperation as you can possibly expect at this time.

Time heals all wounds. It also lessens the impact of rent increase notices.

I first learned how effective this extended lead time could be when I bought a new property and had to raise one tenant's rent 50% in order to get it to something approaching market level. The tenant, of course, was irate about the whopping increase. I explained to him that he had been enjoying especially cheap rent for a long time under the old owners but that I couldn't afford to let him stay there at such a low rent. I told him, "You probably don't know how cheap your rent's been because you haven't needed to look at places for rent for a long time. I tell you what. I'll give you a full sixty days before your rent goes up. You can look around for forty-five days to see whether you can beat the value you're getting here at the increased rent. If you can, give me just fifteen days notice that you're going to be moving, and I'll be happy."

He did some looking and quickly became convinced that he couldn't beat the rent he would be paying when the rent increase took effect. He didn't move out. Nope, he didn't move a thing. What's more, he actually thanked me for giving him the extra time to look around. I had raised his rent 50%, and here he was thanking me!

Be aware that in some parts of the country legislators have been looking closely at how little time tenants have to vacate when they're faced with an involuntary move caused by a rent increase. Finding a new dwelling and moving into it require more than a month, say the legislators, so landlords ought to give tenants an extra month to move and give the tenants this extra month at the lower rent.

If you elect to give your tenants thirty days notice of a rent increase rather than sixty, check to see whether your legislators have already granted your tenants who decide to move as a result of the increase, what amounts to the extra lead time anyway. If you elect to give your tenants sixty days notice, you should already be in compliance with any such law.

■ **More Acceptable Numbers**—Having carefully prepared for the increase, you will know what rents are reasonable for your rentals and you will also then know approximately how much the raise should be. Because you have to take many factors into consideration when you calculate any rent increase and because your final figure will usually be the result of numerous compromises, you may want to select an increment which is psychologically more acceptable to your tenants. The more acceptable numbers are those which are not multiples of five. $12, for example, is better than $10, and $18 is better than $15. Such figures lead tenants to believe that their increases have been carefully calculated to match actual increases in operating expenses rather than to include still more arbitrary profit for the owners rounded up, of course, to the nearest $5.

■ **Reasonable Increments**—You are taking a calculated risk of creating vacancies with any raise you give, but that risk increases somewhat if the rent increase exceeds either 10% or the consumer price index, whichever is greater. If you have timidly lagged behind the marketplace and you now have to raise your rents higher than those guidelines to approach a reasonable rent schedule, you may want to do so even knowing full well that some tenants are going to vacate. Wish them well, and then don't get yourself into the same bind again.

Raise your rents on an annual basis from then on.

■ **Amicable Notices**—Besides preparing carefully, timing properly, coming up with acceptable numbers, and calculating reasonable increments, you should announce your raises officially in writing using honest, sympathetic notices. The notice itself is the culmination of all your work, and it should reflect the great care you have put into all the preparation thus far. The notice should soften the blow with some reasons for the raise and an expression of your personal concern about the possible hardships the increase might cause.

Use a cold, impersonal legal notice like the Notice of Change in Terms of Tenancy if you want, but add to it your own personal message. Mention the tenant by first name in a handwritten aside and apologize for the increase, saying that you are trying to maintain the tenant's dwelling as best you can, but that it is impossible to do so unless you raise rents.

Or you might want to type up your own complete notice using personal wording like this—"As you know, we are living in inflationary times, and even though I do my best to keep costs down, there's no way I can reduce the expenses of this building back to what they were a year ago. I have absorbed these increases as long as I could, but now I am forced to increase your rent by $_____, or _____%, from $_____ per month to $_____ per month, effective _____, 20_____."

Remember that if you use any rental agreement or lease form which has a discount provision, the increase should be based on the gross or non-discounted rental figure and not on the discounted amount that you are accustomed to collecting when the tenant pays on time. You might want to remind the tenant of this situation by stating it directly on the notice, asterisking the rental figures and explaining below as follows: "*When rent is paid on or before the third day following the rent due date, you may take a $20 discount."

Remember also that if you or a previous landlord collected your tenants' last month's rent when they moved in, the sum you originally collected won't be sufficient to cover the increased rent which will be in effect during their last month of tenancy. To avoid misunderstandings later, advise them that they should pay the increase for that last month's rent as soon as the new rent becomes effective. Otherwise you will have a difficult time collecting the difference between what they paid as last month's rent when they moved in and what the rent happens to be when they move out. Their having paid their last month's rent when they moved in does not entitle them to get their last month's rent at that lower amount. They owe you the difference, and you should collect it whenever you raise the rent.

■ **Personal Delivery**—You may deliver a rent increase in person or by mail, but personal delivery is preferable because it provides an opportunity to discuss the reasons for the increase with your tenants on a personal level. If you can't serve it personally, send them the notice, and post one on their door, too. You must rest assured that they have received at least the minimum time required by law for such notices, and your sending them a copy by first-class mail won't give you that assurance unless you give the notice plenty of time to reach them. Should you suspect that your tenants might deny on a stack of comic books that they ever received their notice, have somebody else deliver it. Then you will have a third party's word for verification. Go with the third party if you like.

Controlling Rents

Can you imagine any politician proposing wage controls without price controls (trade unions might bicker among themselves about some matters, but this would unite them like iron filings on a magnet)? Can you imagine any politician proposing ceilings on the prices which homeowners are allowed to sell their single-family dwellings for (homeowners would take up their Saturday-night specials to defend their right to sell their castles at fair market value)? Both are such absurd proposals that any politicians espousing them today would be stripped of their brown shirts and whisked off to asylums to babble and cavort with the other lunatics.

Yet, how many politicians are there who seriously propose rent control as the solution to rising rents, a scheme every bit as illogical as controlling wages without controlling prices and as utterly ridiculous as putting a ceiling on the price of houses? In effect, rent control does both. It limits landlords' "wages" without affecting their expenses, and it artificially limits the value of their rental property. That's what I call "landlord bashing."

Politicians who support rent control don't see it that way, however, and they don't see themselves as fascists either. They see themselves as Robin Hoods, championing the cause of impoverished, victimized renters in the interminable and righteous struggle against wealthy landlords. Them's you and me, remember. They hear the caterwauling of their tenant constituents lamenting the hardships of living on a fixed income and decide that the simplest way to appease these people is to limit the obscene profits, fix the income, of the monopolistic, money-grubbing property owners. You and me again. Although do-gooder politicians are only greasing the squeaky wheels in their communities when they act to control rents and are ignoring the long-term ramifications of what they are doing, they are in truth attempting to silence those noisy tenants the only way they can, with a specious solution to a large and complex problem.

The problem we all face, tenants, politicians, and rental property owners alike, is not constantly increasing rents, and the solution to constantly increasing rents is not rent control. The real problems are a shortage of housing and an increase in the many expenses involved in landlording, from toilet parts to garbage rates. The only real solutions are to build more housing, control inflation, and subsidize the housing of those who are truly poor. Obviously these are formidable solutions, ones which local politicians cannot effect easily or inexpensively, if at all.

Rent control, on the other hand, is easy to enact and relatively inexpensive to administer, and it provides immediate relief. So what if it does exacerbate the real problems? So what if it does victimize those who own rental property? So what if it does favor all tenants regardless of their financial need? It appeases the people with the votes. Therefore, it is an ideal political solution for harassed politicians struggling to cope with what appears to be a local problem they feel they can handle, and it is a solution which is off-budget and unseen. Why not? It offers something for nothing. It appeals to people's greed.

Whenever it becomes an issue in your area, you would be wise to become involved in the political process which will determine whether rent control will be adopted, and if so, what form it will take. Any talk of rent control should bring you to your feet before rent control itself brings you to your knees. Support the political efforts of your rental housing association. Attend hearings.

Ask the reference librarian at your local library to help you find some of the many studies on the subject. Search the web. Contact the Pacific Legal Foundation (see SOURCES & RESOURCES), which has been fighting rent control in the courts for years and has had some notable victories lately.

For anecdotal information, read *Live Rent-Free for Life and Other Incredible Revelations About NYC Rent Control* (see SOURCES & RESOURCES), and learn something about the woes of one poor landlord who tried for ten years to be a scrupulous landlord in New York City and ran afoul of a deeply entrenched rent control bureaucracy and six refined tenants.

Write letters to your politicians and to the editor of your local newspaper citing certain rent control case studies and outlining your own views relative to the local situation. If, at last, you sense that some form of rent control is inevitable, become involved with the shaping of the measure so it will be easier to live with. Face the fact that we live in a world which is more consumer-oriented than ever before, and expect to have to give a little.

Odious as rent control sounds to us landlords, conjuring up images of abandoned properties and bankruptcy, it may be written as a compromise to everyone involved. Tenants fear quantum leaps in their rents, increases of 30% and 50% a year, and you can hardly blame them. Landlords fear being forced to maintain rents at certain base levels *ad infinitum* and eventually losing their buildings. But some form of rent control might assuage both those fears.

Would you balk, for example, at rent control which would apply only to buildings with six or more units and would allow owners to pass through all increased expenses and prorations of improvements, as well as to increase rents by 15% per year? That wouldn't be hard to live with, would it? Well, that is rent control just as much as is a measure which requires you to roll back your rents to what they were twelve months ago and then keep them there forever. Compromises are possible, even desirable at times, in order for everyone involved to save face.

Finally, if rent control is adopted in any area where you own rental property, take the time to learn all you can about it. Are certain sizes of rental dwellings exempt from controls? Under what circumstances may you raise rents? What procedures are there for grievances? How are evictions affected by the controls? The rent control regulations and the bureaucrats who administer them will answer these and other pertinent questions you might have. Be more familiar with these regulations than your tenants are. Be cooperative with the authorities, work within the law, and seek to change it whenever possible.

Don't panic. Don't give up. Shrewd owners study such predicaments thoroughly and learn how to profit from them. There's usually a way.

But don't invest any more of your money in rent control areas. Invest it elsewhere. You don't need a "partner" who's telling you what you can and cannot do, while looking over your shoulder all the time, assuming no responsibility, and contributing absolutely nothing toward providing better rental housing at a reasonable cost.

Some Last Words

Rents are the lifeblood of the landlording business. Setting them, raising them, lowering them, and collecting them are subjects you must know well if you're going to succeed. Return here now and then to reread this chapter so you will be ever mindful of these subjects.

By all means, remember that your raising rents doesn't suddenly metamorphose you into a greedy, unscrupulous monster of a landlord. Rather, it means that you are a good business person who understands the nature of the business you are in. You understand that you can lose money in this business if you want to, just as you can in any other business, and that no one will care, least of all your tenants. You understand that no one is going to nominate you for the "Landlord of the Year Award" just because you leave your rents low, nor is anyone going to tell you that your rents are too low.

When was the last time one of your tenants told you the rent was too low and offered to pay more? Don't wait for it to happen. It won't. Tenants who offer to pay higher rents are as rare as one-armed violinists. Just because they don't volunteer to pay more, however, doesn't mean that the dwellings they occupy aren't worth more rent and that they can't pay more rent.

You are the only one to judge what is the right rent based upon market conditions, and you alone must take the initiative necessary to raise your rents. Set up a schedule for raising rents. Mark the dates on your calendar. Then do it.

7
Keeping Good Tenants

Although some high fallutin landlords like to think of themselves as manor-born aristocrats, while at the same time they think of their tenants as serfs and underlings, people born to be kicked around, they are utterly wrong in that persuasion, just as wrong as those high-and-mighty tenants are who think of landlords as their natural-born enemies.

You, landlord, are a businessperson. Your tenants are your *customers*. Never forget that. Your tenants are your customers. They're not serfs. They're not underlings. They're not people to be ignored, stepped on, or kicked around. They're customers, and they're not merely one-shot, single-purchase customers, either. They're repeat customers, loyal customers, the very best customers any businessperson could hope to have. Month after month, they pay you good money to occupy the shelter you own and maintain.

When was the last time you heard the businessperson's credo, "The customer is always wrong"? No, I've never heard it either. Yet that's the way some landlords treat their very best customers. They act as if their tenants are always wrong. They act as if they would be better off having no tenants at all. Bunk, balderdash, bull, and baloney! There's no doubt that we would be better off without certain tenants—the sneaks, the complainers, the deadbeats, the gossips, the noisemakers, the pigs, the agitators, the rebels, the thieves, the screwups, and the crazies—but that doesn't mean we'd be better off having no tenants at all. No, we wouldn't, not by a moon shot!

We landlords need tenants just as tenants need us. We are mutually dependent.

The Importance of Tenants

Tenants are important to this business. In fact, they are crucial to this business. Perhaps you've never stopped to consider just how crucial your tenants really are. Let me explain.

You probably already know from your reading about real estate that there are four ways in which you as an investor can make money in the residential income property business.

First, there's *appreciation*, also known as *capital gain* (as a result of the natural inflation caused by the government's 'round-the-clock printing of paper money or the forced appreciation caused by your having improved the property somehow, your property should be worth more when you sell it than when you bought it).

Second, there's *equity buildup* (your loan principal decreases every time you make an amortized loan payment, and as a consequence, your equity in the property increases).

Third, there's *tax shelter*, sometimes called *depreciation* (at tax time you deduct a portion of your property's improvements and consider them paper losses to offset your income).

And fourth, there's *cash flow*, that is, positive cash flow (this is the money left over from rental income after you have paid off all the bills).

Although one or several of these four ways might be more significant than others for a certain property, all of them are important to the overall business we are in.

Of these four ways, however, only one of them will keep working for you regardless of how you treat your tenants. Only one of them will work for you if you neglect tenant matters to the point where tenants stop paying you their rent and start tearing the building apart, window by window, door by door, wall by wall, toilet by toilet. That one way is tax shelter.

Sometime after you first acquire a residential income property, you or your accountant will set up a depreciation schedule for the building, and each year you will depreciate it for tax purposes using whichever method of depreciation is most advantageous to you. You will continue depreciating the building on paper regardless of whether the building is shipshape or dilapidated, occupied or vacant. It makes no difference whatsoever. As far as tax shelter is concerned, tenants are as unimportant to an owner as bag ladies are to a fashion designer.

Ah, but things are very different for the other three ways we make money with rental property—appreciation, equity buildup, and cash flow. In order for appreciation to work for you, you and your tenants together have to keep their dwellings livable, even attractive, so the property will increase in value. In order for you to pay off your loan every month and take advantage of equity buildup, your tenants have to keep paying you their rent so you can make those loan payments. And if you are ever to have any cash flow, it will have to come from your tenants. They are the ones who pay you the money that pays the bills and accumulates in your wallet, purse, or bank account.

Can you afford to cut yourself off from three of the four ways to make money in residential income property? If you can, then go ahead and neglect your tenants all you want to. That's your prerogative. But you should be asking yourself why in the world you're in this business anyway. You really ought to be enjoying yourself clipping your bond coupons, fondling your gold coins, debating which Rolex to wear, driving around in your Rolls, admiring your diamonds, wearing your designer clothes, and taking cruises throughout the sunny climes of the world. You ought to think about getting out of the landlording business altogether or at least delegating the management of your property to someone else who has more landlording savvy than you have. You're giving the rest of us a bad name.

If, on the other hand, you cannot afford to cut yourself off from three of the four ways to

make money in residential income property, you should, by all means, not neglect your tenants. You cannot really succeed in this business if you do unless, perhaps, you decide to invest in that one kind of residential income property where tenant problems are minimized, cemeteries. Those tenants you could neglect. They don't complain. They don't plug toilets, break windows, mark up walls, hold noisy parties, fight with one another, or refuse to pay their rent. No matter what you did, you'd have them for keeps, forever and ever, and you could concentrate most of your energies on keeping the property itself in tip-top condition.

Come to think of it, running a cemetery isn't the only way to avoid tenant problems entirely and keep your rental property in tip-top condition. You could simply not rent it out at all just as the state of California did for years with its governor's mansion. Keep the place empty. You'd have no tenants to worry about, none whatsoever. You could get along perfectly well without tenants, couldn't you? Who couldn't? So why not let your building age and weather gracefully without subjecting it to all that tenant abuse and without subjecting yourself to all those tenant problems? Sound interesting? It is, except that without any tenants at all you'd lose out on one of the most time-honored and most important ways to make money in this entire business. You wouldn't have any positive cash flow. There would be cash flow all right, but it would be flowing in the wrong direction. It would be negative cash flow, flowing out of your bank account and into the property instead of out of the property and into your bank account. Of course, you would get the old standby, tax shelter, and you might get some appreciation, but not as much as you would be getting if you had good tenants occupying your property. Buyers would question the value of a residential property which houses nobody. "What's wrong with the place?" they would ask. "Is it haunted?" Haunted properties don't command good prices in the marketplace. Buyers for such properties are limited. Well, what about equity buildup? You'd get some, naturally, but because the loan payments would be coming entirely out of your own funds every month, the equity buildup couldn't be considered a way to make money. You'd merely be robbing Peter to pay Pauline, taking money from one of your bank accounts and putting it into another. That'll never make you rich.

All things considered, then, renting to good tenants and keeping them content enough to stay right where they are for a very long time is surely the best way to run a landlording business. You need those tenants and they need you.

Besides, good tenants also help to determine the value of every rental property you can possibly imagine, that is, with one exception, the house or duplex which buyers want to occupy themselves. Even in that case, although the buyers may want to displace the tenants and don't care two fig leaves about rental values, they'll pay more if good tenants have been keeping the property in good condition. Prospective buyers who have no intention of displacing existing tenants will always pay more for a rental property which already has good long-term tenants living there, tenants who pay their rent on time, respect the property of others, and respect other people as well. Such tenants are prime assets. You cannot get along without them. Treat them well, these good customers of yours. They are the layers of your golden eggs.

How to Keep Good Tenants

Recognizing that good tenants are indeed important to you and that losing them will cost you hundreds of dollars, if not thousands, you are wise to consider various ways to keep those tenants living right where they are for as long as you possibly can, while you're still charging them market rents.

You can increase your chances of keeping your good tenants longer by being friendly with all of them, though friends with none, by being reasonable at all times, and by making an extra effort to please them at certain times.

To be more specific, I have come up with the following list of things you can do to keep your good tenants longer—

■ **Change locks upon move-in**—When tenants first move in, change all the door locks right before their very eyes so they will know that previous tenants have no access (see chapter 17 for hints on changing locks; usually the best time to change locks is when you're reviewing the Condition & Inventory Checksheet).

■ **Change locks when requested**—Continue to provide your tenants with that same sense of security during their tenancy by changing their locks again whenever they reasonably request a change, after a roommate moves out or they lose their keys or their home is burglarized. (NOTE: Because you are responsible to each tenant who has signed your rental agreement, you may not change the locks to exclude any one of them. If you do, you will have to provide access to that person later anyway so long as his or her name appears on the agreement. Before you go to the trouble of changing the locks, therefore, advise the remaining tenant of this responsibility you have. Of course, if the excluded tenant has not signed the agreement or if the remaining tenant can show you a restraining order, you have no responsibility to provide access to the excluded tenant.)

■ **Give a maintenance guarantee**—Give your tenants some extra assurance that you will take care of maintenance problems promptly. Give them a written guarantee that you will take care of maintenance problems within a reasonable period of time or else you will stop charging them rent.

Sound pretty radical? At first, it may sound radical, but it's not, not really. Well, maybe it would sound radical to some landlords, those who promise their tenants anything and everything and then never perform, but for the rest of us, for us scrupulous landlords, it's not at all radical. It only makes good sense, and it's a good way to keep good tenants.

As landlords in America, we have a responsibility to provide our tenants with dwellings which are livable according to modern American standards. These dwellings must have heat, water, sewage, and power, and they must be able to keep out the wind and the rain. When our dwellings cannot provide these basic amenities, we shouldn't be charging any rent at all because we

TIMELY MAINTENANCE GUARANTEE

The management responsible for maintaining the dwelling located at the address given below hereby guarantees to repair any defects discovered in the dwelling which are hazardous to life, health, or safety within seventy-two hours (three days) following notification by the tenants who occupy the dwelling. Tenants' notice may be either verbal or written, but it must be *acknowledged* in writing by someone whom management has authorized to accept such notice.

Should management fail to repair the defects, either temporarily or permanently, within seventy-two hours (three days), tenants shall be relieved of the responsibility for paying rent for every day or portion thereof during which the defects go unrepaired following the initial seventy-two-hour (three-day) period allotted for completing this work in a timely manner. Tenants' responsibility for paying rent shall begin again once the defects have been repaired.

To receive the benefit of any rent abatement owed to them under this guarantee, tenants must be current in their rent payments and must pay their next rent in full when due. Whatever rent abatement is owed will then be paid to them in the form of a rebate within forty-eight hours following receipt of their rent payment.

This guarantee applies only to those defects which are the responsibility of management to maintain as mandated by law and/or as outlined in the applicable lease or rental agreement.

This guarantee does not apply when a portion of the dwelling becomes uninhabitable as a result of flooding, fire, earthquake, or an act of God, and the tenants choose to remain in residence during reconstruction. In such cases, management and tenants will negotiate a fair rent covering the reconstruction period.

This guarantee shall remain in effect so long as there is a valid lease or rental agreement between the parties below covering the dwelling located at the address given below.

Dated ___2/2/xx___ Address ___999 Charm Lane___

Tenants ___CAMERON MITCHELL___

Owner/Manager ___Lester Landlord___

aren't providing our tenants with what we agreed to provide them in the first place.

Remember, we are supposed to be providing our tenants with more than just an address, more than just four walls and a roof. We are supposed to be providing them with a place to live, a place where they won't have to do battle with the elements when they're indoors, a place where they can take care of their bodily needs safely and comfortably.

The Timely Maintenance Guarantee commits to writing what we landlords are supposed to be doing anyway, maintaining our rental dwellings, except that it goes two steps further. It gives time limits, and it gives consequences.

Under the terms of the Timely Maintenance Guarantee, should you fail to fix an inoperable water heater, a leaky roof, a broken entrance lock, or some other significant defect within seventy-two hours following notification of the problem, your tenants will start getting a rent abatement. In other words, your income as a landlord will be cut off if you fail to do your job.

Tenants love this guarantee. Good tenants love it all the more. It's something which puts smiles on their faces because it offers them "satisfaction guaranteed or their money back," something they're not accustomed to getting when doing business with ordinary landlords, certainly not something they're used to getting in writing.

Under normal circumstances, when good tenants can't get their landlord to keep things in good repair, they will start looking around for another place to live rather than fight to get satisfaction. But they know as well as anyone else that moving costs money, and they don't want to have to move just because they can't get their landlord to maintain their property properly. Under the terms of the Timely Maintenance Guarantee, they don't have to worry about whether their landlord will maintain their property properly. They know that it will be maintained, or the landlord is going to suffer. They also know that they shouldn't have to fight their landlord to take advantage of this guarantee. After all, their landlord was the one who offered it to them in the first place. If he had no intention of standing behind the guarantee, he never would have taken the initiative himself and given it to them.

This guarantee, then, is a goodwill, public-relations gesture from you to your good tenants, something which can gain you an edge in doing business without really costing you anything. What's more, it's a stimulus to you to get necessary maintenance work completed quickly.

In the lingo of the real estate seminar gurus, the Timely Maintenance Guarantee is strictly "win-win." Good landlords win when they use it, and good tenants do, too.

■ **Make portable heaters and coolers available for emergencies**—Whereas the Timely Maintenance Guarantee gives you seventy-two hours to make either a temporary or a permanent repair, sometimes you should respond even faster. Recognize as certainties that the heaters at your rental properties will malfunction only on the coldest Sunday of the year and that the air conditioners will malfunction only on the hottest holiday. Naturally, there will be neither parts nor repairers available to fix the heating or cooling equipment right away, and your tenants may think that you are somehow to blame for the delay. Keep cool. Anticipate that such problems will occur regardless of how good your preventive maintenance is, and prepare for them. Buy a good portable electric heater which the building's electric circuitry can reasonably be expected to accommodate, and lend it to your freezing tenants until their broken heater can be repaired. Likewise, buy a portable cooler or a large-bladed box fan and lend it to your sweating tenants until their air conditioner is back in service. Such thoughtfulness will convince your tenants that you do care about whether they are freezing or sweating and that you are attempting seriously to remedy the problem.

■ **Make a plumber's helper and a garbage disposer wrench available**—Make available to your tenants both a plumber's helper (plunger) and a garbage disposer wrench. They're so low on most thieves' requisition lists and they're so inexpensive that you needn't worry much about whether they'll disappear from an accessible location. They're handy, easy-to-use tools, and their availability to your tenants may save you a few maintenance trips.

■ **Memorize tenants' names**—Memorize all of your tenants' names, even the pets' and kids', and try to remember a few specific things about each tenant which you might use later in conversation. Everyone responds better to the personal touch, and what's more personal than a name?

Maintenance Request

Tenant _Jerome Peters_
Unit _1012 Park Street_
Home Phone _244-4444_   Work _246-8888_
Date of Request _10/12/XX_ Time _5:15PM_
Maintenance Request _Toilet loose in master bathroom_

Permission to Enter _OK_
Best Time _anytime_
Request Submitted By _Jerome Peters_

Work Order

Work Order No _XX-101_ Status _Complete_
Work Authorized By _JJ_
Date Work Attempted _10.13.XX_ Time Begun _9:15A_ Ended _9:45A_
Date Work Completed _____ Time Begun _____ Ended _____
Work Completed _Toilet bowl itself was securely bolted to the floor. Seat hinge was broken. Replaced entire seat._

Materials Used _Toilet seat._

COST	
Labor	∅
Materials	12.32
Services	∅
TOTAL	12.32

Percentage of Work
Charged to Tenant _0%_
Work Performed By _JJ_

Tenant Notice

We entered your dwelling today for necessary repairs, maintenance, and/or inspections.
The work is _complete_
Incomplete work, if any, resulted from a lack of the following:
☐ tools. ☐ parts. ☐ time. ☐ assistance.
We expect to return on or about _____

Thank you for your cooperation.
Date _10.13.XX_   _Jennifer James_

■ **Listen to your tenants**—Give an ear to your tenants when they come to you with their concerns. Unless they're talking while you've got your head under their sink, look them straight in the right eye and concentrate on what they're saying. To show them you've been listening, ask them questions every so often and express some agreement. Always let them do more talking than you do. Take time to listen to the bores as well as everybody else. After a while you'll know which tenants have the sense to limit their own chatter themselves and which ones you'll have to limit. If you've been reasonably patient in listening to your tenants all along, they will listen to you more readily when you come to them with your concerns.

■ **Encourage use of Maintenance Request form**—Give your tenants a blank Maintenance Request form and encourage them to use it whenever they have a routine maintenance problem. Explain to them that the form is actually a three-in-one form. It's a maintenance request, a work order, and a tenant notice. When they submit it, they need complete only the upper section. The maintenance person will then do the work and return the form to them with details about what was done.

■ **Hire tenants**—Whenever possible, hire tenants to work for you, doing such things as cleaning, yardwork, and painting. Tenants appreciate the opportunity to pick up some extra money without having to travel any distance from their home, and they take more pride in the place where they live if they have contributed some of their own labor to make it look more attractive. My best groundskeepers have always been tenants who lived on the premises. My best vandalism deterrents have always been those troublesome teenager tenants I've hired to do odd jobs for me (be advised that teenagers working for you do require supervision and that you must have workers' compensation insurance for everybody you hire).

■ **Help tenants find housing assistance**—Become familiar with the various kinds of rental housing assistance available through public agencies and other charitable organizations. Help your tenants who might qualify for this assistance to apply for it and run the bureaucratic maze to get it. Many tenants who should be getting assistance are totally unaware that it exists or are too timid or too proud to apply. There may be some tenants you'll encounter who cannot read or write well enough to fill out even the simplest of the necessary forms and are too embarrassed to admit their handicap. Your help could make the difference between their remaining as your good tenants and their moving to less expensive and less desirable quarters.

■ **Pay interest on deposits**—Sometime during the holiday season, send your tenants holiday greetings, express your gratitude for their having been your good tenants for whatever length of time they have lived there, and enclose a check which equals the bank interest earned during the year by their security/cleaning deposits. Some states and municipalities have laws on the books requiring owners to pay interest on tenants' deposits. In those places, your payment is no more than compliance with the law rather than a goodwill gesture. When the payment is made voluntarily, however, you will find that it makes a pleasing, long-lasting impression on the recipients. Remember, too, that the interest on a $500 deposit at 6% is only $30, and that $30 will pay a bigger dividend when paid to your tenants than it would if it were to remain in your own bank account.

■ **Send greeting cards**—Remember your tenants' special days with greeting cards. People in service businesses have known for years the public relations value of sending personal greetings to their customers on special occasions, and you'll find that tenants like to be remembered by their landlords as well.

■ **Feed your mourning tenants**—Order a catered platter of food or some other token of your concern delivered to those tenants who are mourning the death of a loved one they have been living with. Times of death are awkward times. They're also times when hordes of people suddenly descend upon the survivors with their condolences; hungry people they are, too. A platter of food materializing out of nowhere is always welcomed, and you will find yourself welcomed later when you pay a visit to express your sympathy once again and learn how the death will affect the survivors' tenancy.

■ **Use good tenants to find other good tenants**—Include your good tenants in your efforts to secure other good tenants. Enlist them in your word-of-mouth advertising campaign (see chapter 3), for they have as much of an interest in

For Your Information:

<u>Important Numbers</u>

Police___911___   Telephone Co.___555-1000___

Fire___911___   Gas Co.___555-2000___

Ambulance___911___   Electric Co.___555-3000___

Paramedic___911___   Water Co.___555-4000___

Doctor___911___   Manager___555-0413___

The best time to contact the manager is _8AM-6PM Mon-Fri_.

In an emergency, when you cannot get hold of the manager, call ___555-0240___.

<u>Helpful Hints</u>

1) A fire extinguisher is located _under Kitchen sink_
Use short bursts aimed at the base of the fire. Never use water on
a grease fire; either use the extinguisher provided or throw
baking soda on it.

2) The main electrical shutoff for your dwelling is located
___JUST OUTSIDE BACK DOOR___.
Check there to see whether a fuse has blown (have an extra on
hand) or a circuit breaker has tripped. Restore service by
replacing any fuse which appears to be blown (use one with the
same number on it) or by flipping the circuit breaker switch back
and forth once.

3) The main gas shutoff for your dwelling is located
___N.E. CORNER OF BUILDING___,
but there may be an individual valve on the line supplying each
appliance as well. Shut off the gas by turning the valve 90
degrees, that is, so it crosses the direction of the supply line.

4) The main water shutoff for your dwelling is located
___JUST OUTSIDE BACK DOOR___,
but you may be able to shut off the water to an individual faucet
by turning off the supply valve below your sink or toilet (not
your tub or shower). If hot water is leaking anywhere, shut off
the valve on top of the hot water heater.

5) Whenever you defrost the refrigerator, turn it off or set
the control knob to defrost. Place a pan to catch the water and
empty it when necessary. Do not try to break up the ice with any
implement like a knife or an ice pick. Let it melt on its own or
speed it up by placing a pot of hot water in the freezing
compartment. Dry the floor thoroughly when you have finished.

FOR YOUR INFORMATION - Page 2

6) Whenever you use the garbage disposer, if you have one, feed garbage in gradually along with lots of cold water, and let the water run for half a minute after you turn off the switch. Use the disposer only for those things which are edible, but don't put either cooking oil or grease down it; put them and everything else except toxic liquids in the trash. Keep metal objects out of the sink while using the disposer and turn off the switch immediately if you hear any loud metallic noises. Do not put your hand into the disposer (use tongs to retrieve objects) and do not use any chemical drain openers. If the disposer stops running on its own and you haven't heard it make any strange noises, something may have gotten stuck. Try turning the blades with a disposer wrench. Then push the reset button. After you have tried all this and you find that it still doesn't work, call the manager.

7) Whenever you want to dispose of any liquids which aren't edible, please see the manager. Many liquids are toxic and should not be put down the drain or into the trash. They must be disposed of carefully so they will not contaminate the soil or the water supply in this area. Included in this list of hazardous household wastes are the following: oven cleaners, ammonia-based cleaners, drain cleaners, floor wax, furniture polish, deodorizers, spot removers, medicines, paint, thinners, paint removers, wood preservatives, art supplies, photographic chemicals, antifreeze, car waxes, crankcase oil, fuels, radiator flushes, rust inhibitors, engine cleaners, insect sprays, weed killers, and swimming pool chemicals.

8) Whenever water rises in the toilet bowl, do not try flushing the toilet again. The bowl can hold just one tank of water at a time. More water from the tank will only cause the bowl to flow over. Use a plunger first, and then try flushing it again. Do not try to flush feminine napkins or paper diapers down the toilet. They may disappear from the toilet bowl, but that's no guarantee they'll clear the sewer pipes completely. They could require a plumber's visit, and that'll cost you money.

9) Whenever you have showered or bathed, please take a moment to mop up the excess water on the bathroom floor. A dry floor is a safe floor.

10) Whenever you want to hang anything from, or stick anything to, the walls or ceilings in your dwelling, please ask the manager to explain how to do it acceptably.

11) Whenever you want to remove the screens from your windows, please ask the manager how to do it properly. Some screens have to be removed from the inside and some from the outside. The manager will show you how.

COMPLAINT

We understand that every so often you may have a complaint which you want to make known to the management. We want to hear about it so we can take care of it or if we already know about it, so we can tell you what we're doing about it. Please use this form to register your complaint with us.

Type of complaint: [ ]   Against management

                            [X]   Against another tenant

                            [ ]   Regarding general conditions

If your complaint is against a particular person, please give that person's name and address.

Name _*Anne Noyance*_

Address _*251 Grace Avenue*_

Give details about the incident, complaint, or problem (include date, time, and place as applicable):

Noise is always coming from her apartment. I can hear her tv when I am trying to sleep. She also puts her garbage in my garbage can.

What action do you suggest that management should take?

Tell her to stop playing the TV so loud and to stop putting her garbage in my can.

Please note that management cannot promise complete confidentiality if this complaint is raised against another tenant.

Submitted by _Heidi Tidi_   Date _November 11, xxxx_

*   *

Received by _Charles DeRoge_   Date _11-11-xx_

Action taken _Arranging for a meeting of both tenants, to be held before Thanksgiving, to discuss the complaint_ who their new neighbors will be as you do. Generally they welcome the opportunity to participate in the search for new tenants and make a conscientious effort to find good ones.

■ **Provide useful written information**—Provide your tenants with useful written information for coping with some of life's little emergencies and for doing various things around their home. Here's a two-page form which you might want to use for this very purpose. It has space for your name (as manager) and telephone number along with other important telephone numbers, numbers which should all be readily available in one place. There's also space you may use to indicate where the utility shutoffs are and how to shut them off, and there are some suggestions for coping with such problems as plugged toilets and ice-jammed refrigerators. Many times you will assume that your tenants understand how to use, say, a garbage disposer or a fire extinguisher when, in truth, they don't have a clue because nobody has ever taken the time to explain how to use one before and they themselves are too embarrassed to ask. Whether you make this information part of your move-in procedure or distribute it later is up to you.

■ **Provide a tenant Complaint form**—Provide your tenants with a tenant Complaint form and encourage them to use it. One of the worst things that can happen to a conscientious landlord is to lose good tenants over a matter which could have been corrected had the landlord known about it in time to do something about it.

Some good tenants are too timid to say a single word about those things which irritate them until after they have moved or made irrevocable arrangements to move. Sometimes even then they don't say anything, and you never do learn the real reason why they moved.

Sometimes the source of their frustration surfaces quite fortuitously when you happen to be talking with them about their future while they're moving their things into a U-Haul truck parked in the driveway. Once you learn the real reason why they're moving, you want to whack yourself on the forehead for not having made an effort to find out beforehand, when you could have done something about it and kept the good tenants.

Sometimes good tenants will move because of problem tenants who live nearby and are causing them grief, but they don't say anything to

you about the problem tenants. In fact, all you know is that the problem tenants have stopped paying you their rent. You don't know that your good tenants have been so vexed by the problem tenants that they have decided to move, and your good tenants don't know that they don't have to move to get away from the problem tenants. You know that you are in the process of evicting the problem tenants, and you know that they will be gone within a few weeks. The good tenants don't know. You would have told them had you only known why they're moving.

You want to know when things are going right around your rental properties, and you need to know when things are going wrong. You need to know so you can make adjustments as necessary. This tenant Complaint form is the communications device which will put you "in the know." It makes complaining easy on your tenants who have a complaint. They don't have to sit down and compose a letter, worrying about form and content. They merely fill in the blanks. It's all content, and it's as easy as painting by numbers.

Now look at the form itself and notice how its nine basic elements fit together to make a whole. All of the nine elements except one are either neutral or they encourage the tenant to submit the complaint. That one element is the caveat that management cannot promise complete confidentiality if the complaint is raised against another tenant. Like it or not, you need to include this caveat to protect yourself from grief should there be an unfortunate incident between the tenants involved. It may not even be related to the complaint, but if it might be, you can be sure that it will be considered as such and that you will be targeted as a cause of the incident for having revealed the source of the complaint. You should try your best to protect the confidentiality of the person who submitted the complaint, but you may not succeed, especially because the person who is the target of the complaint will probably figure out who made the complaint anyway.

The only other form elements of note here are those beneath the line of asterisks. They're for the landlord to complete–the one, an acknowledgment of receipt; the other, a description of action taken. Both are especially important in case there should be any litigation. The acknowledgment shows that you actually received the complaint. The description of action taken shows how you responded. A litigious tenant bent on proving that you are an irresponsible landlord could produce a bundle of tenant complaints and claim that you had failed to do anything about them, but if you hadn't at least acknowledged receipt, you could argue that you never received them. Problem tenants can and will twist anything to their advantage.

When a tenant submits a written complaint, sign it and make a copy for the tenant. After you take action and complete the description of the "Action taken," make another copy and give it to the tenant. You'll have a paper trail and so will the tenant.

■ **Redecorate occupied units**—Offer to redecorate your good tenants' dwelling if it hasn't been done for a few years and the place is beginning to look shabby. All too frequently good tenants feel compelled to move because their landlord expects them to tolerate living in a dwelling which needs new linoleum in the bathroom, paint in the living room, drapes in the bedroom, and carpeting in the hallway. When they decide not to tolerate such conditions any longer and they move away to a dwelling which has been completely redecorated by a new landlord, their former landlord is forced not only to redecorate but to lose rent while the place is vacant and then to bear the expense and suffer through the process of finding new tenants who may or may not be as good as the old ones.

That former landlord would actually have saved money by redecorating to keep the good old tenants instead of redecorating to attract good new ones. You cannot afford to be oblivious to the condition of your occupied rentals any more than you can afford to be oblivious to the condition of your vacant rentals.

Some Last Words

You may be a greedy, myopic, misanthropic landlord if you want to be, one who pooh-poohs any act of cooperation or kindheartedness, but your tenants will move out more frequently than will those of benevolent, circumspect landlords who value their good tenants and cater to them whenever possible, while still being formidable enough, when need be, not to permit any tenant to kick sand in their faces.

Remember that as a landlord you are managing both buildings and people. Buildings are easy. Any simpleton can manage them. People are not so easy. They require management with care, loving care mixed with caring discipline.

8
Helping Tenants Move Out

Tenants come and tenants go with some degree of frequency. Every year throughout the United States, almost half of all the tenants who live in unfurnished rentals will move on to other quarters. When you happen to be the landlord whose tenants are moving out, you have certain responsibilities which you should be aware of and be prepared to carry out.

You know pretty well what those responsibilities are when tenants move in, and you probably pay close attention to them then, but chances are good that you know only superficially what your responsibilities are when tenants move out, and furthermore, that you pay little attention to them.

Except in the most perfunctory ways, we landlords tend to neglect helping tenants move out because we are generally disappointed by their moving and regard it as a desertion of sorts. In addition, their moving is overshadowed by our simultaneous preparation for new tenants, something we consider much more important to our business.

While the pitfalls you face when tenants move in may indeed be more momentous and also more numerous than those you face when they move out, pitfalls do exist when they move out, too, pitfalls which can cause you unnecessary aggravation and cost you plenty in terms of wasted time, energy, and money.

Ask a sampling of small claims court judges about the landlord-tenant cases they hear most frequently, and they will tell you that almost all such cases involve disputes which arise over what occurs at the conclusion of the landlord-tenant relationship, when the tenants move out and somebody feels cheated. Sometimes the landlord will feel cheated and bring the case into court. Sometimes the tenants will feel cheated and file suit, but almost always the cases are related to the tenants' moving out.

Many things can happen at move-out time to cause a dispute serious enough to wind up in court.

Either the deposits aren't refunded as they should have been, or the deposits aren't sufficient to cover the charges owed for damages and cleaning, or there are misunderstandings about the condition of the dwelling when the tenants moved in as compared to its condition when they moved out, or there are misunderstandings about the meanings of the expressions "reasonably clean and undamaged" and "normal wear and tear," or there are misunderstandings about how much the landlord charged to repair a hole in the wall and replace a missing light fixture, or there are misunderstandings about the ownership of certain contents of the dwelling, or there are misunderstandings about whether the deposits may be used for last month's rent.

That's altogether too much misunderstanding, if you ask me, and even though it cannot all be avoided, most of it can be avoided so long as you know what steps to take to avoid it and so long as you follow those steps as best you can.

Ten Steps for Avoiding Move-Out Misunderstandings

The ten steps given here for avoiding move-out misunderstandings require a little extra preparation, a few extra forms, and some extra effort in communication, but they work. They work well.

Follow them, and they will make your landlording life a little bit easier.

1) Prepare at move-in time for the move out.
2) Provide a written Notice of Intention to Vacate form for your tenants to fill out, sign, and give to you when they decide to move.
3) Advise your departing tenants of what they can do to get their deposits back.

Rental Agreement

Dated <u>January 15, XXXX</u>

(Month-to-Month)

Agreement between <u>Lester Landlord</u>, Owners, and <u>RICHARD and ROSE L. RENTER</u>, Tenants, for a dwelling located at <u>456 Sweet Street, LITTLETOWN, CALIFORNIA</u>.

Tenants agree to rent this dwelling on a month-to-month basis for $<u>778</u> per month, payable in advance on the <u>1ST</u> day of every calendar month to Owners or their Agent*, <u>X X X X X X</u>, whose address is <u>453 Sweet Street, Littletown, CA 09090</u>.

When rent is paid on or before the <u>4th</u> day of the calendar month, Owners will give Tenants a (discount) (rebate) of $<u>20</u>.

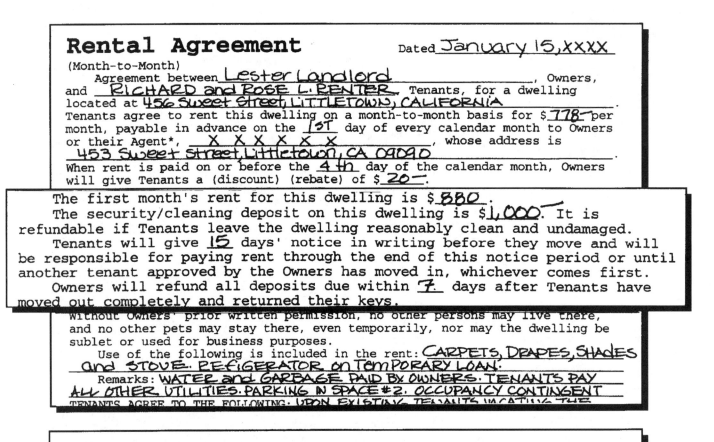

The first month's rent for this dwelling is $<u>880</u>.

The security/cleaning deposit on this dwelling is $<u>1,000</u>. It is refundable if Tenants leave the dwelling reasonably clean and undamaged.

Tenants will give <u>15</u> days' notice in writing before they move and will be responsible for paying rent through the end of this notice period or until another tenant approved by the Owners has moved in, whichever comes first.

Owners will refund all deposits due within <u>7</u> days after Tenants have moved out completely and returned their keys.

Without Owners' prior written permission, no other persons may live there, and no other pets may stay there, even temporarily, nor may the dwelling be sublet or used for business purposes.

Use of the following is included in the rent: <u>CARPETS, DRAPES, SHADES and STOVE. REFIGERATOR ON TEMPORARY LOAN.</u>

Remarks: <u>WATER and GARBAGE PAID BY OWNERS. TENANTS PAY ALL OTHER UTILITIES. PARKING IN SPACE #2. OCCUPANCY CONTINGENT</u>

TENANTS AGREE TO THE FOLLOWING. UPON EXISTING TENANTS VACATING THE

Rent Payment Procedure—Tenants agree to pay their rent in the following way: <u>in person to manager</u>

Deposits—Tenants agree to deposit with the Owners the sum of $<u>1,100</u>, payable before they occupy the premises. Owners may withhold from these deposits only what is reasonably necessary to cover the following tenant defaults: 1) damages to the dwelling; 2) certain cleaning costs following Tenants' departure; and 3) unpaid rent and various other accrued and unpaid charges. Tenants may not apply any part of these deposits to their last month's rent.

Refund of Tenants' Deposits—Within <u>7</u> days after Tenants have moved out completely, Owners shall provide a written accounting of the disposition of the Tenants' deposits and shall at the same time return all deposits remaining.

Occupants—In addition to the Tenants mentioned above, only the following persons may live in this dwelling: <u>X X X X X X X X</u>

No one else may live there, even temporarily, without Owners' prior written permission.

Guests—Tenants may house any single guest for a maximum period of fourteen days every six months or for whatever other period of time the law allows. Provided that they maintain a separate residence, nurses or maids required to care for Tenants during an illness are excepted from this provision.

Subletting and Assignment—Tenants shall not sublet the entire premises or any part of the premises, nor shall they assign this Agreement to anyone else without first obtaining the Owners' written permission. Owners shall not withhold permission unreasonably.

4) Establish what constitutes actually "moving out," and settle upon how the keys will be returned.

5) Give the tenants your "list prices" for move-out charges.

6) Recognize the difference between "normal wear and tear" caused by ordinary comings and goings and "damage" caused by carelessness, abuse, mysterious disappearance, thievery, accident, rules violation, or special request.

7) Inspect the dwelling and itemize its various deficiencies.

8) Calculate the charges fairly.

9) Get the keys.

10) Return the deposits promptly, but not too promptly.

These ten steps don't sound so very difficult, do they? They're not. You probably know enough already to be doing many of them automatically. Still, let's look at each of them more closely. The more you know about move-out misunderstandings, the more you'll be able to avoid them.

1) Prepare at move-in time for the move out.

Avoid this kind of misunderstanding:

"Mrs. Lilliput, we're going to be moving to Houston next Tuesday, and we'd like to use our deposits to pay for the balance of the rent we still owe you from last month, plus whatever else we'll owe you when we leave. That'll just about balance everything out, won't it?"

"I can't believe what you're saying, Mr. Runfree! You give me five days' notice that you're moving and you want me to apply your deposits to the rent? I can't do that. You're supposed to get your deposits back after I've inspected your place and found it to be reasonably clean and undamaged. Right now you owe me $65 on last month's rent, and since you're giving notice today, legally you owe rent for a full one month from today as well."

"Oh, don't you worry your little head about it. We'll leave everything spic 'n' span. You'd be refunding our money anyway. We'll even be saving you the postage you'd have to pay to send the refund to us at our new address."

When your tenants first moved in, you were already preparing for them to move out, whether you ever thought about their moving out at some future time or not. You stipulated how much notice they should give when advising you that they were going to be moving. You asked for

proper notice in writing. You inspected the dwelling with the tenants before they took possession, and you noted its condition and inventoried its contents in writing. You collected adequate deposits, and you informed the tenants that those deposits were not to be considered last month's rent. You did each of these things for one very good reason—to avoid misunderstandings when the tenants were about to move out.

Should you fail to establish these things at the very beginning of your relationship, you will have to expect misunderstandings later, for you cannot expect tenants to know what they should and should not do when they move out unless you inform them at the first opportunity and remind them at every later opportunity.

Unless you tell them otherwise, isn't it logical for them to assume that their deposits should cover their final rent payment, especially if the two are identical sums? Isn't it logical for them to expect to receive all of their deposits back as soon as they move out so long as they clean up after themselves? Why should they have to wait two or three weeks? Why should they have to wait even one single day? And why should they have to give you any notice at all? You'll only re-rent their place the very next day anyway, won't you? Ain't nothin' to this landlording business but cashin' checks!

Discuss the end-game rules with tenants before you ever rent to them, and put those rules in writing in terms which cannot be misunderstood. That done, moveout time will be no trouble at all.

2) Provide a written Notice of Intention to Vacate form for your tenants to fill out, sign, and give to you when they decide to move.

Avoid this kind of misunderstanding:

"Hello, Lester? This is Raymond Renter. I just called to let you know we're all moved out and we'd like to get our deposits back."

"That's news to me, Raymond. You never gave me any notice."

"Come on, man! I did, too! Don't you remember last month when I told you we were planning to move before school started? Isn't that notice enough?"

"No way! I remember when you told me you might be moving sometime soon, but you never said exactly when you'd be moving. How was I to know you'd be out today?"

Notice of Intention to Vacate

TO: _LESTER LANDLORD_

FROM: _RICHARD and ROSE RENTER_

Dated _9/13/XX_

Please be advised that on _SEPTEMBER 30, XXXX_ we intend to move from our residence at _456 SWEET ST, LITTLETOWN_.

We understand that our Rental Agreement calls for _15_ days' notice before we move and that this is _17_ days' notice. We understand that we are responsible for paying rent through the end of the notice period called for in the rental agreement or until another tenant approved by the management has moved in, whichever comes first.

We understand that our deposits will be refunded within _7_ days after we have moved out completely and returned our keys to the management, so long as we leave our dwelling reasonably clean and undamaged.

Reasons for leaving: _We bought a duplex!_

Forwarding address: _1610 Igloo Ave., Littletown_

In accordance with our Rental Agreement, we agree to allow the management to show our dwelling to prospective tenants at any and all reasonable times.

Tenant _Richard Renter_

Tenant _Rose Renter_

Received by _Lester Landlord_

Date _9/13/XX_

The primary reason for requiring written notice from your vacating tenants is to tie them down to a specific moveout date so you can start making preparations to re-rent the dwelling to someone else without delay. Written notice is always better than verbal notice because it's definite, it's incontestable, and it's useful in those cases which wind up in court with the tenant claiming one thing and the landlord claiming quite another.

Some tenants will take the time to compose a thoughtful letter of their own to advise you dutifully of their plans to move out. Accept it so long as it includes the following three necessary particulars: anticipated moveout date, the address of the place they're renting from you, and the signatures of those who signed the rental agreement. But because few people either learn or remember how to communicate anything in writing anymore, you should be prepared to provide a ready-made form for your tenants to complete in order to make your written notice requirement easier for them to satisfy. When they give you verbal notice, supply them with one of your forms and ask them to fill it out then and there if possible.

If you don't have a form handy when they give you verbal notice, use a blank sheet of paper and write down as much of the verbiage as you can remember, making certain that it includes the three necessary particulars. Then have them sign it. You want to tie them down to a specific moveout date as soon as possible following their verbal notice so you won't have to bother chasing them down with the form later.

The form provided here includes space for the necessary information plus space for the tenants to indicate why they are leaving, information

which might prove useful to you in case there's something you might do to get them to stay, should you be so inclined. It's also information which may enable you to improve your landlording operations in general.

3) Advise your departing tenants what they can do to get their deposits back.

Avoid this kind of misunderstanding:

"What do you mean you're going to deduct $75 from my deposit? The place is spotless! I spent $15 on cleaning supplies and $5 on washing and drying the draperies, and I cleaned in there myself for at least six hours! I scrubbed the kitchen and bathroom floors on my hands and knees. They were never that clean when I moved in. I found a good spot remover for the carpet and removed some spots that were there when I moved in. I cleaned the oven so it shines like new. Why, you could rent the place to Martha Stewart, and she wouldn't have to do a thing before moving in!

"I admit that on the whole the apartment's clean, but just look at those drapes! They were new only last year, and now they look so threadbare that I wouldn't even wear them to a toga party! You weren't supposed to wash them. They have to be dry cleaned."

"Well, how was I supposed to know they needed to be dry-cleaned? You never told me what to do. I thought they would come clean in one of those commercial washers down at the laundramat. You gotta admit I tried."

"You tried. I can see that, but you ruined the drapes, and I just have to charge you something for the replacements.

Some of the conditions you impose on your tenants for the return of their deposits are necessarily subjective and open to interpretation. You may have explained what those conditions were

September 13, XXXX

Dear **Margaret and Charlie,**

Moving time is always a busy time, and you will have lots of things on your mind now that you have given notice you are moving. One of those things undoubtedly is how to get your deposits back promptly. In your case, they amount to $ __1,250__ .

Contrary to what some tenants believe, we WANT to return your deposits, and we WILL return them to you so long as you leave your place "reasonably clean and undamaged." That's what your rental agreement says and that's what we will do. You're probably wondering, however, what "reasonably clean and undamaged" means, so we'd like to tell you how we interpret it and tell you also what you should do to get your deposits back.

"Reasonably clean" to us means as clean as you would leave your dwelling if you knew your best friend or your favorite aunt were going to move in after you. To get it that clean, we expect you to clean the appliances, stove hood, and cabinets (under sinks, too) both inside and out; remove all non-adhesive shelf paper; use an appropriate cleanser on the showers, tubs, toilets, sinks, mirrors, and medicine cabinets (inside as well); dust the ceilings (for cobwebs), baseboards, window sills, and closet shelving; wash the kitchen and bathroom walls and spot-clean the walls in the other rooms; wash the light fixtures and windows inside and out; vacuum the floors; scrub the floor tile or linoleum; sweep the entry, patio, storage enclosure, and garage; remove all personal belongings (including clothes hangers and cleaning supplies); and dispose of all trash. PLEASE DO NOT CLEAN THE DRAPERIES, SHAMPOO THE CARPETS, OR WAX THE FLOORS. We prefer to do those cleaning chores ourselves, and we will not deduct anything from your deposits for our doing them.

"Reasonably undamaged" to us means that items which we have supplied should not be missing (including light bulbs) or broken; that there should be no new burns, cracks, chips, or holes in the dwelling or its furnishings; and that the paint on the walls should be sufficient to last at least two years from the time they were last painted. PLEASE DO NOT REMOVE ANYTHING YOU HAVE ATTACHED TO THE WALLS OR CEILING WITHOUT FIRST TALKING TO US, and please try to avoid nicking the paint in the halls and doorways as you move things out.

Please note that until you have returned your keys, you have not "officially" moved out, and you are still liable for paying rent. Make sure that you give us your keys as soon as you move out.

After you have moved out, we would like to inspect your dwelling with you to check it for cleanliness and damage. We will refund all deposits owed to you within seven days thereafter.

We expect you to have moved out completely by **September 30, XXXX** Because we are making arrangements for new tenants to move in after you move, we would appreciate hearing from you immediately if your moving plans should change.

We hope your moving goes smoothly, and we wish you happiness in your new home.

Sincerely,

Hate to lose you!

Leslie Landlady

way back when the tenants first moved in, but since time tends to muddle recollections and since the tenants were hardly thinking then about moving out now, you should review your conditions once more when they are thinking much more specifically about moving out and are more concerned about getting their deposits back.

Discuss your conditions with them in person or send them a letter like the one shown here outlining the conditions, or, better yet, do both. Whatever you do, remind them of the amount of their deposit which is at stake and convince them that you will refund it promptly. They want as much of their deposit back as they can get. You can't blame them. You would, too.

If they refuse to believe that you are a scrupulous landlord who returns deposits, give them the name of somebody who moved out recently and received his deposits back. Tell them to contact that person to learn what kind of treatment they can expect to receive from you when they move out.

Even if you are legally entitled to keep all or most of their deposits because they have accumulated lots of late charges during their tenancy and have adamantly refused to pay them or because they have already failed to meet certain of your move-out conditions, you should still establish some refundable amount which you will pay them no matter what, provided that they return the place to you reasonably clean and undamaged. Give them an incentive to do just that. Don't try to squeeze a few extra dollars out of them at move-out time. That's not in your interest. Bend over backwards, reach into your pocket, and hand them a few dollars after they move out. You don't want them to avenge themselves on your property because you failed to be reasonable.

As for cleaning the place, you know that tenants will seldom clean the draperies, shampoo the carpets, wax the floors, or remove their wall and ceiling attachments to your satisfaction, so you should give them precise instructions for performing these jobs or tell them not to bother at all. Well-meaning tenants may attempt a job and bungle it so badly that you will have to spend extra time and money setting things right, and the tenants, for their part, will expect a full refund regardless of the extra work they have caused you or the extra expense they have cost you. That kind of situation frustrates everyone involved and can easily be avoided through good communication before they move out.

4) Establish what constitutes actually "moving out," and settle upon how the keys will be returned.

Avoid this kind of misunderstanding:

"When we moved out on the last day of the month, we cleaned and cleaned and left everything spotless. We left the keys inside the apartment where anybody could find them and locked all of the doors behind us. That's what we always do when we vacate a motel room.

"The next thing we know, we get our deposit back minus two days' rent. That's not fair!"

"You did do an excellent job of cleaning. I'll grant you that, but I never got your keys back until the second day of the month because I was expecting you to bring them over to me. Vacating a motel room where you've spent a night or two and vacating an apartment where you've lived for an entire year are two different matters. Each has different procedures. You ought to know that technically you haven't moved out until you've returned the keys.

"It was just by chance that I happened to go over to your old apartment on the second of the month to ask you when you would have everything moved out. That's when I learned from your former neighbors that you had already moved out and left the keys behind. You should have told me that that's what you were going to do with the keys. I'd have gone over there earlier, and I wouldn't have had to charge you for those two extra days."

"You didn't say anything to us about what you wanted us to do with the keys. How were we supposed to know?"

Just as your handing the keys over to the tenants when they moved in symbolized your transferring possession to them, their returning the keys to you after they have vacated the premises symbolizes their transferring possession back to you. This transferring of the keys is more than symbolic, however. It constitutes the final step in the termination of the tenancy. Upon returning the keys, the tenants have "officially" moved out.

Inform them of the importance of returning the keys both in the move-out letter and verbally. Tell them that they would be charged extra rent if they were to move out completely and keep the keys because the keys would give them access to the dwelling and essentially leave them still in possession.

Move-Out Charges

Here's what we charge for most of the things we have to do when tenants move out and leave their dwelling in need of something or other. Please note that these charges are averages. Sometimes the actual charges are higher; sometimes they're lower. But most of the time they are exactly as shown. We give allowances for normal wear and tear, of course, and for the length of time something has been in use. Replacement charges include parts and labor.

Cleaning

Clean refrigerator	20.—
Clean stove top	10.—
Clean oven	30.—
Clean stove hood	20.—
Clean kitchen cabinets	20.—
Clean kitchen floor	35.—
Clean tub/shower and surround	15.—
Clean toilet and sink	15.—
Clean bathroom cabinets & floor	20.—
Vacuum throughout dwelling	40.—
Clean greasy parking space	20.—

Flooring

Remove carpet stains	80.—
Deodorize carpet	85.—
Repair carpet	75.—
Repair hardwood floor	90.—
Refinish hardwood floor	580.—
Repair linoleum	45.—
Replace kitchen linoleum	375.—
Replace bathroom linoleum	225.—
Repair floor tile	30.—
Replace kitchen floor tile	250.—
Replace bathroom floor tile	150.—

Walls

Remove mildew and treat surface	12.—
Cover crayon marks	35.—
Repair hole in wall	45.—
Remove wallpaper	135.—
Repaint (per wall/ceiling)	15.—

Doors

Repair hole in hollow-core door	45.—
Repair forced door damage	65.—
Replace door (inside)	125.—
Replace door (outside)	225.—
Replace sliding glass door (sgl)	150.—
Replace sliding glass door (dbl)	250.—
Rescreen sliding door screen	25.—
Replace sliding door screen	45.—

Electrical

Replace light bulb	1.50
Replace light fixture globe	12.—
Replace light fixture	45.—
Replace electrical outlet/switch	5.—
Replace electrical cover plate	1.50

Plumbing

Replace kitchen faucet	50.—
Replace bathroom faucet	45.—
Replace faucet handle	7.50
Replace faucet aerator	3.50
Replace shower head	12.—
Replace toilet tank lid	15.—
Replace toilet	130.—
Replace garbage disposer	80.—

Locks

Replace key (door or mailbox)	2.—
Replace cylindrical doorlock	25.—
Replace passage doorlock	15.—
Replace deadbolt lock	25.—
Replace mailbox lock	6.50

Windows & Window Coverings

Replace window pane (sgl)	75.—
Replace window pane (dbl)	125.—
Replace Venetian blind	75.—
Replace window shade	15.—
Replace drapery rod	25.—
Replace drapery (sill length)	75.—
Replace drapery (floor length)	150.—
Rescreen window screen	10.—
Replace window screen	18.—

Miscellaneous

Replace refrigerator shelf	25.—
Paint refrigerator	75.—
Replace stove/oven knob	6.—
Repair ceramic tile	85.—
Replace ceramic tile countertop	450.—
Repair plastic countertop	35.—
Replace plastic countertop	275.—
Replace cutting board	15.—
Replace mirror	45.—
Replace medicine cabinet	75.—
Replace towel bar	12.—
Replace shower curtain rod	15.—
Replace shower/tub enclosure	150.—
Repair porcelain	135.—
Replace thermostat	60.—
Recharge fire extinguisher	20.—
Replace fire extinguisher	30.—
Fumigate for fleas	125.—
Remove junk and debris	55.—

Settle upon a convenient time and place for the transfer of the keys. Try to combine the transfer with the move-out inspection if possible, but if you can't, just make sure that both you and the tenants understand precisely where and when the transfer is going to take place. There's nothing wrong with letting the tenants leave the keys on the kitchen counter or with somebody on the premises when they depart, so long as you know that you can expect to find the keys there. Tenants who are moving are frequently in a hurry and don't want to wait around for somebody to show up. Neither you nor they have the time to be playing "hide and seek" when you're transferring the keys.

5) Give the tenants your "list prices" for move-out charges.

Avoid this kind of misunderstanding:

"Hey, Edith, this accounting of my security deposit sure is outrageous. It says right here that you kept $20 to clean the refrigerator and $24 to pay for two missing towel bars in the bathroom and $12 to pay for eight burned-out lightbulbs and $45 to repair a hole in the wall. That's a lot of money for those things."

"Those things cost a lot of money nowadays, Mr. Joad. We're not living back in the depression, you know."

"I know that. It's just that if I'd've known how much you were going to charge me for all these things, I'd have seen to 'em myself. I could've gone down to Wal-Mart and bought a perfectly good chromed towel bar for $6.99. You charged me $12 for the replacement you put in there, and it's no better than the one I'd have bought. That's highway robbery!"

"Call it whatever you want. I think those charges are fair and reasonable. They're what I had to pay, and I have the receipts to prove it."

"Not in my book they're not fair! I'm gonna see you in court!"

Business establishments as diverse as dry cleaners, auto repair shops, legal offices, and dental clinics all have list prices for the various routine services they offer. When you bring a lady's two-piece suit to a dry cleaners, for example, the person at the counter will consult a price list and tell you immediately how much you'll have to pay to have it cleaned and pressed. When you take your Ford pickup truck to a shop for an alternator replacement, the mechanic will consult a price list and tell you how much the job will cost. When you ask an attorney how much an uncontested eviction will cost, you'll learn the "list price." When your dentist schedules a visit with the dental hygienist for a cleaning, you will receive a quote for the service if you want one. In each of these cases, you find out in advance exactly how much the work will cost, provided, of course, that there are no complications.

Why not do the same thing with your routine move-out charges? Let your tenants know in advance of their moving just how much your move-out charges really are. If they know what charges they face at move-out time, they'll be less argumentative when you start deducting certain sums from their deposit. They'll be expecting to pay $12 for a towel bar and $75 for having the refrigerator painted.

Try it and see what happens.

Itemize the many things you might have to do to a place when tenants move out, and assign a dollar figure to each (use the form shown here with the prices shown here if you can live with these numbers; if you can't live with these numbers, use the second version of the form which has no prices, and enter other prices which reflect more accurately the labor and parts costs prevalent in your area). Then give these "list prices" to your tenants when they first rent from you and again later when they give you notice that they're moving (the prices may have changed during a long tenancy), and you'll detect a difference in their attitude when you give them an accounting of their deposits. They'll be less defiant, and you won't have to be so defensive about your charges.

Be aware that even though you have a well-defined, realistic, and comprehensive price list for move-out charges, your tenants may still haul you into court to dispute those prices. They may dispute your charging them anything at all to clean the greasy stove and foul-smelling refrigerator they left behind.

Be aware that a judge may disregard your price list, too, especially if you did the work yourself. Judges respond better to actual costs incurred rather than to approximations. If you hired somebody to do the work for you and you have receipts to show for the labor and materials, you have a much better chance of convincing a judge that the departing tenants should pay you those sums than you will if you merely point to your

"WEAR AND TEAR" OR "DAMAGES"?

"Normal wear and tear" caused by ordinary comings and goings	"Damage" caused by carelessness, abuse, thievery, mysterious disappearance, accident, rules violation, or special request
Well-worn keys	Missing keys
"Sticky" key	Key broken off inside lock
Balky door lock	Door lock replaced by tenant without management's permission
Depressurized fire extinguisher with unbroken seal	Depressurized fire extinguisher with broken seal (not used to put out fire)
Worn pattern in plastic countertop	Burn in plastic countertop
Rust stain under sink faucet	Sink discolored by clothing dye
Loose, inoperable faucet handle	Missing faucet handle
Rusty refrigerator shelf	Missing refrigerator shelf
Discolored ceramic tile	Painted ceramic tile
Loose grout around ceramic tile	Chipped or cracked ceramic tile
Carpet seam unraveling	Carpet burn
Threadbare carpet in hallway	Rust marks on carpet from indoor plant container
Scuffing on wooden floor	Gouge in wooden floor
Linoleum with the back showing through	Tear in linoleum
Wobbly toilet	Broken toilet tank lid
Rusty shower curtain rod	Kinked shower curtain rod
Rust stain under bathtub spout	Chip in bathtub enamel
Tracks on doorjamb where door rubs	Hole in hollow-core door
Door off its hinges and stored in garage	Missing door
Plant hanger left in ceiling	Two-inch-diameter hole in ceiling
Stain on ceiling caused by leaky roof	Stain on ceiling caused by popping champagne or beer bottles
Cracked paint	Crayon marks on wall
Chipped paint (minor)	Walls painted by tenant in dark color necessitating repainting
Pleasing, professional tenant wallpapering	Amateurish tenant wallpapering
Mildew around shower or tub	Mildew where tenant kept aquarium
Urine odor around toilet	Urine odor in carpet
Discolored light fixture globe	Missing light fixture globe
Odd-wattage lightbulbs which work	Burned out or missing lightbulbs
Light fixture installed by tenant which fits its location	Light fixture installed by tenant which must be replaced
Window cracked by settling or high wind	Window cracked by movers
Faded shade	Torn shade
Paint-blistered Venetian blinds	Venetian blinds with bent slats
Sun-damaged drapes	Pet-damaged drapes
Drapery rod which won't close properly	Drapery rod with missing parts
Dirty window screen	Missing, bent, or torn window screen
Ants inside after rain storm	Fleas left behind by tenant's pet
Scrawny landscaping which was sparingly watered due to drought conditions	Neglected landscaping which must be replaced with similar plantings
Grease stains on parking space	Caked grease on parking space

price list and tell the judge that you charged the tenant exactly what was on the price list, no more and no less.

6) Recognize the difference between "normal wear and tear" caused by ordinary comings and goings and "damage" caused by carelessness, abuse, mysterious disappearance, thievery, accident, rules violation, or special request.

Avoid this kind of misunderstanding:

"Lonnie, I'm afraid I'm going to have to take something out of your security deposit to get this fire extinguisher recharged. The gauge says it's completely discharged. I know it was fully charged when you moved in, and I know you didn't use it on any fire. Somebody in your household must have been playing around with it."

"Let me see it. You're right, Mr. Sims, it is discharged, but nobody in my family ever touched this extinguisher. It must have become discharged all on its own."

"How can you be so sure?"

"Well, take a look at the seal. It's still there, see, right where it's always been. If the seal were broken, then I ought to have to pay to get the extinguisher recharged. Since it's not broken, I shouldn't have to pay. It lost its charge on its own."

"Okay, so the seal is still there, and maybe nobody in your household played around with it, but somebody's got to pay to have the extinguisher recharged or replaced, and I can't see why I should be the one to pay. I always charge tenants whenever they move out and I find that their fire extinguisher is discharged."

"That's not right. As you can see with your own eyes, I didn't do anything to it. The seal is still there. I shouldn't have to pay for something I didn't damage."

"Hmm. Well, let me think about this situation for a while, and I'll get back to you."

Look at the two lists on the opposite page. They show the sometimes subtle differences between "wear and tear" and "damage," things you shouldn't charge your tenants for and things you should. Note that sometimes the results are identical, such as the discharged fire extinguishers and the cracked windows, but the causes are different. The *causes* of a particular condition really ought to determine who's responsible for paying the bill in some cases.

In other cases, the *extent* of the "damage"

ought to determine who's responsible. A plant hanger left in the ceiling is "wear and tear," but if the tenant rips out the hanger and leaves a hole of some consequence, then it becomes "damage."

In still other cases, the presence or absence of an item ought to determine whether you consider the matter "wear and tear" or "damage." Take a faucet handle, for example. If the handle were so loose and corroded that it couldn't turn the faucet on or off, it would be "wear and tear," but if the same handle were missing, it would be "damage." Missing handles cannot be fixed, whereas there's always a chance that a corroded handle can be. Anything which is supposed to be in the dwelling but turns up missing is "damage."

You might want to advise your tenants how you distinguish between "wear and tear" and "damage," so they will come to understand that you're not being entirely arbitrary when you calculate how much you're withholding from their deposits. You might even want to give them a copy of the lists so they can judge for themselves whether you're correct in your assessments.

As for that discharged fire extinguisher with its seal still intact, the landlord must take the responsibility for having it recharged and paying the bill. The tenant didn't cause the extinguisher to discharge. Its gasket failed and allowed the gas inside to escape.

7) Inspect the dwelling and itemize its deficiencies.

Avoid this kind of misunderstanding:

"That oven was much dirtier when I moved in. I hardly even used it."

"I know it was clean when you moved in, Marge Renter, because I remember cleaning it myself. It was a 'two-cans-of-Easy-Off' job, and it took me half a day to make it sparkle after the previous tenants moved out."

"Well, I cleaned it after I moved out, too. I know that much, and I say you aren't going to charge me for a dirty oven! I'll take you to court! You can't prove anything anyway. It's your word against mine."

If you can possibly arrange for the vacating tenants to accompany you when you inspect their dwelling to determine deposit refunds, do so. You can then explain precisely what is wrong with the place, and you can give them the choice of correcting those deficiencies themselves or paying

Condition & Inventory Checksheet

Tenants: RICHARD and ROSE RENTER   Dated: JAN. 15, XXXX

Address: 456 SWEET ST., LITTLETOWN

Date Moved In: 1/15/XX   Notice Given: _____   Moved Out: _____

Abbreviations:

Air Cond, AC	Clean, Cl	Drape, Drp	Hood, Hd	OK, OK	Table, Tbl
Bed, Bd	Cracked, Cr	Dryer, Dry	Just Painted, JP	Poor, P	Tile, Tl
Broken, Brk	Curtain, Ctn	Fair, F	Lamp, Lmp	Refrigerator, Rf	Venet'n Blind, VB
Carpet, Cpt	Dinette, Din	Good, G	Lightbulb, LtB	Shade, Sh	Washer, Wsh
Chair, Ch	Dishwasher, Dsh	Heater, Htr	Linoleum, Lino	Sofa, Sfa	Waxed, Wxd
Chest, Chst	Disposer, Dsp	Hole, H	Nightstand, Ntst	Stove, Stv	Wood, Wd

Circle rooms; enter abbreviations	Walls, Doors		Floors		Windows		Lt. Fixtures		Inventory: Appliances, Furniture		
	cond.	chgs.	cond.	chgs.	cond.	chgs.	cond.	chgs.	Item	cond.	chgs.
(Living Rm)	OK		Cl Cpt.		wind-cr scrn-ok Drp-ok		–∅–		–∅–		
Dining Rm											
(Kitchen)	OK				scrn-ok sh-G	scrn mending 18⁰⁰	L+B ok		STV, Hd Ref (on loan)	Cl Cl	
(Bath 1)	JP										
Bath 2											
(Bedroom 1)	OK	hole in wall 45⁰⁰	Cl. Cpt.		scrn-ok Drp-cl		L+B ok		–∅–		
Bedroom 2											
Bedroom 3											
Other											
Itemized Charges	45		–∅–		18		∅				∅

TOTAL ITEMIZED CHARGES $63.00

Other Charges Not Itemized
(Dirty garage, etc.
Explained on Backside) _____

Deduction for Improper Notice _____

Deduction for Missing Keys $2.00

TOTAL DEDUCTIONS $65.00

TOTAL DEPOSITS $850

minus (-) TOTAL DEDUCTIONS 65

equals (=) DEPOSIT REFUND $785
or (Amount Owed)

☑ Tenants acknowledge that the smoke detector was tested in their presence and found to be in working order and that its operation was explained to them. Tenants agree to test the detector at least every other week and to report any problems to Owners in writing. If the detector is battery operated, Tenants agree to replace the battery as necessary with a new ALKALINE battery (unless applicable laws require otherwise).

Tenants hereby acknowledge that they have read this Checksheet, agree that the condition and contents of the above-mentioned rental dwelling are without exception as represented herein, understand that they are liable for any damage done to this dwelling as outlined in their Lease or Rental Agreement, and have received a copy of this Checksheet.

Lester Landlord   _Richard Renter_
Owner   Tenant _Rose Renter_
                          Tenant

BY Person authorized to represent Owners

pg. 2 of 3

for the corrections.

Tenants' conceptions of what their dwellings looked like when they moved in are as likely to be mistaken as yours, but from quite the opposite perspective. That's why a proper move-out inspection requires a record of a prior inspection attested to by the tenants. If one is lacking, there is no standard for comparison.

Did the vacating tenants put twelve burns in the carpet or only nine? Did they break the toilet tank lid or did their predecessors do it? Were the lightbulbs working in every fixture when they moved in or were the bulbs mostly burned out? Was the kitchen floor really new when they moved in?

To prove whether the current tenants are at fault, take whatever records you made of the place before the tenants moved in—written, photographic, or videographic—and compare them with what you see now.

Although clear photographic and videographic records are important, sometimes even crucial, when you have to prove your case to a skeptical judge, they aren't as important as a written record when you have to account for a dwelling's deficiencies to tenants. Consider photographic and videographic records as evidence to supplement what appears in your written record.

Your written record should be something like the Condition & Inventory Checksheet. It should have been filled out in triplicate before the tenants moved in, one copy for the tenants to keep, and two for you to use now at move-out time. Retrieve those same two sheets from your files and itemize in duplicate all the various deficiencies you notice this time around during your tour of inspection, from holes in the screens to holes in the walls. Then you can make direct line-by-line comparisons of the place's previous condition with its current condition, and you can ana-

lyze the discrepancies. If you have to refresh the tenants' memories as to its previous condition, show them whatever visual records you have.

8) Calculate the charges fairly.

Avoid this kind of misunderstanding:

"How come you kept $350 out of my deposit for cleaning?"

"You didn't leave the place clean."

"I suppose you're right, but that's still an awful lot to charge me for just a little cleaning. I don't think it's fair."

"We had to do more than a little cleaning, Buster. You're no housekeeper. The stove and refrigerator were a mess, and the bathroom looked like it hadn't been cleaned since we cleaned it ourselves before you moved in two years ago. You're lucky we didn't charge you any more than we did. We had to go through your place with every cleaning product known to soap opera fans. Two of us spent a whole day in there working. We busted our fingernails and sucked more dust into our lungs in that one day than my vacuum sucks out of my house in a whole year. That's how bad your place was. Anybody cleaning up after you oughta get hazard pay."

"All right, all right, I get your drift. All the same, $350 is too much to charge anybody for cleaning something as small as a one-bedroom apartment."

Having itemized the rental's deficiencies, you can begin calculating approximately how much to charge the departing tenants to restore their dwelling to its original splendor, minus normal wear and tear, of course. These calculations ought to be based upon some list of charges as suggested in step 4, but lacking such a list, you should be as realistic as you can be in your estimates.

Household incandescent lightbulbs don't cost $2 apiece just yet, and oven cleaning, no matter how dirty the oven, shouldn't take anyone twelve hours to do. Be reasonable.

Remember that you should charge tenants only for the useful life remaining in an item which is broken or missing, not for its full replacement cost. If two-year-old draperies are missing, charge tenants for only half, rather than all, the cost of the replacements. Likewise, because interior paint jobs should last two years when people are moving in and out, charge for just half of a new paint job when tenants move out and leave their walls, which were painted one year before, looking like the walls in a flophouse. After all, you got half their useful lives out of those drapes and that paint job before the tenants did them in.

Just as you want to be fair to tenants when you calculate the charges to be deducted from their deposits, you want to be fair to yourself.

Remember that not all the charges against tenants' deposits are necessarily for cleaning and damages to the dwelling. You may charge them for accumulated late charges which they were always refusing to pay. You may charge them for having given you too short a notice that they intended to move. You may charge them for certain utility bills which they hadn't paid when they moved out and which you must now pay.

Be especially wary of tenants' unpaid utility bills, whichever ones they paid directly themselves. In some areas, utility companies hold the landlord accountable for the bills tenants leave behind, especially water, sewage, and garbage bills. Just assume that you are liable. Ask your

tenants for proof that they have paid their closing bills so you're not hit with those bills yourself as a big surprise sometime later after you have returned the tenants' deposits and have no hope of getting the tenants to reimburse you.

9) Get the keys.

Avoid this kind of misunderstanding:

"What do you mean, you threw away the key? You only 'throw away the key' when you jail a mass murderer or a crooked politician, not when you vacate an apartment."

"Come on, I know that you always change the locks whenever a new tenant moves in. That's a well-known fact around here. I never thought you'd want my old key. I never thought it'd be important."

YOU'D BETTER GIVE SAMSON BACK HIS DEPOSIT TOMORROW, LESTER. HE SEEMS A LITTLE UNHAPPY ABOUT HAVING TO WAIT 14 DAYS...

Be wary of keys on the loose. They can cause you terrible trouble later, particularly in those situations where you can't change the locks on a rental dwelling for some reason, say, because your rental house is old and has an antiquated mortise deadlatch. You don't want former tenants to retain access to their dwelling after new tenants have moved in. Anything could happen, and you'd be held responsible for not having taken the reasonable precaution of getting the former tenants to return their keys.

Keys on the loose can also cause trouble later when you're moving locks around as you should be, and a key surfaces which opens a totally different dwelling. No, such things don't happen often. They happen just often enough to be a worry.

Make a special effort to get the keys from your departing tenants so you can consider them as having officially moved out and so you don't have any key problems later.

Also, ask your departing tenants to give you any additional keys that they may have in their possession over and above the keys which you gave them originally, and ask them whether there's anyone else, a friend or a relative, who still has a key to the dwelling. If there is, make a special effort yourself to retrieve that key. Don't expect the tenant to retrieve it. Get an address and phone number, and initiate the contact yourself.

10) Return the deposits promptly, but not too promptly.

Avoid this kind of misunderstanding:

Scene 1. Telephone conversation.

"Where's our deposit, Les? It's been three days since we moved out."

"I've been so busy I haven't had a chance to check your apartment. Is everything all right there? Nothing's damaged?"

"Everything's perfect."

"OK, I'll send you the money tomorrow."

Scene 2. Courtroom.

"But, your honor, I sent them back their deposit right away before I had a chance to check out their apartment. Later, when I did check it, I found all this damage that I never expected to find. It was a surprise to me. As you can see from the bills there, I spent over $700 repairing things after they moved out. They owe me that money."

"Mr. Landlord, you are to be commended for returning your tenants' deposits so promptly, but you should have inspected the apartment first. I can't possibly award you a judgment for $700 because when you refunded your tenants' deposits, you acknowledged that you were accepting the condition of their dwelling and were settling all debts with them, whether you understood that or not. Be more careful next time. The law allows you twenty-one days to return the tenants' deposits, and you should take what you need of that time to figure out everything the tenants owe you. Don't be so hasty. Don't try to be such a nice guy."

Do not return tenants' deposits until you are absolutely certain that you have calculated everything which might possibly be deducted from those deposits, including their unpaid utility bills and a charge for a pest exterminator to rid the place of their dog's fleas which emerged from hiding to attack the painter four days after the tenants vacated. If you have already returned the deposits and you later learn that the tenants have neglected to pay a $25 water bill or left fleas behind, you have no legal grounds for collection, and as a practical matter, you might as well forget it, too.

Most laws which govern rental deposit refunds allow you a very reasonable fourteen or twenty-one days to return and account for the deposits after tenants move out. There's no reason why you should need that much time, but there are reasons why you need at least some time before returning the deposits. Take the time. Ten days should be enough. That's only a portion of the time which is most likely coming to you anyway. Take it. Take it because you're entitled to it and you don't want to get burned.

Some tenants will pressure you to return their deposits the very day they move. Resist. Tell them simply that you will be sending them their deposit check within ten days. Tell them that you need a few days to determine whether there's anything which you may have overlooked in your assessment of charges, something which just hasn't surfaced yet. If they insist on learning what you've found so far, tell them what your preliminary assessment of charges is, and tell them that you hope you won't find anything else to deduct.

Then ask them to confirm their forwarding address, the address where they want you to send their deposit refund check. On the Notice of Intention to Vacate, there's a blank for the tenants to supply their forwarding address, but many tenants can't supply a forwarding address a month or even two weeks before they move. They don't know then exactly where they're moving to. Make sure you have the address now.

Remember that those tenants' deposits you hold are not yours. They have been entrusted to you in good faith to insure tenants' compliance with the terms of their rental agreements. If the tenants have indeed complied and you feel certain that you have determined everything which might be deducted from those deposits, then there's no reason to keep the money any longer. Refund it promptly.

Some Last Words

You'll have to forgo an acquaintance with your local small claims court judge if you follow these ten steps for fulfilling your responsibilities when tenants move out, but you'll be well compensated. You'll be saving yourself a great deal of aggravation, as well as time, energy, and money, and you'll be earning yourself a reputation as a fair landlord, too. That's good business. People will remember your fairness and will recommend your rentals to others, and the tenants who remain with you will feel relieved of any worry about whether they will get their own deposits back when the time comes.

9
Dealing with Problem Tenants

Problem tenants are the bane of the landlording business. They are always testing you. They're the last ones to pay and the first ones to gripe. They're the ones who paint all their interior walls and woodwork flat black, adopt stray animals and leave food out for the poor skunks and squirrels, leave their preschool kids home alone to look after one another, report you to the environmental health department when their garbage can overflows with disposable diapers which stink to low heaven, pull up the new wall-to-wall carpet and dispose of it because they prefer wood floors, call the plumber to unplug their toilet and make sure that the bill gets sent to you, change their own locks and refuse to give you a key, invite their latest friends to move in with them, and part out a car in the front yard, all without ever saying one word to you first.

They can be noisy, contrary, destructive, malevolent, or hypocritical all at the same time or at various separate times. They enjoy their music one way, loud, especially between midnight and sunup, and they can cuss as well as any guttersnipe, but what they seem to enjoy most of all is misquoting landlord-tenant laws to you. They love those incredulous looks on your face when they tell you what your legal responsibilities are as their landlord and what their rights are as your tenants.

Have you ever encountered such people? Let's hope not.

Unless you inherit them from a previous owner, you'll never have the displeasure of encountering them yourself if you practice prevention whenever possible, that is, if you select tenants carefully, enforce agreements assertively, and collect rents promptly.

Remember that in landlord-tenant relations, an ounce of prevention is worth many pounds of cure, for cures are costly, agonizing, time-consuming, crisis-oriented, and sometimes downright dangerous to life, limb, and property. Prevention methods, on the other hand, are not particularly cheap, but they are definitely not costly. They may cause dyspepsia at times, but they are hardly agonizing. They do take some time to perform, but they save much time in the long run. What's most important, though, is that they serve to eliminate crises altogether, and they never endanger anyone or anything.

Fortunately, only a small percentage of all tenants are truly problem tenants, and if you happen to be lucky, you may never encounter them at all during your landlording career, although you may encounter ordinary tenants with an inclination toward becoming problem tenants. If you do, you'd better be ready to deal with them head-on before they cause you grief. Here are some suggestions.

Identifying Problem Tenants and Outwitting Them

The full moon isn't the only thing that makes some people difficult to deal with. Some people are difficult during every phase of the moon. They're difficult all the time. They don't know any better.

You can deal with them much better if you know their type. That's right, difficult people come in different types, and they require different responses according to their type. To learn how to identify and outwit them, read *Coping with Difficult People*. It's a gem of a book, a seminal work written by somebody who has studied the subject for a long, long time.

From reading it, you might learn that you have been using the wrong approach in dealing with a particular tenant. He's really a "Sherman Tank" type, and you should be standing up to him rather than bending over backwards to agree with him.

He senses weakness in those who agree with him, and he will take every advantage of the weak. You need to face up to him and deal with him aggressively, whether that's your style or not, so that he will ultimately come to respect you and be a good tenant.

You might learn why you shouldn't expect too much from a "Super-Agreeable" type who will promise you anything and everything but won't follow through.

Of course, this one book isn't going to turn you into a perfect judge of people and a savvy negotiator, but it will get you thinking about the many things you might do to outwit and tame problem tenants.

Giving Problem Tenants One Last Chance—Mediating

When seemingly irreconcilable marital differences arise between spouses, and these differences threaten to destroy the marriage, husband and wife generally seek guidance from a marriage counselor before filing their divorce papers. If they haven't sought any counseling by the time their case gets to court, the judge will make a strong recommendation that they do. As an impartial third party trained to deal with marital disputes, a marriage counselor listens to both sides, sorts out the issues, and initiates discussions designed to help open each spouse's eyes to the real problems as seen through the other spouse's eyes. Once both spouses understand the problems, they can begin to work on solutions. Divorce may be the solution they ultimately settle upon, but at least they will have considered others with the help of someone knowledgeable in these matters.

Divorces and evictions are somewhat similar proceedings, and just as there are impartial third parties available to help spouses settle their differences, there are impartial third parties available to help landlords and tenants settle theirs. These impartial third parties who help landlords and tenants help other people settle their differences, too, people who have problems with neighbors, friends, relatives, or businesses. The problems might involve barking dogs, spite fences, loud music, short changing, shoddy merchandise, broken promises, view-obstructing trees, or anything else which might be a source of discontent. These impartial third parties are called mediators. They're a kind of community Peace Corps.

Mediators come from all walks of life. Most are retired and volunteer their services through a charitable organization which coordinates the people involved, the places, and the scheduling. They receive some training in handling disputes, but it is far from a college education in mediation. The truth is that mediators don't really need a college degree in mediation. They need common sense much more, as well as a love of people, a willingness to listen, and a lifetime of good and bad experiences to draw from. As you might imagine, good landlords make good mediators. They have the "right stuff."

Like a judge, the mediator listens to both parties state their positions, but instead of rendering a verdict, he asks questions to gain more information and tries to get the parties to discuss their differences frankly and work out a solution between themselves.

A judge, you see, has the long arm of the law available to insure compliance, so he can make unilateral rulings, and the disputants must comply or else.

The mediator has neither the position nor the authority of a judge and makes no rulings himself. Because he's not hamstrung by legal procedures and courtroom mumbo jumbo, he is in a position to let the disputants "slug it out," figuratively, of course. He is more like a referee who is trying to insure a fair fight. He gives the disputants as much time as they need to talk about their problems one-on-one, something they can't do in court. And he relies not on any threat of force for compliance but on the disputants' perception of the fairness of "their" agreement. They make the agreement, and they feel responsible to abide by it.

Should you feel that mediation might work to help settle some dispute you're having with a problem tenant, locate the nearest mediation center first. Check the Yellow Pages under "Mediation" for listings. If none appear there, call either the United Way or the office of the county's public defender and ask for the whereabouts of the nearest center. When you finally find it, inquire into the services available. Mention the nature of your problem, and be sure you ask about scheduling, charges, and the background of those who ordinarily act as mediators. You definitely don't want to have to wait more than two weeks to be heard. You don't want to be surprised to learn that you're supposed to pay more for the service than you expected. And you don't want to have some whippersnapper legal aid attorney with minimal life experiences acting as the mediator, either.

After you establish these details, contact the tenant and offer to submit your dispute to mediation. Tell him as much as you know about the mediation process yourself, and tell him that you'd like to try resolving the dispute this way if possible because you think that it would be fair to both of you. Remember, you have to get him to agree to come. You might be able to drag someone before a judge, but you cannot drag anyone before a mediator. Mediation is strictly voluntary. The mediator isn't going to issue a default judgment or a bench warrant if the tenant fails to appear.

If the tenant agrees to attend, set up the meeting, and hope that you'll be able to reach a mutually satisfactory agreement.

At the meeting, be prepared to convince the tenant of the merits of your case, and be as reasonable as you can be in understanding the tenant's point of view. Negotiate if you have to, but emphasize why you maintain the position you do. Say that you, after all, have to look after the concerns and welfare of a number of people, not just yourself or this tenant, and that you aren't on some kind of a power trip. You're just trying to be realistic. The tenant has to behave in a certain way, or you can't tolerate having him around any longer. If the two of you can come to an agreement, put it in writing. You might each want to write down what you've agreed upon and sign it. Then you give your tenant a copy of what you've written, and he gives you a copy of what he's written.

Give the tenant a chance to abide by the agreement, but don't waste any time in evicting him if he doesn't.

Getting Problem Tenants Out; It's an Easy Choice—Them or You

When you recognize that you have problem tenants who do not respond to your best efforts to deal with them fairly and you know for certain that mediation won't work, you cannot think in terms of prevention any more. You have to think in terms of cures. You have no choice really. Either you get rid of them or you'd better begin preparing yourself for complaints from the neighbors, deterioration of your property, departures

of your good tenants, your bankruptcy, your capitulation, or all five. Humor these problem tenants no longer, ignore them no longer, pacify them no longer. Marshal your forces, steel your will, and think in terms of getting them out.

You can get them out, you know. While you're at it, be mindful of the following—

✔ Be more interested in getting recalcitrant problem tenants out than in teaching them a lesson. No matter what their IQ's happen to be, they simply do not learn.

✔ Be pragmatic and businesslike with nonpaying tenants rather than feeling wronged and challenged. You will either lose the challenge or pay a big price to win. Suppress your feelings. Contain your ego. This is purely a business matter.

✔ Try to stop losing rent money as soon as possible instead of relying solely on the certainty of an eviction to cut your losses later. Be relentless. Hound those tenants.

✔ Heed the adage, "Spare the evictions, spoil the tenants," but recognize that "evictions" can mean alternative eviction methods as well as the conventional ones which use the judicial system full-strength.

Considering the Legal Alternatives to Eviction

You can always hope that a Notice to Pay Rent or Quit (used when tenants are in arrears), a Notice to Perform Covenant (used when tenants break their rental agreement), or a Notice to Terminate Tenancy (used when you wish to terminate a rental agreement for any reason at all; check its legality in your area) will precipitate the response you desire, but don't bet any big money on it. Like all consumers nowadays, tenants are better informed than ever before, and many know that you simply cannot legally put them out on the street in just a couple of days. Consequently, they tend to linger beyond the period specified in the notice, and you then seemingly have only one alternative—a full-scale eviction.

Even if you handle an eviction yourself the legal way, it will cost you somewhere between $50 and $250 in out-of-pocket expenses for filing and process-serving fees, not to mention what the lost rent will amount to. It will take you time to prepare all the papers and time to present the papers

Agreement to Vacate   Dated June 15, xxxx

   Agreement between Jay and Linda Wilson   , Tenants,
who occupy a dwelling located at 101 Parrott Ave, Downtown, IL
and Dennis Lee   , Owners, who are the
owners of this dwelling.

   Tenants acknowledge that no one other than those listed above currently
occupies the dwelling.

   Tenants occupy this dwelling under a rental agreement dated 12/1/xxxx .
This agreement is (X) month to month; ( ) a lease expiring _____.

   The current rent for this dwelling is $ 932.xx . The current late fee
is $ 20.xx .

   As of this date, tenants have paid rent through the following date:
  4/30/xx . They owe owners a total of $ 1,864.xx , itemized as follows:
  Rent for May and June   .

   Tenants agree that they have no excuses or defenses for failing to pay
what they owe.

   Tenants agree to vacate the dwelling on or before 6/20/xx
at 7 pm/am.

   If tenants DO vacate as agreed above, owners agree to the following:

   (1) to apply the tenants' security/cleaning deposit to the amount owed
and to waive the balance of any amount owed; any excess remaining from the
security/cleaning deposit after the full amount owed has been paid in full
shall be returned to the tenants after they have moved out completely,
provided that they leave the dwelling reasonably clean and undamaged;

   (2) to release tenants of any further obligation to pay rent under the
lease (if any);

   (3) to make no report to any credit reporting agency regarding tenants'
credit;

   (4) to make no report to any eviction reporting agency regarding tenants'
tenancy.

   If tenants DO NOT vacate as agreed above, this agreement shall be null
and void, and owners may begin eviction proceedings immediately.

   Tenants agree to keep this agreement confidential between the parties
involved. If tenants fail to keep this agreement confidential, this agreement
shall be null and void.

Owner Dennis Lee   Tenant Jay Wilson

By_____   Tenant Linda Wilson

to the court, too. Finally, when it's all over with, after you have painstakingly followed every single obligatory legal step, from serving the proper notice to accompanying the sheriffs or marshals as they put the widows and orphans out on the street, you begin to realize that you and your tenants have been duped because all of you have wound up losers in one way or another.

Take heart. There are other perfectly legal alternatives you might try when you want to get problem tenants out without ever going to court, alternatives which might seem to be unreliable at first because they follow neither a clear-cut procedure nor a precise timetable and, in addition, require a somewhat artful approach. Some might even say they require a bit of chicanery. Maybe they do. Still, they usually work surprisingly well, and, what's more, they don't make losers of everyone involved. These other alternatives you might try are talking, bribery, intimidation, and throwing a temper tantrum. On third thought, forget the last one. It's legal all right, but generally it's not very effective. Let's consider just the first three: talking, bribery, and intimidation.

Remember that with any of these methods you are trying essentially to convince your tenants that it is more advantageous for them to leave than to stay put. After all, if it *is* more advantageous for them to stay put, they will do exactly that. Wouldn't you?

■ Talking

All right, how do you convince tenants to vacate merely by talking to them? Go to their dwelling. Do not summon them to yours like some pompous potentate, and do not talk with them by telephone except to arrange a meeting. Make sure when you arrive that the decision-maker of the group is there. Ask them to explain first of all what has happened, why they have broken their agreement with you, and give them plenty of time to answer without interrupting them. Listen to them. Listen to them intently. Show them how serious you are about what they have to say by taking notes, whether they're saying anything noteworthy or not, and, when you aren't taking notes, by making steady eye contact.

Then say, "Let me see whether I understand you. You are saying blah, blah, blah. Is that about right?" Only after you can state their position in a way acceptable to them should you go ahead and state your own. With that done, outline the situation matter-of-factly as you understand it and suggest some alternatives. Ask them what they would do if they were in your shoes. If they offer up some unacceptable solution, tell them frankly why it wouldn't work and pose your own. Try to be understanding and try to reach an agreement that allows them to save face. Give a little, take a little, all the time being both reasonable and businesslike.

If you can reach an agreement, you ought to formalize it in writing. A written agreement will be most helpful to you if the tenants do not vacate when promised and you have to evict them through court action. You will have something signed by the tenants to prove certain facts to the court and also prove that you were trying to be reasonable. Otherwise, the tenants may deny ever having agreed to anything, and you won't be able to prove that they had agreed to anything. You don't want to get yourself into a your-word-against-theirs situation.

Your agreement may be handwritten or typed, giving the exact terms you and the tenants have agreed upon, or it may follow the format of a standard notice form such as the various notices shown later in this chapter.

If the tenants agree to vacate, use the Agreement to Vacate form shown here. It establishes exactly who is living in the dwelling so they can't say later that you failed to serve everybody with eviction papers and therefore you can't evict anybody. It establishes the particulars about the rental agreement and the tenancy, including the agreement's type and date, the current rent, the late payment consequences, the date through which their rent has been paid, the amount owed, and an itemization of what is owed. It further establishes that the tenants have no excuses or defenses for not paying what they owe and that they will vacate the dwelling by a specific time and date.

In exchange for the tenants' agreeing to vacate and keep the agreement confidential, the owner agrees to apply the security/cleaning deposit to what the tenants owe, release the tenants from further rent obligations, and forego reporting the tenants to credit bureaus and eviction reporting services. In other words, the tenants would be leaving with a clean slate so they could get on with their lives somewhere else.

Considering that such an agreement could save you court costs, legal services fees, more lost rent, and lots of aggravation, it's a pretty good deal, especially if your chances of collecting a court judgment against the tenants are slim to none.

If you simply cannot reach an agreement which you consider fair, tell them you are left with no alternative but to evict them through the courts. Tell them you are loathe to go to that extreme because they will then be identified to the local rental housing association as having been evicted, and it will be all the more difficult thenceforth for them to rent in the area. Not only that, state-wide eviction reporting services which search court records for the names of people who have been evicted will identify them and make the information widely known. Even their credit rating will suffer because credit bureaus include court judgments in their credit reports. And lest they think that they'll be able to avoid paying whatever they owe you by being evicted, tell them that a bill collector will begin hounding them to collect the judgment. In addition, they will never again be able to answer honestly on rental applications that they have not been evicted.

After stating these consequences candidly, see if the tenants still persist in being unreasonable. If so, depart and say, "I'm disappointed that you have left me no choice. I had very much hoped we could work something out." Don't get into an argument. Don't leave in a huff. Just go.

Your success or failure in using this maneuver will depend upon the kind of relationship you have already developed with your tenants, as well as upon your skills of persuasion. Tailor the appeal to the people you are dealing with. Above all, be firm and polite. Don't antagonize them. Don't call them names or impugn their ancestry. You may believe strongly in your heart of hearts that they are doing you wrong, but remember that your doing them wrong will only make you feel better. It won't help matters in the least. In fact, it will make matters worse, much worse. So resist all of your basic urges to "punch them out." Keep your head. Swallow your pride. Keep the dialogue open-ended. If you cut off the dialogue, your impending eviction lawsuit will be all the more difficult to pursue. You want the tenants to be available to be served with court papers as the case progresses. You don't want to alienate them so much that they will fight you at every step, avoiding service and delaying your case in any way they can.

Talking can work well for some landlords. I know one who successfully persuaded a motor-cycle gang leader and his savage-looking retinue to vacate a house they had rented under false pretenses. That's right, he did it with talk. Well, not entirely. Here's what happened.

One evening the landlord brought over a case of beer (their brand) and cannily convinced them that he was entirely sympathetic with their wanting to remain but that he was being harassed so much by the neighbors who were telephoning at all hours to tattle about what was happening at his rental house that he was falling asleep at work and was in danger of losing his job. He apologized about asking them to move out, but he said that he just couldn't see any other way to end the neighbors' wee-hour phone calls. The gang moved out the following weekend. When the neighbors called to report that the motorcyclists were actually moving their things out, he rushed right over there with two more cases of beer and gave them his heartfelt thanks. They left the place spotless. Of course, talk alone didn't do the trick; the beer helped.

For more suggestions on how to settle landlord-tenant disputes by talking, read the classic little book called *Getting to Yes*. It resulted from years of systematic study into how people reach agreement in negotiations. It includes a full discussion of positional bargaining and negotiation jujitsu, as well as some specific examples of landlord-tenant negotiations. You don't even have to read the whole book all the way through to get the gist of it. The seven-page analytical table of contents in the back of the book summarizes everything.

Perhaps you have already tried talking your tenants into leaving, or you feel that your talking to them just wouldn't work. Well, how about bribery?

■ Bribery

Some people gasp and then start whispering at the mere mention of the "B" word, as if it were illegal or somehow wrong. In some situations it may be both, but not here. Here it's a motivating factor, nothing more. It's a motivating factor because it appeals to one very basic human instinct, greed, an instinct which problem tenants seem to be so richly endowed with. The more your bribe excites their greed instinct, the faster they'll react.

Besides being fast-acting, bribery can be inexpensive. It might even be free! That's right! It might cost you absolutely nothing! If you required enough in deposits from your tenants before they moved in, you would, if you were to act fast, have money enough available from these very deposits to pay the tenants for leaving. This possibility that they might stop paying you their rent was one of the reasons for requiring a deposit in the first place, wasn't it?

Obviously, should you succeed in suing to evict them, the money judgment, including court costs, would be subtracted from their deposits, and they could expect to receive little or no money back. In fact, they'd probably owe you some money. An offer to return what's left of their deposits after you deduct something for the rent they owe you might be enough to get them moving, and it wouldn't cost you anything!

Calculate approximately how much a full-scale eviction and the rent lost during the eviction would cost you, especially if you hire an attorney to handle the case, before you make your offer, and you'll likely find that a bribe will cost you far less. Even if you do have to sweeten the offer somewhat out of your own pocket because you have delayed so long that there's only a paltry deposit balance remaining of, say, less than $100 (few tenants will move for less), you will come out way ahead by bribing them to leave, and so will they.

Greed triumphs again! Oh, who cares? Each of you wins, wouldn't you say? Your tenants get a few bucks, and you get your rental property back.

There are some good variations on the bribery gambit, too. You might offer to store the tenants' goods in one of your garages or pay the rent on a self-service storage unit for a few months. The tenants would then be free to stay with friends or relatives until they are able to get back on their feet, and you'd have a dwelling available for a paying customer.

You might offer to arrange and pay for a U-Haul® van and a small crew to move the tenants' possessions anywhere within fifty miles or so.

You might cut a $100 bill in half right before the tenants' eyes, give them half, and keep half yourself until they have moved out completely on or before a designated date, or you might leave the entire $100 bill with a trusted neutral party who has instructions to give it to the tenants if they move by a certain date. This ploy is pretty dramatic for most tenants who can't come up with their rent money. It's dramatic enough to work, and it also circumvents many tenants' natural skepticism about whether you will really pay off or not. Naturally, you should never pay off until you have verified that they have, in fact, vacated.

You might offer to buy the tenants' TV, stereo, appliances, and furniture if they have fallen on hard times. This would unburden them enough so the move would be easier and so they would have the funds needed to pay their other persistent creditors. Before consummating your purchase, however, you would be wise to determine whether the tenants' possessions are still being paid for and are being used as collateral for a loan. If you're unconvinced that they have been fully paid for, ask the tenants for written permission to run a credit check. It will tell all. If you're convinced that the possessions have been fully paid for, ask for a bill of sale.

Be creative. Be practical. Bribe your tenants to leave if the numbers make sense. You'll be free of them sooner rather than later.

■ **Intimidation**

Another maneuver which is perfectly legal and ofttimes prompts tenants to vacate without your ever having to resort to the courts is intimidation. I don't mean hiring goons or gorillas to scare your tenants out. I mean hiring the sheriff, marshal, or constable to scare your tenants out. How? Have the local law-enforcement officer serve your notices. Sure, you can serve the notices yourself, but you're too familiar a face to your tenants. You're simply not intimidating enough. You cannot possibly impress them with the gravity of the matter as much as can an armed and uniformed law-enforcement officer who's handing out a notice signed by you stipulating

that the tenants have a fixed number of days to clear out. That is quite intimidating to most people. They simply do not want to get mixed up with the law if they can help it, and they will sometimes mistake your notice for one from a court which actually sets a firm date for their eviction. It all seems so official and imperative. That's precisely the impression you want to leave with them.

For $30 or so you may be able to arrange to have your notice served by the law-enforcement officer who customarily serves the legal process papers in your area (check into the availability of this service; some law enforcement agencies no longer provide it). The officer will understandably take a few days longer to get around to serving the notice than you would if you were to do the serving yourself, but official service is more effective in getting action out of most tenants, and the nominal delay may be worth the results.

A variation of this method involves the direct hiring of an off-duty law-enforcement officer to serve your notices. In many areas, officers may wear their uniforms while off duty and may act as process servers on their own. Inquire whether officers moonlight doing this in your area. If you can find someone who does perform this service, your notices will be served more promptly than

they ever will be if you have to work through a bureaucracy to enlist an officer's services.

In those situations involving tenants who are breaking their rental agreement, you may find that you can intimidate them and gather evidence to build a case against them all at the same time. Here's how.

Make a sound recording or take some photographs of the tenants or their dwelling, and do so openly. Try to be seen in the act of recording their loud music or photographing their messy yard and prohibited pet. Do everything possible to arouse their interest in what you are doing, and once you have it, tell them that you are gathering evidence for the court case you are preparing against them. You may find them more cooperative after that, and then again you may not, but even if this activity does not serve to intimidate them into changing their ways, you still would have managed to gather some pretty incriminating evidence to introduce into court should you have to go to the mat with your case.

Recognizing Which Alternatives Are Illegal

In some respects, it's fortunate that there are laws to keep us landlords from acting rashly when we're trying to force problem tenants to move out. After being frustrated repeatedly, some of us might be driven to near distraction and feel compelled to take the law into our own hands. We might lock tenants out, toss them out, turn off their utilities, barge in and take their belongings, poison their animals, threaten them with bodily harm, harass them mercilessly, or even damage the dwelling we own so as to render it uninhabitable.

Why do laws keep us from carrying out such "perfectly reasonable acts"? These acts disturb the peace. That's why. They enrage tenants and endanger the lives and limbs of everyone concerned, yours too, to say nothing of the possible property damage they might cause. People get hurt when they're being tossed out on their ears without due process. People become infuriated when their belongings are peremptorily confiscated. People become incensed when someone locks them out of their homes. They strike back blindly. Tempers flare. Problems grow out of all proportion, and the police have to be called in to quell the disturbances. Right behind the police, of course, are the media mongers, ready to broadcast to the world how mean and hateful landlords can be.

Illegal self-help eviction methods are to be avoided. Do not resort to them. The penalties can be extremely severe, resulting in horrendous fines and even imprisonment. Some states fine headstrong landlords $100 *per day* for every day tenants remain in their dwellings with the utilities shut off. Fines of $15,000 and more in these cases are not unheard of, and naturally, there's no rent accruing during such times, either. The electric company can shut off the electricity if customers aren't paying their bills, but you can't deprive tenants of utilities if they stop paying their rent, not even when the utilities are included in the rent. You have to swallow the losses until you can finally evict the tenants.

That's not fair, you say. No, it's not fair. Neither life nor landlording is fair, but we have to live with the laws governing our business whether we think they're fair or not.

Once more then, please, what may you not do on your own initiative to force problem tenants out?

- You may not lock them out or lock them in.
- You may not toss them out on their ears and throw their belongings after them.
- You may not turn off their water, electricity, or gas.
- You may not stop up their sewers intentionally.
- You may not take their belongings.
- You may not petnap their Fido or give arsenic to their Felix.
- You may not threaten to break their kneecaps or their skulls.
- You may not disturb their peace and quiet in order to make life there so unpleasant that they'll move.

- You may not remove a door, a window, a staircase, or a toilet, nor may you do anything else to violate their "warranty of habitability."

These eviction methods are all illegal. They can get you into big trouble and cost you big bucks.

Yet, I know of some landlords who do resort to such methods when they believe the circumstances are right for quasi-illegal self-help methods to work, that is, when they anticipate no complications. Generally they're street-wise people dealing with other street-wise people, people who don't use the courts to settle their disagreements anyway. The secret to using self-help methods successfully, they say, is to keep a low profile, know exactly what you're doing, know full well the kind of tenant you're dealing with, stay utterly alert, and be a convincing bluffer.

I also know of tenants who goad their landlords into taking illegal steps to evict them just so they can collect big judgments.

The film "Pacific Heights" reveals the ways of a professional con man who preys on unsuspecting landlords and makes a handsome living exploiting them. Rent the film from your neighborhood video store and learn from it. You'll be surprised to discover that it's actually sympathetic to landlords! Even watching it in the company of tenants, you'll be able to root for the landlords. They're the good guys in this film! Honest, they are!

Taking Legal Steps

When you have tried and failed to rid yourself of problem tenants by hook or by crook, you have no alternative but to try an eviction by the book. You need legal clout to get them out.

Before you begin, however, you should know that in some areas evictions are handled in small claims courts as well as in other courts, but small claims courts have one major disadvantage. In a word, they are slow. Whenever you hear of a case involving a landlord who has been trying to evict a tenant for three months or more, chances are good that the case was filed originally in small claims court.

Don't use small claims court for your evictions. They waste much too much time.

Each day tenants spend in your dwelling costs you money. Figure it out. A house renting for $930 a month is costing you $31 a day in lost rent, money you might as well forget about ever

Notice to Perform Covenant

TO: _HENRY AND GLADYS LEVNO_

and all other tenants in possession of the premises described as:

460 SWEET STREET
LITTLETOWN, CA 09001

PLEASE TAKE NOTICE that you have violated the following covenant(s) in your Lease or Rental Agreement:

TENANTS AGREE NOT TO PAINT OR ALTER THEIR DWELLING WITHOUT FIRST GETTING THE OWNERS' WRITTEN PERMISSION.

YOU ARE HEREBY REQUIRED within __3__ days to perform the aforesaid covenant(s) or to deliver up possession of the above-described premises which you currently hold and occupy.

If you fail to do so, legal proceedings will be instituted against you to recover said premises and such damages as the law allows.

This notice is intended to be a __3__ day notice to perform the aforesaid covenant(s). It is not intended to terminate or forfeit the Lease or Rental Agreement under which you occupy said premises. If, after legal proceedings, said premises are recovered from you, the owners will try to rent the premises for the best possible rent, giving you credit for sums received and holding you liable for any deficiencies arising during the term of your Lease or Rental Agreement.

Dated: ___3/5/xx___   _Lester Landlord_
                                    Owner/Manager

PROOF OF SERVICE

I, the undersigned, being at least 18 years of age, declare under penalty of perjury that I served the above notice, of which this is a true copy, on the above-mentioned tenant(s) in possesssion in the manner(s) indicated below:

☒ On ___4/5/xx___, I handed the notice to the tenant(s).

☐ On _____, after attempting personal service, I handed the notice to a person of suitable age and discretion at the residence/business of the tenant(s).

☐ On _____, after attempting service in both manners indicated above, I posted the notice in a conspicuous place at the residence of the tenant(s).

☐ On _____, I deposited a true copy of the notice in the United States Mail, in a sealed envelope with postage fully prepaid, addressed to the tenant(s) at his/her/their place of residence.

☐ On _____, I sent by certified mail a true copy of the notice addressed to the tenant(s) at his/her/their place of residence.

Executed on _APRIL 5, XXXX_, at the City of _LITTLETOWN_,
County of _SADDLEBACK_, State of _CALIFORNIA_.
                    Served by _Lester Landlord_

seeing again. Ten days of that rent would easily pay all of your costs in those courts which expedite evictions. If it's summary justice you want, don't go to small claims court. Go instead to whatever other court acts on such cases in your area, be it municipal court, superior court, justice court, county court, or circuit court.

You should also know before you begin that you may represent yourself in an eviction case or you may be represented by an attorney. Most of the time you'll be able to handle everything yourself because evictions are little more than a formality requiring that certain forms be filled out properly and that certain time limits be observed carefully. Attorneys seldom do this work themselves anyway. They delegate it to their secretaries, and their secretaries select the appropriate form from a form book which, by the way, you may consult free of charge in your court's law library, and then they fill in the blanks. That's all they do, and you can surely do the same (California landlords who want to do their own evictions may use *The Eviction Book for California*; see SOURCES & RESOURCES).

Besides, you will devote more attention to your own eviction case than will attorneys who may have some 50 to 150 other cases vying for their attention. You will certainly get the tenants out sooner yourself because you have an incentive which attorneys don't. You are losing money every day a nonpaying tenant remains. Attorneys aren't. Regardless of how long an eviction action takes, attorneys will charge you the same sum for their services. In fact, if your eviction takes longer and presumably takes more of your attorney's time, he will charge you more. Yes, I know, he ought to charge you less the longer it takes, but that's not the way the system works.

Be shrewd enough, though, to recognize when you do need to engage the services of an attorney. Generally you need one when your tenants have hired an attorney themselves, when your tenants in an apartment house have organized against you, when your tenants have filed a serious written answer to your complaint or affidavit, or when there are any complications you don't understand. That's when you should hire yourself an attorney, and remember that even though you have begun an action on your own, you may always hire an attorney to assist you whenever you feel you need one as the case progresses.

Although the procedures and time limits for evictions do vary considerably from area to area, here is some information on evictions which should prove useful to you as you wend your way through the legal maze to get problem tenants out, no matter where you live and do business.

■ Notices

Every legal eviction must begin with a notice advising the tenants of your intentions. It must be properly filled out and properly served. The notice should include the number of days the tenants have in which to comply (minimums are set by laws governing such matters in the area where your rental property is located), the tenants' names and the names of any other adults living there (if you don't know their names, call them "Does I through X" until you can discover who they are), the address of the rental dwelling, the amount of rent due through the current rental period (applicable only in evictions for nonpayment of rent), the period for which this rent is due, the date of the notice, and your signature.

Personal service is better than what attorneys call "nail and mail" (affixing the notice to the door and mailing a copy) because longer waiting periods apply in substituted service situations. You may serve the notice yourself if you want to, but you may be smart to have someone else serve it for you if you think you may be dealing with a perjurer. Some tenants will deny under oath that they ever received the notice, and the judge then has to weigh your word against theirs.

To circumvent this problem, you can always hire an intimidator to do the job for you, or you can serve the notice yourself along with the Payment Pledge introduced in chapter 6. That particular pledge is designed for nonpayment-of-rent situations, but by changing a few words here and there, you could use it in other situations. What's important about the pledge here, though, is that the tenant acknowledges service of the notice when signing the pledge, so the tenant would have a hard time denying in court that he ever received the notice.

■ Waiting Periods

In most places, you may count weekends and holidays when determining the waiting periods in an eviction, but the final day for the tenants to pay the rent, vacate, or answer the complaint must be a day when the courthouse is open for business. Find out from the court clerk whether you may count weekends and holidays. If you may

Notice to Terminate Tenancy

TO: _ANN PHELAN_

and all other tenants in possession of the premises described as:

462 SWEET STREET
LITTLETOWN, CA 09001

PLEASE TAKE NOTICE that you are hereby required within _30_ days to remove from and deliver up possession of the above-described premises, which you currently hold and occupy.

This notice is intended for the purpose of terminating the Rental Agreement by which you now hold possession of the above-described premises, and should you fail to comply, legal proceedings will be instituted against you to recover possession, to declare said Rental Agreement forfeited, and to recover rents and damages for the period of the unlawful detention.

Dated: _3/31/xx_   _Lester Landlord_
                                                          Owner/Manager

PROOF OF SERVICE

I, the undersigned, being at least 18 years of age, declare under penalty of perjury that I served the above notice, of which this is a true copy, on the above-mentioned tenant(s) in possesssion in the manner(s) indicated below:

☒ On _3/31/xx_, I handed the notice to the tenant(s).

☐ On _____, after attempting personal service, I handed the notice to a person of suitable age and discretion at the residence/business of the tenant(s).

☐ On _____, after attempting service in both manners indicated above, I posted the notice in a conspicuous place at the residence of the tenant(s).

☐ On _____, I deposited a true copy of the notice in the United States Mail, in a sealed envelope with postage fully prepaid, addressed to the tenant(s) at his/her/their place of residence.

☐ On _____, I sent by certified mail a true copy of the notice addressed to the tenant(s) at his/her/their place of residence.

Executed on _MARCH 31, XXXX_, at the City of _LITTLETOWN_,

County of _SADDLEBACK_, State of _CALIFORNIA_.

Served by _Lester Landlord_

count them, you will save quite a bit of time in expediting your case.

■ Best Times to Serve

Whenever weekends and holidays may be counted in determining the waiting periods, there are certain especially good days for serving 3-day notices in order to take advantage of weekends and holidays in the count. Those best days are Sunday and Monday. Delaying service of a 3-day notice until Tuesday will, believe it or not, cost you at least five extra days in the whole process.

In those areas where weekends and holidays do not figure into the count, there are no "best" days for serving 3-day notices. They're all good.

The best time to serve a Notice to Perform Covenant or a Notice to Terminate Tenancy is always right after the rent has been paid. After being served, the tenant's will to pay rent diminishes drastically. You may actually create an eviction-for-nonpayment situation by serving the notice at a "wrong" time, although that may be a blessing in disguise because an eviction for nonpayment of rent is easier to win than an eviction for any other reason.

■ Copies

Spend a few cents more to produce enough extra copies of all your eviction papers, including the notices, and you will avoid much disappointment and aggravation later. The copies needed will vary, depending upon the type of form and the number of defendants you have to serve. If you produce an original and three copies of each, though, you will be reasonably certain to have enough of every form to go around.

■ Accepting Rent

You must accept rent offered to you by someone who is responding to your Notice to Pay Rent or Quit within the period specified in your notice. After that time you may accept rent if you want to, but you don't have to. Be aware that if you accept so much as one dollar at any time following service of the notice, you may have to begin all over again from the beginning by serving another notice. For this reason, you should not accept any rent after you have spent the money to file your complaint or affidavit, unless the tenant agrees to pay the entire back rent plus your out-of-pocket filing expenses as well.

Should your tenant offer to pay you a substantial sum which is still only part of the total rent owed, and should you want to take it with-

out risking the loss of your court case in the future after all the time and money you've spent to get into court, secure a formal court agreement with the tenant. Stipulate in the agreement that you may obtain a court judgment for eviction if the tenant fails to pay the balance of the rent or vacate by a certain date. In this way, you get some rent money at least, and you retain your priority for evicting the tenant if he doesn't pay or vacate.

■ Records

Whether or not you expect the tenant to appear in court, take with you into court all the records you possess on the tenant you are evicting. These should include whatever is applicable from the following list: rental agreement or lease, pet agreement, condition and inventory checksheet, waterbed agreement, correspondence, certified mail receipts, invoices covering repairs of damage, collection records, notices, photographs, videos, and even a chronology of the events in your deteriorating relationship.

Such records will strengthen your case much more than anything you are likely to say in court. Judges don't really want to hear you and the tenant vent your spleens. They want hard-and-fast evidence.

■ Bankruptcies

Deadbeat tenants who know all the angles have found that by declaring bankruptcy at the very last minute they can delay their eviction by at least a month. Some even file bankruptcy more frequently, a lot more frequently, than every seven years as the law allows because they know that nobody will discover what they're doing until after they have achieved their objective anyway, that being to delay the eviction as long as possible.

Bankruptcy judges know just how prevalent these ploys are, and one judge has written an opinion known as *In re Smith* 105 B.R. 50 (Bkrtcy.C.D.Cal. 1989), which you should examine if you ever suspect that one of your tenants has declared bankruptcy to get an automatic stay of execution. This opinion concludes that bankruptcies should not stay evictions whenever the tenancy itself is of no value. A rent-controlled tenancy is one which generally does have some value and would be included among the tenant's assets whereas an ordinary tenancy would have no value and should have no part of bankruptcy proceedings whatsoever.

■ Lesson

A final eviction notice on one door of an apartment building serves as a convincing lesson to other tenants that you know how to evict and will evict when necessary.

Leave the notice on the door long enough for at least one other tenant to see it and then remove it yourself. The word will spread quickly. Don't leave the notice up for an extended period (an afternoon should suffice), however, because you don't want other owners in the area to see it. They will wonder what's wrong with your building and will depreciate its value in their minds.

The final eviction notice on the door of a single-family dwelling should be removed as soon as the tenants' belongings are cleared out. It serves no useful purpose after that.

Some Last Words

Remember that not getting rid of problem tenants is much more aggravating than all the aggravations of actually getting rid of them. Go on. Get it over with. Get rid of those problem tenants. Then get on with your business.

10
Managing the Rental House

The rental house business as described in Dave Glubetich's book, *The Monopoly Game*, and Robert Allen's book, *Nothing Down*, both of which were popular when house prices were skyrocketing throughout the U.S. during the 1970's and 1980's, is a little like the Rent-A-Wreck® used car rental business which enables used car dealers to realize a steady income from the cars in their inventory.

Any car sitting on a used car lot is only costing the dealer money because he has money tied up in it which is no longer earning him interest, because he has to provide valuable space on his lot for displaying the car, because the car is depreciating in value as it becomes older and more outdated, and because he has to look after the car to keep it from deteriorating physically. The longer he keeps it, the more costs he incurs, so he tries to buy cars which will sell quickly and sell for considerably more than what he paid for them. Normally his profit is the difference between what he paid for the car and what he sold it for minus his various expenses.

By renting the car out while it's waiting to be sold, though, the used car dealer increases his income and exposes the car to potential buyers who pay him to take it out for "test drives." His expenses increase a little because he has to pay for oil changes and tune-ups and extra insurance and paperwork, but his income increases a lot. That's good business.

Most rental houses are waiting around to be sold, too. The longer their owners hold onto them, the more the holding costs accumulate, but presumably the more the houses will be worth down the road as any number of factors drive up the price of houses. While a house is "in inventory," the owner rents it out so he doesn't have to bear all the costs of holding onto it until he finally sells it.

The rental house business varies widely from place to place around the country. You can see this variance in the ratio of market prices to rents. If you're lucky enough to be doing business in an area where you can buy good houses for $60,000 with little effort and you can rent them out for $600 or more per month (or a similar 100:1 ratio between purchase price and monthly rent) with little effort, you have yourself a "cash cow," and you ought to be counting your blessings every month. You have positive cash flow. You don't need to "feed" your houses. They're feeding you. That's what they're supposed to be doing.

On the other hand, if you're among those who have to pay $160,000 for each of the houses you buy, and you can't rent them out for more than $1,000 per month, you have a "cash crocodile" on your hands. You have negative cash flow. You are paying every month for the privilege of being your tenants' landlord. To some people that may not seem like a smart thing to do, but then again it may turn out to be as smart as buying Microsoft, which has never paid a dividend to its shareholders, and Callaway Golf when those stocks first came to market, especially if you learn how to handle your negative-cash-flow problems adeptly and you sell the houses when there's an upswing in their market value.

Whether your rental house "business" consists of one house or one hundred, whether it's a Cowboy Bob or a Crocodile Dundee operation, you need to know more about how to increase its positive cash flow. Here I call the subject "handling the negative-cash-flow problem" because most owners of rental houses are wrestling negative cash flow; they're wrestling crocodiles. Of all the problems in rental house investing and management, that's the most dangerous to your financial well-being, but there are some solutions to it, and there are some solutions to the other rental house management problems, too.

Handling the Negative Cash Flow Problem

People who, for any number of reasons, prefer to invest in single-family houses rather than multiple-family dwellings have wrestled with the negative-cash-flow problem for some time now and have come up with some pragmatic solutions worth examining. Here are ten, most of which are a combination of investment and management strategies—involving tenants as partners through lease-options, actually sharing the space with a number of tenants, creating a duplex out of a house, renting the house out on a short-term basis, renting out the parts of a house, building more houses on the same lot or buying property with more than one house on a lot to begin with, sharing the ownership with silent partners who want to invest in real estate but don't want to be directly involved with rental property themselves, tinkering with the financing, investing in the least expensive single-family residences available, and "stealing" the house.

Let's examine these solutions in some detail. Perhaps there's one of them you might use.

■ **Involve tenants as "partners"**—Many rental house tenants would like to buy a house but don't have the necessary funds to make the down payment or the necessary expertise to find a good low-money-down deal themselves. The short-term lease-option would seem to work well in those situations for both you and them. It's good for you because the tenants pay a little more in rent every month, enough to cover the house's negative cash flow, and it's good for them because they get the right to buy the house at some future time for either a certain fixed price or an appraised price less whatever credits they have accumulated for their higher monthly payments.

Of course, there's another benefit to using short-term lease-options. Tenants who have an option to buy tend to think of themselves more as owners than as tenants, and they tend to take better care of the property. As a result, your management headaches practically disappear.

See Robert Bruss's book, *The Smart Investors Guide to Real Estate,* for the in's and out's of lease-options. Mr. Bruss uses them himself quite effectively in his own rental house business. He

has also written about them in the report—"How to Buy or Sell Your Home (or Investment Property) with a Lease-Option," #99300 (Robert J. Bruss, 251 Park Road, Burlingame, CA 94010, 800.736.1736).

I should mention here that there's a contrarian point of view about lease-options expressed by John Reed in his "Single-Family Lease Options Special Report" (John T. Reed, 342 Bryan Drive, Alamo, CA 94507, 925.820.6292). He maintains that today's typical lease-option, which credits the tenant with money toward the purchase of the property and is too seldom exercised by the tenant, has such an unclear legal standing that it should be considered more of a gamble than a sure thing. He admits that many people continue to use lease-options today quite successfully, but he's afraid that their glory days won't last when attorneys take up the fight for the poor tenants who too frequently lose large equities when they can't exercise their options. The courts could also recharacterize lease-options as sales. If that happens, landlords would have big problems with their ownership position, their financing, their income taxes, their property taxes, and their financial obligations. Nothing, mind you, has happened as yet. Nothing may ever happen, but the situation does bear watching.

Should you wish to use a lease-option, secure a well-written lease-option agreement. Professional Publishing includes one in their sample forms book (see SOURCES & RESOURCES). Study it carefully. Then seek legal guidance from a local real estate attorney if you have any doubts about whether you ought to use this technique.

Knowing what I know, would I use a lease-option for a rental house of my own? Yes, I would. In fact, I do. I handle them entirely myself without using an agent, and I try to structure them so that the tenant can exercise the option 90% of the time.

■ **Share the space**—In her book, *Managing Your Rental House for Increased Income,* Doreen Bierbrier explains precisely how she rents out the rooms in her rental houses to people who do not know one another initially. They're perfect strangers. She collects more rent from all of these tenants combined than she could possibly collect otherwise if she were renting to a single household.

Perhaps you shared a house or an apartment with a group of friends when you were younger.

Five of you might have rented a house together with each one of you being responsible for paying an even 20% share of the rent and utilities. When one of you got married and moved out, that left the remaining four to pay 25% shares of the rent and utilities. That's the traditional way for groups to rent and share a commodious dwelling.

Bierbrier has come up with a variation, one which has advantages for the rental house owner and for single tenants alike. She sets up what resembles a rooming house operation in each house she acquires, but she does not live on the premises. Even so, she rents out the individual rooms herself in consultation with the people who live there, and she assumes the responsibility for filling every one of the rooms herself as well. No matter how many rooms are rented out, each tenant pays a set rent every month.

Her tenants like the arrangement because they don't have to pay any more rent during vacancies and because they get to help select the new tenants. She likes the arrangement because she gets a higher aggregate rent and a positive cash flow while she still gets all the other benefits of rental house ownership.

Please recognize that this arrangement necessitates much more owner involvement than the normal rental house arrangement, and it works only for certain kinds of houses in certain kinds of locations. One reader of an earlier edition of this book tried it and rued the experience in a six-page chronicle he sent me titled "101 Reasons Not to Split a Single-Family House into Room Rentals." Don't try it yourself without reading Bierbrier's book first. Then proceed deliberately and cautiously.

■ **Create a duplex out of a house**—A good friend of mine fixed up the spacious trunk of his big ten-year-old American car and was actually living in it during his penurious college days. One day another student knocked on the trunk lid and inquired about accommodations for rent in the area. They struck up a deal. My friend rented out the trunk of his car and moved into the back seat. He had created a duplex out of a car, possibly a first in recorded American history!

When that friend began investing in rental property, he specialized in creating duplexes out of houses. With minimal renovation work and minimal expense, he was able to increase his cash flow in just a few years to a point where he could

leave his job as a school teacher and retire on the comfortable and secure income from his rental houses. Poor guy, he never got a real baptism in rental house ownership. He never found out what negative cash flow was. All his cash flow was positive. It still is.

Creating several separate living units out of an opulent old house is nothing new. Every city with housing stock from bygone eras has its examples of such renovations, most made necessary by a change in people's life-styles over the years. These conversions entail radical changes in the existing living areas and permanently transform the houses into multiple-family dwellings.

You wouldn't want to create a duplex out of an ordinary rental house by chopping up the interior space that way if you ever expect to capitalize on the sale of the house to an owner-occupant who will pay a high price for the home of his dreams. No, what you should be doing is creating a duplex while leaving the house itself intact as much as possible, creating an additional living unit out of unused or underused space such as a basement, a rumpus room, an attic, a garage, an outbuilding, or an expandable crawl space (houses on the sides of hills are excellent candidates for a crawl space conversion).

Good as the idea of creating a duplex out of a house may sound at first as a means of increasing cash flow, you should not go to any great expense to create a second living unit unless you can expect a good return on your investment while you own the property because the money you put into the extra living unit may not make the house worth any more when you go to sell it. If the conversion is as simple as installing some used kitchen appliances in a basement which already has a small bathroom and an outside entrance and for this outlay of $500 you are able to collect $500 per month in rent, obviously it makes great sense. If the conversion is going to cost $12,000 and yield $500 per month in extra rent, it would be worth the outlay only if you're going to hang onto the property for at least three years. Otherwise you should consider everything very carefully.

Check around with people who know property values in the area and ask them how the addition of an income unit would affect the value of your particular property.

Often a second living unit is called an in-law apartment because owners used to create them for aging relatives who lacked either the funds or the ability to live completely on their own, and often these in-law apartments were bootlegged, that is, illegally constructed. Owners didn't want to have to deal with building inspectors and zoning ordinances. The zoning ordinances may even have prohibited such conversions altogether. Because of today's housing shortage, however, many areas are more lenient about creating independent living units in existing houses, and the units don't have to be bootlegged anymore. They're legal. Make some anonymous inquiries before you start building yours.

Believe it or not, there's an entire book devoted to this subject, and it happens to be a good one. Called *Creating an Accessory Apartment* and written by two land-use planners, it's a must-read for anybody who's remotely interested in adding rentable self-contained space to a house (currently out of print, the book is available in libraries).

Remember, two self-contained living units with the same square footage as an equivalent single living unit will always yield greater rents than the single unit, and greater rents translate into more cash flow month after month after month.

■ **Rent the house out on a short-term basis**— Just as there is a need for rentals on a long-term basis, there is a need for them on a short-term basis. Companies transfer their employees or put them to work miles from home. Vacationers want to stay in a home away from home rather than in a hotel or motel room. Couples want to try living together for a time before they give up their own digs and commit themselves to a long-term relationship.

In any of these situations and the many others which create a demand for short-term rentals, tenants are willing to pay more for every day they stay in a short-term rental, from twice to five times as much as they would pay per day for a long-term stay. That's the upside of short-term landlording. The downside is the additional time and money required for advertising, cleaning, furnishing, scheduling, bookkeeping, and greeting the tenants upon arrival.

It's more of a hands-on business than long-term landlording, that's for sure, but it can and does pay off well, especially when the location is good, when you are renting several such houses on a short-term basis, and when you are using the web to promote them inexpensively.

Take a look at the website I created for a townhouse my wife and I used to own in San Francisco (landlording.com/townhouse) and rented out by the week. We furnished the place; promoted it with a brochure, a membership in the convention and visitors bureau, and our website; and rented it regularly to short-term visitors. Eventually, we sold the townhouse at a profit, having also realized a profit during our ownership from renting it out on a short-term basis.

■ **Rent out the existing "parts" of a house separately**—Houses frequently come with space which a tenant either doesn't want or doesn't use. In that case, the space is worth nothing to the tenant who is occupying the house, whereas it may be worth quite a bit to somebody else. So go ahead and rent it out to somebody else. Garages are the most likely "house parts" which might be rented separately, but don't overlook other candidates such as parking spaces, storage cellars, basements, gardening areas, back yards, flat roof space, decks, and yes, even swimming pools.

Plenty of people are interested in renting garages, storage cellars, basements, and gardening areas. Who might be interested in renting the swimming pool of a house where he doesn't live? Try the next-door neighbors. To them the pool next door is always bluer.

If you do decide that you can rent out the existing parts of a house separately, be sure that the house tenant is apprised of the arrangement in advance. You don't want to aggravate him and perhaps lose your primary source of income from the property by trying to squeeze out some secondary income. And if you have always included the use of all the house parts in a tenant's rent, you might want to give him a slight rent reduction to gain his cooperation in your efforts to rent out those parts which he had considered his, even though he never used them.

Also, be aware that some communities specifically prohibit the segmenting of house parts for rental purposes. Find out whether your community has any such laws before you make commitments to anybody and then act accordingly.

■ **Put more houses on the lot or buy property which already has more than one house on its lot**—When you want to increase the income from your properties while playing a good competitive game of Monopoly®, you add houses to the matched properties you own. Right? Many times you can do the same thing in the rental housing game as well except that you don't have to wait until you've acquired a full matched set of properties. You need only one property which lends itself to development.

Two or more houses on one lot require no more land investment than one house on that same lot. Yet each one of them adds again as much rent as the one house. Those additional houses help to generate positive cash flow.

When you're looking for investment houses, look for those which have lots large enough to accommodate another house or two somewhere on the property and also have the proper zoning, or look for properties where several houses share the same lot already.

■ **Share the ownership with a silent partner**— People with sizable incomes frequently want to put part of their investment monies into real estate which has good potential for appreciation. Yet they're so busy doing what they do to make their sizable incomes that they don't want to take the time to look after any rental property.

In exchange for a portion of the capital gain when the property sells, they may agree to pay your rental house's negative cash flow every month.

Sounds pretty good, doesn't it? Well, sometimes it is and sometimes it isn't. Be aware that silent partners who have to continue making cash contributions to an investment month after month may decide to stop making those contributions after a while and jeopardize your own ownership position.

Make the payments as painless as possible for your silent partner so the partner doesn't even think about them. Automatic bank transfers or a year's supply of postdated checks may work to keep the payments coming.

■ **Tinker with the financing**—The largest percentage of the rental house owner's expenditures goes to the loan payment. Reduce that loan payment, and you increase the cash flow.

There are many ways to reduce a loan payment, but unless they involve a longer term, a lower interest rate, or a partial forgiveness of the debt, they will increase the amount of the loan principal. You'll be eliminating the negative cash flow all right, but you'll be creating negative amortization. In effect, you'll be taking out a small loan every month to help with the expenses and put money into your pocket. You get positive cash flow at the expense of having to pay off a larger loan balance later.

There's nothing wrong with taking out a small loan every month so long as you understand that that's how you're creating your positive cash flow. If the value of your rental house is appreciating more than the loan principal, you'll do well. If it isn't, be prepared to suffer the consequences later.

■ **Invest in the least expensive "houses" available**—Mobilehomes, known to some people as "tornado targets" and to others as trailers or manufactured housing, are the least expensive housing to build and to buy. Because they compete in the rental market with much higher priced housing stock, however, these inexpensive investments can and do command good rents. Rental mobilehomes don't have negative cash flows, not when you can buy them for $10,000 and rent them out for $200 a month. That's the equivalent of renting out a $100,000 house for $2,000 a month, and I don't know of anybody anywhere who's able to do that.

The truth is that the mobilehome you can buy for $10,000 will usually rent for more than $200 a month. $300-400 a month would be about right. The extra money pays for the mobilehome park's space rent if the mobilehome happens to be located in a park; otherwise, it compensates the property owner for the use of the land where the mobilehome sits and for whatever utilities and services are provided.

Before you rush out to buy a dozen mobilehomes to start your rental fleet, you should know that there are some drawbacks to consider. Financing mobilehomes isn't always easy, and when money doesn't come easy, you know it's going to cost more. Expect to pay one to five percent more to finance a mobilehome than you'd pay to finance a "stick-built" house. Maintaining mobilehomes tends to cost more because the least expensive models have cheap fixtures which can't take much abuse and soon require replacement. Replacement parts aren't always available at the neighborhood hardware store, either. They may have to be purchased from a mobilehome parts supply house, or else you may have to do some adapting so that readily available parts will fit. Dealing with mobilehome park management can be trying, too, especially if the management is

Property Viewing
& Keys Agreement

With my signature below, I hereby acknowledge receipt of the key(s) to the dwelling located at __456 SWEET ST.__ __LITTLETOWN, CA__ .

I intend to use the key(s) for the express purpose of viewing the dwelling to consider whether it is suitable for me to rent, and I will neither disturb nor remove anything found there.

As a courtesy, I will report to the owner/manager whatever appears to be amiss at the dwelling.

I have given the owner/manager, whose acknowledgment appears below, a deposit of $ __20—__ , and also a valuable personal item consisting of __DRIVERS LICENSE__ , both of which will be returned to me when I return the key(s).

I promise to return the key(s) by __4:00__ (~~a.m.~~) (p.m.) TODAY to the owner/manager at EITHER

      (X) the same place where I picked them up OR

      ( ) the following place _____.

Should I fail to do so, the owner/manager is entitled to keep the deposit to pay for changing the locks on the dwelling but will return my valuable personal item to me when asked.

I understand that this agreement gives me no occupancy rights whatsoever and that I must complete a rental application if I want to be considered as an applicant to rent this dwelling.

Signed __Rose Renter__

Current Address __1510 Zebra - Littletown, CA__

Current Telephone Number __555-1988__

Date & Time __Jan. 6, xxxx   2:00 P.m.__

Acknowledged by __Leslie Landlady__
                            Owner/Manager

fickle about allowing non-owner-occupied mobilehomes in the park.

Still, there are benefits to investing in mobilehomes other than the cash flow which they generate. They generally have aluminum siding on the outside and some sort of paneling on the inside, neither of which requires much maintenance. They are mobile and can be moved when economic or political conditions warrant moving them. Apartment house owners would love to put wheels under their buildings and move them when a major employer closes down or when local politicians enact rent control! They are 100% depreciable. They're depreciable over a period of only ten years. And because they're inexpensive, they're relatively easy to sell. After all, they're the least expensive housing available.

■ **Steal the house**—Some rental house investors spend far more of their time shopping for property than they ever spend managing it. They're as close as any real estate investors come to being real used car dealers. They try to buy at wholesale from anyone who wants to get rid of a house in a hurry at any price. They hold onto it awhile. Then they sell it for as close to the retail price as they can get.

Now if you can buy $80,000 houses for $60,000 with reasonable terms and rent them out for $650 per month, you'll have solved the negative cash flow problem all right, but you're going to be working mighty hard looking for those deals. They're not available at the sales office of every new housing tract, you know. You'll have to hunt them down, and that's work in itself.

If stealing houses sounds to you like a good way to eliminate negative cash flow and you'd like to try it, just be sure that you don't neglect management so much that you rent your wholesale houses to people who turn you into someone who wants to get rid of a house in a hurry at any price.

Handling the Vacancy Problems

Vacancies are more worrisome to the rental house investor than they are to the multiple-housing investor. One vacancy in a fourplex means that the building is 75% occupied, whereas one vacancy in a rental house means that the building is 0% occupied. As the owner of that rental house, you're quite aware of the income implications of not having any tenants occupying the property, and you're going to be trying whatever you can to increase the occupancy level from 0% to 100% as soon as possible, but there are some other implications, too. You need to do more than hunt for new tenants during your rental house vacancy.

■ **Take special precautions when showing your rental house**—As a rental house owner, you are by definition an absentee owner, not living on the premises, so whenever you have to show a vacancy, you have to cover some distance to reach your rental house and show it off to prospective tenants. Dropping whatever you happen to be doing and going over there to meet people who want to look at it becomes awfully tiresome after a time. Do what any other landlord might do. Schedule the showings at a particular time when you will open the house to any and all lookers, or else tell those who respond to your advertising to drive by the place first before you schedule a showing for their eyes only.

What else might you do to cut your involvement in showing the place to a minimum? Ask a cooperative neighbor to keep the keys and either unlock the door for anyone who wants to see the place or else take the people through. Many neighbors are delighted to help, some just to get a good look at their prospective neighbors, some just to get a courteous "thank you," and some just to earn a few extra bucks.

Lacking cooperative neighbors, you might ask those who are interested in seeing the place to come over to your house or place of business, pick up the housekeys, and show themselves through the house. This do-it-yourself showing may work smoothly in many situations forever, but it is somewhat chancy. There's always the danger that the people won't return the keys, that they will copy the keys so they can gain access later, or that they will brazenly move into the house without your ever getting a dollar out of them. If they did move in, they wouldn't be considered trespassers either, because they had your permission to enter, so you'd have a hard time getting rid of them. You couldn't merely summon the police to remove them from the premises. You'd have to evict them. For these reasons, I do not recommend giving the keys to prospective tenants and letting them view your rental house on their own unless you take four special precautions.

First, prepare and have them sign a simple

agreement which outlines the conditions for your giving them the keys and allowing them to look through the house on their own. Use the one shown here if you like.

Second, request that they give you a deposit of at least $50 in cash, all of which is completely refundable when they return the keys to you as agreed.

Third, request that they leave with you one item of special value to them, something which they will surely return to retrieve. A major credit card or their driver's license would qualify. Don't take a credit care or a driver's license which has expired, of course. Look at the expiration date to make sure that it's current, and look at the item closely to be sure that it's theirs.

Fourth, give them a time limit for returning the keys. Consider approximately how much time they'll need to travel to and from the house and add about an hour to give them enough time to look around. If they haven't returned the keys within an hour after they should have, make haste to the house and change the locks.

Should you choose to give prospective tenants the keys, make sure that you change the keyed locks on the outside doors just before your new tenants move in. That way, nobody who had access to the keys during the vacancy will have easy access to the house during the tenancy, and you will protect yourself from a potentially damaging lawsuit brought by tenants who claim that your supposedly lax handling of the keys to their home enabled a criminal to get in and commit a crime there. Be cautious with keys.

■ **Safeguard your vacant rental house**—Take special pains to make sure that your rental house is well looked after during any vacancy period. You want to make it attractive enough to prospective tenants, while at the same time you want to keep it from deteriorating.

Transfer the billings for all the utilities into your own name. Having utilities available when you're repairing, cleaning or showing a vacant house is convenient, to say the least. It also enables you to keep up the exterior of the property properly. What's more, it saves potential breakdowns in gas-fired space and water heaters, for they tend to be temperamental when you try to light them after a period of inactivity.

Make it look occupied. Keep the lawn mowed and watered. Keep newspapers and advertising circulars picked up. Empty the mailbox if it's located someplace where the accumulation of mail could advertise that the place is unoccupied. Keep window coverings on the windows. Install a timer to switch on a lamp at night. Do everything you can to discourage the vandals, thieves, burglars, squatters, and buzzards who prey on properties which appear to be unoccupied.

■ **Be sure you're fully insured during extended vacancies**—Whenever any dwelling is totally uninhabited, it becomes more vulnerable to some of the various calamities which owners insure their places against. Insurance companies know this. They know that the risks of fire, flooding from burst pipes, and vandalism, for example, all increase when there's no one around to discover such disastrous developments in their early stages and when there's no one who can act quickly to contain the damage.

They understand that their exposure to property losses is greater during vacancy periods so they are sometimes careful to exclude themselves from certain losses if a single-family dwelling is vacant for an extended period.

Check your insurance policy to be sure. Look for clauses lurking somewhere which exclude coverage during vacancies.

If you'd rather not tax your eyes and addle your brain by reading the small print in your policy, discuss the matter with your insurance agent directly. Be frank. Don't hide a thing.

Don't ignore the possibility that your insurance policy might contain such a clause and then plead ignorance later if you should have a claim. Discuss the matter with your insurance agent in advance. That, after all, is what you're doing when you secure insurance in the first place, isn't it? You are anticipating that you might conceivably have a problem in the future.

If you are supposed to contact your insurance company every time you have an extended vacancy so you can buy additional insurance, then do so. Buy the added insurance whether your lender requires it or not.

Handling the Neighbor Problem

Many times people go out of their way not to become involved with their own neighbors. They try to remain as aloof as possible so they won't be bothered by people who are always close by. They want to preserve their privacy.

As a rental house owner, you're in a somewhat different position because you aren't going to be around much to bother the neighbors in person. You lack the potential to become a 24-hour nuisance. The neighbors think of you differently, and you should think of them differently. Don't think of them as a problem. Think of them as a solution. Without the usual fears neighbors have of one another, you can become friendly with them and you should.

You should go out of your way to establish a relationship with the neighbors. Knock on their doors and meet them. Tell them who you are and tell them a little about yourself. If they don't understand that they have a stake in your operation, then enlighten them. Tell them that even though you don't live in the neighborhood, you are still concerned about keeping it up because the condition of the neighborhood affects your property value, too. Tell them that you may want to enlist their help now and again when you have to pick new tenants. Be sure you give them your telephone number so they can be your "first-alert" system in case your tenants try to pull any shenanigans.

In other words, "employ" the neighbors who live around your rental house. Keep them abreast of what's happening at your end, and ask them to keep you abreast of what's happening at their end.

Handling the Restrictions Problem

Before you ever rent out any dwelling located in a condominium complex, planned unit development, co-operative apartment project, or mobilehome park, apprise yourself of what's been written to govern the tenancy and conduct of anyone living there, owner or tenant. This written word might be called rules, regulations, by-laws, conditions, restrictions, or covenants. Whatever they're called, they're all "restrictions" of some sort or another.

You may sometimes get away with paying scant attention to these restrictions in a complex when you're planning to live there yourself, but when there are tenants involved, you have to pay close heed. Both you and your tenants are bound by them, and you may be held responsible for things that your tenants do against the restrictions unwittingly.

These restrictions can vary widely, too. Some mobilehome parks allow no renting of mobilehomes at all. Others don't care. Some co-operative projects allow unlimited renting. Others allow renting for a limited time, but only if the renter satisfies a screening committee. Some co-ops won't admit ex-presidents or rock stars as owners, let alone truck drivers or hairdressers as tenants. Some planned unit developments have restrictions about animals, landscaping, business uses, satellite dishes, paint colors, recreational facilities, and the like, any of which might affect your tenants. You can't know what's allowed and what's not allowed unless you take the time to read up on these things.

Having become familiar with the restrictions yourself, you must inform prospective tenants of their responsibilities to the development, park, or homeowners' association. They cannot be held responsible unless they are informed. You'll be the one held responsible instead, and that can become a most frustrating situation because you'll have to take the blame and pay the bills for someone else's transgressions.

By the way, always inform the "powers that be" in one of these restricted living environments that you have tenants occupying your dwelling. They may need to know in order to extend recreational or parking privileges or somesuch to your tenants.

Handling the Bookkeeping Problem

As far as bookkeeping goes, you have a choice. Handle each rental house separately or lump them all together. You get to choose.

Why would you want to handle them separately? You would then be able to determine exactly how well each house is doing so you could decide whether to keep or dispose of a particular one.

Why would you lump them all together? Because lumping them together is easier than keeping them separate. Instead of prorating expenditures for all of your properties, you merely list things once. Instead of hassling with a number of spreadsheets or ledger sheets, one for each property, you hassle with only one for all the properties.

Unless all the properties share some common denominators, such as a number of houses on the same lot or a number of mobilehomes in one park, I would recommend that you keep your single-family houses separate. Sure, it's more work to begin with, but it gives you the numbers you need to analyze and control what's happening with each individual house. Whereas it may seem a trifle ridiculous to have only three entries on one house's ledger sheet for the entire month, those entries have special meaning and can best convey that meaning when they aren't lumped together with the expenditures for your other rental houses.

Lumping all of your single-family houses together would be like lumping the statistics for an entire college football team together and not keeping track of the individual players at all. That wouldn't please the fans, the coach, the players, the scouts, or the conference.

There's nothing wrong with having only one checking account for a number of rental houses. That makes good sense. Every time you write a check, merely identify in the checkbook register which house's expenditures it

HOW COME YOU CAN ALWAYS TELL WHICH ONES ARE THE RENTAL HOUSES?

should be posted to. Then post it separately later. Or use Quicken, an outstanding computer program, for your checkwriting. So long as you identify the property associated with a particular expenditure, Quicken can separate the expenditures out of a single account easily when it compiles reports.

Handling the Maintenance Problem

Rental house tenants expect less maintenance service than apartment house tenants, and they will do more things for themselves without bothering the owner. You can encourage them even more in that direction by offering either some sort of ownership participation arrangement like the lease-option already mentioned or some sort of remunerative arrangement like a cash discount on their rent.

Some owners give their tenants a flat $50 rent

discount every month so long as the tenants take care of all the minor maintenance and repairs ("minor" means less than $100), pay their rent promptly, don't call the owner unless there's a major problem, and tend to all the gardening themselves. In a sense, those owners are hiring their tenants to manage the property in the same way a property management company would. It's a good idea, but it has the same primary drawback that hiring a property management company has. It distances the owner. To make it work right, you should require a large enough deposit to begin with so that any maintenance the tenants defer during their tenancy will cost them, not you, when they move out.

Handling the Gardening Problem

Did you know that there's a vegetarian cult on this planet which sincerely believes that lawn mowing causes grass to suffer pain? Well, there is. Tell your tenants that you have a list of all known members of this cult and that unless you can find their names on that list, they'd better keep their grass mowed or you'll be forced to hire a gardening service and raise their rent to pay for it.

That's one way to handle the "gardening problem" at your rental house. There are others.

Consider using the discounted rent policy mentioned above.

Consider installing low-maintenance landscaping. You can't expect a rental house tenant to look after a rose garden. It may be beautiful to look at, something anyone might enjoy, but it's not a practical landscaping choice. It's high maintenance. Study the low-maintenance possibilities and try them.

Consider providing the proper tools and supplies for your tenants to keep the yard weeded, fertilized, and trimmed.

Consider installing an automatic sprinkling system which will keep the landscaping watered without any effort on your tenants' part. They can't have much of an excuse for not watering if there's a sprinkling system available to do it effortlessly.

At least consider yourself lucky that you do have some gardening choices. Owners of multiple-family housing have none. They simply supply gardening service. For them it's "master metered." In most complexes it can't be done any other way for there's no practical way to divide up the gardening so that each tenant would look after a plot of lawn or a few shrubs.

Some Last Words

If someone driving down the street where you own a rental house can pick out that one house of yours from all the others which are themselves owner-occupied, then you're doing something wrong. You're not managing the place properly, and the value of your investment is declining. You do not want its value to be declining. You want it to be appreciating at the same rate as every other house in the neighborhood.

Keep looking for ways to instill a "pride of tenantship" in your tenants while at the same time you put some money into your own pockets from the property.

11
Legal Matters

You may have thought that window screens were merely supposed to keep out pesky mosquitoes, horse flies, gnats, and moths. After all, screens are pretty flimsy things, especially the fiberglass variety with the aluminum frames used so widely today. They could hardly be expected to challenge a charging elephant, a sharp-clawed pussy cat, a wily cat burglar, or even an errant baseball, now could they? Nah, anybody with even a lick of common sense could see that.

Don't be so naive. In these days of the "Twinkies Defense" and the convoluted legal machinations performed in front of TV cameras for all to see, when some people get away with hot-blooded murder in spite of all the facts marshalled against them, common sense doesn't count for very much. Every time you go to court, you check your handgun and your common sense in at the courtroom door.

Some time ago a court decided that window screens were supposed to keep out rapists. That's right! A fiberglass netting less than a thirty-second of an inch thick was supposed to have been sufficient to keep out a man with rape on his mind. I kid you not! Because the screen was missing on the very window through which the rapist had gained entry and because the landlord had failed to replace it, the landlord was negligent and therefore responsible for the rape. The landlord was to blame for the tenant's misfortune. The landlord had to pay the tenant's claim.

Was the landlord really to blame for what had happened? Not in my book he wasn't. Others were to blame, but they weren't available for prosecution and if they had been available, they wouldn't have had the assets or the insurance to compensate the victim. The landlord was capable of compensating the victim, and what's more, the landlord was available. So the landlord became the target of the lawsuit.

People today have been led to believe that there is no such thing as an accident or a misfortune which is nobody's fault. There has to be somebody to blame, somebody with the means to pay up, even if that person is only a teensy-weensy bit at fault.

People no longer harbor dreams of striking it rich in the gold or oil fields or in the dot-com companies. That's the stuff of movies like "Gold Rush," starring Charlie Chaplin; "Giant," starring James Dean; and "Startup.com," starring the real people who rode a dot-com roller coaster. That's the stuff of yesterday.

Today all people need do is watch the nightly news and they see ordinary Janes and Joes striking it rich by winning either a big lawsuit or a big lottery jackpot. The media trumpet these wins across the land. People watch and read about them and dream of making their own fortunes this new-fashioned way. You can hardly blame them for trying to seize their share of the winnings, especially when it costs virtually nothing to get into the game and it's so easy to play.

Unfortunately, there is another side to those dreams of gaining wealth through litigation, and that is the nightmare of losing wealth through litigation. You, landlord, are among those people who have to worry about losing their wealth through litigation. You are a target. You are especially vulnerable to lawsuits because you have what some attorneys call "deep purses" and others call "deep pockets." Presumably these purses and pockets contain plenty of money to pay off the injured party and, of course, all the attorneys involved. You have to take special precautions to protect yourself and your assets from lawsuits.

To us landlords, a lawsuit is like a breath of stale air. Lawsuits are stultifying, time-consuming, costly, tedious, and unnerving. Except in eviction matters, you aren't going to win anything from your tenants in a courtroom. Don't bother trying. Tenants have little or nothing that you can hope to win from them anyway. Most of them are "judgment-proof." They don't have the resources to pay a judgment which does go against them. Yet, they'll bring discrimination suits, liability suits, habitability suits, contract suits, statute violation suits, wrongful eviction suits, security deposit suits, sexual harassment suits, class-action suits, and just plain old nuisance suits against you time and time again because they think that you have plenty to lose and they have plenty to gain.

You're at a double disadvantage in a courtroom as a defendant because you have assets to lose and you have that persistent stereotype of the greedy landlord to contend with. As if that's not bad enough, you're also going to have to spend time and money defending yourself, and you're going to be worrying yourself

sick about the uncertainty of it all. Those are not pleasant prospects. Since you cannot hope to gain any advantage over your tenants in court, you can hope only to keep yourself from being taken full advantage of, nothing more.

Taking Steps to Reduce Legal Difficulties

Short of throwing up your hands and letting your tenants help themselves to your assets, there are some steps you can take to reduce your overall legal difficulties and to keep yourself from being taken full advantage of.

■ **Become aware of the laws relevant to landlording in that part of the country where your rental properties are located**—Lawmakers at the federal, state, and local levels have been busy for a long, long time passing law after law to help keep society running smoothly and peacefully, and they haven't neglected landlording.

There are laws at the federal level, including the Fair Housing Act (sets antidiscrimination standards); the Occupational Safety and Health Act (commonly known as OSHA, this act sets standards for safety on the job); the Fair Credit Reporting Act (sets standards for credit information and availability); the Soldiers' and Sailors' Civil Relief Act (sets special leasing provisions for military personnel); and the Truth-in-Advertising Act (sets advertising standards).

There are laws at the state level which govern tenancies at every stage, from the creation of the tenancy through the duration, termination, and aftermath. State laws tell you what your rights and responsibilities as a rental property owner are and what your tenants' rights and responsibilities are. They outline the proper procedures for evictions. They expand upon the federal antidiscrimination standards. They go into contracts, deposits, notices, employer/employee relationships, liens, vehicle towing, maintenance, subletting, abandonment, bad checks, retaliation, health matters, and safety concerns. In short, state laws cover almost every conceivable aspect of landlording.

There are laws at the local (county or municipal) level, too, which affect what you do as a landlord. They generally add further restrictions to federal and state laws and can be the most hobbling of all. Some zealously pro-tenant communities have virtually doomed their stock of rental housing by making landlording practically a criminal activity.

You can know how these laws will affect you only if you have a look at them, admittedly no easy task for somebody who has never opened a law book before. Let's take a look at one of these laws ourselves.

Here are some important words in the Fair Housing Act, the law of the land about housing discrimination. Check them out for clarity—

Sec. 803. [42 U.S.C. 3603] (b) Nothing in section 804 of this title (other than subsection (c) shall apply to —

(1) any single-family house sold or rented by an owner: Provided, That such private individual owner does not own more than three such single-family houses at any one time: Provided further, That in the case of the sale of any such single-family house by a private individual owner not residing in such house at the time of such sale or who was not the most recent resident of such house prior to such sale, the exemption granted by this subsection shall apply only with respect to one such sale within any twenty-four month period: Provided further, That such bona fide private individual owner does not own any interest in, nor is there owned or reserved on his behalf, under any express or voluntary agreement, title to or any right to all or a portion of the proceeds from the sale or rental of, more than three such single-family houses at any one time: Provided further, That after December 31, 1969, the sale or rental of any such single-family house shall be excepted from the application of this subchapter only if such house is sold or rented (A) without the use in any manner of the sales or rental facilities of any real estate broker, agent, or salesman, or of such facilities or services of any person in the business of selling or renting dwellings, or of any employee or agent of any such broker, agent, salesman, or person and (B) without the publication, posting or mailing, after notice, of any advertisement or written notice in violation of section 804(c) of this title; but nothing in this proviso shall prohibit the use of attorneys, escrow agents, abstractors, title companies, and other such professional assistance as necessary to perfect or transfer the title, or

(2) rooms or units in dwellings containing living quarters occupied or intended to be occupied by no more than four families living independently of each other, if the owner actually maintains and occupies one of such living quarters as his residence.

You wouldn't have to deliberate long if someone were to ask you whether mud or these words were clearer.

Most laws affecting this business appear to have been drafted by the same anonymous drudges who produce the incomprehensible instructions for income tax returns. Laws do not make for easy reading, and they are not something you want to read all the way through or commit to memory. Attorneys don't even do that. Don't you do it either. Do become generally familiar with them, though, so you will know just enough about them to be able to consult specific laws whenever you have a specific question.

Where do you find these laws? How can you consult them? Call your local rental housing association and ask for suggestions. Some state associations have done their members the service of gathering all the applicable federal and state laws together into a single volume. That's just what the California Apartment Association's *Managing Rental Housing* reference book is (see SOURCES & RESOURCES). Buy a copy of your state's equivalent and keep it handy. If such a convenient source isn't available, your association can probably direct you to several books which include the applicable laws.

Because these books tend to be expensive, you may want to use library copies. When you know what you're looking for, call your public library and ask whether they have the titles. If they don't, call your county law library. Almost every county courthouse has a law library nearby. They're not always as conveniently located as public libraries are, but they'll have the books.

As an alternative to using books, you may want to try using the Internet. Do a Google (google.com) or Yahoo (yahoo.com) search on the words "[your state] + codes" or "[your state] + landlord-tenant laws"; you may be surprised by what appears on your search list. If you get a list of all the state codes, go to the property codes and to the civil proceedings codes, and look there specifically for landlord-tenant or rental property codes. Copy the files from the Internet onto your computer's hard drive or print them out for reference.

All of California's codes are now available on

the web, and they're up-to-date. Your state's may be as well. More and more state, county, and city codes are becoming available all the time. Check the Landlording website (landlording.com) for help in locating the laws for your state.

To give you some idea how ignorance of the law can affect your landlording business, consider what happened to me some years ago.

I was evicting a ne'er-do-well tenant who had stopped paying his rent. This fellow never made any effort to explain himself. He just stopped paying. What's more, he went out of his way to avoid meeting me and played hard to find. I sensed that he was digging in and was going to make every effort to extend his rent-free stay as long as he could. I finally had him served with a summons and complaint to get his eviction moving through the courts, and he answered my complaint stating that I wasn't providing him with enough heat in his steam-heated apartment. He even quoted some law to that effect. Well, I knew nothing of any such law, so I looked it up and sure enough, there it was in black and white ten-point type. My hands trembled as I read it. The law stated that I had to provide my tenants with heat at a minimum of 60°F three feet above the floor twenty-four hours a day. Yes, the law was that specific!

I knew that I was providing plenty of heat during the hours that mattered but not twenty-four hours a day. There was a timer controlling the boiler, and it shut everything down during most of the hours when everyone was at work.

After reading the law, I felt bloodied and beaten. Then I started to think about the matter further and realized that the tenant had never complained to me about the heat, nor so far as I could tell, had he ever complained to any public agency as he was supposed to do by law. Fortunately, my initial ignorance of the law didn't cause me to lose the eviction because the tenant had indeed made that fatal mistake. He had not registered his complaint when he should have, before the eviction began. The judge saw through the tenant's transparent ploy to gain as many days of free rent as he could possibly get, and the tenant lost.

Following that scare, though, I decided that some knowledge of the laws affecting me as a landlord was important. No, it was essential.

■ **Stay informed**—Laws are one thing. How they're interpreted is quite another. No matter how hard lawmakers try to draft unambiguous laws and enough of them to circumscribe every possible situation, there's always something they didn't think of. They're human, too. Court decisions which settle the disputes arising out of these overlooked or unclear situations affect us as much as laws do. Court decisions interpret and amplify the laws on the books and become the authority for later decisions in other courts.

Interpretation of these laws can differ markedly from state to state, from court to court, and from time to time.

In New York, there was a case regarding a landlord who refused to rent to someone for one reason only, because that person was an attorney. The attorney-applicant sued, arguing that wholesale discrimination against attorneys was illegal. The landlord responded that attorneys eat landlords for breakfast, that as a whole they are more argumentative and more likely to sue than other people; hence they are more likely to make bad tenants. Amazingly enough, the court sided with the landlord in the case, and that decision made national news (perhaps the case merely showed that attorneys are even less sympathetic figures than landlords).

As a landlord yourself, you might have thought after hearing about the New York case that you could discriminate against an applicant only because he was an attorney, counterfeiter, minister, male stripper, or ballet dancer, in other words, on the basis of occupation alone. After all, you already know that you may not discriminate on the basis of race, color, religion, sex, national origin, age, or physical handicap. That's made clear by federal law. So you might think after hearing about the New York case that you could discriminate legally according to someone's occupation because that's not one of the protected categories in the federal law or in your state or local laws. Why not? If it's not specifically prohibited, then it should be all right, eh? Maybe yes and maybe no!

The next thing you know, the California Supreme Court rules that its state's Unruh Act, which is about discrimination in business and does apply to the landlording business, must be construed to mean that discrimination is prohibited against *any* classification of people when that classification has nothing to do with the business at hand. Wow! That really changes things! Because an applicant's occupation in itself has nothing to do with whether someone will be a good or a bad tenant, landlords may not discriminate on the basis of occupation. Wages, assets, negative recommendations, and the like do have something to do with whether someone will be a good tenant. They are categories of legal discrimination, whereas occupation is not.

Had you read nothing about the California decision and had you attempted to refuse to rent to an attorney applicant on the basis of the New York decision, you could have been in trouble, depending upon where your property is located. In some jurisdictions you might have won in court; in others, you might have lost.

This is all interpretation, remember. You're not going to find a law which specifically prohibits you from discriminating against applicants by height, weight, shoe size, or handwriting, but you might find a court decision which has interpreted some other law as prohibiting you from discriminating in these ways. When you think about these as criteria for tenant selection, they sound pretty illogical, don't they? To refuse to rent to an applicant on the basis of shoe size? Come on! That doesn't really have anything to do with being a good tenant, does it?

In that window-screen rape case mentioned earlier, there was no law cited which absolutely required window screens for the protection of the occupants against physical assault, for there is no such law. The plaintiff's attorney successfully created the impression that an unscreened window was an invitation to enter, and the defendant's attorney didn't argue convincingly enough that it wasn't. That's how the case was decided.

By staying informed of what's happening in the courts, you will know better what you can do to stay out of trouble yourself. You'll make sure that all of your windows have screens. Right?

Read all the relevant, up-to-date information on rental housing that you can possibly lay your hands on. The following are good sources of legal information—daily newspapers (more to make you aware of what's happening than to provide accurate information); rental housing association periodicals (national, state, and local associations publish news of relevance to their members); various independent newsletters published specifically for the attorney who handles landlord-tenant matters and for the interested layman (see what's available at your county law library); and the Internet (search on "rental housing information" or go directly to the sites listed in SOURCES AND RESOURCES).

Attend seminars which focus on the legal aspects of the rental property business. These seminars may be sponsored by rental housing associations, a particular attorney, the state bar association, or a local institution of higher learning. Some may be intended for attorneys in general practice (these are generally open to anyone interested in the subject, not just to attorneys), and some may be intended for landlords.

Seek out several people who take landlording seriously and ask them questions to clarify fuzzy matters and to relieve any specific doubts you might have.

You're in a changing business which absolutely requires that you stay informed.

■ **Inspect your property and enlist others to help**—Most people consider a site inspection of their property by their own insurance company as an imposition at the very least. They think that the company is spying on them, that it's trying to find some reason to cancel their policy. So they're inclined not to cooperate and may even try to conceal whatever's faulty. That's not the right attitude.

First of all, remember that your insurance company is on your side. It's for you, not against you. It wants your business. It doesn't want to cancel your policy. It doesn't make any money by canceling its customers' policies. It simply doesn't want unnecessary or excessive risk. It doesn't want to pay claims which could have been avoided had somebody taken the precaution of surveying the property to search for dangerous conditions and then taken the steps to remedy those conditions. That's all.

Second, any company which is concerned enough about its own exposure to send an inspector to look at your property is a company you want to do business with. They're trying to keep their expenses down. Lower expenses for them translate into lower premiums for you.

Third, if they don't send an inspector out, ask them to. You should know what you can do to make your property as safe as possible.

If you can't get your insurance company to send out an inspector, inspect your property yourself, especially the common areas. Look for anything which might possibly trigger a liability lawsuit. Look for exposed electrical wiring, uneven

May 01, XXXX

Dear Richard and Rose Renter,

    We want to make the place where you live as safe as it can be. We are constantly on the lookout for anything around your home which might prove hazardous to life, limb, or property. But hard as we try, we cannot uncover every potential danger all by ourselves. We need your help.

    Because you are around your home much more than we are, you have a greater opportunity to notice hazards. Please report to us anything you notice which you think might prove hazardous to you or anyone else. We promise that we will investigate the hazardous condition and remedy it if we possibly can.

    Please complete the bottom section of this letter and return it to us with your next rent payment.

    Thank you for your cooperation in making your home a safer place to live.

                 Sincerely,

                   Leslie Landlady

= =

[X] We know of nothing which appears to be unsafe in or around our home, but we will alert you whenever we do notice something.

[ ] We would like to call your attention to the following unsafe conditions in or around our home:

_____

_____

_____

_____

We suggest that you take the following corrective action:

_____

_____

_____

_____

Signed *Richard Renter*   Dated *May 8, XXXX*

walkways, missing or broken railings, slippery floors, potholes in the parking lot, inadequate lighting, faulty locks, sharp protrusions, poorly ventilated heaters, rotted footings, loose toilet seats, and the like.

By inspecting your property yourself and enlisting the aid of your insurance company to do the same, you'll find most of the obviously hazardous conditions around your property, but you're not going to find all of them, and you're not going to be giving your tenants and their attorneys second thoughts about suing you. That's why you should involve your tenants in your inspection. "Deputize" them to be on the alert at all times for hazardous conditions. Make them responsible for advising you whenever they notice something which could prove to be hazardous.

An attorney who specializes in personal injury cases and frequently represents tenants who are injured in slip-and-fall cases told me he would have a difficult time winning many of his cases if rental property owners would just send their tenants a letter every year asking them to report hazardous conditions. Tenants would be hard pressed to argue that their landlords were negligent if the tenants themselves didn't notice a particular hazard.

On the opposite page is the letter he wouldn't like you to use. Use it once a year, and follow up on it. Keep copies of your tenants' responses together with their applications, agreements, and checksheets. They're important, very important. They're part of your insurance policy against a lawsuit calamity.

■ **Do your paperwork properly and promptly**—Act as if it's inevitable that you're going to be dragged into court on some tenant matter or other, and start building your case in advance. Put in writing all of the understandings and transactions that you have with your tenants. Use written rental applications, written rental agreements, written house rules, written condition-and-inventory checksheets, and written receipts. Make an entry in a logbook every time you respond to tenants' complaints or calls for assistance. Put your own complaints about tenants in writing instead of merely talking to the tenants. Insist that your tenants put their complaints in writing, too, and that they use a written notice to advise you that they're moving.

If your tenants turn out to be lawsuit-happy,

if you have to evict them, or if they leave owing you money, this paperwork will be more essential to you than a figleaf in a nudist camp. Judges tend to be "paper slaves" themselves, and they look kindly on good documentation.

■ **Maintain your property well**—Whenever you become aware of anything on your property which might be considered unsafe, take care of it as soon as possible. No, don't fix it as soon as possible. Fix it *now*. As long as you allow a hazardous condition to continue, you are exposing your tenants to injury and yourself to lawsuits, and at the same time you could be allowing the situation to worsen. You know that you'll have to fix it sometime. Why not fix it now? Fixing it now is always less expensive than fixing it later.

■ **Use common sense**—Common sense may not seem to count for very much in a court of law nowadays, but it still counts for something in the real world of landlording. Laws frequently acknowledge the thoughts and actions of "reasonable people," and they mention "reasonable care" again and again. These are other ways of saying that laws cannot cover every eventuality, and when something arises which they don't cover, judgment will be based on whether the people involved acted reasonably. Did they use the good common sense which reasonable people are supposed to have?

Tenant relations require you to use all the common sense you can muster. Be as reasonable as you can be when tenants are being unreasonable. Don't show anger. Don't act rashly. Don't be stubborn. People get hurt and court cases get filed when you take leave of your common sense and do something you'll regret later.

■ **Join "HALT"**—The day appears to be fast approaching when we will have no choice but to consult an attorney before we advertise a vacancy, reject an applicant, say hello to a tenant, repair a broken window, or pick up a scrap of paper. I don't look forward to that day myself, and I'm sure you don't either. To try to change this impending state of affairs, think about joining HALT. HALT stands for "Help Abolish Legal Tyranny" (see "Associations & Organizations" in SOURCES & RESOURCES). It's an organization of legal reform advocates who really believe that our legal system can be reformed.

I believe that it has to be reformed myself, and I believe that it will be reformed one of these days when people begin to realize how expensive the system is and how it benefits such a narrow spectrum of people rather than American society as a whole. Then, and only then, will it get reformed.

As a landlord who has been victimized by the legal system more than once, I would like to climb up on my soapbox and make two recommendations for reform. They aren't complex, and they aren't ridiculous. They're practical. They make sense. They make so much sense that other civilized countries handle legal matters just this way. We should as well.

The recommendations are these—

● *Make the losing plaintiffs pay the costs of the winning defendants.* If tenants sue you and they lose, they should have to pay what you have to pay to defend yourself. Time and time again I have been sued over something patently frivolous, and my insurer will settle rather than spend the money to put up a defense. There's a name for this dirty game which so many plaintiffs and their attorneys play with abandon. It's called extortion. I don't care whether it's legal or not. It ain't right!

● *Put time limits on lawsuits and on court hearings.* Civil and criminal cases clog the courts because the attorneys involved don't care how long they take. Most attorneys are paid by the hour. The longer a case takes, the more they earn. They thrive on delays, patently ridiculous delays, which do nothing but run up the legal bills. That ain't right! By the way, do you know how much time the United States Supreme Court allocates to each case it hears? ONE HOUR! Each side has half an hour to present its arguments. If the Supreme Court can do it...

Right now our legal system has a blank check, a check which we Americans have unwittingly written thinking that the system will somehow produce justice for all. All we have to do is make the check good. Nobody seems to keep track of what figure goes into the blank check every year. We all know that it's huge. We just don't know how huge.

We also don't quite know whether the system produces any justice. We have only a sneaking suspicion that it doesn't. We don't have any proof.

Join HALT and have some input into where our legal system is going.

Until the system is reformed, however, you'd better come to know those attorneys who can help you with the problems which plague you now and probably will tomorrow.

■ **Identify attorneys suited to handle your particular problems**—Whenever I think about hiring an attorney, I remember the little old lady who was overheard saying, "I don't want an attorney. I want to tell the truth."

Attorneys do have to contend with a reputation as truth benders. They have been known to speak with forked tongues at times. Yet, representing clients in court in the best possible light is a small part of what they do. They can help you with their good advice, intercede for you when you seem to be getting nowhere with an adversary, review your contracts with their eagle eyes, and otherwise keep you from getting into trouble.

Like many other professionals, attorneys have specialties. One might know bankruptcies. One might know wills and trusts. One might know divorces from the husband's point of view, and another might know them from the wife's. One might know landlord-tenant law from the landlord's viewpoint; another from the tenant's. Find an attorney who specializes. One who doesn't specialize may be legally qualified to represent you but actually may know less about landlord-tenant matters than you do. Don't pay for that attorney's education.

You won't find attorneys who specialize in landlord-tenant law advertising on television along with the sharkskin-suited personal injury attorneys. You will find them advertising in the Yellow Pages, and that's as good a place as any to start your search for a landlord-tenant specialist. The attorney guide there, which follows the Yellow Pages' "attorney" classification, lists them by field of law, so you can go directly to those who specialize in landlord-tenant law instead of having to look at every attorney advertisement in the book.

Other sources for attorney references are the Internet, your local rental property association, and fellow landlords. If you're looking for an attorney to handle an eviction for you, call the office of the court which handles evictions and ask for the names of the attorneys who file most of the evictions in that court.

Incidentally, HALT publishes a useful manual called *Shopping for a Lawyer*, which will help you when you're trying to find a suitable attorney.

■ **Insure yourself adequately**—No matter how conscientious you are about following the previous suggestions for preventing landlording's legal difficulties, you cannot eliminate the risk of lawsuits entirely. You cannot become a Teflon® landlord. That's why you need insurance.

There's no law requiring you to have any insurance at all except workers' compensation, and you don't need that unless you employ someone to work for you, but you could be very, very sorry that you didn't protect yourself with insurance when you get summoned into court to defend yourself on some matter or other and then have to pay an outrageous settlement for something you could not have foreseen and had no control over.

Because lawsuits are expensive, and settlements are expensive, insurance is expensive, but not having it can turn out to be more expensive still. It can precipitate financial disaster, your financial disaster. You cannot afford that, so insure yourself adequately. See chapter 16 for some suggestions.

■ **Watch yourself when you give tenant recommendations**—We landlords are in the same quandary as employers when we're called upon to give recommendations. On the one hand, we want to *get* honest recommendations from somebody else when we're checking on an applicant and trying to decide whether to initiate a relationship; on the other hand, we're reluctant to *give* honest recommendations ourselves because we're afraid that we might be sued for saying the wrong thing.

Much as you might like the world to know what sort of a scalawag a particular tenant was when he was your tenant, you could be exposing yourself to a lawsuit by actually telling the world all of the details. If the tenant is able to convince a court that you and he merely had a personality conflict and that you in your vindictiveness had given him bad recommendations and made it impossible for him to find another place to live, he could be successful in dipping into your deep pockets.

So, what do you do?

You can't go wrong by verifying a tenant's dates of occupancy, his address, his rent, his pay-ment history, and the circumstances of his departure when called upon to do so. Them's the facts, ma'am. That's useful information which another landlord may draw his own conclusions from in determining whether to rent to your tenant. That's not a recommendation. That's information, and so long as it's accurate, it would be difficult, if not impossible, to refute in a court of law.

Let the tenant take you to court and try to prove that you were being vindictive in supplying another landlord with information about the number of late notices you gave the tenant during his occupancy; you have copies of the notices themselves to show the court. Let the tenant take you to court and try to prove that he vacated owing you nothing; you can show the court your records to the contrary. Don't concern yourself about these possibilities. They ain't gonna happen.

Go ahead and supply a fellow landlord with information which you can prove, information which you would like to receive if you were checking out an applicant. You can't go wrong doing that.

But you can go wrong by supplying anecdotal remarks about a tenant, especially if those remarks are judgmental and detrimental. Don't say things about the tenant that you cannot prove.

If another landlord calls and presses you to reveal what you don't want to reveal about one of your departed or departing tenants, say "No comment!" That response, used widely by personalities who want to protect themselves from pesky, prying reporters, says everything and nothing at the same time.

You might even say something like this, "I have been advised not to give recommendations on any of my tenants because you might sue me if I give them a good recommendation and they turn out to be bad tenants for you, and they might sue me if I give them a bad recommendation and they are able somehow to prove me wrong."

Although you really don't want to say such a thing and you certainly don't want to hear it, in these litigious times, it's an understandable statement.

Some Last Words

An acerbic old attorney once told me that there are only two kinds of landlords—those who have been sued and those who will be. That might sound pretty pessimistic to you. It's not. It's much more realistic than you might think. You should be pessimistic about lawsuits. Resign yourself to the inevitability of your being sued for something or other sometime, and you won't get too upset when you find a process server on your doorstep, there to serve you with your tenant's formal complaint and summoning you to court.

If you're doing most of what is outlined in this book, you will be reducing your exposure to lawsuits and other legal hassles drastically. Unfortunately, you cannot eliminate them entirely, no matter what you do, no matter how careful you are, but at least you will be able to sleep well at night if you insure yourself adequately.

12
Decisions, Decisions

Solomon's decisions may have been more momentous, but they were certainly no more numerous than the landlord's. There's always some decision or other to be made, and there always seems to be so little time and help available when you have to make those decisions that you might as well be plucking daisy petals or flipping quarters to help you make up your mind about what to do.

I can only hope that the alternatives presented in this chapter will contribute something toward helping you make a few of those many decisions more knowledgeably, so you'll be able to improve your profitability and perhaps even begin to enjoy landlording a little. Landlording can be enjoyable, you know; really it can.

Should You Do It Yourself?

Do-it-yourself books never discuss whether you ought to consider hiring someone else to do "it" for you. Why should they? That's a subject beyond their province, and besides, they're too involved with explaining *how* you can do things yourself to discuss *whether* you ought to be doing them yourself at all. They assume that doing things yourself is more enjoyable and less expensive than hiring help, and such an assumption will generally prove correct for most do-it-yourselfers unless they botch a job so badly that they add to its complexity and have to pay that much more for professional help or unless they cut off an ear or crush a toe and have to pay big medical bills.

This do-it-yourself book is different, however, because landlording is different. In landlording it is often good business, for a variety of reasons, *not* to do everything yourself. You can even ask yourself a few questions when you are trying to make the decision. Here are some of those questions, some obvious and some not so obvious, which take into account the special nature of this business and may help you decide whether you

ought to do certain things yourself or hire them done for you.

■ **Are you able and knowledgeable enough to do it yourself?**—You know what expertise you have, and you know what you're capable of doing both physically and mentally. Can you do this job? It may necessitate climbing up the side of a two-story building on an extension ladder that sways in the wind. Are you afraid of heights? It may involve knowledge of the latest tax laws about depreciation. Have you been keeping abreast of the field? It may mean testing electrical connections with the power on. Do you know enough about electricity to avoid electrocuting yourself and shorting the circuits?

If you suspect that you can't do the work properly or at all by yourself, hire it done.

■ **Do you want to do it yourself?**—Some jobs, like cleaning ovens, painting bedrooms, mowing lawns, and unplugging toilets, are tedious or repetitious or mundane or loathsome, and you may have no desire to do them yourself even though you know that you are able to do them.

If you simply don't want to do them yourself, hire them done.

■ **Do you need some company while you do it yourself?**—You may be knowledgeable, ready, willing, and able to do certain work all by yourself, but if you tend to work rather slowly when you work alone, perhaps you should consider hiring someone else to work along with you. You may find yourself becoming more productive when there's a high school or college student working alongside you because you are trying to set a good work example and also trying to compete with the student's work pace.

If you suspect that you would work better and faster working alongside someone else, hire a helper.

■ **Do you have the time to do it yourself?**—Count 'em and you'll find that there are only 168 hours in a normal week. Abnormal weeks have 168 hours, too. Even though you may at times think that you're superhuman, you still cannot cram any more hours into your weeks, whether they're normal or not, and no matter how eager you are to do everything yourself, your body demands that you spend some of those 168 hours sleeping.

If you don't have the time to do a job, hire it done.

■ **Relative to the other landlording work you have to do, how much would this job cost if you were to hire it out?**—You can figure the relative cost of a job by the type of work involved. Plumbing generally costs more than painting, and painting costs more than housecleaning. If you have a kitchen gusher on a Sunday morning, don't call the plumber and pay his $60-per-half-hour minimum for weekend work. Fix it yourself, that is, unless you figure your own time is worth more.

Sometimes the work you do yourself and the work you hire done should be determined strictly on the basis of cost so long as you are able to do both and have the time to do one or the other. Painting, gardening, yard maintenance, and housecleaning are all relatively inexpensive to hire done, whereas work such as plumbing, electrical, and appliance repair are relatively expensive.

If you have a choice, do the expensive work yourself and hire the inexpensive work out.

■ **Do you have the money to pay for hired help?**—In the beginning of your landlording career you will have more time than money and you will have to do much more work yourself whether you want to or not.

If you don't have the money available to hire work done, do it yourself.

■ **Will you lose any additional rental income by doing certain work yourself?**—Some landlords refuse to hire any help at all because they think "it costs too much" or "you can't trust workers nowadays," or they come up with some other reason that suits their fancy. There are plenty.

That kind of attitude sometimes winds up costing them plenty because they haven't considered one very important factor–the rent penalty–which is the rent lost when a dwelling isn't ready to be occupied.

If preparing a vacated unit for renting will take you twenty-one days to do yourself in your spare time and the rent you may expect to get for the place is $900 per month or $30 a day, then your rent penalty for doing the work yourself is $630. If, on the other hand, you hire the work done for $480 (labor only) and it takes six days, your rent penalty is only $180. Adding the rent penalty to the labor costs in each case yields sums of $630 and $660, a difference of $30. In other words, you would be spending three weeks of your spare time, say, 48 hours approximately, and you would be earning all of $30 or 63¢ an hour for your efforts!

Why, that's below the minimum wage, way, way below! You'd better report yourself to your state's employment development department and go directly to jail! Do not pass GO! Do not collect a savings of $480!

You didn't save that much by doing the work yourself. Did you? You saved a mere $30, chump change for someone in the landlording business who must always be looking at the bigger picture.

The advantage of hiring help would vary somewhat, of course, if there were no immediate demand for your rental, if the rent were more or less than $900, if the work took more or less than 48 hours, or if your helpers demanded more or less than $10 per hour. Be that as it may, this example serves to illustrate just how shortsighted some landlords can be when they ignore the rent penalty and try to do everything themselves only to save themselves a few bucks. Little do they realize how few are the bucks which they're actually saving!

If your rent penalty approximates the cost of hiring help, then hire the help. That's using your head! That's working smart! That's looking at the bigger picture!

■ **Is the work tax-deductible?**—Every expense related to your landlording business is tax-deductible, naturally. If the labor for a landlording job will cost you $200, and you're in the 28% tax bracket, you might say that the job is really costing you the equivalent of $144 in taxable dollars.

Well, let's suppose now that you have two jobs to do, one involving exterior painting at your rental property and the other involving exterior painting at your own home. You have a $550 bid on the rental property paint job and a $450 bid for the paint job on your home, but you know you have enough time to complete only one. Which one should you do?

Do the one at home. Why should you? Even though it appears on the surface to cost $100 less, the paint job at home would actually cost you more if you were to hire it out because it's not tax-deductible. The home paint job would cost you $450 in pre-tax dollars and in after-tax dollars, while the rental property job, because it is tax-deductible, would cost you around $550 in pre-tax dollars but only $396 in after-tax dollars if you happened to be in the 28% bracket.

If you must choose between doing several jobs, then, be sure you calculate what their tax consequences are before you decide whether to do them yourself or hire them out.

■ **Is there anyone available to do the work?**— Sometimes you will have decided to hire help, but because it's Big Game Weekend, New Year's Eve, Mardi Gras week, or the first day of elk season, there's just no one available to work for you.

If there is indeed no one available, you'll just have to groan and moan, stall until someone is available, or do it yourself. What other alternative is there?

■ **Is much travel required?**—Those rental properties you own which are located at a distance from your home require a certain amount of time and expense to reach, and you should calculate approximately what both of them are.

If they are anywhere near the sums necessary to hire a job done and if you have no other good reason to visit the property, pick up the phone, hire it done, and save yourself the travel expense, the time, and the bother of doing it yourself.

■ **Are your personal relationships going to suffer if you do it yourself?**—A divorced landlord once told me that no marriage could survive more than ten rental properties, be they houses or apartment buildings. His number may or may not be accurate, I don't know, but he knew from firsthand experience that his own marriage couldn't survive the fourteen rental houses and two sixplexes he and his wife had accumulated. It couldn't survive because he was trying to do everything himself. Looking back on his own experience, he felt that ten would have been the magic number to keep his own marriage intact. Ten may be the correct number for some people, and it may be two or twenty-six for others. The number is relatively unimportant. What is important are the demands which you allow your rentals to place upon your time. Spending all your spare time and energy on your rental properties would strain any personal relationship to the breaking point and would probably strain you, too, even if you could draw your family into the business to help.

If you persist in accumulating rental properties, you must begin to hire help in order to preserve your personal relationships and your own sanity as well. Don't try to do it all yourself. You'll succeed only in becoming a lonely millionaire, sick at heart, and begrudging every alimony check you pay your former spouse.

Should You Hire a Property Management Company?

Country folk have a saying which goes, "Ain't no fertilizer like the farmer's footsteps." Landlording is no different from farming or any other business in the relationship of the owner to the farm or the business. Nobody can do the job of looking after your rental property that you can; absolutely nobody. You knew that already, didn't you? Sure. It's the truth.

When you start swearing at your tenants more than you feel you should, however, and you know that you want to hang onto your rental property because you're convinced that it's a sound investment, a good place to keep your money, you start thinking about hiring a property management company to relieve you of the headaches and get you to stop swearing so much. The ads for property management companies certainly do sound enticing. They promise to take care of everything for you and send you a check every month so that you needn't bother about a thing. That they can do.

In fact, property management companies are set up to handle management on three different levels.

At the most detached level, they can handle *asset management*, which involves fact-finding and decision-making about the acquiring, holding, and disposing of properties. It might be characterized as year-to-year management.

Then there's *off-site management*, which involves the hiring and supervision of on-site employees, contracting of work with independent contractors, purchase of larger items, checkwriting, bookkeeping, and the handling of evictions. It's pretty much month-to-month or week-to-week management.

Finally, there's *on-site management,* which involves showing vacancies, selecting tenants, purchase of smaller items, minor maintenance, tenant relations, collecting rents, and banking deposits. That's day-to-day management.

Institutional investors, such as insurance companies and real estate investment trusts, hire property managers for all three management levels, but most individual investors handle their own asset management because it involves consequential decisions which can make or break those whose assets are involved. It's the other two which individuals hire property management companies to take care of, the off-site and the on-site management.

The charge for off-site management generally ranges from a low of 3% to a high of 10% of the gross; 3% for the largest complexes on up to 10% for single-family dwellings. Of course, this doesn't include the on-site manager's wages. They're extra.

A charge of 5% for looking after a twelve-unit apartment building doesn't sound exorbitant, does it? It's not. That's just what I figure I'm earning when I do my own off-site management. Ah, but don't forget that no company is going to look after your property the way you would. That percentage of the gross may be all you're *paying* the property management company, but it may not be all that their service is *costing* you.

It'll cost you extra if they create problems which have to be remedied. It'll cost you extra if they don't shop around for good prices. It'll cost you extra if they receive kickbacks from certain service companies and suppliers. It'll cost you extra if they hire on-site managers who discriminate illegally. It'll cost you extra if they write

checks for supplies and then get refunds in cash. It'll cost you extra if they collect rent for units which they're reporting as vacant.

Temptations abound for property management companies to siphon off funds. Situations abound for them to make blunders. I suppose you have to expect certain "inefficiencies" whenever you hire help and especially when you are at some distance from their work. People are people, and business is business.

Do you really think that a property management company could relieve you of your landlording worries? The truth is that some of them can. Some of them are indeed forthright and honest, but you must be careful in picking a property management company, just as careful as you would be in picking a surgeon for your heart transplant. Select one recommended to you by more than one satisfied client who stands to gain nothing from the endorsement. Select one that is sworn by rather than sworn at.

After all this, the question still remains—Should you hire a property management company? Yes, you should if you are too disinterested, too busy, too wealthy, too distant, too exasperated, too decrepit, or too haughty to look after your rental property yourself.

As for me, the answer is no. I shouldn't hire a property management company, and I won't, no matter where I'm investing, no matter how much I'm worth. I want control. I want to be able to hire an on-site manager I can trust instead of having another layer of management between myself and the property. I want the on-site manager to know me and be responsible to me. I want to have my bookkeeper handling the receipts and disbursements and the accounting reports. I want to see the bids for painting the outside of the building and for trimming the 29 palms. I want to have my finger on the property's pulse. I want to know what's going on. I want to be making the important decisions. All of this is important to me. It's important to my investment.

Yes, off-site management does require some of my time, but that's really minimal and unimportant. What is important is freedom. Off-site management doesn't tie me down to a place or a time. I still have my freedom.

The real time demands in property management are on the site. Hiring somebody to handle on-site management makes good sense under most circumstances.

Off-site management is different. I feel that being my own off-site manager yields the greatest return for the time involved than anything else I might do in managing my rental properties.

Why not be your own property management company for your own properties? Plant your footsteps around them and watch everything grow and grow and grow!

Should You Own up to Being the Owner?

Shortly after I purchased my first fourplex, a friend mentioned in casual conversation that he knew a landlord who would never ever admit to his tenants that he was, in fact, the owner. He would call himself the manager but never, never the owner. To someone who had just become a landlord, such a posture was inconceivable. I was proud of my units and denying ownership would have been tantamount to denying paternity of a firstborn child. Not only did I feel that I couldn't do it, I couldn't really see the point of the ruse unless, perhaps, one owned tenements and didn't want to be bothered with all the attendant problems.

Years later, I came to understand the value of this polite fiction, this "buck-stops-there" approach to management, and I have come to use it with some properties successfully myself.

Invariably something will come up that a tenant wants to do which you know you don't like, but you're on the spot, and you can't think of a good reason for refusing the request outright. Tomorrow you will think of a good reason in hindsight, no doubt, and you'll kick yourself for not having thought of it sooner, but then it will be too late to do anything about it. If you are known as the "manager" or as one of the "part-

ners," though, you merely say that you will have to consult with the owner or your partner. Then you will have the time necessary to think up a good excuse, or, if you wish, you can simply refuse the request after having consulted the "owner" and not offer any excuse at all for the refusal. When asked for details, you simply say you're awfully sorry but there's nothing you can do about the matter. You tried, but your partner couldn't be budged.

Calling yourself the manager can even work when you, the owner, live on the premises and look after everything there yourself. You are the "manager," aren't you? That's no lie.

Should You Rent It Furnished?

There is extra money to be made in renting furnished dwellings, no doubt about it, but it requires extra effort and investment, and sometimes it brings extra grief. Actually it adds yet another "business," furniture rental, to the one you're already in, so it should be thought of as a sideline which has certain advantages and disadvantages all its own.

Consider these advantages and disadvantages of renting furnished dwellings—

Advantages
• More income
• Lower vacancy factor
• Increased depreciation available for tax purposes
• Less redecoration required when people move (furnished dwellings, when vacant, still look lived in and distract the eye from the walls)
• Less wear and tear on the property caused by tenants' careless moving of their own heavy furniture and appliances

Disadvantages
• Greater investment required
• More tenant turnover
• Muscles needed for moving furniture about
• More repairs
• More maintenance (excluding redecorating)
• Increased risk of damage
• Greater theft potential
• Storage area required for surplus furniture
• Added recordkeeping and bookkeeping
• Purchasing time needed (you have to select the furniture)
• Obsolescence (furniture goes out of style)

Seemingly, the disadvantages of renting fur-

Roommate Agreement Dated June 16, xxxx

(Addendum to Rental Agreement)

    This Agreement amends, is incorporated into, and forms a part of
the Rental Agreement dated 11/30/XX between Margaret Judge,
Owners, and Phylis Browne, Tenants.

    Tenants, also known here as "Roommates," desire to rent the
premises on a "roommates arrangement." Owners agree to this
arrangement under the following terms and conditions:

ROOMMATE APPROVAL AND SUBSTITUTION--Every person who wishes to
become a Roommate under this Agreement, whether as an original
Roommate or as a substituted Roommate, must first submit a Rental
Application and be approved by Owners in writing. Owners, at
their option, may require substituted Roommates to sign the
existing Rental Agreement or may require an entirely new agreement
to be signed by the substituted Roommates and the remaining
Roommates. Upon substitution of Roommates, Owners may elect to
increase the deposit.

FINANCIAL RESPONSIBILITY--Each Roommate agrees to be jointly and
severally liable to the Owners for the entire rent and the entire
amount of any other charges incurred under the Rental Agreement.

DEPOSITS--Roommates agree to pay deposits to Owners in the form of
a single certified check or money order. Owners will hold all
deposits until the entire dwelling has been vacated completely.
Owners may make deposit refunds in the form of a single check made
payable jointly to all Roommates with rights to the deposits.
This check and the itemized accounting of deposit deductions may
be sent to any one of the Roommates with rights to the deposits.

DEPARTING ROOMMATES--Roommates who move out while this Agreement
is in effect continue to have financial responsibility under this
Agreement unless Owners release them from this responsibility in
writing or unless they are replaced by substituted Roommates
approved by Owners. Upon being relieved of financial liability,
departing Roommates relinquish all rights to the deposits.

MAXIMUM NUMBER OF ROOMMATES ALLOWED--Without the prior written
approval of Owners, Roommates may at no time exceed 4 in
number.

GUESTS--Tenants may house any single guest for a maximum period of
fourteen days every six months or for whatever other period of
time the law allows. Guests may at no time exceed 2 in number.

COMMUNICATIONS--Whenever Owners give a notice to one Roommate, it
shall be considered as having been communicated to all Roommates.
Whenever one Roommate gives a notice to the Owners, it shall be
considered as having been communicated from all Roommates.

Owner Margaret Judge   Roommate Lucille Melander

By Phylis Browne   Roommate Ellen Nott

                                        Roommate Sylvie Broenke

Page 3 of 3

nished dwellings outweigh the advantages. They certainly outnumber the advantages. What's more important, though, in this comparison is whether you would be adequately compensated for assuming the burden of all the disadvantages, and that comes down to numbers. If the added furnishings can produce, say, a 100% return on the investment over a twelve-month period without becoming trashed during that time, then renting furnished dwellings might actually be an attractive proposition. It can be done, you know. Such a return can even be surpassed.

One landlord friend of mine has found that renting one-bedroom apartments furnished with his own sturdy homemade furniture yields him a 100% return in six months on the furniture and more than compensates him for the extra effort and investment. His turnover is slightly higher, but his vacancy factor is nil, and his cash flow is phenomenal. Renting furnished apartments has paid off handsomely for him.

If you are fully cognizant of both the advantages and disadvantages of renting furnished dwellings and if your own rentals lend themselves to being rented furnished, such as those catering to singles, armed services personnel, students, business people on assignment, or vacationers, you might try furnishing one rental as an experiment before you furnish them all. See for yourself if you like the furniture rental business and see if you can make any money at it. Then either sweep through Furniture Depot on a buying spree, or call the Salvation Army and have them haul the stuff away.

If you'd rather not experiment at all, recommend to those people who come to you to rent furnished dwellings that they contact a furniture rental company (listed in the Yellow Pages under "Furniture Renting & Leasing") and rent their furniture separately from those who specialize in that business. The big advantage to them in renting the furniture separately is choice. They get to be their own decorators and choose the furniture they want to live with, instead of subjecting themselves to someone else's taste and choices.

If you happen to acquire a building which has unattractive, out-of-date, or abused furniture, and it obviously isn't adding enough income to compensate you for the trouble of looking after it, get rid of it. Don't let the frustrations of handling a furniture rental business interfere with your more important activities as a landlord.

Unless the furniture is "Antiques Roadshow material," offer to sell it to your tenants at attractive prices. If they don't want it at any price, give it to a charitable organization and take its agreed-upon value as a deduction on your income tax return.

Should You Rent to Roommates?

Nowadays you can hardly avoid renting to roommates. More and more unrelated groups of people are living together in a single household than ever before. There's no good reason why you shouldn't rent to them. In fact, you have to rent to them so long as they meet your legitimate tenant selection standards.

Because roommate living arrangements present special problems for the landlord, you need to know what the problem areas are and you need to take measures in advance to deal with them.

Basically, the problem areas all pertain to the loose nature of the roommates' relationship. When they're first looking around for a place to live, they think that they're going to get along well and live together for a long, long time, but when one of them hogs the bathroom every morning and leaves dirty dishes in the kitchen sink every night, the other roommate has second thoughts about the living arrangement and moves out. The landlord is left with an inconsiderate slob who doesn't have enough income to pay the entire rent himself and a departing tenant who wants his share of the deposit back. To afford the rent, the slob finds another slob to move in with him, and soon thereafter the second slob loses his job and can't come up with his share of the rent money. The soap opera goes on and on with the landlord becoming more and more frustrated as the situation deteriorates.

You can't avoid all of the frustrations of renting to roommates by using my Roommate Agreement, but it sure helps because it addresses the seven primary problem areas—roommate approval and substitution, financial responsibility, ownership and disbursement of deposits, departing roommates, number of roommates, guests, and communications.

More than likely, these are concerns which roommates never think about before they decide to room together. Just like newlyweds, they assume that the living arrangement will work out satisfactorily. If it doesn't, they'll merely come to some mutually satisfactory agreement to deal with problems as they arise. You know that some problems will inevitably arise, and you know that the roommates are going to expect you as their landlord to sort them out. You can sort them out much more readily if you begin the relationship with a written agreement. Look at the agreement yourself to see how it addresses common problems to the benefit of everybody involved.

One thing the agreement does for your benefit as a landlord is exercise control over everyone who is allowed to move in, both original roommates and substituted roommates. You don't want to wind up housing human trash whose names you don't even know after all of the original roommates have moved out. Evicting no-names can prove to be complicated, frustrating, expensive, time-consuming, and sometimes even ugly.

Incidentally, whenever you do approve a roommate substitution, you should amend the old rental agreement. Delete the old roommate from the agreement and add the substituted roommate. The wording could be something like this: "AMENDMENT TO RENTAL AGREEMENT originally dated xx between xx and xx. As of xx date, Sam Spade is replacing John Doe in this agreement and is assuming the latter's residency rights and responsibilities. Further, John Doe is relinquishing all rights to the deposits, is no longer financially responsible for any rents or charges incurred under this agreement, and is not residing in this dwelling." This clearly worded amendment should be signed and dated by all of the roommates and by you.

Clear words in your Roommate Agreement will help the roommates understand exactly how their relationship with you is supposed to work. Basically, the agreement says that when you deal with their deposits, rent monies, and communications, you want to deal with them as a group, not as individuals, but when they fail to live up to their financial responsibilities, you will hold them "jointly and severally liable." This legal phrase makes each of them liable for the entire amount owed by the group, and it keeps you from been dragged into their money squabbles.

All told, the Roommate Agreement makes roommates more like a unitary family to the landlord. They can still move out one by one, of course, but you have that situation covered completely. You needn't worry if one of them should leave in a hurry without finding a replacement. You won't have to make any special rent or deposit adjustments. They will have to work out those details themselves without your involvement. That's their responsibility to one another.

Review the Roommate Agreement with all of the roommates before they move in. They need to know their responsibilities as soon as they assume those responsibilities.

Should You Allow Your Tenants to Sleep on Water?

We landlords tend to be pretty protective of our property. We resist anybody and anything that might pose a threat. We don't want pets. We don't want teenagers. We don't want motorcyclists. We don't want attorneys. We don't want welfare recipients. We don't want students. We don't want musicians. And we certainly don't want waterbeds. We seem ornery, suspicious, misanthropic, negative.

Yet, we become that way honestly. We start out as innocents determined to be trusting and determined to be unlike any grouchy, greedy landlord we ever knew. Then we have experiences. We learn slowly, incredulously, but we learn. After we have cleaned up the filth and repaired the damage left behind by more than one unscrupulous tenant who has vacated owing us rent, we become less trusting of people and more protective of our property. We tend to regard people and things guilty until proven innocent.

So when waterbeds first swept into faddish favor in the late '60s, we landlords considered the perils of allowing one-ton water balloons to lie on the floors of our bedrooms, and we acted quickly to protect our interests. We banned them.

Inevitably, some tenants sneaked them in, and just as inevitably our worst fears were realized. Those early waterbeds stained our carpets and buckled our hardwood floors, necessitating expensive repairs. We swore never to allow them, and we wrote into our rental agreements carefully worded clauses to cover future developments, too. We prohibited all liquid-filled furniture, not just waterbeds.

But waterbeds are no longer a fad. They are here to stay, for there are some people who find them essential to a good night's sleep. Nor are waterbeds any longer the flimsy water bags they once were. They have become thick (20-mil; the toughest trash bags are only 5-mil) water containers adequately safeguarded against accidental spillage, so that today a properly designed and installed waterbed is perfectly safe for use in most rental dwellings.

They are so safe and acceptable that California landlords didn't even protest a law promoted by the waterbed industry to govern the acceptance of waterbeds in rentals throughout the state. This law applies only to buildings built since 1973, and it contains certain reasonable safeguards—the tenant must provide liability insurance, must have a quality waterbed which will put no undue strain on the building, and must install it according to accepted standards. The landlord may, in turn, increase the security deposit no more than the equivalent of half a month's rent. Sounds good to me!

In the absence of any law, what's a landlord to do? Strike that "no liquid-filled furniture" clause from the contract and let the waterbeds pour in? Absolutely not!

Waterbeds are still capable of damaging your building. Flimsy waterbeds and waterbeds without frames or liners are still around, and they could cause you the same grief today that they caused people years ago.

What should you do? Above all, be protective. Either continue banning all liquid-filled furniture from your rentals (remember that you may or may not be within your rights in doing so), or adopt a well-considered policy which will enable you to rent to tenants with waterbeds at minimum risk.

Communicate this decision, to ban waterbeds or to accept them on well-defined terms, clearly to both prospective tenants and existing tenants. Begin when you first qualify prospective tenants by determining whether they intend to have a waterbed or not. Make no assumptions about

what they will be sleeping on. Bring the matter out into the open for frank discussion, and you will virtually eliminate unauthorized waterbeds that tenants try to sneak in, beds which expose you to damages you're not protected against.

Before you ever adopt a policy to admit waterbeds, if you choose to, you should determine whether your building can indeed support their weight structurally. Residential buildings built to current construction standards will withstand around 60 pounds per square foot on suspended floors and can safely support most any waterbed. Poured concrete floors, of course, pose no problem at all. If you have any doubts, first pay a visit to a local waterbed dealer (look in the Yellow Pages under "Waterbeds-Dealers") and ask there for information about waterbed floor loading. They should be helpful and have some printed information to give you. Second, check with your local building department about the floor loading limits for your building. Third, if you still have reservations, hire a structural engineering firm (look in the Yellow Pages under "Engineers-Structural") to determine the weight per square foot which your building can safely support. Compare that with the weight per square foot of each waterbed in question, and you will be able to tell whether your building can take the weight.

Waterbeds vary in total weight, from around 360 pounds for a twin-sized hybrid (urethane/water combination) bed to about 2,500 pounds for the large, round, all-water variety. You can estimate the total weight of any waterbed yourself by making some simple calculations. Multiply the water capacity in gallons by 8.33 pounds and then add 4% for the miscellaneous waterbed parts if it's an all-water type or 20% if it's a hy-

Waterbed Agreement   Dated Jan. 15, XXXX

(Addendum to Rental Agreement)

   This agreement is attached to and forms a part of the Rental
Agreement dated January 15, XXXX between Lester Landlord ,
Owners, and Richard Harvey and Rose L. Renter, Tenants.
   Tenants desire to keep a waterbed described as queen size
   combination foam and water   in the
dwelling they occupy under the Rental Agreement referred to above, and
because this agreement specifically prohibits keeping waterbeds without
the Owners' permission, Tenants agree to the following terms and
conditions in exchange for this permission:

1) Tenants agree to keep one waterbed approved by Owners for this
   dwelling. Waterbed shall consist of a mattress at least 20 mil
   thick with lap seams, a safety liner at least 8 mil, and a sturdy
   frame enclosure made of plywood or solid natural wood only, no
   particle board.

2) Tenants agree to consult with the Owners about the location of the
   waterbed. They agree to hire qualified professionals to install and
   dismantle the bed according to the manufacturer's specifications
   and further agree not to relocate it without the Owners' consent.

3) Tenants agree to allow Owners to inspect the waterbed installation
   at any and all reasonable times, and Tenants agree to remedy any
   problems or potential problems immediately.

4) Tenants agree to furnish Owners with a copy of a valid liability
   insurance policy for at least $100,000 covering this waterbed
   installation and agree to renew the policy as necessary for
   continuous coverage.

5) Tenants agree to pay immediately for any damage caused by their
   waterbed, and in addition, they will add $ 50 to their
   security/cleaning deposit, any of which may be used for cleaning,
   repairs, or delinquent rent when Tenants vacate. This added
   deposit, or what remains of it when waterbed damages have been
   assessed, will be returned to Tenants within SEVEN days after
   they prove that they no longer keep this waterbed.

6) In consideration of the additional time, effort, costs, and risks
   involved in this waterbed installation, Tenants agree to pay   RH
   additional rent of $ 3.50 , which /includes/does not include RR
   the premium for the waterbed liability insurance policy referred to
   in item 4.

7) Tenants agree that the Owners reserve the right to revoke this
   permission to keep a waterbed should the Tenants break this
   agreement.

Owner Lester Landlord   Tenant Richard Renter

By _____   Tenant Rose Renter

Page 2 of 2

brid.

More important than total weight, though, is floor loading or weight per square foot, for these are the figures which structural engineers use to determine the stress the waterbed puts on the floor. Again, you can estimate the weight per square foot quite accurately yourself. Simply divide the total weight of the bed by the square footage of its base (unless the bed rests on a pedestal base which is smaller than the surface, the base and the surface dimensions will be the same).

Let's take, as an example, the most common size waterbed, the queen size (60"x80"), and we'll figure its weight per square foot. The all-water type (9" fill) has a water capacity of 196 gallons; the hybrid, 72 gallons. 196 gallons times 8.33 pounds per gallon plus 4% equals 1,698 pounds total weight for the all-water queen-size waterbed. 72 gallons times 8.33 pounds per gallon plus 20% equals 720 pounds, total weight for the queen-size hybrid. To find the pounds per square foot for a queen-size waterbed, assuming that the base and surface dimensions are the same, multiply the length (80") times the width (60") and divide by the number of square inches in one square foot (144). That's 80"x60" or 4,800 square inches; divided by 144, it's 35 square feet. Next, divide the weight, 1,698 pounds, by 35 and you get 48.5 pounds, which is the weight per square foot of an all-water queen-size waterbed. Divide 720 pounds by 35 and you get 20.5 pounds, which is the weight per square foot of a hybrid queen-size waterbed. That wasn't hard, was it? You can do the same for any size waterbed.

Once the weight question is answered to your satisfaction and you know the floor loading limits for your building, you may want to consider renting to tenants who sleep on water. If so, take these seven items into consideration for each individual waterbed— specifications, components, installation, inspection, insurance, deposit, and agreement.

■ **Specifications**—Waterbeds differ considerably. Learn the size, weight, and type of each waterbed your tenants wish to have. Using these specifications, calculate whether each bed falls within the floor loading limits for your building. Reject those which might seem perilous to you, and suggest that the tenants consider lighter beds.

■ **Components**—The minimum allowable com-

ponents, as far as you are concerned, should be a mattress at least 20 mil thick with lap seams (preferably less than three years old so it has more flex-fatigue resistance), a safety liner at least 8 mil, and a sturdy frame. If made of wood, the frame should be at least 2"x10", the deck should be at least 1/2" thick, and neither the deck nor the pedestal should have any particleboard components (plywood or solid natural wood only).

■ **Installation**—To prevent floods and minor catastrophes when they are most likely to occur, insist that professional installers (every waterbed store has its own service department) do the installation, and insist that you be present to supervise the eventual dismantling. If, for some reason, professional help is unavailable and you feel confident enough in your own abilities, help the tenant yourself by overseeing the installation while you consult the manufacturer's printed instructions. Proper installation will validate the insurance policy and give you peace of mind.

■ **Inspection**—Make your first inspection just after the waterbed has been installed. Check its location, which should be along a load-bearing wall and away from intense heat sources. Check its problem potential, which should include feeling the frame for protrusions which might puncture the mattress. Check for water spillage from the installation, and direct the tenant to clean up any water immediately. After that, you might wish to check the waterbed periodically, say, every six months or so, for possible damage and signs of potential damage.

■ **Insurance**—Responding to popular demand, a number of insurance companies now write waterbed liability insurance designed specifically for tenants, and they make it available through agents and waterbed stores. The annual premium is minimal (around $35) for a policy with a $25 deductible clause and a liability limit of $100,000. Require your tenant to secure such a policy. It covers damage to the building and to the property of other tenants, but it specifically excludes fire damage; damage to buildings which do not conform to governing building codes; and damage resulting from failure to follow the manufacturer's specifications for assembling, installing, filling, emptying, locating, and maintaining the waterbed. Because these policies expire after twelve months, make certain that the tenant renews for continuous coverage.

■ **Deposit**—Require at least an extra $25 deposit from the waterbed tenant to cover the deductible should the insurance policy have to cover damages. Add this deposit to the total security/cleaning deposit so it need not be restricted in use to waterbed damages alone. That way it's available to be used for any kind of damage, for cleaning, or for rent.

■ **Agreement**—Cross out and initial the liquid-filled furniture exclusion, if any, in the rental agreement you use, and add to the agreement the terms under which you are allowing the waterbed. These terms could be included in the remarks section of the agreement; they could be written or typed on the back of the agreement and signed by all parties concerned; or they could be written as a separate agreement and referenced to the main rental agreement. Written succinctly into the remarks section, the wording might be as follows: "Tenants have one waterbed approved by Owners for this dwelling. Waterbed shall consist of mattress, liner, and frame; shall be kept insured for liability of $100,000; and shall be installed according to manufacturer's specifications."

This entire waterbed-acceptance procedure involves additional time, effort, costs, and risks which other tenants should not have to subsidize. Therefore, consider adding a nominal sum to the waterbed tenant's rent to compensate you for all this, and consider including in the sum enough to pay the premium yourself on the tenant's waterbed liability policy so you are certain the policy is kept current.

Waterbeds may not be what you want in your building, but if you do, and if you follow these guidelines, you will be able to rest well at night yourself no matter what you sleep on.

Should You Allow Pets?

Just as there is no federal law yet compelling you to rent to tenants with waterbeds, there's none compelling you to rent to tenants with pets, guide and signal dogs excepted, and you might be wise to exclude both waterbeds and pets from your rental property. It's your prerogative, your right, to come up with your own policy here, but in adopting a dogmatic, hidebound policy, you are excluding not just waterbeds and pets but also all of the people who go along with them, some of whom make very good tenants. By excluding pets, in fact, you are halving the number of people who can qualify to rent from you, for more than half of all American households have some kind of pet. By excluding pets, you are making the task of finding good tenants that much more difficult because you have fewer people to choose from.

If finding good tenants without accepting pets is easy for you, then continue excluding pets altogether because pets undeniably do pose problems, but if you are having problems finding good tenants and if you have a building which is suitable for pets (buildings suitable for dogs and cats are those with yards or patios and with little or no wall-to-wall carpeting), consider accepting good tenants who have good pets.

According to one university study, pet owners as a group are supposed to be friendlier, richer, smarter, and more attractive than those who have no pets. Surprised? I was, too. Yet, when we think about pet owners as renters, we tend to think first about the stereotype of the inconsiderate pet owner who's never heard of pooper scoopers and doesn't believe in leashes. That's the same as people thinking first about unscrupulous landlords whenever they think about landlords. You're an example of a scrupulous landlord, aren't you? Well, there are lots of examples of scrupulous pet owners, too.

Scrupulous pet-owning tenants save you money because they tend to be more permanent residents, and they make you money because they will pay higher rent for their accommodations than will tenants without pets. My own experience with an admittedly small sample has shown that tenants with pets stay on average twice as long as those without pets and they will pay $10 to $35 more per month for a place to live where they can keep their pets. They realize that finding another place which accepts them and their pets is difficult at best and is sometimes altogether impossible, so once they move in, they tend to stay a long time and they will pay more in rent while they stay there.

Whereas some landlords think that pets never add to the value of a rental dwelling, they're thinking with blinders on. They're thinking strictly about the pets of inconsiderate owners and about the additional management and maintenance problems such pets cause. That's one way to look at the situation. There is another way. Since pet owners will pay more rent and since higher rents translate into higher property values, pets can

---

PET POLICY

No pets of any kind may be harbored on the premises, even temporarily, no matter what they are and no matter who owns them.

No stray animals may be fed or kept on the premises.

If you should notice any pet or stray animal on the premises, please report the sighting and its particulars to management immediately.

PET POLICY

Subject to approval, tenants may have pets in any ONE of the following categories:
1. Caged birds (maximum of two)
2. Fish (as many as can survive happily in a fifty-five gallon acquarium)
3. House cats (one, spayed or neutered, at least three months old
4. Dogs (one, spayed or neutered, at least nine months old; no pugnacious breeds)
5. Other animals (permitted only on a case-by-case basis)

Tenants shall bring all prospective pets to management for approval beforehand.

Tenants shall have a Pet Agreement covering the keeping of their pet.

Tenants shall neither feed nor keep any stray animals on the premises.

---

actually increase the value of a building. Have you ever thought about that? Twenty dollars more per month for each unit in a sixplex adds up to additional income of $1,440 per year and equals an added property value of $10,080 at only seven times the gross income. That ain't pet feed!

If you do decide to rent to pet owners, set the rent high, advertise that you accept pets, and you'll be so inundated with applicants that you'll wonder why you hadn't thought about accepting pets before.

Here's a caution. Some landlords require their pet owning tenants to pay a flat surcharge upfront. Don't follow this practice. Surcharges lead pet owners to believe that damages caused by their pets, whatever they may be, are already paid for, so the pet owners tend to be more irresponsible in cleaning up the messes. Charge higher rents and higher deposits instead (higher deposits should not exceed the legal limits for all the deposits which are set for your area, and they should not be designated as "pet deposits" because any deposit so designated must be used only for pet damages; they may not be applied to rent, cleaning, or breakage unrelated to the pet; designate them as deposits, plain and simple).

Whether you choose to rent to people with pets or not, you must have a pet policy. Actually you have one already whether you realize it or not, but you may not have formalized it in writ-ing. You may have been telling your tenants all along that you do not accept any pets, and they may be interpreting that to mean no fish, fowl, mammals, insects, or reptiles. Then again they may interpret it to mean that certain fish, fowl, and insects are acceptable, but not mammals or reptiles. Just what do you mean by "no pets" anyway? Would you allow someone to have a twenty-gallon aquarium or three parakeets in one cage? They're all pets. Would they violate your policy?

Spell out what you mean when you say "no pets" or "pets OK" by putting your policy in writing and making it fair to your tenants, their pets, the neighbors, and yourself. Specify in your policy the type, age, number, and reproductive capability (if appropriate) of the pets you will accept or not accept and outline these specifications clearly. Don't bother with size or weight limitations. They don't seem to be relevant to whether a certain pet will be a nuisance around the property. The age of a pet is far more important. Older pets are less likely to cause trouble.

Take a look at the two pet policies above.

You may wish to include in your list of acceptable pets only caged birds or only house cats, or you may wish to exclude every conceivable animal, no matter what it is. That's your decision to make. You have great flexibility in determining your policy and you have some flexibility in ap-

Your Pet and You

Please provide us with a photograph of your pet, plus some specifics about your pet and you. This information will help us make an informed decision when we are considering your pet and you as tenants for our rental dwelling.

Your name Suzanne Tenant   Date 3/26/xxxx

Description...pet's name, breed, age, weight, size (give height and length), activity level, and traits

Jessie, Doberman, 11 years, 77 pounds, 26" high × 38" long; child friendly; non-cat chasing; alert; quiet; gentle

Training...obedience school or other training (give dates, too)

Weiss Dog Obedience School — Certificate of Successful Completion, June - October xxxx

Activities...exercise (give type and frequency)

Walks three times a week, daily play, constant attention

Health...spayed or neutered; vaccinations; health exams (give schedule); veterinarian (give name and phone number)

Spayed female with all vaccinations; annual vet exams and vet visits as needed. Veterinarian, Charles Aldrich, 555-1111

Grooming...schedule of grooming; groomer (give name and phone number)

Monthly shampoo and monthly medication for flea prevention at the Petall Dog Laundry, 555-9999

Care arrangements...caretaker during absences (give name and phone number)

1-3 days absence — Norma Constantin, 555-6666; more than 3 days absence - Bates Pet Motel, Norman Bates, 555-6789

Commitment...duration of relationship with this pet; pet license particulars; membership in animal protection organizations such as the S.P.C.A. (Society for the Prevention of Cruelty to Animals); willingness to put up an additional deposit

Jessie has been part of our family for more than ten years; annual dog license; lifetime SPCA members; willing to put up a pet deposit

References...people who know your pet and you (give names and phone numbers)

Daniel McGowan (neighbor), 555-9768

Gracie Colton (friend), 555-4321

plying it, but you should be astute enough to recognize that whatever pet policy you adopt will have to apply equally to everyone in a building or at least to everyone in a very distinctly designated area. You cannot extend a privilege to some tenants and not to others. They won't stand for it. I know.

As a consequence of acquiring a fourteen-unit complex some time ago, I happened to inherit a situation involving an elderly lady who had been allowed by the previous owner to have a small house dog. It was her constant companion, her security system, her confidant, and her first love. I was averse to giving her the choice of dog or dwelling since that dog meant so much to her and since she had already lived there for fifteen years. I let her keep the dog.

Still, I was adamant about not allowing anyone else to keep a dog there because the building was being improved with new carpeting and other amenities which the wrong dog could easily lay waste.

Three of the thirteen other tenants who lived there defied me by getting their own dogs. When confronted with my no-pets policy, which I had already discussed with them, all three referred to the little old lady's dog. "If she can have one, why can't we?" they asked almost in unison. Indeed, why couldn't they?

The crucial difference between them and the little old lady as far as I was concerned was that she had the dog long before I assumed ownership and before I instituted the no-pets policy. Her dog was "grandmothered" in. The other tenants couldn't have cared less how I rationalized the situation. As far as they were concerned, there was no difference whatsoever between her and them. If she were allowed a dog, then they should be as well. One of those tenants had to be evicted over this matter. The other two finally relented and gave their pets away, but they struggled hard. So did I. I had to.

By the way, if tenants ever do break your rental contract by acquiring a pet which you distinctly prohibit, you should confront them about the matter immediately and give them no more than three days to get rid of it. If you give them any more time, they will only dillydally in getting rid of the pet and become attached to it in the process, and you'll wind up having to evict them in the end. If you fail to approach them at all when you first learn about their pet, you have in effect given them your tacit approval, and you'd better be prepared to fend off your other tenants. They'll want one, too. This is another one of those little landlording problems which only become more difficult to deal with if you procrastinate in handling them.

Because you never know quite how tenants will react when you approach them about a forbidden pet, consider how one savvy landlady handled tenants who claimed that they were merely sheltering a pit bull which had showed up on their porch. She bought "Bubba" for $10 and got them to agree that they wouldn't get another dog. Then she took the little bruiser off to the pound.

It worked once. It could work again. It's worth a try.

Oh, and if you have reason to suspect that a tenant might have acquired a dog on the Q.T., you can find out for sure without getting a search warrant and conducting a midnight hunt. All you need is a silent dog whistle which you can buy at a pet store. Blow it outside the tenant's dwelling, and listen for dog sounds from inside. Even docile lap dogs will respond by whining or barking.

Having a pet policy which you can enforce when necessary is one thing, but finding good pet owners with good pets is another. It's a process requiring circumspection and deliberation. You will want to determine whether the owners you interview are devoted enough to their pets to care for them faithfully and whether the pets are of a type and temperament to cause you and your other tenants no grief.

Use the form, "Your Pet and You," on the opposite page to help you make this determination. It enables the pet owning tenant to create a "pet résumé" of sorts, covering most of the specifics about the pet and the pet owner's commitment to it.

You want to separate the casual or accidental pet owner from the committed, the dedicated pet owner. This form will help you with that task.

Another way to find good pet owners with good pets is to ask questions such as "Will you rent this place if we do not allow you to keep your pet?" and "Who will be taking care of your pet in your absence?" and "Will you pay a larger refundable security/cleaning deposit of $100?" and "Can you live by our pet agreement which says the following...?" and "Who's your veteri-

Pet Agreement

Dated APRIL 6, XXXX

(Addendum to Rental Agreement)

This agreement is attached to and forms a part of the Rental Agreement dated 1/14/XX between LESLIE LANDLADY, Owners, and DORTHY MAE MAHONEY, Tenants.

Tenants desire to keep a pet named "FANG." and described as LHASA APSO in the dwelling they occupy under the Rental Agreement referred to above, and because this Agreement specifically prohibits keeping pets without the Owners' permission, Tenants agree to the following terms and conditions in exchange for this permission:

1) Tenants agree to keep their pet under control at all times.
2) Tenants agree to keep their pet restrained, but not tethered, when it is outside their dwelling.
3) Tenants agree to adhere to local ordinances, including leash and licensing requirements.
4) Tenants agree not to leave their pet unattended for any unreasonable periods.
5) Tenants agree to clean up after their pet and to dispose of their pet's waste properly and quickly.
6) Tenants agree not to leave food or water for their pet or any other animal outside their dwelling where it will attract other animals.
7) Tenants agree to keep their pet from being unnecessarily noisy or aggressive and causing any annoyance or discomfort to others and will remedy immediately any complaints made through the Owners or Manager.
8) Tenants agree to provide their pet with regular health care, to include innoculations as recommended.
9) Tenants agree to provide their pet with an identification tag.
10) Tenants agree to get rid of their pet's offspring within eight weeks of birth.
11) Tenants agree to pay immediately for any damage, loss, or expense caused by their pet, and in addition, they will add $ 100 to their security/cleaning deposit, any of which may be used for cleaning, repairs, or delinquent rent when Tenants vacate. This added deposit, or what remains of it when pet damages have been assessed, will be returned to Tenants within SEVEN days after they have proved that they no longer keep this pet.
12) Tenants agree that this Agreement applies only to the specific pet described above and that no other pet may be substituted.
13) Tenants agree to furnish Owners with a picture of their pet.
14) Tenants agree that Owners reserve the right to revoke permission to keep the pet should Tenants break this Agreement.

Owner *Leslie Landlady*   Tenant *Dorthy Mae Mahoney*

By _____   Tenant _____

Page 4 of 4

narian?" and "Is your pet properly licensed?" Their answers to these questions will indicate quite clearly how important their pet is to them and how faithfully they will care for it after they move in.

The pet itself, which you ought to meet at some point before you agree to accept it, should fall within your pet policy guidelines and should be reasonably friendly, healthy, and well-behaved.

If your screening of the owners and their pet raises any doubts in your mind about their ability and willingness to respect your property, refuse to rent to them. You have every right to be discriminating in this matter, and furthermore, you should be discriminating.

Refusing applicants who have unacceptable pets or are themselves unacceptable is pretty straightforward. Refusing existing tenants who have no pet and want one is much the same, especially when you suspect that they might prove to be indifferent toward the pet they choose. The only way to determine their attitude is to impose upon them the same set of conditions which you impose upon newcomers with pets. Caution your tenants that you will allow them to have a pet only if they discuss the matter with you in advance and only if you approve.

When they approach you, review your pet policy with them first to make certain that they understand what kinds of pets you allow. Then go over the entire Pet Agreement item by item. Tell them that you treat all pet owners alike and that all of those tenants who now have pets have submitted their pets to you for approval, signed pet agreements, and increased their security/cleaning deposits. So long as your existing tenants will do likewise, they will be allowed to have a pet, too. Emphasize that your refusal of any particular pet has nothing to do with their own tenancy but that keeping an unauthorized pet will certainly result in an eviction of both the tenants and the pet.

All of your tenants should understand that they have no right to have a pet on the premises unless you grant them the privilege under well-defined conditions. If they should fail to live up to those conditions, you will be forced to withdraw the privilege.

Should you allow pets?

Considering your building, its vacancy factor, and your own inclinations, what do you think?

The decision is yours.

Should You Furnish the Major Kitchen Appliances?

You don't always have a choice about whether to supply your tenants with stoves and refrigerators in your unfurnished rentals because sometimes these appliances are already built in and sometimes the rental market is so fiercely competitive that you have to supply them if you want to keep your rentals occupied. When you do have a choice, however, either don't furnish them at all or tell your new tenants that you no longer supply these appliances in unfurnished rentals but that you would be willing as a favor to supply a stove or refrigerator on loan for a few months.

Tenants are far less likely to complain about the minor faults of their appliances when they are using a stove or refrigerator "on loan" than if you tell them the appliances are included in the rent. Tenants fear that each time you see the appliances you'll be reminded of the loan agreement and may ask for them back, so they keep mum about the little problems. Fiddling with temperamental stoves that bake lopsided cakes and explaining why milk freezes and ice cream melts in some crazy refrigerators takes far too much of your valuable time. Supplying these major appliances and providing what amounts to a full maintenance contract on them to boot seldom pays off.

Should You Leave Them Plain or Fix Them Fancy?

Cosmetics people market hope. Automobile people market freedom. Clothing people market style. Wine people market status. Appliance people market convenience. Vitamin people market health.

What do you market, landlord? The blahs? Plain-Jane housing with off-white walls? How pedestrian! Shame on you! You could do better, you know, much better.

Don't get me wrong now. There's nothing wrong with renting out clean, functional dwellings with heating, electricity, carpets, drapes, and indoor plumbing, but it's just so, well, so practical. That's all. And "practical" doesn't sell or rent for very much. Chevrolets are practical, too, but they don't sell for what Cadillacs do. People will rent your functional dwellings in tight housing markets no matter what, to be sure, but they will always pay more in any market if they believe they are getting more for their money, and you can give them more for their money without spending much more of yours.

With a little extra work and very little investment, you could be marketing the same kinds of illusions that Cadillac customers so willingly pay extra money for. What illusions? Individuality, class, style, luxury. "All that in my rental property and with very little investment? Surely you're putting me on." Not in the least. Here's how.

Put on your interior decorator hat, size up your rental dwelling from the inside out, and consider the following suggestions for what they might add to the place. Choose particular colors, patterns, and items which would add the most dazzle for your dollar. Install them. Increase the rent 5% or 10% above what you had intended to charge. Expose the place to potential tenants, and see what happens. You will be surprised.

Here are some "dazzlers" which work for me and others I know. Tailor them to the kind of property you have and the kind of tenant you want to attract.

■ **Wallpaper a wall**—Wallpapering only one prominent wall either opposite the front door or opposite the entrance to the kitchen makes a big impression on prospective tenants as they walk in and begin visualizing themselves living there. Yet, vinyl-coated, prepasted wallpaper costs surprisingly little, is easy to apply, and is easy to care for. Watch for bargains in wallpaper remnants, but make sure you buy enough to complete the job because you may not be able to buy any more later.

■ **Paste a decorative paper border along the walls in a room or two**—Perhaps the least expensive dazzler around and certainly the easiest to install is the decorative paper border. Paint and

wallpaper stores sell these borders in rolls as narrow as three inches and as wide as eight inches. You paste them horizontally around the walls of a room at waist or ceiling height. Then you stand back and admire how much your colorful, decorative border accents whatever else is on the wall. Tenants don't need to know how little it cost.

■ **Paint some rooms with two or three attractively contrasting colors**—Tenants are so used to seeing plain white walls in rental properties that they almost gasp with surprise when they come upon a dwelling which has rooms painted any other way. Select one or two of the living-area rooms in your rental dwelling, and make the walls and trim stand out with pleasing two-tone or even three-tone paint jobs. Ask your paint supplier for color suggestions, and make sure that the painting work itself looks professional.

■ **Put up a woven shade**—A woven shade on any window which requires some kind of window covering anyway dazzles beholders into believing that they are getting something extra for their money, something fancy. Woven shades are fancy. They are special, and they are colorful. They can also be inexpensive. You don't have to spend a lot of money on those fancy Roman shades made of wood. They're costly and no more decorative than the vinyl varieties which sell for approximately what you'd pay for ordinary window shades.

■ **Hang mini-blinds in several rooms**—Like woven shades, mini-blinds provide a decorator's touch to windows. Unlike woven shades, they can be adjusted precisely to compensate for outside lighting conditions. If you're combining woven shades and mini-blinds, use mini-blinds on the side of the building where the sun shines most. They're more durable when exposed every day to direct sunlight. They will let the tenants make infinite adjustments for light, and they come in a full range of colors and stock sizes. Should your windows be odd sizes, either mount stock mini-blinds which are larger than the casement on the outside of the casement rather than waiting for a special order sized to fit inside the casement or else choose some other window covering. Special orders are expensive and take more time than you're likely to have.

Be aware that some vinyl mini-blinds contain lead and that the lead will appear as a powder on the surface of those blinds which have deteriorated after much exposure to the sun. If you suspect that you have any of these blinds, replace them with new ones labeled with words like "nonlead formula" or "no lead added."

■ **Put full-length mirrors on bedroom closet doors**—Mirrors and smoke are so much the stuff of illusions that magicians couldn't get along without them. Forget about providing smoke illusions to dazzle your tenants. Leave them to the magicians. Stick to using mirrors instead. Mirrors make attractive rooms look all the more attractive and also look larger. As a consequence, people like them. Because full-length, single-piece mirrors can be pricey, though, consider using mirror squares instead. They don't have quite the luxury look of single-piece mirrors, but they don't have quite the price tags either. In addition, they have another big advantage when used in rental properties. They are both easier to install and easier to replace. Tenants who break a large mirror won't believe you when you tell them how much they'll have to pay for the replacement, whereas they'll breathe a big sigh when you tell them how little a broken mirror square or two will cost them to replace.

■ **Mount a curtain-rod valance over the shower bath**—A shower-bath curtain-rod valance made of 1"x6" fir or pine and painted with a simple design or covered with fancy Contact Paper® spruces up drab bathrooms as if by magic. Mounted just in front of the rod itself, the valance hides the curtain rod and lends a special illusion of warmth and luxury to the place.

■ **Switch to oak toilet seats**—Everybody likes home furnishings made of real wood, and there's no wood better liked than oak. It's solid and durable, and it fits into almost every interior decorating scheme tenants might fancy. An oak toilet seat stands out in an otherwise sterile white-and-chrome bathroom. It's a "statement." The statement is, "Somebody here cares about the details and wants to make the surroundings especially livable."

■ **Replace a ceiling light fixture with an inexpensive ceiling fan**—Nostalgia and luxury are the trademarks of the ceiling fan, that special fixture which conjures up memories of romantic places like the Raffles Hotel in Singapore and old movies like "Casablanca." In case you haven't noticed, ceiling fans are back. People love them. Not only do they lend a special decorative touch to any room, they do a pretty good job of circulating warm air in winter and cool air in summer to the very recesses of the room. They may be slightly harder to install than an ordinary light fixture but not all that much, and they're well worth the effort. They're charming. Everyone from Sears to K-Mart and the big-box discount stores carries them.

■ **Install some distinctive lighting fixtures**—Distinctive lighting fixtures seem to add the most to kitchens and bathrooms because the fixtures there are more used than in other rooms. What people seem to like most in kitchens and baths are track lights. They're appealing, I suppose, because they have a high-tech, modern look about them, and since they can be adjusted to illuminate work areas, they have a real practical value as well. Become well acquainted with the selection of lighting fixtures available through your lighting supplier, and pick up some fancy ones when they go on sale. Be especially watchful for track lights which require no special wiring, that is, those which can be wired into existing ceiling electrical boxes (avoid track lights with halogen bulbs; they're juice hogs).

All of these dazzlers together shouldn't cost the do-it-yourselfer any more than $450, and yet they should yield around $50 more per month in increased rental income. Think of what that does to the value of your property. At seven times the annual gross, $50 of additional rental income increases the value by $4,200! Even for a hard-boiled capitalist like you, that's a decent return on your money, isn't it? That's better than nine times its cost!

Try these dazzlers or be imaginative and think up others of your own, and capitalize on people's willingness to pay extra for illusions. Just make sure that whatever dazzler you try is fashionable, uncomplicated, inexpensive, easy to care for, and easy to replace.

Do make sure that you use dazzlers tastefully. Too many in one room will make it look cluttered and cheap, you know, like the inside of a film-set bordello.

Of course, you must always keep your dazzlers in like-new condition. Shabby dazzlers make a place look even more tawdry than shabby basics. What, after all, looks worse than a millionaire's mansion which has gone to ruin? Designed to impress and delight, it only depresses. You don't want your dazzlers to depress anybody. Keep them looking like new, and replace them as soon as they start to lose their appeal or go out of style.

Should You Outfit the Laundry?

An apartment-house laundry room can be a blessing or a curse. It can pay off as handsomely as a small casino full of slot machines, or it can be simply another welfare case for you to support. Mostly there are two factors which determine whether you will "win" or "lose" in your laundry room—how much the machines are used and who owns them.

■ **Use**—All things considered, your laundry room will pay off handsomely if it's used frequently enough. Although you cannot tell for certain whether your tenants will indeed do their laundry there or how many loads they will wash per week, you can make a good educated usage guess based on the number of people or the number of bedrooms in the building. If you have a fourplex, for example, and you have four families living there with two children in each, you have sixteen people in all, and they will surely produce enough dirty laundry to support one coin-operated washer and one dryer. On the other hand, a fourplex tenanted by singles and couples, no matter how clean they happen to be, just will not support a washer and dryer.

The rule of thumb I use to determine whether I ought to outfit a laundry room at all and, if so, with how many machines, is this—*Sixteen people or twelve bedrooms (even the smallest dwelling counts as one bedroom) will support one washer and one dryer.* If a building meets either of these minimums and if its laundry machines are set to charge competitive rates, those machines should produce

liberal returns.

■ **Ownership**—Some landlords feel that they have better things to worry about than laundry machines and would rather let someone else handle them completely. They have that choice and so do you if you have an apartment-house laundry room. If you contract with a vendor to supply the machines on a lease or commission basis, you will be relieved of all the ownership worries. The vendor will supply, insure, and service the machines while you provide the laundry room itself, the necessary plumbing, hookups, and, of course, the utilities. He will write a one-to five-year contract to assure himself a profit and then split the leavings with you.

If you supply the machines yourself, you will have to take care of the repairs and maintenance, count the coins, worry about vandalism and other calamities, see that they're insured, and you'll have to pay about a twelve hundred dollars for each washer-dryer pair you buy, but you'll have the only access to the coin boxes, and you'll get to depreciate the machines over a reasonably short period of time, or, if you wish, you may elect to expense them as IRS Section 179 business equipment in the very first year.

What choice should you make? That depends. If you are pretty clumsy or helpless about maintenance matters, if you don't think you'd enjoy the business, if you own an apartment building with fewer than sixteen occupants or twelve bedrooms, if your building is located in an area prone to break-ins and vandalism, *or* if you intend to dispose of your building within two years, don't buy your own machines. Contract with someone else to supply them.

■ **Dealing with an outside vendor**—Should you decide to have someone else supply the machines, ask other landlords to recommend trustworthy companies, and then shop around for the best available terms. They vary a lot, and I do mean *a lot.*

There are two primary contract types—straight-commission and lease-commission. Straight-commission contracts allocate a certain percentage of the gross receipts to the property owner and another percentage to the vendor, from the very first quarter to the very last. I have seen these percentages be as low as 40% and as high as 75% for the property owner. That higher percentage wasn't at an enormous property with numerous machines, either. It was at a twenty-unit complex. The owner had simply done some tough bargaining, knowing that the laundry vendor business is very competitive and that there's room for negotiation.

Under a lease-commission arrangement, the vendor retains a fixed sum each month and splits the balance with the property owner, again according to some predetermined percentages, so if the machines produce only enough to cover the supplier's fixed sum, you, property owner, get nothing, but lemons, oranges, and grapes; no cherries. Tough luck!

A straight-commission arrangement generally nets you more than a lease-commission arrangement because some money will accrue to you with each load washed, regardless of how many.

Life with a laundry room vendor isn't all cherries, I can assure you. You have to be naturally suspicious when dealing with vendors because there's more than one way that they and their employees can cheat you.

Take a look at this one clause which appears in fine print at the end of a five-year laundry equipment lease I inherited from the previous owner of a property—"This lease shall be automatically renewed for the same period of time unless canceled in writing by either party at least 90 days prior to expiration by registered mail." What's that verbiage mean? It means that if I fail to notify the vendor that I want to cancel the lease three months before it expires, I'll be stuck with it for another *five years*. Now that's what I call a cheater clause! Some wily lawyer must be congratulating himself over sneaking that one into the contract. It's entirely one-sided. The burden of canceling the contract is mine, not the vendor's, and if I'm forgetful, I could have an unwanted contract on my hands virtually forever. Read your laundry equipment lease carefully. Don't be caught without your reading specs at lease signing time, or you may be taken to the laundry.

Incidentally, every laundry equipment lease I have ever seen is automatically transferred to the new owner upon change of ownership. Selling a property releases the seller from the lease but binds the buyer exactly as it did the previous owner. Whenever you are negotiating to acquire a property with leased laundry equipment, review the lease, and if you find that it has restrictive terms, make them part of your negotiations.

To make certain that buyer and seller are both well aware of the lease, some vendors will record the lease against the property in county records without your knowledge, as one did in my case. The vendor considered the lease valuable enough to record and wanted to make certain that it could not be ignored.

Consider, then, whether you are giving away something valuable when you sign a laundry equipment lease. After all, it's an exclusive right to put coin-operated laundry machines on your property for a given period of years. You might not think it's worth much when you sign the lease, but the vendor thinks differently. The vendor knows it's valuable. The vendor will protect it in every way possible, and the vendor will require you to pay him to break the lease before it expires if you decide you want to install your own machines.

Be wary of laundry leases. Be very wary. Read the fine print. Read the large print. Read the italics. Read the handwriting. Read the white space.

The other primary way you might be cheated when dealing with an outside vendor is through underreporting of income. If a vendor supplies you with laundry machines, the vendor also empties the coin boxes and counts the coins. The amount of income you receive depends upon how much income the vendor reports. Remember when several large oil companies were exposed on *Sixty Minutes* for underreporting the amount of oil they were pumping from Indian lands? It ran into the millions of barrels. Trucks were loading crude oil from wellhead sites at all hours and bypassing the flow meters. In comparison to that enormity, vendors' underreporting of laundry machine income is dime-and-quarter stuff, to be sure, but the situation is no different. The potential for underreporting income is much the same for laundry machines as it is for oil wells or a city's parking meters, for that matter. Only the amounts differ. Coins there for the taking are pretty tempting to some people, be they the vendors themselves, their employees, or your own managers.

Lest you think that those laundry coins don't amount to very much, get out your calculator and multiply the cost of one coin-machine wash-and-dry times the number of loads you do every month at your home times the number of families in your apartment house. Those coins pile up into heaps of dollars!

One response to this underreporting problem by at least one vendor is the non-resettable counter. Mounted directly inside the timer access plate, it tallies each actuation of the laundry machine's coin slide. When the machines are emptied, your manager or you accompany the vendor's route collector as he empties the coin boxes, and you both take the readings from the counters so you both know how much revenue the machines have generated. It's a good idea and appears to work pretty well.

Another response is what's known in the trade as "verified accounting." Your manager or you are called upon to witness the collection of the coins as they are removed from the machines. After that, you witness the weighing of the coins on one of the new, highly sensitive, portable coin scales which give precise totals in dollars and cents of all the coins being weighed, even when they're mixed. The route collector then writes a receipt for the amount collected.

If your vendor offers neither of these verification methods, you will have to resort to a self-help method to keep from being cheated. Try one or both of these methods. The first one involves insisting that your manager or you be present when the coins are emptied, but that's not all. Because you can't know what sum of coins you're looking at unless you have some sort of quick-count method, get yourself a scale which will weigh as much as fifty pounds pretty accurately. Weigh the coins as they're emptied, write down the weights on a scratch pad, and later do the calculations to determine just how much the machines coughed up. If the coins are all quarters, as they frequently are nowadays, your calculations will be easy. If they're a mixture of quarters, dimes, and nickels, you'll have to work with the numbers a bit to come up with the right proportions, but when you do, you won't be far off.

The second method echoes one which is used by IRS agents to check the false reporting of coin laundry income at launderettes, which are so notorious for "laundering money" that they have given their name to the practice of reporting inaccurate income, in some cases overreporting the income and in others underreporting. IRS agents call the washing machine manufacturer to find out how much water one wash load takes and then examine the launderette's water bill. After allowing for a certain margin of error, say 10%, they can calculate approximately what the launderette's income ought to be and compare that with what's being reported as income.

You can do the same thing yourself even if your water in the laundry room is master metered along with the entire building's. Find out where the water line comes in to service your entire laundry room, and install a water meter right there. Yes, you as an individual may buy water meters, volt meters, watt meters, gas meters, light meters, practically any kind and size of a meter you might want. Unless it's particularly large, a water meter is reasonable priced, too. A 3/4" water meter in a quantity of one should cost less than $50. When you consider how much underreporting of income you might be suffering, that's nothing. Let your vendor know that you've installed a water meter, and watch your income post an immediate increase for some strange reason. In one instance, when I'd inherited a lease from a previous owner, my laundry room income jumped around $200 per month after a water meter installation.

Perhaps the most important aspect of your efforts to be treated fairly by your laundry machine vendor is the interest you show in the whole operation. Too many apartment house owners regard their laundry rooms as beneath them. The laundry room is nickels, dimes, and quarters, and they're interested only in big bucks. They don't particularly care whether the laundry room is profitable or not. When the vendor recognizes this attitude and knows he's under no scrutiny, he'll do as he pleases, but when you've gone to all the trouble of installing a water meter in the laundry supply line and/or weighing coins as the machines are emptied, and the vendor knows you've gone to these lengths, he has to treat you honestly. He's afraid not to.

If yours is a small building, you're not going to get rich from laundry proceeds even with a desirable contract. Consider the laundry room more of an amenity than a money-maker and hope that you'll be able to recover your utility costs.

If yours is a large building, your laundry room proceeds will add more than pocket change to your income. They will be a factor in the property's value. The more desirable the contract you negotiate, the more your property is worth.

■ **Going it alone**—If you are the least bit handy, if you believe you'd enjoy looking after your own coin-operated laundry machines, if you own an apartment building with at least sixteen occupants or twelve bedrooms, *and* if you intend to keep your building at least two years (naturally you can take them with you if you want to, but be sure you specify that in your property sales agreement), then, by all means install your own machines. You will be pleasantly surprised to see just how much money they can make, and soon you will understand why so many firms are in the business of supplying laundry machines on a commission basis, why they offer to paint laundry rooms for "free," why they invest in non-resettable counters, why they buy expensive coin scales for account verification, why they advertise so heavily in rental housing association publications, and why they offer various inducements to managers and owners of large complexes. It can be a lucrative business.

Should you decide after due consideration to install your own laundry machines in your apartment house, you need to know something about buying laundry machines, setting rates, changing rates, getting a decent return on your investment, and counting coins.

■ **Buying coin-operated laundry machines—** As with so many other big-ticket buying decisions, when you're in the market for coin-operated laundry equipment, you need to decide upon the best brand and the best dealer.

For general brand information, consult *Consumer Reports*. It regularly tests laundry machines designed for domestic use in its own laboratories under rigorous conditions and then rates them. Coin-operated machines, one old codger many years in the business told me, have innards exactly like the domestic machines. "Only the tops are different," he said. "When my bottoms wear out, I junk 'em and put my old tops on the cheapest new domestic machines made by the same manufacturer. They last just as long as new coin-operated models." If the two are indeed that similar, then the manufacturers of good domestic machines also make good coin-operated machines.

When making your own brand decisions, visit several coin-operated laundries in your area and see what brands of machines they use. If every one in the vicinity uses General Electric equipment, then you should be able to get General Electric parts and service readily, and you might want to consider purchasing General Electric equipment for this reason alone.

In addition to merely visiting the various laundries to see what kind of equipment they have, try to talk with the owners of the laundries themselves and ask them for their opinions on the various brands. Because so many coin-operated laundries are unattended, however, you might have to wait around for a long time before an attendant appears who could answer your questions. Don't waste your time waiting. Look around for a sign which lists the telephone number of a person to call in case of trouble. Usually that person is the owner. Call the number and ask your questions. The primary questions you should ask when inquiring about equipment brands ought to cover reliability, durability, utilities consumption, parts availability, service availability, warranty, and initial cost.

Ask also about equipment dealers because you'll want to call several dealers who sell the same machines. Prices do vary somewhat on coin-operated machines from dealer to dealer. Make sure, though, for the purposes of comparison that you are asking for quotes on the same model of machine (most companies seem to make two commercial models, one with frills and one without), the same type of coin slide (it should be fully adjustable), the same kind of warranty (the factory warranty on commercial machines may be practically nonexistent, but nonetheless, you will want to establish what it is, how long for labor and how long for parts), and the same kind of delivery (curbside delivery, delivery and uncrating, or delivery and complete installation).

Be aware that the firms which advertise under "Laundry Equipment" in the Yellow Pages likely sell and lease machines. They may sneer at you when you tell them that you want to buy your own coin-operated laundry machines because their primary business may be leasing. They may try to convince you that you're making a big mistake to buy your own machines. Tell them that unless they're willing to put machines into your laundry room on a 75/25 split (75% to the property owner and 25% to the machine supplier) that you'd just as soon install your own machines. Don't be dissuaded from buying machines once you've chosen to do so.

I have been very satisfied with Speed Queen and Kenmore machines myself. They have given good service over long periods of time, and they both wash well.

Kenmore, which is a Sears brand, seems to be

the low-price leader in coin-operated laundry equipment. No matter what other brands you are considering, do check the prices at Sears, but do not bother checking the prices at a regular Sears store. They may have the machines all right, but they won't have the best prices. Check the prices through the Sears Contract Sales National Appliance Operations Center (1-800-359-2000), a special department set up to handle the needs of contractors and rental property owners.

Because coin-operated laundry machines do not come with the same guarantees as their domestic counterparts, some nervous Nellies are tempted to buy extended maintenance contracts. My own experience has shown that these contracts are priced higher than the repairs themselves cost without a contract. I don't bother with maintenance contracts. I consider them a rip-off, something you have to be sold, not something you'd buy.

You're much better off learning how to fix the machines yourself or to have your handyman trained. Inquire when you're purchasing machines whether the dealer has maintenance manuals and maintenance classes available. Laundry machines are pretty simple to repair, but any suggestions for repairing them will surely save time and aggravation. Buy the manuals and attend the classes (they're either very cheap or free). Unlike maintenance contracts, they are good value.

My biggest problem with coin-operated laundry machines couldn't be solved by any maintenance contract, that's for sure. Every so often tenants have called me to complain that the washers or dryers weren't working and I've arrived with my tools only to find that the one thing wrong with them was that I had forgotten to empty the coinboxes. So I'd "fix" the machines by emptying almost $200 from each pair. That's what I call a jackpot!

One important consideration when you're selecting machines is whether to buy gas or electric dryers. In most areas, gas dryers are quite a bit less expensive to operate, so if you have natural gas available, you should give some thought to paying the little extra that gas dryers cost initially in order to save on operating costs over the years. Before making your final decision, however, be sure you check with your local utility companies about the relative costs of operating gas and electric dryers. They'll have the current, local information you need for making your decision.

By the way, don't bother looking around for used coin-operated laundry machines unless you know their complete history or don't mind rebuilding them yourself. Used machines are available, to be sure, but they're far more trouble than they're worth because most owners simply won't part with them until they've been through the wringer.

■ **Setting rates**—Since you with your laundry room are actually providing a convenience for your tenants rather than competing directly with coin-operated laundries in the area, you should set your machines at rates slightly higher, say, 10¢ or 25¢ higher, than the prevailing scale for local laundries. Your machines will need more repairs and wear out faster with frequent use, so you don't want to stimulate too much use by keeping the rates low. Keep them just low enough so the machines will be used fairly often, yet not so high that they won't be used often enough to justify your investment.

■ **Changing rates**—My first laundry machines had coin slides which were set to charge 25¢ to wash and 10¢ to dry. If I were to charge those rates today, I wouldn't break even. As it was, I kept them much too long at those prices because the coin slides were fixed to accept only quarters and dimes, and finding adjustable coin slides took me a while. Adjustable slides enable you to change the rates to any multiple-coin combination in minutes with only a screwdriver. These slides may be purchased by themselves from most laundry machine suppliers and retrofitted to most existing machines. If you're ordering a new laundry machine, be sure you specify adjustable slides rather than fixed slides, to allow you the flexibility of adjusting your income to offset leaping utility costs.

When you do change rates, label the machines with the new rates so users know exactly what you're charging this week to wash and dry a load.

■ **Getting a decent return on your investment**—Income from the machines should cover your utility costs, purchase of the machines, repair service, and a fair return on your investment. The return should be very fair, believe me. One of my eightplexes, all two-bedroom units, paid for its new washer and dryer and all of the overhead in just eleven months. Ever since then, those machines have simply churned out profits, never missing a beat. Over a five-year period, the return on that investment has been in excess of 95% per year; not bad in anybody's book, I'd say.

Do keep an eye on your utility costs, though, for they can, in certain situations, gobble up all your profits and then some. I had one laundry room where the water heater and the dryers all operated on propane gas, and the gas bill alone each month amounted to more than the machines were grossing. I raised the rates, and that helped some, but then I hit upon the idea of shutting off the water heater entirely when I learned that the heat for hot water generally accounts for between 75% and 90% of all the energy used to wash clothes. After switching to cold-water washing only, I posted a sign to that effect, lowered the rates, and began enjoying a good return on my investment.

■ **Counting coins**—Those coins you remove from your laundry machines are all mixed up and require sorting, counting, and wrapping before being deposited. It's a pleasant chore, counting stacks of your very own coins, one which you can do almost without thinking while you watch TV in the evening, but if you find the laundry business profitable enough to install more than one washer and dryer, you will notice that counting coins becomes increasingly tedious. When that happens, buy a coin sorter for your counting house and restore some of the old pleasure to the chore.

There are coin sorters which whirl and tinkle and even tally their coins digitally, and they cost pretty pennies, too. You'd certainly need such a machine if you had a vending machine route or a casino, but you don't need the fanciest sorter available to help you count a few hundred dollars in coins every month. A simple, inexpensive sorter will handle the chore quite well.

Fortunately, there is one. It enables you to sort,

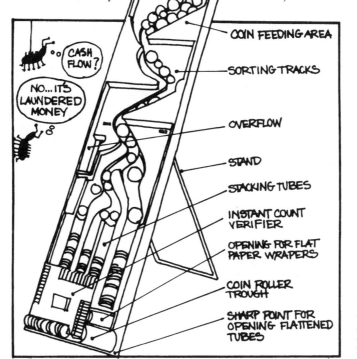

count, and wrap coins quickly and accurately, and it works without moving a single part. Gravity makes it work rather than electricity (they do have an electric "shaker" model; I prefer the "gravity" model myself). After you feed the coins in at the top, they sort themselves by following tracks of varying widths until they wind up sorted into calibrated stacks at the bottom. Little nubs in the stacking tubes raise the 41st or 51st coin, depending on the denomination, to mark full rolls, which can then be removed, checked with the instant count verifier, and wrapped (most banks provide coin wrappers free of charge as a service to their customers).

This marvel of simplicity and utility is called the Nadex Coin Sorter and Packager, Model 607. It's available through larger stationery and business-supply stores or directly from the manufacturer, Nadex Industries, 145 Ontario St., Buffalo, NY 14207. Telephone 716-873-6600.

Should You Pay the Garbage and Utility Bills?

Landlords frequently pay the garbage and water bills themselves for their single-family rental properties rather than leaving that responsibility to their tenants, and with good reason. Paying the garbage bill means that the garbage will positively be picked up and the property will be kept reasonably tidy. Paying the water bill means that the yard will probably be watered and the landscaping won't die of thirst. Paying both means that the tenant can offer no excuse for poor groundskeeping at least, and the place should look reasonably presentable when you drive by.

These arguments make sense for the house rental, but what about the apartment house which has no yard? Whenever I'm lucky enough to have separate water meters for each apartment, I require that the tenants pay their own bills. They should know what their water costs so they'll conserve more.

Garbage is another matter entirely. Personally, I prefer to pay the garbage bill for all of my rentals unless some other satisfactory precedent was established by a previous owner. Some tenants either forget to pay their bill or discontinue service claiming that they would rather haul it to the dump themselves to save paying the bill, and then their cans begin to overflow and there's a constant mess for you to look after.

Control of the garbage area is always easier if you pay. If the tenants pay separate bills, there's bound to be friction caused by the invasion of one tenant's garbage can by strange garbage. It gets tossed aside and then begins a great garbage battle. Finally, there's more of a mess than you can cope with. You pay and you control. Make them pay, and you're likely to be plagued by a continuous garbage war. You have better things to do with your time than participate in garbage wars.

There are ways to save on garbage bills, and you should be well aware of what they are. Garbage bills have risen dramatically because of increasingly restrictive governmental regulations on sanitary landfills. See the garbage handling alternatives at the end of chapter 15 for suggestions.

Also see the section on itemizing rents at the beginning of chapter 6 for a suggestion on how to recoup garbage bill increases when they occur rather than waiting until the next rent increase.

Should You Convert a Master-Metered Building?

As for the utilities in an apartment house, my practice is to have the tenants pay for their own so long as they are on separate meters, and if they are not on separate meters, I try to convert their units to separate meters.

One situation which had me puzzled for a while involved a big, old fourplex with steam heat produced by one common boiler which was connected to a gas meter with dials that spun faster than a moon rocket's altimeter. I was paying the bill for that one meter myself, and with sharply rising utility rates, the bill soon rose to equal one quarter of the building's total rental income! As if that weren't bad enough, one tenant kept complaining that he never had enough heat, and I

had to turn the controlling thermostat up to 80 degrees just to keep his place around 68. Every unit but one then had to keep the windows open night and day to avoid being bathed in steam heat. Consequently, much of the heat that I was paying so dearly for was literally going out those windows.

What could I do? I knew that I couldn't raise the rents to a level where the increased utility costs would be covered. That would have necessitated an increase substantially higher than market conditions warranted. Fortunately, because each unit already had its own gas meter for an individual kitchen stove and water heater, I could install new direct-vent heaters in each unit and connect them to the individual meters already in place. In less than twelve months, those heaters paid for themselves in utility-bill savings, and my tenants' heating complaints evaporated into thin air that I wasn't paying to heat. Hooray and hallelujah! Problem solved!

Tenants are more interested in lower rent, I believe, than in the inclusion of utilities, and when they have to pay their own utility bills, they conserve energy as they should.

Fortunately for me, my fourplex was not a fully master-metered building. Fully master-metered buildings are dinosaurs, no longer being built today because they do not encourage utility conservation and because few owners want to speculate in gas and electricity futures. They require more work and more money to convert than my old fourplex did, but they may be worth converting all the same.

If you happen to be stuck with such an animal, seek out other owners who have already dealt with the problem themselves and learn what you can about their experience. Don't forget to confer with your utility company. Many offer their customers low-interest loans for energy conservation measures. Perhaps you can convince them that the conversion of your master-metered building qualifies.

Once you know what the conversion costs are, consider how long a time you'll have to wait to get your money back. Less than three years is very good; three years is good; more than three years is questionable. Also consider whether the conversion will make the building worth any more, and include that in your payback calculations, too.

Don't just sit there fretting and sweating over

the bills. Do something. There's a lot you can do. Take your choice.

Should You Charge for Providing Lockout Service?

You and I know that landlording is at least a 24-hour-a-day job. Night and day we're on call with our little tool boxes just as family doctors used to be in the old days with their little black bags. We don't like to be called out in the middle of the night to repair a leaky roof or fix a balky furnace, but we go anyway because we feel responsible for providing our tenants with housing which is fit to live in.

When something goes awry with the building, that's one thing. We are responsible. When tenants do something foolish, that's quite another thing. We're not responsible. They are.

Yet, when tenants do something as foolish as lock themselves out, they expect us to drop everything we're doing and hurry over to let them in. They know we have a duplicate set of keys on hand, and they assume that one reason we have those keys is so we can provide lockout service. They think of us as the keeper of their spare set of keys.

Nobody minds letting a tenant in when a lockout occurs at a convenient time, but all too often tenants find themselves locked out at odd hours, times when the "keeper of the keys" is otherwise occupied or unavailable.

There are several ways to handle lockouts—provide the service as a courtesy, charge a fee every time you let a tenant in, or install a key safe.

Most landlords provide lockout service as a courtesy whenever they're called upon to do so. There's nothing wrong with this approach if your tenants seldom ask you to let them in and appreciate your efforts when you do. It may score you a few Brownie points, but if they're constantly asking you to let them in, and you're tired of being at their beck and call, consider changing your approach.

Unless you have agreed with your tenants that their rent money covers a variety of special services like hauling off their dried out Christmas tree, taking their extra garbage, replacing their broken windows, unclogging their sewer stoppages, and providing lockout service, you can charge them for each of these things, that is, in the absence of any law which compels you to do otherwise. Understand that you are not charg-

ing for these services in order to gather additional revenue. You are charging in order to shift the responsibility for these services to the tenants, where it belongs.

Before you charge them anything, though, you should advise them in writing of your policy because they might be expecting you to provide lockout service free of charge and become incensed when they learn that you don't. The best way to advise them of your charges is to include a clause in their rental agreement. Lacking that, an ordinary letter or a Notice of Change in Terms of Tenancy will do.

For lockout service between the hours of 8 a.m. and 6 p.m., Monday through Saturday, excluding holidays, the fee might be $10. At other times, $20 would seem adequate. You shouldn't make the fee so high that they would be tempted to break in. It should be just high enough so they will feel more responsible in looking after their keys and won't be calling you immediately upon discovering that their keys are missing.

Another way to handle lockouts is to install a key safe, the modern-day equivalent of keeping a key under the doormat. A key safe resembles the lock box which real estate salespeople use when they want to provide many agents with access to many houses for sale and they don't want the hassle of duplicating and distributing the keys for every house. Each agent has one master key which fits all the lock boxes in town, and inside each lock box are the keys for the house where the lock box is located.

You don't need a master key to get into a key safe, however. That would defeat their purpose. Key safes are for people who can't keep track of their keys. Instead of a master key, a key safe uses a combination, a combination which both you and the tenants know. You install the key safe in an inconspicuous place, set the combination, and after that, whenever the tenants find themselves locked out, they open the key safe and use the spare set of keys to get in.

Key safes come in two mechanism types, the dial type which opens like a school locker when you dial in three letters or numbers and the pushbutton type which opens when you push any combination of ten buttons. I prefer the pushbutton type myself. They're easier and quicker to open and easier to change.

Key safes cost about $30 and work especially well at rental houses and small complexes where the keeper of the keys lives some distance away.

They also have another advantage. They relieve you of having to rendezvous with contractors who are working on the dwelling while it's vacant. You give the contractors the combination to the key safe, and they use that key while they're working. When they're finished, they return the key to the key safe, and you change the combination.

Should You Allow Nails in Your Walls?

When you come across tenants who don't want to attach your walls to their pictures because they don't want to damage your walls, let me know, and I'll personally recommend that they be enshrined in the "Tenants' Hall of Fame." The Hall still has lots of room.

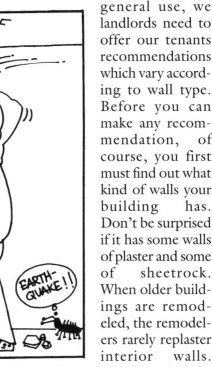

For all those other tenants, you have several decisions to make. What should you allow them to use to attach your walls to their pictures, clocks, and other lightweight stuff? Should you let them hang the heavier stuff at all, stuff like birdcages, bookcases, lamps, planters, wall systems, and bulletin boards?

First, let's consider the lightweight stuff. Remember the olden days when tenants could cause their landlord to have a crying jag if they tried banging a nail into the wall and got caught? Why the concern? Because one nail in a plaster wall would sometimes cause a tiny crack which would grow into a fissure, and then chips and chunks of the plaster would start falling down, and finally there would be a lath wall showing where once there had been one of plaster. Fortunately, along came some creative person who invented adhesive wall hangers, and the problem was solved. The adhesive hangers would hold light burdens

without disturbing the plaster wall at all. Landlords invariably recommended them and most tenants dutifully used them.

But things changed again with the advent of sheetrock, also known as plasterboard, wallboard, and gypsum board. A nail wouldn't crack the sheetrock as it would the plaster, but the adhesive wall hangers, when removed, would peel off both the paint and the paper surface of the sheetrock, leaving a broad, ugly scar underneath which was difficult to conceal.

Since both plaster and sheetrock walls are in general use, we landlords need to offer our tenants recommendations which vary according to wall type. Before you can make any recommendation, of course, you first must find out what kind of walls your building has. Don't be surprised if it has some walls of plaster and some of sheetrock. When older buildings are remodeled, the remodelers rarely replaster interior walls. They sheetrock 'em. Once you know what the walls are made of, you may confidently make your recommendations. For plaster walls, recommend that your tenants use adhesive hangers wherever possible, and if they must use a nail, recommend that they drill a pilot hole first to avoid any cracking which might be caused by the impact of banging too hard on the brittle wall. For sheetrock walls, recommend that your tenants use nails tapped in carefully and that they avoid using those adhesive hangers or tapes altogether. Holes left by nails in sheetrock may be filled neatly with spackling compound and do not even have to be painted in most cases.

How about the heavier stuff? Here you should think as much about the psychological aspects of the heavier stuff as you should about the damage that hanging it could possibly cause. Because tenant turnover is costly, you want your tenants to feel well rooted in your units so that, all things being equal, they will stay a long time. If they are comfortably ensconced in one of your rentals midst all of their hanging plants, their swag lamps, their wall systems, and their pet parakeets, they likely will stay a long time. Swallow hard and let them hang these things.

There is always the danger in their hanging this heavier stuff from your walls, that they'll use an inadequate fastener and that chunks of your walls will come tumbling down when their heavies and your walls part company, but you may avoid this danger by recommending that they first try to find a concealed stud to screw or nail into. Show them how to do it with one of the readily available electronic stud finders. You might want to make one available to lend out for this very purpose. Attaching directly to a stud is by far the best way to hang heavy things from either plaster or sheetrock walls. If it's absolutely impossible to do, however, recommend that your tenants use an anchor (show them what you mean by an "anchor") designed to support at least twice the weight of what they're hanging.

By all means, discuss your "hanging policy" thoroughly with your tenants before they move in because few of them will approach you for permission or advice later on. They'll just go ahead and hang things any which way they please, assuming that you don't really care how they hang things because you never broached the subject to them, but if you have discussed the matter with them in advance, most of them will try to follow your advice and hang their things your way.

Let's hope so.

Should You Cover Those Naked Windows with Draperies, Shades, Blinds, or Bedsheets?

Yes, yes, yes, yes! Cover their nakedness with something!

Every type of window covering has its place. A fancy dwelling which rents for a handsome sum should have handsome appointments, to include fine draperies, woven wood shades, vertical slat blinds, or wooden mini-blinds, whatever's in fashion, sometimes supplied by you and sometimes by your tenants. Neither you nor your tenants want anything but the best for those places.

Average rental dwellings don't need the best

window coverings. They do need window coverings of some sort. Contract draperies are an excellent choice for average rentals. They work wonders to enhance appearances and keep tenants happy.

No matter how fancy the rental dwelling happens to be, though, don't overlook roller shades as a window covering possibility. They help to insulate. They are cheaper than drapes, longer lasting, easier to install, and easier to keep clean. They never need to be taken down for dry cleaning, they don't get threadbare, and except on sliding patio doors, both shades and drapes can co-exist on the same windows at the same time.

This dual window treatment is a good one to try in average dwellings. It can be perfectly adequate while saving you money in the short run and the long run. You supply the roller shades and drapery rods yourself, and you let your tenants supply their own drapes. The initial cost is less and so is the maintenance cost. What's more, tenants who supply their own draperies tend to stay put longer than those who don't.

As for blinds, count yourself lucky if you already have Venetians in your rentals, and unless they are too dated, leave them right where they are because they should last a long time without requiring any further capital outlay. When kept cleaned and repaired by professionals (listed in the Yellow Pages under "Venetian Blinds–Repair & Cleaning"), Venetians cost surprisingly little to maintain.

So-called mini-blinds have already been mentioned as "dazzlers." They are. They have been popular with decorators for years, but they haven't always been as inexpensive, as available, or as durable as they are today. Many paint stores, department stores, hardware stores, and variety stores have ready-made sizes in stock. Because they can be mounted either inside or outside window casements, stock mini-blinds can accommodate most window sizes. That's especially convenient for you when you need a window covering right away. Just go to a nearby store, buy one, and hang it. What could be simpler? Give mini-blinds a long, hard look as a window-covering alternative which will fit well into almost any rental unit and do some dazzling. You'll find that they are more decorative, easier to clean, and easier to maintain than draperies, and they look every bit as good.

Above all, do use some kind of window cover-

ONE-WAY DRAW	
Window Opening	**Drapery Size**
5' x 6'8"	64" x 84"
6' x 6'8"	78" x 84"
8' x 6'8"	102" x 84"

TWO-WAY DRAW			
Window Opening	**Drapery Size**	**Window Opening**	**Drapery Size**
3' x 3'	42" x 44"	6' x 6'8"	78" x 84"
4' x 3'	52" x 44"	8' x 3'	102" x 44"
4' x 4'	52" x 56"	8' x 4'	102" x 56"
4' x 6'8"	54" x 84"	8' x 5'	102" x 68"
5' x 4'	64" x 56"	8' x 6'8"	102" x 84"
6' x 3'	78" x 44"	10' x 4'	126" x 56"
6' x 4'	78" x 56"	10' x 6'8"	126" x 84"
6' x 5'	78" x 68"		

ing when your rentals are vacant, yes, even if it has to be a bedsheet. The obviously vacant dwelling with naked windows is a prime target for vandals and squatters.

Should You Measure for and Install Draperies Yourself?

Any time you require somebody to come out to your rental property site to perform some kind of service there, you're going to pay dearly for that service.

You can measure for and install draperies yourself in a minimum amount of time, and you don't need to buy any special equipment to do it, so why should you pay somebody to come out to your rental property? Just take the following quick lesson before your first attempt.

- First, measure the distance across the front (face) of the installed rod or across where you want the rod installed. This measurement is called the drapery width and is always expressed first.
- Second, measure the distance from the top of the rod to one inch above the floor for floor-length draperies, or measure from the top of the rod to four inches below the window sill for apron-length draperies. This measurement is the drapery length and is always expressed second.
- Third, indicate whether the drapery is to be a

panel (one-way draw opens from one side) or a pair (two-way draw opens from the middle).

Do not measure and include in your measurements either the rod projections (distance at each end between rod and wall) or the center overlap. Contract drapery shops make allowances for them.

Do not measure an old drapery's exact dimensions and submit them for duplication. Drapery sizes, strange as it seems, are not actual drapery measurements.

Do not add any height above the top of the rod up to that point where you think the drapery will extend.

Do not be afraid to inquire whether this is the very method used by your drapery supplier. Whereas contract drapery suppliers do use this method, suppliers who deal with the general public may use another. To find a contract drapery supplier, look in the Yellow Pages under "Draperies-Whsle & Mfrs." Yes, they will sell to you. Give them one of your business cards, and they will probably even set you up with a billing account. (See SOURCES & RESOURCES for information on a contract drapery firm which sells nationwide.)

If there's no drapery rod in place and you have to install one, install it so you can take advantage of the standard sizes which contract drapery shops keep in stock. Standard sizes will cost you much less and will not require you to wait those precious days while custom draperies are being made up to your specifications, something that is especially important when you have just finished redecorating a dwelling, have advertised it for rent, and then you learn that the draperies won't be ready for another two weeks. The bedsheets, old draperies, bedspreads, or drop cloths you'll then have to put on the windows will detract noticeably from that rental's appearance during the very time when you want it to look its best.

Shown here in tables are the standard contract sizes generally available (width x length), together with the common window openings they fit.

As you can calculate from these tables, the ends of the rod should normally extend three inches on either side of the window opening, and the top of the rod should be three and a half inches above the window opening. Such a rod installation will be firmly anchored in the wood of the window framing. If, because of an odd-sized window opening, you have to fudge a little to create a standard size, by all means, fudge. Use plastic or nylon anchors for mounting the rod brackets so you can avoid having to order a custom size.

Likewise, if there is a drapery rod already installed and it isn't exactly standard in length, don't despair. You can usually fit a drapery size which is an inch too big or too small without having to move the brackets. If, however, a standard-size drapery varies too much to fit your existing rod installation, just move the rod brackets so the standard size will fit and use anchors as necessary. Stay with the standard sizes whenever you can.

Should You Carpet Those Floors?

Understand, first of all, that there is no such thing as a perfect floor covering for rental dwellings. Each one has its disadvantages, but there is one floor covering which has fewer disadvantages and more advantages for most rentals, excluding kitchen and bath areas, than any other floor covering you might consider, and that one is wall-to-wall carpeting.

Besides the other attributes it has, carpeting adds tremendously to the soundproofing and income of any rental, and I can testify that it adds to the warmth and rentability as well. After working two weeks on one apartment unit, installing a new kitchen counter, sink, built-in oven, and vanity, and then painting the walls and doors

throughout, I thought I'd really made great changes, but all that work was nothing compared to the change that the carpet installer made in only three hours. Wowee! That apartment was transformed from stark, cold, colorless housing with bland asphalt tile on all the floors into an inviting, warm, cheerful place which someone would delight in calling "home," and it rented easily for a substantial sum. No wonder tenants prefer wall-to-wall carpeting and will pay more for it!

Before you buy any carpeting, however, think about a few important considerations to determine whether you ought to make the investment at all. Consider roughly how much the carpeting will cost (draw and measure the floorplan, determine the yardage required, and multiply that by a telephone quote); consider how much additional rent you can expect if you add carpets (make a brief marketing survey); consider how much your income property will increase in value if you add carpets (use prevailing rules of thumb for determining the market value of income property and see whether the addition of carpets will more than offset the cost); and consider whether the condition of the present floors warrants either adding carpets or recarpeting (look them over carefully).

After you have considered those investment questions and have decided to go ahead with the carpeting, you'll still have decisions to make about areas, colors, patterns, piles, yarns, pads, prices, suppliers, and installers. Read on for some help in making those decisions.

■ **Areas**—Since one of your major concerns is the overall expense, you might save by carpeting only a portion of a unit, perhaps just a living room, because it will cost a mere fraction of a fully carpeted installation and yet you will have "wall-to-wall carpet" to tout to prospective tenants. Another possibility for savings involves laying durable sheet goods (linoleum, tile, or vinyl) by entrances (usually in a three-foot square) and in hallways where traffic is heavy and the carpet tends to wear and spot quickly. You won't notice any savings by doing this right away, but you will in time because you won't have to replace an entire room full of carpeting to eliminate the eyesore of small worn areas.

■ **Colors**—Carpets come in all the colors God made and in some which only man could concoct, many of which you can summarily reject for rental units. No matter what color you choose, you'll manage to choose one that clashes with some tenant's taste, so don't worry too much about it. In general, avoid light and bright colors and choose those which are relatively neutral. Medium shades of gold and brown are the most neutral, but some greens and blues work well, too. Darker colors naturally show less dirt and fewer spots, while lighter colors are more cheerful and make rooms look larger. Select darker colors for rentals where you can expect kids, pets, and less responsible tenants, and use lighter colors in places where you can expect sun fading and more responsible tenants.

■ **Patterns**—There may be some doubt about what carpet color is best for rental properties, but there's no doubt about what pattern of carpet is best for most rental units. Tweed is. Dirt, stains, wear areas, crumbs, toenail clippings, ashes, swatted flies, and swift cockroaches just don't show up as much on a tweed background. They blend right into its randomness.

■ **Piles**—Carpets have piles, too. Carpet "pile" refers to the shape of the yarn. While the most durable carpet pile you can buy is level-loop, the most camouflaging is short shag (3/4" yarn), sometimes called "cabled plush." Both are good for use in rentals. Short shag in solid colors, and especially in tweeds, will camouflage anything that tweeds will by themselves, and what's more, it will camouflage cigarette burns as well, but it shows traffic wear more than level-loops do. A 20-ounce (face weight measures the weight of the yarn in one square yard and determines, more than any other single factor, a carpet's price) level-loop will actually outwear a 50-ounce shag. Use shag in living rooms and bedrooms which have a moderate amount of traffic and avoid using it in heavy traffic areas like hallways. Those are best covered with sheet goods in shag installations (avoid mixing carpet piles and colors within a single dwelling; it looks tacky). Because they are so tightly woven, level-loop carpets wear well and may be installed in heavy traffic areas, but they will definitely show burns. If traffic wear is your primary concern, then choose either level-loop carpeting by itself or short shag combined with sheet goods. If burns are your primary concern, choose short shag.

■ **Pads**—Remember that the pad you select is every bit as important as the carpet itself because it is the pad which gives carpeting that luxurious, substantial feeling underfoot and at the same time extends a carpet's life. Use a half-inch rebonded polyurethane pad or else a polymeric pad, and avoid jute, rubber, and light polyurethane pads. Rebonded and polymeric pads are in the lower, not the lowest, price range and are well worth the money. They will last through several changes of carpet.

■ **Prices**—Don't buy expensive carpet for rentals, no matter how much more wear the salesperson says you'll get from it. It will look just as shabby as any inexpensive carpet after tenants have used and abused it for five years. When combined with a good pad, nylon carpeting which sells in the lowest third of the price range will give at least as good service as expensive carpeting.

■ **Suppliers**—Carpet peddling is a very competitive business, and you can take advantage of this competition by shopping around. When you shop, don't limit yourself to the same sources the typical homeowner uses, retail stores with salespeople who work on commission, because you as a landlord have two additional types of suppliers available to you—contract carpet firms and the mills themselves.

To keep an eye on the overall carpet market, check now and then on the prices at the biggest, most advertised retail supplier for the home market, but don't expect that firm to offer the cheapest carpets suitable for the rental market. They generally operate on a 40-60% markup, depending upon their advertising expenses and their sales volume.

Usually you will find better buys by dealing with small contract carpet firms which supply building contractors with lots of yardage and will deal fairly with you as a landlord because they consider you a source of repeat business. Typically, they operate on a 20-25% markup. Ask several building contractors for the names of their carpet suppliers. Also, check the ads in the Yellow Pages under "Carpets & Rugs, Dealers–New" (look for suppliers which state in their ads that they sell to contractors).

You will find that contract carpet suppliers will give you especially good deals when you structure a "clean deal" for them, that is, when you take your own measurements (saves them a trip), tell them exactly what you want when you examine what they have in stock (saves them time), buy their remnants and excess stock (saves them storage costs), pay cash on the barrelhead (saves them billing hassles and carrying charges), and have it installed by "your own installer" (saves them employee hassles on the one part of their business where they make little or nothing). Contract carpet suppliers like clean deals. Offer them one, and you'll see how flexible they can be on price.

Carpet mills offer their wares directly to landlords, too, at what appear to be bedrock-bottom prices. Before yielding to the temptation of these low prices, however, you should consider a number of factors and ask yourself why building contractors who buy a whole lot more yardage that you ever will, do not deal directly with the mills themselves.

First, there's the time problem. You have to plan your carpet purchases long in advance because there's going to be a time lag of a month or more between when you place your order and when you receive it. Second, there's the delivery problem. Mills ship via common carrier, and either you pick up the goods on their dock or you'll have to set aside a large block of time when the common carrier's local delivery truck will try to get it to you. Third, there's the off-loading problem. Carpet rolls are big and heavy, real big and real heavy. You need to have a "rhino" forklift available to handle one, to get it off the truck and move it to a convenient location. Handling it is like trying to park a Boeing 747 in your garage. It ain't easy. Fourth, there's the storage problem. Do you have the storage space needed to store full carpet rolls? If so, do you want to devote that storage space to carpet rather than renting the space out to somebody else? Fifth, there's the payment problem. Some mills require payment up-front prior to shipment. Are you ready to pay for something long in advance of when you'll be able to use it? Sixth, there's the quantity problem. When you buy from a mill, you'll have a *whole roll* of the same kind of carpet on your hands. You won't have any flexibility if it turns out to be unsatisfactory. And seventh, there's the problem of quality. Defects are an ever-present problem with new carpets. How are you going to handle them when you're dealing with a distant mill?

Get the idea?

Buying carpet directly from a mill is too much like starting another business. It creates more problems than it solves without really saving you that much money. When you consider all the problems, you may find that you're better off dealing with a local supplier.

■ **Installation**—Hire your own carpet installer rather than use whoever happens to be working for your carpet supplier. You'll get better overall prices from the supplier, and you'll get consistently better installations once you identify a good installer. Many installers moonlight, and you should be able to find a good one through "services offered" classified ads, one who will install your carpet for less than the price of the so-called "free installation" included in a package deal.

Be sure you understand who's paying for the tackless strip and the metal threshold pieces. Some installers will quote you a price per yard which includes these items, and others will charge you for them separately later.

If you're a real diehard do-it-yourselfer, you might want to learn how to install carpet yourself by working alongside your installer on one job and reading some words on the subject. It's not rocket science. Moreover, the installations you're likely to encounter in rental properties tend to be the simpler ones, and the specialized equipment you need is available for less than $300 from Maintenance Warehouse.

Be sure you understand that installing carpet yourself puts heavy physical demands on your back and knees. You'll be lifting and dragging heavy materials. You'll be crawling around on your knees, and you'll be kicking with your knees. Protect your back and knees with proper safety and prophylactic devices.

My advice on carpet installation is this—Learn enough so that you can do the work yourself in a pinch and so that you can make repairs. Leave the big jobs and the complex jobs to the professionals. They're better conditioned to do the work.

■ **Measurements**—Measure the areas you want carpeted yourself, and learn from your carpet supplier how to translate those measurements into yardage which minimizes waste. Avoid having an installer measure for you because installers love seamless installations. They charge by the yard, not by the hour, and prefer the easiest possible installation. They don't care about waste. You're paying for that waste. They're not. If you do have an installer take measurements, ask him to show you the cuts and justify his yardage figures.

■ **Squeaks**—Before you have anyone install carpeting for you, tread splayfooted, like Charlie Chaplin playing "The Little Tramp," over every square foot of the installation area to find all the squeaks that have been caused over the years by a loosening of the nails in the subflooring. Then nail the squeaks out with 2 1/2" cement-coated screw or ring nails placed strategically alongside the squeaky culprits.

Squeaky floors annoy tenants upstairs and downstairs and detract from the image of your building. Eliminate them.

Some Last Words

Hamlet, that prince of Denmark, would have made a terrible landlord. He talked too much and he couldn't make decisions. The decisions in this chapter alone would have taken him dozens more plays just to contemplate. By then, his tenants would have either left in disgust, fallen fast asleep, or taken over. You can do better. You must.

Sure, the questions in this chapter themselves are mundane—To allow pets or not to allow pets? To carpet or not to carpet? These questions are not nearly as grand or poetic as Hamlet's "To be or not to be?" Are they? Nobody's going to write a play about real-world landlording decisions and the disturbing perplexity you go through whenever you make them, but you'll stay in this business a long, long time, and you'll prosper in it, too, so long as you can make prompt and mostly correct decisions about what will work and what won't.

Take enough time to think over the implications of your decisions, make up your mind, and then act. Sometimes you'll be right and sometimes you'll be wrong. When you're right, congratulate yourself. When you're wrong, don't chide yourself. Learn, and make the right decision next time.

13
Hiring Help

Having decided to hire help to assist you in your landlording business (see "Should You Do It Yourself?" in chapter 12), you become a boss perhaps for the first time in your life.

Suffer no great trepidation over this new role. Simply prepare for it. You survived being called "landlord" didn't you? Surely you will survive being called "boss."

The truth is that as a landlord who hires help, you are more than just a boss supervising people. You're the personnel, accounting, payroll, legal, and executive departments of your business all rolled into one. Sounds impressive and also a little forbidding, doesn't it? Don't worry. If you have shown yourself to be a competent landlord, you'll be a competent employer as well. It only takes some common sense, some understanding of people, and some acquaintance with certain applicable laws, practices, procedures, and forms.

These next few pages are not meant to tell you all you need to know about hiring help. That is an enormous subject in itself, and there are entire books devoted to it alone. The information provided here is intended merely to get you started in the right direction and keep you out of trouble as you face a number of responsibilities and tasks which are altogether different from the usual ones involved in do-it-yourself landlording and probably altogether different from your normal workaday world, too, unless you already happen to be self-employed and have people working for you.

You'll notice that the information in this chapter pertains more to on-site property managers than it does to the other workers you might hire. On-site property management work is different from most other work in a number of ways. It's different because it generally necessitates residency on the premises. There's both work and housing involved. It's different because on-site property managers don't work under direct supervision. There's nobody around to tell them what to do most of the time. It's also different because on-site managers need to be willing and able to work whenever a need arises. There's no telling when a drain line might plug or some tenants might drink too much and start a noisy fight.

As a consequence, the hiring process needs to be more thorough. You need to know more about the people you're considering for on-site property management before you hire them. You need to know whether they'd make good tenants *and* good workers. You need to know whether they have the awareness to see what needs to be done, the discipline needed to get things done whenever they need to be done, and the honesty not to steal from you when they have the opportunity.

If you're hiring other workers, that is, workers who are under your direct supervision and who don't have to live on the premises, you may still follow the procedures outlined here for hiring on-site managers. Merely modify them as necessary.

Settling the Independent Contractor-Employee Question

You have undoubtedly hired help in the past without even thinking much about it. You were hiring help when you hired a roofer to repair a leaky roof, just as you were when you called a plumber to install a new commode, but that was contractual hiring rather than employee hiring. In other words, those who did the work were not your employees. They were performing services for you while being either self-employed or employed by somebody else. You agreed to pay them a flat fee or an hourly rate, and they gave you a bill for their work. You may have blanched at their bill, but you had no hidden costs, no obligatory reports due to governmental agencies, no increased insurance burden, and no extra bookkeeping chores, all of which you would have had if the roofer or plumber had been your employee.

Because of the benefits inherent in contractual employment and because contractual employees can be expected to do good work without requiring much supervision, many landlords prefer to hire only bonded contractual help, that is, commercial gardeners, window washing specialists, artisan house painters, professional electricians, plumbing contractors, carpet cleaning services, and the like. These landlords may pay more, but they avoid the hassles of being an employer. Besides, independent contractors generally get the work done well and quickly.

Some landlords have tried to avoid the legal obligations and paperwork involved in being employers in another way, by drawing up contracts for those they employ and by calling their employees "independent contractors." Years ago this stratagem worked, but it doesn't work anymore, not since the government discovered that many so-called independent contractors had joined the underground economy. They weren't reporting any income, and naturally, because they weren't reporting any income, they weren't paying any income taxes. More than anything else, this increasingly widespread evasion of taxes by workers who were being paid their full wages without any deductions being taken out, prompted a government crackdown on would-be independent contractors. Our government doesn't like to be cheated out of taxes any more than Mother Nature likes to be fooled.

You may *avoid* paying taxes as we landlords do when we take advantage of the depreciation provisions in the tax law and also when we exchange properties to avoid paying capital gains tax, but you may not *evade* paying taxes as some people do when they fail to report income. Tax evasion is enough to get the government mad at you. It's enough to get the IRS involved in your life on a familiar, first-name basis.

As employers, we don't particularly care whether the workers we hire pay their income taxes or not. That's as much our concern as whether they say grace at the dinner table. We have other concerns when we hire people to work for us. Still, we cannot afford to overlook the government's distinction between "employee"

and "independent contractor" unless we want to risk paying some punitive penalties ourselves.

When you hire an employee, then, don't try to convert that person into an independent contractor unless he undeniably is one. It's not worth the worry and the potential trouble. Bite the bullet. Yes, you are saddled with the same burdens as any other employer. Yes, you do become an income tax collector for the government, and yes, you pay a premium for the privilege. Do it, whether you like it or not. It comes with the territory.

If you're ever wondering whether someone you hire is really an employee or an independent contractor, you may apply some simple tests. Here's the primary one. If you control both *what* work is to be done and *how* it is to be done, then the person doing the work is your employee and not an independent contractor.

Other tests to determine whether workers are independent contractors are these—

- Do the workers have a business license or a contractor's license?
- Do they pay their own deductions including self- employment tax?
- Do they assume legal liability for their work?
- Do they come and go whenever they want?
- Do they qualify as specialists who work without your having to supervise them?
- Do they have a verbal or written contract for the work being performed?
- Do they carry appropriate insurance?
- Do they provide their own tools, equipment, and materials?
- Do they work for other people?
- Do they advertise their services?
- Do they realize a profit or a loss as a result of their services?
- Do they have business cards and stationery?

If the answers to these questions are mostly, if not entirely, affirmative, the workers may be considered independent contractors, and your only responsibility would be to pay them whatever they charge. If not, you must consider them your employees, no matter what name you give them and no matter how carefully you draft a self-serving contract which both of you sign. The government has ruled, "An employee by any other name is still an employee."

Should someone you hire legitimately as an independent contractor turn out, unbeknownst to you, to be using the independent contractor status to evade paying taxes, you may be penalized for not having paid the employer's share of taxes for this "employee." To protect yourself from this possibility, give him an IRS 1099-MISC form (if you paid him $600 or more) at the end of the calendar year, listing his name, his Social Security or federal employer identification number and how much you paid him over the year.

Do not hire anybody to work for you in any capacity and for any length of time without first securing either a Social Security number or a federal employer identification number so that you have the information you need to complete an IRS form if you must.

Should you ever force an employee to be an independent contractor in order to avoid the added employer expenses and responsibilities, you are exposing yourself to dire consequences, especially if that worker is injured on the job or wants to begin claiming unemployment or Social Security benefits after having worked for you.

Keep in mind that on-site property managers, the helpers you are most likely to hire, are *always* considered employees no matter what ruse you use to metamorphose them into independent contractors. Therefore, you might as well resign yourself to having an extra paperwork and expense burden whenever you hire a manager.

You may get away without assuming this burden if you discount a tenant's rent a few dollars for doing yard maintenance around an apartment house or if you pay a few dollars every month to a resident who acts in your stead as, say, rent collector and resident keeper of the keys, but even then you should secure both workers' compensation and non-owned automobile insurance coverage.

The potential liability for not having this minimal insurance when you hire help is too draconian for you to bear yourself. If your yard maintenance worker were to put his own eye out quite by accident, you would have to pay all the medical bills and compensate him for his pain and suffering as well. If you had workers' compensation coverage, it would pay everything. If not, you'd learn something about pain and suffering yourself. If your manager were to injure someone in a crosswalk while driving to the bank to deposit the rent money, you would be held partly responsible because the manager was on an errand for you. If you had non-owned automobile insur-

ance, it would take care of the matter. If not, you might as well sign over your properties to the injured party.

As an employer, you assume a variety of attendant responsibilities, responsibilities which add approximately 30% to the actual wages you pay your employees, a heavy burden indeed. In other words, an employee whom you pay $10 an hour will really cost you $13.00. It's no wonder, then, that landlords try to interpret certain work relationships as contractual, and it's no wonder that the government has pursued the matter doggedly to recover taxes and to protect the welfare of employees.

As for doing the burdensome paperwork involved in hiring employees, that will depend pretty much on whether you are hiring casual helpers or regular helpers and on how much money they are earning over a given period of time. If you wonder whether you ought to be doing the paperwork, call the governmental agencies involved with collecting taxes on wages and ask them. Be frank with them and you'll stay out of trouble.

Complying with Employment Laws

As an employer, you must comply with a variety of laws designed to protect employees and employ countless bureaucratic minions. To find out how these laws apply to you, contact your state department of employment. Tell them that you want whatever materials they have which relate specifically to rental property management. They will supply you with the proper instructions, employer numbers, tables, timetables, and forms necessary for compliance.

Because rental property management work involves strange hours and sometimes long hours, what you decide to pay a manager may not comply with the applicable minimum wage standards. Should disgruntled former managers challenge you for having compensated them with something less than their entitlements, you may be forced to pay back wages and fines, that is, unless you can produce time sheets to prove that you did pay the minimum wage or more. The burden of proof is on you as the employer. Find out what those standards are.

Keeping time sheets is a chore for your managers and for you, that's certain, but they will keep you from running afoul of the labor laws.

By the way, you needn't bother with time sheets for any manager earning a salary above a set figure. That manager is exempt from the laws governing minimum hourly wages and overtime. Ask your state's department of employment for the current figure.

Setting the Pay and Defining the Job

Whenever people consider taking a job, they always have at least two questions in mind. "What's the pay?" and " What's required of me?" You should have answers at the ready to both those questions and to others as well before you ever begin looking for help, casual or permanent, full- or part-time.

As for compensation, some landlords pay their managers a flat rate per unit per month, say, $20, and some pay a percentage of the rent collected, say, 5%, but neither of these methods for determining managerial compensation is fair to both landlord and manager because neither one reflects the actual time required to perform the tasks involved.

I know some properties where $20 per unit per month would be a windfall for the manager because the properties practically run themselves. I know others with the same number of units where it would be a pittance because there's always something for the manager to do.

Consider, for example, the difference between managing a complex tenanted mostly by retirees and managing another complex tenanted mostly by working families who average 1.8 kids apiece. The manager of the one complex may do little more than police a cement-covered courtyard and write rent receipts, while the manager of the other complex may have more to do than old Mother Hubbard. Neither a flat rate nor a percentage of the gross is fair compensation for management as far as I'm concerned.

Another, much fairer method of compensation involves paying for the work you can expect the manager to do at a particular property. The job might include as little as collecting rents when due, showing vacancies, and keeping the keys, or it might include all that plus pursuing late payers, checking applications, selecting tenants, banking, keeping records, doing minor maintenance and repairs, caring for the pool, cleaning, gardening, painting, and handling tenants' complaints.

List the tasks you expect your managers to perform and also try to establish the amount of time you think they should be spending on those tasks during the average month. Collecting rents when due, you might figure, would average ten minutes per dwelling per month, and so on. Set the pay by multiplying an hourly rate, pegged somewhat above the minimum wage, times the anticipated number of hours you expect the managers to work, but guarantee to pay them a certain salary every month.

Review your time estimates after the managers have been on the job a while to make sure that you haven't underestimated or overestimated the time involved.

Here are some suggestions about paying those you hire and defining their jobs—

✔ Inquire into local practices for compensating full- and part-time managers. Ask your rental housing association for some figures. If the association itself can't help you, its members can. Ask around.

✔ Never, ever, say that you are giving a manager "free rent"; the correct expression is "rental compensation." Rent is "free" only if you are giving it away, expecting nothing in return. If you are giving it away, you're a philanthropist, not a landlord.

✔ If you do compensate a manager by providing a residence, do not agree to pay the utilities, too, unless the whole building is master-metered. You cannot predict how much the manager's utilities will cost every month, and you wouldn't be encouraging energy conservation either.

✔ Pay your helpers after they have done their work, not before.

✔ Compensating part-time managers in the form of rent constitutes advance payment. Collect full rent from them, the same as from other tenants, and then pay them a salary at the end of the month. Otherwise, being human, they will tend to regard their discounted rent after a while as a birthright and not as a compensation for services.

✔ Compensate full-time managers with salary and rent only if that is the accepted practice. Check into the special tax rules which apply to the portion of a manager's income attributable to the residence.

✔ Pay the members of a management couple

separately for the work which each one performs so that each of them will receive Social Security credits.

✔ Do not expect your employees to put forth a reasonable effort for unreasonable wages.

✔ Raise the manager's compensation every time you raise rents by the same percentage as the rent increase. Remember that the manager is on the front lines and has to take the flak whenever there's a rent increase. Give him an incentive to implement increases, maybe even to push for them.

✔ Do not give the manager so much to do that he cannot do it all adequately. If, in addition to everything else, you want your manager to paint and prepare every unit which becomes vacant, you may be saving a little money over hiring somebody else to do the work, but you may be losing a lot more money by keeping your available rentals off the market while the work is either being done or waiting to be done. Pitch in yourself or get some outside help to get those rentals ready to rent and back on the market as quickly as possible.

Establishing a Worker Profile

Recognizing that ignorant, careless maintenance workers and bigoted, caustic, timid, lecherous, hot-tempered, forgetful, disorganized, or thin-skinned managers all will cost you time and money and good tenants, too, you should try to establish a profile of the ideal worker your job requires and then identify the categories of people who might most likely fit that profile.

Managers for multiple-family dwellings, for example, should be fair, honest, reliable, used to dealing with people, intelligent, self-assured, unflappable, willing to learn, handy, helpful, thrifty, neat, clean, inquisitive, organized, modest, pleasant, and patient homebodies who can speak with an air of authority and who resemble the residents of the property they manage.

Who is most likely to fit a profile like that? Few humans I know of. But those with service-oriented backgrounds would be the most likely to fit it. Some owners go out of their way to hire school teachers as managers because teachers know how to think on their feet, are accustomed to keeping records, are used to dealing with people, are used to disciplining, have spare time during the afternoon and summer, are profes-

sional in their outlook, work without close supervision, and could use the extra money. Some owners say that former farmers make good managers because they have good work skills and habits, are used to dealing with adversity, and tend to be honest and friendly. Other owners look for people who have any kind of a service-oriented background, such as nursing, sales, hair care, janitorial work, or gardening.

Chances are good that you'll have to compromise in your choice, so decide which of the managerial qualities already mentioned are most important for the job as you see it and which are the least important. Rank them.

Don't overlook the last criterion, either, that the managers resemble the residents of the property they manage. Hiring a young couple to manage a building tenanted mostly by pensioners is courting trouble, just as hiring a pensioner to manage a student complex would be, or hiring a bigoted redneck to manage a black-ghetto property. Managers who resemble their tenants can understand those tenants' unique problems and deal with them properly.

Finding Management Help

Whenever you're looking for management help, consider your existing tenants first. They already have a familiarity with the property and its occupants, and they are known to you, so you needn't be particularly apprehensive about their character. After all, you have already entrusted them with a dwelling worth $75,000 or more, and they have not been found wanting. The chances are good that they will be equally as reliable when looking after more of the same if they have the basic managerial attributes. Good tenants whom I have approached about becoming managers have invariably become good managers, even for as many as 113 units.

One good tenant I approached about managing an eightplex refused the job outright without offering any explanation. He simply said he wasn't interested. I considered each of the seven other tenants for the job and decided against offering it to any of them. A week after he'd refused the job, I went back to this one tenant who seemed so right for the job and offered it to him again. This time I asked him why he'd refused the job before and whether he would reconsider. I learned then that he did want to look after the building all right, but that he didn't want ten-

Employment Application

>>APPLICANT<<
Name __EARL A. LACY__   Home Phone __555-0222__   Work Phone __555-2787__

Social Security No. __517-40-6535__   Driver's License No. __2900123__

Present Address __333 DUTCH St., FUNSVILLE, NV__   Own ___ Rent __✓__   How long at this address? __1 YR.__

Present/Last Occupation __LABORER__ Employer __UIC TECH__   How long with this employer? __3 YRS.__

Reason for Leaving? __STILL EMPLOYED__ Monthly Gross __1275__ Name of Supervisor __JOHN TECH__ May we contact? __Y__ Phone __(200)123-5500__

Previous Occupation __LABORER__ Employer __SWIFT DELIVERY__   How long with this employer? __1 YR.__

Reason for Leaving? __BETTER PAY__ Monthly Gross __900__ Name of Supervisor __Pete Swift__ May we contact? __Y__ Phone __(200) 333-5500__

How many years of schooling have you had? __12__   Course of study __GENERAL__   What languages do you speak fluently? __ENGLISH__

>>SPOUSE/PARTNER<<
Name __GLENDA LACY__   Social Security No. __200-00-3000__   Driver's License No. __Q375521__

Present/Last Occupation __CLERK__ Employer __MM's Italian MARKET__ How long with this employer? __5 YRS__

Reason for Leaving? __STILL EMPLOYED__ Monthly Gross __1126__ Name of Supervisor __Dario Miglia__ May we contact? __Y__ Phone __(200) 345-1111__

Previous Occupation __NONE__ Employer __NA__   How long with this employer? __NA__

Reason for Leaving? __NA__ Monthly Gross __NA__ Name of Supervisor __NA__ May we contact? __NA__ Phone __NA__

How many years of schooling has spouse/partner had? __12__   Course of study __GENERAL__   What languages does spouse/partner speak fluently? __ENGLISH, SPANISH__

>>APPLICANT AND SPOUSE/PARTNER<<
What are your skills related to this job? __Plumbing, some electrical, bookkeeping__

What experience have you and your spouse/partner had related to this job? __our jobs and managing APT. HOUSE__

What tools do you and your spouse/partner have which might be useful on this job? __Electrical DRILL, SAW, hand tools__

What transportation do you and your spouse/partner have which might be useful on this job? __small PICKUP__

How many dependents do you and your spouse/partner have? __0__   What do you and your spouse/partner receive monthly from pensions, alimony, etc.? __0__

What health insurance do you have? __BLUE CROSS__   What do you and your spouse/partner pay monthly for debts, alimony, child support, etc.? __900.__

Are you and your spouse/partner bondable? __YES__ Previous bonding? __NONE__

Savings or Checking Account Bank Name __COMFORT SAVINGS__ Branch __MAIN__   Account Number __0011-11-9910__

Credit Reference __SEARS__   Account Number __S-500018910__   Balance Owed __635__   Monthly Payment __72__

Personal Reference __GEORGE JUDGE__ Address __1 JAMES Rd., Bath, NV__ Phone __(200)123-5432__

Personal Reference __BRIAN NUNN__ Address __77 Nuke Ct. Bath, NV.__ Phone __200)123-6541__

Contact in Emergency __DAN ROBINSON__ Address __207 BOXER AV, CIRCLE, NV__ Phone __200) 223-6114__

Have you ever been convicted of a felony or serious misdemeanor? __NO__ Will you take a drug test? __YES__ When are you available for this job? __Now__

I/we declare that the information above is true and correct, and I/we hereby authorize verification of this information and a thorough background check.

Date __5-7-XX__ Signed __Earl A. Lacy__

ants banging on his door at all hours. We made a deal that he would be called the "caretaker" rather than the "manager," and that he would keep the keys, show vacancies, and clean up around the building, but that tenants would send their rent payments to me directly and call me with their complaints. The arrangement worked beautifully for both of us for years until I finally sold the property.

You might be surprised about the pool of talent that most residential income properties have, and you should not be averse to using it.

If you cannot identify one of your good tenants as a managerial candidate, advertise the position through the help-wanted classifieds, state employment offices, management schools' employment offices, agencies, your rental housing association, and the Internet. You'll likely be besieged with applicants, for there seem to be many people who find the work agreeable.

Even though this kind of work typically doesn't pay much, it offers certain advantages which many people prize—discounted housing, independence, autonomy, and a short commute.

Finding Maintenance and Repair Help

When you're looking around for maintenance and repair help, consider your tenants second on your list of prospects. Whom should you consider first? Your relatives and friends, of course. Haven't you ever heard of nepotism?

After eliminating your relatives and friends as prospects, look to your tenants for this kind of help, and only as a last resort should you have to advertise or call the local office of your state employment development department.

One good outside source too often overlooked is the local retirement community, which might be a mobilehome park for seniors, an RV park for snowbirds, a HUD complex for low-income retirees, or a ritzy housing development for well-to-do seniors who enjoy golf and tennis. Post a notice on the community's bulletin board and see what happens.

The job might interest a healthy, skilled retiree looking for something to do.

Inheriting Managers

Just as you will usually inherit tenants when you acquire a multiple-family dwelling, you will also frequently inherit managers, and you will be faced with the decision of whether to keep the old managers or find your own. Unless there are obvious reasons to let them go right away, agree to keep them on for a month or two until you become familiar with the place and can make an informed decision whether to retain them on a permanent basis or not.

Whatever you do, don't rely solely upon the previous owner's recommendations. The managers may have been duping the owner for years.

Be aware that this takeover period is the perfect time for dishonest managers to abscond with funds. They may have been using a scam which had gone undetected by the previous owner and fear that you as the new owner will find them out. So they will sometimes leave in a hurry and try to cover their tracks. Look carefully through the rental payment records of any property you are acquiring which already has managers. Ask plenty of questions until you understand precisely who owes what and when it is owed. If you have good reason to doubt the managers' honesty, let them go immediately.

If you decide to keep the managers, consider how much they are being paid. Talk over the job as it's being performed. Calculate the time involved and determine what the job is worth to you as the new owner. You may find that, based on the actual workload, the previous owner was overpaying the managers and couldn't tell the difference because he had owned the property a long time and had had an easily assured and gradually increasing cash flow. Consequently, he may have been reluctant to upset the situation by reviewing the managers' pay. If that's the case, you'll probably have to begin looking around for new managers. Not many people will accept a decrease in pay while continuing to do the same work they've been doing all along.

On the other hand, you may find that the previous owner was underpaying the managers. Even a small increase in pay may be incentive enough for them to work harder to prepare vacancies more quickly and to keep the property looking its best all the time.

Inheriting a Property Management Company

When you acquire a building which has been managed for the previous owner by a property management company, you are under no obligation to continue using that company yourself.

Management Agreement   Dated <u>April 20, XXXX</u>

Agreement between <u>Duke and Lady Milquetoast</u>, Owner, and <u>Earl and Glenda Lacy</u>, Manager, for management and maintenance of property located at <u>2100 Main St. Bigtown</u>.

Compensation for Manager shall be in the form of a lodging credit and cash payments. The lodging credit shall be $<u>550.—</u> per <u>Month</u> (must not exceed credit allowed by state law). The combined rate of compensation shall equal $<u>7—</u> per hour (must equal or exceed minimum wage). Owner may adjust the lodging credit and hourly rate upon notice to Manager.

In spite of rental property management's irregular and variable hours, Manager is responsible for planning and carrying out assigned duties so as to work no more than eight hours per day and forty hours per week. Overtime hours will be compensated provided that Manager obtains Owner's permission in advance or, in case of an emergency, provided that Owner is notified within 48 hours afterwards. Manager shall take a ten-minute break for every four hours of work and take an unpaid meal break of at least thirty minutes after every five hours of work. Manager shall record working hours on timesheets provided, one timesheet for each person, and shall submit signed timesheets at the close of each pay period to certify that the hours recorded were actually worked and that no unrecorded hours were worked. Paydays will be <u>Monthly, by the fifth of the month.</u>

Other compensation shall be as follows: <u>hourly pay for additional tasks.</u>
Manager shall have days off as follows: <u>Tuesdays and Wednesday</u>
Manager shall have vacation time as follows: <u>one day per month (accumulating)</u>
Manager shall have sick leave as follows: <u>one day per month (accumulating)</u>
Manager's duties and responsibilities shall be as follows: <u>clean grounds; keeps keys; collects rents; show vacancies; handle minor maintenance.</u>

(Either party to this Agreement may request a review of compensation, days off, vacation, sick leave, duties, responsibilities, etc. Any changes superseding the Agreement must be in writing and must be signed by all parties.)

Manager shall receipt all monies collected on the Owner's behalf and shall deposit or transfer them within <u>two days</u> of collection as follows: <u>Call owners to report collections; make deposits to "Milquetoast Properties"</u>

Manager shall spend, or commit to spend, no more than $<u>100—</u> on the Owner's behalf without first obtaining permission.

Manager agrees to reside on the premises of the property as an employee and not as a tenant. Manager is an at-will employee who may be terminated at any time. Either Manager or Owner may terminate this Agreement upon <u>seven days</u> written notice. Immediately upon termination, Manager shall surrender all keys, records, supplies, equipment, and other items related to the position and shall vacate whatever lodging Owner supplies as a condition of employment. In no event shall Manager vacate later than 72 hours following termination.

(THIS PARAGRAPH APPLIES ONLY IF INITIALED BY BOTH PARTIES. Initials: Owner <u>DM</u>; Manager <u>EL gL</u>.) Manager and Owner agree to submit all disputes that cannot be resolved between them, except failure to vacate, to arbitration. The party seeking to arbitrate a dispute shall begin arbitration by serving a written demand to arbitrate on the other party and on the Judicial Arbitration and Mediation Services (JAMS). Arbitration costs shall be shared equally by both parties, and the costs shall be estimated in advance.

Any item in this Agreement found to be illegal, invalid, or unenforceable shall be considered null and void, and it shall not affect the validity of any other item in the Agreement.

As written, this Agreement constitutes the entire agreement between Owner and Manager. They have made no further promises of any kind to one another, nor have they reached any other understandings, either verbal or written.

Manager hereby acknowledges that he/she has read this Agreement, understands it, agrees to it voluntarily, and has been given a copy.

Owner <u>Duke Milquetoast</u>   Manager <u>Earl A. Lacy</u>

By _____   Manager <u>Glenda Lacy</u>

Even if the company has an extended contract to manage the property, it should be nullified by the sale of the property. The management contract is between the owner and the management company. It doesn't remain with the property.

Sort out the matter during the negotiations to acquire the property. Ask to see the property management contract, and examine the termination clauses. One of them should state that the contract terminates upon the sale of the property. If you cannot find such a clause, ask specifically about termination, and settle the matter with the seller before you take title to the property.

Prior to closing on the property, contact the property management company to advise them of your plans. Tell them who it is you intend to handle the on-site management and who it is you intend to handle the off-site management. The two do not necessarily go together. You may terminate the property management company and still keep the on-site manager, that is, if the on-site manager wants to work for you directly. If you terminate the property management company, the on-site manager may give notice. Be prepared for that possibility.

Prequalifying

If you are considering relatives, friends, or acquaintances for a job, you have already prequalified them in your mind before you ever approach them about it, but if perfect strangers are inquiring about a particular job, you should take a little time to prequalify them first before going ahead with an interview. Otherwise, you'll be wasting their time and yours. At a minimum, each interview takes half an hour, so interviewing ten people will easily take a full day. That's much too much time. Unless you genuinely enjoy conducting interviews and have the time to do it, there's no reason for you to spend that much time at it. Shortcut the procedure by selecting two or three prime candidates to interview.

To select them, prequalify all the respondents by requesting written resumes. Read the resumes carefully and try to imagine each of these people working for you in the particular job you have available. Call only the ones who appear to be the most promising. If the position involves resident management, ask them the same questions you'd ask to prequalify tenant applicants. Then ask them the same questions you'd ask of any employee applicant, questions about their experience, salary requirements, and availability. If they appear worth pursuing, set up an interview. If not, tell them you'll "get back to them."

Interviewing

Arrange employment interviews at the property itself preferably. Make note of anything which might provide clues as to the people's suitability for the job. Try to determine whether they "have a drinking problem." Note especially their promptness, overall appearance, bearing, habits, sense of humor, body odor, speech, smile, and hands.

Outline the job first, including its responsibilities, its advantages, and its drawbacks. Tell applicants whether their living in a certain dwelling is a prerequisite for the position. Explain what the compensation is and when it's paid. Tell them whether there are raises which might be expected after a trial period, and so on.

Ask them whether the job appears attractive to them and whether they feel themselves capable of handling it. If so, proceed to ask them questions using the Employment Application as a guide, and transcribe the information yourself so you can measure their responses and let them talk freely. In addition to the questions on the application, you might want to ask such questions as how they feel about living in close proximity to people as manager and not being able to be good friends with anybody, how they would describe themselves to a stranger, what accomplishments they are most proud of, whether they own any real property, whether they know anything about the laws governing the rental housing business, and why they feel they should be considered for the job. Tell them that you are going to conduct a thorough background check, and ask whether they know of anything unflattering which might turn up in the check that they'd like to explain now. Establish good eye contact with them during the interview. Be friendly, attentive, and helpful, and encourage them to talk frankly about themselves while you take notes.

When you have finished the interview, take a few minutes to show them around the property. Then make a promise to call them back within the next couple of days to inform them of your decision. Letting them know your decision as soon as possible is only fair. Selected or not, they need to be making plans for themselves.

WHAT DO YOU KNOW ABOUT RENTAL PROPERTY MANAGEMENT?

1. How do you determine the market rent for a vacant apartment?

2. If an applicant must have a gross income of three and a half times the rent, how much of an income does the applicant need in order to qualify to rent a house which rents for $1,250 per month?

3. We always collect an entire month's rent and all the deposits whenever a tenant moves in, and we prorate the rent for the second month when it comes due. Let's say that some tenants move in on the twentieth of August. Their rent is $900 and their deposits are $975. How much do you collect from them before they move in, and how much do you collect from them when their September rent comes due?

4. Give several legal reasons you might use for refusing to rent to someone.

5. Under what three circumstances may you enter a tenant's dwelling when the tenant is not at home?

6. Our rental agreement states that the rent must be paid by check or money order, not in cash. How do you respond to a late-paying tenant who offers to pay everything up in cash on a Friday afternoon?

7. What's a realistic late fee for an apartment which rents for $750 per month?

8. How do you begin an eviction for nonpayment of rent?

9. When a tenant calls to give you notice that she's moving, what should you do above all?

10. Prioritize the following tasks which need to be done before a certain vacant apartment can be re-rented: "steam" clean the carpets, dry-clean the draperies, re-key the locks, patch a doorknob hole in a bedroom wall, advertise, replace a broken window, paint the rooms which need painting.

Selecting

If you haven't already done so during the prequalifying step, call the employer references directly and try to verify the information you have on the applicants. Ask about the circumstances surrounding their departure, if they have left their previous job already, and ask quite frankly whether the employer would consider hiring them again.

Give little credence to letters of recommendation which thicken applicants' resumes. Anyone writing such a letter knows that the subject of the recommendation will see it, so there won't be anything negative included. To learn what a former employer really thinks about an employee, call and ask direct questions.

After calling employers, run a credit check on the applicants, and also see what you can learn about their driving records through either your insurance company or your state's department of motor vehicles. Then, if everything appears satisfactory and you are still interested in hiring them, make an appointment to talk with them where they currently reside.

When you see where they live and how they live, you will be able to decide whether to hire them or not. If you don't like what you see, tell them you have other applicants to visit before you make your decision, and then leave. If you do like what you see, show them a blank copy of your Management Agreement and go over it with them. Be certain they understand those provisions in the agreement which call for them to submit their hours of work regularly on a time sheet. If the job means that they will be moving into a manager's dwelling, show them a copy of the Rental Agreement, too, and review it. Then complete both agreements, making sure that you state in the Rental Agreement that their occupancy is dependent upon their management job.

Once you have made your decision, don't continue keeping the unsuccessful applicants in limbo. Call or write them, whichever you prefer. Thank them for their interest and wish them good luck in finding an even better job.

Testing

Because the whole process of hiring an employee is rather subjective, you might want to consider including a slightly more objective step in the whole process. You can, you know. Available to you as well as to large employers are tests specifically designed to assist in employee selection.

Pre-employment testing fell out of favor during the civil rights era because some thought testing was racially discriminatory. Perhaps some tests back then were discriminatory. I don't know. I do know that the psychologists who create these tests today go to great lengths to eliminate racial and cultural biases. I also know that university studies have shown that testing is far and away the best predictor of success in employment. It's even considerably better than the next best predictor, a tryout on the job.

I am not referring here to intelligence tests. No, I'm referring to tests which probe personality characteristics and attitudes. Perhaps the word "test" isn't even the right word to use, for these "tests" are really questionnaires. There are no right or wrong answers. The answers given help to shape a personal profile which enables you to compare your applicant's profile with the profiles of others who have been successful in that particular line of work.

Now, you wouldn't think too seriously of going to all the trouble of testing the applicants you're interviewing to manage a fourplex, but when you're looking for somebody to manage thirty or more units, you have a lot more to lose if you mistakenly hire inept managers. Testing might help you make the right decision.

Two pre-employment tests are available from the National Apartment Association. The PIC (Performance Improvement Corporation) Personality Plus Indicator measures how assertive, organized, flexible, sensitive, and imaginative a person is. The Wilkerson Pre-Employment Audit measures one's attitudes about theft and substance abuse. Wouldn't you like to know these things about the person you're thinking of hiring?

If you'd like to know what practical knowledge manager applicants have about the job, you might want to give them the "quick and dirty" test shown here. It's split into two parts, rental property management and landlording maintenance.

Here are the questions and some possible corresponding answers. You know the answers, but just in case you forgot, here they are again.

■**What Do You Know About Rental Property Management?**

1. How do you determine the market rent for a

WHAT DO YOU KNOW ABOUT LANDLORDING MAINTENANCE?

1. How do you repair a toilet which cycles on and off all by itself every twenty minutes or so?

2. How do you repair a burn in a kitchen counter made of Formica® laminate?

3. How do you repair a four-inch hole in a hollow-core door?

4. How do you remove a bathtub spout without putting any permanent marks on it?

5. A new tenant calls to report that half of an electrical outlet doesn't work. How do you fix it?

6. What's the difference between fuses and circuit breakers?

7. Describe the function of each of the following: closet auger, drum auger, Teflon® tape, hack saw, saber saw.

8. What determines whether a doorknob lock is installed right-side up or upside down?

9. Where should you be sure to install a smoke detector?

10. Prioritize the following maintenance tasks: sweep the parking area, unclog a garbage disposer, replace an outside light, paint a bathroom in a vacant apartment, change locks for a tenant whose boyfriend moved out yesterday.

vacant apartment? *Do a market survey by checking the competition, that is, the current vacancies. Occupied apartments are not the competition.*

2. If an applicant must have a gross income of three and a half times the rent, how much of an income does the applicant need in order to qualify to rent a house which rents for $1,250 per month? *Multiply $1,250 by 3.5; the answer is $4,375.*

3. We always collect an entire month's rent and all the deposits whenever a tenant moves in, and we prorate the rent for the second month when it comes due. Let's say that some tenants move in on the twentieth of August. Their rent is $900 and their deposits are $975. How much do you collect from them before they move in, and how much do you collect from them when their September rent comes due? *Collect $1,875 from them before they move in; collect $300 from them when their September rent comes due.*

4. Give several legal reasons you might use for refusing to rent to someone. *The applicants lied on the application; they have been evicted; they don't earn enough; they have bad credit; they have unsatisfactory recommendations from a previous landlord.*

5. Under what three circumstances may you enter a tenant's dwelling when the tenant is not at home? *You may enter with permission, upon giving 24 hours' notice, or in an emergency.*

6. Our rental agreement states that the rent must be paid by check or money order, not in cash. How do you respond to a late-paying tenant who offers to pay everything up in cash on a Friday afternoon? *Take the tenant somewhere nearby where he can buy a money order. Return with the money order in hand, and write the tenant a receipt. Tell him that he knows now where to buy a money order, and he can go there on his own next time.*

7. What's a realistic late fee for an apartment which rents for $750 per month? *Five percent of the monthly rent is realistic.*

8. How do you begin an eviction for nonpayment of rent? *Give the tenant a "notice to pay rent or quit."*

9. When a tenant calls to give you notice that she's moving, what should you do above all? *Have the tenant put her "notice of intention to vacate" in writing.*

10. Prioritize the following tasks which need to be done before a certain vacant apartment can be re-rented: "steam" clean the carpets, hang the dry-cleaned draperies, re-key the locks, patch a doorknob hole in a bedroom wall, advertise, replace a broken window, paint the rooms which need painting. *If spare keys might be floating around somewhere or if the former tenants might try to move back in surreptitiously, re-key the locks straightaway. Then advertise, replace the broken window, patch the doorknob hole in the bedroom wall, paint the rooms which need painting, "steam" clean the carpets, hang the dry-cleaned draperies, and re-key the locks again if any independent service people have had a key during the make-ready interim.*

■What Do You Know About Landlording Maintenance?

1. How do you repair a toilet which cycles on and off all by itself every twenty minutes or so? *Replace the flush valve and check the valve seat. If the valve seat is corroded, install a stainless steel liner with epoxy.*

2. How do you repair a burn in a kitchen counter made of Formica® laminate? *Make the burn area level with the rest of the counter, and cover it with a glued-down cluster of ceramic tiles or a glued-down synthetic cutting board.*

3. How do you repair a four-inch hole in a hollow-core door? *Using double-sided tape, cover the hole with at least one 12-inch-square mirror tile; better still, add three more mirror tiles to make the mirrored area larger and more useful.*

4. How do you remove a bathtub spout without putting any permanent marks on it? *First, grip it with your hands as close to the wall as possible and try turning it counter-clockwise; if it won't budge, use a strap wrench.*

5. A new tenant calls to report that half of an electrical outlet doesn't work. How do you fix it? *Likely half of the outlet is wired to work all the time; the other half is wired to work with a wall switch. Tell the tenant to flip the wall switch to turn on the switchable half of the outlet.*

6. What's the difference between fuses and circuit breakers? *Fuses self-destruct when electri-*

SITE VISIT
Property Name: Earl Lacy, Manager 1328 Sutter   Date: 3-28, XXXX

Needs Attention: garbage/trash area must be cleaned daily, Maybe even twice a day. One outside light in carport burned out.

Safety Concerns: Railing across from Apt. 2 is loose. Check batteries in apartments smoke detectors this month and at the same time check the smaller fire extinguishers.

Comments: Apt. 14 has been vacant too long. Find out what other similar places are going for and lower the rent if necessary.

Paperwork/Logbook: Daily entries in logbook complete - NICE WORK! Its neat and very legible.

Looks Good: Front of the building shows much improvement in apperance with new landscaping - you carried through on some good ideas! Tenants even commented on improvements.

Vacancies (circle if ready to rent): 2, (14)

Visitor's Followup: Return with latest Grainger Catalog. Look into a good supplier for durable garbage cans which aren't noisy. get Buster a cordless phone, the smaller, the better.

Visited by: Margaret Rubli   Time: 4:15-6P 1¾ hr.   Expenses: car only cal current greater than their amperage rating flows through them; they must be replaced. Circuit breakers trip to their off position when excess amperage flows through them; they may be reset and reused.*

7. Describe the function of each of the following: closet auger, drum auger, Teflon® plumber's tape, hack saw, saber saw. *A closet auger is a short, stout snake for clearing toilets. A drum auger is a snake for clearing drains; this snake coils inside a drum when not in use. Teflon® plumber's tape seals threaded pipe joints. A hack saw is a hand saw with a narrow, fine-toothed blade used for cutting metals primarily. A saber saw is an electric saw with a reciprocating blade supported on one end only so it can be used for plunge cuts.*

8. What determines whether a doorknob lock is installed right-side up or upside down? *A doorknob lock is installed correctly, right-side up, when the key inserted to open it has its keycuts pointing up.*

9. Where should you be sure to install a smoke detector? *Always install a smoke detector near the bedrooms.*

10. Prioritize the following maintenance tasks: sweep the parking area, unclog a garbage disposer, replace an outside light, paint a bathroom in a vacant apartment, change locks for a tenant whose boyfriend moved out yesterday. *Whenever possible, take care of tenant requests first, security and safety tasks second; preparation of vacant units third; and common-area maintenance last. Change locks for a tenant whose boyfriend moved out yesterday; unclog a garbage disposer; replace an outside light; paint a bathroom in a vacant apartment; sweep the parking area.*

Supervising Managers

If one of your employees were to discriminate against a prospective tenant illegally, give a tenant a black eye, fire another employee improperly, commit to have the parking lot fog-sealed by a fly-by-night crew, or even cause an automobile accident while on the way to the bank with your rent receipts, you as their employer would be held responsible. You can ill afford such problems.

Managers should save you time and worry, not cost you both. Take the time, therefore, to let your managers know how much discretionary authority they have to act on their own, how much money they can spend without asking for your approval, which suppliers and service people you prefer them to patronize, what constitutes an emergency, what necessitates their calling you right away, how they should go about selecting new tenants, how you would like existing tenants to be treated, what your rent collection policy is, and how they should handle time sheets.

After you have told them what you want them to do and how you want them to do it, let them do it. Never undermine your manager's authority either by allowing tenants to approach you behind the manager's back or by making deals without the manager's knowledge. Tenants will try to divide and conquer. Don't let them get away with it. Sometimes they will have legitimate grievances which aren't being addressed by the manager, though, so at least listen closely to what they have to say whenever they go to the trouble of contacting you directly, but then talk with the manager and either let the manager reply to them or arrange a three-way discussion. Never go to see tenants by yourself without first consulting the manager. Work *with* your managers, not *around* them.

Every time you pay a business visit to a property which you have entrusted to a manager, you'll be discussing all kinds of things about the condition and operation of the place. You'll forget most of your discussion soon after you leave and you'll muddle the rest, but you'll expect the manager to remember everything, of course. You'll also expect the manager to do everything you told him to do by the time you return for your next business visit. When you do return, you'll wonder why the manager didn't do something you were sure the two of you had discussed, and then you'll learn that the manager doesn't remember your ever discussing it. The manager, for his part, will wonder why you didn't return with that whatchamacallit you'd promised to bring.

In order to circumvent these frustrations and become more effective as a supervisor of managers, use the Site Visit form shown here. It helps you focus on what's important when you visit a property. It helps you remember from visit to visit what you last discussed with the manager, and it helps you create a written history of your visits. What's more, it gives you a good excuse to mention things which need attention and things which

Time Sheet

ALFRED GOOD
Employee's Name

al good
Employee's Signature

450 SWEET ST.
Property

Pay Period 3/1 to 3/15

Date	Times		Hours	Description of Work Performed	Contract Amount
3/1	5:00 5:30	5:15 7:45	2½	ground keeping, rent collection	
3/2	5	6	1	"	
3/3	5:20	6:30	1⅙	" "	
3/4	5	5:15	¼	" "	
3/5	12— 3:00	1:00 5:00	3	" & dump run with my truck	10.00
3/6	5:15	6:00	¾	" "	
3/9	5:00	5:30	½	plumbing repair, apt. 4	
3/10	10:00	11:30	1½	court apperance-eviction #3	
3/13	6:00	7:20	1⅓	cleaning # 3	

Total Hours 12
Rate 7.00
Hourly Gross 84.00
Contract 10.00
Total Gross 94.00

Total Contract 10.00

Approved by *Duke*

Date 3/16/XX

are safety concerns, neither of which you might think is important enough to point out to your managers otherwise.

My managers have told me that they like the form. They say that they like to know what I notice when I pay them a visit because they don't look at the property the same way I do. They're too close to it, for one thing, and they recognize that they sometimes need their eyes opened. The form makes me open my eyes, too, and forces me to comment on what I see.

Fill it out in duplicate and leave one copy with the manager. Take the other copy with you and do the things under "Visitor's Followup" which you're supposed to be doing yourself after the visit. Bring this copy back with you on your next visit and check to see whether the manager has completed everything under "Needs Attention" from the last visit.

Since all people like to know that their work is being appreciated, show your employees that you like what they're doing for you. Praise them sincerely when they do good work, make note on the Site Visit form of whatever looks good at the property, and remember them on their birthdays and during the holiday season.

Likewise, if they are not handling the overall job as you wish it handled, tell them the source of your dissatisfaction and give them an opportunity to improve. Document what you say to them so you'll have ammunition to use in case any of your employees accuse you of terminating them illegally. A succession of Site Visit forms repeating items which need attention will go a long way toward proving that they're not doing their job.

Doing Payroll

Doing payroll is no simple matter because it requires more than simply calculating an employee's hours, making the payroll deductions, and writing the checks. It requires all that plus the completion and submission of quarterly data, the periodic deposits of employer and employee taxes, and the preparation of year-end forms, including the W-2's.

Some employers find the task too daunting or too time-consuming and turn it over to a payroll service which handles everything for a fee.

If you prefer to hire out your payroll, even for a single employee, you will find any number of companies, from local bookkeeping services to nationwide payroll services, willing and able to do the job. You will find local and some nationwide bookkeeping services in the Yellow Pages under "bookkeeping service" and "payroll service." You will find all kinds of payroll services by using an Internet search engine and searching on "payroll services [your state]."

Ask fellow landlords for recommendations.

Be sure to analyze how each company charges for its services. You can always save on their fees by paying your employees less frequently. You will save by paying them monthly rather than semi-monthly or by paying them biweekly rather than weekly.

If you prefer to do your payroll yourself, go ahead and do it. As soon as you get through the learning curve and into the routine, you might even enjoy doing it. It's not trigonometry or even algebra. It's basic math, nothing more. If you do your own income taxes, you'll find doing payroll much the same thing. It's a routine.

Using both the time sheets which your employees submit at least once a month and the figures for deductions provided by governmental agencies, calculate your employees' gross earnings and all their necessary deductions. Write those figures in duplicate on a statement of earnings and deductions form (Rediform 4H416 is one of several available at stationery stores for this purpose) for each employee. Tear out the original and give it to the employee along with your check for the employee's net earnings. Leave the copy of the statement attached to the pad as a record of payment and then transfer those figures to the Payroll Record sheet you keep for each employee (see sample in chapter 18).

Do not deceive yourself into thinking that the employee's deductions are all you need to keep track of and pay to the government. You must contribute, too. Be sure to indicate in the "Employer FICA" column the contribution you must make as an employer. This sum, almost equal to the employee's Social Security contribution, was not reflected in the statement given to the employee, but you must keep track of it nonetheless, and you must forward it, along with the monies collected, to the various governmental agencies involved at either monthly or quarterly intervals. Failure to do so will result in a response much swifter than any made to the person who fails to file an individual income tax return. For instructions about forwarding these monies, ask the IRS and your state tax collecting agency to send you their free employer booklets.

Want to handle payroll on your computer? You can do an adequate job using Quicken, but Quicken does not calculate the deductions automatically. You have to consult tables to find the appropriate figures, and you have to keyboard them whenever you write paychecks. The job is easy if you pay an employee the same amount every pay period because you consult the tables once and save that information for the next time (until the tables themselves change). It's a bother if you pay your employees different amounts every pay period because you will have to consult the tables every time you write paychecks and then keyboard the figures. Quicken is a big help when you're preparing your state and federal tax deposits, however, because it will provide you with the summary figures you need to make those deposits. That's where it shines as opposed to doing everything by hand.

QuickBooks is another option for handling payroll. It's a more complicated program than Quicken, but then it does more. It calculates payroll deductions automatically once you load the latest tax tables and set everything up for each of your employees.

For good, practical advice on using Quicken or QuickBooks for payroll, consult their respective user's guides.

Thwarting Thievery

Not all on-site property managers are honest. Some are outright dishonest and will even create opportunities to steal from you, while some are easily tempted when opportunities present themselves. To thwart thievery, eliminate the opportunities and watch for certain danger signs.

The primary opportunity for thievery is the handling of cash. The simple solution to eliminating this opportunity is to keep cash out of your manager's hands. Let your tenants know that they must pay by check or money order or credit card or bank transfer, never in cash, and be strict about enforcing this policy.

If there's some important reason why you must allow your manager to handle cash, make sure that the cash gets deposited soon after it's received. Have the manager get two bank deposit receipts, one for the manager and one for you.

Adopt a shingle or a triple-receipt system for receipting rents. The tenant, the manager, and you should each have some uniquely numbered record of every payment.

Eliminate or minimize the petty cash fund you make available to your manager to pay for little purchases. Instead, set up accounts at local merchants and authorize the manager to buy there. Examine every charge slip you receive before you pay it, and check periodically to make sure that the manager didn't return items later for a cash refund.

Watch for these danger signs that a manager might be stealing from you—extended vacancies (some managers will report a unit as vacant when it's actually occupied and they have pocketed the move-in monies); delayed deposits (an enterprising thief will scheme to "borrow" your funds and delay the deposit until new rent monies come in); sloppy bookkeeping (a thief will claim that his unbalanced totals were honest mistakes); a reluctance to take a vacation and leave the bookkeeping to somebody else (some managers may seem extremely conscientious; they're never absent; they're never absent because they don't want anybody else to look closely at their bookkeeping); and a change in the manager's financial status (thieves are not Robinhoods; they spend their ill-gotten gains on themselves, on gambling, booze, drugs, jewelry, clothes, or cars). Keep an eye on them.

No, keep two eyes on them.

Terminating

Sometimes a management arrangement just doesn't work out, and you find yourself faced with the unpleasant task of terminating managers, something rendered all the more awkward because they live on the premises as a condition of employment. You are terminating them, and you are evicting them. Until they go, you don't even have a place for the new managers to live.

Under these circumstances, time is of the essence. You want them to vacate as quickly as possible. Offer them some incentive to leave within twenty-four hours, perhaps two hundred dollars. Reclaim the keys, bookkeeping records, equipment, and supplies immediately. Ask a trusted tenant to look after things for the time being, but do not divulge to anyone the details surrounding the termination. If any announcement is in order, it might center around the transfer of managerial responsibilities and nothing more.

Believe it or not, I have acquired good properties at below-market prices from owners who sold out because they were unwilling or unable to terminate their incompetent managers, admittedly an unpleasant task, but definitely achievable.

When you have to do it, do it.

Giving References

From time to time, you will be called upon by other employers to furnish information about former or even current employees who are looking around for other employment. You'll want to give good employees a good recommendation, and giving them a good recommendation presents no problem at all. On the other hand, you'll want to give bad employees a bad recommendation, but

doing so presents a definite problem. You leave yourself open to a lawsuit whenever you say anything negative about an employee which you couldn't prove conclusively in a court of law.

Go ahead and give concrete details about salary and length of employment whenever you're asked for that information legitimately. It can't be disputed and won't get you into any trouble. But whenever you're asked to give information which is subject to interpretation and which might be construed as negative, say, "No comment!" It speaks volumes and won't get you into any trouble at all.

Some Last Words

In spite of all the complications involved in hiring help, you will find that your landlording business will prosper so much more with help than without it and that you will feel liberated enough to enjoy some of the advantages of the business. You cannot do all the work yourself. Don't die trying!

14
Participating in the Section 8 Housing Program

Every inveterate M*A*S*H rerun watcher has heard the term "Section 8" often enough. Corporal Max Klinger keeps dressing up in outrageous female garb and concocting outlandish schemes to get out of the U.S. Army on a Section 8. That Section 8, a release for psychological reasons, bears scant resemblance to the Section 8 of this chapter. They just happen to share the same section numbers in their respective government documents. That's all.

The Section 8 of this chapter does bear a remarkable resemblance to something else which has the stamp of GOVERNMENT all over it, however, and that is the food stamp program.

The Section 8 housing program is to rental housing what food stamps are to groceries. Both are federal government assistance programs, and both enable the poor to live better than their incomes would otherwise allow them to. Through these programs, they get to enjoy meat, potatoes, milk, and indoor plumbing on a gruel, bread, water, and shantytown pocketbook.

Section 8 differs markedly from the other types of government housing programs which I maligned in the introduction to this book. Those are essentially *housing*-based assistance programs. Tenants must live in a particular place to get their assistance under those programs. Section 8 is a *tenant*-based program. It requires that tenants qualify financially just as the other programs do, but it doesn't restrict them to living in housing which is government-owned, government-financed, or government-operated. They could be living in rental housing belonging to anybody, even to you or to me. When they move from one rental dwelling to another, their assistance goes with them.

Whereas other government housing programs operate outside the competitive marketplace, Section 8 operates inside it. In fact, Section 8 includes a monitoring of the competitive rental housing market which is supposed to make its local administrators better informed about what's happening in the market than many landlords and managers. Its administrators need to know the current market rents in their areas so they can attract landlords and managers to the program by offering them fair market rents and certain program benefits in exchange for renting to tenants who themselves don't have enough income to qualify as renters under normal circumstances.

The program's full official title is the "Section 8 Tenant-Based Assistance Housing Choice Voucher Program." Bureaucrats within the U.S. Department of Housing and Urban Development (HUD), which manages the program at the federal level, call it the "housing choice voucher program" for short. Here we'll simply call it what the po' folks call it, "Section 8."

Established by the 1974 Housing and Community Development Act, Section 8 is now a major federal program involving billions of dollars and thousands upon thousands of people. So far, it has had a salutary effect upon the rental housing business, and though changes lie ahead for the program as legislators tinker with it, it likely will continue to have a salutary effect on the business for years to come.

As a free-enterprising landlord, you may be one of the three key local elements in the program if you want to be, but you certainly don't have to be. Unlike poor, frustrated Klinger, who wanted desperately to become a Section 8 soldier, you have a choice about whether to become a Section 8 landlord.

Interested or not, you really ought to know something about this government program and how it operates. Knowing something about it will help you answer those loopy liberals who propose rent control in your community as the perfect solution to the high cost of housing for the poor, when what they really want to do is bash landlords and transfer the burden of providing inexpensive housing for the poor from the public sector, where it belongs, to the private sector, where it doesn't.

Our government has programs to help the poor live cheaply in decent housing, and well it should, because the poor *are* the government's responsibility. They are not the responsibility of one segment of the population. They are not the responsibility of landlords alone, in spite of what some people think, those same people who don't mind giving away property, so long as it's other people's property.

Section 8 is just one of our government's housing programs, and it seems to be working as well as any government program with noble goals can work. Unlike rent control, it is not a scattergun approach to making rental housing affordable. It does not help everybody, rich or poor, who happens to live in rental housing in a particular area. It is a targeted approach. It helps those who need help. It helps the poor, and it helps them in a way that integrates them in the real world with everybody else rather than isolate them with other poor people in overcrowded, poorly maintained housing projects too frequently dominated by criminal elements.

The "Right Kind" of Housing

Just as there are no special "food stamp groceries" in the supermarket, there is no such thing as special Section 8 housing.

Yet there is a "right kind." It may take many forms, from tract houses to townhouses, from mobilehomes to apartments.

The right kind of housing must also meet minimal size, amenity, and condition requirements.

At the very least, it must have a separate and private bathroom, a living room, and a separate kitchen or a kitchen area in the living room. In other words, a studio or efficiency apartment would do nicely. A hotel room without a private bath and without facilities for food preparation would not.

As a general rule, Section 8 housing must have one bedroom for every two people. It must have walls, floors, ceilings, windows, roof, wiring, plumbing, heating, and locks, all in good condition, and there must be no lead-based paint anywhere about. That's one thing the government is adamant about in any residential housing it subsidizes. Simply put, it should be what Section 8 materials repeatedly call "decent, safe, and sanitary" housing.

Abe Lincoln's log cabin would not qualify as the "right kind" of housing for Section 8 tenants today.

HUD'S Role

HUD bankrolls the entire cost of the program, from the costs of administering it at every level to the funds allocated for the housing assistance payments made to those landlords who elect to participate.

In addition, HUD acts as a watchdog of the local administrators of the program to ensure that they follow the rules adopted at the federal level for implementing the program at the local level.

Roles of the Three Local Parties

Three parties make Section 8 work at the local level, and they are all three key parties. Without any one of them, there would be no program. The three are tenants, landlords, and local public housing agencies.

Tenants qualify to participate according to income and family size; landlords qualify by having the right kind of rental housing available and by being willing to participate; and local public housing agencies "qualify" by having the necessary funds funneled through to them by the federal government and by having the personnel available to run the program.

Qualified tenants may be young or old, normal or handicapped, active or lethargic, single or multiple, bright or dull, married or not married, but they may not be rich or poor. They may only be poor, not necessarily dirt poor, mind you, just poor enough according to the federal government's latest poverty level definition. Right now the so-called "truly needy" or very low income people who qualify for Section 8 assistance must have an income amounting to less than half the median income for their given family size located in their particular part of the country. These figures vary from time to time, from family to family, and from place to place.

Currently, a family of four in the Oakland, California, area will qualify if their yearly income is less than $32,850. That's not quite as poor as church mice in Oakland, I'm sure, but it's only as poor as you have to be to qualify for Section 8 assistance there. After qualifying initially, that family of four must not exceed $47,800 in yearly income to continue receiving assistance.

Incidentally, a "family" for Section 8 qualification purposes consists of one or more persons who have established a stable relationship and have lived together for a minimum of ninety consecutive days.

As you might imagine, there are more people applying for Section 8 assistance who qualify as "truly needy" than there is assistance available, so the local housing agency has to put qualified applicants on waiting lists until funds become available. It gives preference on these lists to applicants according to various criteria which it determines. Generally, those whose income falls below 30% of the area's median income, those who are paying more than 50% of their income in rent, those who are homeless or living in substandard housing, those who are veterans, those who already reside in the area, those who are single and pregnant, those who are disabled or handicapped, those who are at least 62 years old, and those who are being displaced from their homes through governmental action receive some preference.

For landlords to qualify to participate in Sec-

tion 8, they must have the right kind of housing available. They must be willing to accept tenants who are poor enough to qualify. They must be willing to sign a year's lease with the tenants and a year's assistance payments contract with the local public housing agency. They must be willing to have the property inspected by the housing agency. They must be willing to maintain the property according to minimal standards. And they must be willing to set the rent at or below the fair market value as determined by HUD for that county or metropolitan area.

The third key party, the local public housing agency, identified as the "PHA" in HUD documents, is the local administrator of the program. It acts as the liaison with HUD, as the conduit for the funds, and as the "inspector general." It is directly responsible to the federal government and takes care of all the paperwork involved in making the program work at the local level. It qualifies the tenant-applicants, inspects the housing, negotiates the rent, signs the assistance payments contract, calculates the tenants' contributions, collects the federal monies, pays the landlords, and polices the abuses. As you might imagine, it has plenty to do.

How the Program Works

All three parties have to be involved for Section 8 to work, but they don't all have to begin their involvement at the same time. The housing agency is the first to become involved because it has to work together with HUD to set up the program at the local level and secure the monies. Once that's done, it solicits tenants to apply.

Tenants apply for admission to the program by proving that they're poor enough to participate. They submit information on family income, assets, and family composition. If that information proves they qualify, either they receive an assistance voucher which entitles them to the assistance right away or they receive a place on a waiting list with others who qualify for Section 8 assistance but can't get it just yet because there's none available.

For those lucky enough to receive a voucher, there's still more to do before they can move in somewhere and start living a better life. They have to go scouting for rental housing on the open market like everyone else. When they find something they like which would seem to fit the Section 8 guidelines for their family size, they must

Tenancy Addendum
Section 8 Tenant-Based Assistance
Housing Choice Voucher Program

**U.S. Department of Housing
and Urban Development**
Office of Public and Indian Housing

(To be attached to Tenant Lease)

1. **Section 8 Voucher Program**
    a. The owner is leasing the contract unit to the tenant for occupancy by the tenant's family with assistance for a tenancy under the Section 8 housing choice voucher program (voucher program) of the United States Department of Housing and Urban Development (HUD).
    b. The owner has entered into a Housing Assistance Payments Contract (HAP contract) with the PHA under the voucher program. Under the HAP contract, the PHA will make housing assistance payments to the owner to assist the tenant in leasing the unit from the owner.

2. **Lease**
    a. The owner has given the PHA a copy of the lease, including any revisions agreed by the owner and the tenant. The owner certifies that the terms of the lease are in accordance with all provisions of the HAP contract and that the lease includes the tenancy addendum.
    b. The tenant shall have the right to enforce the tenancy addendum against the owner. If there is any conflict between the tenancy addendum and any other provisions of the lease, the language of the tenancy addendum shall control.

3. **Use of Contract Unit**
    a. During the lease term, the family will reside in the contract unit with assistance under the voucher program.
    b. The composition of the household must be approved by the PHA. The family must promptly inform the PHA of the birth, adoption or court-awarded custody of a child. Other persons may not be added to the household without prior written approval of the owner and the PHA.
    c. The contract unit may only be used for residence by the PHA-approved household members. The unit must be the family's only residence. Members of the household may engage in legal profitmaking activities incidental to primary use of the unit for residence by members of the family.
    d. The tenant may not sublease or let the unit.
    e. The tenant may not assign the lease or transfer the unit.

4. **Rent to Owner**
    a. The initial rent to owner may not exceed the amount approved by the PHA in accordance with HUD requirements.
    b. Changes in the rent to owner shall be determined by the provisions of the lease. However, the owner may not raise the rent during the initial term of the lease.
    c. During the term of the lease (including the initial term of the lease and any extension term), the rent to owner may at no time exceed:
        (1) The reasonable rent for the unit as most recently determined or redetermined by the PHA in accordance with HUD requirements, or
        (2) Rent charged by the owner for comparable unassisted units in the premises.

5. **Family Payment to Owner**
    a. The family is responsible for paying the owner any portion of the rent to owner that is not covered by the PHA housing assistance payment.
    b. Each month, the PHA will make a housing assistance payment to the owner on behalf of the family in accordance with the HAP contract. The amount of the monthly housing assistance payment will be determined by the PHA in accordance with HUD requirements for a tenancy under the Section 8 voucher program.
    c. The monthly housing assistance payment shall be credited against the monthly rent to owner for the contract unit.
    d. The tenant is not responsible for paying the portion of rent to owner covered by the PHA housing assistance payment under the HAP contract between the owner and the PHA. A PHA failure to pay the housing assistance payment to the owner is not a violation of the lease. The owner may not terminate the tenancy for nonpayment of the PHA housing assistance payment.
    e. The owner may not charge or accept, from the family or from any other source, any payment for rent of the unit in addition to the rent to owner. Rent to owner includes all housing services, maintenance, utilities and appliances to be provided and paid by the owner in accordance with the lease.
    f. The owner must immediately return any excess rent payment to the tenant.

6. **Other Fees and Charges**
    a. Rent to owner does not include cost of any meals or supportive services or furniture which may be provided by the owner.
    b. The owner may not require the tenant or family members to pay charges for any meals or supportive services or furniture which may be provided by the owner. Nonpayment of any such charges is not grounds for termination of tenancy.
    c. The owner may not charge the tenant extra amounts for items customarily included in rent to owner in the locality, or provided at no additional cost to unsubsidized tenants in the premises.

7. **Maintenance, Utilities, and Other Services**
    a. **Maintenance**
        (1) The owner must maintain the unit and premises in accordance with the HQS.
        (2) Maintenance and replacement (including redecoration) must be in accordance with the standard practice for the building concerned as established by the owner.
    b. **Utilities and appliances**
        (1) The owner must provide all utilities needed to comply with the HQS.
        (2) The owner is not responsible for a breach of the HQS caused by the tenant's failure to:

ask you as the landlord whether you would be willing to participate in the Section 8 program yourself and whether you would be willing to accept them as tenants, even though they do not qualify to rent from you on economic grounds. If you respond positively to both questions, you and the tenants sign a request for tenancy approval form provided by the agency.

Acting on the request, the housing agency dispatches an inspector to look the place over and negotiate lease terms. If the housing qualifies and you can agree on terms, you and the tenants sign a lease, which may be your own, so long as it conforms with certain guidelines provided in HUD's tenancy addendum. Where it doesn't conform, the HUD addendum takes precedence (its first page appears here; you may examine the complete addendum by asking your local agency for a copy or by going to an Internet search engine and searching on the words "Section 8 Tenancy Addendum"; one of the selections on your found list will direct you to the HUD or HUDCLIPS website where you will find the addendum in a readable format). As an alternative, you may use a lease provided by the housing agency for this purpose.

Then you and the housing agency sign a Housing Assistance Payments Contract, known to bureaucrats as the HAP Contract (its first page appears on the next page; to examine the complete contract, contact your local agency or search for it on the Internet). Finally, you collect the advance monies, the tenants move in, and you all live happily ever after, well, presumably for a year at least.

If your housing does not pass inspection, you may make the repairs and improvements to remedy its deficiencies and try again, or you may refuse to try again. That's up to you. No Section 8 tenants may move into any rental dwelling until it does pass inspection, though, and they aren't allowed to fix it up themselves so that it will comply. You must do the work.

As a landlord-participant, you will receive directly from the tenants that portion of the rent which they are responsible for and directly from the housing agency that portion of the rent which it has promised to pay. Should your Section 8 tenants fail to pay you their share of the rent when it's due, you may still assess them late penalties and evict them if necessary, just as you would any other tenant. That doesn't change. You also

receive the security/cleaning deposit directly from the tenant, and you handle that just as you would a deposit from any other tenant.

If you as a landlord wish to participate in the Section 8 housing program and you don't have a qualified tenant already lined up, you may contact your local housing agency and request that your name be placed on the referral list of available dwellings. Tenants who are looking for housing under Section 8 will know in advance that you are familiar with the program and are willing to participate. They will contact you directly about your vacancy.

Advantages and Disadvantages

There are certain advantages and disadvantages to your participating in Section 8, of course, and you'll have to weigh them against one another as you decide whether you want to participate.

The primary advantage is that you get to enjoy the benefits of having a strong co-signer, the federal government, on the hook for the tenants' financial obligations to you. This co-signer seldom has to step in and pay for the tenants' obligations, however, because Section 8 tenants are more motivated to pay whatever they owe you than the average low-income tenant is. They know that they're getting something for nothing, and they want to hold onto a good thing. They also know that big government is involved now. If they break their lease, not only is their landlord going to become provoked and evict them, but big government is going to become aware of what's going on, too, and they're going to have to explain themselves all the more thoroughly when they next try to qualify for financial assistance from a government agency.

If Section 8 tenants don't pay and you have to evict them, the program will continue to pay its share of the rent during eviction proceedings and even afterward. It will pay a portion of the entire rent for a period of up to thirty days following the last time the rent was paid under the program. The same holds true if the tenants break their lease and vacate all of a sudden. You'll still be getting something from Section 8 after they leave. In addition to those advantages, the program will also help to reduce your vacancy losses because you'll be able to rent to a greater number of potential tenants.

The primary disadvantage of participating in Section 8 is that you're hampered somewhat more

**Housing Assistance Payments Contract
(HAP Contract)
Section 8 Tenant-Based Assistance
Housing Choice Voucher Program**

U.S. Department of Housing
and Urban Development
Office of Public and Indian Housing

Part A of the HAP Contract: Contract Information

(To prepare the contract, fill out all contract information in Part A.)

1. **Contents of Contract**

    This HAP contract has three parts:

    Part A: Contract Information

    Part B: Body of Contract

    Part C: Tenancy Addendum

2. **Tenant**

    Martin C. McDougal
    Sharon B. McDougal

3. **Contract Unit**

    1533 Oak Street
    Seawind, KY   41702

4. **Household**

    The following persons may reside in the unit. Other persons may not be added to the household without prior written approval of the owner and the PHA.

    Martin C. McDougal
    Sharon B. McDougal
    Bertie B. McDougal
    Shelly F. McDougal
    Malcom J. McDougal

5. **Initial Lease Term**

    The initial lease term begins on (mm/dd/yyyy): _____ 11/1/XXXX _____

    The initial lease term ends on (mm/dd/yyyy):   _____ 10/31/XXXX _____

6. **Initial Rent to Owner**

    The initial rent to owner is: $ _ 1,200. _____

    During the initial lease term, the owner may not raise the rent to owner.

7. **Initial Housing Assistance Payment**

    The HAP contract term commences on the first day of the initial lease term. At the beginning of the HAP contract term, the amount of the housing assistance payment by the PHA to the owner is $ 900. _____ per month.

    The amount of the monthly housing assistance payment by the PHA to the owner is subject to change during the HAP contract term in accordance with HUD requirements.

Previous editions are obsolete   Page 1 of 10

form **HUD-52641** (3/2000)
ref Handbook 7420.8

than otherwise. You're hampered because you have to commit your property to the program for at least a year. You're hampered because you have to handle more paperwork and take the time to deal with a third party which isn't known for being swift to act or having much common sense. And you're hampered because you have to rent to low-income people who tend to be more ignorant and less responsible than tenants who can afford to pay the entire rent themselves.

You won't notice these disadvantages at all if you'd normally be plagued with vacancies, evictions, and damage losses, but you might notice them a lot if such woes have never bothered you before.

An Important Distinction

In whatever rental agreement you sign with Section 8 tenants, make sure you distinguish between the rent paid by the tenants and the housing assistance payments paid by Section 8. In other words, do not label the funds paid by Section 8 as "rent." Label it "housing assistance payments." You might even want to mention specifically that the housing assistance payments are *not* to be considered rent. This seemingly unimportant distinction may become an important distinction later should you ever have to evict your Section 8 tenants.

Let's say that you give a proper notice-to-terminate-tenancy to some Section 8 tenants because they won't keep their dog under control. You have warned them and warned them, but their dog continues to bark at all hours and escape regularly from its backyard pen to terrorize neighborhood children. Your other tenants in the duplex are fed up, and so are you. You decide to evict the dog's owners. Upon giving them their notice, they stop paying their rent, but Section 8 continues to make payments on their behalf, and you accept the payments.

The tenants decide to fight their eviction in court. They argue that you continued accepting rent from Section 8 after the notice period expired, so the notice you gave them is meaningless. They claim that you waived your right to evict them.

You argue that you did indeed stop accepting rent from them. You continued to accept only the housing assistance payments. They're not rent at all. The Housing Assistance Payments Contract, which is between the housing agency and

you, even says that the housing agency agrees only to make assistance payments. It does not agree to pay rent. Besides, neither HUD nor the housing agency administering the local Section 8 program is a party to the rental agreement. They have no right of possession, and because they have no right of possession, they cannot be making any *rent* payments. Rent payments are paid by *tenants* for the purpose of using and possessing a property.

You cannot be absolutely certain that this argument will sway a judge, but you stand a much better chance of prevailing if you make the distinction between rent and housing assistance payments in whatever rental agreement you sign with Section 8 tenants.

Some Misunderstandings

Landlords often misunderstand two aspects of the Section 8 program. They tend to think that a tenant needs no further screening after being qualified as acceptable by the public housing agency, and they tend to think that the "published" fair market rent figures are the actual rents which they can charge. Neither happens to be the case.

The housing agency screens tenants according to need primarily, and it may screen them according to other criteria, too, such as prior tenant history and landlord references, but its screening procedures and yours may be very different. You cannot rely upon the agency to do your screening. You must do it.

You must qualify Section 8 tenants in exactly the same way you qualify any other tenant on every criterion except financial capability. That's only good management, and good management goes hand in hand with the whole Section 8 program.

The other common misunderstanding involves the fair market rent figures which you may see published in your local newspaper. Don't get all excited when you see that Section 8 will pay $75 per month more for two-bedroom places than what you're currently charging for your two-bedroom places. The figures are misleading. For one thing, they include a utility allowance for water, garbage, electricity, and gas. When you eliminate payment for these items, the "fair-market rent" which you as the landlord stand to receive, declines accordingly. For another thing, the published rents are the top rents approved for dwellings with that number of bedrooms. The housing agency's inspector will negotiate with you to determine what rent you may charge a Section 8 tenant for your particular dwelling. You are not automatically assured that you will get the top rent allowed.

Fair Market Value

The primary bone of contention most landlord-participants have with the program is the tendency of the housing agency to undervalue the market rent for a given dwelling. The agency has an obligation to set the rent at fair market value, but even with lots of data and professional guidance available, they may still come up with what you consider to be a low number for your dwelling.

You as a landlord-participant need to be prepared to justify your own determination of fair market rent for your particular rental dwelling. In order to do that, you need to do your homework. You need to be able to show the agency some proof that the rent you are charging is indeed fair market rent and not some number you arbitrarily decided upon in order to take advantage of the same government which pays high dollars for hammers and toilet seats included in defense contracts.

For the single-family dwelling, you need to identify every feature, big and not so big, including things such as a double-car garage with an automatic door opener, laundry hookups, spacious kitchen, and convenient public transportation, so that you can factor in the value of such features when making comparisons with other properties currently listed for rent. Show the agency's property inspector how you arrived at your valuation.

For the multi-family dwelling, you need to identify the unit with the highest rent which is most similar to the one you want to make available under Section 8. That rented unit in the same building will provide perfect justification for the current market rent.

If you and the agency don't agree that your rent is reasonable, the Section 8 tenant may still decide to rent from you and pay the difference between what you want to charge and what the agency will subsidize.

The Future

As a landlord, you might be hesitant about participating in Section 8 because of its uncertain future as a federal government welfare program. Don't be. Future administrations, no matter how conservative, are not going to succeed in cutting back Section 8 funding anytime soon. Its future is probably more assured than that of some of our businesses and industries. Do expect the program to change, though. Presumably it will become more like the food stamp program in that it will provide subsidies to tenants which they may spend on housing pretty much as they see fit. That prospect bodes well for the landlord.

Some Last Words

Face it. This is a welfare program, one of those government giveaway programs which some taxpayers resent and rail against. If you personally feel that welfare programs are wrong and that welfare recipients are lazy, good-for-nothing chiselers, then don't participate. Your attitude would surface eventually, and you'd probably find yourself saying or doing something which would put you behind the Section 8 eightball before long.

If you're either ambivalent about or supportive of government welfare programs, consider participating, but don't commit yourself initially to more than one Section 8 tenant. Try one and get a feel for the operation of the program first. Then if you find you like the way it all works, commit yourself to more. Otherwise, limit your participation to that one tenant or stop participating altogether.

Whether you participate or not is up to you. Whether you continue to participate or not is up to you as well.

15
Fattening
The Bottom Line

Fattening your own bottom is a whole lot easier than fattening your bot-tom line in the landlording business, but no matter. The truth is that you can indeed fatten your bottom line in landlording. All you have to do is increase your income and decrease your expenses. It's that simple.

Simple? Ha! Only a simpleton would call it simple. It's simple to say but not quite so simple to do. It's like a stock market advisor saying that you should buy low and sell high. It's like a presidential candidate saying he's going to balance the budget by lowering taxes and increasing the spending on the latest fashionable government enterprise. Hey, wait a minute! That sounds simple all right, but it also sounds suspiciously like "voodoo economics," doesn't it? We all know what happened as a result of twelve years of that kind of economic thinking. The federal budget went further out of whack than it's ever been, and

Well, you don't have to practice any voodoo economics to fatten your bottom line in landlording, but you should be aware that fattening the bottom line in the landlording business is not only a matter of increasing income and decreasing expenses. That improves the cash flow all right, but it's just one of the ways to fatten the bottom line. There are four all told, each tied to one of the four ways to make money in this business. Remember them? They were mentioned in chapter 7. Let's see, besides the cash flow which results from your income exceeding your expenses, the other three are making your property worth more (appreciation), saving more money on your income taxes (tax shelter), and paying off your mortgage with more dollars going to principal (equity buildup) and less to interest.

Each one of them has a bottom line of sorts, and all of them together contribute to the big bottom line, which is the sum of the differences between the following—net sales price and net purchase price, income tax savings and income tax penalties, positive cash flow and negative cash flow, original loan amount and payoff loan balance—over the entire period of ownership. That's the overall bottom line. That's the big picture.

Keep all of the bottom lines in mind. You can hardly do otherwise because they're so interrelated that you can scarcely do something about one of them without affecting another. Try to fatten all of them whenever you can, but recognize that in this chapter we're referring to one bottom line primarily, the cash-flow bottom line. That means increasing income and decreasing expenses.

Increasing Income

Other *Landlording* chapters mention only incidentally a variety of things you can do to increase a rental property's income, from raising rents to lowering rents (amazing but true), to outfitting the laundry room with your own machines, marketing illusions by installing dazzlers, setting up interest-bearing checking accounts, shortening turnover time by not trying to do everything yourself, adding furniture, infilling your land with another dwelling or two, and so forth. Those aren't the only things you might do to increase your income. There are other ways to do it as well.

Some of these ways require a certain expertise to make them pay off best. Some require additional capital investment, which may not come easily. Some require certain existing facilities or space to work. Some require more labor and attention. But all of them yield a good return under the right circumstances.

If you're running on empty for ideas, think about these.

275

STORAGE AGREEMENT
THIS CONTRACT LIMITS OWNER'S LIABILITY--READ IT

PARTIES--THIS AGREEMENT, dated ___June 16, XXXX___, is by and between

___Brian Nunn___, "Owner," and

___Sophie Sorenson___, "Occupant,"

for storage of a vehicle, boat, trailer, or other personal property located at the following address:

___2232 Thornbird Avenue, Buffalo, IA 52000___.

OCCUPANT'S ADDRESS: ___16 Tradeway St., Muscatine, IA 52111___

OCCUPANT'S ALTERNATIVE ADDRESS: ___3506 Scotts Blvd., Jimtown, IA 52666___

[X]   INDOOR STORAGE--Unit: ___6___

[ ]   OUTDOOR STORAGE--Personal Property to be Stored--

Type: _____

Description (Color, etc.): _____

Dimensions: _____

Identification Number: _____

License Number (State, too): _____

Legal Owner (Name, Address, Phone): _____

_____

Registered Owner (Name, Address, Phone): _____

_____

TERM--Occupant agrees to rent the space for storage on a month-to-month basis beginning ___June 16, XXXX___.

RENT--Occupant agrees to pay Owner, without deduction, the sum of $___110___ per month, payable in advance, on the first (1st) day of each month of the term hereof. Rent paid more than ___10___ days following the due date is subject to a late fee of ten percent (10%) of the month's rent. Under no circumstances will prepaid rents be refunded.

CONSIDERATION FOR EXECUTION OF AGREEMENT--Owner hereby acknowledges receipt of $___165___ from Occupant which covers the first full month's rent under this agreement and any prorations necessary to pay rent to the first of the following month, plus any other sums here identified ___None___. Payment pays rent through ___July 31, XXXX___.

TERMINATION--Either party may terminate this agreement by giving the other party thirty days' written notice, and the rent shall be paid through that date.

■ **Don't give away the space you might be charging for**—As a landlord, you are renting out living space primarily, but you probably own other space which you consider so incidental to your primary business that you may be giving it away. This other space I'm referring to is parking and storage space.

Are you giving away parking and storage space to those who rent living space from you, whether they have any need for it or not? Parking and storage space has value no matter where it is. It's just more valuable in some places than it is in others, and it's more valuable to some people than it is to others.

Tenants with cars need garages more than tenants without them. Pack rats need storage space more than marsupials.

Look carefully at the allocation of the parking and storage space on your rental property. Try to determine how much rent you're getting from it now, even if it is bundled together with the rent you're charging for living space. Then try to determine how much you could be getting for it if you were to separate it out and rent it to either the same tenant who's using it now or to somebody else.

You might find that you could increase the income from your parking and storage space by charging separately for it. If so, why not do just that?

Lest you be reluctant to wrest space away from a tenant who's been "paying" for it all along and isn't using it, consider reducing that tenant's overall rent somewhat. Then rent the space out to somebody else who's ready to pay you what it's really worth on the open market.

■ **Convert carports into garages**—Most tenants will pay more for a carport than they will for a mere parking space, and they will pay more for a garage than they will for a carport. Take advantage of this potential for increasing your income. Convert parking spaces into carports or garages. Convert carports into garages.

Converting a carport into a one-car garage isn't much work and doesn't require much money. All that this kind of a conversion requires is three walls and a door forming the fourth wall. The roof's already in place. For less than $1,500 in most cases, you can hire someone to do the converting and in the process create an income of around $75 or more per month. That's a twenty-month payback and an increase in the

value of your property of around $6,300. That's what I'd call an excellent return on a minimal investment!

Before you pooh-pooh this idea as being somehow beneath you because you think of yourself strictly as an owner of residential rental property, consider the phenomenal success of the self-service storage complexes which have sprung up across the country.

A knowledgeable real estate appraiser once told me that he could not believe the return on investment which these extraordinarily simple complexes produce. He said that they yield a better return than any other kind of income-producing real estate he's ever appraised, from office buildings to strip shopping centers to apartment houses to mobilehome parks. In the suburbs near where I live, the going rate for a 5'x5' cubicle is $41 per month and for the most popular size, 10'x10', it's $99! Your single-car garage, at about 10'x20' is twice that in size and would rent for $127, but even producing a rent of only $75 a month, you'd be doing well. Check the rents in your area. Take the hint! Get with it! There's more money to be made here than you might think.

By the way, always use a separate storage agreement, something like the one shown here, whenever you rent out storage space. Understandings about the rents, insurance, use of the space, applicable laws, refunds, and liability need to be in writing.

■ **Create your own self-storage complex on unused land at your multi-family property**—Your tenants are big renters of self-storage units, and in most cases they have to leave home to get to their units. They'd rent units closer to home if they could, if units were available.

You know that you have a built-in customer base, and you know that self-storage units make money, so why not make units available to your tenants, why not put units on that piece of unused land in the back corner of your multi-family property?

Sound enticing? Ready to give it a try? Where do you start?

From personal experience, I can tell you one place not to start, and that is with a set of plans which you submit to your city or county building department, thereby setting in motion the bureaucratic machinery which grinds down developers with red tape and fees and time delays. Start there only if you have lots of land and want

USE OF SPACE--Occupant agrees to use the space only for the storage of property wholly owned by Occupant and to store said property under his/her own supervision and control. Occupant shall not store or use or produce on the premises any materials which are classified as hazardous or toxic under any local, state, or federal law or regulation. Occupant shall not store illegal substances, perishables, food items, explosives, paint, varnish, thinner, gasoline, and/or other highly flammable materials. Occupant shall not use the space for any business or for manufacturing or production, nor for human or animal occupancy. Occupant shall not create a nuisance or permit creation of a nuisance on or near the storage premises. Occupant shall remove all trash brought onto the space. Occupant shall not use any electricity in the space for any purpose whatsoever other than for lighting and then only while Occupant is present. Occupant shall turn off lights when leaving space.

OCCUPANT'S AFFIRMATIVE COVENANTS--Occupant agrees to the following:
  1) To lock the personal property and keep it secure,
  2) To drain all water lines during the wintertime in order to prevent any damage that may be caused to same due to low winter temperatures, and
  3) To obtain insurance to cover the property and contents thereof as Occupant is hereby informed that Owner does not carry such insurance. To the extent that Occupant does not maintain insurance, Occupant shall be completely "self-insured" and shall bear all risk of loss or damage.

WAIVER OF LIABILITY--Occupant, as a material part of the consideration under this agreement, hereby waives all claims against Owner for any damage or loss from any cause, other than the negligence of Owner, arising at any time, including but not limited to fire, theft, acts of God, vandalism or any physical damage while the Occupant's personal property remains in the storage area. Occupant does hereby agree to indemnify and hold Owner harmless from and on account of any damage or injury to any person, equipment, or personal property arising from any cause, other than the negligence of Owner, or from the negligence of Occupant, Occupant's family, or Occupant's guests.

SELF-SERVICE STORAGE FACILITY LAWS--This storage agreement is governed by the laws applied to self-service storage facilities in this locality.

ILLEGAL PROVISIONS NOT AFFECTING LEGAL PROVISIONS--Whatever item in this Agreement is found to be contrary to any local, state, or federal law shall be considered null and void, just as if it had never appeared in the Agreement, and it shall not affect the validity of any other item in the Agreement.

ACKNOWLEDGEMENT--Occupant hereby acknowledges that he or she has read this agreement, understands it, agrees to it, and has been given a copy.

_____   _____
          Owner   Occupant

_____   _____
BY Person authorized to represent Owner or Occupant

STORAGE AGREEMENT--Page 2 of 2

to build a permanent self-storage structure with lots of units anchored to a concrete-slab floor.

I once tried to build such a structure, consisting of twenty-five self-storage units, on some unused land at one of my multi-family properties. I had plans drawn up. I paid the application fees. I notified the neighbors. I attended the hearings. I took the plans to the various departments which needed to approve them. I did everything I was supposed to do in the proper sequence and according to schedule.

Then, just before everything came together, the fire marshal demanded that I locate a new fire hydrant within fifty feet of the units. The cost for that one hydrant alone amounted to a third of the cost for the entire project!

I argued that the units were all steel and concrete. They wouldn't need a fire hydrant nearby. I cried foul. I tried a political end run. Nothing worked. The fire marshal prevailed, and the project was snuffed out.

Sometime later I came across those plans and thought about alternatives for building self-storage units in that same location. The best alternative I could think of happened to be portable steel sheds built in a factory, trucked to the site, and set up on a level dirt pad made more solid with a layer of road base. Even without a foundation, these sturdy metal sheds are almost rooted in place. They have 26-gauge steel siding which is galvanized and then painted and cured, inch-and-an-eighth tongue-and-groove plywood floors, and substantial I-beam steel skids. A tornado might pick them up and set them down somewhere on a farm in Kansas, but otherwise they're not going anywhere.

I checked with the building department and found that these portable sheds were perfectly legal in my area. So long as they weren't bolted to a foundation, they could be brought in as personal property, and nobody, not even the fire marshal, couldn't object to them, nor could he demand that we put a fire hydrant nearby.

I did the numbers and determined that these units could pay for themselves in two years. They did.

They also increased the value of the entire property by more than three times their cost.

To locate a supplier in your area, check "Sheds" in your Yellow Pages or search for "[your state or local area] steel sheds" using an Internet search engine.

■ **Make unproductive space productive**— Have you ever stopped to consider how much rent you could be charging for those three garages you've reserved for yourself? At $75 per month apiece, you could be getting $2,700 per year for all three.

Don't hog all of that storage space yourself. People are willing to pay you for it. Consolidate in one garage all the things you've been hoarding in three garages. Hold a garage sale to dispose of the stuff you don't really need. Or, better still, call the Salvation Army to pick up the items they might be able to sell and get them to give you a receipt for your donation. Get the junk out of there. Get some heavy-duty storage racks from Grainger and organize the tools and supplies of your trade better, so they require less floor space. One garage is plenty for storing what you really need.

At the very least, realize how much those extra garages are costing you. Is that old bulky stuff you've been saving for years really worth all that much? Sure, you might have some need for it someday, but remember that every month you keep it, you're adding onto its cost to you. You might think that your garage full of the stuff which tenants have left behind didn't cost you anything. Well, it may not have cost you anything to begin with, but now it's probably costing you $75 every month, and that mounts up in a hurry. The stuff had better be worth something because it's free no longer.

Garages aren't the only unproductive space you might make productive. Offices and storage rooms have potential as well.

I'm always amazed at how many relatively small apartment complexes have large offices which some architect with no apartment management experience thought would be a good idea to include back when the building was still on the drawing board. Nobody questioned the space then and nobody questioned it for years afterward.

Ask yourself whether you really need an office at your complex? What are you using the office for? Might it be rented out as office space to an insurance agent, a bookkeeper, or someone else, or might it be turned back into an apartment if that's what it once was? Do you really want employees of yours spending time in an office when they could be "on call" in their own home on the premises?

Just remember that office space is not free even to you as the owner, not when it could be generating income. As one room in the manager's apartment, an office makes sense, but as a totally separate space, and especially if it's an apartment which has been converted into an office, it may not make any sense at all.

Is there any other spare room or space on the premises of your rental property which isn't getting the use it should? Might it be converted into rentable, productive space? That's your business, remember, renting out space.

■ **Keep looking for other income possibilities**—Vending machines, amusement machines, satellite television systems, pay phones, special Internet services, and coin-operated car washing facilities all offer the apartment house owner other income possibilities, as does renting otherwise unused space for billboards and cellular telephone transmitters. Many times these possibilities promise more than they produce, unfortunately, for all kinds of reasons, from unfavorable contracts and increased utility costs to technological changes and demands on your time. Ask advice of others who have had experience with such ventures in similar situations before you commit yourself.

My own best income producer from the list above has been a soda vending machine. It's like having your own automated lemonade stand. You don't need to be a great genius at math or finance to understand that buying sodas for 25¢ and selling them for 75¢ holds profit potential. Why, after all, are the soda companies so anxious to place their vending machines on your property?

Of course, you do need to do some careful estimating before you buy your own machine because you might not sell enough soda to make

the machine pay for itself. Like a coin-operated laundry machine, it ought to pay for itself in less than three years.

My own worst income producer from this list has been a satellite television system. After working the numbers and installing the system at considerable expense, I had to compete with the falling prices of the small satellite dishes and their broader range of program offerings. Not only did I lose customers to the small dishes, but I had to continue paying on a three-year contract for a larger customer base than my satellite system was serving.

Expect to win some. Expect to lose some. Keep trying to put more on that bottom line than you lose from it and you'll be a happier landlord.

Decreasing Expenses

Trying to fatten your bottom line by increasing income holds greater potential than trying to fatten it by decreasing expenses. There aren't that many things you can do to decrease expenses, and there's a limit beyond which you cannot go. That limit is zero. You cannot save more than $22,213 in expenses on any property where the expenses are $22,213 per year. You'd be hard pressed to come anywhere near that, of course.

Nevertheless, you should never overlook what opportunities there are to decrease expenses. There are almost always some.

Besides questioning your insurance coverage and its cost, picking the right things to do yourself while hiring out the others, converting master-metered buildings to separate meters, paying the manager according to some realistic measurement of the work involved, watching advertising costs, and decreasing expenses in other ways mentioned elsewhere in this book, you still ought to look at some other possibilities. Here are a few.

■ **Monitor your mortgage interest**—Look at your expenses for any property and rank them, biggest ones first. Unless you're making abnormally large down payments or paying cash for your property, right at the top will be mortgage interest. It's a major expense, one you need to monitor in order to keep as low as possible.

Lenders don't call their borrowers to offer better loan terms when interest rates decline. You as a borrower have to take the initiative. You have to monitor current rates yourself and compare your rate to them. You have to shop around for new financing which will lower your interest expense. Nobody else is going to do it for you.

Before you even consider shopping for a new loan to lower your mortgage interest, however, you must examine your loan documents to see whether the existing mortgage contains a prepayment penalty. If it does, factor the penalty into your calculations. You'll trigger the penalty when you pay off the existing loan, and that can make a substantial difference in the calculations.

Besides the prepayment penalty, you need to know the other costs you'll incur in obtaining the new loan, from the appraisal fee to the points, right on down to the notary fees.

Finally, you need to have some idea how long you intend to keep the property. In some cases, the costs involved in obtaining a new loan at a lower interest rate make it unattractive unless you plan to keep the property for more than three years. If you intend to sell the property in one year, you shouldn't get such a loan because its advantages evaporate when it's paid off in a year's time, and they wouldn't be realized for three years. You want new financing to pay for itself in short order, and sometimes it can.

If you're currently borrowing $100,000 at 10%, a new loan for that same amount at 8% will reduce your interest expense the first year by $2,000 (assuming for the sake of simplicity that there's no amortization). If the costs involved in obtaining that new loan at the lower interest rate amount to $2,000, and you expect to keep the property longer than a year, you will definitely fatten your bottom line by obtaining the new loan.

Do the numbers yourself on your property and the available loans.

■ **Fool yourself into thinking your cash flow is negative**—Ordinarily you shouldn't be trying to fool yourself. Fooling oneself carries bad con-

notations. People say that you're only fooling yourself if you think you can keep up with the Joneses on half their income, if you think a movie star on location in your hometown is going to fall in love with you, if you think money buys happiness, if you think you're going to beat the odds in Atlantic City, if you think your no-name dot-com stocks will rise from their ashes, or if you think that your next cigarette is going to be your last. Those don't sound like good ways to fool yourself, do they?

They're not. They're not realistic. They're not productive.

There is at least one good way to fool yourself that I know of, one which helps you watch your rental property expenses more carefully. Fool yourself into thinking that you have a negative cash flow. Some of you may not have to fool yourself. You already have a negative cash flow, and you'd be delighted just to break even. This method for decreasing your expenses won't help you in the least, but you can surely understand from first-hand experience how it works.

If you have an honest-to-goodness negative-cash-flow property, you know how closely you watch your expenses. They're supremely important to you because you have to dip into your own pocket every month to support the property. You're depriving yourself of the opportunity to use those funds for other purposes. On the other hand, if your property is generating a positive cash flow, you don't pay nearly as much attention to the expenses. You simply pay them out of the available income.

You can see how this attitudinal difference works whenever you buy a rental property which in the previous owners' hands was either completely paid off or mostly paid off. You'll notice that they were lax in raising their rents and lax in controlling their expenses. "Easy come, easy go!" was their attitude. With a big new mortgage payment facing you every month, you'll be looking for all kinds of ways to make that property pay, and you'll discover them.

To keep yourself from becoming inattentive to your own expenses, fool yourself into thinking that your positive-cash-flow property is poorer than it actually is. It's a simple thing to do. You just transfer that property's excess funds out of its operations account once a month so that the balance is never very high. That's all. You'll be fooling yourself into thinking that the property

Notice of Change
in Terms of Tenancy

TO   Sam and Barbara Brooks   , Tenant in Possession

3104 Dogwood Drive

Bigtown, CA 09601

YOU ARE HEREBY NOTIFIED that the terms of tenancy under which you occupy the above-described premises are to be changed.

Effective   August 5   , XXXX, there will be the following changes:

• Tenants must pay for repairs of all damage, including drain stoppages, which they or their guests have caused.

• Tenants must pay for any windows broken in their dwelling while they live there.

Dated this 2nd day of   July   , XXXX .

Clyde Woodard, Manager
Owner/Manager

This Notice was served by the Owner/Manager in the following manner (check those which apply):

(X) by personal delivery to the tenant,
( ) by leaving a copy with someone on the premises other than the tenant,
( ) by mailing,
( ) by posting.

has little money available to pay its bills, and as a consequence, you'll be watching those expenses a little more closely. It works for this old fool.

■ **Question your property tax bill**—Perhaps you have seen one of those "QUESTION AUTHORITY" bumper stickers on an ancient, beat-up Volkswagen bus. You shake your head and lament the further decline of the old-fashioned values you were brought up with. Yet your own attitude toward authority could be costing you some big bucks.

You may be questioning all of your other land-lording expenses and trying every which way to control them, but you may not even have thought about questioning your property taxes, and they're always a major expense.

You may have thought your tax bill was sacrosanct because it comes to you on an official computer-printed form and appears to be based on a "Higher Authority" or at the very least upon some mandated formulas.

Whoa now, don't get carried away! That tax bill of yours may have some very exact figures on it, and it may be printed on an official form, but it is definitely open to question. Go ahead and question it. Take the time once a year to examine your tax bill for each property. Make sure that the bill is for the property you own, first of all, and not for some other property which the county has mistakenly linked to your name. Make sure that you understand the bill, and then see whether you agree with the figures. You want to be certain that the law is being applied to you fairly, that the formulas for calculating the value of your property are correct and that the tax rate has been applied to your property correctly.

If anything appears to be out of line, question the authorities. If you see the error of their ways but you can't quite convince them of their errors yourself, consider whether the sums involved warrant your hiring an "authority" of your own to represent you. There are knowledgeable people who specialize in challenging property tax assessments. They expect to be paid well, of course, but what they expect for their efforts is a portion of your tax savings. They profit only if you profit.

■ **Transfer costs**—When you rent out residences, you are furnishing your tenants with more than a roof over their heads. You are providing them with certain services, too, services which cost you money. Some of these services, such as maintenance and repairs, you absolutely have to provide and pay for because laws require you to, but that doesn't mean you have to provide and pay for maintenance and repairs when tenants are negligent or destructive. You don't. You may want to provide the service so the work gets done promptly, but you shouldn't be paying for it as well.

When a tenant shoots a shotgun through the ceiling and it blows a hole right through the roof, you go ahead and repair the damage, but you expect the tenant to pay for it, don't you? Sure, the tenant has damaged the building. Who cares whether it happened accidentally or on purpose? The tenant caused the damage. The tenant should have to pay.

If that roof had started to leak as a result of weathering or a windstorm, you would have paid for the repairs. That leak wouldn't be the tenant's fault, and repairing it is your responsibility under the "warranty of habitability" which you provide as a landlord.

When a tenant plugs up a toilet or breaks a window, do you get it fixed and pay for the damage yourself, or do you make the tenant pay? Are plugged-up toilets and broken windows your responsibility or are they your tenant's? In my book, they're the tenant's responsibility, and the tenant should pay. You didn't plug up the toilet. You didn't break the window. No defect, no normal wear and tear caused the damage. It didn't happen through an act of God. It doesn't always happen through an act of your tenants. I'll grant you that. It could have been a neighbor's kid who put a rock through the window. But if you tell your tenants that they must pay for only those windows which they break and that you will pay for all the others, then you can be sure that no window broken in their place will ever be their fault, and they won't know who broke it. You'll be paying for every broken window. Why should you pay automatically? Why should you in effect let them charge every plugged-up toilet and every broken window on your MasterCard?

Sure, if there are some special circumstances, then you can make a deal with your tenants. Get them to pay a portion and you pay the rest. That's reasonable. Just don't pay every time. Make your tenants responsible. Transfer the costs of dealing with these problems to them.

The rental agreements in this book do just that, and you should do the same. If you and your tenants have an existing agreement which fails to mention payment for broken windows and plugged drains, you don't have to switch rental agreements to make this change. All you have to do is give your tenants a Notice of Change in Terms of Tenancy which shifts the responsibility from you to them in thirty days (could be longer if you want to play Mr. Niceguy), provided, of course, that your existing agreement and the landlord-tenant laws in your area allow you to.

Transferring these costs to your tenants will definitely decrease your expenses. Look around. Ask yourself whether there are any other services which cost you money but which you are providing free of charge to your tenants? Might you get them to pay for these services? Once they are, you've eliminated another expense and fattened your bottom line a little bit more.

■ **Practice sensible energy conservation**— You're a lucky landlord if you have a building where you pay none of the utilities, where everything is on separate meters, and there are no common areas requiring heat or lighting or water.

I had such a building once, the first rental property I ever purchased. It was a fourplex with a stucco exterior which never needed painting, a pitched roof which shed water like a doorman's umbrella, a concrete yard area which never needed mowing, and four separate meters for electricity, four separate meters for gas, and four separate meters for water. I still dream of the place and its minimal expenses. I bought it from the builder who had built it and owned it for fifteen years. He had built it to be cheap to own. He was right on the mark.

Unfortunately, such buildings are about as scarce as modesty among film stars. Most rental buildings create utility bills for their owners, and those bills can be whoppers, potentially very damaging to your financial health. You can't expect much relief from the people who contribute to those bills, your tenants, but you can expect to find some relief from the people who send you the bills every month, the utility companies. Seek their advice.

You will find that most utility companies have conservation advisors who specialize in helping customers reduce their energy consumption. At the very least, they will give you booklets on energy conservation. Many offer much more help than that, though. They may give you conservation devices like shower flow restrictors and toilet tank water displacement bags. They may subsidize the cost of low-flush toilets. They may come out and conduct an energy audit of your building and make suggestions for conservation. They may even offer you low-interest loans so you can make building changes which will conserve energy, changes such as installing efficient space and water heaters, thermal windows, fluorescent lighting, and extra insulation.

Take advantage of these programs. Become better informed about energy conservation, and make those changes which offer a good payback and will show up before long on your building's bottom line.

■ **Foster conservation, recycling, and reuse of "solid waste"**—Not only do conservation (using less of anything), recycling (reprocessing used products into new products), and reuse (using something over rather than throwing it away) make good sense ecologically, they make good sense economically, especially for landlords. The more you do to reduce the solid waste which your tenants throw into the garbage, the more you do to reduce your garbage bills.

Encourage your tenants to recycle their newspapers, magazines, cardboard, glass, aluminum, beverage containers, and plastics. Make it easy for them to do so by providing a place where they can sort their recyclables and separate bins where they can deposit their sorted items. You might even be able to make your recycling effort pay for itself by giving a tenant the responsibility of looking after your building's "recycling center" in exchange for getting to keep whatever monies the recyclables bring.

A conscientious recycling effort will reduce the garbage your tenants generate by at least one-half. Think of what your building's bottom line would look like with its garbage bill cut in half!

■ **Investigate garbage-handling alternatives**— Solid waste disposal is big business. It's expensive business. It has become especially expensive because garbage is no longer so easy to get rid of. You can't just burn it in an incinerator, bury it in a landfill, or ditch it in the ocean. You have to dispose of it properly in accordance with myriad governmental regulations. As a result, dumps nowadays are expensive to open, to maintain, and to close. And because few people want to have a dump in their neighborhood, new dump sites are further than ever from populated areas. New York

City's garbage leaves the city on barges and in railcars destined for dumping grounds hundreds of miles away.

Garbage charges vary dramatically from place to place for any number of reasons. My most expensive garbage bill averages twice what the lowest one averages per dwelling, even though I've made every effort to reduce it. Had I not been careful, it would have been higher still. Watch carefully how much you're paying for garbage and investigate various garbage-handling alternatives when you notice your garbage bill growing.

Here are some cost-saving alternatives you might want to investigate—switching from one hauler to another (most haulers have community monopolies, and you may have no choice); installing a compactor for an entire complex (compacted garbage qualifies for a cheaper rate per yard than loose garbage); switching to smaller cans (some households produce less than 20 gallons per week; why should you provide a more expensive 30 gallon can?); switching from individual cans to a dumpster (do the calculations); switching from a dumpster to individual cans (do the calculations again); and hauling your own garbage (where local regulations allow my staff to haul the garbage in a covered utility trailer, they do; my garbage bill is cut in half; they get half the savings; I get half the savings, and we're both happy).

Some Last Words

Take neither your income nor your expenses for granted. Be alert to the opportunities which exist all around you for increasing your income and decreasing your expenses, but don't forget that your primary objective is to fatten your bottom line. It is not merely to increase your income or decrease your expenses, not when the one will have an adverse effect on the other. Increasing your monthly income by $5 while at the same time increasing your monthly expenses by $6 isn't any way to fatten your bottom line, not even when you multiply those numbers many times. Remember the old joke about the fellow who lost money on every sale but made it up on volume. Don't follow suit.

16
Insurance

Believe it or not, General Motors' biggest single expense is not payroll, steel, tires, aluminum, or even plastic. It's insurance, insurance of every kind imaginable. GM, with its considerable assets, has to proceed with caution in a society overrun by people who are quick to place a highly inflated dollar value on stubbed toes and kinked necks, people who pursue their fortunes through litigation.

As a rental property owner with assets somewhat less than GM's, you need not follow GM's example by spending more on insurance than on anything else, but you should nevertheless be well covered by various kinds of insurance. You become increasingly vulnerable to losses as you build your property assets. You have a lot to lose if a building of yours burns to the ground when it's half paid for. You have a lot to lose if someone files a lawsuit against you just when you've taken early retirement to live off your rental income. Litigants and their legal counsel don't care how hard or how long you've worked to gather your assets. That's of no consequence to them. They show no mercy when they're fighting to get their hands on your money. They just want everything they can get out of you, and, of course, they know you're wealthy because, after all, you own income property. You're a landlord.

Because you do own income property, you have special insurance needs above and beyond those of people who don't. You should know something about the many kinds of insurance available to you to serve those needs. You should know something about exercising prudence whenever you're thinking about insurance, and you should know something about selecting a solid company to insure you.

In addition, you should know something about getting a fair settlement, responding to accidents, settling claims yourself, and helping your tenants understand renters' insurance. These are the subjects of this chapter.

Becoming Acquainted with the Many Kinds of Insurance Available

In the not too distant past, there was only one kind of insurance which we had to consider as rental property owners. That was fire insurance. We still buy fire insurance today, at least as much as ever, but because we are exposed to so many more types of liability and danger, we need more kinds of insurance, lots more. Here are eighteen kinds of insurance you should know something about if you want to protect your assets from calamity.

■ **Fire**—Kids shouldn't play with fire, and rental property owners shouldn't play with fire insurance. Fire insurance is serious business. Even lenders know that.

Lenders require you to protect their interest in your building with a fire insurance policy at the very least because they figure that they cannot afford to risk a loss should the place go up in flames. Were that to happen, they'd lose the collateral for their loan and the income as well because they know you'd stop making the payments.

That's all understandable, but what about your share of your building? Shouldn't you have fire insurance on it, too?

Absolutely yes! You should be even more cautious than your lender because your equity in a building represents a much greater proportion of your total assets than what one building represents of a lender's assets. In addition, your interest in that building keeps growing as appreciation pushes the value up and your equity payments push the loan balance down. With more to protect virtually every month, you should be so cautious about your fire insurance that whenever your premium comes due, you make certain that your building is covered with a policy large enough to pay current replacement costs. Anything less, and you'd be playing with fire. Anything more, and you'd be wasting your money, for $250,000 worth of coverage on a building which costs $200,000 to replace will pay only $200,000, no matter what.

Note that you should insure only your building, its contents, and the other improvements on the property which might be damaged by fire. Do not insure the land. It'll still be there when the fire dies down.

Being the conservative folks they are, lenders may tell you that you have to carry enough fire insurance to cover the entire amount of their loan, even when that loan amount exceeds the replacement cost of everything a fire could possibly damage. They don't seem to understand that some of their loan might be secured by land. Enlighten them. Don't pay for an expensive policy with higher than necessary coverage just to appease a nervous, hidebound lender.

I once had a lender demand that I secure a $300,000 fire insurance policy to protect a first mortgage for that amount on a trailer park. Only after I produced evidence showing that no fire could possibly do more than $75,000 worth of damage to the park did the lender relent and allow me to reduce the policy to $75,000. As you might imagine, my premium for a quarter of the original coverage took a significant drop, and the savings were mine alone to keep.

Just as you should avoid being forced into buying too much insurance by an ignorant lender, you should avoid buying too little insurance in order to save yourself a few dollars on the premiums.

There's more than one drawback in having too little insurance. There's the obvious drawback, of course. With $150,000 worth of coverage on a $200,000 building which burned to the ground, you wouldn't be able to collect enough for a replacement. But there's another less obvious drawback. It involves compliance with something called the *co-insurance* clause, also known as the *average clause* or the *reduced-rate-contribution clause.*

Here's how it works. Suppose you decide to insure your $200,000 building for $100,000 because you read somewhere that most fires are extinguished before they destroy an entire building. You figure that you'll get the insurance com-pany to assume the risk for the first $100,000 worth of damage and you'll assume the risk for the second $100,000. So far, so good. You stand to save a fair amount of money on premiums by assuming a risk for the same amount of money as the insurance company when you're actually taking a much smaller risk. The first half of a building always burns before the second half, doesn't it? And the first half is insured.

You'd be right except for one little thing. Insurers ain't completely stupid. They know some people think this way, so they include a co-insurance clause in their policies. This clause requires you as policy holder to insure your building for at least 80% of its replacement cost in order to collect the entire amount of any damage up to your policy limits. If your $200,000 building is insured for $100,000, and you have a loss of $50,000, the policy will pay only $25,000 (50% of the loss) even though you have $100,000 worth of coverage. Under the co-insurance clause, the *percentage* of coverage you have, not the amount, applies to losses. $100,000 of coverage on a $200,000 building translates into 50%. By insuring that $200,000 building for at least 80% of its replacement cost, or $160,000 in this case, you'd avoid being caught by the clause, and you'd receive a full $100,000 in the event of a $100,000 loss.

Don't get caught with your coverage down! You might become a big loser by trying to save a little on your premiums.

■ **Extended Coverage**—Most insurance companies offer what they call "extended coverage" (sometimes called "comprehensive coverage" or a "package policy") along with their standard fire insurance policies, and they price this coverage at very attractive rates. It may include damage caused by hail, explosions, windstorms, aircraft, vehicles, smoke, burst pipes, rioting, vandalism, falling trees, freezing, collapse, landslides, or accidental water discharge. Look into it. It's good coverage to have when a hard freeze breaks water pipes in a vacant rental house you own, and comes the thaw, water squirts everywhere through those burst pipes, ruining the flooring throughout the house.

■ **Earthquake**—Extended coverage policies do not extend far enough to include earthquake coverage. It's always a separate policy. Even with a high deductible and lots of exclusions, it's not cheap, but you shouldn't be without it in any area prone to earthquakes where you own improved property. One earthquake, just seconds-long, could destroy your lifelong landlording work.

On the other hand, an insurance consultant told me that he is wary about earthquake coverage because he believes that insurance companies' exposure is too great. They could be wiped out by a major earthquake and be unable to pay their policyholders' claims even after having accepted hefty premiums for years. He advises certain of his clients to take whatever physical precautions they can take to minimize earthquake damage to their property and then self-insure ("self-insuring" and "insuring yourself" mean that you act as your own insurer; you don't buy coverage from anyone else). He advises other clients to select a company which has abundant assets and little exposure itself to earthquake claims in a single area.

You might want to discuss the subject in detail with your insurance agent or with an independent insurance consultant before you commit yourself to spending any money on an earthquake policy.

■ **Flood**—Water damage is water damage, isn't it? Yes it is, but water damage has lots of causes, and as far as water damage and insurance coverage are concerned, what's most important is what causes the damage. You could find yourself "high and dry" one of these days upon discovering that your insurance policy covers only water damage caused by accidental leakage and not water damage caused by flooding, high water, or sewage backups. Ask for the coverage you want according to the likelihood of these calamities' occurring where your property is located, and don't assume that you have flood insurance unless you see it written in your policy. Like earthquake insurance, flood insurance doesn't come packaged with other coverage. It's separate.

In areas prone to flooding, which present too much risk for the average insurer, the National Flood Association will still provide coverage and at nominal rates.

■ **Other Improvements**—Property improvements other than buildings, including such things as swimming pools, parking lots, walks, fences, and signs, may sustain direct damage from a flood, fire, ice storm, or other disaster, too, but they won't be covered by your standard building policy unless you include them specifically under extended coverage. Examine what your insurer offers for coverage and decide whether the peace of mind is worth the premiums.

Many owners insure themselves for damage to their non-building property improvements because they regard the potential risk of damage, extent of damage, and consequences of damage to be minimal in relation to the other exposure they have.

■ **Vandalism and Malicious Mischief**—Should anyone damage your property, say, by tearing your laundry machines apart for the coins or by laying waste a vacant apartment, your vandalism and malicious mischief insurance would pay to repair the damage. You hope you'll never have occasion to use such coverage because damage like this is pretty demoralizing to a conscientious owner, but if it should happen, you ought to have the right insurance to pay for the repairs. When included in a package policy, it can be quite inexpensive.

■ **Liability**—Up until thirty years ago, not every rental property owner bothered to obtain liability coverage because few people filed liability claims and even fewer collected. Today that's all changed. Today you can't afford to be without liability insurance any more than obstetricians can afford to be without malpractice insurance.

No longer does the age-old maxim, "Caveat emptor!" ("Let the buyer beware!") apply to business dealings. Now it's "Caveat venditor!" ("Let the seller beware!") You are expected to be the perfect landlord and to supply the perfect rental property. That's quite a burden to bear, an impossible burden for any individual businessperson like yourself.

Both the number of liability cases and the types of cases have increased, as have the awards. It's not just the personal injury case caused by your supposed negligence that you have to worry about nowadays. It's the discrimination case, the wrongful eviction case, the invasion-of-privacy case, the crime-on-your-property case, the strict liability case, the failure-to-maintain case, the failure-to-keep-me-happy case. Those are ever-present worries.

The worries keep growing, too. "Strict liability" applied to landlording is something new. In case you haven't heard, courts are beginning to rule that tenants need prove only that your "product" was defective and that as a result of the defect they were hurt. They do not have to prove that you were negligent in the least.

This policy of strict liability has been applied to manufactured products for some years here in the U.S. It has caused some companies to go out of business entirely and others to stop making certain products. Cessna Aircraft, for example, stopped manufacturing the popular 152 trainer when its product liability insurance reached $17,000 for each one of these little $40,000 airplanes, the smallest of any they made and one of the safest airplanes ever built.

At that rate (42.5%), your insurance bill on a $600-a-month apartment would be $255 a month, pretty steep for only one type of coverage, wouldn't you say? We can only guess how the application of strict liability is going to affect the landlording business.

Don't go the self-insurance route for this risk. Buy insurance which will cover every liability you can think of, and while you're at it, buy enough. Buy the highest limits available, or add to your liability policy's limits with an umbrella policy. You will find that a million dollars' worth of coverage costs little more than a hundred thousand dollars' worth, and it could save you from the poorhouse, for the awards people manage to get in liability cases, especially when they involve a personal injury, tend to be high.

Expect your liability premiums to become a more noticeable expense than they have been in the past. Complain all you want to about the rising rates, but don't neglect paying them.

■ **Loss of Rents**—If a fire or some other mishap should render your rentals uninhabitable for a time, your tenants will stop paying you their rent immediately and you won't have any income to use for paying those many fixed expenses which keep right on accumulating. You'll have to pay those continuing bills out of your own savings unless you have loss-of-rents insurance coverage. In that case, your insurance company will compensate you for the loss of rental income over a reasonable period of time while your building is being repaired.

With all the other problems you're likely to have if a major mishap should occur at your property, you don't need financial problems, too, not when you can protect yourself for a small premium.

■ **Contents**—Your own belongings which you keep at your rental property, belongings such as mowers, tools, laundry machines, furniture, appliances, supplies, and the like, would be covered against a variety of losses by most comprehensive rental property owners' insurance policies (check yours to make sure), but your tenants' belongings would not be covered at all.

■ **Workers' Compensation**—Even though you may hire only casual help or deduct just a few dollars from a tenant's rent in exchange for minor management or maintenance services, you are an "employer" and you *must* have workers' compensation insurance. If that worker of yours were to require medical attention or become incapacitated while on the job, even while driving to the bank to deposit rent monies, you would be held liable. You would have to pay those bills, no matter how large or how small.

You don't have to be the least bit at fault to be held liable. In fact, your clumsy worker could be totally at fault for throwing out his back after tripping over a paint bucket which he had carelessly left lying around and you'd still be liable for his medical bills. Fault doesn't matter. Workers' compensation insurance is "no-fault" coverage.

While he was out doing some yard work, one of my managers was bitten by a rare spider and nearly died from the resulting complications. Neither he nor I was at fault. We couldn't have done anything to prevent this spider bite. It just happened. I was sick at heart about the whole thing, but I'd have been a lot sicker if I hadn't had a workers' compensation policy to pay for his care. It cost some big bucks.

Don't assume this risk yourself. You know what medical bills can run nowadays, and you probably know what awards juries are making to people who become disabled on the job, even when the disability is only 10%. Whatever the medical bills, whatever the disability, you cannot afford to pay for these things yourself directly. You need workers' compensation insurance to pay for them for you.

Don't assume that any all-inclusive insurance policy you buy for your rental property also includes workers' compensation. It doesn't. Workers' compensation insurance is a separate policy altogether.

Most states require every employer to have workers' compensation insurance, and because it's required, the rates are reasonable. They're based upon how much your workers earn and upon the type of work they do. The rates are a percentage of earnings, and the percentage increases as the riskiness of the work increases. The rate for somebody who does office work is around 1.2%, while the rate for somebody who does deep sea diving is over 100%.

Rates do vary, and you will find that you can save something on your premiums by taking a little initiative. Rather than approaching an insurer on your own, go through a group if you can because they usually get the most attractive rates. Check to see whether your rental housing association offers some sort of a group plan. Many do.

Rather than letting the insurer arbitrarily classify your workers, make sure you classify them correctly yourself according to the kind of work they do most. For a manager who does little more than clerical work, you should be paying around 1.2%. For a manager who does a little bit of everything, including both sedentary work and maintenance work, you should be paying around 12%. Don't pay too much or too little by classifying your workers incorrectly.

By the way, workers' compensation insurers conduct audits periodically to ensure that you are paying the correct premiums, so don't think you'll be able to get away with something by classifying your handyman as a clerical worker just to pay a cheaper rate. Besides, if your handyman is classified as a clerical worker and he gets injured using an electric drain auger, you'd better be prepared to do some fast explaining. Cheating doesn't pay.

Rather than buying multiple policies, one for each of your properties, buy a single policy to cover all the workers at all of your properties, and divide up the costs among the properties yourself when you pay the bill.

■ **Mortgage**—Two completely different types of insurance coverage have come to be known as "mortgage insurance." The object of both types is the same, to pay off the balance of the outstanding mortgage when trouble strikes, but the beneficiaries are definitely not the same.

The first type benefits the property owner. It's pretty much the same as decreasing term life insurance, the decreasing sum being the mortgage balance. It's especially popular with homeowners because they want to protect themselves in case

death or disability puts an end to some or all of the income used to make their house payments. The mortgage would then be paid off in full. Such insurance is available to cover rental property mortgages as well, and it may be just as important for some rental property owners to have as it is for homeowners, especially when a rental property is running a negative cash flow and one person is contributing income from a job to support it.

When determining whether you should get this insurance coverage, consider both the salary and the time contributions of each person involved with the property because you may find that hired help would be needed to compensate for the work done by one of those people involved, and that, of course, would increase the negative cash flow still more. If you do choose to buy this kind of mortgage insurance for your income property, consult your tax adviser for advice on whether it is tax-deductible as a business expense in your situation. It may or may not be.

The other type of mortgage insurance will pay off the mortgage all right, but it won't benefit you as the property owner in the least. It protects your lender should you default on the mortgage and should the property be sold off for less than the balance owing. The policy would pay the lender the difference between the two.

Although your lender may require that you pay the premium on such a policy, don't suppose that you're getting the same coverage as the other kind of mortgage insurance. You're not. When the first one pays off, you or your heirs wind up with assistance in making your loan payments or with a property which is free and clear. When the second one pays off, neither you nor your heirs get a thing. The lender gets the policy's proceeds.

■ **Fidelity**—In some businesses where dishonest employees have the opportunity to steal cash and/or goods, wary employers buy fidelity insurance, that is, they "bond" their employees to protect themselves from pilferage and embezzlement.

The employees you hire to manage and maintain your rental property have an opportunity to steal from you. Of that there is no doubt. They might appropriate your tools or supplies for their own use. They might under-report occupancies. They might charge higher rents than they report to you. They might withhold more from tenants' security deposits than they tell you about. They might find more than a few coins on the floor after they've counted the laundry money. They might be even more audacious and abscond with an entire month's rent receipts. All of these things have been known to happen to suspecting and unsuspecting owners alike. They could happen to you, too.

If you are inclined to put your properties on "automatic pilot," to let your manager run everything for months at a time, checking only now and then to see whether there's any money in the property account down at the bank, you need fidelity insurance. You need it desperately.

But if you are looking over your manager's shoulder on a random basis and you believe that you have a pretty good handle on your income, don't bother. The premiums for this kind of insurance are really much too high for the limited amount of exposure you have.

Rather than pay fidelity insurance premiums for a policy which will pay careless employers for their carelessness,

save the money and insure yourself by being careful. Reduce the opportunities managers have to steal from you. See that they handle little or no cash. See that they provide you with weekly income and occupancy reports. And see that you select your managers carefully in the first place.

Note that fidelity insurance covers losses you sustain as a result of your own employees' mishandling of funds. It would not cover losses caused by a manager working at your property if that manager were responsible to a property management company rather than to you. To protect yourself from that kind of loss, insist that any property management company you use, supply a bond of its own.

■ **Auto**—To protect your property assets, you should obtain the highest liability limits available for your own automobiles. Minimum liability in-

surance may be quite sufficient for your tenants. If they're hit with a $500,000 judgment, their insurance carrier would pay out the limits of the policy, their few assets would be liquidated, and they would simply declare bankruptcy. It's done every day. But what if you, a person of property, get hit with a $500,000 judgment, and you have only $100,000 in coverage? Kiss everything goodbye. Caveat, dear landlord!

■ **Non-Owned Auto**—Non-owned auto liability insurance does not protect you from liability when you're driving a car other than your own. Your regular automobile policy should do that.

No, non-owned auto protects you in case anyone you hire, even temporarily, is driving his own automobile and running errands for you when he becomes involved in an automobile accident. When the injured's attorney learns that your employee, while driving to the hardware store to pick up some towel bars for you, caused the accident which injured his client, you will be added to the list of those being sued. Insurance to protect you under such circumstances is reasonably inexpensive and well worth the cost.

■ **Umbrella**—Umbrella insurance coverage has nothing at all to do with those umbrellas we hold up to keep raindrops from falling on our heads. No, umbrella insurance, which is also known as blanket or excess insurance, keeps covering us when we reach the limits of our other liability policies. Those other policies cost more per dollar of coverage than an umbrella policy does because they pay off more. They pay the smaller claims. Umbrella policies pay only the larger claims and only the higher amounts of the larger claims. On a $465,000 claim, for example, the primary policy might pay the first $300,000, while the umbrella policy might pay the rest, the $165,000.

Investigate the possibility of keeping the limits of your individual liability policies around $300,000 for each property and then buying an umbrella policy for $300,000 to a million or more. You should find that that practice will be less expensive than buying individual policies for a million dollars or more each.

To be most effective, your umbrella policy should leave no gaps between the upper limits of your various primary liability policies and the lower limit of the umbrella policy itself. It should also cover you for at least double the value of your personal assets.

Buy it from the same company which wrote most of your primary liability policies, and you'll avoid potential squabbling between two companies which have different ideas for settling a single lawsuit.

■ **Boiler and Machinery**—You can imagine how horrendous the explosion of a boiler could be. The deaths, injuries, and property damage could result in some very costly claims. But the risk of claims isn't the only reason you should consider this type of insurance if you have the kind of equipment it covers: boilers, heavy machinery, pressure tanks, large air conditioners, or large compressors. You should consider it because the insurer becomes a partner with you in keeping losses to a minimum by inspecting the equipment regularly and making sure that it is well maintained and safe to operate.

Other insurers ought to spend as much of their premium dollars on loss prevention as boiler and machinery insurers do. They'd have fewer claims to pay.

■ **Waterbed**—Your tenants with waterbeds are the ones who ought to provide waterbed insurance, but face it, they're not going to remember to keep it in force unless you keep reminding them. You'd be wise to charge them enough extra rent to pay for the policy, and then pay the premiums yourself if you want the coverage.

■ **Title**—When you learn that title insurance companies pay out less than ten cents in claims out of every dollar they collect in premiums, you're inclined to think that you ought to stop whatever you're doing and become a title insurer yourself, whatever it is that title insurers do. After all, the house take in Vegas doesn't approach

ninety cents out of a dollar. If it did, gamblers wouldn't return to the tables.

Well, then, should you buy title insurance yourself on your newly acquired properties? Why does title insurance pay out so little? What is title insurance anyway?

First of all, title insurance protects buyers against other people's claims to a property which might result from any number of unexpected occurrences, such as forgeries, mistaken identical names, and undisclosed heirs. Title insurance guarantees that nothing out of a property's past will catch up with you and deny you ownership now or in the future. It guarantees that you have clear title, that you and no one else truly owns the property.

Title insurance companies pay out so little in claims because they go to great lengths to discover problems with the title, and these protective measures are included in the price of the policy. If fire insurance companies operated similarly, they'd install an automatic sprinkler system in every building they cover and include the cost of the system in the price of the policy.

As to whether you should buy title insurance or not, you may not have much of a choice. Institutional lenders require you to buy enough title insurance to cover their loan. But the policy they require is strictly a lender's policy, not a buyer's policy. It's like the mortgage insurance which some lenders require borrowers to buy to protect the lenders. It doesn't pay you at all. It does benefit you somewhat, however, because it pays for the insurer's exhaustive title search, and consequently, the buyer's title insurance premium, which you may choose to buy or not, is less expensive than it would otherwise be.

When you're trying to decide whether to buy a buyer's title insurance policy, you should remember that you pay for it only once, when you first acquire the property, and then both you and your heirs are covered for as long as you or they own the property. You never pay another premium after that.

Whatever you do, don't acquire any property without having someone search the title at the very least, even if no lender's involved and you're paying for it in cash, yes, even if you win it in a poker game. That title search is an absolute must. It could reveal mechanics' liens, attachments, and old loans which the owner told you nothing about and which could trouble you for years to come.

Exercising Prudence

Insurers play the odds just as bettors do, just as you do when you gamble on renting to a certain applicant or on buying a particular property. You should play the odds when you buy insurance, too. Although there is some kind of insurance available for every conceivable risk connected with landlording, if you want to pay for it, and there are a great many insurance agents around who would be delighted to sell it to you, you don't want insurance to become your number-one expense as it is for General Motors. Seize the opportunity to save money every time you review your insurance needs.

Naturally you might be prudent in trying to save or you might be imprudent.

Here's how to be prudent—

* Select only the kinds of coverage you need for your location and situation. ("Are there all that many hurricanes in Billings, Montana?")
* Calculate carefully the amount of coverage you need. ("Do you really need $380,000 worth of fire insurance for your $160,000 duplex?")
* Shop around for coverage two months before the renewal date on your policy, and do it every time. ("$285? Why, Gerry wants $450 for the very same thing!")
* Price package policies. ("You mean that fire, vandalism, liability, loss of rents, and contents coverage all together are only $80 more than fire insurance alone?")
* Consider policies with deductibles you can live with. ("Does earthquake insurance with a $25,000 deductible clause really have a premium $222 lower? Does liability insurance with a $500 deductible really cost $93 less every year?")
* Hire an insurance consultant (see Yellow Pages under "Insurance Consultants") who sells no insurance himself to review your properties and your coverage and make suggestions for reducing your insurance costs. ("Will adding two more fire extinguishers really save me $65 in premiums?")

Here's how to be imprudent—

* Buy only the kinds and amounts of coverage your lender and the law require. ("The tenant in Apt. 112 wants how much for tripping on that broken step?")
* Buy whatever coverage your agent sells you. ("You think I need glacier coverage? OK, if you say so. The winters have been getting colder around here. Write it up.")
* Buy only from your bridge partner who sells insurance on the side. ("Can you get me a good deal, Gerry?")
* Buy separate policies for each kind of peril. ("Is it $85 more for contents and $18 for loss of rents or vice versa?")
* Buy non-deductible coverage. ("You want to settle my claim about the dent in my commercial washing machine for $52?")
* Trust insurance agents to give you money-saving suggestions. ("Did you say that you drove by the property and everything looked all right?")

Selecting a Solid Insurance Company

Not so long ago we needn't have concerned ourselves about the ability of our insurance company to pay a claim. We simply shopped for the best price and took for granted that the company we selected would be sound enough to pay whatever claims we might have.

Today, some companies, having put their hoarded premiums into failed investments and having had to pay numerous big settlements, are finding themselves on ground shakier than a southern California earthquake fault, unable to pay claims without digging deep into their assets. Even the venerable Lloyd's of London has been in trouble and many of the "names" who back the Lloyd's policies with their personal fortunes have suffered their own Dust Bowl Depression and lost everything.

Lucky for us, we don't have to depend upon flacks and advertising agencies for information about insurance companies. Their assets are not cloaked in secrecy. It is public information. Insurance companies are rated by an independent company, A.M. Best, and you may consult these ratings at your local library.

Understand that the ratings change as the companies' fortunes change. What was a solid company two years ago may be jelly today. Be sure you're looking at the very latest ratings.

Getting Your Fair Settlement

Some insurance companies don't pay claims very willingly or fairly. They make you jump through their flaming hoops before they will pay you even a pittance. Should you feel that your insurance company isn't treating you equitably when handling your claim, secure the services of a public insurance adjuster. Their business is to represent policyholders. They know how much claims are worth because they're involved with them all the time. For a percentage of your claim, they get bids, do the paperwork, make the phone calls, and argue on your behalf. They will make sure that you get every cent your insurance company owes you and that you get it promptly. You'll find them listed in the Yellow Pages under "Adjusters."

Responding to an Accident

Whenever an accident on your property results in an injury, see that the injured party receives proper medical attention right away. Immediately after that, contact your insurance agent and complete an accident report. As time goes by, the witnesses and the injured party tend to forget what actually happened, and you can be sure that their muddled memories are not going to favor their landlord as they struggle to reconstruct the mishap.

Settling Tenants' Claims Yourself

Because they don't want their premiums raised or their coverage canceled, motorists will sometimes try to settle "fender-bender" claims themselves rather than turn them over to their insurance companies.

For these same reasons and a few others, I have tried to settle tenants' claims myself at times. The results have been mixed. In most cases, the tenants took what I offered and went away pleased. In one case I well remember, the tenant took what I offered and acted pleased. Then, without any warning or attempt to discuss the matter further, she went to an attorney and filed suit. I was not pleased.

Just as greed among heirs surfaces when estates are being settled, greed among tenants surfaces when damage claims are being settled. Greed, you must recognize, feeds upon itself in some people. No matter how much you offer to settle a claim, it won't be enough. They expect a lifetime annuity for a hangnail, but if you offer them a lifetime annuity straightaway, they'll hold out for a life-after-death annuity, too, and expect you to deliver it wherever they happen to be.

If you are inclined to settle a claim yourself, be cautious every step of the way, but do act fast and do document everything. Determine, first of all, whether you are at fault for what has happened. Listen to what everybody has to say. Get statements from witnesses if possible, and decide whether you ought to bother making an offer at all. Sometimes the best thing you can do is ask the tenants what they think is fair for you to do under the circumstances. Take your cues from them. They might surprise you and say something reasonable.

Tailor your offer to the type of tenants you're dealing with (do not even bother approaching "difficult" tenants; let an insurance adjustor deal with them), the type of incident (stick with property damage cases and cases involving minor medical expenses), and the severity of the incident (do not bother with any "serious" cases; turn them over to your insurance company immediately).

Be aware that if you do turn a claim over to your insurance company after you have given your tenants some compensation, the insurance company will not reimburse you for whatever you have given the tenants.

Whenever you give your tenants some compensation, get a statement from them in writing, whether it will stand up under close scrutiny or not, stating that they have been fully compensated for whatever has happened. Although a wily attorney can poke holes in any statement you ask your tenants to sign, most tenants feel inclined to abide by what they sign, and they feel disinclined to take the matter any further. They consider the matter settled, and they will thank you for treating them fairly and quickly in a time of need.

Helping Your Tenants Understand the Benefits of Having Renters' Insurance

Only a third of all tenants have some kind of insurance to protect themselves from calamity in case their possessions go up in smoke or they're flooded out when the creek rises or their child burns the building down while playing with matches. Your owners' policy would pay to repair or replace the building if something were to happen to it, but your policy would not cover the tenants' possessions nor the tenants' liability if they were found to have caused damage to the property.

February 25, XXXX

Dear *Richard and Rose Renter,*

As we do every year when the premiums come due, we have been reviewing our insurance policies, and we thought that you might like to know how you are affected by the insurance we carry.

Basically, our policies cover only the building itself where you live. They do not cover any of your belongings against damage or disappearance, nor do they cover you for negligence should you, for example, leave a burner going under a pan and start a fire which damages the kitchen.

To protect yourself against these calamities, you should get a tenant's insurance policy. Most insurance companies and agents will write such a policy for you, and we would strongly urge that you inquire about getting one.

For the peace of mind that it gives, a tenant's insurance policy is reasonable indeed.

Sincerely,

Leslie Landlady

This state of affairs raises any number of questions, and you should have some answers so you can help your tenants understand renters' insurance and buy it if they wish.

Why do so few tenants purchase renters insurance?
- They erroneously believe that their landlord carries insurance which will cover them and their belongings.
- They have never given it even a first thought because nobody has ever made them aware of such a thing.
- They think they can't spare the money.
- They think their assets are too insignificant to be concerned about
- They'd rather gamble that the premiums which they would pay over time would exceed whatever benefits they would receive.

Why should you as a landlord even be concerned about whether your tenants have a renters' insurance policy?
- You should show a positive, caring attitude toward your tenants whenever you can. After all, you are a scrupulous landlord, aren't you?
- Tenants who have insurance are less likely to sue their landlords after a calamity than tenants who don't have insurance. Tenants who have insurance don't have to turn to you for compensation. They turn to their own insurance company for compensation.

What does a renters' policy cover?
- It may cover fire damage only or fire damage plus lots more.
- It may cover tenants' personal goods which are damaged or stolen on the premises.
- It may cover losses to their goods when they are off the premises, such as golf clubs or a camera stolen out of their locked car.
- It may cover them in case someone mugs them on or off the premises where they live, forges their checks, or steals their credit cards.
- It may cover personal liability in case they are negligent as tenants and cause damage to the dwelling.
- It may cover personal liability for non-auto bodily injury claims brought by others.

Where can tenants buy a renters' policy?
- Almost all the big general insurance companies sell it–State Farm, Allstate, Safeco, Farmers.
- Tenants might start their search by asking the

company which insures their car.
- Tenants who know how to use the Internet need only go to a search engine like Google and search on "renters insurance" to find the websites of companies which write it. "Leasingdesk.com" is one of those websites. It lists owners as "additionally insured" and notifies them via email when there's any change in the status of the policy, including cancellation for lack of payment.

How much does it cost?
- Rates vary by regions; one company I know of in particular has different rates for nine different regions in a single state.
- Typically, a renters' policy will cost between $8 and $25 per month for $25,000 worth of coverage with a $250 deductible. Personal liability on such a policy is $300,000.
- Policies which offer minimal coverage cost as little as $96 per year and go up from there.

Can tenants pay in installments?
- Most insurers offer a variety of payment plans–monthly, quarterly, semiannually, and annually. Ask. Of course, there is a service charge for the extra paperwork in handling installment payments.

What discounts are available?
- Discounts are available for those who have any combination of the following–a deadbolt lock, a smoke alarm, a fire alarm, a sprinklered dwelling, or a fire extinguisher.

How can you best make your tenants aware of the benefits of a renters' policy?
- Mention when you first rent to them that they should secure a renters' insurance policy if they want coverage.
- Remind them of their exposure every so often in a note included with their rent receipt. Use a letter like the one shown here.

How can you convince them that they ought to have renters' insurance?
- Make them aware that their possessions are indeed worth something, probably more than they think.
- Tell them that they would be liable if they caused a fire at the property, and the place burned down. A renters' policy would cover them.
- Tell them that a renters' policy includes much broader coverage than they might think.

Are there any ways you can help them get a renters' policy?

- You may buy a policy for them in their name and include its cost in their rent. Remember that it becomes their policy. Should they move out six months after you paid the annual premium and should you then ask the company for a refund, the tenants will get the refund, not you, because the policy has to be in their name.

Will the insurance company notify the landlord when the renters' policy lapses?

- If you ask to be notified, you will be notified. Leasingdesk.com lists landlords as "additionally insured" and automatically notifies them via email when there's any change in the status of a renters' policy, including cancellation for lack of payment.

Some Last Words

Be prudent whenever you buy insurance affecting your income property business. You'll save on the premiums and you'll protect your assets so that someday you'll be able to enjoy those assets yourself.

Also, make your tenants aware of the benefits of having a renters' policy and then help them get one.

17
Providing for Security & Safety

True security and absolute safety are utterly impossible to achieve in this world. They always have been and they always will be. Metal detectors, luggage X-ray machines, and sharp-eyed security people at airline passenger terminals around the world have helped to curtail, but not eliminate, airplane hijackings and bombings. Mandatory fire sprinkling systems installed at great expense in gleaming high rises usually prevent small fires from becoming conflagrations, but not always. Even the most sophisticated electronic alarm systems and round-the-clock Secret Service agents cannot protect the President of the United States from harm.

All we landlords can hope to do is provide a modicum of security and safety for our tenants and ourselves by taking reasonable precautions. That's what this chapter is about, taking reasonable security and safety precautions to provide as much security and safety for our tenants as we can at a reasonable cost.

Learning More About Fire Safety

Now and then television lives up to its potential, and you see a program which teaches you something you never knew before, something important, in fact, something so important that you know it could save your life. Such a program is "On Fire: A Family Guide to Fire Safety." Look for it on your public television channel, but don't despair if you miss it because you may buy a videotape of this illuminating 60-minute program for $19.95 (plus shipping and handling) directly from the PBS station which produced it, KCET in Los Angeles, by calling 800.343.4727. I bought a copy myself and lend it to anyone who will take the time to watch it. It should be mandatory viewing for everybody, especially every landlord.

What's so special about this tape?

It shows graphically how to prepare for fires,

how to survive fires, and how to fight fires, no matter where you happen to be, in familiar or unfamiliar surroundings. It points out people's misconceptions about firefighters' ladders, nets, and rescue bags. It notes the differences between real fires like the devastating Las Vegas MGM Grand Hotel fire back in 1980 and the fictional portrayal of fires as shown in the film, "The Towering Inferno." It shows how "flashover" can turn a small fire into an all-consuming fire in minutes. It shows proper techniques for using fire extinguishers. It advises what type of stairwell to look for when you're trying to exit a burning multi-story building. It tells why you should never re-enter a burning building, even to save your precious pets. It shows what you should be doing all the while you're trapped inside a room in a burning building.

That's not all. There's more to be seen here, more to be learned.

View "On Fire: A Family Guide to Fire Safety" yourself, and review it periodically so it's fresh in your mind. You'll want to make it available to your tenants and to your friends and relatives, too. It will help to provide for your safety and their safety. Anyone acting upon the information in it may save a life.

Picking and Placing Fire Extinguishers

Why it is that insurance companies don't absolutely require fire extinguishers for all the buildings they insure, I certainly don't know. I do know that no rental building I have ever purchased has had them. As soon as I take possession, the first thing I do is place fire extinguishers everywhere. Whether your insurance company cares enough about your having fire extinguishers available to require them shouldn't matter. You need them. Your tenants need them. All us sinners need them.

Although you are undoubtedly violating local fire ordinances if you do not have extinguishers available at your rental properties, the enforcement of such ordinances is so lax that chances are good you won't be fined or even warned if you fail to supply them. But why should you wait for a fire safety inspector to tell you to install extinguishers before you buy them? They are so important that you should rush out to buy and install them as soon as you read this section on fire extinguishers. Remember that your property and your tenants' lives and their property are all endangered if there's no extinguisher available when it's needed.

Also, remember that if anybody should perish or be injured in a fire on your property, you would most definitely be considered negligent in a court of law for having failed to provide legally required extinguishers. Even a hard-drinking, incompetent plaintiff's attorney could nail you on that one, and of course, you'd be chastising yourself until the end of your days because your oversight, your mistake, led to somebody's horrible death or injury.

You need witness only one fire in your rentals to become completely convinced that you need extinguishers, but by then, of course, it's too late. If you haven't witnessed any fires in your rentals lately, consider the following scenario.

After cooking a big breakfast for her family, your tenant is cleaning up the kitchen when she hears familiar music introducing her favorite morning television program. In her haste to watch, she inadvertently turns the electric burner beneath the pan of bacon grease to high heat, one click from off, and hurries into the living room. Ten minutes later, all of a sudden, the grease ignites into flames high enough to scorch the kitchen cabinets and set the walls on fire. The tenant notices the fire and springs into action. She rushes about looking for an extinguisher nearby, and finding none, she tries dousing the flames with water. Naturally, that only feeds the flames. Finally realizing her plight, she grabs her portable TV, scrambles out, and screams "FIRE!" Someone calls the fire department, but by the time the fire trucks arrive and fire fighters can put out the blaze, the entire apartment, as well as the one next to it, are rendered uninhabitable.

Then what happens? The insurance adjuster surveys the damage. You get estimates for repairs, and sometime later the work begins. Three

months after the fire, you're looking around for new tenants to move into the two repaired apartments. You have lost three months' rent on the two apartments, you've spent hours of your own time planning and supervising, and you've gone through the uncertainties again of selecting more new tenants. In other words, you're out of pocket a considerable amount of money for expenses and you've wasted a considerable amount of your valuable time. Even if you do have a rent-loss coverage provision in your insurance policy and it will pay for every dollar of the repairs, you still suffer a loss because you've had to spend so much time on the project, time you cannot possibly be compensated for.

As a landlord, you need fire extinguishers. There's no doubt about it. They're every bit as essential as locks on a bank vault. The only question is what type should you buy?

The extinguisher you buy should be effective in fighting all kinds of fires. It should be easy to carry and use. It should not leave a catastrophe to clean up after. It should be durable. It should be rechargeable. And it should be modestly priced.

There are two types which fit these guidelines fairly well, but first let me warn you about two types of extinguishers which are still found around rental properties and should be avoided as if they were incendiary bombs. Soda-acid and pressurized water extinguishers they're called. They are easy to recognize because they look like "real fire extinguishers." They're shiny chrome or brass cylinders about two feet tall and eight inches in diameter. They're rather impressive in appearance to somebody who knows nothing about fire extinguishers. You'll notice them around many older apartment houses. I suppose they're still used because grandpa and grandma once used them, and I suppose they're still all right if you happen to have a stationery store, a lumber yard, or a yardage shop because they're great for putting out paper, wood, and natural fiber fires, but they're as messy as untrained quintuplets to clean up after. They're also heavy, and they only aggravate other types of fires because their extinguishing agent is water, hardly the best thing to put out a small electrical or grease fire.

Around your rental properties, you should use either dry chemical or Halon fire extinguishers. Dry chemical extinguishers are filled with a mono-ammonium-phosphate-base powder or its equivalent as an extinguishing agent and will work on any class of fire. These extinguishers fit the guidelines well. The five-pounder, rated 2A, 40B, and C is ideally suited for most rental property installations. It's called a five-pounder because the firefighting chemicals inside it weigh just that. Its total weight is around ten pounds, still light enough so that almost any tenant can wield it.

Halon extinguishers are filled with invisible, odorless Halon gas and work especially well on grease and electrical fires. They are the only kind of extinguisher recommended for use in computer rooms and on aircraft because they leave no residue which might damage or corrode sensitive parts. Many restaurants use them, too, though they're as secretive about using Halon extinguishers as they are about using their microwave ovens. Some have been known to extinguish a flaming steak with a Halon extinguisher and then serve that same steak to an unsuspecting customer who couldn't tell the difference.

Because Halon is a gas, extinguishers charged with it lose none of their ability to extinguish fires when they have been partially discharged. When dry chemical extinguishers are partially discharged, they might as well have been totally discharged. They must be recharged again or they're useless. A Halon extinguisher, on the other hand, continues to work until the gas is totally exhausted.

Halon extinguishers retain their charge for as long as twenty years without requiring attention, whereas dry chemical extinguishers should be checked at least once a year and should be turned upside down and given a little shake periodically to keep the powder inside from caking. Halon extinguishers work best indoors where the gas can concentrate on depriving a fire of the oxygen it needs to burn. Outdoors the gas tends to disperse quickly.

Unfortunately, Halon extinguishers are much too expensive for general use. They're more than double the price of their dry chemical counterparts, but they're well worth the money for use in any areas housing computers or other sensitive equipment.

Halon extinguishers have almost disappeared from the market because, good as they are for fighting fires, they use a gas which some believe is harmful to the earth's ozone layer. The U.S. and certain other countries have banned the making of the gas as it used to be formulated, so now

Halon gas suppliers are working to modify their formulas to remedy this problem. Don't be surprised to find newly formulated Halon extinguishers or something like them available soon.

For now, you will have to resort to aviation parts suppliers such as WagAero (wagaero.com) and Sportys (sportys.com) to find them. Owners of airplanes large and small won't use anything else.

Check the letters and numbers on any extinguisher you are considering in order to determine the class and size of fire it can effectively extinguish. The letters stand for classes of fire. "A" firefighting agents will put out fires fed by wood, paper, cloth, rubbish, and some plastics. "B" firefighting agents will put out fires fed by flammable liquids, paint, grease, or cooking oil. "C" firefighting agents will put out live-wire electrical fires.

The number appearing before each class was assigned by Underwriters' Laboratories (UL) and indicates the size fire in that class which the extinguisher will put out. The larger the number, the larger the fire it will put out, and hence the greater is the extinguisher's effectiveness. A "1A" extinguisher, for example, will put out 50 burning pieces of wood which are 2"x2"x20"; a "2A" extinguisher will put out a fire twice that size, and so on. A "1B" extinguisher will put out a fire fed by 3.25 gallons of naphtha (a solvent) blazing away in a 2.5 square-foot pan, and, likewise, a "2B" extinguisher will extinguish a blaze twice that size. Only the "C" class has no numerical rating. "C" means that the chemical in the extinguisher does not conduct electricity and is therefore safe for use on electrical fires.

The big soda-acid and pressurized water extinguishers have a "2A" rating, and that's all. They're totally worthless on flammable liquids and on electrical fires, whereas a five pound dry chemical extinguisher is just as effective on Class "A" fires as the water monsters are, besides having a "40B" and a "C" rating, too.

Having selected a suitable type, you will still have to decide where to place your extinguishers, what size to buy, what brand to buy, and whether or not to house them in glass-fronted boxes which require either a key or breakage of the glass for access.

Generally speaking, one five- or ten-pound dry chemical extinguisher is enough for four to five single-story apartments if their doors are within thirty feet of the extinguisher's location. If you have a fourplex with entrances on two levels, install two extinguishers, one on each level, and be safe. If you can't decide where to place them outside, try mounting one small extinguisher in every kitchen underneath the sink or on a wall in a conspicuous place, but never above the stove. Sometimes this course is more economical anyway because you don't then have to install clear-panel-fronted boxes (you'll find fire extinguisher cabinets available in the Maintenance Warehouse catalog for $25-45 apiece, depending upon the dimensions), something I always do when mounting extinguishers outside.

Two-pound dry chemical extinguishers with a rating of "1A:10BC" run somewhere between $12 and $30 each, while the five-pounders with a rating of "2A:40BC" are $30 to $40. Ten-pounders, with a rating of "4A:60BC" are $50 to $60. Small Halon extinguishers start around $35 and go up from there. Shop around and compare prices because extinguishers are often discounted.

The cautions which follow all resulted from costly or painful experiences I have had with fire extinguishers myself. I hope you may learn the lessons involved without having to repeat the experiences.

✔ **Caution ONE**—You would think that extinguishers which are labeled "rechargeable" would, in fact, be rechargeable. Well, technically they may be, but in a practical sense they may not be rechargeable at all. They may be able to hold only their original factory charge, whereas they cannot hold one they get in the field for a reasonable period of time. When their charge has been spent on a fire or they have lost their pressure spontaneously over time, you might try to have them recharged at an extinguisher service shop only to learn that what you purchased are really disposable extinguishers rather than rechargeable ones because the service shop won't recharge them for you. The shop doesn't want you blaming them when the charge doesn't last, and the fault lies not with them but with the materials used in the extinguisher. If you expect your extinguishers to last a long time and take recharging, then before you buy, ask the advice of someone trustworthy who recharges extinguishers for a living, preferably someone who does not also sell extinguishers. Lacking the advice of an expert, select an extinguisher which has an all-metal head over one made of plastic. I have yet to encounter an extinguisher with an all-metal head which couldn't be recharged, while I have encountered many extinguishers with plastic heads which couldn't be.

✔ **Caution TWO**—If you do buy the smaller extinguishers, be wary about placing them in any exposed areas, including shared laundry facilities. They're the perfect size for use in cars, trucks, boats, planes, and recreational vehicles, and they sometimes mysteriously develop legs. To discourage people from taking them, engrave them with your name or your property's name and a distinguishing number, such as the address where they're located, and also paint them with some sort of colored marker, perhaps some blue dots or a black band. Then, if they do a disappearing act for a time, you will be able to make a positive identification when they ultimately reappear.

✔ **Caution THREE**—Heads, bare fists, and feet were not made to break glass, filmed barroom brawls notwithstanding. Instruct your tenants to use a shod foot or any hard object that doesn't bleed when they have to break a glass pane in an emergency to get at an extinguisher.

✔ **Caution FOUR**—No extinguisher lasts very long. Nine to twelve seconds is all that a five-pounder will last in a sustained blast. It's made to be used in short two-second bursts rather than all at once, and though it certainly will not extinguish a burning house, it should extinguish any small fire your tenants are apt to have.

✔ **Caution FIVE**—Most fire extinguishers carry instructions warning users to stand back a certain distance from a burning target while attempting to put it out. One reason for this warning is obvious. The closer you are to the flames, the greater are the chances that you'll get burned. The other reason is not so obvious. The pressure of the extinguisher's stream can act like a blast of air and actually blow away some of whatever's burning, thereby spreading the fire to another area. If your extinguisher says, "Stand back 6 feet and aim at base of fire," do so. Don't doubt the wisdom of that advice. You can be sure that some lab technicians have tested the extinguisher under controlled conditions and have determined that six feet is the optimum distance for effectiveness. Don't figure that you know better and that the extinguisher would be more effective up close.

Keeping a Firefighter on Duty In the Kitchen 24 Hours a Day

Most residential fires start in the kitchen when an unattended burner on the stove gets too hot and ignites something flammable on or near the burner. To put out such fires in restaurant kitchens, fire codes require that the stove hoods be outfitted with fire extinguishing systems which activate automatically when the temperature rises to a dangerous level. Until now, anyone wanting an automatic extinguishing system in a residential kitchen would have to install the same kind of expensive system used in restaurants.

Now there's a new extinguisher on the market designed specifically for residential kitchens. Although not as powerful as a restaurant's system, the FireStop™ Automatic Fire Extinguisher works well enough to extinguish stovetop fires soon after they start, and it works without human intervention. It works automatically.

Either a direct flame or a temperature above 277 degrees Fahrenheit will activate the extinguisher. It then does two things. It makes a very loud popping sound to alert anybody within earshot that something has gone terribly wrong in the kitchen, and it releases its full load of siliconized bicarbonate soda, a non-toxic powder, directly onto the fire.

As you might imagine, fires start small and grow large quickly. The sooner you attempt to extinguish them, the better are your chances of putting them out. Because these extinguishers attack the fire as soon as they sense that there is a fire, and because they work automatically, like an automobile's airbag, they can be most effective. They're almost like keeping a firefighter on duty in the kitchen 24 hours a day.

These extinguishers are very easy to install. They come with a built-in magnet which clings to the underside of the vent hood and keeps them mostly, if not completely, out of sight. There's no drilling and no sawing required. There are no bolts and no screws, just magnets. What could be easier to install than that?

They are a little pricey at $24.50 each (quantity one), especially when you need two of them for a four burner stove, and they must be replaced every five years, so that adds to their overall cost as well, but with the average kitchen fire causing $3,000-$4,000 worth of damage and with fire insurance premium discounts available on buildings where they are installed, they may not "cost" anything at all in the long run.

Quantity discounts will bring the unit price down by as much as 40%. With that big of a discount available on quantity purchases, you should offer to pool people's orders at the next meeting of your rental housing association so that all of you will get these firefighters-in-a-can at a wholesale price.

For more information, go to the manufacturers' website (stovetopfirestop.com).

The extinguishers are available directly from the manufacturer (Williams-Pyro; 888.616.PYRO) or from Maintenance Warehouse.

If you're inclined to be skeptical about purchasing these extinguishers for all of your properties, try a set of them in your own kitchen, and also try them in your rental dwellings occupied by the disabled, by anyone who has had a kitchen fire in the past, and by the elderly who live alone. They are the ones most at risk.

These extinguishers will make a believer out of you when they save a life or save a building. They're the best kind of "fire insurance" you can buy. They actually put out fires before there's any damage to life, limb, or property.

Supplying Smoke Detectors

Surely some landlord must have invented paint rollers. Who else besides a professional painter has to paint so often? Who else benefits so much from rolling paint instead of brushing it? Likewise, some landlord must have invented smoke detectors because they provide the rental property owner the great benefit of minimizing exposure to fire danger and damage when even the most klutzy and irresponsible tenant is around.

Because tenants tend to be a little more careless about handling fire-causing agents than you would be in your own home and because you can't possibly keep watch over them constantly, smoke detectors are ideal watchdogs to protect life, limb, and property. They aren't fire sprinklers or extinguishers, mind you. They can't put out fires, but they do do a good job of warning the living that there is fire danger.

Now that so many manufacturers make them, perfectly adequate smoke detectors are available for as little as $10 and as much as $35. At such prices, there's no good reason for any rental dwelling to be without them, and there's no good reason for the landlord not to replace them quickly when they malfunction.

There are two fire detection techniques used in the smoke detectors readily available today, ionization and photocell. Each has distinct advantages. Ionization detectors, which sound an alarm when smoke interferes with an electric current flowing constantly through an ionization chamber, are better at detecting rapidly burning, flaming fires. Photocell detectors, which sound their alarm when smoke deflects a beam of light to a photocell, are better at sensing slow, smoldering fires.

In order to detect both types of fires in their earliest stages, you need to have both types of smoke detection. You'll find that Sears offers a detector which combines both ionization and photocell detection in a single unit. It is my first choice in smoke detectors.

My second choice would be two different types of detectors mounted in two different locations. The photocell detector might be located near bedroom areas because that's where smoky fires tend to start, and the ionization type might be located nearer the kitchen because that's where blazing fires tend to start.

My third choice would be a photocell detector alone. Photocell detectors, it is true, are slower in detecting rapidly burning fires, but only by mere seconds, whereas ionization detectors are slower by minutes in detecting smoldering fires.

My fourth choice would be an ionization detector alone. They do work satisfactorily, and they are the least expensive detectors on the market. Though they're not the best detector available, they're a whole lot better than no detector at all.

As for location, if you're installing only one detector, mount it near the bedrooms where it will awaken the sleepyheads. They're the ones who really need the warning so they can get out

alive. Avoid locating any detector in a kitchen because cooking is bound to cause some nuisance alarms, and you don't want your tenants disarming the alarm altogether in order to stop those nuisance alarms.

All detectors require an electrical power source. Some run on house current, and some run on batteries. Those which run on house current are preferable because they don't depend upon the uncertain reliability of a battery and they're less likely to be disabled by tenants who are tired of hearing their burning steaks sound the alarm. Unless your building is being constructed or rewired, however, you might as well forget about installing a detector which runs on house current. Retrofitting new electrical outlets in the unusual locations which are best suited for detectors is simply too expensive. On the other hand, battery-operated detectors can be mounted practically anywhere.

Select a detector which uses a readily available battery like the standard 9-volt battery used in transistor radios. They're a whole lot less expensive to replace than uncommon types. Use only alkaline batteries like Duracell or the Energizer, not the cheap carbon ones which have been known to fail prematurely without warning. Alkaline batteries last much longer and drain slowly enough to be able to send out proper warnings when they need replacing. Don't use nicad rechargeable batteries. They tend to die too quickly at the tail end of their charge and aren't able to send out warning signals for very long.

Detectors using long-lasting lithium batteries, which should last five years or more, are now available. They perform no better than other detectors. They simply have longer lasting batteries and higher price tags. Their advantage is convenience, and it's a big advantage. Once installed, they function so long that you can practically forget about them. Their disadvantage is convenience, and it's a big disadvantage, too. You change their batteries so infrequently that you are more likely to forget all about them, scheduling neither testing nor battery replacement on a regular basis. I still prefer the conventional detectors myself because they don't let me forget about them. I have to remember to change the batteries on a regular basis.

Unless you are a really conscientious Smokey the Bear and will take the time to monitor the batteries in your smoke detectors carefully, schedule the batteries for testing and replacement, if necessary, once every year. Put a label on the outside of each detector and write on it when the battery is next scheduled for testing. Put this date in your maintenance records, too, where you can't miss it.

Before you buy any detector, familiarize yourself with your community's recommendations and/or regulations. Some require a particular type and some require a certain number of detectors to be installed in certain locations. Find out what those regulations are and comply.

Every time you conduct orientations for new tenants, give instructions in smoke detector care. Show them where each detector is, tell them why each was located there, show them how to conduct a functional test, explain to them how to shut off the detector when it's sounding a nuisance alarm, and demonstrate how to replace the battery. Make sure that each detector is in working order when they move in, and have them initial the smoke detector paragraph on the Condition & Inventory Checksheet, but don't rely entirely on them to check the functioning of each detector. Do it yourself periodically.

Setting Water Heater Temperature

Here's the scenario—A groggy tenant steps into her shower and inadvertently turns the hot water to high. You have a good recirculating hot water system in your apartment building, so the shower immediately blasts the tenant with scalding water. Before she can think clearly enough to do anything about it, she has sustained skin burns and requires a trip to the emergency room. She looks to you to cover her medical bills and compensate her for her pain and suffering and for the time she misses from work. Your insurance company settles for $25,000 and cancels your policy.

The simple act of turning down the thermo-

stat on the building's hot water heater would have changed this scenario. She would not have been burned, and your insurance policy would not have been canceled. Moreover, you would have saved money on your energy bill every month.

Water heaters have thermostats just as space heaters do, and you may set the temperature yourself according to the manufacturer's recommendation, which is 120 degrees Fahrenheit (49 degrees Celsius). You should. That's less than the 150 degrees Fahrenheit (65 Celsius) dishwashers require, but it's more than the 100 degrees Fahrenheit (38 degrees Celsius) people require for their baths and showers.

Dishwashers have their own internal heaters to boost water temperature, so lowering the water temperature to the water heater manufacturer's recommendation presents no problem in cleaning dishes hygienically and thoroughly.

Some clothes washers have internal heaters, too, to bring the water temperature up to 140 degrees Fahrenheit (60 degrees Celsius), but they still wash satisfactorily at 120 degrees Fahrenheit (49 degrees Celsius). Again, there's no problem.

There is one little problem you'll need to be aware of before you set the thermostat to the recommended temperature. You'll likely find that the markings on the water heater's thermostat will be the words, "Warm," "Hot," and "Very Hot," rather than actual temperature numbers in Fahrenheit or Celsius. These relative designations are too subjective. What's warm to one person may be hot to another. You want as precise a setting as you can get, and for that you'll need a thermometer to insert directly into a stream of water flowing from a faucet which is attached to or close by the water heater.

The first time you check the water temperature, you'll know whether to turn the thermostat up or down, but once you do, you won't know exactly how close the setting is to the desired temperature. Because of the volume of water already in the tank, any change you make in the setting won't be reflected right away. You'll need to return later to recheck the temperature and reset the thermostat as necessary. Set it as close to the manufacturer's recommendation as you can even if it requires more than two visits. This job is worth doing right.

Should you be skeptical about how the reduction of the water temperature will save you money, consider that there will be less heat loss as the water sits in the tank and as it circulates through the pipes. That alone translates into lower energy costs for heating the water. During periods of minimal use, which is, after all, most of the time, the heater won't turn on as often. During periods of maximum use, it will stay on longer because more water will be flowing through the heater as users mix a larger amount of hot water to achieve the temperature they prefer for washing themselves, but the heater still won't have to raise the temperature as much.

Talk about a winning combination! This is a good one. You provide for the safety of your tenants, and you save money at the same time.

Changing Locks

Give your new tenants the assurance that the locks on their dwellings have been changed so that previous tenants couldn't possibly use old keys for access. You needn't hire a locksmith for this job. You can do it yourself. If you can turn a screwdriver, you can change locks.

The simplest way to make this change, if you lack the expertise and equipment to rekey lock cylinders, is to keep several spare locksets on hand. They should be exactly like the old ones if possible (locks from the same manufacturer shouldn't require changing either the spring-loaded latches or the striker plates, nor should you have to worry about adjusting the door cutout sizes). In most cases, you can change locks simply by zipping out two screws with a screwdriver, removing the old lock, putting a new one in its place, and securing it by zipping the two screws back in again. That's all there is to it.

To keep dust and water from settling inside the pin chambers and gumming up the works, always install locks so that the flat edge of the keyway is on the bottom. In other words, the key cuts should point up whenever a key is inserted. To reverse their keyways, Kwikset locks, America's most popular doorlocks, require a special cylinder removing tool, an inexpensive item available from your hardware store or locksmith shop. Buy one.

What do you do with the old locks? Play "musical locks" with them, of course. No one need know where they went. If people ask, tell them they went to "Lock Heaven."

Whether you install new or resurrected locks doesn't seem to matter at all. What is most important to tenants' feeling of security is knowing that no former tenants of that particular dwelling have keys.

While you're changing the locks on their doors, you might want to inform your tenants exactly who does have access to their home. You may be the only one, or you may have a resident manager and a maintenance person who have full sets of keys or master keys. Tell the tenants. They have a right to know.

Selecting Padlocks

To gain access with just one key to all the padlocked garages and storage enclosures where you keep your landlording equipment and supplies, buy padlocks which are keyed alike. All padlock manufacturers make them and most regular hardware stores carry them in stock. Just ask. Maintenance Warehouse carries them, too.

Don't use keyed-alike padlocks for those applications at multiple-family dwellings where every tenant needs access, applications such as gates and common storage areas. You don't want to have to issue still another key to each of your tenants. For those applications, use a special kind of combination padlock called the Sesamee Keyless Padlock (Master Lock makes a version as well). Its four dials may be set to any of ten thousand combinations and may be reset very simply at any time. Set it to an easily remembered number, like a building address or the current year, and your tenants will all have access when they need it without having to fumble for keys.

Any padlock used by more than one tenant will soon disappear, however, unless you attach a chain to its shackle. Ask at your hardware store for a special padlock chain restraint made by the Master Lock Company which fits most padlocks and eliminates this lost-padlock problem.

Installing Peepscopes

Some entrances to dwellings are blind, that is, there's no way for the occupants to see who's at the door. Occupants have to either talk through the door or open it a crack to answer. Sometimes people attach security chains to their doors and door jambs to limit the door's movement and hence restrict access, but these chains provide more psychological than physical security because they pull loose from their mountings in response to the slightest blow and expose the occupants immediately to outside danger.

A far better way to solve this problem is to

install a peepscope right in the door itself so that occupants can see who's out there knocking on the door without jeopardizing their own safety. Peepscopes cost less than $5 each and take less than five minutes to install. Take care to install yours low enough, say around four and a half feet from the door bottom, so little people will be able to peep through without having to use a stepstool and big people will be able to peep through without getting a backache.

Tenants need peepscopes. Tenants use peepscopes. Tenants appreciate peepscopes.

Helping to Deter Break-Ins and Burglaries

You will want to try what you can to prevent break-ins and burglaries from occurring at your rental property because every one reflects negatively on the property itself and scares off better tenants, but you hardly have unlimited funds to spend for prevention, and you must recognize that no measure you take will be 100% effective, no matter how much it costs.

Before you go out and spend the big bucks to hire an around-the-clock security service or install decorative iron grillwork all around your building, try taking other much less expensive measures which your tenants will surely appreciate, measures like strategically located outside lighting and "Operation Identification" as deterrences and the closet safe as a damage-control measure.

■ **Outside Lighting**—When the sun goes down, criminals seem to come to life. They use darkness as a shield to protect themselves from being noticed while doing their dastardly deeds. Because burglars, robbers, muggers, rapists, and vandals all tend to avoid well-lit areas, you have to provide good lighting to keep them at bay. If you don't and a crime should occur on your rental property in a location where some attorney tells a sympathetic jury that you, you penny-pinching landlord, "should have installed adequate lighting," you will be held responsible for the crime just as surely as if you had slipped on your black nylon windbreaker, your rubber gloves, and your panty hose (over your head, of course) and taken up your Saturday night special to go out and do wrong.

You're left with no choice but to provide good lighting.

As for the lighting itself, you have many, many choices. When making your choices, be aware of these considerations—location, vandalism resistance, operating cost, initial cost of the installation, lumens, and availability of the replacement lamps and other parts.

Location is of primary importance for every kind of real estate, and it's most important for an outside security light. Ask the tenants who would be most affected by the installation just where they would locate a light to do the most good. They'll usually make good suggestions because they're the ones who walk that area at night. Go with them at night yourself and examine the area. You'll be showing them you care, and you'll be getting some good ideas. Be somewhat practical when you're selecting the location, of course. It should have readily available electricity, and it should be far enough out of reach to frustrate the garden variety bulb-snatcher. (Do you know how the New York subway authority frustrates bulb-snatchers? All the subway's incandescent bulbs have left-hand threads. They won't fit normal light fixtures.)

Keeping the light fixture out of the bulb-snatcher's reach will go a long way toward eliminating common vandalism, but you may have to go a step further. You may have to install a fixture with a polycarbonate (Lexan®) lens so kids won't be able to shoot out the bulb with their pellet guns. Lexan lens fixtures are more expensive, to be sure, so you might want to try a more ordinary fixture first.

These are the most common lamp types, together with their lumen output per watt—incandescent (15-20 lumens per watt), tungsten-halogen (18-25 lpw), mercury-vapor (40-60 lpw), fluorescent (55-100 lpw), high-pressure sodium (75-140 lpw), metal halide (80-125 lpw), and low-pressure sodium (around 200 lpw).

The higher the lumens per watt, the more efficient is the source, and the lower will be the operating cost. Incandescent lamps have the highest operating cost, and sodium-vapor lamps have the lowest operating cost. In fact, a 60-watt high-pressure sodium vapor produces five to seven times more lumens than the 60-watt incandescent. It's that much more efficient.

Efficiency has its price, naturally, so you'll want to do some calculations to determine whether you can save enough over three years to justify the higher cost of more energy-efficient fixtures.

Factor into your calculations the cost of the fixtures themselves, the bulb life-expectancy, and the price you pay for electricity. Where electricity is expensive, the extra efficiency of sodium-vapor lighting easily pays for the higher cost of the fixtures.

Any one of the commonly available lamp types, from incandescents to sodiums, is available in a size which will provide the lumen output you need to illuminate areas adequately. Match the output to a particular application carefully. Make sure that you will get enough lumens to illuminate what you want to illuminate when you mount the light source at a certain height, too. The higher the light source is, the fewer the lumens on a given area. Don't mount your light fixtures so high that they light more of the sky than they do of the ground.

As you know, the lightbulbs you use around your house all have the same screw-type bases, whether the bulbs are 60-watt or 150-watt, whether they're floodlamps or reading lamps, and you can install low- and high-wattage bulbs in the same socket interchangeably. In the case of most other lamp types, the bulb is matched to the fixture. When you buy a fixture, that fixture will accommodate only one particular bulb and no other. So don't try to put a 70-watt sodium-vapor bulb in a 50-watt sodium-vapor fixture. It won't work. The ballast differs and the base may differ as well.

W.W. Grainger offers an extensive selection of light fixtures and lamps in its regular catalog and also publishes a special lamp and ballast ordering guide. Don't even consider buying any fixture unless Grainger carries the replacement lamp. Incidentally, both Grainger books are full of useful information about lamps and fixtures.

Light as much outside area as you can with energy-efficient lighting, and you'll be marking your property as a poor target for nighttime burglars, as well as assisting your tenants in their nocturnal peregrinations.

■ **Operation Identification**—"Operation Identification" involves engraving every item of value with the owner's name and driver's license number to prevent burglars from fencing it easily. Burglars might be able to keep this marked booty for their own use and have no problems, but whenever they try to convert it into cash, they encounter difficulties. Fences certainly don't want stuff which is plainly identified because it is just too easy to trace. Burglars can try to eradicate the engraved marks by grinding them off, but that's too much like work and it leaves marks which diminish the item's value to anyone buying stolen goods. Whenever they come upon engraved goods, then, burglars tend to leave them behind because there's plenty of other stuff around for the taking that won't cause them a bit of trouble.

Many urban police departments lend engravers and supply warning decals which can be placed near every likely burglary access to strike the fear of "Operation Identification" into any burglar who's casing the joint. You might consider buying an engraver yourself (they're less than $20), identifying all of your own tools and valuables, and then lending it to your tenants. They'll appreciate it, and you'll all find that it works. By the way, for less laborious, better-looking engraving, try using cursive script rather than printing each letter separately.

■ **Closet Safe**—The closet safe is a damage-control measure designed more to lessen the impact of burglaries than to prevent them from occurring altogether. It involves creating a closet safe where tenants may secure their valuables right at home. A closet safe is merely a closet with a lock on it which is intended to delay burglars, forcing them to spend more time and make more noise than they would like to, many times frustrating them completely and causing them to leave with far less than what they came for. The lock on a closet safe might be a doorknob or a deadbolt lock keyed like the entrance locks, or it might be a padlock which the tenants supply themselves.

Having tenants supply their own padlocks is preferable, of course, because it relieves you of the responsibility of looking after still another lock and key. The usual padlock hardware is a little unsightly, I know, and you might shake your head at the thought of installing it on an inside door, but Master No. 60 Padlock Eyes, which are designed to be used on any ordinary household door, are almost unnoticeable. Yet they, together with a good door and a strong padlock, create a reasonably secure closet safe, one which is quite capable of providing some extra protection for your tenants' valuables.

Whatever else you can do to thwart burglars and give your tenants a sense of security will help you keep good tenants longer, and that's good business.

Hiring a Security Service

Even though "rent-a-cops" earn low wages, a security service can cost a landlord plenty as an on-going monthly expense. Having had several experiences with such services, I have come to understand when to use them and how to use them.

Use them when there's a drug problem in your complex or when so-called "criminal" elements are at work there. Then hire a security service to position a guard on your site during nighttime hours to record people's comings and goings and report them to the police. Before long, likely within a week, you should find that the drug problem and the criminal elements have vanished, and you can have the security service remove the guard. The cost to you for the service during that period won't amount to much, and it will be a one-time expense rather than an on-going monthly expense.

Avoid signing up for a regular security patrol service. It's nothing more than a drive-by every few hours and is a waste of money for a residential complex. It's something which might be useful for an office complex where there are no people about during the night, but residential complexes are full of people at night, and the eyes of those people who may be awake at any time are better for noticing and reporting criminal activity than the two eyes of one guard who happens to drive by every few hours.

"Neighborhood Watch" works better than a security patrol service, and its price is better, too. Use whatever influence you have with your tenants to get one started and then support it.

Neutering Tenant Identification

To thwart the criminal types who prey on single, defenseless people, identify your tenants on their mail boxes, bell buttons, and tenant directories with their last names only or with their last names and first initials only.

Do not give would-be intruders a clue as to the sex or number of people living in any dwelling.

Selecting "Harmless" Employees and Tenants

Whenever you select employees and tenants, be especially deliberate in determining whether they might possibly pose a physical threat to others. Whether they appear to be harmless or suspect on the surface, investigate them as thoroughly as you can before you hire them or rent to them because once you begin doing business with them on a regular basis, you take on a certain responsibility for their actions.

If they should ever harm a tenant physically during an argument or run down a tenant's child while driving drunk or use their master key to waylay a tenant and if there happened to have been something in their past which you should have discovered, something which would have indicated that they might indeed hurt somebody, and you didn't even attempt to discover it, you will be held responsible for having hired them or rented to them in the first place. You will be called upon to compensate their victims.

When you check out their applications, look for missteps in their past. If you find anything suspicious, reject them. Don't take pity on people who have checkered pasts, thinking that you're the one who ought to give them a second or a tenth chance. You're not in the business of rehabilitating people who've gone wrong. You're in the business of providing secure, safe housing to good people.

If you find no missteps while checking into your applicants' backgrounds, but they go sour anyway while they're working for you or renting from you, at least you can't be faulted for having failed to investigate them to begin with. You tried.

Let's suppose that you did try, but you still made a mistake. You hired a handyman who drinks too much and drives recklessly. You rented to a tenant who is showing signs of pedophilia. Don't wait for something bad to happen. Deal with the situation immediately. Learn the details, ascertain the truth, and act quickly. Do whatever you have to do to get rid of them legally. Don't put your good tenants in any kind of physical jeopardy because of anything you did or failed to do. Keep your tenants out of harm's way.

Taking Safety Precautions When Handling Rent

You are a wise landlord to insist on cash, a money order, or a cashier's check for a tenant's initial rental payment. You have to be absolutely certain that you're not giving a new tenant the keys to a $50,000 dwelling in exchange for a bum check or some worthless collateral. After that, however, you should be more concerned about the risk involved in handling cash, for you could lose your property's entire monthly income all too easily by misplacing it or getting robbed, and since there's no commercially available and affordable insurance policy to protect you from the loss, it would be yours alone to bear. Take the precaution, therefore, of refusing to accept cash.

Some tenants will want to pay you their rent in cash, and since cash is legal tender for all money transactions, you will have to take it unless you stipulate with adequate notice in advance that you won't. State in your rental agreement or take-over letter that rent must be paid by check or money order and insist on it! Some contrary tenants who deal strictly in cash may wave a fistful of greenbacks in your face and say, "Take it or leave it," and you'll have to weigh all the factors of the situation before deciding what to do. If you accept it, they will probably continue trying to pay you in cash month after month, and if you decline it, you may never collect their rent at all. I usually accept their cash and patiently explain each time why I prefer rents to be paid by check or money order, until they finally tire of hearing my repeated explanations and give in.

Even though you are resolute about not accepting cash, you may face a loss if someone robs you and gets away with your rent checks and money orders, because even stolen checks and money orders can be negotiated by a thief who knows how. Add one extra safety precaution—the "Little Old Rubber Stamp Trick."

Invest a few dollars in deposit stamps for yourself and any manager who handles rent for you so that stolen checks and money orders cannot be negotiated easily, if at all. As soon as a tenant hands you a check or a money order, stamp the back with a rubber stamp which might read like one of these—

FOR DEPOSIT ONLY
to the account of
Lester Landlord
Leslie Landlord

or

PAY TO THE ORDER OF
BIG BANK
Lester Landlord
Leslie Landlord
011-123456
FOR DEPOSIT ONLY

Stamped on the backs of your checks and money orders, such a deposit stamp renders them virtually worthless except as deposits to your own bank account. No one can cash them by trying to impersonate you at the corner liquor store or market. They can only be put into your account.

These same deposit stamps are also handy for marking the coin wrappers you use for rolling all those quarters, dimes, and nickels generated by your coin-operated laundry machines. Banks usually insist that rolls of coins be identified in case they're found wanting.

If using the "Little Old Rubber Stamp Trick" saves you just one unauthorized check cashing, it's well worth the small cost.

Taking Personal Safety Precautions

We landlords tend to neglect our own personal safety because we are so conditioned to thinking about the safety of our tenants first and foremost. We also think that we can take care of ourselves no matter what happens. We've been "around the block" once or twice, and we think we've seen everything. Why should we be concerned?

Wake up. Bad things do happen to good people nowadays because there are all too many drugs, guns, gangs, hoodlums, loonies, and no-accounts loose in our society. There are so many opportunities for weak-willed people to get into trouble that they yield to temptation sooner rather than later, and the chances that a miscreant will be apprehended and then punished for a single criminal act are so slim that they can expect to get away with many such acts before anything happens to them.

We landlords are more vulnerable to "bad things" than most people because we're more exposed. We sometimes alienate people who have short fuses, people who think nothing of venting their frustrations upon us directly because they have nothing to lose. We sometimes find ourselves alone with people who have just come off the street, strangers we know nothing about. We also sometimes have tempting amounts of cash money on hand, and we're not the only ones who know we have it.

Pay heed to the newspaper accounts of the landlord who was attacked by an irate tenant and the landlady who was assaulted by someone posing as a prospective tenant. Take some personal safety precautions, and if you have people working for you, help them to do likewise. Don't become a chalked body outline on the pavement.

Here are some precautions you might want to take to reduce the risk of your becoming a crime statistic—

✔ Whenever you are going to show a vacancy to a prospective tenant, day or night, tell somebody else exactly where you're going and when you'll be returning. If there's nobody to tell, at the very least leave a note somewhere in plain sight.

✔ Whenever you're working in a vacant dwelling, hang something on the windows so you can't be seen by passersby, and keep the doors locked so you won't be surprised by somebody who walks in on you.

✔ Work together with a second person if possible. Criminals who work alone and are bent upon committing robbery or assault tend to be intimidated by the presence of more than one person. They're afraid of being overwhelmed by that extra person and losing control of the situation while they're victimizing you. They're also afraid of being identified by a corroborating witness should they ever be hauled into court for their crimes.

✔ Keep a personal security device with you at all times. These devices, which are generally available from gun shops and stores like Radio Shack, Target, Wal-Mart, and K-Mart, are meant to startle, disable, or mark the person who is threatening you. My favorite is a device about the size of a beeper. Pull its pin, and it explodes with a shrill 110-decibel wail which demands immediate attention. It startles the criminal and attracts the attention of anybody in the vicinity who might give help or summon help.

✔ Have a communication device, such as a walkie-talkie or a cordless telephone, handy so you can call for help in an emergency.

✔ Buy a small cellular phone, and keep it with you wherever you go. Cellular phones aren't quite the size of Dick Tracy's two-way wrist radio yet, but they're getting close. My own is only a bit larger than a pack of cigarettes, weighs all of eight ounces, is just as durable as a football helmet, and works well virtually everywhere. It slips right into my pocket and enables me to call for help wherever I am. It's a marvel. I wouldn't want to be caught dying without it.

Cellular service providers practically give these phones away now to their new customers as premiums for signing up. Costs do vary from company to company, and each company has a variety of rate plans and promotions available. Check several before deciding which one fits your needs best.

If you do plan to rely upon a cellular phone for emergency calls, find out how 911 calls are routed in your area. They may not reach operators who can provide you most quickly with the emergency service you need. In other words, your 911 call may go to a distant clearing house which takes calls from a large geographical area, and the clearing house operator may have to route your call before it reaches a dispatcher who can send actual help out to you. Instead of relying upon 911, you may want to program your cellular phone with the numbers of the local police, fire, and ambulance services, and use those numbers rather than 911 to minimize the response time.

✔ Whenever you have to confront a tenant with something unpleasant and you suspect that things could get nasty, rehearse what you're going to say in advance. Choose your words carefully, recognizing that the exact words you use could get you hurt or even killed but that they could also have the opposite effect. They could disarm the tenant and defuse the whole situation.

Go see the tenant and take someone with you as a witness, preferably someone of the opposite sex (instruct your witness to keep quiet, no matter how intense things become). Be friendly and personal in your approach. State your business briefly, mentioning only the important reasons why the tenant should be cooperative. Then let the tenant talk and talk and talk. Remain calm. Do not raise your voice or make any threats, even though the tenant is shouting threats at you at an ear-damaging volume.

If things do get intense, say something disarmingly crazy, something like this, "Maybe we're both getting a little too worked up over all this. Why don't we just stop for a minute and take three deep breaths? Come on now. One, two, three. That's good. That's good. How about three more? One, two, three. Okay, now where were we?" Sure, this sounds crazy. It is crazy, but so are loud arguments, and they never help matters. They just get people upset, perhaps upset enough to reach for their weaponry and harm somebody they had no intention of harming. Doing something as idiotic as taking six deep breaths together with an irate tenant may be enough for you and the tenant to smile at one another and recognize how idiotic your disagreement is. It might be enough for the two of you to begin seeking common some grounds for settling your disagreement.

Maybe you'll succeed, and maybe you won't. Leave the scene as soon as you realize that words and ploys won't help and that the tenant is going to remain obstinate. You've tried all you could. The time has come to make everything impersonal.

Get somebody else to deliver a written notice appropriate to the situation within 48 hours, and pursue the matter through intermediaries. Keep out of it.

✔ Whenever you do anything at your rental property, ask yourself whether you're taking needless risks and whether you can do something, anything, to reduce those risks.

Coping with Lead-Based Paint

Lead is good for paints because it makes them last longer. It's good for gasolines because it makes them burn evenly and longer rather than simply exploding quickly. It's good for plastics because it gives them stability. It's good for crystal because it adds brilliance and weight. It's good for shielding because it stops X-rays and radiation. It's good for batteries because it reacts with acid to store an electrical charge efficiently. It's good for solder because it connects electronic components reliably. It's good for wine bottle caps because it keeps rodents from gnawing the corks. It's good for roofing, especially flat roofing, because it will last easily for sixty years when exposed to the elements.

Lead is good for many, many things, but it is not good for humans. Lead in humans, whether ingested by mouth, inhaled through the nose, or absorbed through the skin, can be just as damaging as a lead bullet. It simply acts more slowly. It can cause neurological damage, high blood pressure, headaches, joint pain, and all kinds of other medical problems. Children are especially vulnerable to lead poisoning because their bodies tend to absorb more of it and they are more sensitive to it.

Many dwellings built prior to 1978 have lead-based paint in them, and we landlords who own any of these older dwellings must comply with the federal regulations requiring us to disclose to our tenants whatever we know about lead hazards on the property. The mandated disclosure form for this purpose appears in chapter 4. You must give a copy of the form and the EPA booklet, "Protect Your Family from Lead in Your Home" (see FORMS), to everyone who rents a pre-1978 dwelling from you (give new tenants the form and booklet when they move in; give existing tenants the form and booklet as soon as possible, but no later than when the terms of their tenancy change) unless any of the following apply—

• The units have zero bedrooms, such as studios and lofts;
• The occupancy is expected to last less than 100 days;
• The housing is for the elderly (unless children also live there);
• The housing is for the handicapped (unless children also live there); or
• The housing has been found by a certified inspector to be free of lead-based paint.

The primary question here, though, is this, "What should we as landlords be doing to minimize our own and our tenants' exposure to whatever lead-based paint hazards might be on any property we own which was built prior to 1978?"

First, we should assume that all of the existing gloss and semi-gloss paint is lead-based, whether it is or it isn't. The truth is that we don't want to know for sure because if we know, we have to disclose what we know. If we know nothing, we merely state that we know nothing.

Second, we should make no effort to remove any of the existing paint unless we absolutely have to. Hiring experts to remove it properly is expensive and adds no value to the property. Hiring just anybody to remove it exposes them to danger and us to liability. Removing it ourselves exposes us to contaminated fumes or dust and may expose others as well. Don't take the chance.

Third, we should maintain all of the existing paint according to the highest standards, that is, we should keep it clean, and we should repair any surfaces where the paint is peeling, chipping, chalking, or cracking. Repairing might involve repainting the surface with an unleaded paint or covering the surface with wallpaper, paneling, sheetrock, or siding.

By being aware of the possible presence of lead-based paint, by being careful not to disturb it, and by complying with the federal guidelines, we are acting responsibly in coping with whatever lead-based paint might be on our property.

Coping with Asbestos

Like lead, asbestos used to show up in all kinds of products because of its desirable properties. It is very durable and very heat-resistant. When it was found to be especially dangerous to humans, however, it disappeared from many of those products entirely. Around dwellings, those products include electrical and thermal insulation, caulking putty, floor tiles, linoleum, acoustical plaster, ceiling tiles, and roofing. You won't find asbestos in any of those products made today.

Let's say that your rental property has asbestos in its acoustical ceiling, its floor tiles, and its steam heating system's insulation. That's bad news, of course, but it's not a complete catastrophe. Just remember that short of spending more than the property is worth on removing it, you cannot rid the property of asbestos entirely. You shouldn't try. You needn't try.

What you want to do is cope with the asbestos, make it safe to be around. That's neither particularly difficult nor particularly expensive. It does require knowledge of the danger, periodic inspections, and cautious repair when necessary.

The danger in asbestos lies partly in its near invisibility and partly in its great durability. When asbestos fibers are visible to the naked eye, they are bound together, stable, and safe to be around. When they are disturbed, they become dangerous. They become "friable," that is, they separate like a windblown dandelion seed puff into tiny individual fibers and escape, generally becoming airborne. So tiny are they that you'd have to bundle 1,200 of them together to equal the thickness of one strand of human hair! Being that tiny, they tend to float in the air a long, long time before they settle somewhere or get sucked into something like a human lung, where they remain forever and begin causing health problems. That's the danger they pose to us humans. Compounding that danger is the long period of time (10 to 30 years) between exposure to friable asbestos and the appearance of the symptoms of diseases caused by the asbestos. In other words, you could be removing the stuff from your property without using proper safety techniques and breathe enough of it into your lungs to cause health problems twenty years later.

Periodic inspection of your property's suspect areas is the best course to take to keep asbestos under control. Look to see that the asbestos-containing material is solid in appearance and to the touch and that it appears to be in good condition. If it is, then it presents no problem, for it is not releasing any of its tiny fibers into the air where they may be inhaled.

Should you find deterioration in any asbestos-containing material, chances are that it can be repaired. In fact, you will want to repair it rather than remove it because removal will only disturb the material and release more asbestos fibers into the air. Repair may involve something as simple as coating it with paint to seal the fibers or filling the damaged areas with a commercial product designed for containment. You will find suppliers of commercial products for dealing with asbestos problems in the Yellow Pages under "Safety Equipment and Clothing."

For more information on coping with asbestos, get a copy of the EPA pamphlet called "Guidance for Controlling Asbestos-Containing Materials in Buildings," otherwise known as the "Purple Book," USEPA 580/5-05-084. Call

312.353.2211 to order it or go to the EPA website.

Some Last Words

Go ahead and provide every security precaution and safety measure in the book which appears reasonable and appropriate for the kind of property you have and where it's located, but don't advertise your property's security and safety features. Don't even mention security and safety features when you're showing prospective tenants around the premises. Let them make up their own minds about the security and safety of the property.

You don't want to be sued by a tenant who becomes the victim of a crime or some medical malady and claims to have developed a false sense of security and safety after having been misled by your advertising or your verbal remarks.

18
Keeping Records

For some people the most onerous chore of landlording is keeping records. They'll care for their properties with vigor. They'll look after their tenants with delight. They'll show their properties with pride. But speak to them about keeping records, and they'll laugh nervously, perhaps they'll point to a dog-eared, old rent receipt book and a stack of shoeboxes stuffed with miscellaneous slips of paper, and they'll say that they just don't have time to sit down and shuffle papers. They have more important work to do. Besides, they have an accountant who does all that stuff for them. Sound familiar? Have any more excuses to add?

Unfortunately, people who neglect recordkeeping don't seem to recognize what's truly important in this business. Since they keep their records haphazardly, they don't know what's really happening at all and they can't possibly make good decisions because their decisions aren't informed decisions. They don't know whether their rents are covering their expenses, so they haven't a clue whether a rent raise is warranted. They don't know how much they're spending on utilities compared to previous periods, so they have yet to consider conserving utilities as a cost-saving measure. They don't keep any figures on their coin-operated laundry machines, so they're still charging 25¢ to wash and 10¢ to dry. They don't even know when they'll be making the final payment on a second mortgage. Consequently, they can't know when to expect an increase in cash flow. When can they buy that new Cadillac? They can't say.

These things are truly important in this business. Sure, you have to do a great many other important things, but few are ever quite so important as recordkeeping, and none will assist you in both managing your property day by day and satisfying the requirements of the IRS. You can-

not afford to neglect it. Don't neglect it.

Landlording without recordkeeping is like playing baseball without keeping score. Nobody would know what was going on. If the teams didn't know their scores and the innings remaining, they couldn't adjust their strategies, and the fans wouldn't know whether to get excited or go home. Batting, fielding, and pitching are only parts of the game. Recordkeeping *is* the game. Sports almanacs have more baseball statistics than *The Wall Street Journal* has financial statistics. Baseball fans study those statistics and compare players, teams, stadiums, leagues, and years one with another. You ought to be at least one-tenth that diligent with the recordkeeping and statistics for your landlording business because they affect you much more directly than baseball statistics could ever affect a fan.

To do your own recordkeeping, you may use a quill pen, ink pot, eye shade, sleeve garters, and leather ledger if you want to; you may use a fancy computer with a speedy processor, a capacious hard disk, more RAM than ewes ever see, and the best software available; or you may use some combination of low-tech and high-tech bookkeeping. That doesn't matter. What does matter is that you have some recordkeeping system, preferably one which you can understand yourself. The one outlined in this chapter might be considered rudimentary by some standards, but it is wholly sufficient for landlords who do their own recordkeeping. Some people have used it for just one rental house, and others have used it for more than three hundred rentals. It's a flexible system, simple to follow, easy to crosscheck, and exhaustive enough to lead into tax preparations. It's based on forms which are designed to be read vertically and to fit into a standard 8.5"x11" binder. Best of all, it's all right here in your hands. You can get started using it right away by making copies of the forms included in the back of this book or by making equivalents of these forms on your computer.

Before we get to the forms themselves, though, let's consider a way to keep those miscellaneous slips of paper out of your old shoeboxes.

Filing

You handle so many important written records in your landlording business that you have to organize them so they are readily accessible when needed or you will become hopelessly bogged down in futile searches for lost records again and again. A simple filing system will help.

For each property, make up three file folders (use folders of a different color for each property so they're readily distinguishable). Label each folder with the property's address or some other designation and "RECORDS," "TENANT RECORDS," or "RECEIPTS."

● In the RECORDS file folder, keep the property's insurance policies, title papers, termite reports, tax information, deeds, notes, loan records, and anything else pertaining to the property as a whole that you're not already keeping in your safety deposit box.

● In the TENANT RECORDS file folder, keep completed Rental Applications, Rental Agreements, Leases,

Condition & Inventory Checksheets, and any other papers pertaining to the property's tenants, including those tenants who have moved out.

● In the RECEIPTS file folder, keep the paid receipts for expenses related to the property. As soon as you get a receipt, circle the amount paid and mark it with the date of payment, the method of payment (a "$" for cash, a "✓" and a number for a check, and a "CC" for credit cards), and a property identifier, so you'll be able to identify it easily if it happens to get mislaid. If the receipt does not already include a description of the item or service paid for, write a description right on it.

Prorate on an itemized or percentage basis those receipts which cover expenses for more than one property so that each property pays its own share. If two properties are involved, make a duplicate receipt for one property's share and reference it to the original bill, which should be adjusted and then inserted into the other property's file. For unreceipted expenses, such as casual labor, make up your own receipt with the important information, get a signature if you can, and file it with the other expense receipts.

Arrange all receipts chronologically in the file folder so they will be easier to post.

Arranging them is easy unless you get very far behind and your receipts become mixed up. Just put the receipts face up in the back of the folder, oldest first and most recent last, and you won't have to bother sorting out them later. They'll be in proper sequence already. Keep all the receipts for one month together and slip them into a folded sheet of paper which is identified with the month and the year. When you finish recording the receipts for the month, staple them together inside the folded sheet and leave them in the folder.

At the end of the year, empty the RECEIPTS folder of that year's receipts and put them, along with the year's income and expense sheets referred to later, into a large envelope for storage. Because you never can tell when the IRS will want to audit your tax returns and you'll need to produce evidence in support of your numbers, you would be wise to keep them for a long time to come (ever since some seven-year-old records helped net me a $20,000 income tax refund windfall, I recommend keeping them seven years at least).

If you begin accumulating more and more properties, you will want to add more folders to your filing system to accommodate the greater volume of paperwork and to keep it more nar-

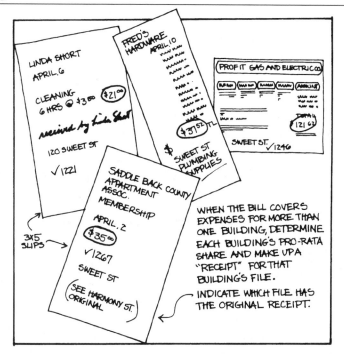

rowly divided. The following folders might prove useful—INCOMING, UNPAID BILLS, BANKING, LOANS, PAYROLL, and RENTAL APPLICATIONS (all except those of your current tenants, which should remain with the tenants' other papers). You'll surely find plenty of stray items to keep safely and neatly tucked away inside these folders.

That's all there is to keeping your written records organized. Read on to learn how to use these records in doing your bookkeeping.

Bookkeeping

The loose-leaf binder kept for recording purposes has the following five sections—TENANTS, INCOME, EXPENSES, SUMMARIES, and LOANS/INSURANCE.

Properly filled out and kept up to date, the forms in these sections will give you quick access to most of the information you need as you look after your rental property.

Form blanks for every sample form shown in these sections appear in the back of this book. Use the form blanks as originals and copy them for your own loose-leaf binder. Do not write on the original forms themselves. Write only on the copies.

Tenant Record   Property 456-64 Sweet Street

Unit	Tenant	Phone	Date Moved In	Out	Rent Date	Rent	Deposit	Bank/Chkg. Acct. Nos.
1	456	Richard + Rose RENTER	555-2207	1/xx		1st	750-	610-	BIG BANK 570-66-301
2	458	Lu MELANDER	555-4137	3/xx		✓	700-	550-	MAIN BANK 151193-461
3	460	Kathy + Rick BODEN	555-6916	10/xx		✓	700-	623-	BIG BANK 6397810-2
4	462	Nelly BUNN	555-0812	7/xx	3/xx	✓	650-	350-	
5	464	Jan + Jennifer BROWN	555-3771	4/xx		✓	750	650-	SAFE BANK 0210-006.89
6									

■ **Tenants—Tenant Record**

The first section, the one for tenant information, has only one form. It's called the Tenant Record. Record information on it which you'll need to refer to occasionally, information such as rent due dates and tenants' telephone numbers.

Nowadays so many people have unlisted phones that you may not be able to get your tenants' numbers from a directory or from the information operator. Having the numbers handy will save you lots of fumbling, frustration, and wasted trips.

Although you hope that you won't ever have to take advantage of such information, you may use the Tenant Record form to keep track of your tenants' current checking and savings account numbers, too. Then you'll know exactly where to go to attach these assets if you ever have to collect a money judgment against them. The savings account number should be on the Rental Application, and the checking account number will be written in those funny-looking magnetic numbers at the bottom of the tenant's rent check. Be prepared!

Because you will be referring to the Tenant Record repeatedly and because these sheets should last for years, you may wish to keep them clean with a transparent page protector which slips on and off easily and is available in stationery stores. When tenants move, cross them off the Tenant Record using a squiggly line or a yellow highlighter felt pen. Both still give you access to the old information if you need it. The highlighting just looks neater.

Add new tenants to the bottom of the list. Even though they won't be in sequence according to their dwelling number or letter designation, their information will be readily accessible.

Use a separate Tenant Record sheet for every multiple-family property. Use a separate one for

Monthly Rental Income   Page 1
Property SWEET ST. & NEAT ST.
Period XXXX

	Unit	January	February	March	April	May	
1	456 SWEET STREET	750-	750-	750-	750-	750-	1
2	458 " "	700-	700-	700-	700-	700-	2
3	460 " "	700-	700-	700-	700-	700-	3
4	462 " "	650-	650-	650-	750-	750-	4
5	464 " "	750-	750-	750-	750-	750-	5
6	TOTAL	3550-	3550-	3550-	3650-	3650-	6
7							7
8							8
9	125 NEAT STREET	875-	875-	875-	875-	875-	9
10							10
11	TOTAL BOTH BLDGS	4425-	4425-	4425-	4525-	4525-	11

a small collection of rental houses.

■ Income—Monthly Rental Income Record

The second bookkeeping section, INCOME, includes three different forms—Monthly Rental Income Record, Laundry Income, and Other Receipts and Income.

Unless you have quite a few properties, one of each form should suffice. For example, if you are Lester Landlord and you have one duplex, half of which you occupy yourself, and one fiveplex, you can easily list both properties on a single Monthly Rental Income Record.

If you do enter more than one property on a form, use a highlighter pen to highlight the "TOTAL" lines all the way across both sheets, and you'll be able to spot the totals more easily.

If you have room, you might even use the same record sheets for subsequent years by listing the properties again further down the sheets and indicating on each "TOTAL" line which year you are recording. One advantage in recording your rental income this way is that you have instant access to past years' rental income for comparison purposes. You'll know when you last raised rents and how much of a vacancy factor you created by doing so. You can use this information to help you prepare for the next rent increase.

After using these sheets to record rental income for a full year, calculate the total year's income for each dwelling and enter it in the "Year's Totals" column. Total that column so you can crosscheck the monthly totals for all buildings on the sheets. If your figures don't match, find out why they don't and correct your error.

This kind of crosschecking is easy work with an electronic calculator. Get yourself a printing calculator which produces a paper tape record of its entries. Sometimes just one slightly incorrect entry will cause an error and you'll be able to find it without painstakingly adding each item again merely by comparing the tape, item for item, with the Monthly Rental Income Record figures.

■ Income—Other Receipts & Income

Like the Monthly Rental Income Record, the form called Other Receipts & Income requires two sheets to span a full year. It is used to record miscellaneous income, or income considered incidental to the primary business. In the residential landlording business, that's anything which doesn't count as rental income from dwellings.

Other income items which may be included are added appliances or furniture, deposit forfeits, interest on deposits, late charges (unless you use the discounted rent policy, in which case both gross and net rents could be recorded as regular rental income), laundry collections, laundry commissions, soda machine revenues, pay phone receipts, garage rent, etc. Those income items which are normally included in the rent should be recorded as rental income and not here. Rents for furnished apartments, for example, need not be itemized separately, nor should a garage rent be recorded separately if it's normally included in the dwelling's rent. If, however, you bill tenants separately for their garage, refrigerator, or any-

Other Receipts & Income

Added Appliances or Furniture, Deposit Forfeits, Interest, Late Charges, Laundry, Garages, etc.

Page 1
Property SWEET ST. + NEAT ST.
Period XXXX

	Description of Income	January	February	March	April	May	
1	SWEET STREET						1
2	Laundry	8 6 75	8 5 50	9 2 25	7 8 75	8 6 75	2
3	Garage(s)	4 5 –	4 5 –	3 0 –	4 5 –	4 5 –	3
4	INTEREST on deposit account				1 8 86		4
5							5
6	TOTAL	1 3 1 75	1 3 0 50	1 2 2 25	1 4 2 61	1 3 1 75	6
7							7
8	NEAT STREET						8
9	Late Rents						9
10	INTEREST on deposit accounts				3 90		10

Laundry Income

Property _SWEET STREET_
Period _KKKK_

	Date	Washer	Dryer	Both	Cumulative Totals	Monthly Totals
1	1/05	22 50	21 25	43 75	43 75	
2	1/24	19 50	23 50	43 00	86 75	86 75
3	2/05	18 25	14 75	33 00	119 75	
4	2/21	24 00	28 50	52 50	172 25	85 50
5	3/09	22 75	25 25	48 00	220 25	
6	3/23	26 75	17 50	44 25	264 50	92 25

thing else, then you may wish to include those separate amounts here.

Still, don't worry yourself much about where to include an item. Worry instead about whether you have inadvertently recorded any income on both the Monthly Rental Income Record and the Other Receipts & Income record. Do avoid that! Only the laundry income should be recorded in two places, the Laundry Income sheet and the Other Receipts & Income sheets.

Although tenants' deposits may seem like some kind of income when you receive them, they're not. They're deposits to be held by you for insuring the tenants' compliance with the Rental Agreement. Upon receiving them, do not record them here or anywhere else as income. Instead, record them as deposits on the Tenant Record form. When the tenants move out and you have to use part or all of the deposits to pay for back rent, cleaning, or damages, that's when you list as income the portion you keep. After all, that's when deposit monies do become income, not before.

Last month's rent and any other rents paid in advance are another story. The IRS tells us that they must be considered as income when received. There's no choice. Take the hint. Don't ask incoming tenants for last month's rent. Increase their deposits by the equivalent of what you'd otherwise be charging them for last month's rent. The move-in costs remain the same, but you need list as income right then only what you label as rent.

One Other Receipts & Income form may last you a year or it may last you several, depending on the number of properties you have. Fill it out pretty much the same way you fill out the Monthly Rental Income Record, grouping all the items for one building together.

■ Income—Laundry Income

Owners of coin-operated laundry machines may use the Laundry Income form as an interim record or as a basis for a more detailed analysis of what's happening in the laundry room.

To use it strictly as an interim record, make only a "Date" entry and a "Both" entry for every time you empty the coin boxes. Then post the monthly totals to the more permanent Other Receipts & Income sheets once a month. The "Both" entry, of course, would be your total for each collection from both the washer(s) and the dryer(s).

If you don't use something like the Laundry Income form, you'll have to save little scraps of paper, each representing one collection, until you have a full month's worth of collections and can make the monthly entry. Those scraps may very well get lost in the wash if they remain too long in your pockets.

To use the form as a basis for a more detailed analysis, complete more of the form's seven columns. The other columns provide quite useful information to anyone who bothers to take the time to complete them. The separate washer and dryer columns tell you how much each machine is used. From these figures you can determine each machine's exact number of loads. Use this information to check on a machine's reliability whenever it needs repair. Perhaps, because of this information, you'll want to change brands of machines when they need replacement or when you purchase a set for another location.

The separate washer-dryer columns also provide a revealing ratio of use for the machines. If a tenant claims that the dryer is requiring twice as many coins to dry each load as it used to, you can calculate whether it is or it isn't by checking for a change in the income ratio between the machines. You'll have a quick clue whether the machine really does need a good cleaning or maintenance or repair or whether the tenant is foaming at the mouth.

The "Cumulative Totals" column tells you at a glance whether your investment is paying off. Let's say that your machines cost you $1,000 and you take in a minimal $200 in the first six months. At that rate, recouping your capital investment would take two and a half years, but that's not including the utilities needed to run them or the cost of the repairs. Still, that's a decent return. Anything which pays for itself in three years or less is a good investment.

If the machines last ten years and on a projected basis take in $70 a month or $8,400 in all, $2,500 of which goes for utilities and $800 for repairs, you'll make a return on your investment of 51% per year simple interest. That's a spectacular return! I'll take that kind of a return any old time. Wouldn't you? That's the kind of a return a casino owner might hope to get out of the one-armed bandits in the casino's best locations.

The "Monthly Totals" column is a convenience expressly for the purpose of entering the necessary figures on the Other Receipts & Income sheets, but these figures will also let you compare month-by-month laundry receipts if your collection dates are fairly consistent and frequent. Remember that not every line requires a monthly entry in this column. Only those which represent the last collection for the month require an entry.

■ Expenses—Expense and Payment Record

There are three forms in the expense section of the loose-leaf record binder—the Expense and Payment Record, the Depreciation Record, and the Payroll Record.

The first one, the Expense and Payment Record, is undoubtedly the most used of all the forms in the binder. Remember all those receipts you moved from your shoeboxes and shopping bags into a neat file folder labeled "RECEIPTS," which you then organized by date of payment? Well, here's where you record them all.

The entries are made chronologically and should include all the expense receipts in the RECEIPTS folder, plus the payroll expenses from the Payroll Record and the loan payments which are recorded on the Loan & Note Record sheets.

Besides being chronological, the entries are separated into eleven different categories which enable you to refer easily to certain kinds of expenses whenever you want to find out where all your money's going. You may find some surprises when you examine the categories, surprises that appear only when you examine a series of similar expenditures rather than just one bill. Might you, for example, have inadvertently paid your property taxes or your insurance twice? Don't laugh. It happens. Here's where you can check on your own absentmindedness.

Filling out these expense sheets can cause drowsiness, and you might not want to operate heavy machinery afterwards, that is, unless you make a conscious effort to concentrate on what you're doing. Tell yourself that these numbers you're working with are important stuff and that they have to be accurate. Mistaking one number for another here, transposing two numbers there, adding an extra digit somewhere else will all skew the outcome of your hard work. You cannot afford to make mistakes while posting.

Posting the loan payments requires even more concentration than other entries. Loan payment entries are a little tricky because one payment might have to be distributed to three columns, column 2 for interest, column 11 for mortgage principal, and column 12 for nondeductible impounds. Column 2 is the only one of the three which is deductible as an expense. Column 11, which is the amount you pay on the principal of your loan, represents an increase in your net worth rather than an expense. Yet, since it is definitely money paid out, it should be recorded as such. Likewise, an impound amount, which should be posted to column 12 as a nondeductible item, goes into a "savings" account. It's called an impound account, and it's forced savings, to be sure, but it's still a savings account. The mortgagor uses an impound account to pay taxes and insurance, and the funds you pay into an impound account are not an expense, strictly speaking, until they're actually used.

When the mortgagor uses your impounded funds to pay taxes or insurance, you then record the payment like any other and stipulate in the "How Paid" column that funds for payment came out of the impound account.

I know. I know what you're thinking. You're thinking this means that the amount in the "Total Paid Out" column is actually more than what you will have paid out. Trust me, though, and

I'll show you on the Summary of Business and Statement of Income form how everything evens out again. Just don't worry about it for now, and don't worry about the matter at all if you're not paying into an impound account with a portion of your mortgage payment.

Now let's take a look at the procedure for ordinary entries. After you complete the information called for in the first five columns, you come to the columns with the eleven different headings. Choose whichever one best fits each expense and put the amount in that column. Be sure, however, that it's all on the same horizontal line. Even though the lines are numbered four times on the two sheets, sometimes your eyes will play tricks on you and you may inadvertently post some figures on the wrong line. Use a straight edge if you have trouble finding the right places to put your figures. Even a piece of paper will work as a straight edge.

Don't deliberate too much about the proper categories for ambiguous expenses. If you can't easily decide whether something should be called a "service" or not, then it can't matter much, and since you identify each item in the "For" column anyway, you always have backup information in case you want to change categories later for some reason or other.

If you find that you have no use for a certain column heading, if, for example, you have no payroll to enter, change the heading to something more useful to you. Other possibilities are travel/telephone, advertising/rental fees, and non-employee labor.

Now look again at the sample Expense and Payment Record for Lester Landlord's fiveplex. Note that the distribution of the mortgage payments is broken into three categories—interest, mortgage payment, and nondeductible (impounds). Note also that the first line of these sample sheets has the totals brought forward from the previous sheets. You must do this on every page except the first one for the year (corresponding left and right sheets should have the same page numbers).

After you have entered your final expenditure for the year, total the last sheet and you'll have your annual expenditures for the property.

Let me caution you here, though, about two important no-no's related to your Expense and Payment Record sheets.

No-No Number One...Never include as a regular deductible expense the items which the government considers "depreciable."

No-No Number Two...Never include as a regular deductible expense the money you pay yourself.

"Depreciable items" are property used in your landlording business (a utility trailer, for example) or property replacements (new roof) or property improvements (new patio), all of which have long useful lives and cost more than $750. Unless these items qualify as "Section 179" property (five- and seven-year depreciables qualify; check a current tax book for details because there are any number of restrictions) and can be expensed in the year they were purchased, you have to "depreciate" them, that is, you have to write them off

Expense & Payment Record

Page **3**
Property **SWEET STREET**
Period **APRIL XXXX**

	Date Paid	How Paid	To Whom Paid	For	1 Total Paid Out	2 Interest	3 Taxes, Licenses	4 Insurance	
1			BAL FWD		4956 29	1949 96	24 80		1
2	4/02	267	BIG BANK	1ST. MORT.	879 00	521 20			2
3	✓	268	S. MONEY BAGS	2ND. MORT.	250 00	135 12			3
4	4/06	269	LITTLETOWN HDWE	ELEC SAW, EXT. CORD	48 59				4
5	4/07	270	SADDLEBACK CNTY	PRORTAX 3RD PYMT	674 31		674 31		5
6	4/07	271	MONOPOLY GAS + ELEC	3/1 - 31	86 12				6
7	4/11	272	KMART	SHADES	12 26				7
8	4/12	273	LITTLETOWN WTR DIST.	3/1 - 31	58 20				8
9	✓	274	CARTEL GARBAGE	3/1 - 31	102 00				9
10	4/15	275	PHONEY PAINT	PAINT + SUP.	32 64				10
11	4/15	276	BIG BANK	1ST QTR PAYROLL TAXES	31 10				11

little by little over a period of years (the IRS specifies the period according to the item's type).

You might think that a new fence and some new appliances are items which you should be able to charge off against this year's income. After all, you had to pay for them this year, didn't you? Shouldn't you be able to write them off this year, too? Normally you can't, but whether you can or you can't, whether they qualify for first-year expensing or they don't, you should still enter these expenditures in column 10 so you can keep track of them in a special way as depreciable items. You'll see in a moment how they're treated.

By the way, there's no difference as far as depreciation is concerned between items which you bought and paid for completely this year and items which you bought this year and are paying for over any number of years, having borrowed the money to pay for them. Depreciables bought with entirely with cash and depreciables bought entirely or partly with borrowed money are treated in exactly the same way.

Money which you pay yourself from your property's income is called a personal draw. It is definitely not an expense, and it is not the least bit deductible. It's personal income withdrawn from the business. If you wish to keep track of any money you pay yourself out of your property account, and you would be wise to do so, enter it on the Expense and Payment Record, but be sure to list it as a nondeductible item in column 12. It is not deductible in the least by any stretch of a landlord's vivid imagination.

■ Expenses—Depreciation Record

The Depreciation Record is a worksheet which enables you to keep track of the amount of depreciation available to you for every year you own something which is depreciable. It will serve to remind you years after you have paid for something depreciable whether you still have any depreciation coming to you and precisely how much it is. It will also help you calculate your adjusted basis and the amount of depreciation which must be recaptured when you dispose of some property.

As mentioned already, depreciable items are the various kinds of property used in your landlording business, as well as the replacements and improvements made to your property. They include everything except the land itself. Land is not depreciable. Here are some examples of depreciable items—big buildings, little buildings, equipment, appliances, air conditioners, roof replacements, carpeting, linoleum, grading, swimming pools, laundry machines, vending machines, replumbing, rewiring, remodeling, and draperies.

With these depreciable items in mind, do you think that either an $80 sander or a $30 kitchen faucet replacement would be depreciable? No, they wouldn't. They do have long useful lives, but they're not expensive enough to bother with. In general, you should depreciate an item only if it costs more than seven-hundred-and-fifty dollars and has a useful life of more than two or three years. Painting is an exception. Even if an exterior paint job costs you $3,500, improves the

Expense & Payment Distribution Page 3

	5 Utilities	6 Services, Rep., Maint.	7 Merch., Supplies	8 Payroll	9 Misc.	10 Depreciable	11 Mortgage Principal	12 Non-deduct.	
1	549 40	399 39	153 70	197 60	16 90		1417 04	247 50	1
2							357 80		2
3							114 88		3
4		48 59							4
5									5
6	86 12								6
7		12 26							7
8	58 20								8
9		102 00							9
10			32 64						10
11					31 10				11

Depreciation Record

Property or Capital Improvement
Location and Description OAK STREET - CARPET, DRAPES, LINOLEUM

Date Acquired or Converted to Business JUNE, XXXX   New or Used NEW

Method of Depreciation ACCELERATED   Useful Life 7 YEARS

Cost or Other Basis $ 1,683.55

minus (-) Land Value or 1st Year Expensing $ Ø

equals (=) Depreciable Basis $ 1,683.55

	Tax Year	Prior Depreciation	Depreciable Balance	% Year Held	% Bus. Use	Rate	Depreciation This Year
1	XX		1,683.55	—	100	.1428	240.41
2	XX	240.41	1,443.14	—	—	.2449	412.30
3	XX	652.71	1,030.84	—	—	.1749	294.45
4	XX	947.16	736.39	—	—	.1249	210.28
5	XX	1,157.44	526.11	—	—	.0893	150.34
6	XX	1,307.78	375.77	—	—	✓	✓
7	XX	1,458.12	225.43	—	—	✓	✓
8	XX	1,608.46	75.09	—	—	.0446	75.09
9							
10							
11							
12							
13							
14							
15							

Depreciation Record

Property or Capital Improvement
Location and Description OAK STREET

Date Acquired or Converted to Business 10/1/XX   New or Used USED

Method of Depreciation STRAIGHT LINE   Useful Life 40 YEARS

Cost or Other Basis $ 382,000

minus (-) Land Value or 1st Year Expensing $ 114,600

equals (=) Depreciable Basis $ 267,400

	Tax Year	Prior Depreciation	Depreciable Balance	% Year Held	% Bus. Use	Rate	Depreciation This Year
1	XX		267,400.00	.25	100		1,671.25
2	XX	1,671.25	265,728.75	100	✓		6,685.00
3	XX	8,356.25	259,043.75	✓	✓		✓
4	XX	15,041.25	252,358.75	✓	✓		✓
5	XX	21,726.25	245,673.75	✓	✓		✓
6	XX	28,411.25	238,988.75	✓	✓		✓
7	XX	35,096.25	232,303.75	✓	✓		✓
8	XX	41,781.25	225,618.75	✓	✓		✓
9	XX	48,466.25	218,933.75	✓	✓		✓
10	XX	55,151.25	212,248.75	✓	✓		✓
11	XX	61,836.25	205,563.75	✓	✓		✓
12	XX	68,521.25	198,878.75	✓	✓		✓
13	XX	75,206.25	192,193.75	✓	✓		✓
14	XX	81,891.25	185,508.75	✓	✓		✓
15	XX	88,576.25	178,823.75	✓	✓		✓

appearance of your rental property 100%, and lasts nine years, you can and should expense it.

Remember that expensing is better than depreciating because it allows you an immediate deduction from income instead of your having to wait for it. You don't get any bigger deduction by depreciating, so if you have some doubt about whether to expense or depreciate an item because of its cost or useful life, go ahead and expense it. For example, carpet that cost you $739 ought to be expensed, as should some $596 worth of replacement draperies.

On the other hand, $739 worth of carpet which is part of a larger carpet replacement order totaling $1,863 ought to be depreciated.

Before you fill out a Depreciation Record for any depreciable, you will need to know its particulars—its description, its purchase price, its date of acquisition, and its percentage of business use. You will also need to know the IRS classification it falls under. Then you will have to decide which depreciation method to use.

At present, there are six primary classifications of interest to rental property owners—5-year property (computers, light trucks), 7-year property (appliances, water heaters, carpets, draperies, furniture), 10-year property (residential mobilehomes), 15-year property (land improvements such as landscaping, paving, and site lighting), 27.5-year property (residential buildings), and 39-year property (non-residential buildings). The first two of these classifications correspond roughly to what you might expect their items' useful lives to be. The last four are flights of fancy. They don't correspond to anything within reason. After all, who can say that a mobilehome has a useful life of ten years or that landscaping will last fifteen?

As for methods, there are really only two you should know something about, accelerated and straight line.

Accelerated depreciation uses percentages which change every year according to a set schedule. Were you to depreciate 7-year property using an accelerated schedule, for example, you would get 14.28% of the full purchase price as your depreciation for the first year, 24.49% for the second, 17.49% for the third, 12.49% for the fourth, 8.93% for the fifth through the seventh years, and 4.46% for the eighth year.

Were you to add up the percentages, you would find that the first four years provide more than 68% of all the depreciation available over the entire eight years. That's how "accelerated" depreciation works. It allocates more depreciation to the early years, so you get a greater benefit earlier than you would with straight-line depreciation. You would also find by adding up all the percentages that they total 100%. Accelerated depreciation doesn't offer you any more or any less than straight-line depreciation. It merely enables you to take more depreciation in the early years.

The depreciation allowable for each property classification is simple to calculate from prescribed percentages. Use the tables provided for this purpose in IRS Publication 534 or in current editions of any general-interest tax book.

The sample Depreciation Record for carpet, draperies, and linoleum illustrates how accelerated depreciation works for 7-year property. Note that all of the 7-year depreciable expenditures made during the year for the one rental property are lumped together on one Depreciation Record sheet. You needn't fill out a separate sheet for each item and then do separate calculations. That would be a major waste of your time.

The "straight line" method lets you write off a depreciable at a constant rate and, if you prefer, over a longer period of time than accelerated depreciation provides. The sample Depreciation Record for the Oak Street apartment house illustrates how straight line works when applied to a property being depreciated over forty years, something an owner would do only in certain tax situations where smaller amounts of depreciation spread over many years would prove beneficial.

The Oak Street owners deducted the presumed land value from the acquisition cost and got their depreciable basis. Then they divided their basis by 40, the useful life they selected, and multiplied that by 25%, the percentage of the first year they held the property, and they came up with their depreciation for the first year. For the next year and all successive years, except the final one, their depreciation equals 1/40th or 5% of the original basis. The final year (the 41st) picks up the balance for those months they didn't own the property during the first year.

That's pretty easy, isn't it?

Once you begin filling out a Depreciation Record, you should complete it for the item's entire useful life so you will know exactly how much depreciation you can expect every year.

Payroll Record Property _456-64 SWEET STREET_

Employee _ALFRED GOOD_ Social Sec.No. _100-00-000_

Pay Rate _$6.00/HR_ Exemptions _2_ Married ☒ Single ☐

	Period	Base Wages	Lodging	Fed Whldg	Employee FICA	Medicare	Employer FICA	Medicare	State Disblty	State Whldg	Other	Net	Chk No	
1	1/01-31	300.00	0	0	18.60	4.35	—	—	1.50	0	0	275.55	218	1
2	2/01-28	294.50	0	0	18.26	4.27	—	—	1.47	0	0	270.50	243	2
3	3/01-31	312.00	0	0	19.34	4.52	—	—	1.56	0	0	286.58	271	3
4														4
5	1ST QTR	906.50	0	0	56.20	13.14	—	—	4.53	0	0	832.63		5
6	TAX DEP.				56.20	13.14	56.20	13.14				138.68	287	6
7														7
8														8
9														9
10														10
11	4/01-30	332.00	0	0	20.58	4.81	—	—	1.66	0	0	304.95	295	11

■ Expenses—Payroll Record

For each employee you hire, you will have to keep some sort of a Payroll Record. It's absolutely essential because it shows a complete breakdown of the various categories of payroll deductions, as well as the employer's contributions. Fortunately, it's a relatively simple form to use.

Once you have calculated the employee's various payroll deductions and have prepared the statement-of-earnings-and-deductions form to accompany each payroll check (see chapter 13), post those figures onto the Payroll Record, and then add to all that the employer's contribution to Social Security and Medicare. Remember that you do not deduct the employer's contributions from the employee's gross. It's an expense item for you, not for your employee. You merely keep track of it here so that you will know how much you need to pay out of your own pocket every quarter.

Refer to this form whenever you have to prepare monthly, quarterly, or annual reports for the government agencies involved.

■ Summaries—Annual Summary of Expenses and Payments

The summaries section includes two different forms. The first one closely parallels the Expense and Payment Record and is solely for the purpose of gathering together the expenditures for several properties. If you have only one property, you would already have figured your expenditures for the year on the final Expense and Payment Record page, and you would not need to use this form.

The only difference between the regular Expense and Payment Record form and this Annual Summary of Expenses and Payments form is that "Unit(s)" takes the place of the first four columns, "Date," "How Paid," "To Whom Paid," and "For," and there's a thirteenth col-

Expense & Payment Record Page _1_
Annual Summary Property _SWEET ST & NEAT STREET_
Period _XXXX_

	Units	1 Total Paid Out (2-12)	2 Interest	3 Taxes, Licences	4 Insurance	5 Utilities	
1	456-64 SWEET ST.	21576.73	6496.72	2930.71	1348.62	648.12	1
2							2
3	125 NEAT ST.	4915.68	1358.69	1002.48	593.87	261.74	3
4							4
5	TOTAL	26492.41	7855.41	3933.19	1348.62	909.86	5
6							6

umn for recording both regular and supplemental depreciation.

List each property's location on the form first and then record the total expenses just as you have calculated them on the final Expense and Payment Record sheets for each property. That accomplished, you will be prepared with the figures needed for the next form.

■ Summaries—Summary of Business and Statement of Income

The Summary of Business and Statement of Income form brings together all income and all expenses for a final reckoning. Use them monthly if you want to and you'll be exceedingly well informed about the financial status of your property. Though desirable, monthly summaries are hardly indispensable, however, and most landlords use them just once a year unless they're using a computer bookkeeping system such as the one shown in chapter 20. It gives monthly and year-to-date totals automatically.

Whether you use this summary form on an annual or a monthly basis, you will make some important calculations using it. Here's where you subtract from your expense totals the depreciable items you paid for this year, the amounts cred-

Summary of Business & Statement of Income

Property __SWEET STREET__ Period __XXXX / APRIL__

#									
1									
2									
3	INCOME								
4	Rental				3	6	5	0	00
5	Other					1	4	2	61
6	TOTAL INCOME				3	7	9	2	61
7									
8									
9									
10									
11									
12	EXPENSES & PAYMENTS								
13	Interest					6	5	6	32
14	Taxes, Licenses					6	7	4	31
15	Insurance					8	8	6	54
16	Utilities					1	4	4	32
17	Services, Repairs, Maintenance					1	7	1	08
18	Merchandise, Supplies						3	9	70
19	Payroll					1	1	3	18
20	Miscellaneous Expenses						1	6	38
21	Depreciable					1	5	9	74
22	Mortgage Principal					4	7	2	68
23	Non-deductible					2	0	0	00
24									
25									
26	TOTAL EXPENSES & PAYMENTS			3	5	3	4	25
27	minus Non-deductible (line 23)				2	0	0	00
28	TOTAL			3	3	3	4	25
29	minus Depreciable (line 21)				1	5	9	74
30	TOTAL			3	1	7	4	51
31	minus Mortgage Prin. (line 22)				4	7	2	68

ited to your loan principals, as well as your sundry non-deductibles (including impounds). And if you haven't done so already, here's where you have the opportunity to deduct as business expenses your telephone, the office space used in your home (use great discretion with this one; be prepared with proof), and your mileage (log your landlording trips for substantiation). When you have completed all of these calculations, you'll have a net expense figure ready for your income tax return.

What's more, when you take the difference between your total expenditures and your non-deductibles and you subtract this figure from your total income, you will know what your actual cash flow is, that is, what you actually took in minus what you actually paid out.

Note that this cash flow figure includes as "expenses" what you paid out for both mortgage principal and depreciable items. Even though what you paid toward mortgage principal represents a kind of forced savings account and what you paid for depreciable items will be deducted for tax purposes over a number of years, you still had to pay out that money this year. What's left over for spending, saving, or investing after you've

Loan & Note Record

Property 456-64 SWEET STREET
Noteholder BIG BANK, P.O. BOX 678, LITTLETOWN   Loan Number 01-2345
Original Loan 214,114   Interest Rate 10%   Payment 1,879.00   Due Date 8/01/XX

	Date Paid/Ck.#/New Payment if Changed	Interest	Principal	Impounds & (Imp.Disb.)	Impound Balance	Principal Balance	
1	BAL FWD					209770.26	1
2	3/01/xx ✓ 567	1748.09	130.91			209639.35	2
3	4/01/xx ✓ 631	1746.99	132.01			209507.34	3
4	5/02/xx ✓ 672	1745.89	133.11			209374.23	4
5	6/01/xx ✓ 694	1744.79	134.21			209240.02	5
6	7/01/xx ✓ 716	1743.67	135.33			209104.69	6
7	8/01/xx ✓ 729	1742.54	136.46			208968.23	7
8	9/01/xx ✓ 747	1741.40	137.60			208830.63	8
9	10/03/xx ✓ 762	1740.26	138.74			208691.89	9
10	11/01/xx ✓ 788	1739.10	139.90			208551.99	10
11	12/01/xx ✓ 797	1737.93	141.07			208410.92	11
12	1/02/xx ✓ 811	1736.76	142.24			208268.68	12
13	2/01/xx ✓ 832	1735.57	143.43			208125.25	13
14	3/01/xx ✓ 847	1734.38	144.62			207980.63	14
15	4/03/xx ✓ 860	1733.17	145.83			207834.80	15
16	5/01/xx ✓ 879	1731.96	147.04			207687.76	16
17	6/01/xx - 893	1730.73	148.27			207539.49	17
18	7/02/xx ✓ 914	1729.50	149.50			207389.99	18
19	8/03/xx ✓ 930	1728.25	150.75			207239.24	19
20	9/01/xx ✓ 943	1726.99	152.01			207087.23	20
21	9/30/xx ✓ 959	1725.73	153.27			206933.96	21
22	11/02/xx ✓ 975	1724.45	154.55			206779.41	22
23	12/02/xx ✓ 987	1723.16	155.84			206623.57	23
24	1/03/xx ✓ 1012	1721.86	157.14			206466.43	24
25	2/01/xx ✓ 1020	1720.55	158.45			206307.98	25
26	3/03/xx ✓ 1031	1719.23	159.77			206148.21	26
27	4/01/xx ✓ 1053	1717.90	161.10			205987.11	27
28	5/01/xx ✓ 1062	1716.56	162.44			205824.67	28
29	6/01/xx ✓ 1071	1715.21	163.79			205660.88	29
30	7/02/xx ✓ 1090	1713.84	165.16			205495.72	30
31	8/01/xx ✓ 1106	1712.46	166.54			205329.18	31
32	8/30/xx ✓ 1115	1711.08	167.92			205161.26	32

paid all your expenses is in one sense the true cash flow produced by the property. But it's not the same as the "cash flow" which has been referred to elsewhere in this book along with the other three ways to make money in the landlording business. If you want to calculate that cash flow, you don't include either the mortgage principal payments (they're really contributing to your "equity buildup," remember) or the cost of the depreciable items. You include among the ordinary expenses only the amount of this year's depreciation on the depreciable items you paid for during this year and prior years. That's the classic way to calculate cash flow, but it results in an unreal figure, if you ask me. It's not really the money you get to pocket. Personally, I think the other figure is more meaningful. Use whichever one makes more sense to you.

■ Loans/Insurance—Loan & Note Record

The Loan & Note Record form enables you to keep tabs on your loans, an activity some might say is akin to the miser's counting his stacks of gold and silver coins. It ain't necessarily so. Actually, this form provides you with information which is very useful when you're renegotiating a loan, when you're double-checking a lender's interest calculations, or when your payment book is lost in the mail. Everything's here, the original amount of the loan, the interest rate, the payment, the principal balance, etc., and filling it out takes just a moment after you receive your payment book back from the lender.

Come to think of it, filling out this record is kind of fun, too, because you can watch the equity in your property gradually building up every time you fill another line with figures. Maybe misers do have more fun. Well, in this business you'd better take your fun when and where you can get it.

■ Loans/Insurance—Insurance Record

This last form keeps track of the insurance policies for your properties, all of your properties. It's not an absolutely essential part of your records, and you won't get any jollies out of keeping it up to date or reading it when you have nothing else to do, but you will find that having all of your insurance information in this one place is convenient when you begin wondering how soon a policy is due or what coverage you still have on a certain property. Insurance policies themselves don't yield that kind of information quickly. Typically you have to read through lots of fine print before you discover the information you're looking for. Read the fine print only once and record the pertinent information here. Then you'll have it handy when you need it.

Insurance Record Property __456-64 Sweet Street__

Company and/or Agent	Type of Policy	Policy Number	Limits	Premium	Expiration Date
Comfy Insur. 555-2845	Workers' Comp.	00479	—	$136 - 5/10/xx '1063	6/01/xx
Driver Friendly Glenda Lacy 555-1181	Auto	2YA-30454	1,000,000 liability	$483 - 10/20/xx '1149	11/12/xx
Wholesale Insur. Vernagae Lee 555-1068	Apt. Owners	FI-778 1101	1,000,000 liability	$886.54 4/20/xx '1279	4/30/xx
Driver Friendly Glenda Lacy 555-1181	(Pick-up) Auto	2V.A.30864	1,000,000 liability	$321 - 3/26/xx '1212	11/12/xx
Major Carrier Victor Wong 555-3050	Earthquake	099837L	37,000 Deduct.	$867 5/11/xx '1292	6/01/xx

Some Last Words

Do your recordkeeping regularly at least once a month, and you'll find that it's practically tolerable. It will also give you the current information you need when you're curious about how well your properties are doing or are applying for financing or refinancing.

Better still, get yourself a computer and follow the suggestions in chapter 20 for computerizing your operations. Even a homegrown computer bookkeeping system will save you lots of drudgery and time, and it should motivate you enough to keep on top of all your recordkeeping instead of sinking beneath it.

19
Doing Taxes

During the first two weeks of April every year, many adults seem to suffer from the same malady, the dreaded DT's. They wobble a little and complain a lot, and their eyes grow bug-eyed and red. They start imagining all sorts of devils and demons and beastly beasties, and it isn't until after the fifteenth of the month that the symptoms finally disappear, because not until then do they finish DOING TAXES.

Landlord, if you're among these seasonal sufferers, you should be ashamed of yourself! Income tax time is an especially good time for you, and you should enjoy the opportunity to snicker a little over your good fortune. Don't wait until April 15th to file your return. Do it as soon as you can, so you'll have your income tax refund check in hand when everyone else is suffering those dreaded DT's. Besides, you need that check by April to help pay your property taxes.

You get to snicker over your income taxes because at tax time you may take advantage of one of the four ways to make money in landlording—depreciation. (If you don't remember the other three, look back at the beginning of chapter 7.)

Here's how depreciation works for rental property owners. Every year, little by little, you get to deduct from your property's income a portion of the value of the capital improvements just as if they were honest-to-goodness, out-of-purse expenses incurred during the year. "Capital improvements" include everything but the raw land where the property is located. Many times, even though the property is producing a positive cash flow, these extra deductions will shelter that cash flow and create a paper loss on the property besides. You as owner may then apply this loss to your other income (within legal limits naturally) in order to reduce your overall income tax burden. When you finally sell the property, you then pay income taxes on the "depreciation recapture" (the amount of depreciation you took while you owned the property) and the "capital gain" (the difference between the net sales price and the net purchase price).

Here's a straightforward example. Let's say that you bought a fourplex for $125,000 (this sum would be your purchase price) and you depreciated it down to $75,000 (this sum would be your depreciable balance) over the years you owned the property. During that time, you avoided paying taxes on $50,000 of your income. If you now sell the property for $300,000 (to learn about the impending tax consequences every time you plan to acquire or dispose of income property, spend a few bucks and consult a knowledgeable, aggressive accountant or tax attorney), you'll have a depreciation recapture total of $50,000 and a capital gain total of $175,000.

Neither of these sums is earned income. Depreciation recapture and capital gain fall under tax classifications which are treated more favorably than earned income. In other words, even though you were sheltering earned income with depreciation and you profited handsomely from the capital gain you received when you sold the property, you pay less in taxes on those sums than you would have if they had been earned income.

That in itself is an advantage, but the real advantage you enjoyed in depreciating this property for tax purposes is that you didn't have to pay taxes on the $50,000 you took as depreciation during the years you owned the property. If the property generated that amount or more in cash flow while you owned it, then you paid no income taxes whatsoever on $50,000 of its cash flow. If it generated less than that amount in cash flow, then it enabled you to pay no taxes on the cash flow the property did generate, and the excess depreciation sheltered some of your regular income as well, provided, of course, that you qualified to use it according to the IRS income and activity requirements.

Remember that a dollar in your pocket today is worth more than a dollar in your pocket next year. If you can postpone paying a bill today and pay it with the same amount of money years hence, that is, without having to pay any interest on the amount you owe, then you get to put that money to use for your own benefit, and it costs you nothing to do so. Such a deal! You are essentially borrowing money from a bank which doesn't charge any interest!

Consider how much money you'd have if you could somehow retrieve every dollar you ever paid in income taxes and you could use that money to buy more rental property. You'd be worth a lot more than you are today, wouldn't you? Well, the situation is similar when you consider that depreciation for tax purposes enables you to keep a portion of your income from being taxed. You get to use the tax money you would otherwise be paying. It becomes part of your net worth. Such a deal!

Here's an even better deal. What if you could save some or all of the money you pay in income taxes every year and not just postpone paying those taxes but never pay them at all? Yes, yes. You can, you know.

You can if you exchange your property. Exchanging is the best way available to avoid depreciation recapture and capital gains taxes altogether when you want to get rid of one rental property and acquire another. In fact, exchanges are easier to arrange now than ever before because they don't have to be simultaneous. The IRS has given them a specific designation and, what's more, has given them its blessing. They're called Section 1031 exchanges.

Here's how they work. You sell your property and put the proceeds into an exchange account

which requires your signature plus the signature of another qualified person for withdrawal. You then have forty-five days to identify as many as three properties to purchase. You may purchase one or more of the three, but what you do purchase must have an equal or greater value than the property you sold in order for you to pay no taxes at all. Having identified the property, you have six months to consummate the acquisition using the exchange account funds. Each transaction merely needs to have the proper verbiage to indicate that it is part of an interdependent sale and reinvestment.

For practical information about doing 1031 exchanges with or without pricey assistance, see "How to Do a Delayed Exchange." It's a 38-page special report written by John Reed, the author of *John T. Reed's Real Estate Investor's Monthly* (John T. Reed, 342 Bryan Drive, Alamo, CA 94507, 925.820.6292, johntreed.com). He calls them "the granddaddy of all real estate tax breaks." He's right. They certainly are.

Bob Bruss has written about 1031 exchanges in his newsletter as well—"How to Profit from Starker Delayed Tax-Deferred Exchanges," #00315 (Robert J. Bruss, 251 Park Road, Burlingame, CA 94010, 800.736.1736, bobbruss.com). Incidentally, every year the *Robert Bruss Real Estate Newsletter* comes out with a special issue covering the latest real estate tax tips. It's well worth reading.

In the case of the fourplex which you sold for $300,000, you would get to reinvest all of the proceeds from that sale in another property without paying any taxes on your considerable capital gain or on the recapture of the depreciation so long as you set up the transaction as a 1031 exchange! If the loan balance on the old property were $70,000, and the sales commission and costs were $16,000, you'd have $214,000 in untaxed cash to reinvest, and you should be able to purchase a new property selling for $650,000 to $1,000,000.

Had you not exchanged, you'd have had to pay something like $73,000 of your proceeds in state and federal taxes. Consequently, you'd have had only $141,000 to reinvest, and you'd have been limited to smaller properties in the $425,000 to $700,000 range. The 1031 exchange would have saved you $73,000!

Invested in good income-producing real estate with a cap rate of 9 (remember now—"cap rate" is the return generated by a property exclusive of debt service; it's really a percentage figure derived from dividing the net operating income by the value of a property; higher numbers are better), that $73,000 should be making you an extra $547 per month, month after month after month for the rest of your life!

Where does all this end?

If you continue exchanging and exchanging, you may defer the payment of taxes until you finally sell off your properties, or you may keep exchanging properties and keep avoiding the payment of taxes on the capital gains forever.

When your heirs assume ownership of your property, they do so at its then current value, not at its old basis or depreciable balance. By exchanging, therefore, you avoid paying the capital gains taxes while you are alive, and so do your heirs when they acquire it upon your death. Tax-deferred exchanges can become true tax-free exchanges!

Is your mind boggled? It should be. Think about this. You can be increasing your net worth year after year every time you depreciate your property for tax purposes while at the same time the property itself actually appreciates in value. Yet you are not liable for income taxes on the resulting increase in your net worth, not even when you sell one property and use the proceeds to buy another! That's more amazing than any pickled two-headed billy goat I've ever seen and a heck of a lot more important to you and me as real estate investors.

Ah, but you say, "I've only got a fourplex, and I just want to learn how to prepare the tax forms I need to submit along with my income tax return. I can't be wasting my time dreaming about exchanging my property and becoming wealthy while I sleep. I have all the rental property I can handle right now. One place is plenty. Heck, most of the time it's more than plenty!"

Okay, okay. Here's how to do your return, and here are some sample tax form sheets completed for Lester Landlord (he's no millionaire either). He has a duplex and a fiveplex.

Doing Your Own Taxes by Hand and Calculator

Begin preparing your taxes by completing a Depreciation Record sheet (see chapter 18) for every building you own and for the various expenditures you have to depreciate, including those which qualify for first-year expensing as Section 179 property (only five- and seven-year depreciable items qualify).

Check a current tax reference book such as *The Ernst & Young Tax Guide* to determine what useful life is appropriate, whether a depreciable item may be expensed in its first year, and how much depreciation you may take for every year you own a property.

Use the same form for all of your buildings and depreciable expenditures, but use one sheet for each building and one sheet for each classification of depreciable expenditures made for a particular building. For example, Lester should have one sheet for the new roof he put on his duplex and another one for the new roof he put on his fiveplex several years later. He should have one sheet for all the five-year items he bought for his duplex in one year and another sheet for all the seven-year items he bought for his fiveplex that same year. All of these Depreciation Records should remain in his three-hole recordkeeping binder for reference whenever it's time to do taxes.

Next comes the biggest job of all for procrastinators, completion of the annual summary reports for all rental property held. You may do them manually with the forms provided in chapter 18. You may do them with a spreadsheet template like the one shown in chapter 20. You may do them with a computer checkwriting program like Quicken. How you arrive at the summaries doesn't matter so long as they're accurate. Once you have completed the summaries, keep them close at hand. Together with the depreciation sheets, they comprise the primary source of data essential from here on.

Now make blank copies of tax forms E-3, D-1, and SD in the FORMS section of this book

| Form E-3 | **RENTAL INCOME AND EXPENSE** | | | | | | | YEAR KXXX | |

| NAME(S) OF TAXPAYERS | LESTER LANDLORD | | | | SOC. SEC. NUMBER | 123 | 45 | 6789 | |

PROPERTY LOCATION & DESCRIPTION								GROSS INCOME
Property A	123 NEAT ST.				LITTLETOWN			10,500.00
Property B	456-464 SWEET ST.				✓			42,600.00
Property C								
Property D								
Property E								
Property F								
Property G								
					TOTAL GROSS INCOME			53,100.00

EXPENSES	A	B	C	D	E	F	G	Totals
Interest	3,643.06	7,312.78						
Taxes, Licenses	1,648.62	1,374.42						
Insurance	741.80	886.54						
Utilities	490.07	2,177.60						
Serv,Rep,Maint.	232.31	1,407.90						
Merch., Supplies	387.91	489.27						
Payroll	—0—	790.60						
Misc. Expenses	248.72	92.79						
Other: Tel	138.48	—0—						
Travel	149.70	—0—						
Subtotal	7,680.67							
% Business Use	50%							
Subtotals	3,840.33	14,540.90						18,381.23
Deprec. (D-1)	1,426.08	3,465.00						4,891.08 *
Deprec. (SD)		412.30						412.30 *
Totals	5,266.41	18,418.20						23,684.61

*Sum of D-1 and SD Depreciation Totals 5,303.38 *

Form D-1	**DEPRECIATION WORKSHEET**		YEAR XXXX

NAME(S) OF TAXPAYERS	LESTER LANDLORD	SOC. SEC. NUMBER	123 45 6789

PROPERTY LOCATION & DESCRIPTION

Property A 123 NEAT ST., LITTLETOWN

Property B 456 - 464 SWEET ST.,

Property C

Property D

Property E

Property F

Property G

	A	B	C	D	E	F	G	Totals
Date Acqd. or Conv. to Bus.	2/XX	10/XX						
New or Used	USED	USED						
Cost or Other Basis	112,356	198,000						
Land Value	34,000	59,400						
Salvage Value	O	O						
1st Year Special Depreciation	O	O						O
Depreciable Basis	78,356	138,600						
Prior Depreciation	25,669.43	18,191.25						
Depreciable Balance	52,686.57	120,408.75						
Method of Depreciation	ACCEL	SL						
Useful Life	27.5	40						
Full Year Depreciation	2852.16	3465.00						
Percentage of Year Held	100	100						
Percentage of Business Use	50	100						
Depreciation This Year	1426.08	3465.00						4,891.08

PAGE TOTAL 4,891.08

Form SD	SUPPLEMENTAL DEPRECIATION							YEAR XXXX

NAME(S) OF TAXPAYERS *LESTER LANDLORD*   SOC. SEC. NUMBER 123 45 6789

CAPITAL IMPROVEMENT LOCATION & DESCRIPTION

1 456-464 SWEET ST., CARPETING, DRAPERIES, LINOLEUM

2

3

4

5

6

7

	1	2	3	4	5	6	7	Totals
Date Acqd. or Conv. to Bus.	6/XX							
New or Used	NEW							
Cost or Other Basis	1683.55							
Salvage Value	Ø							
1st Year Special Depreciation	Ø							
Depreciable Basis	1,683.55							
Prior Depreciation	240.41							
Depreciable Balance	1,443.14							
Method of Depreciation	ACCEL							
Useful Life	7							
Full Year Depreciation	412.30							
Percentage of Year Held	100							
Percentage for Business Use	100							
Depreciation This Year	412.30							412.30

PAGE TOTAL 412.30

(these forms, by the way, could be made into computer spreadsheet templates as well; in fact, Landlording® on Disk (The Forms) includes several such templates, the same ones I use myself every year), and using applicable information from your Depreciation Records, fill out D-1 and SD. Use D-1 for buildings only and SD for anything else depreciable, from furnaces to roofs.

Enter the appropriate property location and description information on form E-3 and post each building's depreciation for the year from form D-1 to E-3. Add all the supplemental depreciation as noted on SD for each property and post the figures onto E-3 in the space marked "Deprec. (SD)." Remember that all of the supplemental depreciation for each building must be added together before it's posted.

After you post both regular and supplemental depreciation for your properties onto E-3, enter the gross income as calculated on the Summary of Business and Statement of Income form. Then post the expenses from the summary sheet to E-3 (you'll notice that the categories are the same on both forms) and calculate the totals. Remember to add the two asterisked boxes and post their sum in the bottommost box on the form.

Using all of this information, you can easily fill out Form 1040, Schedule E, otherwise known as the "Supplemental Income and Loss Schedule." In Part I of Schedule E, simply write "SEE ATTACHED FORM E-3" where it won't be missed, perhaps where you might otherwise identify the location of "Property A." Then post the TOTALS from E-3 to the corresponding lines of Schedule E. Post the total income (rents received) where indicated and the total expenses where indicated. You needn't go to the trouble of itemizing the expenses again on Schedule E; just post the total expenses. Use the "Property A" column for these figures, and make sure that you post an income figure and an expenses figure separately. Do not combine them before posting them on Schedule E. By all means, do remember to post your depreciation total on its proper line. Then follow the instructions printed right on Schedule E for adding the expenses and the depreciation together and subtracting them from the rents received. Also at this time, write "SEE FORMS E-3 AND SD FOR DEPRECIATION CALCULATIONS" across the bottom of the form to advise the reviewer of your return where to look for your depreciation information. If the other parts on page 2 apply to you, include their totals with your Part I total in the summary section under the final part. If they don't, merely transfer the total from Part I to the designated line on Form 1040.

Should you show a loss from your rentals, check the tax booklet's instructions for Schedule E to determine whether you're eligible to apply the loss to your other income. The rules for eligibility keep changing, so even though you might not have been eligible before, you might be now. Keep checking the rules, and take whatever losses you can. Hey, they're a gift! Gifts from the IRS are almost as scarce as winning tickets in a state lottery. Take 'em when you can get 'em.

From this point on, just go ahead and finish your tax computations as you normally do, snickering as you go, and remember to attach forms E-3, D-1, and SD to Schedule E when you submit your return.

Doing Your Own Taxes by Computer

What would you say if I told you there's a computer program available which automatically transfers the total from your Schedule E to the proper line on your 1040? What's more, it calculates your taxes any which way you want. If you wish, it will step you through the return with plain-English questions. It offers plenty of online advice. It prints on blank paper very readable facsimiles of the IRS forms which you may sign and submit, and it won't let you forget to check a box you're supposed to check. What's that? Did you say that if there were such a thing you'd really and truly consider doing your own taxes?

Well, there is such a program. It's called MacInTax® in its Macintosh version and TurboTax® in its Windows version, and it's stunning! It does all the above and a whole lot more (see SOURCES & RESOURCES). It makes manual tax preparation seem like washboard laundering.

No longer do you have to concentrate so intently on making sure that you do every calculation on your return correctly, that you post the right total from one box on one form to a corresponding box on another form, and that you be consistent with the names and social security numbers on every form you submit. No longer do you have to redo your return when you discover belatedly that you forgot to include the

```
===============================================================================
  DEPRECIATION STATEMENT
===============================================================================
     YEAR: XXXX                                          NAME: Lester Landlord
  PROPERTY: 456-464 Sweet St., Tarrytown          SOC SEC NO: 123-45-6789
-------------------------------------------------------------------------------
```

Description of Property	Date Acq	Cost/ Basis (less land)	Sec. 179 Election This Yr	Prior Dep (Fed)	Prior Dep (State)	Re- maining Cost (Fed)	Re- maining Cost (State)	M t h d	Life in Yrs	Fed Rate	State Rate	Prtn Yr Held	Fed Dep This Yr	St Dep This Yr
5-Plex Bldg	10/1/XX	138,600		18,191	18,191	120,409	120,409	SL	40			1	3,465	3,465
Cpt, lino	6/2/XX	1,684		240	240	1,444	1,444	A	7	0.2449	0.2449	1	412	412
						0	0						0	0
						0	0						0	0
						0	0						0	0
						0	0						0	0
						0	0						0	0
						0	0						0	0
TOTALS		140,284		18,431	18,431	121,853	121,853						3,877	3,877

Methods:
  SL, straight line; A, accelerated

second payment you made on the property taxes for one of your rental houses. Add that figure into the expenses for that house, and these programs will take care of all the necessary recalculations right on down the line.

These programs remove most of the grunt work from tax preparation and give you the opportunity to analyze your return to see whether you might save on your taxes by readjusting your investments. They let you play "what if?" with the numbers.

The only thing they don't do is sign the return. You still have to do that.

Not only can these programs produce your federal return, they can produce your state return as well. They will transfer the appropriate data from your federal return, which you should always do first, to your state return and help you fill it out correctly. Even with all their many capabilities, they're bargain-priced. They sell for less than $50. They're so good and so easy to learn that even though you have no intention of buying a computer, you might want to think about buying either program anyway and giving it to a friend who does have a computer in exchange for some time on his machine. Then both of you could use the program to do your returns.

Lacking a friend with a computer, you could still buy the program and then buy some computer time somewhere. Computers are available

for rent from certain computer stores and from stores which offer copying and desktop publishing services, especially those near college campuses. You could generate your return, print it out, and save it to a floppy disk just in case you needed to make some changes later.

Another way to enlist the aid of a computer, virtually any computer, for doing your taxes is to use an electronic spreadsheet program to create your own spreadsheets according to the patterns of the forms shown in this chapter. Once you have them set up to your liking, you can use them year after year with little alteration. They won't be nearly as automated as MacInTax or TurboTax, but they will be very useful.

The printout above shows how the forms D-1 and SD might look as a computer spreadsheet. Here they're combined and arranged horizontally to show all the depreciation on one property for a single year. The spreadsheet includes formulas which calculate the federal and the state depreciation, if they're different, and then add the totals at the bottom.

Some Last Words

There are those naysayers you'll encounter in this world who will say you're a pig-headed fool for doing your own taxes. They'll say you should have a sorcerer in tax matters do them for you, someone who's thoroughly experienced in doing income taxes for propertied folk, someone who knows all the latest loopholes applicable to your situation, and those naysayers may be right. It all depends on your ability and your inclination.

Some people have the good sense to invest in rental property, but they lack the capacity to deal with numerical data and somewhat complicated instructions. People like that should leave their taxes to the experts.

Some people have the good sense to invest in rental property and are good with numbers, but they find tax preparation too boring to do themselves. They'd rather spend their time looking after their properties, looking for more properties to acquire, or learning more about the landlording business. People like that should leave their taxes to the experts, too.

If you happen to be a landlord who possesses the ability and has the inclination to prepare your own taxes, you ought to do them yourself, by all means, but once you have finished with them, get a second opinion from a specialist by buying an hour or two of professional advice. You can-

not possibly keep abreast of the volumes of current tax laws, and you could unknowingly be throwing money away by overlooking perfectly legitimate tax angles.

Whereas you may not be foolish for preparing your tax return yourself, you certainly would be foolish for submitting it to the tax collector without first reviewing it with someone who knows the subject intimately. At the very least, have your self-prepared returns reviewed by a professional preparer every three years, when you may still amend any of those returns to change items reported in error or omitted on the original return.

Whether you have your taxes prepared for you or whether you do them yourself, try to get a feel for the tax principles which affect the landlording business. Read about taxes in periodicals. Get a copy of *Aggressive Tax Avoidance for Real Estate Investors*, and read it from cover to cover. Jot down questions for your tax consultant. Then make an appointment for a consultation. A capable professional will save you money and give you a tax education at the same time.

20
Using a Computer

If you have a computer already, you may find in this chapter several ways to put it to better use.

If you don't have a computer, you may find in this chapter some reasons why you might want to consider buying one.

BUT, just as it's all right not to drink alcohol, it's all right not to have a computer. Really, it is! In spite of what the ads say, or your neighbors, or your kid's teachers, or the media, or the computer store salesperson, there's nothing a computer can do for you that you can't also do some other way without one. It's just that a computer will definitely save you time once you've learned the basics, and it will motivate you to do some of those things that you either don't do at all or don't do when you should do them because they're so tedious and take so much time.

Few Americans nowadays would exchange their Buick for a horse and buggy. They've become so used to the advantages of having an automobile that getting along without one would be unthinkable. Automobiles have been around a long time, and their advantages are pretty obvious. Every fifteen-year-old with a learner's permit knows those advantages by heart. In comparison, computers haven't been around very long, and their advantages are not so obvious to one and all.

When the first edition of this book appeared back in 1975, which was the same year, believe it or not, that Volkswagen stopped selling the original "Beetle" in the U.S. and America got out of Vietnam, there was no such thing as a personal computer. Computers were monstrosities which cost a small fortune to acquire, a small staff to operate, a small priesthood to program, a small utility company to power, and a small throne room to house. They weren't available to mere mortals. The closest thing to a personal computer

then were word processing machines which cost $15,000 a copy and were little more than the electronic typewriters of today.

In the years since then, a lot has happened in the computer world. Fortunes have been made and lost, companies have come and gone, innovators have surfaced and vanished, and reputations have waxed and waned, but now, if you want to, you can enjoy the fruits of many, many creative people's extensive labors. We have available to us today some very powerful, very compact, very useful, and very inexpensive computers, computers which are now also very easy to use compared to their predecessors.

Whereas the average person can't easily justify spending the money necessary to buy a computer simply in order to play games or send and receive email, you, landlord, are more fortunate. You don't have to think very hard about what you could do with a computer to justify buying one. There's plenty you can do with one, from creating your own forms and letters to doing your own bookkeeping, tax returns, and financial statements. Like never before, you can keep track of your business with accuracy and ease, just like one of the big Fortune 500 companies.

Useful though they are in rental property management, computers still require a certain initial commitment in terms of time and resources. That commitment isn't so great anymore because we have better computers nowadays and better programs to make them work, but it is still a commitment nonetheless, and you have to be willing to make that commitment if you want to become more productive.

If you're the type of person who balked at automating with a rubber stamp and a hand-cranked adding machine, then you definitely shouldn't commit any of your time or resources to computerize. Stick with what you've been

341

doing all along. Don't change. If you're the type who hates to spend time or resources on anything without getting an immediate reward, then you shouldn't computerize either. But if you're the type who is always looking for better ways to do things, and you recognize that you're going to have to commit some time and some resources upfront to make your landlording business run better in the future, then you should definitely computerize. Not doing so would hinder your progress in landlording.

Am I a proselytizer of computers in landlording? You bet. As far as I'm concerned, they're as useful in landlording as they are in conquering space. As far as you are concerned, well, you have to make that decision yourself.

Should you have any fears or doubts, should you wonder about the language computer people speak, should you wonder how a computer might help you, read on.

Fear Not

Computers are stupid. They're so stupid that they're practically brain dead. When tested, they always reveal IQs of either 0 or 1. You're much smarter than that. I know you are. Why, computers are so stupid, so obedient, that they will do exactly what you tell them to do every time and they're do it in exactly the same way every time! Be honest now. When was the last time you got a tenant to do that? So, why should you be afraid of computers?

Computers are passive, too. In spite of what you may have seen in some science-fiction film or other, computers have never been known to attack people. Why be afraid of them? There's nothing they can do to hurt you or you to hurt them.

You can hit every key on a computer's keyboard all day and all night long and in every conceivable combination, and you won't get executed, you won't start a nuclear war, you won't even break into American Airline's reservation system or a Citibank payroll file, not accidentally you won't. Have no fear of that.

Ordinary people did have something to fear about computers a few years ago. Computers were different then. They were primitive beasts, tough to tame, and requiring lots of patience, technical knowledge, concentration, and logical thinking to operate. They could do a lot of work for you, but as often as not, they would make work for you.

All that's changed now. Now they come pretty much tamed and housebroken, and you have nothing to fear from having them around. What's more, you don't have to spend all that much time learning how to use one anymore.

If you haven't yet seen the new breed of computer and computer software yet, visit a computer store and take a good look at a Macintosh or a Windows machine. They are truly different from their predecessors. They use something called a graphical user interface. Rather than memorizing and using cryptic keyboard commands to accomplish tasks, you merely manipulate a pointing device, such as a mouse or a trackball, and press a button to tell your computer what to do. They're so simple to use that you can be fearless around them.

If you're embarrassed to learn anything about computers because you don't want to appear ignorant around little kids who seem to grasp these newfangled machines so quickly, don't be. Most kids and most adults, too, who are computer "junkies," love to show others what they can make their computers do, and they love to show others how neophytes can work wonders with a computer. They show and tell and teach computers with joy and hope that they will awaken the computer nerd in everybody.

Remember that everybody's been a computer beginner sometime. If you don't know diddlysquat about computers right now, so what! Now's the time to get started, no matter how young you are or how old you are. I have helped people in their seventies and eighties learn how to use a computer and become more productive as a result. One of these days I'm sure I'll come across some intrepid souls in their nineties who want to learn how to use a computer. I'll show them what they need to know, and they'll be so delighted by all they can do that they'll want to extend their lease on life for at least another decade.

But What Can You Really Do with One?

What can you, dear landlord, really do with a computer?

For starters, you can write checks with it. When you write your checks using your computer, you enter the numbers only once rather than two or three times. You eliminate the inevitable errors which creep in when you transcribe check amounts to the check register by hand and later when you post them by hand to a spreadsheet. Computer checkwriting programs automatically post the original amounts entered on the checks themselves. Reconciling your monthly statement becomes a pleasant task instead of a frustrating one, and preparing the expense reports for your properties is a snap.

You can analyze your expenses using percentages and graphs. Are you spending too high a percentage of your expenses on insurance, for example? You can't tell that without using a computer unless you take a lot of extra time to produce comparable figures. A computer can do it for you in a jiffy.

You can analyze the occupancy rates of your various-sized dwellings so you can tell whether the rents for your one-bedroom units are too high or too low. If they're showing an 80% occupancy rate over the same period of time that your two-bedroom units are showing a 96% rate, your one-bedroom rents are probably priced too high and should be adjusted. The rental market is always speaking to you. All you have to do is listen and interpret what it's saying.

You can make up professional-looking rental agreements and pay-rent-or-quit notices to suit your particular needs, and then you can change them whenever you choose.

You can keep track of your tenants' addresses, phone numbers, bank account numbers, birthdays, rents, deposits, payment history, and rent raise anniversaries. You can create rent statements and receipts and maintenance requests and work orders.

You can create letters as fast and as perfectly as the best legal secretary who's still using an ordinary typewriter.

You can set up a year's budget in advance and try to stay within it. When have you ever been able to do that before?

You can analyze the potential of a property which is being offered for sale and calculate a fair offer. When you get ready to sell your own property, you can calculate a fair sales price based upon the detailed operational figures you've assembled.

You can run the numbers applicable to any number of different IRS Section 1031 delayed exchange scenarios so that you can select the best one. Once you've run the numbers, you can also determine the depreciable basis for your new property without having to hire an accountant to do it for you.

You can complete your own tax return almost painlessly. You won't need an eraser or a calculator or any midnight oil to help you do it either.

You can produce loan payment schedules for all your loans, including those held by private parties, those with variable interest rates, those with irregular payments, and those with balloon payments.

You can update your financial statements regularly so you'll understand fully how well you're doing in your financial dealings and know when you've joined the Millionaire Club of America.

You can access the Internet and verify information on rental applications, order credit reports and eviction reports, locate former tenants who skipped out owing you money, check out the latest in fair housing laws, download and read the current state codes applicable to rental properties, research market rents in your area, retrieve an unusual IRS form you didn't know you needed until late on April 15th, search for the obscure manufacturer of a heater part, shop for more rental properties, and even chat with other landlords.

That's pretty heady stuff, isn't it? Believe it or not, you can do all of these tasks with the various programs mentioned in this chapter.

A Little Jargon

Before you start thinking much about using a computer in landlording, you really ought to learn a little computer jargon, some "tech talk."

Jargon helps people engaged in similar pursuits understand each other quickly. As a real estate investor, you unwittingly use jargon sometimes, and few outsiders would understand what in the world you're talking about. "COE" (close of escrow), "REO" (real estate owned by note holders who have foreclosed), "paper" (mortgages or notes in lieu of cash), "points" (percentage points charged by lenders to make a loan), "boot" (difference between equities involved in a trade), "DOS" (due on sale), "recording" (placing a document on file with the county for all to see), "wrap" (a combination of existing loans and a new one carried by the seller), and "title" (evidence of someone's right to a property) are all terms which mean something special to you, something quite different from what they mean to John and Jane Doe.

Computer people use jargon just as you unwittingly do. They use so much of it that one group of computer people using one type of computer frequently cannot understand their colleagues who use another type of computer. Four words they all understand, though, are "hardware," "software," "programs," and "files," and you should understand what they mean, too. They're essential terms.

"Hardware" in computer jargon is anything you can see and touch. That includes the computer which sits on your desk, the central processing unit (CPU) and the random access memory (RAM) inside, the monitor you stare at, the keyboard your fingers tap on, the mouse you use to scurry your pointer around the monitor's screen and execute commands, the printer which gives you print on paper, and the modem which connects you to the Internet. "Hardware" also includes the drives which store information on disks much as videotape machines store information on tape cassettes.

"Software" in computer jargon is anything you can't see or touch. Computer programs which do word or number processing are "software" as are instructions which tell the computer where to find what's stored in its memory. Software is essential to making hardware work the way you

want it to work. A movie stored on a videocassette is software. You can't see it unless the videotape player interprets it for you, and you can't touch it. Yet you know the movie is there. The same is true with computer software. You know that something is in there interpreting your commands. You just can't see it. That's the software at work.

"Programs" are software. You can't see them or touch them. They're stored on magnetic disks, magnetic tape, CD-ROMs (compact disks, read-only memory), and computer memory "chips." They are very detailed instructions written by computer programmers to make computers act in certain ways in response to user commands. Programs turn computers into many different things. There are programs which make personal computers act like office calculators, flight simulators, electronic typewriters, typesetters, speed reading machines, filing cabinets, telephone dialers, fax machines, video arcade machines, drawing boards, musical instruments, utility usage monitors, photograph retouchers, animation editors, et cetera. The list goes on and on.

"Files" are software, too. They're what you, the computer user, save on disk. When you write a letter using a computer or enter a whole series of numbers that you want to save, you save them on a disk as a file. Once they're stored on disk, you can retrieve and use them whenever you wish, so long as you have a program which can open them.

Whew, that's enough jargon for now! Don't you agree?

The Power Programs

Let's take a look at how you might use computer programs for word processing, number handling, data management, Internet access, and other specialized uses.

■ **Word Processing**—Word processing programs enable you to manipulate words easily and quickly. With a word processor, you may type away on your computer's keyboard to your imagination's content and then move those words around to suit your second thoughts.

The two primary uses for word processing in landlording are correspondence and forms creation.

Correspondence is obvious enough. Whenever you "feel a letter coming on," you sit down at your computer and bang away on the keyboard.

When the letter looks pretty good to you on the screen, you tell the program to print it out on paper. If it looks good to you on paper, you send it. If it doesn't, you go back to the same letter on the computer screen and change it to your liking without having to type it all over again or use correction tape. You add a comma here, move a paragraph there, delete a word in paragraph two, and change an abbreviation at the end. Then you print the letter-perfect version. That done, you save the letter in a file on your computer's disk if you think you might want to use parts of that same letter again sometime, or else you go ahead and trash it.

Forms creation isn't that much different from correspondence. It involves either making up your own forms from scratch or using someone else's like the ones in this book. All you do is create a word processing "template" for each form you want to use repeatedly. You may take a "standard rental application" and a "standard rental contract" and adapt them to fit your locale, the type of tenant you cater to, the type of dwelling you rent out, and the times, and then print copies whenever you need them.

You may also personalize your agreements for each of your tenants if you want to, using a form you set up with what are called "fields" in place of the variable data, shown otherwise as underlined blanks to be filled in. These fields accept data from another file when the two are "merge-printed." The data file contains only such things as the tenants' names, their address, the amount of the rent, and anything else specific to the tenancy. The result is a beautiful looking personalized document with no blanks to fill in except for the signature blanks. The computer program "fills in" all the other blanks with data.

■ **Spreadsheet Programs**—Spreadsheet programs are not the only computer programs which process numbers, but they're the easiest for ordinary people like us to learn and use. Usually the second business application program mastered by the personal computer user, they do more to justify the use of a computer by landlords than any other program because they're so versatile and powerful. They can do so much.

What's surprising is that the computer spreadsheet program is such a recent innovation that even my unabridged edition of *The Random House Dictionary of the English Language*, which was copyrighted in 1971, lacks an entry for the word "spreadsheet."

The grandaddy spreadsheet program of them all, VisiCalc, first appeared on the scene in 1977 and worked only on the Apple II computer. Because so many businesspeople recognized its potential right away, that program alone sold thousands upon thousands of Apple II's and helped to establish Apple as a computer company.

Today, many people consider the computer spreadsheet program one of the most innovative ideas of the 20th century. I would readily agree. Spreadsheet programs now run on every personal computer, and they are so much improved that they make the first version of VisiCalc seem as crude as a crystal set.

A computer spreadsheet program consists of what resembles a large piece of graph paper inside the computer. Each one of the graph paper's little boxes, or "cells," as they're called, may be addressed individually with a column and row designation, like every good seat in a college football stadium. The very first cell in the upper left-hand corner of a spreadsheet is A1 ("A" is the column and "1" is the row). The very last one in the bottom right-hand corner, depending on how many cells your spreadsheet program has, might be BK63 ("BK" is the column and "63" is the row).

Now, if these carefully identified cells could hold only numbers, they'd be about as useful as a curl of calculator tape in a wastebasket. We'd have to keep asking ourselves what the numbers meant, just as we'd be asking ourselves what a radio sportscaster meant in announcing, "We have two great basketball scores for you, folks, 89 to 88 and 106 to 104!" You'd have to admit that those were great scores indicating close games, exciting games, but they wouldn't mean anything to anybody without team names attached to them.

So, spreadsheet programs allow you to put words into their cells as well as numbers, but what's more important, they allow you to put formulas (add up what's in cells A6 through AH6 and put the sum in cell G6) and cell references (look at another cell and put its value or formula in this one) there, too. These formulas and cell references are what make spreadsheet programs so versatile and powerful.

Because a blank computer spreadsheet has so many cells waiting to be filled and so many capabilities waiting to be used, it has tremendous

Income and Expense Spreadsheet with Dummy Data

	A	B	C	D	E	F	G	H	I	J	K	L	M	N	O	P	Q	R	S	T
1																				
2	PROPERTY NAME: SWEET ST					INCOME AND EXPENSES -				MONTH: April					SWST	PAGE 2				
3																				
4	Date	Ck #		Paid To		For	Total	Adverts	BnkChg	Car Exp	Dues&Pub	Garbage	Insurance	Interest	Lgl&Prof	Lic/Perm	OfcSupls	OutSrvs	Pstg&Frt	Promo
5																				
6	4/2	267		Big Bank		1st mortgage	579.03							311.42						
7	"	268		S. Moneybags		2d mortgage	122.00							53.34						
8	4/6	269		Littletown Hdw		hdw account	43.29													
9	4/7	270		Saddlebk Cnty		prop taxes	674.31													
10	4/10	271		Monopoly Util		3/1-4/1	57.12													
11	4/11	272		K-Mart		shades	24.42													
12	4/12	273		Lttletwn Water		April water	41.30													
13	"	274		Monopoly Garb		April service	22.50					22.50								
14	4/15	275		Phoenix Paints		paint & suppl	8.23													
15	"	276		Lester Landlord		pers draw	280.00													
16	"	277		C. Goodfolks		payroll	30.00													
17	4/19	278		" " P/C		plumbsupp	20.52												4.40	
18	4/20	279		USA Insurance		annual prem	286.54						286.54							
19	4/21	280		LittltwnOffSup		copying	5.47										5.47			
20	4/25	281		Seeres Co.		water heater	443.64													
21	4/31	282		C. Goodfolks		payroll	74.13													
22							0.00													
23	4/15	$$$		Mtn Oaks Hdw		pnt brushes,	17.40													
24	4/22	$$$		Littletown Rag		ad to rent apt	6.50	6.50												
25							0.00													
26							0.00													
27							0.00													
28							0.00													
29							0.00													
30							0.00													
31							0.00													
32							0.00													
33							0.00													
34							0.00													
35							0.00													
36							0.00													
37							0.00													
38							0.00													
39							0.00													
40							0.00													
41							0.00													
42							0.00													
43							0.00													
44							0.00													
45							0.00													
46							0.00													
47							0.00													
48							0.00													
49							0.00													
50							0.00													
51							0.00													
52							0.00													
53							0.00													
54							0.00													
55																				
56				THIS MONTH'S TOTALS			2736.40	6.50	0.00	0.00	0.00	22.50	286.54	364.76	0.00	0.00	5.47	0.00	4.40	0.00

NOTES:

These facing pages show what an income and expense spreadsheet looks like when completed for a single month.

Designed to print on three 8.5"x11" pages, this spreadsheet has been condensed here to fit onto two pages. The page breaks should come where you see the solid black vertical lines.

This sample includes row and column headings for easy reference. For better looking results, don't print the headings on your final copy.

Column G, you'll be happy to note, requires no user input. It adds whatever you enter in columns H through AG and puts that total where it belongs.

Columns AE through AG include expenditures which are not, strictly speaking, expenses, at least not for tax purposes. Nonetheless, because they do come out of the property's checking account and do relate to the property, you have to keep track of them somewhere. This is the place.

Column AJ starts with zeros in January. Other months show the year-to-date figures from the previous month's spreadsheet.

Column AK automatically picks up the current month's totals for each category of expenditures. You have to enter the income figures for the month here.

	Repairs	Sewer	Supplies	Txs,EPT	Txs,Pay	Txs,Prop	Tel	Trv&Ent	Util	Wages	Deprec	Princpl	Non-Ded		Prior Month	This Month	Yr to Date	% Ttls
2								SW ST	PAGE 3							SUMMARY		
4	Repairs	Sewer	Supplies	Txs,EPT	Txs,Pay	Txs,Prop	Tel	Trv&Ent	Util	Wages	Deprec	Princpl	Non-Ded		Prior Month	This Month	Yr to Date	% Ttls
6												267.61		Income:				
7												68.66		Rental	6,398.00	2,314.00	8,712.00	94%
8	43.29													Laundry	264.50	78.75	343.25	4%
9						674.31								Storage	120.00	45.00	165.00	2%
10									57.12					Other	0.00	18.86	18.86	0%
11			24.42															
12									41.30					TOTAL INCOME	6,782.50	2,456.61	9,239.11	100%
14	8.23													Expenditures:				
15													280.00	Advertising	12.50	6.50	19.00	0%
16										30.00				Bank Charges	0.00	0.00	0.00	0%
17			16.12											Car Expenses	0.00	0.00	0.00	0%
18														Dues&Publications	0.00	0.00	0.00	0%
19														Garbage	90.00	22.50	112.50	2%
20											443.64			Insurance	0.00	286.54	286.54	5%
21										74.13				Interest	1,104.39	364.76	1,469.15	28%
22														Legal&Professional	0.00	0.00	0.00	0%
23			17.40											Licenses&Permits	10.00	0.00	10.00	0%
24														Office Supplies	1.37	5.47	6.84	0%
25														Outside Services	35.00	0.00	35.00	1%
26														Postage&Freight	4.40	4.40	8.80	0%
27														Promotion	0.00	0.00	0.00	0%
28														Repairs	74.39	51.52	125.91	2%
29														Sewer	0.00	0.00	0.00	0%
30														Supplies	152.33	57.94	210.27	4%
31														Taxes, Employer'sPay	7.40	0.00	7.40	0%
32														Taxes,Payroll	7.40	0.00	7.40	0%
33														Taxes,Property	0.00	674.31	674.31	13%
34														Telephone	25.67	0.00	25.67	0%
35														Travel&Entertainment	0.00	0.00	0.00	0%
36														Utilities	193.73	98.42	292.15	6%
37														Wages	97.60	104.13	201.73	4%
38														Depreciable	0.00	443.64	443.64	8%
39														Mortgage Principal	990.64	336.27	1,326.91	25%
40														Non-Deductible	247.50	280.00	527.50	
42														TOTAL	3,054.32	2,736.40	5,790.72	
43														Less Non-Deduct	247.50	280.00	527.50	
45														TOTAL EXPENDITURES	2,806.82	2,456.40	5,263.22	100%
47														Income	6,782.50	2,456.61	9,239.11	
48														Less Expenditures	2,806.82	2,456.40	5,263.22	
50														**CASH FLOW**	3,975.68	0.21	3,975.89	
52														Tot Exp less Debt				
53														Serv & Deprec as	10%	53%	22%	
54														% of Tot Income				
56	51.52	0.00	57.94	0.00	0.00	674.31	0.00	0.00	98.42	104.13	443.64	336.27	280.00	Checkbook Balance		359.14		

Column AL adds columns AJ and AK to get figures reflecting the entire year through the current month.

Column AM calculates some important percentages. Examine them to see in relative terms where the property's money is coming from and where it's going. If one appears to be out of proportion to the others, find out why.

Row 50 is the actual cash flow from the property after the total expenditures have been deducted from the income. This figure is not the same as the net income for tax purposes. To get that figure, you'd have to add back what was paid for depreciable items and what was paid on the mortgage principal.

Row 53, like column AM, calculates a percentage. This time the percentage excludes debt service and depreciable items and shows what proportion of the income the expenses are. Use these percentages to compare one month with another and one property with another. This percentage is useful because it strips properties of their debt service so you can compare them on an equal basis. By the way, can you tell why the percentage for April is so high when compared with the previous months?

The checkbook balance, cell AK56, is strictly a reference figure which you enter from your checkbook register at the end of the month. It puts everything into perspective so you know whether to add money to the property account, whether to take money out as a personal draw, or whether to leave it alone.

Income and Expense Spreadsheet Template

	A	B	C	D	E	F	G	H	I	J	K
1	=	=	=	=	=	=	=	=	=	=	=
2	PROPERTY NAME:					INCOME AND EXPENSES				MONTH:	
3	=	=	=	=	=	=	=	=	=	=	=
4	Date	Ck #		Paid To		For	Total	Adverts	BnkChgs	Car Exp	Dues&Pub
5	-		-	-		-	-	-	-	-	-
6							=SUM(H6:AG6)				
7							=SUM(H7:AG7)				
8							=SUM(H8:AG8)				
9							=SUM(H9:AG9)				
10							=SUM(H10:AG10)				
11							=SUM(H11:AG11)				
12							=SUM(H12:AG12)				
13							=SUM(H13:AG13)				
14							=SUM(H14:AG14)				
15							=SUM(H15:AG15)				
16							=SUM(H16:AG16)				
17							=SUM(H17:AG17)				
18							=SUM(H18:AG18)				
19							=SUM(H19:AG19)				
20							=SUM(H20:AG20)				
21							=SUM(H21:AG21)				
22							=SUM(H22:AG22)				
23							=SUM(H23:AG23)				
24							=SUM(H24:AG24)				
25							=SUM(H25:AG25)				
26							=SUM(H26:AG26)				
27							=SUM(H27:AG27)				
28							=SUM(H28:AG28)				
29							=SUM(H29:AG29)				
30							=SUM(H30:AG30)				
31							=SUM(H31:AG31)				
32							=SUM(H32:AG32)				
33							=SUM(H33:AG33)				
34							=SUM(H34:AG34)				
35							=SUM(H35:AG35)				
36							=SUM(H36:AG36)				
37							=SUM(H37:AG37)				
38							=SUM(H38:AG38)				
39							=SUM(H39:AG39)				
40							=SUM(H40:AG40)				
41							=SUM(H41:AG41)				
42							=SUM(H42:AG42)				
43							=SUM(H43:AG43)				
44							=SUM(H44:AG44)				
45							=SUM(H45:AG45)				
46							=SUM(H46:AG46)				
47							=SUM(H47:AG47)				
48							=SUM(H48:AG48)				
49							=SUM(H49:AG49)				
50							=SUM(H50:AG50)				
51							=SUM(H51:AG51)				
52							=SUM(H52:AG52)				
53							=SUM(H53:AG53)				
54							=SUM(H54:AG54)				
55	-		-	-		-	-	-	-	-	-
56				THIS MONTH'S TOTALS			=SUM(G6:G54)	=SUM(H6:H54)	=SUM(I6:I54)	=SUM(J6:J54)	=SUM(K6:K54)

NOTES:

These pages show the words and formulas used to create the template which forms the basis for what you see on the previous two pages.

Because of space limitations, columns L through AG have been omitted. Except for their "totals" cells in row 56, which reflect a particular column letter designation, they look just like columns H-K shown here.

Rows 1, 3, 5, and 55 all have symbols which repeat across the pages. The symbols look like single or double lines when they're set to fill out their cells.

Columns C, E, and AH are narrow spacer columns.

They separate entries to prevent confusion in the final printout.

The "=" sign in this particular spreadsheet program, which happens to be Excel™, identifies a cell as a formula cell. Cell G6, for example, totals everything in cells H6 through AG6. Cell H56 totals everything in cells H6 through H54.

To get the prior month's figures for column AJ, copy the figures, NOT THE FORMULAS, from the previous month's column AL and paste them into column AJ for the current month.

	AH	AI	AJ	AK	AL	AM
1	■	■		■	■	■
2			SUMMARY			
3	■	■	■	■	■	■
4			Prior Months	This Month	Yr to Date	% Ttls
5	-		-	-	-	-
6		Income:				
7		Rental			=SUM(AJ7:AK7)	=AL7/AL12
8		Laundry			=SUM(AJ8:AK8)	=AL8/AL12
9		Storage			=SUM(AJ9:AK9)	=AL9/AL12
10		Other			=SUM(AJ10:AK10)	=AL10/AL12
11		-		-	-	-
12		TOTAL INCOME	=SUM(AJ7:AJ10)	=SUM(AK7:AK10)	=SUM(AL7:AL10)	=SUM(AM7:AM10)
13						
14		Expenditures:				
15		Advertising	0	=H56	=AJ15+AK15	=AL15/AL45
16		Bank Charges	0	=I56	=AJ16+AK16	=AL16/AL45
17		Car Expenses	0	=J56	=AJ17+AK17	=AL17/AL45
18		Dues&Publications	0	=K56	=AJ18+AK18	=AL18/AL45
19		Garbage	0	=L56	=AJ19+AK19	=AL19/AL45
20		Insurance	0	=M56	=AJ20+AK20	=AL20/AL45
21		Interest	0	=N56	=AJ21+AK21	=AL21/AL45
22		Legal&Professional	0	=O56	=AJ22+AK22	=AL22/AL45
23		Licenses&Permits	0	=P56	=AJ23+AK23	=AL23/AL45
24		Office Supplies	0	=Q56	=AJ24+AK24	=AL24/AL45
25		Outside Services	0	=R56	=AJ25+AK25	=AL25/AL45
26		Postage&Freight	0	=S56	=AJ26+AK26	=AL26/AL45
27		Promotion	0	=T56	=AJ27+AK27	=AL27/AL45
28		Repairs	0	=U56	=AJ28+AK28	=AL28/AL45
29		Sewer	0	=V56	=AJ29+AK29	=AL29/AL45
30		Supplies	0	=W56	=AJ30+AK30	=AL30/AL45
31		Taxes, Employer'sPayroll	0	=X56	=AJ31+AK31	=AL31/AL45
32		Taxes,Payroll	0	=Y56	=AJ32+AK32	=AL32/AL45
33		Taxes,Property	0	=Z56	=AJ33+AK33	=AL33/AL45
34		Telephone	0	=AA56	=AJ34+AK34	=AL34/AL45
35		Travel&Entertainment	0	=AB56	=AJ35+AK35	=AL35/AL45
36		Utilities	0	=AC56	=AJ36+AK36	=AL36/AL45
37		Wages	0	=AD56	=AJ37+AK37	=AL37/AL45
38		Depreciable	0	=AE56	=AJ38+AK38	=AL38/AL45
39		Mortgage Principal	0	=AF56	=AJ39+AK39	=AL39/AL45
40		Non-Deductible	0	=AG56	=AJ40+AK40	
41		-	-	-		-
42		TOTAL	=SUM(AJ15:AJ40)	=SUM(AK15:AK40)	=SUM(AL15:AL40)	
43		Less Non-Deduct	=AJ40	=AK40	=AL40	
44		-	-	-		-
45		TOTAL EXPENDITURES	=AJ42-AJ43	=AK42-AK43	=AL42-AL43	=SUM(AM15:AM39)
46						
47		Income	=AJ12	=AK12	=AJ47+AK47	
48		Less Expenditures	=AJ45	=AK45	=AL45	
49		-	-	-		
50		* * CASH FLOW * *	=AJ47-AJ48	=AK47-AK48	=AL47-AL48	
51		-	-	-		
52		Tot Exp less Debt				
53		Serv & Deprec as	=(AJ45-(AJ21+AJ38+AJ39))/AJ12	=(AK45-(AK21+AK38+AK39))/AK12	=(AL45-(AL21+AL38+AL39))/AL12	
54		% of Tot Income				
55	-					
56		Checkbook Balance		0		

Column AK requires original input for the income figures, cells AK7 through AK10, but it takes its expenditure figures from row 56 across the spreadsheet. Cell AK15, for example, picks up the total spent for advertising during the month. It appears as "=H56," which means repeat here exactly what appears in cell H56.

Column AL merely adds columns AJ and AK to produce the year-to-date figures.

Column AM divides each category of expenditure except Non-Deductible by the total amount of expenditures so far this year to get a percentage.

The percentages in row 53 are different from those in column AM. Look at the formula in cell AL53 to see what I mean. It lumps all the expenditures together except Non-Deductible, cell AL45, deducts the total paid for debt service and depreciable items, cells AL21, AL38, and AL39, and divides that by the total income, cell AL12, to show what percentage of total income the property's expenses are.

potential in and of itself, but you won't see the true extent of that potential until you have filled some of those cells with a carefully prepared layout which you can use over and over again. These cell layouts are called "templates," just like their word processing counterparts. They're actually nothing more than words and formulas which you use frequently.

Rather than begin each computer spreadsheet session with a blank spreadsheet and put into it the same words and formulas you've used before and know you'll use again, you use a template, one you make up yourself or one you buy from someone else (ExPress sells them; see "Landlording® on Disk (The Forms)" in SOURCES & RESOURCES).

Except for one essential difference, a spreadsheet template is much like any of the bookkeeping forms in this book. The big difference is that the spreadsheet template has a "calculator" built right into it, and you can tell this calculator to perform its mathematical calculations automatically or upon command.

Were you manually posting a series of numbers on a paper bookkeeping form, you'd first have to enter the numbers on the form and then you'd have to run a calculator tape to total them. You'd be entering every number twice, once on the paper form and once on the calculator, and doubling your odds for making errors. Using a spreadsheet program and a template, you enter the numbers only once. The built-in calculator takes over from there, so you have fewer opportunities to make mistakes.

Is it any wonder, then, that accounting firms today, which have to be extremely accurate in their calculations, cannot be without their personal computers, spreadsheet programs, and templates?

You could create all sorts of these templates for yourself if you wanted to. You could create them for loan tables, property analyses, tax schedules, financial statements, bookkeeping, and anything else which involves numbers.

The expense-and-payments-record template shown on the previous pages is a good example of a useful template which you could use with any spreadsheet program. The first two pages include a month's data so you can visualize what it looks like when it's in use. The two pages after that show what the template looks like with its formulas exposed.

To create this template yourself, you'd enter into your spreadsheet program what appears in the cells on the second two pages. Doing so is not nearly as hard as it may first appear because many of the cell entries are repeated with only slight modifications. The program itself will sense what you're trying to do and make the cell address adjustments automatically. Enter a formula and command your spreadsheet genie to copy that one to other cells. G56, for example, is copied with adjustments into all the cells from H56 through AG56.

Once you set up an expense and payment record template like this one, you don't have to do it again. That's the beauty of it. All you do after that is call up the template, enter the appropriate property designation and dates in row 2, and go to cell A6 to enter the date for the first expenditure. Follow across the row and enter the check number, the payee, and a description of the expense or payment item itself. Then you select the column heading which best describes the item you're posting and enter the dollar amount there. As you do that for each of the month's entries, the spreadsheet program will insert the total for the line into column "G," total the columns, and place the column totals into the proper positions for the cumulative summary over in the "This Month" column (AK), all automatically.

But wait, there are several more steps you ought to take to get full advantage of the really important information the template can provide for you. After you've posted all expenditure entries as outlined, enter the income for the current month in cells AK7 through AK10. Then load the "Year to Date" column from the previous month's spreadsheet into the "Prior Months" column (AJ) on this month's spreadsheet, and the program will figure everything else out for you, right down to cash flow and percentages. That's useful information, easily produced!

I would like to caution you here to examine closely every spreadsheet template you create. Once you've created a template and are using it, you needn't worry much about data entry errors because they'll be noticeable. Ah, but a simple formula error in one cell will be magnified whenever that formula affects another cell. The error will just keep being repeated. Neither the computer nor the program knows any better. If, for example, you inadvertently tell the program to put the sum of every cell from H7 through H54 into cell H56, when you meant to include cell

H6, too, you're going to have a problem. The problem may not surface for a while if you seldom enter a number in cell H6, and even when you do enter a number in H6, you may not notice what's wrong in H56 right away. There won't be any bells tolling or error messages appearing on your viewing screen. The error will just creep in quietly, on little rat feet.

If that ever happens, you'll know why computer people are so mindful of their oft repeated saying, "Garbage in, garbage out!" Do be careful. Spreadsheets are powerful, but they're also unforgiving. Check and double-check your work.

■ **Database Management Programs**—Database management programs are essentially filing programs with search, sort, and math functions added. Your telephone book is a large database, and all the names in it are filed alphabetically according to last names. If you wanted a list of all the people who have a certain telephone prefix and live on a certain street and you weren't using a database management program, you'd have to sit down and laboriously make a list of them one by one. Ah, but if you had your whole telephone book entered into a database management program, all you'd have to do to get a list of the people who live on Tewkesbury Street and have a 555 telephone prefix is ask for it. The program would find everyone with those two things in combination, and it would list them in any order you specify, that is, by last name, street address, or telephone number.

Database management programs are powerful, but they have been difficult to master in the past. Without attending intense seminars or lengthy classes or pouring over some fairly technical material and learning some cryptic commands, you couldn't become proficient in using most database management programs.

Fortunately, the newer database management programs like FileMaker are much easier to learn and use, and they're far more versatile. With FileMaker, you as a non-programmer could design an entire recordkeeping system to keep track of just about everything for your rental properties. Ultimately, it would be even easier to use on a monthly basis than a spreadsheet template, though it would take more time to design.

■ **Integrated Programs**—Sometimes likened to Swiss Army knives because they are capable of doing many different tasks, integrated programs can do word processing, spreadsheet work, database management, and more. Some of them even have a paint and a draw function.

Although the early versions of these programs were anemic, the more recent ones are powerful, and what's more, they're inexpensive. You needn't buy copies of Word and Excel for your ordinary landlording chores. They're overkill. They have far more features than you'd ever use. Integrated programs can do everything you as a landlord need to do with a computer, and they're practically "road kill" in cost. Many computers come with them already loaded on the hard drive at no extra cost. MicrosoftWorks and AppleWorks are good examples of capable integrated programs.

■ **Canned Programs**—So-called "canned programs" are different from word processing, spreadsheet, database management, and integrated programs. Canned programs are not nearly so flexible as other programs. They are not written to be flexible; they're written to perform specific tasks. In that, they might be said to resemble the combination of a spreadsheet program and a particular spreadsheet template. They do one thing, and they should do it well because they can't be modified to do anything else.

Good examples of good canned programs are TurboTax, MacInTax, and Quicken (see SOURCES & RESOURCES). They're easy to master, and they do a great deal with a minimum amount of input from you.

There are, however, a lot of canned business programs on the market which are, quite simply, terrible because they take a long time to learn, because they contain a lot of bugs and do strange things for no apparent reason, or because they don't do very much of what you want them to. They're simply not well conceived or well written.

Buyer of canned programs, beware!

If you are inclined to purchase any canned program for more than a few hundred dollars, make arrangements to try it out first before you buy. Ask about the availability of a demo disk or a demo download from the company's website. Ask for a list of customers whom you could call or email for some frank words about the program. I have a canned program which cost me over $2,000 and is now sitting on a shelf gathering dust. It didn't work out for me, and I couldn't get my money back when I finally discovered that it wouldn't do what I wanted it to do. That expensive lesson from Hard Knocks College you needn't learn the expensive way.

Be wary. You want to buy software which will work as advertised and will make your life easier, not harder. Be wary, by all means, of the program which is sold as the "complete property management software package." First, such programs are not going to be cheap. Second, they're not going to do all that you want them to do. Third, they're going to be difficult or impossible to change. They're set up to do things one way and one way only. You can't change them. You can hope that the people who developed them will listen to your suggestions and complaints and eventually make successive versions more to your liking, but don't place a big bet that they will.

■ **Internet Access**—With so much useful landlording information readily available over the Internet these days, you ought to have some means of accessing it yourself. Not only should you be accessing this information yourself, you should be advertising your vacancies on the Internet where appropriate and using it for sending and receiving email, too.

Here are a few recommendations regarding your using the Internet as a landlord.

Subscribe to a true Internet service provider (ISP) rather than to a proprietary online service such as AOL or CompuServe. Each has its advantages, of course, but now that connecting to an ISP is easier than ever, now that there's so much content available over the Internet to anybody with access, and now that many ISPs provide nationwide toll-free access numbers, there's little reason to use a proprietary online service with its obtrusive advertising.

When selecting an ISP, inquire about their ratio of subscribers to ports; the lower, the better. A lower ratio means that fewer subscribers will be trying to log on when you are, so the likelihood of your getting a busy signal is smaller.

Be well aware of how much time you spend logged onto the Internet, and remember that whenever you're logged on, your phone line is unavailable for both incoming and outgoing calls. As soon as you can, determine how much time you'll be using the Internet regularly, and decide whether to install a separate phone line strictly for Internet access. One alternative to installing another line is to use your fax line for Internet access, that is, if you have a separate fax line. Another alternative is to use call forwarding from your primary line to your cell phone, so you won't miss any incoming calls when you're logged onto the Internet.

Try to access the Internet on a home phone line rather than on a business phone line. Your phone company may be charging business line customers one message unit for every minute the line is connected to a local phone number. Even casual Internet users who are dialing up their access provider over a business line which is assessed connect charges, will find a surprising item on their monthly bill.

If you're using a modem and a dial-up, read and write your email off line so you're not tying up a phone line when you don't really need to. You should be able to log on, collect and send your email in a matter of seconds, and then log off, that is, unless you're using a web-based email service such as HotMail or YahooMail, in which case you're receiving, composing, and sending your email while online.

HotMail and YahooMail email accounts, by the way, are free for the registering, and you ought to set one up just in case you cannot access your regular email account from a computer not your own. HotMail and YahooMail are accessible through any computer with an Internet connection anywhere in the world.

Spoil yourself with a speedy Internet connection. With high-speed DSL (digital service line) and cable access now available in many areas and high-speed satellite Internet hookups available everywhere, consider using one of them as your access to the Internet. They're more expensive than dial-ups, and they have been known to be quirky, but they're improving, they're coming down in price, they're much faster than dial-ups, and they don't tie up a phone line. You don't have the time to wait and wait while graphics and files flow through your modem. You have a landlording business to run and demanding tenants to pamper. You cannot afford to be sitting at your computer waiting for a tortoise of a system to transfer data.

Be aware that Windows is especially susceptible to viruses because hackers enjoy attacking what they consider the "evil empire." Because your Windows computer could inadvertently contract a virus through an Internet connection when you're downloading and because that virus could bring your system to a halt as well as destroy your precious files, be alert and be cautious. Run an updated virus protection program whenever you start up Windows and also back up your most precious files onto a floppy disk, a Zip disk, or a CD-R at least once a day. You won't be sorry you did. You could be very sorry you didn't.

Both Internet browsers, Netscape and Internet Explorer, are excellent, and they keep getting better. Don't be too quick to upgrade to the latest version, however, until you know you need it (some websites may require a later browser than what you have installed and may give you an indication that you need to upgrade) or until you learn from a trusted source that the upgrade runs reasonably well on your machine.

Netscape has "bookmarks," and Internet-Explorer has "favorites." They're the same thing, stored addresses of the websites you expect to frequent. Use them. They're great timesavers.

General Computer Recommendations

✔ Read the hardware and software reviews in magazines such as *PCWorld* and *MacWorld* before you buy. Even though they accept advertising and you might think that their reviews would be slanted toward their advertisers, they appear to publish reasonably unbiased reviews of the computer items they test.

✔ Try to find someone who's using the hardware or software you're interested in acquiring and ask them how they like it. For contacts, call your local rental housing association or attend a meeting of a local computer club.

✔ Attend a computer club meeting. Computer clubs are great support groups where you can find all kinds of practical solutions to your problems. Sometimes software vendors will attend the meetings to demonstrate their software to the group and will offer special deals to whoever wants to buy right then and there. You'll be welcome at these meetings whether you're using a computer already or merely have an interest in using one. The clubs exist for any number of reasons. Some are for people who happen to live in a particular geographic area and merely want to get together to talk computers. Some are for people who have one specific type of computer or computer operating system (like Windows or Macintosh OS or Linux). Some are for people who are using a particular type of software (Excel, Photoshop, Illustrator, or FileMaker). Some are for people who have similar business uses for their computers (real estate appraisers or attorneys). To find an appropriate club, consult the listings in a local computer periodical, ask the people who run your local computer store, or use an Internet search engine.

✔ Do not buy any piece of computer hardware or software until you can see an immediate need for it. There's not one computer or computer-related purchase I have ever made, whether it's been on sale or not when I bought it, which I couldn't buy today for less money than what I originally paid for it. Because you have to spend some time learning how to use each new piece of software for your computer, buying a whole batch of software which you can't use right away is foolish. By the time you get around to using all that you bought, there will be newer, improved versions available, and you'll have to pay extra for the updates.

✔ Do not overlook public-domain software ("freeware," free to everybody) and what's called shareware (software intended for free distribution among users who are under no obligation to pay for it unless they find it useful). You may obtain this software through user groups or via modem from computer bulletin boards, from various Internet websites, and from proprietary on-line services like CompuServe and AOL. (You might wonder why anyone would make software available for little or nothing. Here's why. Writing computer programs is one thing. Writing extensive documentation, packaging the program, marketing it, and supporting it are something else again. Some programmers like to write programs but hate to write documentation and hate to provide support. They're similar to those rental property owners who like to buy property but hate to manage it. These programmers consider themselves noncommercial types and would rather make their work available for little or nothing than either put themselves at the mercy of software publishers or not make their software available to the public at all.)

✔ Although the biggest complaint computer owners have is that they bought too early, don't wait for the right moment to buy the right computer at the right price. That moment will simply never come. Buy now if you feel you need a computer now.

✔ Do not buy any hardware, new or used, unless you know where you can have it repaired and upgraded. Although computer hardware requires repair much too seldom to justify a maintenance contract, it sometimes does require repair, and when it does, you should know where to take it.

✔ To avoid many frustrations, buy a hardware configuration which comes with a pointing device (mouse or trackball) and works with a graphic user interface (GUI). All Apple Macintoshes fit into this category and so do the IBM-PC's and PC compatibles running any version of Microsoft Windows. GUI software takes less time to learn than non-GUI software. That's why it's so popular. It also requires a speedier processor, lots of memory, and more hard disk space. Make sure that your hardware is capable of running GUI software at a reasonable speed.

✔ Consider buying a factory refurbished computer. They may be display models returned to the manufacturer from retail stores or customer returns which cannot be sold as new. Still, they have been checked thoroughly, discounted, and sometimes come with good guarantees. They're as good as new but without the new prices. You'll find them available through computer manufacturers' own websites (dell.com, compaq.com, and apple.com have them) and also through some of the large resellers such as warehouse.com (microwarehouse.com and macwarehouse.com). Know your prices. Sometimes factory refurbished computers sell at minimal discounts and carry a minimal guarantee, and you might as well buy a new one.

✔ Consider buying a used computer. Even the newer computer models appear for sale used, sold presumably by those who have to try the latest of everything without thinking about how much it costs. Used computers are available through your daily newspaper's classified ads, through computer flea markets, through specialty stores which sell only used computers, and through Internet auction sites such as eBay and Yahoo (auctions section). You may also find them listed on bulletin boards at computer stores and elsewhere.

When buying a used computer, be especially wary about whether the price is right, whether it has been stolen, and whether the software included is legitimately yours or whether it's been pirated.

Know prices before you go shopping for a used computer. Many times you'll find one priced even higher than its new equivalent. A used computer ought to be less expensive than a new one because some of its useful life is gone, because it comes with little or no warranty, and because it's likely to be an older, slower model. The prices of new computers keep coming down so much that even though you might think a computer which cost $1,500 two years ago is a good deal at $750, it might not be at all if you can now buy a new one with a faster clock speed, more RAM, a larger hard drive, and a faster modem for $800. That older computer ought to be selling for $300-400. One good place to check current prices for used machines is eBay. It lists lots of used computers for sale, and you'll see what buyers are willing to pay for a particular used computer today.

Be wary about whether the used computer is

stolen. A used computer ought to come with a paper trail establishing that it belongs to the seller, and it ought to come with the manufacturer's serial number intact. Serial numbers on computer equipment are printed on adhesive labels which thieves simply peel off. If you can't find a serial number on the equipment, it's probably stolen, and you'll have to do some mighty fast talking whenever you take it in for repair. You may have to do that fast talking down at the police station, and you may even have your computer equipment confiscated as stolen property if you're not careful. The first thing a computer repairer looks for is that serial number, so it should be one of the first things you look for when you're contemplating the purchase of a used system; no serial number, no purchase.

Another thing to be wary about when buying a used computer is the software included with the machine. Because of software piracy (unauthorized copying), so-called "used" software doesn't have much market value. Yet, new software costs plenty if you have to go out and buy it. With a used machine, you generally get valuable software for little or nothing. If you do acquire any used software, make sure that the seller gives you all the original diskettes and documentation and agrees to help you get the software license transferred into your name. Sometimes sellers will give you the original diskettes and manuals from an early version of some software which they have upgraded and intend to continue using themselves in the later version. In that case, the early version is the same as pirated software in the eyes of the software publisher. Ask for a clarification of what you are getting.

✔ To foil those who traffic in stolen equipment, engrave the manufacturer's serial number, your name, your driver's license number, and your Social Security number on the chassis and case of every separate piece of computer equipment you own. If a thief should happen to steal your well-marked equipment anyway, he won't be able to sell it easily. It'll probably remain in his possession until he's caught, and because it's so readily identifiable as yours, it might be returned to you instead of being auctioned off at the next police auction..

✔ If you already have a computer, so long as it can run a word processing program, a spreadsheet program, a check writing program, and an Internet browser, and so long as you feel comfortable with it, use it. Don't run out every year or so to buy something else which is new and improved and just a little bit faster. Every time you change computers, you face the daunting task of transferring files and loading software which you earlier loaded on your old machine. Plan to set aside a day for these tasks.

On the other hand, if you're still using MS-DOS, Windows 3.1, or a pre-PowerPC Mac, you ought to upgrade to a more current computer. You'll notice a dramatic increase in speed.

✔ Look closely at the PDA's (personal data assistants) now on the market, and ask yourself whether you'd use one if you had it. The Palm® and its brethren are far and away the most popular, and they have the most software available. They're good and well worth a look, but the real comer is the Pocket PC powered by the Windows CE® operating system, primarily because the display is 50% larger than the Palm display. The Compaq iPAQ®, the Hewlett-Packard Jornada®, and the Casio Cassiopeia® all use this operating system. They come loaded with versions of Microsoft Word, Excel, and Outlook. Using a separately available wireless modem, they connect to the Internet so you can send and receive email. For inputting data, they have a virtual keyboard built in and have handwriting recognition capability. They're small enough to fit in your pocket, and paired with a folding keyboard, which compares favorably to a full-size keyboard, yet folds to the size of the Pocket PC itself, they enable users to enter data quickly. They offer great features combined with great mobility. Although they can work independently for keeping address books and calendars, PDA's work best in tandem with a desktop or laptop computer, which have larger displays and connect in more ways to peripherals such as printers and mass-storage devices.

✔ Check your homeowners' insurance policy to make sure it specifically includes personal computers. Some do. Some don't. Some specifically exclude personal computers. If your insurance agent doesn't write computer insurance, ask other computer owners for the name of the agent who writes theirs. It's necessary. It's inexpensive.

✔ Always "back up" your work, that is, make duplicate copies of it on another disk. Power outages, magnetic fields, defective disks, operator error, disk drive problems, software viruses, software bugs, static electricity, and coffee spills all conspire now and then to cause you to lose the precious work which you labored long and hard over. The loony bins are full of people who didn't back up their work. Don't join them. Back up your work regularly.

✔ Some computer manufacturers trumpet the fact that they include thousands of dollars worth of software with their computers. Be aware that you may have no use for any of that software, that it may consist of outdated or "light" versions, and that it may come with none of the documentation it would come with if you were buying the full version. Nonetheless, the bundled software may get you started and entitle you to purchase version upgrades at greatly reduced prices. In fact, companies whose software is included in a bundle hope that you will come to like their software so much that you'll want to upgrade to the full, current version.

✔ Check for competitive upgrades when buying software, especially any software selling for hundreds of dollars. "Competitive upgrades" are greatly reduced prices made available to users of competing products. Let's say that you've been using one database management program for years, but you've heard many good things about another one and you'd like to acquire a copy. Whereas the best street (computer people refer to lower-than-list prices as "street" prices) price you can find after shopping around is $250, you might find that the competitive upgrade price is only $100 or even less. Why pay more when you can legitimately pay less?

✔ Check the auction websites when buying software. Some people buy software and never use it for one reason or another. It sits and sits until they clean out their closets and decide to sell it on an auction website. In general, you don't need to buy the very latest version of a word processing or spreadsheet program when an older version will do. Just make sure when you buy such software that it's legitimate and that you receive the license to use it.

My Own Biased Personal Computer Recommendations

Seasoned computer users tend to be biased in favor of one system over another and in favor of one kind of software over another. These biases can lead to intolerance and belligerence among otherwise intelligent and tolerant adults. I admit to being biased myself, but I don't get fighting mad when people I know buy precisely the system I've advised them not to buy. I just shake my head. I'm a landlord. I'm used to having people do precisely the opposite of what I say.

Although I use both an IBM-PC clone with a fast Pentium processor running Windows and a Macintosh PowerPC with a speedy G3 processor running the MacOS, I prefer the Macintosh. It's still easier to set up and easier to use than Windows machines, even though Microsoft programmers have made great strides in adding some nifty features such as Plug 'n' Play, which usually works as advertised. What I like about the Macintosh is that it hangs up (freezes) less often, and unlike Windows machines, because it was designed for a graphical user interface from the silicon up, you never have to revert to cryptic commands and see a dreaded "C" prompt when problems arise. Also, because Apple insisted that software companies writing for the Macintosh be consistent with certain common commands, users find that they can run most new software right out of the box without even looking at a manual.

Were you to compare Windows with the MacOS in terms of the time required to learn how to use each of them, you'd find that Windows requires at least a third more time to learn, and then the Windows user typically spends more time on file management and data communications. Whereas there used to be a big price differential between the two, today there is none at all for comparably equipped systems.

If you don't have some compelling reason to buy one computer over another and you want to use a computer to help you with your landlording chores without your having to spend much time learning how to use a computer, consider the following recommendations. They are my own biased personal hardware and software recommendations made by a long-time user of all kinds of computers and software in both education and business.

Buy a Macintosh. An iMac is plenty good enough unless you want a larger monitor and don't mind paying for it. One of the iBook laptops is a good choice for anyone who wants a computer which works as well in the home office as it does away from home.

Lest you worry that Mac users are isolated,

you should know that Macs can read, write, and format Windows diskettes. With an inexpensive external Zip or floppy drive, the iMac you have at home for your kids' schoolwork and your landlording business can read the word processing and spreadsheet files you bring home from the office on a Windows-formatted disk. Using equivalent programs, you can work on the files at home on your Mac and return to work the next day with your office work completed.

When buying a printer, consider the output quality, the speed, the paper path (the fewer turns the paper or envelope has to negotiate, the better; a straight-through paper path is best), the initial cost, and the cost of supplies. Some printers are inexpensive initially but may surprise you when you have to buy supplies (shop for supplies over the Internet; you'll find that prices vary dramatically; a generic cartridge distributor may undercut a printer manufacturer's list prices by seventy-five percent).

If you want to print in color, buy one of the low-cost, color-capable inkjet printers made by Epson, Hewlett-Packard, Canon, or Lexmark. They're all reasonably good when printing in black and white, but you'll want to examine their color print quality carefully. See how well they can print a color photo. Sooner or later you're going to be using a digital camera, if you don't already have one, and you will want a good color printer to produce the "prints" from that camera. You might as well buy that printer now.

If you have no use for color, buy a somewhat more expensive laser printer. Affordable laser printers print in black and white only, but their print quality is noticeably better than that of inkjets, and they tend to print faster.

For software, use AppleWorks, an integrated package which has all you're ever likely to need for everyday landlording tasks. Use Quicken, the checkwriting program for writing checks and keeping track of your expenses. Both come already preloaded on iMacs and iBooks. Finally, use Landlording on Disk (The Forms), my own collection of word processing forms and spreadsheet templates.

If you want to automate still further, buy a copy of Pushbutton Landlording, my own canned rental property management program for Macs and Windows machines.

For best prices on hardware and software, call one or more of the computer suppliers listed in SOURCES & RESOURCES and ask them to send you a catalog. They all have toll-free numbers. These same suppliers also have websites which sometimes have special offers not mentioned elsewhere. Of course, they all have two or three delivery options, including overnight delivery, at reasonable prices.

My Even More Biased Software Recommendation– Pushbutton Landlording

In an oft rued weak moment back in 1992 after having already paid many thousands of dollars to programmers to write a stand-alone landlording program and getting no useful results, I decided to write the program myself. I knew what I wanted. I knew what I didn't want.

I didn't want the program to deal with expenses. I didn't want it to write checks. I was using Quicken for those tasks and knew that I couldn't improve on it. I wanted my landlording program to handle the tenant and income side of rental property management. I wanted it to keep track of my properties, my units, and my tenants. I wanted it to write rental agreements, statements, receipts, notices, and maintenance requests. I wanted it to crank out income and occupancy reports. I wanted it to produce a list of late tenants at the push of a button and to produce late notices at the push of another button. I wanted it to be easy to use and attractive to look at. I wanted it to run under Windows and the Mac OS.

Little did I know then that I would be spending two years of my life cooped up in a room filled with computers and computer peripherals. Little did I know then that there would be so many details and problems to deal with that I would be thinking about them every hour of the day and night, every day of the week.

The first version of Pushbutton Landlording emerged from all of this work and thought and did what it was supposed to do, but it wasn't very attractive to look at. In fact, it was downright ugly.

Some years later, I took this ugly program and turned it into a thing of beauty. That's the Pushbutton Landlording available today. We use it ourselves for all of our rental properties, half of them on a Windows machine and half on a Macintosh. The program looks the same and

"Screen Shot" of Pushbutton Landlording's Primary Menu

"Screen Shot" of Pushbutton Landlording's Tenant List

Tenants

Selected tenant, Lane (JHL1), is 1 of 11; entered on 1/16/2001 and modified on 8/11/2001.

One tenant is on a waiting status.   No tenants need their current rent updated.

KEY: Go to links   Go to agree.   Move over   Review/change rents   Export merge data

Print labels   Check leases   Change "waiting"   Update rents   Find tenants

Push button below to go to selected tenant. Push a sort button to sort list. Push sort-status icon to unsort.

Unit	Tenant	Name	Address	Status
HILL1	JHL1	Joe H. Lane	234 Hill Lane, Apt. 1	Current
HILL2	ECV2	Evelyn Carol Venable	234 Hill Lane, Apt. 2	Current
HILL3	MCJ3	Margaret C. Judge	234 Hill Lane, Apt. 3	Current
HILL4	JOP4	Jeremiah Oscar Parker	234 Hill Lane, Apt. 4	Current
HILL5	GIO5	Gene Irwin Olson	234 Hill Lane, Apt. 5	Moved
HILL6	RAW6	Raymond Aaron Winston	234 Hill Lane, Apt. 6	Current
HILL3	ERB3	Ernie Ricardo Schwartz	234 Hill Lane, Apt. 3	Waiting
HILL5	ILR5	Iona Lee Rodham	234 Hill Lane, Apt. 5	Current
HILL3	GGG3	Gary Grice Graves	234 Hill Lane, Apt. 3	Moved
HILL7	JJD7	James Joseph Demming	234 Hill Lane, Apt. 7	Current
HILL8	RAJ8	Rufus Andrew Johnson	234 Hill Lane, Apt. 8	Current

works the same on both platforms.

It's all written in FileMaker, the most popular database management program on Macs and likewise on Windows machines when users are purchasing an unbundled database management program (Microsoft Access is the most popular bundled database management program on Windows machines; it's bundled with Microsoft Office Professional and Office Premium).

Pushbutton Landlording comes with a runtime version of FileMaker so that it truly is a standalone program. It can be networked, but networking requires multiple copies of FileMaker.

It accommodates an unlimited number of properties and units and tenants, and it exports its income data to Quicken, QuickBooks, and Microsoft Money.

Pushbutton Landlording works through a primary menu which directs the user to any number of tasks, from just getting started with the program to exiting and being reminded to back up the data. You will find a screen shot of the primary menu on page 358. You'll find it in color on the landlording.com website, accessible through the site's home page or the software page or directly, using the following URL, landlording.com/pushbuttonlandlording.html. Everything works with the colorful pushbuttons designed so that they indicate what they do when pushed.

Throughout the program there are explanations to guide the user along, and there's always a "Help" button which takes the user to specific help.

For the novice user, there's a "step-through" procedure for entering tenants which includes copious notes. For the experienced user, there's a "fly-through" procedure which has minimal notes.

Elsewhere in this book you have seen printouts from Pushbutton Landlording. The statement, the receipt, and the maintenance request all come from the program.

The program isn't perfect (no software is), and it isn't for everybody (some people can make any program fail), but it's pretty good as it is, it's pretty useful as it is, and it will only get better as users make suggestions for improvement.

Some Last Words

Some day there will be computers available which will repair leaky roofs, collect the rents, do all your bookkeeping chores, discipline your tenants, draw your bathwater, and read you your favorite bedtime stories. While you're waiting for that day to arrive, consider using a computer to assist you in handling some of your more mundane landlording chores. That kind of computer and the programs to run it are available right now, today.

21 Potpourri

This final chapter addresses certain subjects which are very different from one another; hence the title, "Potpourri." That they should share a single chapter here is almost as unthinkable as a hard-drinking, Cuban-cigar-puffing communist's happily sharing a room with a tee-totaling, antismoking capitalist, but here they are nonetheless, these strange chapterfellows. They don't really fit anywhere else.

The first three subjects are awkward or difficult situations which you are likely to encounter at some time or another in your career as a landlord. You ought to have some clue how to handle them when they do occur because making the wrong move in these situations could provoke some disgruntled person to drag you into court. You know you don't want to go there. Courts tend not to treat landlords well.

The fourth subject is a serious matter which you need to keep in mind all the time. It's illegal discrimination during tenancy. An awareness of this subject will make you less likely to commit some innocent, but costly, blunders.

The fifth subject is lease termination. Who's supposed to do what when a lease ends?

The sixth subject is house rules. Most landlords don't bother spelling out their house rules even though most tenants need them. You should spell out yours.

The seventh subject should allow you to step back and look at your landlording efforts in a detached way and assess them realistically using a common yardstick, money. Too few of us landlords step back now and then to evaluate what we're doing and where we're headed. Instead, we simply keep our heads down and plow forward through one difficult situation after another, never knowing whether we're really getting anywhere.

The eighth subject, incorporation, beckons seductively to many landlords with promises of special dispensations. After the seduction comes the realization that Oz and Kansas are very different. Here we look at some of the differences.

The ninth subject is vacation time, something you need to give yourself at least once a year to get your mind off your landlording troubles and put everything in a different perspective.

The tenth subject offers some alternatives to paying a heap of capital gains taxes when you want to retire from landlording and live some of your dreams.

The eleventh subject summarizes this whole book in ten commandments, just in case you need to be reminded periodically whether you're doing the right thing.

We start with a subject which would seem to be a landlord's dream, having two qualified tenants who want to live in the same dwelling.

A stranger to this business might liken the situation to a marriageable young person's having two good-looking suitors who are loving, kind, handy, talented, intelligent, educated, well-read, entertaining, sophisticated, generous, and rich.

Wrong! Wrong! Wrong!

The situation is just another landlording nightmare.

Two Tenants— One Rental Dwelling

Because you want to keep your vacancy losses to a minimum, you will likely begin trying to attract a new tenant to fill an upcoming vacancy shortly after your existing tenant gives you notice that he is leaving. You may advertise, interview prospects, show the place, select a desirable prospect, and sign a rental agreement all before the vacating tenant has packed so much as a toothbrush.

Good for you! That's the way to run a landlording business!

Ah, but what happens if you and the new tenant are both waiting anxiously for the old tenant to vacate so you can make the transition smoothly, and then you learn that the old tenant has decided not to move out after all?

Arrgh! What a revolting development!

Besides strangling the old tenant, praying for an unexpected vacancy in another rental, doubling the tenants up, moving the new tenant temporarily into your recreational vehicle, or hammering together a prefabricated rental overnight, how can you extricate yourself from this predicament which you couldn't have predicted and you didn't cause?

Let's try.

Although you have an agreement with only one of the two tenants at this time, unfortunately it is not with the one who is occupying your rental. His agreement terminated on the date he gave you for moving out, and he is now "holding over." You now have an agreement with the new tenant alone, but you, through no fault of your own, cannot perform according to the agreement. Arrgh! Arrgh!

You could sue the existing tenant for possession and for damages if you wanted to, but you could be sued as well by the new tenant, and, of course, since you probably have real assets to tap, you could still lose on balance even if you won the suit involving the existing tenant and lost the suit involving the new tenant.

There's another problem, too.

Although you would have little trouble bringing a case against your old tenant for eviction (if you were proceeding with an eviction in a situation like this, you need give no notice before filing; that was already given when the tenant gave you notice in writing that he was going to move on a certain date; always make certain that tenants who are moving out give you notice in writing, and if they don't, you should provide a 30-day notice form for them to fill out and sign; otherwise, should complications such as these arise, it's your word against his, and you should assume that he can tell lies better than you can tell the truth), by the time you pursued the case to a successful conclusion several weeks later, the other tenant might no longer want to move in.

To forestall your legal liability for this kind of a problem, always put the clause, "Occupancy is contingent upon existing tenant's vacating premises," in any rental agreement you sign with someone who is renting a dwelling from you which has yet to become vacant. The problem of having two tenants and only one rental dwelling could still arise, but at least then you could go about solving the problem without fearing that you might be sued successfully by the new tenant.

In addition to including the clause, maintain contact with both tenants so you can let the new tenant know immediately if any complications arise which might prevent the change in tenancy from occurring on time. If the departing tenant tells you there's going to be a delay, find out the details, and let the new tenant know. Tenants like to be informed so they can make plans. They will know that you are trying your best to facilitate the transition if you contact them before they feel that they need to call you.

Should you encounter the "two tenants–one rental dwelling" problem unexpectedly and when you had not prepared in advance to deal with it, determine as nearly as you can why the holdover tenant isn't leaving and whether his plight is permanent or temporary. With definite information concerning the nature of his problem and when it will be resolved, you can proceed to resolve your own problems and that of the new tenant with all the finesse of a career diplomat.

If, after explaining to the holdover tenant that he is residing there unlawfully and that the new tenant is rightfully entitled to possession, you cannot resolve the matter to everyone's satisfaction and if you expect to be sued yourself by the new tenant, you will have to coerce the holdover tenant to leave or else sue for possession. On the other hand, you might be able to settle the matter by helping the new tenant find suitable housing somewhere else.

Be sensible and helpful in trying to resolve this kind of a problem, and avoid confrontations which will only exacerbate the problem and result in lawsuits flying back and forth among the three parties.

By the way, you should certainly avoid taking a month's rent from the holdover tenant while you're still trying to settle this matter because your acceptance of rent will automatically entitle him to possession even though the old rental agreement was terminated by his notice of intention to vacate. If you did accept rent from him and you had an agreement with the new tenant, then you would be in real trouble. You would have "agreements" with both tenants and room for only one.

Divorce or Separation

When two of your tenants decide to separate or get a divorce, they seldom remain under the same roof together. This situation presents several unique problems to you as the landlord who rented to them when they were a happy couple.

There is the problem of access to the dwelling, especially if their parting is acrimonious, and the remaining partner wants to keep the other one out.

There is the problem of responsibility for the dwelling and the rent—past, present, and future.

There is the problem of creating a new tenancy and ending the old one.

To help them and yourself deal with these problems, you would be wise to visit the remaining tenant as soon as possible to learn what you can about their inten-

tions. Naturally, you will want to keep your rental dwelling occupied by a responsible tenant, and you will want to explain your position as a landlord who wants to help the surviving tenant insure his privacy and start a new life, regardless of your personal feelings about their breakup.

Explain that you and the tenants, both surviving and departing, are all still bound by the original rental agreement which everybody signed.

Explain that you as landlord must give each of them access to the dwelling unless the surviving tenant has secured a temporary restraining order specifically excluding the other one. You may change the lock on the door for the surviving tenant even without a restraining order, but you would have to give access to the other tenant if it were requested of you.

Explain that so long as the current rental agree-

ment remains in force, both tenants are legally obligated for all of the rent when it comes due, whether they are living there or not.

Explain that you want to try to resolve the matters of dwelling access and rent responsibility by drawing up a new agreement to take the place of the old one, so long as everyone concerned is agreeable, but that because you rented the place to a couple with a combined income sufficient to pay the rent and because you must protect your own interest in the property, you will need the tenant who signs the new rental agreement to submit an application specifically for determining financial ability.

If the surviving tenant does not qualify financially (gross monthly income should be at least three times the rent), require a cosigner. In a pinch, the other tenant could be the cosigner, but the other tenant must understand that the cosigner obligation includes no access privileges. Another reliable and financially capable person would be a better cosigner because the question of access would not be an issue nor would other acrimonious matters surface later.

Whatever you do when you learn that your tenants are separating or divorcing, do not take a "wait and see" position. The tenants don't know how their situation will affect their tenancy. You do. Act quickly to solve the tenancy problems, and hope that you will be able to avoid creating more problems.

You want to avoid a lawsuit against yourself for favoring one tenant over the other or for violating the agreement binding on all of you.

You want to avoid damage done to your property by an irate ex-spouse.

You want to avoid loss of rent because the surviving tenant couldn't afford to live there.

You want to avoid creating another vacancy

because you failed to help out.

Deal with the problem soon after it arises, and you may succeed in avoiding unwelcome and unforeseen trouble later.

Death of a Tenant

Whenever a tenant who has lived alone in one of your rental dwellings dies, you may be besieged by relatives and other strangers, all claiming to be entitled to certain of the deceased's possessions. At a time like this, when there are certain to be attorneys and courts and public agencies involved anyway, you should be careful about complying strictly with the law, even though you want to clear the personal property out as soon as possible and re-rent the place. Be patient and cautious, and you will stay out of trouble.

Here's the chronological sequence of what you should do—

1) Call the fire department as soon as you or anyone else discovers what is believed to be a corpse. Fire department rescue squads are trained and equipped to examine the body for signs of life and foul play, and they will try to save the life if at all possible. They will then contact either the appropriate law enforcement agency or the county coroner, and they will direct you as to what to do next.

2) Keep everyone out of the dwelling. "Everyone" includes friends, neighbors, former roommates, bill collectors, handymen, the curious, even relatives. Consider the place "sealed" just as if it were a crime scene. Be firm in keeping everyone out, but don't be nasty. Later, you'll be asking one of those people you're keeping out now to pay you the rent owed on the place. You don't want to alienate them too much. If asked, explain why you're keeping everyone out. Say, "It's the law, and I have to follow the law so that

—You know, Mabel, I sure hate to see old Simpson go. He was a fixture around here so long that I thought he'd live forever. I always knew they'd have to carry him out of here.

—I'm surprised to hear you say anything nice about him. I thought you two never got along.
—Sure, we had our differences, but he was the only tenant I had who always paid his rent on time.

everything is handled correctly according to the wishes of the deceased."

3) Notify the next of kin, and allow them to remove only the body and the personal effects needed for the funeral, nothing more.

4) Release the deceased's personal property only to the county's public administrator or to a court-appointed administrator or to an executor of the estate who can produce either Letters Testamentary or Letters of Administration, documents giving that person possession of the personal property. If the deceased's estate is worth little, close relatives may qualify to take possession of the personal property without having to get involved in formal proceedings. In that case, make sure that they sign a receipt for the items they remove.

5) Submit a claim for unpaid rent (you are entitled to rent covering the full period that the deceased's personal property remains in the dwelling and makes it unavailable for re-renting) to the probate court clerk. If there is no probate of the deceased's estate, submit a written claim for rent to the heirs or next of kin and hope that they will pay. Do not hold any of the deceased's personal goods until they're ransomed with a rent payment, but do try to make a deal with the heirs or next of kin which might include your receiving some of the deceased's belongings in exchange for what is owed to you, that is, if they claim that there's no money to compensate you otherwise. Put the deal in writing.

Illegal Discrimination During the Tenancy

You already know that you must not discriminate illegally when you're selecting tenants. You must treat every applicant alike. You must discard your personal prejudices and judge every applicant according to the same selection criteria. That's the law.

You also know that you must not discriminate illegally when you are evicting tenants, either.

You may not know that you must treat every tenant alike during the tenancy as well. You must not discriminate against your tenants because of their race, color, religion, sex, national origin, age, familial status, or handicap and whatever other categories apply in your area.

You probably never gave the matter much thought. You probably just assumed that you wouldn't encounter any discrimination problems once you selected your tenants according to the proper procedures and went about the business of landlording in a businesslike manner. Well, you should give the matter some thought, for you could wind up being accused of discriminating illegally when you never meant to at all, and you simply didn't know that what you were doing really was discriminatory.

We're going to assume here that you do know better than to discriminate against your tenants overtly. You know that you can't call them derogatory names because they're handicapped or come from Timbuktu. You know that you can't extend special privileges to all your black tenants and require all your brown tenants to jump through hoops. You must treat all your tenants alike, no matter what. When your Cambodian tenants are late with their rent, you must follow the same collection procedures you'd follow for your Russian tenants. When your blind tenants are having a loud party, you must approach them with warnings to quiet down in the same way you'd approach your sighted square-dancing tenants. Those situations are pretty obvious.

What's not so obvious is the discrimination you may be practicing against people in two of HUD's protected categories, age and handicap. The addition of these two to the protected categories list must cause us to reassess how we treat people of different ages and people with different handicaps.

Let's take "age" first. Simply put, you may not discriminate against your younger tenants any more than you may discriminate against your older tenants.

Nowhere is age discrimination more apparent during a tenancy than it is in the house rules we landlords draft to supplement our rental agreements. Frequently they restrict certain times, ac-

tivities, and areas to adults only. Adults may be in the laundry room; children may not. Adults may be in the swimming pool; children may not. Adults may be in the parking area playing; children may not.

Be very careful in drafting your rules. For example, do not draft a pool rule which sets aside one period of time for family swimming and another period for adult swimming. That would be discriminating against children and would make you vulnerable to a HUD complaint.

You might include a pool rule which limits the pool to lap swimming at certain times and opens it to all kinds of swimming at other times, but even then I would be careful not to allocate too much time to the lap swimmers. Although lap swimmers of all ages would be allowed to use the pool during lap swimming time, somebody might argue that you're really trying to set the pool aside for adults during that period.

To test your rules for age discrimination, substitute a racial group for "child[ren]" every time the word appears and see how the rule sounds. If it sounds discriminating against the racial group, then it would be discriminating against children.

Be careful. Your rules should provide guidelines for all of your tenants, not just certain ones.

Handicapped tenants require special consideration as well, consideration we never thought about giving them before they became a protected category. Here the discrimination would not be apparent in rules. It would be apparent more in the direct relationship between landlord and tenant. You should be careful, then, in what you say to handicapped tenants. A big mouth will get you into big trouble.

First of all, don't offer your handicapped tenants anything that they don't ask for. Approaching them and offering to do something for them, like setting aside a special parking place, might be considered patronizing and might subject you to a discrimination complaint. Let them come to you with their requests.

When they do come to you with a special request, listen to them carefully, and don't ask a bunch of questions. You may not ask about the severity or nature of their handicap, for example. Just assume that they are handicapped enough to need the accommodation they are requesting or they wouldn't be requesting it in the first place.

Whatever they request, you must provide so long as the request satisfies these three require-

LEASE TERMINATION ARRANGEMENTS

Date ___1/31/xxxx___

)ear ___DENISE BERGER_____:

We want you to be aware that the lease under which you occupy

:he premises located at ___1220 DOGWOOD DRIVE, JIMTOWN___

vill terminate on ___3/31/xxxx___.

When the lease terminates...

[ ] you will need to vacate the premises.

[X] you may continue to occupy the premises...

    [ ] upon signing another fixed-term lease for _____ months

       at a new rent of $_____ per month.

    [X] on a month-to-month basis at a new rent of $_1,250_

       per month and...

        [X] all other provisions of your original lease will

           continue to apply to your tenancy.

        [ ] you will need to sign a new agreement, in this

           case a month-to-month agreement.

In order for us to begin making plans, we need to know what

/ou plan to do when your lease terminates. Please let us know by

:ompleting the information below and returning it to us within

:hree days. Thank you.

Sincerely,

Robert Hardy

Manager/Owner

*   *   *   *   *   *   *   *   *   *   *   *   *   *   *   *   *   *   *

[ ] I plan to vacate the premises when the lease terminates.

[ ] If given the choice, I plan to continue occupying the premises

    when the lease terminates.

_____   _____
)ate   Tenant

ments—

1) They must make an actual request;

2) The accommodation requested must give the handicapped tenants an equal opportunity to use and enjoy their dwelling; and

3) The accommodation must be considered reasonable.

Generally, they will ask for reasonable accommodations, such as whether they can modify the entrance to accommodate a wheelchair; whether they can add an alert light to the doorbell; whether they can add grab bars to the bathtub surround; or whether they can have a reserved parking place close to their dwelling.

These requests meet the requirements above and should be granted. If you have any doubts about a particular request or situation, stall the tenants, and call HUD's "Housing Discrimination Hotline" at 800.669.9777 to ask for some help in determining how to handle your tenants' request.

Just remember that handicapped people make excellent tenants, and you'd be wise to accommodate them even if there were no laws compelling you to do so. That they are willing to make modifications to their rental dwelling shows that they want to be long-term tenants. What could possibly be better? Accommodating them is definitely in your interest.

Lease Termination

When their lease term is about to end, tenants are sometimes at a loss as to what their landlord expects of them. Are they supposed to tell the landlord whether they plan to remain or move? Are they supposed to wait for the landlord to say something to them? Are they supposed to wait until the very last day of their lease and then move out without saying anything to the landlord in advance? They need to know what you expect of them. You need to know what they expect of you.

The best thing you can do to clarify matters is provide them with a form letter which tells them what you expect of them, a form letter which also gives them the opportunity to reply.

Send them this letter at least sixty days before their lease term ends so that both of you have plenty of time to prepare.

House Rules

The rental agreement you use, whether it's one page or fifty, tends to be something you and your tenants review only when they move in. After that, you file your copy away with your other important papers for that dwelling, and your tenants file their copy away with their important papers. When the tenants are ready to move out, they look for their copy and try to figure out what they need to do to get their deposits back, and you retrieve your copy to see what all it says about the move-out.

Rental agreements tend not to be words to live by on a day-to-day basis, even though they may contain words aplenty. House rules, on the other hand, *are* words to live by on a day-to-day basis. They are just as legitimate and just as authoritative as rental agreements, but they address practical tenancy concerns in a less formal and less intimidating way. They're useful.

Rental agreements are specific to a particular tenant and a particular dwelling. An agreement for tenants occupying one dwelling does not apply to tenants occupying another dwelling. Their agreements were filled out differently at different times and may even have been based upon totally different forms.

On the other hand, house rules are uniform and egalitarian. They are all the same for a single property, and they apply equally to everyone who lives there.

Whereas you are not absolutely required to have house rules for your rental property, you may find that having them helps your landlord-tenant relationship be more consistent. Your tenants know what's expected of them on a day-to-day basis because they have everything in writing, and they know that it applies to everybody. They can judge you on your enforcement of the rules, and you can judge them by the rules themselves.

I recommend that you create house rules for each of your rental properties and that you examine them periodically and change them as needed.

When you set about creating your own house rules for a property, you'll find that there's no particular form or verbiage sufficient for the job. You have to create them yourself in order to cover the unique characteristics of a property and the procedures you consider important for your tenants to follow there.

Sure, creating house rules is another time-consuming task, but it's hardly a daunting task. They're not all that hard to create so long as you keep a few things in mind.

Keeping in mind what you already know about illegal discrimination, make certain that your house rules do not discriminate against anybody in the protected classes, especially children.

Make certain that your house rules are understandable. Use words that any sixth-grader would understand, and when you finish writing your rules, reread them yourself four or five times over during the space of a week to see whether they make good sense to you. Then ask your tenants whether any of them would like to read your "draft" of the new house rules and comment on them. Some tenants may be eager to read and comment, but even if nobody responds, at least you will have asked for their input, and they can't accuse you of acting like a despot. What's more, some of them may pass along good ideas you hadn't thought of yourself and would like to incorporate in the final version.

Make certain that your house rules are both reasonable and enforceable. "Reasonable" means that your quiet hours, for example, ought to be from 10 p.m. to 8 a.m. rather than from 6 p.m. to 10 a.m. "Enforceable" means that you can and will do something when tenants call you to tattle on their neighbors for breaking the rules.

Make certain that your rules are dated on every page so that the most recent rules won't be mistaken for earlier ones. That's important. Tenants sometimes claim that they don't have to do such-and-such because it's not in the rules. It may not have been in the old rules which were in effect when they moved in, the ones they were referring to, whereas it is most definitely in the new rules they neglected to read and save. Dating the rules helps to differentiate the versions, and it also helps to remind you how old they are, so you will think about reviewing and revising them periodically.

Don't worry about whether your house rules repeat what appears in your rental agreement. They may be repetitious in places. So what! Certain things are important enough in landlord-tenant relations that they should be repeated.

Draft a letter explaining why you have created new house rules and asking for everyone's cooperation in following them. It needn't be a long letter. It might say simply that you felt new rules were needed and that you considered each one of them carefully while you were writing them. Say that you would appreciate feedback, especially if anybody feels strongly about certain ones. Distribute this letter along with the new rules themselves.

As for tenants' signatures, they're somewhat important as an acknowledgment that tenants have received the rules, but because many tenants balk at signing anything you give them to sign after they move in, I don't bother trying to secure signatures. Getting signatures from existing tenants is just too much trouble. I don't even put a blank for the tenant's signature anywhere on the rules. I merely leave blank space somewhere near the bottom where new tenants may sign the rules when they get their copies.

Here are some items you might want to address in your rules, if they're applicable. They're arranged here alphabetically—

- *Alterations*—alterations requiring landlord's permission; alterations not requiring permission
- *Appliances*—responsibility for maintaining landlord-owned appliances; tenant-owned major appliances allowed; care in moving tenant-owned major appliances
- *Deposits*—requirements for return of deposits; handling of deposits when a tenant who has contributed to the deposits moves out and everybody else remains
- *Garbage*—acceptable items; non-acceptable items; recycling possibilities; suitable trash containers; preparation for collection; collection schedule
- *Guests*—length of stay allowed; number allowed; use of common facilities
- *Insurance*—extent of coverage for tenant-caused calamities and tenants' possessions
- *Landscaping and gardening care*—front yard; back yard; changes in plantings; watering; trimming; mowing
- *Laundry room*—hours of operation; accessibility if kept locked; use of the room by non-residents and guests; handling of non-attended laundry; responsibility for lost laundry
- *Locks and lockouts*—changing locks; lockout charges
- *Patios and decks*—items acceptable for storage on patios and decks
- *Pest control*—scheduled service; as-needed service; responsibility for particular kinds of infestations, such as ants, cockroaches, fleas, mice, and spiders

- *Pets*—pets allowed; pet approval procedure; number of pets; separate pet agreement; pet care; pet replacement
- *Playground*—hours; noise; guest usage; play restrictions
- *Quiet hours*—hours when all should be especially quiet
- *Rent*—collection procedure; form of payment; return check charges and consequences; receipt policy; late payment consequences; partial payment
- *Repairs*—making repair and maintenance requests; charges for tenants' failure to report promptly a malfunction or breakage requiring repair; entering the tenants' dwelling for repairs
- *Responsible parties*—determination of tenant responsible for dwelling; procedure when that person leaves
- *Sewer stoppages*—reporting; handling; conditions determining landlord's responsibility and tenants' responsibility
- *Storage space*—availability; location; cost
- *Swimming pool*—hours; times set aside for lap swimming; attire; minimum and maximum number of swimmers allowed; guest usage; poolside activities; swim toys; swimming proficiency requirements
- *Utilities*—changing utilities to tenants' names; responsibility for payment
- *Vehicles and parking*—types and number of vehicles allowed; resident parking areas; guest parking; towing of wrongly parked vehicles; towing of inoperable and unlicensed vehicles; responsibility for oil-leak damage to paving; repairs permitted on the premises; changing of oil; disposal of used crankcase oil; time limitations for repairs; storage of boats and recreational vehicles; vehicle washing
- *Waterbeds*—acceptance according to applicable laws; acceptance according to property's characteristics; separate waterbed agreement
- *Window breakage*—reporting; handling; conditions determining landlord's responsibility and tenants' responsibility

Once you have created your first set of rules and have implemented them, you'll find after a while that you will want to change something. Go ahead. Change the rules. Changing them is a simpler matter than changing rental agreements because you don't have to individualize every

copy as you do with agreements. When you want to change your rules, you simply crank out one original and copy it for everybody. Everybody gets the same thing.

Please note that house rules go into effect sometime after you distribute them. They do not go into effect the very day you distribute them. Generally the lag time is the same as it is for other notices which announce changes in terms of tenancy, that is, unless there's another notice period specifically mentioned in the rental agreement. It would be a week for those tenants who pay their rent weekly, two weeks for those tenants who pay their rent bi-weekly, and a month for those tenants who pay their rent monthly. The "kitchen-sink" agreement introduced in chapter 5 states that new rules take effect upon at least two weeks' notice. Regardless of what their agreement says or how frequently they pay rent, make new house rules effective the same date for everybody living in a complex. Set the effective date at the conclusion of as generous a lag time as anybody gets, and announce the date in your accompanying letter.

Your Score

You already know that there are four ways to make money in this business, but you won't know whether you're actually making any money at any of them unless you sharpen your pencil, uncover your calculator, grab your abacus, or power up your computer and have a session with the numbers now and then.

Naturally, you only have to keep up with your regular bookkeeping to know whether you're getting any cash flow or equity buildup, and you only have to do your income tax return every year to know whether you're getting any tax shelter, but you won't know whether you're getting any appreciation on your properties and you won't know whether you're getting any closer to becoming independently wealthy unless you complete a financial statement. It alone can tell you whether you've really "made it." It's your score.

If you haven't been keeping track of your financial health with a financial statement, shame on you. It's one of the more agreeable undertakings in this entire business. Some landlords say it's the best part by far.

You're in good company if you don't have a clue what your financial health is, though. While being escorted around the newly opened

Disneyland by Walt Disney, one foreign potentate, suitably impressed, remarked that Disney must be a very wealthy man, whereupon Disney replied, "I guess I am. They tell me I owe ten million dollars." He honestly had no idea what he was worth! He never realized he could walk into an automobile showroom and drive out in a snazzy little sportscar until he did just that on a whim sometime later. Fortunately for him, Walt Disney had a brother who kept track of the finances, and he had a banker, A.P. Giannini himself (founder of Bank of America), who kept an eye on the company's fortunes.

Lacking a devoted brother and an astute banker to look after your financial health, you're left to do the job yourself. There's nothing wrong with that. It's not something you ought to have somebody else do for you anyway. Nobody else is going to find the special pleasure in preparing your financial statement that you are. It's more fun than watching the Olympics or the Super Bowl. It's kind of like participating in them.

What you may not realize is that you have probably been doing financial statements for years without even thinking much about them, certainly without enjoying them. That's right! Every time you've applied for a loan and filled out a loan application, you've actually made up a financial statement. That's mostly what loan applications are, you see. They're a picture of your financial health. They tell the lender how much you're worth and whether you have enough income to repay the loan. You haven't been enjoying them because you were forced into doing them. Isn't that right? They were "assignments," required "homework." Ugh!

Go on. Go to your files and get the last loan application form you filled out. See. You had to list your assets and your liabilities, your income

and your expenses, and somewhere on that form you had to calculate what your net worth was at the time. That's all a financial statement is. It's two basic parts—a *balance sheet*, which is comprised of your assets and liabilities, and an *income and expense statement*, which is comprised of your annual income and your annual expenses. Subtract your liabilities from your assets and you can tell whether you're independently wealthy. Subtract your annual expenses from your annual income and you can tell whether you're going to be independently wealthy for very long.

If you don't particularly care what you're worth or you just don't want to know, then continue doing what you've been doing all along. Complete your latest "financial statement" only when you're applying for a loan to buy some more rental property. Don't think much about it, and above all, don't enjoy doing it. In-between-times, go about your business oblivious of your financial health. Press your nose to the window of that Cadillac, BMW, or Lexus showroom and keep on dreaming of the day when you can afford to walk in there and buy the biggest, fanciest model with cash.

Oh, come on! Let a little joy into your life while you can still enjoy it! There's more to life as a landlord than terrible tenants and temperamental toilets. There's little delight in all that, is there? You don't really want to be oblivious to your financial health and spend your time dreaming about a rosy future while you're out there taking flak from tenants and fixing their overflowing toilets, do you?

That sort of plodding, mindless approach to one's lot in life may work for those people who juggle their income and expenses one week at a time and buy lottery tickets with their every spare dollar, but that's not a good approach for anyone who's regularly accumulating assets. That's not a good approach for you. It's chancy and unbusinesslike, and it's terribly shortsighted. You cannot make informed business decisions unless you are informed about your own affairs, and your financial statement is a large part of what makes you informed.

Convinced? Good, good, good! Go to the head of the class, and we'll start calculating what your assets are.

As far as your personal financial statement is concerned, your assets are your rental properties, your house, vehicles, airplanes, boats, stocks, bonds, mutual funds, cash accounts, precious metals, livestock, raw land, partnerships, business interests, personal goods, vested pensions, notes receivable, trusts, and the cash surrender value of your life insurance. They all have a value. They're all worth something if they have to be liquidated. Perhaps they're worth what you have in them, perhaps less, perhaps a lot more.

You may think you have other assets, too, such as straight teeth, a good golf swing, a winning personality, a college degree, and a trim figure, but they're figurative assets as opposed to hard, literal assets. Like family photo albums and bronzed baby shoes, they have personal value but no market value. They can't be converted into ready cash. No one would pay you anything for them, so don't list them on your financial statement.

Establishing the value of all your assets which do have a market value does take some doing, especially since you own real estate. Whenever possible, professional appraisers base their income property appraisals on several approaches, most commonly, *replacement cost* (how much the property improvements would cost to build today, plus a certain market value for the land), *income* (how much the property produces in income times an accepted multiplier which would depend upon property type and whether the income were net or gross), and *comparable sales* (how much other similar properties have sold for recently). Not one of these three can yield an exact figure. Each is merely an approximation, and the final appraisal figure is merely a composite of these approximations.

When you're just trying to figure out approximately what your real estate is worth so you can include it among your assets, you needn't go to all the trouble that professional appraisers do. You're going to be reasonably accurate a great

percentage of the time with just a cursory appraisal using any one of the approaches they use. You won't be right on the money, but then, neither would they. It'll be close enough.

When you're appraising your own property for your financial statement, try to detach yourself from it if you can. Think of yourself as a potential buyer of the property, not as the owner. Look the numbers over, perform some calculations, make a few telephone calls, close your eyes, and ask yourself what you'd pay for the property realistically yourself if it belonged to somebody else. Be honest. Cheating doesn't pay. Base your appraisal on something you can justify.

If it's multiple-family rental property you're appraising, some sort of income formula like a gross rent multiplier will do, whatever applies to your type of rental property. Don't go overboard and value it at ten or twelve times the annual gross income when it ought to be seven, either. That will make a substantial difference in the property's value and will distort your balance sheet and resultant net worth. Find out what the commonly used yardstick is for your type of multiple-family rental property and use it.

If it's a single-family rental property or the house you occupy, comparable sales figures will do well enough. Remember that sales figures are different from listing figures. Sellers may list their properties at whatever price they want to list them for. They don't sell their properties at whatever price they want to sell them for. Properties sell for whatever a buyer is willing to pay and a seller is willing to take. You want sales figures to help you establish the fair market value of your property, and you can get them from a cooperative real estate agent or from county records.

The trouble is that even if you were able to peg the price of your property correctly and a buyer were to give you that price, you wouldn't net that amount in crisp cash money. You'd net something less. Commissions, prepayment penalties, transaction fees, transfer taxes, legal fees, and other costs would reduce the net proceeds you'd realize from the sale. Be that as it may, don't discount your holdings to reflect these costs. A lender might do that a second time upon looking at your figures, and you don't want it deducted twice. You're not looking for a liquidated cash value for your holdings. You're not holding a fire sale. All you need is a market value.

You might want to do a little research to learn

the market value of your other assets, but that'll be easy compared to putting a value on your real estate. Just don't forget anything, not even that timeshare in Orlando you bought in a weak moment.

Whereas your assets may take a little time to calculate, your liabilities won't, so long as there's a semblance of order in your recordkeeping system. The mortgages, loans, and credit card balances you owe are all liabilities, and they all have definite dollar figures attached to them. They're solid figures, but you must remember that they change every day because the interest on your liabilities is accruing daily, and the loan balances are changing as well. Also remember that there may be some liabilities you tend to overlook, such as taxes you owe but haven't paid yet, a mechanics lien on your property, an old school-aid loan, or an interest-free loan from a trusting family member. They're liabilities, too. They reduce your assets. Estimate what they are and include them among your liabilities.

Calculating your net worth is the easiest part of all, once you know what your assets and liabilities are. Simply subtract your liabilities from your assets and presto, you have the all-important telltale figure. That's it. That's your momentous net worth figure. That's your score. Now you know what everybody else would like to know about you—how much you're worth in dollars and cents.

If it's seven figures or more, then you're a millionaire. Congratulations! You've arrived at an important milestone in your life! You've learned a lot from playing Monopoly all those years, haven't you? Now you ought to read *The Millionaire Next Door* to see how you measure up to the other millionaires who live in your neighborhood. Their life-styles may surprise you. Earning your first million is one thing. Keeping it is quite another.

If your net worth is four, five, or even six figures, you're still a lowly thousandaire. Keep working. If it's in three figures and you've been landlording for more than a year, you'd better think about raising your rents and getting a copy of Nickerson's classic book on making money with rental properties, *How I Turned $1,000 into Five Million in Real Estate in My Spare Time*. You need all the help you can get!

Once you've calculated your net worth, you're nearly finished with your financial statement, but you still need to indicate how much you're taking in and how much you're shelling out. That's the income-and-expense portion of your financial statement. Its end result will show whether the cash flow in your life is coming or going, positive or negative.

You might have a substantial net worth and think that you've done pretty well for yourself until you find out that you actually have more money going out every month than you have coming in. Negative-cash-flow properties can put you in that position, you know. They're a slippery business, much like trying to twirl around an ice skating rink on roller skates. One or two such properties may not affect you very much if you have substantial earned income that you want to protect from taxes and if you feel that the properties have good upside potential, but more than that and you could begin to have problems. Watch those properties. They have been known to be more voracious than a Little League baseball team at a pizza parlor after a tough game. They can eat their owners out of houses and homes.

Well, how do your income and expenses look? Are you going to be holding onto your net worth much longer? Let's hope so.

At least you now have a clue as to how you're doing. You have some score to keep in mind when you're cleaning toilets and painting vacant apartments at 3 a.m., and you can make your plans for the future knowledgeably.

Incorporation

Some people think that owning a corporation catapults them into the major leagues. Owners of corporations draw big salaries, fly in private jets or at the very least in first class, smoke the best cigars, maintain several palatial residences, ride everywhere in chauffeured limos, mingle with the rich and famous, and sleep soundly at night because they cannot be sued for something relating to the corporation's business.

Dream on!

Owning a big corporation has its perks and advantages, some of which appear in the list above. Owning a little corporation has no perks and no advantages which appear in the list above.

The biggest carrot dangled in front of anybody who has a few rental properties and a few hundred thousand dollars in assets and is thinking about incorporating is asset protection. Advocates of incorporating say that you should incorporate so that the liabilities you incur as a corporation will not affect your personal wealth. That argument appears sound until you become involved in a Robinhood lawsuit and the attorney suing your closely held corporation convinces the court that the corporation is nothing but a sham, designed strictly to protect you from liability. The attorney pierces your so-called corporate veil, and you and your personal assets are laid bare for the vultures to devour.

Incorporating may succeed in protecting you from liability and then again it may not. Why bother incorporating at all? Wouldn't you be better off keeping your life simple than you would be in complicating it by forming a corporation just to protect your assets?

We're talking major complications. A corporation compounds your legal work (you must abide by the latest corporate laws) and your paperwork (you must have officers, hold meetings, and keep minutes) and your bookkeeping (you must keep a separate set of books for the corporation) and your tax preparation (you must submit a state tax return and a federal tax return for the corporation), and it prevents you from representing yourself in court even for the simplest eviction. You have to hire an attorney to do that for you.

The "keep it simple, stupid" admonition applies here. A corporation simply ain't simple.

If you're worried about your assets, buy enough insurance to protect them from predators. That's what umbrella insurance policies are for.

If you're still unconvinced, still romanced by the notion of incorporating, seek out some people who have incorporated and whose assets are similar to yours in extent and substance and ask them about the advantages of incorporating versus the disadvantages. Ask them whether they would choose to incorporate again if they could. They're more inclined to give you straight answers than someone who stands to profit from your decision to incorporate.

As I see it, incorporating is much like declaring bankruptcy for the protection bankruptcy provides. There's a time and a circumstance for bankruptcy, and as many tenants have discovered after declaring bankruptcy during an eviction, the extra month or two they gained during their eviction wasn't enough of a benefit to warrant declaring bankruptcy. Naturally, they didn't know

that at the time. They suffered later when they needed credit to buy a car or a house and couldn't get it or had to pay more in interest and fees than otherwise.

There's a time and a circumstance for incorporating, too. Make absolutely sure that the time and circumstances are right for you to be taking this step. Make absolutely sure that the rewards are greater than the consequences, for incorporating is a very big step into a very different world, and once you take the step, you cannot easily retreat.

Vacation Time

Landlording can become all-consuming work, sucking up as much of your time as you are willing to give it. There's always something you can do to make your tenants happier or your properties better, and you know that there's nobody who can do all that better than you can.

Don't succumb to the temptation to manage and maintain your properties every hour of every day of every year yourself. Succumb to the temptation to get away from them now and then. Take a vacation.

There are plenty of excuses you might give for staying on the job and not taking a vacation, but there are plenty of reasons why you should get away as well. Not only might you discover some landlording "pearls" when you aren't tending to business and distracted by minutiae, you will find yourself refreshed when you return. You will approach your work with a spring in your step, a smile on your face, a clarity in your mind, and a new tool in your hand.

Of course, you will need to arrange for somebody to look after your properties while you're away. Find another landlord who's willing, able, and trustworthy, and arrange to look after one another's properties during those much deserved vacations each of you needs to take.

Take some vacation time. It will make you a better landlord.

Retirement

Eventually you may conclude that you no longer want to own residential rental properties, and you are going to be looking for ways to reduce or eliminate your personal involvement.

You want to retire and kick back, do some serious traveling, write a chronicle of the black sheep in your family, take up the piano, polish your Russian, follow in the footsteps of Julia Child and study at a French cooking school, circumnavigate the globe in a comfortable sloop, attend film festivals around the world, concentrate on your golf game, build a kitplane and learn to fly it, earn an advanced degree, participate in a yearlong archeological dig in Turkey, become a *Ring* nut and see every complete production on earth every year, clean Mt. Everest of climbers' debris, volunteer at your neighborhood school to teach reading to dyslexics, join a Habitat for Humanity crew, chase rainbows, or catch falling stars. In short, you want to start enjoying life more. You want to enjoy the fruits of your labors at long last.

You'd like to sell your holdings, but there's one thing stopping you, one major thing. You don't want to pay the capital gains taxes on a good portion of your personal wealth.

Let's say that you own $2 million worth of rental properties free and clear, and your basis in them is $200,000. If you sell, you will owe federal and state income taxes on a gain of $1.8 million. Were the combined tax rate on capital gains 35% (state and federal), you would be writing checks to the IRS and to your state income tax collector totaling $630,000. With two strokes of your pen, your $2 million worth of rental properties would drop precipitously to $1,370,000 in cash, and you and your heirs would lose the income-generating potential of that $630,000 forever.

You don't have to lose the income-generating potential of that money forever. You can reduce or eliminate your personal involvement in your rental properties in a number of ways without incurring a huge tax bill.

One way is to keep the properties you have and hire somebody else to manage them for you. Whether you hire a trusted relative, a faithful friend, or a professional management company, you must understand that they will not manage your properties as efficiently as you have. The return on investment will decline, but it won't decline as much as it would if you sold the properties, gave the government its tax money, and put what's left into safe investments.

Another way is to set up a charitable remainder trust. You put the free-and-clear properties (they must be free-and-clear) into the trust, naming one or more of your favorite charities as the beneficiaries of the trust when you die. After put-

ting the properties into the trust, you sell them and put the cash, all of it, into any income-generating vehicle you select. You maintain control of the trust and collect its income as long as you live (whatever money you withdraw from the trust is taxable to you personally). The charities take over the trust when you die. To protect your heirs' inheritance, you may use a portion of your income from the trust to buy as much term life insurance as you want them to receive when you die.

My very favorite way to get out from under the burdens of owning residential rental properties which claim too much of my time is the tax-free exchange. Some people call it a tax-deferred exchange. Call it what you want. It's the same thing. You pay no tax at all when you consummate an IRS Section 1031 exchange and put the entire proceeds from the property you sell into the property you purchase. In other words, when you take no money out of the exchange, it's entirely tax free. You may choose to sell outright later and pay taxes then if you wish, but that's your choice. You'll find a brief explanation of the 1031 exchange in the "Doing Taxes" chapter.

In order to achieve your retirement objective in an exchange, you need to sell your property and use the proceeds to buy another property which requires less management. Look for properties which require less management and have good Cap (capitalization) Rates ("Cap Rate" is the net return on the investment divided by the price of the investment; loan costs are excluded; Cap Rates are expressed in percentages; higher figures indicate a higher return).

Calculate the Cap Rate for your own properties first, so you know how they compare with others. Make sure that you include something for off-site management when you do your calculations. You may not have been paying anything for off-site management, but it's a standard cost included in Cap Rate calculations.

You could trade out of an apartment house with a Cap Rate of nine and trade into a triple-net-leased (triple-net, or NNN, leases require the tenant to pay for property taxes, insurance, maintenance, and utilities) building leased by the U.S. Postal Service with a Cap Rate of nine, and you'd be moving closer to Easy Street. You'd also be preserving your capital, and you'd be benefitting from whatever escalation clauses there are in the lease.

Where do you find triple-net-leased properties and other minimal-management commercial properties for sale? Try a local brokerage firm which specializes in commercial properties, and also look through the listings on the Loopnet (loopnet.com) website.

Loopnet enables you to search for properties by area, type, and price. If you want to find all the Loopnet listings of net-leased office buildings in your state selling for $2m-$5m, enter those parameters, and see what results. To enlarge the list, enlarge your parameters.

You'll notice that Loopnet includes Cap Rates with its listings. Be wary about those figures. Because you don't know whether they're based upon current or proforma data, you must consider them little more than starting points for your property comparisons.

Yes, you can retire from landlording. When you're ready, you should, but you should plan your retirement carefully in order to preserve the capital you have worked so hard to accumulate. Look at the alternatives to selling out and paying the capital gains taxes.

Landlording's Ten Commandments

No, these commandments were not handed down from God to Moses. They were handed down by many wise and successful landlords who had to make them up as they went along to suit the realities of life as a landlord.

Heed them, and you, too, will be successful. Ignore them, and you will perish many times.

1) Thou shalt investigate and qualify every applicant thoroughly, being mindful of discrimination laws and intent upon finding people who will make good neighbors and good tenants.

2) Thou shalt permit no tenants to move in until they have paid every bit of their move-in monies in greenbacks, gold pieces, silver bars, money orders, or cashier's checks.

3) Thou shalt be friendly with all tenants but friends with none.

4) Thou shalt listen to thy tenants; that is "l-i-s-t-e-n," as in open thine ears and close thy mouth.

5) Thou shalt not kill thy tenants in a fit of anger or at any other time, nor shalt thou vent thine anger or frustrations around thy tenants, no matter how angry or frustrated they make thee.

6) Thou shalt keep up with the local market for rents and adjust thine own rents accordingly.

7) Thou shalt consider the payment of rent a mandatory religious ritual and brook no excuses for ignoring it, hounding those who try until they leave in ignominy and with ruined credit.

8) Thou shalt keep thy property in good repair as if thou wert living there thyself.

9) Thou shalt make thy tenants no promise thou canst not keep.

10) Thou shalt commit consequential landlording matters to writing rather than committing them to memory.

Some Last Words

Surely the primary purpose of landlording is to become independently wealthy, and even though many things and many people may conspire to frustrate you from reaching that goal, do not despair. Walk through landlording's "valley of the shadow of death," its perilous minefields, heeding landlording's ten commandments as best you can, and you won't have to fear becoming independently poor. No way, Jo!

Words in Edgewise

Yours is a thankless job, dear landlord and landlady. Just remember that landlording is a business. People are not going to commend you for your efforts, but neither are they going to stop depending on you. People who are too timid, too transient, too insolvent, too young, too feeble, too smart, too stupid, or otherwise too indisposed to own their own housing are all depending on you to provide them with housing. Do just that, and do it as best you can.

There will be times when you will feel distraught over your landlording troubles and trials, times when you will have tried your best and yet you find yourself on the short end. Don't show your anger. Keep a punching bag at home for that. But if you cannot get along with a tenant or a tenant with you, get the tenant out. You know how to do it. Run your business yourself. Don't let your tenants run it for you.

Forms

The forms in this section have been introduced in the text, all, that is, except for the bulk of the rent reminders (only two of the twelve reminders appear in the text) and the EPA lead pamphlet. Blank forms are included here so you may reproduce them on any copier according to your needs.*

If you do plan to copy them, keep them clean and free of marks. These are your originals, re-member. Any marks you make on them will show up on your copies.

To assist you in finding the blank forms you seek, we put small page numbers in the upper corners. When you go to copy these forms, either white-out the page numbers, cut them off, or fold over the corners of the pages so the numbers will not show up on your copies.

The Forms

(Forms appear here alphabetically; bracketed numbers refer to samples in text.)

*NOTA BENE

The author assumes no responsibility for the legality or currency of these forms. Before using them, check with your local housing authorities, your local rental housing association, and/or an attorney knowledgeable about real estate law to determine whether they are appropriate for your use.

The author hereby grants permission to the purchaser of this book to copy any or all of these forms for personal use. Their reproduction for sale or distribution shall constitute an infringement of copyright.

Agreement to Hold Dwelling Off the Market

RECEIVED FROM _____, Approved Applicant,

the sum of _____ $_____.

$_____ of this sum is <u>nonrefundable</u>. It shall be used for the purpose of holding off the market the rental dwelling commonly known as

_____

for the period from _____ through _____ only.

$_____ of this sum is <u>refundable</u> if approved applicant does not move in. If applicant moves in, it shall be applied to move-in monies.

The applicant whose name appears above has been approved to rent the dwelling identified above but for one reason or another cannot take possession now.

The applicant has read and approved the rental agreement but has not paid all of the sums required to move in. The applicant has no right to receive keys or take possession of the dwelling until all of the sums required to take possession have been paid in full.

The owner/manager retains possession of the dwelling under this agreement and is obligated to safeguard it and maintain its condition so that it does not deteriorate during the term of this agreement. If it is materially damaged, applicant shall receive a refund of all monies paid.

At least twenty-four hours prior to the termination of this agreement, the applicant must notify the owner/manager of his/her intentions to take possession or not take possession of the dwelling. Notice must be made in writing and delivered to the owner/manager during normal business hours (9am-5pm) at the owner/manager's address shown below.

Should the applicant fail to notify the owner/manager of his/her intentions to take possession as outlined above, owner/manager will put the dwelling back on the market upon the termination of this agreement.

Should the applicant take possession of the dwelling prior to the termination of this agreement, the applicant will be credited as having paid rent through the termination date of this agreement, and this agreement will then be superseded by the rental agreement.

Should the applicant not take possession of the dwelling prior to or upon the expiration of this agreement, the owner/manager will keep the entire nonrefundable sum paid as consideration for having held the rental dwelling off the market for the time period specified above and will refund the applicant's refundable sum within forty-eight hours.

_____   _____
Date/Time   Approved Applicant--Name / Signature

                             _____
                             Address / Phone

_____   _____
Date/Time   Owner/Manager--Name / Signature

                             _____
                             Address / Phone

Agreement to Vacate   Dated_____

    Agreement between _____, Tenants,
who occupy a dwelling located at _____
and _____, Owners, who are the
owners of this dwelling.

    Tenants acknowledge that no one other than those listed above currently
occupies the dwelling.

    Tenants occupy this dwelling under a rental agreement dated _____.
This agreement is ( ) month to month; ( ) a lease expiring _____.

    The current rent for this dwelling is $_____. The current late fee
is $_____.

    As of this date, tenants have paid rent through the following date:
_____. They owe owners a total of $_____, itemized as follows:
_____.

    Tenants agree that they have no excuses or defenses for failing to pay
what they owe.

    Tenants agree to vacate the dwelling on or before _____
at _____ pm/am.

    If tenants DO vacate as agreed above, owners agree to the following:

    (1) to apply the tenants' security/cleaning deposit to the amount owed
and to waive the balance of any amount owed; any excess remaining from the
security/cleaning deposit after the full amount owed has been paid in full
shall be returned to the tenants after they have moved out completely,
provided that they leave the dwelling reasonably clean and undamaged;

    (2) to release tenants of any further obligation to pay rent under the
lease (if any);

    (3) to make no report to any credit reporting agency regarding tenants'
credit;

    (4) to make no report to any eviction reporting agency regarding tenants'
tenancy.

    If tenants DO NOT vacate as agreed above, this agreement shall be null
and void, and owners may begin eviction proceedings immediately.

    Tenants agree to keep this agreement confidential between the parties
involved. If tenants fail to keep this agreement confidential, this agreement
shall be null and void.

Owner_____ Tenant_____

By_____ Tenant_____

Availability of Information Regarding Registered Sex Offenders

(Addendum to Rental Agreement)

This disclosure is attached to and forms a part of the Rental Agreement dated _____ between _____, Owners, and _____, Tenants.

The following text applies in California only:
Notice: The California Department of Justice, sheriff's departments, police departments serving jurisdictions of 200,000 or more and many other local law enforcement authorities maintain for public access a data base of the locations of persons required to register pursuant to paragraph (1) of subdivision (a) of Section 290.4 of the Penal Code. The data base is updated on a quarterly basis and a source of information about the presence of these individuals in any neighborhood. The Department of Justice also maintains a Sex Offender Identification Line through which inquiries about individuals may be made. This is a "900" telephone service. Callers must have specific information about individuals they are checking. Information regarding neighborhoods is not available through the "900" telephone service.

The following text applies in states other than California:
Notice: The state justice department, sheriff's departments, police departments serving jurisdictions of 200,000 or more and many other local law enforcement authorities maintain for public access a data base of the locations of persons required to register pursuant to "Megan's Law" or a similar statute. The data base is updated on a regular basis and is a source of information about the presence of these individuals in any neighborhood. Contact the state justice department to determine whether it also maintains a telephone service through which inquiries about individuals may be made.

The following acknowledge that the Owner or Owner's Agent whose signature appears below has provided a copy of this Rental Agreement Addendum to the Tenant(s) whose signature(s) appear(s) below.

Date_____ Tenant _____

Date_____ Tenant _____

Date_____ Owner or Agent _____

Co-Signer Agreement

Dated _____

(Addendum to Rental Agreement)

This agreement is attached to and forms a part of the Rental Agreement dated _____ between _____, Owners, and _____, Tenants.

My name is _____.

I have completed a Rental Application for the express purpose of enabling the Owners to check my credit. I have no intention of occupying the dwelling referred to in the Rental Agreement above.

I have read the Rental Agreement, and I promise to guarantee the Tenants' compliance with the financial obligations of this Agreement.

I understand that I may be required to pay for rent, cleaning charges, or damage assessments in such amounts as are incurred by the Tenants under the terms of this Agreement if, and only if, the Tenants themselves fail to pay.

I also understand that this Co-Signer Agreement will remain in force throughout the entire term of the Tenants' tenancy, even if their tenancy is extended and/or changed in its terms.

I am paying the sum of ten dollars ($10) as a consideration of acceptance of this Co-Signer Agreement by all parties concerned.

_____
Co-Signer

_____
Accepted by Owner/Manager

Page_____ of _____

COMPLAINT

We understand that every so often you may have a complaint which you want to make known to the management. We want to hear about it so we can take care of it or if we already know about it, so we can tell you what we're doing about it. Please use this form to register your complaint with us.

Type of complaint: [ ]   Against management

                       [ ]   Against another tenant

                       [ ]   Regarding general conditions

If your complaint is against a particular person, please give that person's name and address.

Name_____

Address_____

Give details about the incident, complaint, or problem (include date, time, and place as applicable):

_____

_____

_____

_____

_____

_____

What action do you suggest that management should take?

_____

_____

_____

Please note that management cannot promise complete confidentiality if this complaint is raised against another tenant.

Submitted by_____ Date_____

* *

Received by_____ Date_____

Action taken _____

_____

_____

Condition & Inventory Checksheet

Tenants: _____ Dated: _____

Address: _____

Date Moved In: _____ Notice Given: _____ Moved Out: _____

Abbreviations:

Air Cond, AC	Clean, Cl	Drape, Drp	Hood, Hd	OK, OK	Table, Tbl
Bed, Bd	Cracked, Cr	Dryer, Dry	Just Painted, JP	Poor, P	Tile, Tl
Broken, Brk	Curtain, Ctn	Fair, F	Lamp, Lmp	Refrigerator, Rf	Venet'n Blind, VB
Carpet, Cpt	Dinette, Din	Good, G	Lightbulb, LtB	Shade, Sh	Washer, Wsh
Chair, Ch	Dishwasher, Dsh	Heater, Htr	Linoleum, Lino	Sofa, Sfa	Waxed, Wxd
Chest, Chst	Disposer, Dsp	Hole, H	Nightstand, Ntst	Stove, Stv	Wood, Wd

Circle rooms; enter abbreviations	Walls, Doors		Floors		Windows		Lt. Fixtures		Inventory: Appliances, Furniture		
	cond.	chgs.	cond.	chgs.	cond.	chgs.	cond.	chgs.	Item	cond.	chgs.
Living Rm											
Dining Rm											
Kitchen											
Bath 1											
Bath 2											
Bedroom 1											
Bedroom 2											
Bedroom 3											
Other											
Itemized Charges											

TOTAL ITEMIZED CHARGES _____

Other Charges Not Itemized (Dirty garage, etc. Explained on Backside) _____

Deduction for Improper Notice _____

Deduction for Missing Keys _____

TOTAL DEDUCTIONS _____

TOTAL DEPOSITS _____

minus (-) TOTAL DEDUCTIONS _____

equals (=) DEPOSIT REFUND or (Amount Owed) _____

☐ Tenants acknowledge that the smoke detector was tested in their presence and found to be in working order and that its operation was explained to them. Tenants agree to test the detector at least every other week and to report any problems to Owners in writing. If the detector is battery operated, Tenants agree to replace the battery as necessary with a new ALKALINE battery (unless applicable laws require otherwise).

Tenants hereby acknowledge that they have read this Checksheet, agree that the condition and contents of the above-mentioned rental dwelling are without exception as represented herein, understand that they are liable for any damage done to this dwelling as outlined in their Lease or Rental Agreement, and have received a copy of this Checksheet.

_____ _____
Owner   Tenant

_____ _____
BY Person authorized to represent Owners   Tenant

Credit Check & Screening Receipt

RECEIVED FROM _____, Applicant,

the sum of _____ $_____

for the purpose of verifying the information submitted on the application to rent that dwelling commonly known as

_____.

Sum received will be used as follows:
1) Cost to obtain credit report, eviction $_____
   report, and/or other screening reports

2) Cost to process and verify information $_____
   (time and associated costs)

It is understood that this sum received is in no way to be considered a deposit to hold the dwelling. The Owner/Manager may take other applications to rent the dwelling and indeed may already have done so.

The sum received is refundable only if the owner/manager selects another applicant to rent the dwelling BEFORE checking Applicant's credit history. Otherwise, this sum is entirely non-refundable.

Date:_____   _____
                                        Owner/Manager
Time:_____

                                  _____
                                        Applicant

                                  _____
                                        Applicant

Deposit Receipt & Agreement

RECEIVED FROM _____, Applicant,

the sum of _____ $_____

for the purpose of verifying information submitted on the application and for holding the rental dwelling commonly known as

_____

until _____ or such earlier time as the undersigned Owner/Manager is able to complete a verification of the information submitted on Applicant's rental application.

This dwelling will be rented to the Applicant provided that:
1) The Applicant's rental application and credit history satisfy the Owner/Manager;
2) Within 24 hours of being approved, the Applicant signs the rental agreement offered by the Owner/Manager, a copy of which the Applicant has received, read, and approved; and
3) Within 24 hours of being approved, the Applicant pays all of the sums necessary to move in.

Should the Applicant be approved to rent this dwelling and meet all three conditions above, all monies received will be refunded except for the sum of $_____, used to process Applicant's rental application, here itemized as follows:
1) Cost to obtain credit report, eviction $_____
   report, and/or other screening reports
2) Cost to process and verify information $_____
   (time and associated costs)

Should the Applicant be approved to rent this dwelling and not do so, none of the monies received will be refunded.

Should the Applicant not be approved to rent this dwelling, the Owner/Manager will refund all monies received except for the sum used to process Applicant's rental application (itemized above).

Date: _____

Time: _____

_____
Owner/Manager

_____
Applicant

_____
Applicant

386

Form D-1	DEPRECIATION WORKSHEET	YEAR		

NAME(S) OF TAXPAYERS		SOC. SEC. NUMBER			

PROPERTY LOCATION & DESCRIPTION

Property A

Property B

Property C

Property D

Property E

Property F

Property G

	A	B	C	D	E	F	G	Totals
Date Acqd. or Conv. to Bus.								
New or Used								
Cost or Other Basis								
Land Value								
Salvage Value								
1st Year Special Depreciation								
Depreciable Basis								
Prior Depreciation								
Depreciable Balance								
Method of Depreciation								
Useful Life								
Full Year Depreciation								
Percentage of Year Held								
Percentage of Business Use								
Depreciation This Year								

PAGE TOTAL

Depreciation Record

Property or Capital Improvement
Location and Description _____

Date Acquired or Converted to Business _____ New or Used _____

Method of Depreciation _____ Useful Life _____

Cost or Other Basis $_____

minus (-) Land Value or 1st Year Expensing $_____

equals (=) Depreciable Basis $_____

Tax Year	Prior Depreciation	Depreciable Balance	% Year Held	% Bus. Use	Rate	Depreciation This Year
1						
2						
3						
4						
5						
6						
7						
8						
9						
10						
11						
12						
13						
14						
15						
16						
17						
18						
19						
20						
21						
22						
23						
24						
25						
26						
27						
28						
29						
30						
31						
32						
33						
34						
35						
36						
37						
38						
39						
40						
41						

Disclosure of Information on Lead-Based Paint and/or Lead-Based Paint Hazards

Lead Warning Statement

Housing built before 1978 may contain lead-based paint. Lead from paint, paint chips, and dust can pose health hazards if not managed properly. Lead exposure is especially harmful to young children and pregnant women. Before renting pre-1978 housing, lessors must disclose the presence of known lead-based paint and/or lead-based paint hazards in the dwelling. Lessees must also receive a federally approved pamphlet on lead poisoning prevention.

Lessor's Disclosure

(a) Presence of lead-based paint and/or lead-based paint hazards (check (i) or (ii) below):

(i) _____ Known lead-based paint and/or lead-based paint hazards are present in the housing (explain).

_____

_____

(ii) _____ Lessor has no knowledge of lead-based paint and/or lead-based paint hazards in the housing.

(b) Records and reports available to the lessor (check (i) or (ii) below):

(i) _____ Lessor has provided the lessee with all available records and reports pertaining to lead-based paint and/or lead-based paint hazards in the housing (list documents below).

_____

_____

(ii) _____ Lessor has no reports or records pertaining to lead-based paint and/or lead-based paint hazards in the housing.

Lessee's Acknowledgment (initial)

(c) _____ Lessee has received copies of all information listed above.

(d) _____ Lessee has received the pamphlet *Protect Your Family from Lead in Your Home.*

Agent's Acknowledgment (initial)

(e) _____ Agent has informed the lessor of the lessor's obligations under 42 U.S.C. 4852(d) and is aware of his/her responsibility to ensure compliance.

Certification of Accuracy

The following parties have reviewed the information above and certify, to the best of their knowledge, that the information they have provided is true and accurate.

Lessor	Date	Lessor	Date
Lessee	Date	Lessee	Date
Agent	Date	Agent	Date

Employment Application

>>APPLICANT<<

Name_____ Home Phone_____ Work Phone_____

Social Security No._____Driver's License No._____

Present Address_____ Own_____How long at
Rent_____this address?_____

Present/Last
Occupation_____Employer_____ How long with this employer?_____

Reason for
Leaving?_____Monthly Gross_____Name of Supervisor_____ May we contact?_____Phone_____

Previous
Occupation_____Employer_____ How long with this employer?_____

Reason for
Leaving?_____Monthly Gross_____Name of Supervisor_____ May we contact?_____Phone_____

How many years of schooling have you had?_____Course of study_____ What languages do you speak fluently?_____

>>SPOUSE/PARTNER<<

Name_____ Social Security No._____ Driver's License No._____

Present/Last
Occupation_____Employer_____ How long with this employer?_____

Reason for
Leaving?_____Monthly Gross_____Name of Supervisor_____ May we contact?_____Phone_____

Previous
Occupation_____Employer_____ How long with this employer?_____

Reason for
Leaving?_____Monthly Gross_____Name of Supervisor_____ May we contact?_____Phone_____

How many years of schooling has spouse/partner had?_____Course of study_____ What languages does spouse/partner speak fluently?_____

>>APPLICANT AND SPOUSE/PARTNER<<

What are your skills related to this job?_____

What experience have you and your spouse/partner had related to this job?_____

What tools do you and your spouse/partner have which might be useful on this job?_____

What transportation do you and your spouse/partner have which might be useful on this job?_____

How many dependents do you and your spouse/partner have?_____What do you and your spouse/partner receive monthly from pensions, alimony, etc.?_____

What health insurance do you have?_____What do you and your spouse/partner pay monthly for debts, alimony, child support, etc.?_____

Are you and your spouse/partner bondable?_____Previous bonding?_____

Savings or Checking Account
Bank Name_____Branch_____Account Number_____

Credit Reference_____Account Number_____Balance Owed_____Monthly Payment_____

Personal Reference_____Address_____Phone (   )_____

Personal Reference_____Address_____Phone (   )_____

Contact in Emergency_____Address_____Phone (   )_____

Have you ever been convicted of a felony or serious misdemeanor?_____Will you take a drug test?_____When are you available for this job?_____

I/we declare that the information above is true and correct, and I/we hereby authorize verification of this information and a thorough background check.

Date_____Signed_____

Employment Verification

TO: EMPLOYER   _____

                           _____

                            _____

RE: EMPLOYEE   _____

      We are in the process of checking out a rental application submitted by the person named above as "EMPLOYEE."

      This person claims to be working for you currently as a _____ earning $_____ per _____. This person also claims to have started working for you as of _____.

      Because time is a factor in our approving this employee to rent from us, we would appreciate your PHONING us as soon as possible with a verification of this information. Our telephone number is _____, and we are generally available at the following times: _____.

      If you cannot phone us, please complete the section below and mail this entire letter back to us at your earliest convenience.

      Thank you.   Signed   _____

                            Address   _____

- -

The above information is correct with the following exceptions: _____ (if none, write "none.")

Is this employment part-time?   or full-time?

Is this employment temporary?   or permanent?

INFORMATION PROVIDED BY

Name_____ Title_____ Date_____

Expense & Payment Record

Page _____

Property _____

Period _____

	How Date Paid		To Whom Paid	For	1 Total Paid Out	2 Interest	3 Taxes, Licenses	4 Insurance	
1									1
2									2
3									3
4									4
5									5
6									6
7									7
8									8
9									9
10									10
11									11
12									12
13									13
14									14
15									15
16									16
17									17
18									18
19									19
20									20
21									21
22									22
23									23
24									24
25									25
26									26
27									27
28									28
29									29
30									30
31									31
32									32
33									33
34									34
35									35
36									36
37									37
38									38
39									39
40									40
41									41

Expense & Payment Distribution Page _____

	5 Utilities	6 Services, Rep., Maint.	7 Merch., Supplies	8 Payroll	9 Misc.	10 Depreciable	11 Mortgage Principal	12 Non-deduct.	
1									1
2									2
3									3
4									4
5									5
6									6
7									7
8									8
9									9
10									10
11									11
12									12
13									13
14									14
15									15
16									16
17									17
18									18
19									19
20									20
21									21
22									22
23									23
24									24
25									25
26									26
27									27
28									28
29									29
30									30
31									31
32									32
33									33
34									34
35									35
36									36
37									37
38									38
39									39
40									40
41									41

Expense & Payment Record

Annual Summary

Page _____

Property _____

Period _____

	Units	1 Total Paid Out (2-12)	2 Interest	3 Taxes, Licences	4 Insurance	5 Utilities	
1							1
2							2
3							3
4							4
5							5
6							6
7							7
8							8
9							9
10							10
11							11
12							12
13							13
14							14
15							15
16							16
17							17
18							18
19							19
20							20
21							21
22							22
23							23
24							24
25							25
26							26
27							27
28							28
29							29
30							30
31							31
32							32
33							33
34							34
35							35
36							36
37							37
38							38
39							39
40							40
41							41

Expense & Payment Distribution Page _____

Annual Summary

	6 Services, Rep., Maint.	7 Merch., Supplies	8 Payroll	9 Misc.	10 Depreciable	11 Mortgage Principal	12 Non-Deduct.	13 All Depreciation	
1									1
2									2
3									3
4									4
5									5
6									6
7									7
8									8
9									9
10									10
11									11
12									12
13									13
14									14
15									15
16									16
17									17
18									18
19									19
20									20
21									21
22									22
23									23
24									24
25									25
26									26
27									27
28									28
29									29
30									30
31									31
32									32
33									33
34									34
35									35
36									36
37									37
38									38
39									39
40									40
41									41

Date: _____

To: _____

Your application to rent from us has been rejected either partly or solely because of information provided by the following sources:

CREDIT REPORT
[ ]   Equifax Credit Information Service, P. O. Box 740241, Atlanta, GA 30374-2041; 800.685.1111

[ ]   Experian Consumer Assistance, P. O. Box 949, Allen, TX 75002; 800.682.7654

[ ]   Trans Union Consumer Relations, P. O. Box 1000, 2 Baldwin Place, Chester, PA 19022; 800.888.4213

[ ]   _____

COURT RECORDS REPORT
[ ]   American Tenant Screen, 131 N. Narberth Ave., Narberth, PA 19072; 610.664.2323

[ ]   _____

BAD CHECK REPORT
[ ]   Telecheck Services, P.O. Box 4513, Houston, TX 77210-4513; 800.366.2425

[ ]   _____

The federal Fair Credit Reporting Act requires us to reveal the source of whatever credit reports figured in the decision to reject you as an applicant. Please note that the agencies checked above only provided information about you. They did not make the decision, nor can they explain the decision.

Under federal law, you have the right to obtain a free copy of your credit report within sixty days from the date when we inquired about your credit. That was ____/____/____.

To secure the report, you must provide the following: your full name, your complete mailing address, your residential address if different from your mailing address, your daytime phone number, your employer's name, your Social Security number, your driver's license number and the state where issued (bad checks only), and the name of the company which rejected you. Our company name is _____.

If you believe your report is inaccurate or incomplete, you may contact the agency to dispute its accuracy and insert a 100-word consumer statement of explanation. Assistance is available at the credit reporting agency to help you with the statement.

You may have additional rights under the credit reporting or consumer protection laws of your state. To find out what they are, you may contact your state or local consumer protection agency or the office of your state attorney general. See the government listings in the white pages of your telephone book.

Sincerely,

Fellow Landlord:

_____ has applied to rent from us and has
identified you as a current or former landlord or rental property
manager having first-hand experience with him/her as a tenant.

We are trying to determine what this person was like when living
at _____ as your tenant and would
appreciate your answering the following questions about him/her:

How long was this person your tenant?
Less than six months [ ] Six months to a year [ ]
One to two years [ ] More than two years [ ]

When did this tenant move out? _____

How much was the rent when he/she moved out? $_____

How many other people were living with this tenant?
None [ ] One [ ] Two [ ] Three [ ] Four [ ] Five [ ] Six [ ]

Did the tenant have any pets?
Yes [ ] No [ ] If so, what kind? _____

How many times did the tenant fail to pay the rent on time?
Once [ ] Twice [ ] Three times [ ] More than three times [ ]

Did you ever have to serve the tenant with a notice to pay rent or
quit? Yes [ ] No [ ]

Did you ever have to serve the tenant with any other notice?
Yes [ ] No [ ] If so, what kind? _____

Was this tenant reasonably quiet? Yes [ ] No [ ]

Was this tenant reasonably clean? Yes [ ] No [ ]

Did the tenant give enough notice that he/she was moving?
Yes [ ] No [ ]

Did the tenant leave the premises clean and undamaged?
Yes [ ] No [ ]

If you withheld any of the tenant's cleaning/security deposit, why
did you withhold it? _____

Did the tenant leave owing you any money?
Yes [ ] No [ ] If so, how much? $_____

On a scale of one to ten, with ten being the most cooperative and
zero being the least cooperative, how would you rate this tenant
in terms of his/her cooperating with you?
10 9 8 7 6 5 4 3 2 1 (Circle only one number.)

If you had the opportunity, would you rent to this tenant again?
Yes [ ] No [ ]

Thank you very much for answering these questions.

Sincerely,

FINANCIAL QUALIFIER
(all figures monthly)

APPLICANT NAME _____

Number of Adults _____

Ages of Children _____

Adults all work? _____

Health plan through work? _____

Child care? _____

Pets? _____

G R O S S   V E R I F I A B L E   I N C O M E
(amounts)   (notes)

Wages _____

Wages _____

Wages _____

Wages _____

Social Security _____

Pension _____

Alimony _____

Child Support _____

Interest _____

Dividends _____

Other _____

_____

TOTAL INCOME _____ (+)

E X P E N S E S   &   D E D U C T I O N S
(amounts)   (notes)

Income Taxes _____ 20% if state inc tax; 17% if none

Credit Card Payments _____

Vehicle Payments _____

Loan Payments _____

Vehicle Expenses _____ $100/fin; $75/not; add $30 hi risk

Gas & Electricity _____ check local utility for sq ft avg

Telephone _____ ask re avg bill; otherwise $25

Cable TV _____

Food _____ $140/person

Health Care _____ $85/person wo paid plan; $25 with

Alimony _____

Child Care _____ $450/child full day; $200 partial

Child Support _____

Pet Care _____ $35/dog; $25/cat

Other _____ $200/adult; $100/child

_____

TOTAL EXPENSES & DEDUCTIONS _____ (−)

SAVINGS ACCOUNT BALANCE _____ add 5% bal to "available for rent"

AVAILABLE FOR RENT _____ (=) ADJUSTED _____
(total income minus total expenses & deductions)

For Your Information:

Important Numbers

Police_____ Telephone Co._____

Fire_____ Gas Co._____

Ambulance_____ Electric Co._____

Paramedic_____ Water Co._____

Doctor_____ Manager_____

The best time to contact the manager is _____.

In an emergency, when you cannot get hold of the manager, call

_____.

Helpful Hints

1) A fire extinguisher is located _____.
Use short bursts aimed at the base of the fire. Never use water on
a grease fire; either use the extinguisher provided or throw
baking soda on it.

2) The main electrical shutoff for your dwelling is located
_____.
Check there to see whether a fuse has blown (have an extra on
hand) or a circuit breaker has tripped. Restore service by
replacing any fuse which appears to be blown (use one with the
same number on it) or by flipping the circuit breaker switch back
and forth once.

3) The main gas shutoff for your dwelling is located
_____,
but there may be an individual valve on the line supplying each
appliance as well. Shut off the gas by turning the valve 90
degrees, that is, so it crosses the direction of the supply line.

4) The main water shutoff for your dwelling is located
_____,
but you may be able to shut off the water to an individual faucet
by turning off the supply valve below your sink or toilet (not
your tub or shower). If hot water is leaking anywhere, shut off
the valve on top of the hot water heater.

5) Whenever you defrost the refrigerator, turn it off or set
the control knob to defrost. Place a pan to catch the water and
empty it when necessary. Do not try to break up the ice with any
implement like a knife or an ice pick. Let it melt on its own or
speed it up by placing a pot of hot water in the freezing
compartment. Dry the floor thoroughly when you have finished.

FOR YOUR INFORMATION - Page 2

6) Whenever you use the garbage disposer, if you have one, feed garbage in gradually along with lots of cold water, and let the water run for half a minute after you turn off the switch. Use the disposer only for those things which are edible, but don't put either cooking oil or grease down it; put them and everything else except toxic liquids in the trash. Keep metal objects out of the sink while using the disposer and turn off the switch immediately if you hear any loud metallic noises. Do not put your hand into the disposer (use tongs to retrieve objects) and do not use any chemical drain openers. If the disposer stops running on its own and you haven't heard it make any strange noises, something may have gotten stuck. Try turning the blades with a disposer wrench. Then push the reset button. After you have tried all this and you find that it still doesn't work, call the manager.

7) Whenever you want to dispose of any liquids which aren't edible, please see the manager. Many liquids are toxic and should not be put down the drain or into the trash. They must be disposed of carefully so they will not contaminate the soil or the water supply in this area. Included in this list of hazardous household wastes are the following: oven cleaners, ammonia-based cleaners, drain cleaners, floor wax, furniture polish, deodorizers, spot removers, medicines, paint, thinners, paint removers, wood preservatives, art supplies, photographic chemicals, antifreeze, car waxes, crankcase oil, fuels, radiator flushes, rust inhibitors, engine cleaners, insect sprays, weed killers, and swimming pool chemicals.

8) Whenever water rises in the toilet bowl, do not try flushing the toilet again. The bowl can hold just one tank of water at a time. More water from the tank will only cause the bowl to flow over. Use a plunger first, and then try flushing it again. Do not try to flush feminine napkins or paper diapers down the toilet. They may disappear from the toilet bowl, but that's no guarantee they'll clear the sewer pipes completely. They could require a plumber's visit, and that'll cost you money.

9) Whenever you have showered or bathed, please take a moment to mop up the excess water on the bathroom floor. A dry floor is a safe floor.

10) Whenever you want to hang anything from, or stick anything to, the walls or ceilings in your dwelling, please ask the manager to explain how to do it acceptably.

11) Whenever you want to remove the screens from your windows, please ask the manager how to do it properly. Some screens have to be removed from the inside and some from the outside. The manager will show you how.

Dear

    As we do every year when the premiums come due, we have been reviewing our insurance policies, and we thought that you might like to know how you are affected by the insurance we carry.

    Basically, our policies cover only the building itself where you live. They do not cover any of your belongings against damage or disappearance, nor do they cover you for negligence should you, for example, leave a burner going under a pan and start a fire which damages the kitchen.

    To protect yourself against these calamities, you should get a tenant's insurance policy. Most insurance companies and agents will write such a policy for you, and we would strongly urge that you inquire about getting one.

    For the peace of mind that it gives, a tenant's insurance policy is reasonable indeed.

                    Sincerely,

Insurance Record Property _____

Company and/or Agent	Type of Policy	Policy Number	Limits	Premium	Expiration Date

Laundry Income

Property _____

Period _____

Date	Washer	Dryer	Both	Cumulative Totals	Monthly Totals
1					
2					
3					
4					
5					
6					
7					
8					
9					
10					
11					
12					
13					
14					
15					
16					
17					
18					
19					
20					
21					
22					
23					
24					
25					
26					
27					
28					
29					
30					
31					
32					
33					
34					
35					
36					
37					
38					
39					
40					
41					

Lease

Dated_____

Agreement between_____, Owners, and _____, Tenants, for a dwelling located at _____.
Tenants agree to lease this dwelling for a term of _____, beginning _____ and ending _____ for $_____ per month, payable in advance on the ____ day of every calendar month to Owners or their Agent*, _____, whose address is _____.
When rent is paid on or before the _____ day of the calendar month, Owners will give Tenants a (discount) (rebate) of $_____.

The first month's rent is $_____.

The security/cleaning deposit on this dwelling is $_____. It is refundable if Tenants leave the dwelling reasonably clean and undamaged.

Upon expiration, this Agreement shall become a month-to-month agreement AUTOMATICALLY, UNLESS either Tenants or Owners notify the other party in writing at least thirty days prior to expiration that they do not wish this Agreement to continue on any basis.

Should Tenants move before this Agreement expires, they will be responsible for paying rent through the end of the term or until another tenant approved by the Owners has moved in, whichever comes first.

Owners will refund all deposits due within ___ days after Tenants have moved out completely and returned their keys.

Only the following ___ persons and ___ pets are to live in this dwelling:
_____
Without Owners' prior written permission, no other persons may live there, and no other pets may stay there, even temporarily, nor may the dwelling be sublet or used for business purposes.

Use of the following is included in the rent: _____
_____

Remarks: _____
_____

TENANTS AGREE TO THE FOLLOWING:
1) to accept the dwelling "as is," having already inspected it.
2) to keep yards and garbage areas clean.
3) to keep from making loud or bothersome noises and disturbances and to play music and broadcast programs at all times so as not to disturb other people's peace and quiet.
4) not to paint or alter the dwelling without first getting Owners' written permission.
5) to park their motor vehicle in assigned space and to keep that space clean of oil drippings and grease.
6) not to repair their motor vehicle on the premises (unless it is in an enclosed garage) if such repairs will take longer than a single day.
7) to allow Owners to inspect the dwelling, work on it, or show it to prospective tenants at any and all reasonable times.
8) not to keep any liquid-filled furniture in this dwelling.
9) to pay rent by check or money order made out to Owners. (Checks must be good when paid or applicable late-payment consequences will apply.)
10) to pay for repairs of all damage, including drain stoppages, they or their guests have caused.
11) to pay for any windows broken in their dwelling while they live there.

Violation of any part of this Agreement or nonpayment of rent when due shall be cause for eviction under applicable code sections. The prevailing party (shall) (shall not) recover reasonable legal services fees involved.

Tenants hereby acknowledge that they have read this Agreement, understand it, agree to it, and have been given a copy.

Owner_____ Tenant_____
*By_____ Tenant_____
*Person authorized to accept legal service on Owners' behalf

LEASE TERMINATION ARRANGEMENTS

Date _____

Dear _____:

   We want you to be aware that the lease under which you occupy
the premises located at _____
will terminate on _____.

   When the lease terminates...

   [ ] you will need to vacate the premises.

   [ ] you may continue to occupy the premises...

      [ ] upon signing another fixed-term lease for _____ months

         at a new rent of $_____ per month.

      [ ] on a month-to-month basis at a new rent of $_____

         per month and...

         [ ] all other provisions of your original lease will

            continue to apply to your tenancy.

         [ ] you will need to sign a new agreement, in this

            case a month-to-month agreement.

   In order for us to begin making plans, we need to know what
you plan to do when your lease terminates. Please let us know by
completing the information below and returning it to us within
three days. Thank you.

                              Sincerely,

                              _____
                              Manager/Owner

* *

[ ] I plan to vacate the premises when the lease terminates.

[ ] If given the choice, I plan to continue occupying the premises
      when the lease terminates.

_____   _____
Date   Tenant

Dear

    We want to make the place where you live as safe as it can be.
We are constantly on the lookout for anything around your home which
might prove hazardous to life, limb, or property. But hard as we
try, we cannot uncover every potential danger all by ourselves. We
need your help.

    Because you are around your home much more than we are, you have
a greater opportunity to notice hazards. Please report to us
anything you notice which you think might prove hazardous to you or
anyone else. We promise that we will investigate the hazardous
condition and remedy it if we possibly can.

    Please complete the bottom section of this letter and return it
to us with your next rent payment.

    Thank you for your cooperation in making your home a safer place
to live.

                Sincerely,

= =

[ ] We know of nothing which appears to be unsafe in or around our
home, but we will alert you whenever we do notice something.

[ ] We would like to call your attention to the following unsafe
conditions in or around our home:

_____

_____

_____

_____

We suggest that you take the following corrective action:

_____

_____

_____

_____

Signed   Dated

Loan & Note Record Property_____

Noteholder _____ Loan Number _____

Original Loan _____ Interest Rate_____ Payment _____ Due Date _____

	Date Paid/Ck.#/New Payment if Changed	Interest	Principal	Impounds & (Imp.Disb.)	Impound Balance	Principal Balance	
1							1
2							2
3							3
4							4
5							5
6							6
7							7
8							8
9							9
10							10
11							11
12							12
13							13
14							14
15							15
16							16
17							17
18							18
19							19
20							20
21							21
22							22
23							23
24							24
25							25
26							26
27							27
28							28
29							29
30							30
31							31
32							32
33							33
34							34
35							35
36							36
37							37
38							38
39							39
40							40
41							41

Maintenance Request

Tenant _____

Unit _____

Home Phone _____ Work _____

Date of Request _____ Time _____

Maintenance Request _____

_____

_____

_____

_____

_____

Permission to Enter _____

Best Time _____

Request Submitted By _____

Work Order

Work Order No _____ Status _____

Work Authorized By _____

Date Work Attempted _____ Time Begun _____ Ended _____

Date Work Completed _____ Time Begun _____ Ended _____

Work Completed _____

_____

_____

_____

_____

Materials Used _____

COST	
Labor _____	
Materials _____	
Services _____	
TOTAL _____	

_____

_____

_____

Percentage of Work _____
Charged to Tenant _____

Work Performed By _____

Tenant Notice

We entered your dwelling today for necessary repairs, maintenance, and/or inspections.

The work is _____

Incomplete work, if any, resulted from a lack of the following:

☐ tools. ☐ parts. ☐ time. ☐ assistance.

We expect to return on or about _____

_____

Thank you for your cooperation.

Date _____ _____

Management Agreement

Dated_____

Agreement between _____, Owner, and _____, Manager, for management and maintenance of property located at _____.

Compensation for Manager shall be in the form of a lodging credit and cash payments. The lodging credit shall be $_____ per _____ (must not exceed credit allowed by state law). The combined rate of compensation shall equal $_____ per hour (must equal or exceed minimum wage). Owner may adjust the lodging credit and hourly rate upon notice to Manager.

In spite of rental property management's irregular and variable hours, Manager is responsible for planning and carrying out assigned duties so as to work no more than eight hours per day and forty hours per week. Overtime hours will be compensated provided that Manager obtains Owner's permission in advance or, in case of an emergency, provided that Owner is notified within 48 hours afterwards. Manager shall take a ten-minute break for every four hours of work and take an unpaid meal break of at least thirty minutes after every five hours of work. Manager shall record working hours on timesheets provided, one timesheet for each person, and shall submit signed timesheets at the close of each pay period to certify that the hours recorded were actually worked and that no unrecorded hours were worked. Paydays will be _____.

Other compensation shall be as follows: _____

Manager shall have days off as follows: _____

Manager shall have vacation time as follows: _____

Manager shall have sick leave as follows: _____

Manager's duties and responsibilities shall be as follows:

_____

(Either party to this Agreement may request a review of compensation, days off, vacation, sick leave, duties, responsibilities, etc. Any changes superseding the Agreement must be in writing and must be signed by all parties.)

Manager shall receipt all monies collected on the Owner's behalf and shall deposit or transfer them within _____ of collection as follows:

_____

Manager shall spend, or commit to spend, no more than $_____ on the Owner's behalf without first obtaining permission.

Manager agrees to reside on the premises of the property as an employee and not as a tenant. Manager is an at-will employee who may be terminated at any time. Either Manager or Owner may terminate this Agreement upon _____ written notice. Immediately upon termination, Manager shall surrender all keys, records, supplies, equipment, and other items related to the position and shall vacate whatever lodging Owner supplies as a condition of employment. In no event shall Manager vacate later than 72 hours following termination.

(THIS PARAGRAPH APPLIES ONLY IF INITIALED BY BOTH PARTIES. Initials: Owner_____; Manager_____.) Manager and Owner agree to submit all disputes that cannot be resolved between them, except failure to vacate, to arbitration. The party seeking to arbitrate a dispute shall begin arbitration by serving a written demand to arbitrate on the other party and on the Judicial Arbitration and Mediation Services (JAMS). Arbitration costs shall be shared equally by both parties, and the costs shall be estimated in advance.

Any item in this Agreement found to be illegal, invalid, or unenforceable shall be considered null and void, and it shall not affect the validity of any other item in the Agreement.

As written, this Agreement constitutes the entire agreement between Owner and Manager. They have made no further promises of any kind to one another, nor have they reached any other understandings, either verbal or written.

Manager hereby acknowledges that he/she has read this Agreement, understands it, agrees to it voluntarily, and has been given a copy.

Owner _____   Manager _____

By _____   Manager _____

Monthly Rental Income

Page _____

Property _____

Period _____

	Unit	January	February	March	April	May	
1							1
2							2
3							3
4							4
5							5
6							6
7							7
8							8
9							9
10							10
11							11
12							12
13							13
14							14
15							15
16							16
17							17
18							18
19							19
20							20
21							21
22							22
23							23
24							24
25							25
26							26
27							27
28							28
29							29
30							30
31							31
32							32
33							33
34							34
35							35
36							36
37							37
38							38
39							39
40							40
41							41

Monthly Rental Income Record

Page _____

	June	July	August	September	October	November	December	Year's Totals	
1									1
2									2
3									3
4									4
5									5
6									6
7									7
8									8
9									9
10									10
11									11
12									12
13									13
14									14
15									15
16									16
17									17
18									18
19									19
20									20
21									21
22									22
23									23
24									24
25									25
26									26
27									27
28									28
29									29
30									30
31									31
32									32
33									33
34									34
35									35
36									36
37									37
38									38
39									39
40									40
41									41

Move-Out Charges

Here's what we charge for most of the things we have to do when tenants move out and leave their dwelling in need of something or other. Please note that these charges are averages. Sometimes the actual charges are higher; sometimes they're lower. But most of the time they are exactly as shown. We give allowances for normal wear and tear, of course, and for the length of time something has been in use. Replacement charges include parts and labor.

Cleaning

Clean refrigerator _____
Clean stove top _____
Clean oven _____
Clean stove hood _____
Clean kitchen cabinets _____
Clean kitchen floor _____
Clean tub/shower and surround _____
Clean toilet and sink _____
Clean bathroom cabinets & floor _____
Vacuum throughout dwelling _____
Clean greasy parking space _____

Flooring

Remove carpet stains _____
Deodorize carpet _____
Repair carpet _____
Repair hardwood floor _____
Refinish hardwood floor _____
Repair linoleum _____
Replace kitchen linoleum _____
Replace bathroom linoleum _____
Repair floor tile _____
Replace kitchen floor tile _____
Replace bathroom floor tile _____

Walls

Remove mildew and treat surface _____
Cover crayon marks _____
Repair hole in wall _____
Remove wallpaper _____
Repaint (per wall/ceiling) _____

Doors

Repair hole in hollow-core door _____
Repair forced door damage _____
Replace door (inside) _____
Replace door (outside) _____
Replace sliding glass door (sgl) _____
Replace sliding glass door (dbl) _____
Rescreen sliding door screen _____
Replace sliding door screen _____

Electrical

Replace light bulb _____
Replace light fixture globe _____
Replace light fixture _____
Replace electrical outlet/switch _____
Replace electrical cover plate _____

Plumbing

Replace kitchen faucet _____
Replace bathroom faucet _____
Replace faucet handle _____
Replace faucet aerator _____
Replace shower head _____
Replace toilet tank lid _____
Replace toilet _____
Replace garbage disposer _____

Locks

Replace key (door or mailbox) _____
Replace cylindrical doorlock _____
Replace passage doorlock _____
Replace deadbolt lock _____
Replace mailbox lock _____

Windows & Window Coverings

Replace window pane (sgl) _____
Replace window pane (dbl) _____
Replace Venetian blind _____
Replace window shade _____
Replace drapery rod _____
Replace drapery (sill length) _____
Replace drapery (floor length) _____
Rescreen window screen _____
Replace window screen _____

Miscellaneous

Replace refrigerator shelf _____
Paint refrigerator _____
Replace stove/oven knob _____
Repair ceramic tile _____
Replace ceramic tile countertop _____
Repair plastic countertop _____
Replace plastic countertop _____
Replace cutting board _____
Replace mirror _____
Replace medicine cabinet _____
Replace towel bar _____
Replace shower curtain rod _____
Replace shower/tub enclosure _____
Repair porcelain _____
Replace thermostat _____
Recharge fire extinguisher _____
Replace fire extinguisher _____
Fumigate for fleas _____
Remove junk and debris _____

Dear

　　Moving time is always a busy time, and you will have lots of
things on your mind now that you have given notice you are moving.
One of those things undoubtedly is how to get your deposits back
promptly. In your case, they amount to $_____.

　　Contrary to what some tenants believe, we WANT to return your
deposits, and we WILL return them to you so long as you leave your
place "reasonably clean and undamaged." That's what your rental
agreement says and that's what we will do. You're probably wondering,
however, what "reasonably clean and undamaged" means, so we'd like to
tell you how we interpret it and tell you also what you should do to
get your deposits back.

　　"Reasonably clean" to us means as clean as you would leave your
dwelling if you knew your best friend or your favorite aunt were
going to move in after you. To get it that clean, we expect you to
clean the appliances, stove hood, and cabinets (under sinks, too)
both inside and out; remove all non-adhesive shelf paper; use an
appropriate cleanser on the showers, tubs, toilets, sinks, mirrors,
and medicine cabinets (inside as well); dust the ceilings (for
cobwebs), baseboards, window sills, and closet shelving; wash the
kitchen and bathroom walls and spot-clean the walls in the other
rooms; wash the light fixtures and windows inside and out; vacuum the
floors; scrub the floor tile or linoleum; sweep the entry, patio,
storage enclosure, and garage; remove all personal belongings
(including clothes hangers and cleaning supplies); and dispose of all
trash. PLEASE DO NOT CLEAN THE DRAPERIES, SHAMPOO THE CARPETS, OR WAX
THE FLOORS. We prefer to do those cleaning chores ourselves, and we
will not deduct anything from your deposits for our doing them.

　　"Reasonably undamaged" to us means that items which we have
supplied should not be missing (including light bulbs) or broken;
that there should be no new burns, cracks, chips, or holes in the
dwelling or its furnishings; and that the paint on the walls should
be sufficient to last at least two years from the time they were last
painted. PLEASE DO NOT REMOVE ANYTHING YOU HAVE ATTACHED TO THE WALLS
OR CEILING WITHOUT FIRST TALKING TO US, and please try to avoid
nicking the paint in the halls and doorways as you move things out.

　　Please note that until you have returned your keys, you have not
"officially" moved out, and you are still liable for paying rent.
Make sure that you give us your keys as soon as you move out.

　　After you have moved out, we would like to inspect your dwelling
with you to check it for cleanliness and damage. We will refund all
deposits owed to you within seven days thereafter.

　　We expect you to have moved out completely by _____.
Because we are making arrangements for new tenants to move in after
you move, we would appreciate hearing from you immediately if your
moving plans should change.

　　We hope your moving goes smoothly, and we wish you happiness in
your new home.
　　　　　　　　　　　　　Sincerely,

Notice of Change
in Terms of Tenancy

TO _____, Tenant in Possession

_____

_____

    YOU ARE HEREBY NOTIFIED that the terms of tenancy under which you occupy the above-described premises are to be changed.

    Effective _____, _____, there will be the following changes:

_____

_____

_____

_____

    Dated this _____ day of _____, _____.

_____
                          Owner/Manager

This Notice was served by the Owner/Manager in the following manner (check those which apply):

    ( ) by personal delivery to the tenant,
    ( ) by leaving a copy with someone on the premises other than
        the tenant,
    ( ) by mailing,
    ( ) by posting.

Notice of Change
in Terms of Tenancy
(Rent)

TO _____, Tenant in Possession

_____

_____

YOU ARE HEREBY NOTIFIED that the terms of tenancy under which you occupy the above-described premises are to be changed.

Effective _____, _____, your rent will be increased by _____ per month, from _____ per month to _____ per month, payable in advance.

Dated this _____ day of _____, _____.

_____
Owner/Manager

This Notice was served by the Owner/Manager in the following manner (check those which apply):

( ) by personal delivery to the tenant,
( ) by leaving a copy with someone on the premises other than the tenant,
( ) by mailing,
( ) by posting.

Notice of Intention to Enter

TO _____, Tenant in Possession

_____

_____

    YOU ARE HEREBY NOTIFIED that at or about _____ (a.m.) (p.m.) on _____, _____, the Owner, Manager, Owner's agent, or Owner's employees intend to enter the premises identified above which you hold and occupy. They should need to stay approximately _____ hour(s).

    The purpose for entry is as follows:

_____

_____

    You are not required to be on the premises to provide access. Whoever comes to enter will first knock and after determining that no one is available to answer, will enter using a passkey.

    If the lock has been changed without proper notice and you have not given management a duplicate key, a locksmith will be called upon to open the door and rekey the locks. Your account will be charged for these services, and you will be provided with a new key.

    This is intended to be a reasonable notice of at least twenty-four (24) hours.

    This Notice was personally served by the Owner/Manager at the following time: _____(a.m.) (p.m.) and date: _____.

_____

Owner/Manager

Notice of Intention to Vacate

TO: _____

FROM: _____

Dated _____

    Please be advised that on _____ we intend to move from our residence at _____.

    We understand that our Rental Agreement calls for _____ days' notice before we move and that this is _____ days' notice. We understand that we are responsible for paying rent through the end of the notice period called for in the rental agreement or until another tenant approved by the management has moved in, whichever comes first.

    We understand that our deposits will be refunded within _____ days after we have moved out completely and returned our keys to the management, so long as we leave our dwelling reasonably clean and undamaged.

    Reasons for leaving: _____

_____

    Forwarding address: _____

    In accordance with our Rental Agreement, we agree to allow the management to show our dwelling to prospective tenants at any and all reasonable times.

                Tenant _____

                Tenant _____

Received by _____

Date _____

Notice to Pay Rent or Quit

TO: _____

_____

and all other tenants in possession of the premises described as:

_____

_____

PLEASE TAKE NOTICE that the rent is now due and payable on the above-described premises which you currently hold and occupy.

Your rental account is delinquent in the amount itemized as follows:

Rental Period: _____ Rent due $ _____

Rental Period: _____ Rent due $ _____

Rental Period: _____ Rent due $ _____

TOTAL RENT DUE $ _____

less partial payment of $ _____

equals TOTAL BALANCE DUE of $ _____

YOU ARE HEREBY REQUIRED to pay said rent in full within_____ days or to remove from and deliver up possession of the above-described premises, or legal proceedings will be instituted against you to recover possession of said premises, to declare the forfeiture of the Lease or Rental Agreement under which you occupy said premises and to recover rents and damages, together with court costs and attorney's fees, according to the terms of your Lease or Rental Agreement.

_____

_____

Dated: _____   _____

Owner/Manager

PROOF OF SERVICE

I, the undersigned, being at least 18 years of age, declare under penalty of perjury that I served the above notice, of which this is a true copy, on the above-mentioned tenant(s) in possesssion in the manner(s) indicated below:

☐ On _____, I handed the notice to the tenant(s).

☐ On _____, after attempting personal service, I handed the notice to a person of suitable age and discretion at the residence/business of the tenant(s).

☐ On _____, after attempting service in both manners indicated above, I posted the notice in a conspicuous place at the residence of the tenant(s).

☐ On _____, I deposited a true copy of the notice in the United States Mail, in a sealed envelope with postage fully prepaid, addressed to the tenant(s) at his/her/their place of residence.

☐ On _____, I sent by certified mail a true copy of the notice addressed to the tenant(s) at his/her/their place of residence.

Executed on _____, at the City of _____,

County of _____, State of _____.

Served by _____

Notice to Perform Covenant

TO: _____

_____

and all other tenants in possession of the premises described as:

_____

_____

PLEASE TAKE NOTICE that you have violated the following covenant(s) in your Lease or Rental Agreement:

_____

_____

_____

_____

YOU ARE HEREBY REQUIRED within _____ days to perform the aforesaid covenant(s) or to deliver up possession of the above-described premises which you currently hold and occupy.

If you fail to do so, legal proceedings will be instituted against you to recover said premises and such damages as the law allows.

This notice is intended to be a _____ day notice to perform the aforesaid covenant(s). It is not intended to terminate or forfeit the Lease or Rental Agreement under which you occupy said premises. If, after legal proceedings, said premises are recovered from you, the owners will try to rent the premises for the best possible rent, giving you credit for sums received and holding you liable for any deficiencies arising during the term of your Lease or Rental Agreement.

Dated: _____   _____
                                                              Owner/Manager

---

PROOF OF SERVICE

I, the undersigned, being at least 18 years of age, declare under penalty of perjury that I served the above notice, of which this is a true copy, on the above-mentioned tenant(s) in possesssion in the manner(s) indicated below:

☐ On _____, I handed the notice to the tenant(s).

☐ On _____, after attempting personal service, I handed the notice to a person of suitable age and discretion at the residence/business of the tenant(s).

☐ On _____, after attempting service in both manners indicated above, I posted the notice in a conspicuous place at the residence of the tenant(s).

☐ On _____, I deposited a true copy of the notice in the United States Mail, in a sealed envelope with postage fully prepaid, addressed to the tenant(s) at his/her/their place of residence.

☐ On _____, I sent by certified mail a true copy of the notice addressed to the tenant(s) at his/her/their place of residence.

Executed on _____, at the City of _____,

County of _____, State of _____.

Served by _____

Notice to Terminate Tenancy

TO: _____

_____

and all other tenants in possession of the premises described as:

_____

_____

PLEASE TAKE NOTICE that you are hereby required within _____ days to remove from and deliver up possession of the above-described premises, which you currently hold and occupy.

This notice is intended for the purpose of terminating the Rental Agreement by which you now hold possession of the above-described premises, and should you fail to comply, legal proceedings will be instituted against you to recover possession, to declare said Rental Agreement forfeited, and to recover rents and damages for the period of the unlawful detention.

Dated: _____   _____

Owner/Manager

PROOF OF SERVICE

I, the undersigned, being at least 18 years of age, declare under penalty of perjury that I served the above notice, of which this is a true copy, on the above-mentioned tenant(s) in possesssion in the manner(s) indicated below:

☐ On _____, I handed the notice to the tenant(s).

☐ On _____, after attempting personal service, I handed the notice to a person of suitable age and discretion at the residence/business of the tenant(s).

☐ On _____, after attempting service in both manners indicated above, I posted the notice in a conspicuous place at the residence of the tenant(s).

☐ On _____, I deposited a true copy of the notice in the United States Mail, in a sealed envelope with postage fully prepaid, addressed to the tenant(s) at his/her/their place of residence.

☐ On _____, I sent by certified mail a true copy of the notice addressed to the tenant(s) at his/her/their place of residence.

Executed on _____, at the City of _____,

County of _____, State of _____.

Served by _____

Other Receipts & Income

Page _____

Added Appliances or Furniture, Deposit
Forfeits, Interest, Late Charges, Laundry,
Garages, etc.

Property _____

Period _____

	Description of Income	January	February	March	April	May	
1							1
2							2
3							3
4							4
5							5
6							6
7							7
8							8
9							9
10							10
11							11
12							12
13							13
14							14
15							15
16							16
17							17
18							18
19							19
20							20
21							21
22							22
23							23
24							24
25							25
26							26
27							27
28							28
29							29
30							30
31							31
32							32
33							33
34							34
35							35
36							36
37							37
38							38
39							39
40							40
41							41

Other Receipts & Income

Page _____

	June	July	August	September	October	November	December	Year's Totals	
1									1
2									2
3									3
4									4
5									5
6									6
7									7
8									8
9									9
10									10
11									11
12									12
13									13
14									14
15									15
16									16
17									17
18									18
19									19
20									20
21									21
22									22
23									23
24									24
25									25
26									26
27									27
28									28
29									29
30									30
31									31
32									32
33									33
34									34
35									35
36									36
37									37
38									38
39									39
40									40
41									41

Payment Pledge

Dear Landlord/Landlady:

On or before _____, I promise to pay you $_____ for rent and other charges now owing on the dwelling which I rent from you located at _____.

I expect to be receiving sufficient funds to pay you from the following sources:

Name   Address   Phone   Amount Expected

_____

_____

_____

Should you wish to, you have my authorization to verify these sources.

If I fail to honor this pledge, I understand that I will be evicted and that this pledge will be used against me as evidence of my bad faith in paying what I owe.

____ I acknowledge receipt of a Notice to Pay Rent or Quit as required by law to begin eviction proceedings. I understand that the Notice may show a balance owed which is different from that given above because a Notice to Pay Rent or Quit can demand only delinquent rent. I also understand that the period mentioned in this Notice is being extended to the date given above, at which time I promise to pay you what I owe. If I fail to pay on or before that date, you have the right to continue the legal eviction procedure against me without having to serve me another Notice to Pay Rent or Quit. I have already been served. I am being given the extra time to pay only as a courtesy and only this once.

Signed _____

Dated _____

Payroll Record

Property _____

Employee _____ Social Sec.No. _____

Pay Rate _____ Exemptions _____ Married ☐ Single ☐

Period	Base Wages	Lod-ging	Fed Whldg	Employee		Employer		State Disblty	State Whldg	Other	Net	Chk No
				FICA	Medcare	FICA	Medcare					
1												1
2												2
3												3
4												4
5												5
6												6
7												7
8												8
9												9
10												10
11												11
12												12
13												13
14												14
15												15
16												16
17												17
18												18
19												19
20												20
21												21
22												22
23												23
24												24
25												25
26												26
27												27
28												28
29												29
30												30
31												31
32												32
33												33
34												34
35												35
36												36
37												37
38												38
39												39
40												40
41												41

Pet Agreement

Dated _____

(Addendum to Rental Agreement)

This agreement is attached to and forms a part of the Rental

Agreement dated _____ between _____,

Owners, and _____, Tenants.

Tenants desire to keep a pet named _____ and

described as _____ in the

dwelling they occupy under the Rental Agreement referred to above, and

because this Agreement specifically prohibits keeping pets without the

Owners' permission, Tenants agree to the following terms and conditions

in exchange for this permission:

1) Tenants agree to keep their pet under control at all times.
2) Tenants agree to keep their pet restrained, but not tethered, when it is outside their dwelling.
3) Tenants agree to adhere to local ordinances, including leash and licensing requirements.
4) Tenants agree not to leave their pet unattended for any unreasonable periods.
5) Tenants agree to clean up after their pet and to dispose of their pet's waste properly and quickly.
6) Tenants agree not to leave food or water for their pet or any other animal outside their dwelling where it will attract other animals.
7) Tenants agree to keep their pet from being unnecessarily noisy or aggressive and causing any annoyance or discomfort to others and will remedy immediately any complaints made through the Owners or Manager.
8) Tenants agree to provide their pet with regular health care, to include innoculations as recommended.
9) Tenants agree to provide their pet with an identification tag.
10) Tenants agree to get rid of their pet's offspring within eight weeks of birth.
11) Tenants agree to pay immediately for any damage, loss, or expense caused by their pet, and in addition, they will add $_____ to their security/cleaning deposit, any of which may be used for cleaning, repairs, or delinquent rent when Tenants vacate. This added deposit, or what remains of it when pet damages have been assessed, will be returned to Tenants within _____ days after they have proved that they no longer keep this pet.
12) Tenants agree that this Agreement applies only to the specific pet described above and that no other pet may be substituted.
13) Tenants agree to furnish Owners with a picture of their pet.
14) Tenants agree that Owners reserve the right to revoke permission to keep the pet should Tenants break this Agreement.

Owner _____   Tenant _____

By _____   Tenant _____

Page _____ of _____

Property Viewing
& Keys Agreement

With my signature below, I hereby acknowledge receipt of the key(s) to the dwelling located at _____

_____.

I intend to use the key(s) for the express purpose of viewing the dwelling to consider whether it is suitable for me to rent, and I will neither disturb nor remove anything found there.

As a courtesy, I will report to the owner/manager whatever appears to be amiss at the dwelling.

I have given the owner/manager, whose acknowledgment appears below, a deposit of $_____, and also a valuable personal item consisting of _____,
both of which will be returned to me when I return the key(s).

I promise to return the key(s) by _____ (a.m.) (p.m.)
TODAY to the owner/manager at EITHER--

      ( ) the same place where I picked them up OR

      ( ) the following place _____.

Should I fail to do so, the owner/manager is entitled to keep the deposit to pay for changing the locks on the dwelling but will return my valuable personal item to me when asked.

I understand that this agreement gives me no occupancy rights whatsoever and that I must complete a rental application if I want to be considered as an applicant to rent this dwelling.

Signed _____

Current Address _____

Current Telephone Number _____

Date & Time _____

Acknowledged by _____
                       Owner/Manager

Protect Your Family From Lead In Your Home

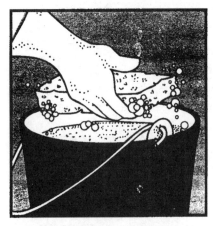

 **EPA** United States
Environmental
Protection Agency

 United States
Consumer Product
Safety Commission

United States
Department of Housing
and Urban Development

U.S. EPA Washington DC 20460
U.S. CPSC Washington DC 20207
U.S. HUD Washington DC 20410

EPA747-K-99-001
April 1999

Are You Planning To Buy, Rent, or Renovate a Home Built Before 1978?

Many houses and apartments built before 1978 have paint that contains lead (called lead-based paint). Lead from paint, chips, and dust can pose serious health hazards if not taken care of properly.

Federal law requires that individuals receive certain information before renting, buying, or renovating pre-1978 housing:

LANDLORDS have to disclose known information on lead-based paint and lead-based paint hazards before leases take effect. Leases must include a disclosure form about lead-based paint.

SELLERS have to disclose known information on lead-based paint and lead-based paint hazards before selling a house. Sales contracts must include a disclosure form about lead-based paint. Buyers have up to 10 days to check for lead hazards.

RENOVATORS have to give you this pamphlet before starting work. (After June 1, 1999.)

IF YOU WANT MORE INFORMATION on these requirements, call the National Lead Information Clearinghouse at **1-800-424-LEAD**.

IMPORTANT!

Lead From Paint, Dust, and Soil Can Be Dangerous If Not Managed Properly

FACT: Lead exposure can harm young children and babies even before they are born.

FACT: Even children who seem healthy can have high levels of lead in their bodies.

FACT: People can get lead in their bodies by breathing or swallowing lead dust, or by eating soil or paint chips containing lead.

FACT: People have many options for reducing lead hazards. In most cases, lead-based paint that is in good condition is not a hazard.

FACT: Removing lead-based paint improperly can increase the danger to your family.

If you think your home might have lead hazards, read this pamphlet to learn some simple steps to protect your family.

Lead Gets in the Body in Many Ways

In the United States, about 900,000 children ages 1 to 5 have a blood-lead level above the level of concern.

Even children who appear healthy can have danger-ous levels of lead in their bodies.

People can get lead in their body if they:

◆ Put their hands or other objects covered with lead dust in their mouths.

◆ Eat paint chips or soil that contains lead.

◆ Breathe in lead dust (especially during renovations that disturb painted surfaces).

Lead is even more dangerous to children than adults because:

◆ Babies and young children often put their hands and other objects in their mouths. These objects can have lead dust on them.

◆ Children's growing bodies absorb more lead.

◆ Children's brains and nervous systems are more sensitive to the damaging effects of lead.

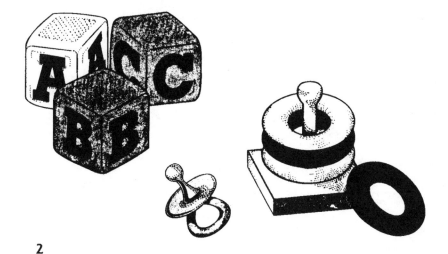

Lead's Effects

If not detected early, children with high levels of lead in their bodies can suffer from:

◆ Damage to the brain and nervous system

◆ Behavior and learning problems (such as hyperactivity)

◆ Slowed growth

◆ Hearing problems

◆ Headaches

Lead is also harmful to adults. Adults can suffer from:

◆ Difficulties during pregnancy

◆ Other reproductive problems (in both men and women)

◆ High blood pressure

◆ Digestive problems

◆ Nerve disorders

◆ Memory and concentration problems

◆ Muscle and joint pain

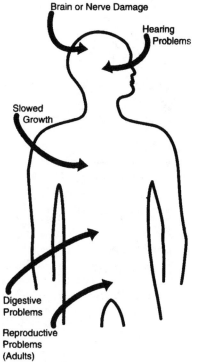

Brain or Nerve Damage

Hearing Problems

Slowed Growth

Digestive Problems

Reproductive Problems (Adults)

Lead affects the body in many ways.

Where Lead-Based Paint Is Found

In general, the older your home, the more likely it has lead-based paint.

Many homes built before 1978 have lead-based paint. The federal government banned lead-based paint from housing in 1978. Some states stopped its use even earlier. Lead can be found:

◆ In homes in the city, country, or suburbs.

◆ In apartments, single-family homes, and both private and public housing.

◆ Inside *and* outside of the house.

◆ In soil around a home. (Soil can pick up lead from exterior paint or other sources such as past use of leaded gas in cars.)

Checking Your Family for Lead

Get your children and home tested if you think your home has high levels of lead.

To reduce your child's exposure to lead, get your child checked, have your home tested (especially if your home has paint in poor condition and was built before 1978), and fix any hazards you may have. Children's blood lead levels tend to increase rapidly from 6 to 12 months of age, and tend to peak at 18 to 24 months of age.

Consult your doctor for advice on testing your children. A simple blood test can detect high levels of lead. Blood tests are usually recommended for:

◆ Children at ages 1 and 2.

◆ Children or other family members who have been exposed to high levels of lead.

◆ Children who should be tested under your state or local health screening plan.

Your doctor can explain what the test results mean and if more testing will be needed.

4

Where Lead Is Likely To Be a Hazard

Lead-based paint that is in good condition is usually not a hazard.

Peeling, chipping, chalking, or cracking lead-based paint is a hazard and needs immediate attention.

Lead-based paint may also be a hazard when found on surfaces that children can chew or that get a lot of wear-and-tear. These areas include:

◆ Windows and window sills.

◆ Doors and door frames.

◆ Stairs, railings, and banisters.

◆ Porches and fences.

Lead dust can form when lead-based paint is dry scraped, dry sanded, or heated. Dust also forms when painted surfaces bump or rub together. Lead chips and dust can get on surfaces and objects that people touch. Settled lead dust can re-enter the air when people vacuum, sweep, or walk through it.

Lead in soil can be a hazard when children play in bare soil or when people bring soil into the house on their shoes. Call your state agency (see page 11) to find out about testing soil for lead.

Lead from paint chips, which you can see, and lead dust, which you can't always see, can both be serious hazards.

5

Checking Your Home for Lead Hazards

Just knowing that a home has lead-based paint may not tell you if there is a hazard.

You can get your home checked for lead hazards in one of two ways, or both:

◆ A paint **inspection** tells you the lead content of every different type of painted surface in your home. It won't tell you whether the paint is a hazard or how you should deal with it.

◆ A **risk assessment** tells you if there are any sources of serious lead exposure (such as peeling paint and lead dust). It also tells you what actions to take to address these hazards.

Have qualified professionals do the work. *There are standards in place for certifying lead-based paint professionals to ensure the work is done safely, reliably, and effectively.* Contact your state lead poisoning prevention program for more information. Call 1-800-424-LEAD for a list of contacts in your area.

Trained professionals use a range of methods when checking your home, including:

◆ Visual inspection of paint condition and location.

◆ A portable x-ray fluorescence (XRF) machine.

◆ Lab tests of paint samples.

◆ Surface dust tests.

Home test kits for lead are available, but studies suggest that they are not always accurate. Consumers should not rely on these tests before doing renovations or to assure safety.

What You Can Do Now To Protect Your Family

If you suspect that your house has lead hazards, you can take some immediate steps to reduce your family's risk:

◆ **If you rent, notify your landlord of peeling or chipping paint.**

◆ **Clean up paint chips immediately.**

◆ **Clean floors, window frames, window sills, and other surfaces weekly.** Use a mop or sponge with warm water and a general all-purpose cleaner or a cleaner made specifically for lead. REMEMBER: NEVER MIX AMMONIA AND BLEACH PRODUCTS TOGETHER SINCE THEY CAN FORM A DANGEROUS GAS.

◆ **Thoroughly rinse sponges and mop heads after cleaning dirty or dusty areas.**

◆ **Wash children's hands often, especially before they eat and before nap time and bed time.**

◆ **Keep play areas clean.** Wash bottles, pacifiers, toys, and stuffed animals regularly.

◆ **Keep children from chewing window sills or other painted surfaces.**

◆ **Clean or remove shoes before entering your home to avoid tracking in lead from soil.**

◆ **Make sure children eat nutritious, low-fat meals high in iron and calcium,** such as spinach and dairy products. Children with good diets absorb less lead.

How To Significantly Reduce Lead Hazards

Removing lead improperly can increase the hazard to your family by spreading even more lead dust around the house.

Always use a professional who is trained to remove lead hazards safely.

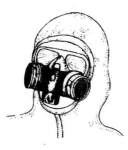

In addition to day-to-day cleaning and good nutrition:

◆ You can **temporarily** reduce lead hazards by taking actions such as repairing damaged painted surfaces and planting grass to cover soil with high lead levels. These actions (called "interim controls") are not permanent solutions and will need ongoing attention.

◆ To **permanently** remove lead hazards, you must hire a certified lead "abatement" contractor. Abatement (or permanent hazard elimination) methods include removing, sealing, or enclosing lead-based paint with special materials. Just painting over the hazard with regular paint is not enough.

Always hire a person with special training for correcting lead problems—someone who knows how to do this work safely and has the proper equipment to clean up thoroughly. Certified contractors will employ qualified workers and follow strict safety rules as set by their state or by the federal government.

Call your state agency (see page 11) for help with locating certified contractors in your area and to see if financial assistance is available.

Remodeling or Renovating a Home With Lead-Based Paint

Take precautions before your contractor or you begin remodeling or renovations that disturb painted surfaces (such as scraping off paint or tearing out walls):

◆ **Have the area tested for lead-based paint.**

◆ **Do not use a belt-sander, propane torch, heat gun, dry scraper, or dry sandpaper** to remove lead-based paint. These actions create large amounts of lead dust and fumes. Lead dust can remain in your home long after the work is done.

◆ **Temporarily move your family** (especially children and pregnant women) out of the apartment or house until the work is done and the area is properly cleaned. If you can't move your family, at least completely seal off the work area.

◆ **Follow other safety measures to reduce lead hazards.** You can find out about other safety measures by calling 1-800-424-LEAD. Ask for the brochure "Reducing Lead Hazards When Remodeling Your Home." This brochure explains what to do before, during, and after renovations.

If you have already completed renovations or remodeling that could have released lead-based paint or dust, get your young children tested and follow the steps outlined on page 7 of this brochure.

If not conducted properly, certain types of renovations can release lead from paint and dust into the air.

9

Other Sources of Lead

While paint, dust, and soil are the most common lead hazards, other lead sources also exist.

◆ **Drinking water.** Your home might have plumbing with lead or lead solder. Call your local health department or water supplier to find out about testing your water. You cannot see, smell, or taste lead, and boiling your water will not get rid of lead. If you think your plumbing might have lead in it:

- Use only cold water for drinking and cooking.

- Run water for 15 to 30 seconds before drinking it, especially if you have not used your water for a few hours.

◆ **The job.** If you work with lead, you could bring it home on your hands or clothes. Shower and change clothes before coming home. Launder your work clothes separately from the rest of your family's clothes.

◆ Old painted **toys** and **furniture.**

◆ Food and liquids stored in **lead crystal** or **lead-glazed pottery or porcelain.**

◆ **Lead smelters** or other industries that release lead into the air.

◆ **Hobbies** that use lead, such as making pottery or stained glass, or refinishing furniture.

◆ **Folk remedies** that contain lead, such as "greta" and "azarcon" used to treat an upset stomach.

For More Information

The National Lead Information Center

Call **1-800-424-LEAD** to learn how to protect children from lead poisoning and for other information on lead hazards. (Internet: **www.epa.gov/lead** and **www.hud.gov/lea**).

For the hearing impaired, call the Federal Information Relay Service at **1-800-877-8339** and ask for the National Lead Information Center at **1-800-424-LEAD**.

EPA's Safe Drinking Water Hotline

Call **1-800-426-4791** for information about lead in drinking water.

Consumer Product Safety Commission Hotline

To request information on lead in consumer products, or to report an unsafe consumer product or a product-related injury call **1-800-638-2772.** (Internet: www@cpsc.gov). For the hearing impaired, call **TDD 1-800-638-8270.**

State Health and Environmental Agencies

Some cities and states have their own rules for lead-based paint activities. Check with your state agency to see if state or local laws apply to you. Most state agencies can also provide information on finding a lead abatement firm in your area, and on possible sources of financial aid for reducing lead hazards. Receive up-to-date address and phone information for state and local contacts on the Internet at **www.epa.gov/lead** or contact the National Lead Information Center at **1-800-424-LEAD.**

11

EPA Regional Offices

Your Regional EPA Office can provide further information regarding regulations and lead protection programs.

EPA Regional Offices

Region 1 (Connecticut, Massachusetts, Maine, New Hampshire, Rhode Island, Vermont)

Regional Lead Contact
U.S. EPA Region 1
Suite 1100 (CPT)
One Congress Street
Boston, MA 02114-2023
1 (888) 372-7341

Region 2 (New Jersey, New York, Puerto Rico, Virgin Islands)

Regional Lead Contact
U.S. EPA Region 2
2890 Woodbridge Avenue
Building 209, Mail Stop 225
Edison, NJ 08837-3679
(732) 321-6671

Region 3 (Delaware, Washington DC, Maryland, Pennsylvania, Virginia, West Virginia)

Regional Lead Contact
U.S. EPA Region 3 (3WC33)
1650 Arch Street
Philadelphia, PA 19103
(215) 814-5000

Region 4 (Alabama, Florida, Georgia, Kentucky, Mississippi, North Carolina, South Carolina, Tennessee)

Regional Lead Contact
U.S. EPA Region 4
61 Forsyth Street, SW
Atlanta, GA 30303
(404) 562-8998

Region 5 (Illinois, Indiana, Michigan, Minnesota, Ohio, Wisconsin)

Regional Lead Contact
U.S. EPA Region 5 (DT-8J)
77 West Jackson Boulevard
Chicago, IL 60604-3666
(312) 886-6003

Region 6 (Arkansas, Louisiana, New Mexico, Oklahoma, Texas)

Regional Lead Contact
U.S. EPA Region 6
1445 Ross Avenue, 12th Floor
Dallas, TX 75202-2733
(214) 665-7577

Region 7 (Iowa, Kansas, Missouri, Nebraska)

Regional Lead Contact
U.S. EPA Region 7
(ARTD-RALI)
901 N. 5th Street
Kansas City, KS 66101
(913) 551-7020

Region 8 (Colorado, Montana, North Dakota, South Dakota, Utah, Wyoming)

Regional Lead Contact
U.S. EPA Region 8
999 18th Street, Suite 500
Denver, CO 80202-2466
(303) 312-6021

Region 9 (Arizona, California, Hawaii, Nevada)

Regional Lead Contact
U.S. Region 9
75 Hawthorne Street
San Francisco, CA 94105
(415) 744-1124

Region 10 (Idaho, Oregon, Washington, Alaska)

Regional Lead Contact
U.S. EPA Region 10
Toxics Section WCM-128
1200 Sixth Avenue
Seattle, WA 98101-1128
(206) 553-1985

12

CPSC Regional Offices

Your Regional CPSC Office can provide further information regarding regulations and consumer product safety.

Eastern Regional Center
6 World Trade Center
Vesey Street, Room 350
New York, NY 10048
(212) 466-1612

Central Regional Center
230 South Dearborn Street
Room 2944
Chicago, IL 60604-1601
(312) 353-8260

Western Regional Center
600 Harrison Street, Room 245
San Francisco, CA 94107
(415) 744-2966

HUD Lead Office

Please contact HUD's Office of Lead Hazard Control for information on lead regulations, outreach efforts, and lead hazard control and research grant programs.

U.S. Department of Housing and Urban Development
Office of Lead Hazard Control
451 Seventh Street, SW, P-3206
Washington, DC 20410
(202) 755-1785

Simple Steps To Protect Your Family From Lead Hazards

If you think your home has high levels of lead:

◆ Get your young children tested for lead, even if they seem healthy.

◆ Wash children's hands, bottles, pacifiers, and toys often.

◆ Make sure children eat healthy, low-fat foods.

◆ Get your home checked for lead hazards.

◆ Regularly clean floors, window sills, and other surfaces.

◆ Wipe soil off shoes before entering house.

◆ Talk to your landlord about fixing surfaces with peeling or chipping paint.

◆ Take precautions to avoid exposure to lead dust when remodeling or renovating (call 1-800-424-LEAD for guidelines).

◆ Don't use a belt-sander, propane torch, heat gun, dry scraper, or dry sandpaper on painted surfaces that may contain lead.

◆ Don't try to remove lead-based paint yourself.

Date: _____

To: _____

We appreciate your applying to rent a dwelling from us. We regret to inform you that you will need to continue looking for a place to live somewhere else for the following reasons:

CIRCUMSTANCES

[ ] Dwelling rented to previously approved applicant

[ ] Unsigned application   [ ] Incomplete application

[ ] Discrepancies on application

CREDIT REPORT (If items here are checked, see attachment.)

[ ] Credit not verifiable   [ ] Bankruptcy filed

[ ] Judgments, garnishments, liens   [ ] Slow pay

[ ] Account(s) sent for collection   [ ] Low credit score

INCOME/ASSETS

[ ] Income not verifiable   [ ] Insufficient income

[ ] Assets not verifiable   [ ] Insufficient assets

EMPLOYMENT HISTORY

[ ] Employment not verifiable   [ ] Unsteady employment

[ ] Temporary employment

TENANCY HISTORY

[ ] Tenancy not verifiable   [ ] Eviction on record

[ ] Late payments   [ ] Insufficient funds checks

[ ] Agreement violation(s)   [ ] Lack of cooperation

PERSONAL REFERENCES

[ ] References not verifiable   [ ] Negative reference

OTHER REASONS

_____

Your application will remain in our files for a minimum of two years. If you would like to discuss it or our reasons above, please contact us for an appointment.

We wish you good luck in finding an even better place to live.

Sincerely,

Rental Agreement

Dated: _____

Agreement between Owners: _____
and Tenants: _____
for a dwelling located at: _____

[Initial ONE of the boxes below to indicate whether this Agreement is month-to-month or fixed term.]

☐ **Month-to-Month Agreement**—Tenants agree to rent this dwelling on a month-to-month basis beginning _____.

☐ **Fixed-Term Agreement (Lease)**—Tenants agree to lease this dwelling for a fixed term of _____, beginning _____ and ending _____.
Upon expiration, this Agreement shall become a month-to-month agreement AUTOMATICALLY, UNLESS either Tenants or Owners notify the other party in writing at least thirty days prior to expiration that they do not wish this Agreement to continue on any basis.

Rent—Tenants agree to rent this dwelling for $_____ per _____, payable in advance. The first month's rent is $_____.

Rent Due/Late Consequences—Rent is due on the _____. It is late on the _____. Owners expect to RECEIVE the rent BEFORE the late date. Should exceptional circumstances prevent prompt payment, _____.

Returned Checks—If, FOR ANY REASON, a check used by Tenants to pay Owners is returned without having been paid, Tenants will pay a returned check charge of $_____ AND take whatever other consequences there might be in making a late payment. After the second time that a Tenants' check is returned, Tenants must thereafter secure a cashier's check or money order for payment of rent.

Form of Payment—Tenants agree to pay rent in the form of a personal check, a cashier's check, or a money order made out to _____.

Rent Payment Procedure—Tenants agree to pay their rent in the following way:

_____

Deposits—Tenants agree to deposit with the Owners the sum of $_____, payable before they occupy the premises. Owners may withhold from these deposits only what is reasonably necessary to cover the following tenant defaults: 1) damages to the dwelling; 2) certain cleaning costs following Tenants' departure; and 3) unpaid rent and various other accrued and unpaid charges. Tenants may not apply any part of these deposits to their last month's rent.

Refund of Tenants' Deposits—Within _____ days after Tenants have moved out completely, Owners shall provide a written accounting of the disposition of the Tenants' deposits and shall at the same time return all deposits remaining.

Utilities/Services—Tenants agree to pay all utilities and services with the exception of the following which Owners agree to pay:_____

Occupants—In addition to the Tenants mentioned above, only the following persons may live in this dwelling:

_____
No one else may live there, even temporarily, without Owners' prior written permission.

Guests—Tenants may house any single guest for a maximum period of fourteen days every six months or for whatever other period of time the law allows. Provided that they maintain a separate residence, nurses or maids required to care for Tenants during an illness are excepted from this provision.

Subletting and Assignment—Tenants shall not sublet the entire premises or any part of the premises, nor shall they assign this Agreement to anyone else without first obtaining the Owners' written permission. Owners shall not withhold permission unreasonably.

Pets—Tenants have received permission to house the following pet(s) on the premises:

_____

Tenants may house no other pet of any kind on the premises, even temporarily, without first obtaining Owners' written permission. "Pets" includes, but is not limited to, both warm- and cold-blooded animals, such as dogs, cats, fish, hamsters, rats, birds, snakes, lizards, and insects. "Pets" does not include animals trained to serve the handicapped, such as seeing-eye dogs, hearing dogs, or service dogs. These animals may be housed on the premises so long as they are in the direct service of those they were trained to serve and so long as Owners are notified in advance in writing of the circumstances.

Liquid-filled Furniture—Tenants agree not to keep any liquid-filled furniture in this dwelling without first obtaining Owners' written permission.

Vehicles—Tenants agree to park their vehicles in assigned spaces and to keep those spaces clean of oil drippings. Tenants agree to keep no more than _____ vehicle(s) on the premises. Vehicle(s) must be both operable and currently licensed. Tenants agree to advise their visitors about parking and to take responsibility for where their visitors park. Only those motorcycles which have exhaust muffling comparable to that of a passenger car are allowed. Only those self-propelled recreational vehicles which are used for regular personal transportation are allowed. Tenants agree not to park boats, recreational trailers, utility trailers, and the like on the premises without first obtaining Owners' written permission. Tenants agree not to repair their vehicle(s) on the premises if such repairs will take longer than a single day unless the vehicle is kept in an enclosed garage.

Appliances—Although the following appliances are presently in the dwelling:

_____

the use of these appliances is not included in the rent. If Tenants wish to use these appliances, they agree to assume all responsibility for care and maintenance. If Tenants wish to use their own appliances, they may request that the owner's appliances be removed from the premises.

Tenant Inspection—Tenants have inspected the dwelling and its contents and agree that they are in satisfactory order, as are the electrical, plumbing, and heating systems.

Notification of Serious Building Problems—Tenants agree to notify the Owners immediately upon first discovering any signs of serious building problems such as a crack in the foundation, a tilting porch, a crack in the plaster or stucco, moisture in the ceiling, buckling sheetrock or siding, a leaky roof, a spongy floor, a leaky water heater, or termite activity.

Reasonable Time for Repairs—Upon being notified by Tenants that there is some building defect which is hazardous to life, health, or safety, Owners shall undertake repairs as soon as possible. Should there be a delay of more than seventy-two (72) hours in making the repairs, due to a difficulty in scheduling the work or obtaining parts or for any other reason beyond the Owners' control, Owners agree to keep Tenants informed about the progress of the work.

Windows—Except for those windows which are noted in writing as being cracked or broken when Tenants move in, Tenants agree to be responsible for any windows which become cracked or broken in their dwelling while they live there. Tenants may repair the windows themselves if they can do the work in a professional manner. Otherwise, they may hire a glazier or submit a maintenance request to Owners. If they submit a maintenance request, Owners will charge them no more for the work than the least expensive written bid for the work which Tenants can obtain.

Drain Stoppages—As of the date of this Agreement, Owners warrant that the dwelling's sewage drains are in good working order and that they will accept the normal household waste for which they were designed. They will not accept things such as paper diapers, sanitary napkins, tampons, children's toys, wads of toilet paper, balls of hair, grease, oil, table scraps, clothing, rags, sand, dirt, rocks, or newspapers. Tenants agree to pay for clearing the drains of any and all stoppages except those which the plumber who is called to clear the stoppage will attest in writing were caused by defective plumbing, tree roots, or acts of God.

Trash—Tenants agree to dispose of their ordinary household trash by placing it into a receptacle for periodic collection. They agree to dispose of their extraordinary household trash, such as Christmas trees, damaged furniture, broken appliances, and the like, by compacting it so that it will fit inside their trash receptacle or by hauling it to the dump themselves or by paying someone else to haul it away.

Outside Placement—Owners reserve the right to place trash receptacles, portable storage units, and the like wherever convenient on the premises. Owners further reserve the right to construct property improvements above or below the ground anywhere on the premises so long as they conform to all building codes.

Damage—Tenants agree to pay for repairs of all damage which they or their guests have caused.

Locks—Tenants agree that they will not change the locks on any door or mailbox without first obtaining Owners' written permission. Having obtained permission, they agree to pay for changing the locks themselves and to provide the Owners with one duplicate key per lock.

Lockouts—Should Tenants lock themselves out of their dwelling and be unable to gain access through their own resources, they may call upon a professional locksmith or the manager to let them in. In either case, they are responsible for payment of the charges and/or damages involved. Management charges a fee of $15 for providing this service between the hours of 8 a.m. and 6 p.m., Monday through Saturday, excepting holidays, and a fee of $25 at other times. This fee is due and payable when the service is provided.

Landscaping—[*This paragraph applies only if it is initialed by both parties.*] Tenants agree to maintain the existing landscaping by watering, weeding, fertilizing, mowing, and shaping it as necessary.

Alterations, Decorations, and Repairs—Except as provided by law, Tenants agree not to alter or decorate their dwelling without first obtaining Owners' written permission. Decorations include painting and wallpapering. Further, Tenants agree not to repair their dwelling or anything belonging to the Owners without first obtaining Owners' written permission unless such repairs cost less than one hundred dollars ($100), and Tenants agree to pay for them. Tenants shall hold Owners harmless for any mechanics liens or proceedings which Tenants cause. When approved by Owners, Tenants' plans for alterations and decorations shall bear a determination regarding ownership. If Tenants are able to convince Owners that Tenants can remove the alterations or decorations and restore that part of their dwelling to its original condition, then Owners may grant Tenants the right to remove them. Otherwise, any alterations or decorations made by Tenants become the property of Owners when Tenants vacate.

Painting—Owners reserve the right to determine when the dwelling will be painted unless there is any law to the contrary.

Access—Owners recognize that Tenants have a right to privacy and wish to observe that right scrupulously. At certain times, however, Owners, their employees, or agents may have to gain access to the Tenants' dwelling for purposes of showing it to prospective Tenants, purchasers, lenders, or others or for repairs, inspection, or maintenance. When seeking access under ordinary circumstances, Owners will schedule entry between the hours of 8 a.m. and 8 p.m., Monday through Saturday, excepting holidays, and Owners will provide Tenants reasonable notice of twenty-four hours, or less than twenty-four hours notice with Tenants' concurrence. In emergencies, there will be no notice.

Peace and Quiet—Tenants are entitled to the quiet enjoyment of their own dwelling, and their neighbors are entitled to the same. Tenants agree that they will refrain from making loud noises and disturbances, that they will keep down the volume of their music and broadcast programs at all times so as not to disturb other people's peace and quiet, and that they will not install wind chimes.

Telephone—If and when Tenants install a telephone in their dwelling, they will furnish Owners with the number within five calendar days. When divulging the number, Tenants shall advise Owners whether the number is listed or unlisted. If it is unlisted, Owners agree to take reasonable precautions to keep it from falling into the hands of third parties.

Prolonged Absences—Tenants agree that they will notify Owners whenever they plan to be absent from their dwelling for more than ten days.

Business Use—Tenants agree to use this dwelling as their personal residence. They agree to conduct no business on the premises without first obtaining Owners' written permission.

Lawful Use—Tenants agree that they will not themselves engage in any illegal activities on the premises nor will they allow others to engage in any illegal activities on the premises insofar as they have the power to stop such activities.

Insurance—Owners have obtained insurance to cover fire damage to the building itself and liability insurance to cover certain personal injuries occurring as a result of property defects or owner negligence. Owners' insurance does not cover Tenants' possessions or Tenants' negligence. Tenants shall obtain a Tenants' insurance policy to cover damage to or loss of their own possessions, as well as losses resulting from their negligence. Tenants agree to show Owners evidence of such a policy within one month from the date of this Agreement.

Insurance Considerations—Tenants agree that they will do nothing to the premises nor keep anything on the premises which will result in an increase in the Owners' insurance policy or an endangering of the premises. Neither will they allow anyone else to do so.

Fire or Casualty Damage—During any time when the dwelling cannot be used because of fire or casualty damage, Tenants are not responsible for payment of rent. Should a portion of the dwelling become unusable due to fire or casualty damage, Tenants are not responsible for payment of rent on that portion. In either case, Owners reserve the right to decide whether the dwelling is usable and what portions are usable. Owners are not responsible for repairing or replacing any improvements made by Tenants if those improvements are damaged. Should the fire or casualty damage have been caused by Tenants' own action or neglect, they shall have not be relieved of the responsibility for payment of rent, and they shall also bear the full responsibility for repair of the damage.

Rules and Regulations—Owners' existing rules and regulations, if any, shall be signed by Tenants, attached to this Agreement, and incorporated into it. Owners may adopt other rules and regulations at a later time provided that they have a legitimate purpose, not modify Tenants' rights substantially, and not become effective without notice of at least two (2) weeks.

Service of Process—Every Tenant who signs this Agreement agrees to be the agent of the other Tenants and occupants of this dwelling and is both authorized and required to accept, on behalf of the other Tenants and occupants, service of summons and other notices relative to the tenancy.

Identity of Manager—The person who is responsible for managing this dwelling and is authorized to accept legal service on Owners' behalf is _____whose address is

_____.

Changes in Terms of Tenancy—[*This paragraph applies only when this Agreement is or has become a month-to-month agreement.*] Owners shall advise Tenants of any changes in terms of tenancy with advance notice of at least _____ days. Changes may include notices of termination, rent adjustments, or other reasonable changes in the terms of this Agreement.

Notice of Intention to Vacate—[*This paragraph applies only when this Agreement is or has become a month-to-month agreement.*] When Tenants have decided to vacate the premises, they will give Owners written notice of their intentions at least _____ days prior to their departure, and they will give an exact date when they expect to be moved out completely.

Holding Over—If Tenants remain on the premises following the date of their termination of tenancy, they are "holding over" and become liable for "rental damages" equaling one/thirtieth of the amount of their then current monthly rent for every day they hold over.

Possession—Owners shall endeavor to deliver possession to Tenants by the commencement date of this Agreement. Should Owners be unable to do so, they shall not be held liable for any damages Tenants suffer as a consequence, nor shall this Agreement be considered void unless Owners are unable to deliver possession within ten (10) days following the commencement date. Tenants' responsibility to pay rent shall begin when they receive possession.

Sale of the Dwelling—If Owners sell this dwelling or otherwise transfer its Ownership to another party, they shall have the right to terminate this Agreement by giving Tenants written notice of at least sixty days, notwithstanding any conflicting occupancy rights Tenants might have under a fixed-term agreement. Should Tenants have conflicting occupancy rights guaranteed them by law, however, those legal rights shall prevail.

Illegal Provisions Not Affecting Legal Provisions—Whatever item in this Agreement is found to be contrary to any local, state, or federal law shall be considered null and void, just as if it had never appeared in the Agreement, and it shall not affect the validity of any other item in the Agreement.

Non-Waiver—Should either Owners or Tenants waive their rights to enforce any breach of this Agreement, that waiver shall be considered temporary and not a continuing waiver of any later breach. Although Owners may know when accepting rent that Tenants are violating one or more of this Agreement's conditions, Owners in accepting the rent are in no way waiving their rights to enforce the breach. Neither Owners nor Tenants shall have waived their rights to enforce any breach unless they agree to a waiver in writing.

References in Wording—Plural references made to the parties involved in this Agreement may also be singular, and singular references may be plural. These references also apply to Owners' and Tenants' heirs, executors, administrators, or successors, as the case may be.

Application Part of Agreement—The rental application Tenants submitted to rent this dwelling forms a part of this Agreement. Falsified information on the application shall be considered a breach of this Agreement.

Entire Agreement—As written, this Agreement constitutes the entire agreement between the Tenants and Owners. They have made no further promises of any kind to one another, nor have they reached any other understandings, either verbal or written.

Consequences—Violation of any part of this Agreement or nonpayment of rent when due shall be cause for eviction under appropriate sections of the applicable code.

Trial by Judge—[*This paragraph applies only if it is initialed by both parties.*] Should any aspect of this Agreement or tenancy be litigated in civil court, Owners and Tenants agree to waive their rights to a trial by jury and have the matter tried by a judge.

Legal Service's Fees—If either party to this Agreement shall bring a cause of action against the other party for enforcement of the Agreement, the prevailing party [*cross out the alternative which does not apply and initial the beginning of this paragraph*] (shall) (shall not) recover reasonable legal service's fees involved.

Other—_____

_____

Acknowledgment—Tenants hereby acknowledge that they have read this Agreement, understand it, agree to it, and have been given a copy.

_____   _____
Owner   Tenant

_____   _____
BY Person authorized to represent Owners   Tenant

Rental Agreement—Page 5 of ___

Rental Agreement

Dated_____

(Month-to-Month)

Agreement between_____, Owners,
and _____, Tenants, for a dwelling
located at _____.
Tenants agree to rent this dwelling on a month-to-month basis for $_____ per
month, payable in advance on the _____ day of every calendar month to Owners
or their Agent*, _____, whose address is

_____.
When rent is paid on or before the _____ day of the calendar month, Owners
will give Tenants a (discount) (rebate) of $_____.

The first month's rent for this dwelling is $_____.

The security/cleaning deposit on this dwelling is $_____. It is
refundable if Tenants leave the dwelling reasonably clean and undamaged.

Tenants will give ___ days' notice in writing before they move and will
be responsible for paying rent through the end of this notice period or until
another tenant approved by the Owners has moved in, whichever comes first.

Owners will refund all deposits due within ___ days after Tenants have
moved out completely and returned their keys.

Only the following ___ persons and ___ pets are to live in this dwelling:

_____
Without Owners' prior written permission, no other persons may live there,
and no other pets may stay there, even temporarily, nor may the dwelling be
sublet or used for business purposes.

Use of the following is included in the rent: _____

_____

Remarks: _____

_____

TENANTS AGREE TO THE FOLLOWING:
1) to accept the dwelling "as is," having already inspected it.
2) to keep yards and garbage areas clean.
3) to keep from making loud or bothersome noises and disturbances and to
   play music and broadcast programs at all times so as not to disturb other
   people's peace and quiet.
4) not to paint or alter the dwelling without first getting Owners' written
   permission.
5) to park their motor vehicle in assigned space and to keep that space
   clean of oil drippings and grease.
6) not to repair their motor vehicle on the premises (unless it is in an
   enclosed garage) if such repairs will take longer than a single day.
7) to allow Owners to inspect the dwelling, work on it, or show it to
   prospective tenants at any and all reasonable times.
8) not to keep any liquid-filled furniture in this dwelling.
9) to pay rent by check or money order made out to Owners. (Checks must be
   good when paid or applicable late-payment consequences will apply.)
10) to pay for repairs of all damage, including drain stoppages, they or
   their guests have caused.
11) to pay for any windows broken in their dwelling while they live there.

Violation of any part of this Agreement or nonpayment of rent when due
shall be cause for eviction under applicable code sections. The prevailing
party (shall) (shall not) recover reasonable legal services fees involved.

Tenants hereby acknowledge that they have read this Agreement, understand
it, agree to it, and have been given a copy.

Owner_____ Tenant_____

*By_____ Tenant_____
*Person authorized to accept legal service on Owners' behalf

Rental Application for (address)_____

Name_____ Home Phone_____ Work Phone_____

Social Sec. No._____ Drivers License No._____ Date of Birth_____

Present Address_____
   How long at this address?_____ Rent $_____ Reason for moving_____

Owner/Manager_____ Phone_____

Previous Address_____
   How long at this address?_____ Rent $_____ Reason for moving_____

Owner/Manager_____ Phone_____

Name and relationship of every person to live with you, even if only temporarily (include ages of minors):
_____
_____

Any pets?_____ Describe_____ Waterbed?_____

Present Occupation_____ Employer_____ Phone_____
   How long with this employer?_____ Supervisor_____ Phone_____

Previous Occupation_____ Employer_____ Phone_____
   How long with this employer?_____ Supervisor_____ Phone_____

Current Gross Income Per Month (before deductions) $_____

List sources and amounts of other income_____

Amount of alimony and/or child support you receive $_____ or pay $_____

Savings Account: Bank_____ Branch_____ Account Number_____

Checking Account: Bank_____ Branch_____ Account Number_____

Major Credit Card_____ Account Number_____ Average Balance_____ Expires_____

Credit Reference_____ Account Number_____ Balance Owed_____ Monthly Payment_____

Credit Reference_____ Account Number_____ Balance Owed_____ Monthly Payment_____

HAVE YOU ever filed bankruptcy?_____ ever been evicted?_____ ever been convicted of a felony?___

Vehicle(s) Make(s)_____ Model(s)_____ Year(s)_____ License(s)_____

Personal Reference_____ Address_____ Phone_____

Contact in Emergency_____ Address_____ Phone_____

I declare that the statements above are true and correct. I authorize verification of my references and credit as they relate to my tenancy and to future rent collections.

Date_____ Signed_____

Verified: SSN____ DL/ID____ CurTenancy____ Prev____ Credit____ Inc____ PersRefs____ By_____

RENTAL APPLICATION INSTRUCTIONS

We appreciate your interest in the rental dwelling we currently have available. Because we want to rent this dwelling to people who are considerate of their neighbors, clean in their living habits, capable of paying the rent, and prompt in paying their bills, we use a rental application to help us determine whether our applicants meet these qualifications.

In order for you to rent from us, you must complete a rental application. We want you to know how to complete the application we use, and we also want you to know what our company does with your application.

When filling out the application, put something in every blank, even if you have to put "None" or "N.A." in some blanks. Try to write so that your entries fit in the spaces provided. If they don't, continue them on the back side. Take your time and look up any information called for on the application which you're at all uncertain about. Don't guess.

Make sure that you read the declaration just above the signature line and agree to it before you sign your name to the application. It states that the information on your application is true and correct, and it authorizes us to verify your references and your credit as they relate to your tenancy now and to your paying rent in the future.

When you have completed your application, read it over carefully to make sure that it is accurate, complete, and legible. Look especially for misspellings and transposed numbers.

Once we receive your application, we verify as much of it as we can. If you look at the last line on the application itself, you will notice all of the things we verify. We verify your Social Security number (SSN), your driver's license (DL) or personal identification number (ID), your current tenancy (CurTenancy), your previous tenancy (Prev), your credit (Credit), your income (Inc), and your personal references (PersRefs). When we have verified each of these items, we put a check mark next to its abbreviation.

We verify this information in a variety of ways. We look at your Social Security card or some other evidence of your Social Security number. We look at your actual driver's license or some other official picture identification which you use whenever you cash a check. We call your current landlord or manager to ask whether the information you put on your application is correct about how long you've been at your current address, how much you've been paying in rent, and why you are moving. Then we call your previous landlord or manager and ask the same questions about your previous tenancy.

At the same time that we order a credit report, we also order an eviction report and a bad check report. The credit report tells us whether you pay your bills on time. The eviction report tells us whether you have ever been evicted and why. The bad check report tells us whether you write bad checks.

Next, we call whoever can verify your source of income to determine how much you generally receive from that source every month and how long you have been receiving it.

Finally, we call your personal references to verify that they know you and that we have their correct addresses and phone numbers so that we can contact them should anything happen to you.

That's the procedure we follow when we check applications.

Now, if you suspect we might discover a "skeleton in your closet" when we check your application and you want to tell us about it before we go to all the trouble of checking you out, please feel free to do so. We'd be glad to talk with you about it. Otherwise, we will expect no surprises when we're checking you out and hope that we will soon be doing business together as landlord and tenant.

| Form E-3 | RENTAL INCOME AND EXPENSE | YEAR | | |

| NAME(S) OF TAXPAYERS | SOC. SEC. NUMBER | | | |

PROPERTY LOCATION & DESCRIPTION		GROSS INCOME
Property A		
Property B		
Property C		
Property D		
Property E		
Property F		
Property G		
	TOTAL GROSS INCOME	

EXPENSES	A	B	C	D	E	F	G	Totals
Interest								
Taxes, Licenses								
Insurance								
Utilities								
Serv,Rep,Maint.								
Merch., Supplies								
Payroll								
Misc. Expenses								
Other:								
Subtotal								
% Business Use								
Subtotals								
Deprec. (D-1)								*
Deprec. (SD)								*
Totals								

*Sum of D-1 and SD Depreciation Totals   *

Request for Verification of Deposit

Instructions: Landlord—Complete items 1 through 7. Have applicant(s) complete item 8. Forward directly to depository named in item 1. Depository—Please complete items 9 through 15 and return DIRECTLY to landlord named in item 2.

Part I—Request

1. To (Name and Address of Depository)	2. From (Name and Address of Landlord)	
3. Signature of Landlord/Manager	4. Title	5. Date

6. INFORMATION TO BE VERIFIED

Type of Account	Account in Name of	Account Number	Balance
			$
			$
			$
			$

To Depository: I/We have applied to rent a dwelling and stated in the rental application that the balance on deposit with you is as shown above. You are authorized to verify this information and to supply the landlord identified above with the information requested in items 9 through 12. Your response is solely a matter of courtesy for which no responsibility is attached to your institution or any of your officers.

7. Name and Address of Applicant(s)	8. Signature of Applicant(s)

To Be Completed by Depository

Part II—Verification of Depository

9. Deposit Accounts of Applicant(s)

Type of Account	Account Number	Current Balance	Average Balance for Previous Two Months	Date Opened
		$	$	
		$	$	
		$	$	
		$	$	

10. Bank Card Accounts of Applicant(s)

Type of Bank Card	Account Number	Current Balance	Average Monthly Payment	Expiration Date
		$	$	
		$	$	

11. Loans Outstanding to Applicant(s)

Loan Number	Date of Loan	Original Amount	Current Balance	Installments		Secured by	No. Late Pmts.
		$	$	$	per		
		$	$	$	per		

12. Please include any additional information which may be of assistance in determination of credit worthiness. (Please include information on loans paid-in-full in item 11 above.)

13. Signature of Depository	14. Title	15. Date

The confidentiality of the information you have furnished will be preserved except where disclosure of this information is required by applicable law. The form is to be transmitted directly to the landlord and is not to be transmitted through the applicant(s) or any other party.

Roommate Agreement Dated _____

(Addendum to Rental Agreement)

This Agreement amends, is incorporated into, and forms a part of the Rental Agreement dated _____ between _____, Owners, and _____, Tenants.

Tenants, also known here as "Roommates," desire to rent the premises on a "roommates arrangement." Owners agree to this arrangement under the following terms and conditions:

ROOMMATE APPROVAL AND SUBSTITUTION--Every person who wishes to become a Roommate under this Agreement, whether as an original Roommate or as a substituted Roommate, must first submit a Rental Application and be approved by Owners in writing. Owners, at their option, may require substituted Roommates to sign the existing Rental Agreement or may require an entirely new agreement to be signed by the substituted Roommates and the remaining Roommates. Upon substitution of Roommates, Owners may elect to increase the deposit.

FINANCIAL RESPONSIBILITY--Each Roommate agrees to be jointly and severally liable to the Owners for the entire rent and the entire amount of any other charges incurred under the Rental Agreement.

DEPOSITS--Roommates agree to pay deposits to Owners in the form of a single certified check or money order. Owners will hold all deposits until the entire dwelling has been vacated completely. Owners may make deposit refunds in the form of a single check made payable jointly to all Roommates with rights to the deposits. This check and the itemized accounting of deposit deductions may be sent to any one of the Roommates with rights to the deposits.

DEPARTING ROOMMATES--Roommates who move out while this Agreement is in effect continue to have financial responsibility under this Agreement unless Owners release them from this responsibility in writing or unless they are replaced by substituted Roommates approved by Owners. Upon being relieved of financial liability, departing Roommates relinquish all rights to the deposits.

MAXIMUM NUMBER OF ROOMMATES ALLOWED--Without the prior written approval of Owners, Roommates may at no time exceed _____ in number.

GUESTS--Tenants may house any single guest for a maximum period of fourteen days every six months or for whatever other period of time the law allows. Guests may at no time exceed _____ in number.

COMMUNICATIONS--Whenever Owners give a notice to one Roommate, it shall be considered as having been communicated to all Roommates. Whenever one Roommate gives a notice to the Owners, it shall be considered as having been communicated from all Roommates.

Owner _____   Roommate _____

By _____   Roommate _____

                                   Roommate _____

Page _____ of _____

SITE VISIT Property Name:_____ Date:_____

Needs Attention:_____

_____

_____

_____

Safety Concerns:_____

_____

_____

_____

Comments:_____

_____

_____

_____

Paperwork/Logbook:_____

_____

_____

Looks Good:_____

_____

_____

Vacancies (circle if ready to rent):_____

_____

Visitor's Followup:_____

_____

_____

Visited by:_____ Time:_____ Expenses:_____

STORAGE AGREEMENT

THIS CONTRACT LIMITS OWNER'S LIABILITY—READ IT

PARTIES—THIS AGREEMENT, dated _____, is by and between

_____, "Owner," and

_____, "Occupant,"

for storage of a vehicle, boat, trailer, or other personal property located at the following address:

_____.

OCCUPANT'S ADDRESS: _____

OCCUPANT'S ALTERNATIVE ADDRESS: _____

[ ]   INDOOR STORAGE—Unit: _____

[ ]   OUTDOOR STORAGE—Personal Property to be Stored—

Type: _____

Description (Color, etc.): _____

Dimensions: _____

Identification Number: _____

License Number (State, too): _____

Legal Owner (Name, Address, Phone): _____

_____

Registered Owner (Name, Address, Phone): _____

_____

TERM—Occupant agrees to rent the space for storage on a month-to-month basis beginning _____.

RENT—Occupant agrees to pay Owner, without deduction, the sum of $_____ per month, payable in advance, on the first (1st) day of each month of the term hereof. Rent paid more than ___ days following the due date is subject to a late fee of ten percent (10%) of the month's rent. Under no circumstances will prepaid rents be refunded.

CONSIDERATION FOR EXECUTION OF AGREEMENT—Owner hereby acknowledges receipt of $_____ from Occupant which covers the first full month's rent under this agreement and any prorations necessary to pay rent to the first of the following month, plus any other sums here identified _____. Payment pays rent through _____.

TERMINATION—Either party may terminate this agreement by giving the other party thirty days' written notice, and the rent shall be paid through that date.

USE OF SPACE--Occupant agrees to use the space only for the storage of property wholly owned by Occupant and to store said property under his/her own supervision and control. Occupant shall not store or use or produce on the premises any materials which are classified as hazardous or toxic under any local, state, or federal law or regulation. Occupant shall not store illegal substances, perishables, food items, explosives, paint, varnish, thinner, gasoline, and/or other highly flammable materials. Occupant shall not use the space for any business or for manufacturing or production, nor for human or animal occupancy. Occupant shall not create a nuisance or permit creation of a nuisance on or near the storage premises. Occupant shall remove all trash brought onto the space. Occupant shall not use any electricity in the space for any purpose whatsoever other than for lighting and then only while Occupant is present. Occupant shall turn off lights when leaving space.

OCCUPANT'S AFFIRMATIVE COVENANTS--Occupant agrees to the following:
   1) To lock the personal property and keep it secure,
   2) To drain all water lines during the wintertime in order to prevent any damage that may be caused to same due to low winter temperatures, and
   3) To obtain insurance to cover the property and contents thereof as Occupant is hereby informed that Owner does not carry such insurance. To the extent that Occupant does not maintain insurance, Occupant shall be completely "self-insured" and shall bear all risk of loss or damage.

WAIVER OF LIABILITY--Occupant, as a material part of the consideration under this agreement, hereby waives all claims against Owner for any damage or loss from any cause, other than the negligence of Owner, arising at any time, including but not limited to fire, theft, acts of God, vandalism or any physical damage while the Occupant's personal property remains in the storage area. Occupant does hereby agree to indemnify and hold Owner harmless from and on account of any damage or injury to any person, equipment, or personal property arising from any cause, other than the negligence of Owner, or from the negligence of Occupant, Occupant's family, or Occupant's guests.

SELF-SERVICE STORAGE FACILITY LAWS--This storage agreement is governed by the laws applied to self-service storage facilities in this locality.

ILLEGAL PROVISIONS NOT AFFECTING LEGAL PROVISIONS--Whatever item in this Agreement is found to be contrary to any local, state, or federal law shall be considered null and void, just as if it had never appeared in the Agreement, and it shall not affect the validity of any other item in the Agreement.

ACKNOWLEDGEMENT--Occupant hereby acknowledges that he or she has read this agreement, understands it, agrees to it, and has been given a copy.

_____   _____
               Owner   Occupant

_____   _____
BY Person authorized to represent Owner or Occupant

STORAGE AGREEMENT--Page 2 of 2

Summary of Business & Statement of Income

Property _____ Period_____

#										
1										
2										
3	INCOME									
4	Rental									
5	Other									
6	TOTAL INCOME									
7										
8										
9										
10										
11										
12	EXPENSES & PAYMENTS									
13	Interest									
14	Taxes, Licenses									
15	Insurance									
16	Utilities									
17	Services, Repairs, Maintenance									
18	Merchandise, Supplies									
19	Payroll									
20	Miscellaneous Expenses									
21	Depreciable									
22	Mortgage Principal									
23	Non-deductible									
24										
25										
26	TOTAL EXPENSES & PAYMENTS									
27	minus Non-deductible (line 23)									
28	TOTAL									
29	minus Depreciable (line 21)									
30	TOTAL									
31	minus Mortgage Prin. (line 22)									
32	TOTAL NET EXPENSES (for tax purp.)									
33										
34	TOTAL INCOME (line 6)									
35	minus line 28									
36	CASH FLOW									
37										
38										
39										
40										
41										

464

SUPPLEMENTAL DEPRECIATION

Form SD

YEAR

| NAME(S) OF TAXPAYERS | | SOC. SEC. NUMBER | | | |

CAPITAL IMPROVEMENT LOCATION & DESCRIPTION

1

2

3

4

5

6

7

	1	2	3	4	5	6	7	Totals
Date Acqd. or Conv. to Bus.								
New or Used								
Cost or Other Basis								
Salvage Value								
1st Year Special Depreciation								
Depreciable Basis								
Prior Depreciation								
Depreciable Balance								
Method of Depreciation								
Useful Life								
Full Year Depreciation								
Percentage of Year Held								
Percentage for Business Use								
Depreciation This Year								

PAGE TOTAL

Dear

    You probably know already that the building where you live has changed hands. Because tenants usually feel some apprehension every time such a changeover occurs, we would like to take this opportunity to clear the air by letting you know just what you can expect in the future about a few things.

    DEPOSITS...One special concern you must have is your deposits. We are concerned, too, and we want to make absolutely certain that all of your deposits are credited to you. To avoid any misunderstandings about your deposits and other matters related to your living here, we would like you to answer the questions on the sheet attached. They are questions which you should be able to answer quickly from memory or by referring to information readily available to you. Please do so as soon as possible and return your answers to us in the envelope provided.

    PAYMENT BY CHECK OR MONEY ORDER...Since it is unwise for anyone to keep or carry cash around in quantities, we request that you pay your rent by check or money order (made payable to us exactly as underlined below). You will be protected and so will we.

    PROMPT PAYMENT...You are expected to pay your rent within three days after the due date. For example, rent due on the first must be paid by the fourth at the very latest. If you anticipate being late beyond that for any reason whatsoever, please let us know beforehand. If you don't, we will assume that you are deliberately avoiding payment, and we will immediately serve you with the notice which starts eviction proceedings.

    MAINTENANCE...We expect you to pay your rent promptly, and you can expect us to respond promptly to maintenance problems. Sometime within the next week, we will visit you to inspect for any building maintenance work that should be taken care of. You can help by starting now to make a list of such work which you notice around the house.

    RENTAL AGREEMENT...We will also stop by soon to explain to you the standard rental agreement we use, and we will leave you with a copy of your own.

    We are reasonable people and we will try anything within reason to make living here enjoyable for you, but naturally we need your cooperation. If we have it, we will get along well together and we can all take pride in this place that you call home.

                Sincerely,

Tenant Information:

Your Name_____

Your Address_____Soc. Sec. No._____

Your Home Telephone Number_____Work Phone_____

Who lives with you? (Include ages of children, please) _____

_____

What pet(s) do you have? _____

Do you have a waterbed? _____

What vehicle(s) do you have? Make(s)_____ License(s)_____

Where do you work? (Company name) _____

Where does your co-tenant work? (Company name)_____

When did you move in?_____

What is your current rent per month?_____

What date is your rent paid up to right now?_____

When is your rent due each month?_____

What refundable deposits have you paid? Keys $_____ Security $_____

    Cleaning $_____ Other (please explain) $_____

When you moved in, you paid your first month's rent. Did you also then

    pay your last month's rent? _____ If so, how much was it? $_____

Which of the following furnishings in your dwelling belong to the

    owners of the building? (Please give room locations where

    appropriate.)

    Carpets_____ Drapes_____

    Shades_____ Blinds_____

    Stove_____ Refrigerator_____

    Other appliances? (Please list)_____

    Other furniture? (Please list)_____

Do you have a rental agreement or lease in writing?_____

    If so, what is the date of the latest one?_____

In case of an emergency, what friend or relative should we contact?

    Name_____ Telephone Number_____

Date _____ Your Signature_____

Tenant Record Property _____

Unit	Tenant	Phone	Date Moved In	Moved Out	Rent Date	Rent	Deposit	Bank/Chkg. Acct. Nos.
1								
2								
3								
4								
5								
6								
7								
8								
9								
10								
11								
12								
13								
14								
15								
16								
17								
18								
19								
20								
21								
22								
23								
24								
25								
26								
27								
28								
29								
30								
31								
32								
33								
34								
35								

Time Sheet

Employee's Name _____   Property _____

Employee's Signature _____   Pay Period _____ to _____

Date	Times		Hours	Description of Work Performed	Contract Amount

Total Hours _____   Total Contract _____

Rate _____

Hourly Gross _____

Contract _____

Total Gross _____   Approved by _____   Date

TIMELY MAINTENANCE GUARANTEE

The management responsible for maintaining the dwelling located at the address given below hereby guarantees to repair any defects discovered in the dwelling which are hazardous to life, health, or safety within seventy-two hours (three days) following notification by the tenants who occupy the dwelling. Tenants' notice may be either verbal or written, but it must be *acknowledged* in writing by someone whom management has authorized to accept such notice.

Should management fail to repair the defects, either temporarily or permanently, within seventy-two hours (three days), tenants shall be relieved of the responsibility for paying rent for every day or portion thereof during which the defects go unrepaired following the initial seventy-two-hour (three-day) period allotted for completing this work in a timely manner. Tenants' responsibility for paying rent shall begin again once the defects have been repaired.

To receive the benefit of any rent abatement owed to them under this guarantee, tenants must be current in their rent payments and must pay their next rent in full when due. Whatever rent abatement is owed will then be paid to them in the form of a rebate within forty-eight hours following receipt of their rent payment.

This guarantee applies only to those defects which are the responsibility of management to maintain as mandated by law and/or as outlined in the applicable lease or rental agreement.

This guarantee does not apply when a portion of the dwelling becomes uninhabitable as a result of flooding, fire, earthquake, or an act of God, and the tenants choose to remain in residence during reconstruction. In such cases, management and tenants will negotiate a fair rent covering the reconstruction period.

This guarantee shall remain in effect so long as there is a valid lease or rental agreement between the parties below covering the dwelling located at the address given below.

Dated _____ Address _____

Tenants _____

Owner/Manager _____

Waterbed Agreement

Dated _____

(Addendum to Rental Agreement)

    This agreement is attached to and forms a part of the Rental Agreement dated _____ between _____, Owners, and _____, Tenants.
    Tenants desire to keep a waterbed described as _____ _____ in the dwelling they occupy under the Rental Agreement referred to above, and because this agreement specifically prohibits keeping waterbeds without the Owners' permission, Tenants agree to the following terms and conditions in exchange for this permission:

1) Tenants agree to keep one waterbed approved by Owners for this dwelling. Waterbed shall consist of a mattress at least 20 mil thick with lap seams, a safety liner at least 8 mil, and a sturdy frame enclosure made of plywood or solid natural wood only, no particle board.

2) Tenants agree to consult with the Owners about the location of the waterbed. They agree to hire qualified professionals to install and dismantle the bed according to the manufacturer's specifications and further agree not to relocate it without the Owners' consent.

3) Tenants agree to allow Owners to inspect the waterbed installation at any and all reasonable times, and Tenants agree to remedy any problems or potential problems immediately.

4) Tenants agree to furnish Owners with a copy of a valid liability insurance policy for at least $100,000 covering this waterbed installation and agree to renew the policy as necessary for continuous coverage.

5) Tenants agree to pay immediately for any damage caused by their waterbed, and in addition, they will add $_____ to their security/cleaning deposit, any of which may be used for cleaning, repairs, or delinquent rent when Tenants vacate. This added deposit, or what remains of it when waterbed damages have been assessed, will be returned to Tenants within _____ days after they prove that they no longer keep this waterbed.

6) In consideration of the additional time, effort, costs, and risks involved in this waterbed installation, Tenants agree to pay additional rent of $_____, which /includes/does not include/ the premium for the waterbed liability insurance policy referred to in item 4.

7) Tenants agree that the Owners reserve the right to revoke this permission to keep a waterbed should the Tenants break this agreement.

Owner _____   Tenant _____

By _____   Tenant _____

Page_____ of _____

"WEAR AND TEAR" OR "DAMAGES"?

"Normal wear and tear" caused by ordinary comings and goings	"Damage" caused by carelessness, abuse, thievery, mysterious disappearance, accident, rules violation, or special request
Well-worn keys	Missing keys
"Sticky" key	Key broken off inside lock
Balky door lock	Door lock replaced by tenant without management's permission
Depressurized fire extinguisher with unbroken seal	Depressurized fire extinguisher with broken seal (not used to put out fire)
Worn pattern in plastic countertop	Burn in plastic countertop
Rust stain under sink faucet	Sink discolored by clothing dye
Loose, inoperable faucet handle	Missing faucet handle
Rusty refrigerator shelf	Missing refrigerator shelf
Discolored ceramic tile	Painted ceramic tile
Loose grout around ceramic tile	Chipped or cracked ceramic tile
Carpet seam unraveling	Carpet burn
Threadbare carpet in hallway	Rust marks on carpet from indoor plant container
Scuffing on wooden floor	Gouge in wooden floor
Linoleum with the back showing through	Tear in linoleum
Wobbly toilet	Broken toilet tank lid
Rusty shower curtain rod	Kinked shower curtain rod
Rust stain under bathtub spout	Chip in bathtub enamel
Tracks on doorjamb where door rubs	Hole in hollow-core door
Door off its hinges and stored in garage	Missing door
Plant hanger left in ceiling	Two-inch-diameter hole in ceiling
Stain on ceiling caused by leaky roof	Stain on ceiling caused by popping champagne or beer bottles
Cracked paint	Crayon marks on wall
Chipped paint (minor)	Walls painted by tenant in dark color necessitating repainting
Pleasing, professional tenant wallpapering	Amateurish tenant wallpapering
Mildew around shower or tub	Mildew where tenant kept aquarium
Urine odor around toilet	Urine odor in carpet
Discolored light fixture globe	Missing light fixture globe
Odd-wattage lightbulbs which work	Burned out or missing lightbulbs
Light fixture installed by tenant which fits its location	Light fixture installed by tenant which must be replaced
Window cracked by settling or high wind	Window cracked by movers
Faded shade	Torn shade
Paint-blistered Venetian blinds	Venetian blinds with bent slats
Sun-damaged drapes	Pet-damaged drapes
Drapery rod which won't close properly	Drapery rod with missing parts
Dirty window screen	Missing, bent, or torn window screen
Ants inside after rain storm	Fleas left behind by tenant's pet
Scrawny landscaping which was sparingly watered due to drought conditions	Neglected landscaping which must be replaced with similar plantings
Grease stains on parking space	Caked grease on parking space

WHAT DO YOU KNOW ABOUT LANDLORDING MAINTENANCE?

1. How do you repair a toilet which cycles on and off all by itself every twenty minutes or so?

2. How do you repair a burn in a kitchen counter made of Formica® laminate?

3. How do you repair a four-inch hole in a hollow-core door?

4. How do you remove a bathtub spout without putting any permanent marks on it?

5. A new tenant calls to report that half of an electrical outlet doesn't work. How do you fix it?

6. What's the difference between fuses and circuit breakers?

7. Describe the function of each of the following: closet auger, drum auger, Teflon® tape, hack saw, saber saw.

8. What determines whether a doorknob lock is installed right-side up or upside down?

9. Where should you be sure to install a smoke detector?

10. Prioritize the following maintenance tasks: sweep the parking area, unclog a garbage disposer, replace an outside light, paint a bathroom in a vacant apartment, change locks for a tenant whose boyfriend moved out yesterday.

WHAT DO YOU KNOW ABOUT RENTAL PROPERTY MANAGEMENT?

1. How do you determine the market rent for a vacant apartment?

2. If an applicant must have a gross income of three and a half times the rent, how much of an income does the applicant need in order to qualify to rent a house which rents for $1,250 per month?

3. We always collect an entire month's rent and all the deposits whenever a tenant moves in, and we prorate the rent for the second month when it comes due. Let's say that some tenants move in on the twentieth of August. Their rent is $900 and their deposits are $975. How much do you collect from them before they move in, and how much do you collect from them when their September rent comes due?

4. Give several legal reasons you might use for refusing to rent to someone.

5. Under what three circumstances may you enter a tenant's dwelling when the tenant is not at home?

6. Our rental agreement states that the rent must be paid by check or money order, not in cash. How do you respond to a late-paying tenant who offers to pay everything up in cash on a Friday afternoon?

7. What's a realistic late fee for an apartment which rents for $750 per month?

8. How do you begin an eviction for nonpayment of rent?

9. When a tenant calls to give you notice that she's moving, what should you do above all?

10. Prioritize the following tasks which need to be done before a certain vacant apartment can be re-rented: "steam" clean the carpets, dry-clean the draperies, re-key the locks, patch a doorknob hole in a bedroom wall, advertise, replace a broken window, paint the rooms which need painting.

Your Pet and You

Please provide us with a photograph of your pet, plus some specifics about your pet and you. This information will help us make an informed decision when we are considering your pet and you as tenants for our rental dwelling.

Your name_____ Date_____

Description...pet's name, breed, age, weight, size (give height and length), activity level, and traits

_____

_____

Training...obedience school or other training (give dates, too)

_____

_____

Activities...exercise (give type and frequency)

_____

_____

Health...spayed or neutered; vaccinations; health exams (give schedule); veterinarian (give name and phone number)

_____

_____

Grooming...schedule of grooming; groomer (give name and phone number)

_____

_____

Care arrangements...caretaker during absences (give name and phone number)

_____

_____

Commitment...duration of relationship with this pet; pet license particulars; membership in animal protection organizations such as the S.P.C.A. (Society for the Prevention of Cruelty to Animals); willingness to put up an additional deposit

_____

_____

References...people who know your pet and you (give names and phone numbers)

_____

_____

Sources & Resources

The information given here was checked for accuracy when this edition of *Landlording* went to press. Surely some of it was outdated already when the book came off the press. If you have trouble locating any of these sources or resources, consult the reference librarian at your local public library or log onto the Internet and go to one of the search engines such as Google or Yahoo. Search there on the name itself or else search on "directories" to find websites which provide current listings for all kinds of organizations and businesses.

For your information, I have no financial relationship with any organization or company mentioned here and stand to profit nothing from your contributions to the organizations or from your purchases of these companies' products, that is, with the notable exception of any purchases you might make of my own books and software, all of which I recommend here shamelessly.

Associations & Organizations

American Association of Small Property Owners. 1101 30th Street, N.W., Suite 500, Washington, D.C., 20007. (aaspo.org) 202.625.8330.

This advocacy group concerns itself with the formidable task of educating politicians at every level about the practical consequences of proposed or already implemented regulations concerning the buying, selling, owning, and managing of real property. Its newsletter informs members about what's happening with matters such as rent control, taxes, inspection fees, and environmental issues. When your state or local politicians are debating some issue which puts still another burden on the small property owner, you can count on this association's experts and advisors to provide you with the best arguments against it which you may use when presenting the rental property owners' side before your leg-

islators or city council. You can also count on this association to argue for you as a small property owner when relevant matters come before Congress.

HALT. 1612 K Street, NW, Suite 510, Washington, DC 20006. (halt.org) 888.367.4258.

HALT stands for "Help Abolish Legal Tyranny." It's a non-partisan membership organization founded in 1977 to reduce the cost and improve the quality of legal services in America. Such modest goals! Methinks that researchers will find cures for cancer and heart trouble long before legal services improve in this country. We have to start sometime somewhere, however, and HALT is a very good start. HALT also publishes a series called Citizens Legal Manuals, one of which is about real estate and another of which is about shopping for a lawyer. They're useful and so is the organization.

National Apartment Association. 1111 14th Street, NW, Suite 900, Washington, DC 20005. (naahq.org) 202.842.4050.

Most state and local rental housing associations are affiliated with the National Apartment Association, which is headquartered in the nation's capitol and acts as lobbyist, trade association, and information repository for rental property owners. Anyone who wants to keep abreast of what Washington is doing to help or hinder our business at a national level would do well to read NAA's monthly *Multihousing Advocate*. Anyone who wants to locate a state apartment association should contact the NAA as well.

Pacific Legal Foundation. 10360 Old Placerville Road, Suite 100, Sacramento, CA 95827. (pacificlegal.org) 888.367.4258.

This nonprofit organization should not be necessary in a free, self-governing society. People living in a free society ought to have enough common sense to realize that private property rights are sacrosanct and absolutely vital to the workings of such a society. Unfortunately, they don't, not even here in the United States, where private property rights are guaranteed by the Constitution. Every day zealous government officials and government agencies appropriate people's property rights through a variety of legitimate and quasi-legitimate means such as rent control, zoning, and environmental regulations. Every day property owners choose not to fight the "taking" of their property because fighting is so costly. They cannot afford to "fight city hall" for years and years. Enter the Pacific Legal Foundation. Its attorneys take on cases involving property rights and personal rights where government has overstepped the boundaries of fairness. They will take cases all the way to the U.S. Supreme Court, too, if they have to, just as they did when they helped a widow fight for eight years for the right to build a house on a lot she owned in a built-out subdivision. If you are concerned about your property rights, if you want to help champion a just cause, if you want to keep abreast of what's happening with legal challenges to rent control, support this organization. It's a good one. What it's doing is right up every landlord's alley.

Books—Investment

When you notice the publication dates for some of the books in this and the following four sections, you might wonder why books more than twenty years old, some of which are out of print, are listed here. They're here because they're good. They're here because they're not as dated as you might think. They're here because they're readily available in libraries and through Internet searches. They're here because new print technology enables publishers to reprint out-of-print books in small quantities profitably. Your interest in these books will awaken publishers to this possibility.

Bruss, Robert. *The Smart Investor's Guide to Real Estate: Big Profits from Small Investments*. New York: Crown, 1989.

Real estate's "Answer Man," the syndicated columnist who answers everybody's real estate questions in his "Real Estate Mailbag" column, has gathered all of his sound advice together here in this one place. To make the book especially understandable, he has spiced his advice with numerous practical examples showing how real estate ideas apply to real-world situations. He has

also included selected answers to the many questions asked of him over the years.

de Heer, Robert. *Realty Bluebook*. 155 N. Wacker Drive, Chicago, IL 60606. (dearborn.com) 800.551.0709: Real Estate Education Company, 2001.

Written primarily for real estate salespeople, it includes some stuff you might not be interested in, but it does have some most helpful tax information and explanations of real estate contract clauses. A newly revised edition comes available every three years. It's now published in two volumes—volume one is sales techniques, financing, checklists, clauses, risk management, and tax information; volume two is tables.

Gardner, Scott. *Live Rent-Free for Life and Other Incredible Revelations About NYC Rent Control*. Box 248, 1173-A Second Ave., New York, NY 10021: Free-Rent Press, 1990.

This book doesn't belong in the category of "Investment Books," not really. It deserves a category all its own. That category should be "Anti-Investment Books," for this is a sad tale of someone who tangled with New York City's rent control establishment and lost big. The tale is uneven, but it's heartfelt and full of clever black humor. You have to sympathize with the poor author who barely escaped with the shirt on his back after enduring ten years as the owner of six units in New York City, all tenanted by professional people. Yes, New York City landlords do have some scary stories to tell, and we all ought to be listening. There but for the grace of God go we.

Hare, Patrick; Jolene Osler. *Creating an Accessory Apartment*. New York: McGraw-Hill, 1987.

The in-law apartment has come a long way, baby! Variously known as an "outlawed in-law" and a "bootlegged apartment" because its very existence so often violated building and zoning codes, the "accessory apartment," as it's called in this book, is seeing a resurgence in popularity. Partly, this popularity is a result of the demand for inexpensive housing, and partly it's a result of a change in the laws. Many communities now permit homeowners to modify their homes and create accessory apartments legally. If you can visualize the possibility of creating an accessory apartment in, under, on, or beside any house you own, read this book before you take the first step. It's written by two land-use planners who have guided homeowners through the process every step of the way. It'll surely save you grief.

Lowry, Albert. *How You Can Become Financially Independent by Investing in Real Estate.* New York: Simon & Schuster, 1982.

The Lowry-Nickerson Real Estate Investors Seminar was a fixture on the American scene for years. I'd be willing to bet that it produced more graduates who went on to become millionaires than the nation's leading school of business produced since the year it was founded. Because Lowry was involved so long with this successful teaching program, you might suspect that he has a lot to say about the subject matter. You also might suspect that the subject matter is going to be pretty well organized. You'd be right on both counts. Lowry's book summarizes on half a page his tested, foolproof formula for becoming financially independent; then it goes on to detail the many do's and don'ts involved in making that formula work.

Maloney, Roy. *Real Estate Quick & Easy.* 1706 Gough St., San Francisco, CA 94109: Dropzone Press, 1999.

Ever have somebody sit down with you and explain patiently and concisely just what "cap rate," "internal rate of return," "gross rent multiplier," "mechanic's liens," "prescriptive easement," "riparian rights," and the "Rule of 72" are? That's what this book does. It explains hundreds of real estate terms and concepts in the simplest way possible, through illustrations, graphs, and a highly condensed text. Use it as you would a real estate dictionary. It has an ample index useful for this very purpose.

Nickerson, William. *How I Turned $1,000 into Five Million in Real Estate in My Spare Time.* New York: Simon & Schuster, 1980.

This book is classic enough so that most buyers of rental property know what a "Nickerson" is (it's a fixer-upper with potential for forced appreciation, yielding at least two dollars of added value for every dollar spent on fixing it up). The book is loaded with sage advice and good information about purchasing, improving, managing, and trading rental properties. Sure, it's an old book, even the 1980 revision, but the techniques it espouses for pyramiding your real estate wealth remain the same today as they did when it was first published in 1959, when you could buy rental properties any day of the month for $5,000

a unit. Anyone who bought the book back then and bought properties according to Nickerson's twenty-year plan couldn't fail to have become a millionaire by 1979. Any edition of the book will do. Just roll your eyes at the numbers in the early editions and pay attention to the formulas. They're still valid today.

Reed, John. *How to Increase the Value of Real Estate.* 342 Bryan Dr., Alamo, CA 94507 (johntreed.com): Reed Publishing; published on demand.

Most people wait around for the value of their real estate to go up, and sooner or later it usually does. That's the slow track. If you'd rather be on the fast track to real estate wealth, you need to know as many ways as possible to force the value of your real estate to go up. Here's a book which examines all kinds of ways, from the obvious to the obscure. Not only does it examine the ways, it provides the mathematics to show you how the ways work.

Scher, Les; Carol Scher. *Finding and Buying Your Place in the Country.* Chicago, IL (dearborn.com): Dearborn Financial Publishing, 2000.

This book does cover country property, but there's so much that urban and suburban property have in common with country property that you'll want to examine a copy of this book even though you never plan to leave West 89th Street. It's very thorough. It tells about dealing with insurance agents, lawyers, lenders, neighbors, partners, real estate agents, sellers, and tax assessors, not so that you can take advantage of them, but so that they won't take advantage of you, whether you're a city hick or a country slicker.

Books—Law & Eviction

The first three books are intended for use only in California.

California Apartment Association. *Managing Rental Housing.* 980 Ninth St., Suite 2150, Sacramento, CA 95814, (ca-apartment.org): California Apartment Association, 2000.

This extensive compilation of "official" residential rental property information includes some text about tenancies, portions of the California codes pertaining to rental dwellings, some legal case citings, a batch of attorney-reviewed forms which have been approved by the CAA, and short explanations of how the forms are to be used.

Because the compilers do not want you to photocopy the forms right out of the book, however, they have overprinted each one with a large "SAMPLE" in shaded letters. You must either buy the forms from your local apartment association or type them out yourself. That drawback aside, I recommend the book as an indispensable reference work for California landlords.

Moskovitz, Myron; Ralph Warner; and Stephen Elias. *California Tenants' Rights.* 950 Parker St., Berkeley, CA 94710 (nolo.com): Nolo.com, 2001.

Some landlords might think that this is the enemy's battle plan and might even regard it offensive. Some of it is. But it is primarily defensive. After all, there are a few unscrupulous landlords lurking about, and tenants do need help in dealing with them. Your reading the book will give you a chance to consider the tenant's point of view for a change.

Robinson, Leigh. *The Eviction Book for California.* Box 1639, El Cerrito, CA 94530 (landlording.com): ExPress, 2001.

It details each step of the entire legal eviction process in California and includes the forms necessary to do an eviction yourself. When you've exhausted every possible method for getting problem tenants to move without resorting to the courts, find a copy of this book and get them out by going into court. It also covers certain other matters related to evictions, such as how to handle tenants who declare bankruptcy, how to handle tenants who stop paying rent for a garage or self-storage unit, how to evict a former owner from a foreclosure property, how to handle squatters, how to handle nonpayment and noncompliance in a mobilehome or RV park, and how to collect a money judgment.

Stewart, Marcia; Ralph Warner; and Janet Portman. *Every Landlord's Legal Guide.* 950 Parker St., Berkeley, CA 94710 (nolo.com): Nolo.com, 2000.

This is not one of those impressively bound tomes which line the walls of attorneys' offices and are dusted more often than they're consulted. This is a frank and friendly law book written by attorneys who are committed to making accurate legal information available to the uninitiated. Go to Nolo's website and read the sample chapter. Included with the book is a CD-ROM with forms.

Books—Maintenance

Ebeling, Walter. *Urban Entomology.* Berkeley, CA: University of California, Division of Agricultural Sciences, Publications Office, 1978.

More than a big book about the bugs plaguing city dwellers, it's over six hundred pages of detailed, factual information about all kinds of cosmopolitan pests, from cockroaches to snakes. It explains where they come from, how they live, and how they die. It may save you from having to hire a professional exterminator when your tenants are demanding that you eradicate an "infestation" of an unfamiliar bug, two of which they saw sauntering across their kitchen counter on a Sunday morning. Though this book is now out of print, you may be able to find a copy at your local library or in a used bookstore.

How Things Work in Your Home (and What to Do When They Don't). Alexandria, VA: Time-Life Books, 1987.

In clear illustrations and tight prose, this book outlines how plumbing, electrical, heating, and cooling systems work. It explains how the various components of these systems operate, and it details ways to troubleshoot malfunctioning heaters, appliances, septic tanks, faucets, and the like.

Reader's Digest New Complete Do-It-Yourself Manual. Pleasantville, NY: The Reader's Digest Association, 1991.

It's a valuable book full of good illustrations and photographs. If you have a job to do, like pouring a cement walkway or repairing a decayed threshold, you can look the subject up in the index and then turn to practical hints for doing the job right the very first time you do it.

Reader's Digest New Fix-It-Yourself Manual. Pleasantville, NY: The Reader's Digest Association, 1996.

Shhh, don't tell anybody, but the "complete" manual above wasn't 100% complete. Here's more of the same, just as good. It was recently republished.

Robinson, Robert. *Complete Course in Professional Locksmithing.* 111 N. Canal St., Chicago, IL 60606: Nelson-Hall Co. 1973.

As the title indicates, this is a training manual for professionals, and it includes much more than you'll ever want or need to know about locksmithing, such as using car opening tools and laying out a locksmithing shop, but it also includes the basics—lock picking, key duplication, master keying, and lock maintenance.

Books—Management

Bierbrier, Doreen. *Living with Tenants: How to Happily Share Your House with Tenants for Profit and Security.* P.O. Box 5602, Arlington, VA 22205: The Housing Connection. 1992.

Anyone who contemplates sharing a house with a roomer should find out how this specialized kind of landlording works. After sharing her house with roomers, Bierbrier has made most of the mistakes and most of the discoveries. You ought to make the most of what she's written on the subject. She also wrote *Managing Your Rental House for Increased Income,* published by Bantam in 1991, in which she writes about tenanting rental houses with single people whose aggregate rent is greater than what a single family would pay.

Bramson, Robert M. *Coping with Difficult People.* New York: Dell. 1988.

Strictly speaking, this is not a rental property management book as are the other books under this heading, but it belongs here anyway because it clearly identifies the various types of difficult tenants we landlords encounter, and it describes various ways of coping with them. Difficult tenants can make your life as a landlord pretty miserable if you let them. They tend to bring out the worst in you and make you do things which you come to regret later. This book helps you understand what's really happening when somebody is being difficult so that you will be able to respond sensibly and solve problems rather than exacerbate them. There's nothing quite like this book. It's a seminal work. Reading it will make you a better landlord.

Cain, Christopher. *Maximize Your Resort Property Investment Business.* 1007 Green Branch Court, Oviedo, FL 32765: Christopher Communications. 1985.

For anyone who rents out a vacation home by the week or weekend and wants help in making it pay, this book is a treasure-trove of good ideas. There are ideas for finding renters on your own, dealing with management companies, handling emergencies from a distance, and keeping people coming back year after year. Be forewarned that if you use all of this book's good ideas, your vacation home will be so booked up that you won't

be able to find accommodations there for yourself. You'll have to rent someone else's. That, I suppose, is the epitome of success in the vacation home rental business.

Edwards, Brian F.; Casey Edwards; and Susannah Craig. *The Complete Idiot's Guide to Being a Smart Landlord.* 201 West 103d Street, Indianapolis, IN 46290 (idiotsguides.com): Alpha Books. 2000.

One of the "Idiot's Guides" series, this book follows the series formula with lots of graphics and lists. If you like the series, you'll like this book. It makes a commendable effort to include specific legal requirements for each state, but you may want to use the Internet to check the current requirements for your state before you bet the farm on them. It includes sixteen blank forms, although they're in a strange multi-page format dictated by the book's physical dimensions.

Griswold, Robert. *Property Management for Dummies.* 909 Third Ave., New York, NY 10022 (hungryminds.com): Hungry Minds. 2001.

Another in the "Dummies" series, this is as good a starting place as any for somebody who knows absolutely nothing about landlording. It makes the reader hungry for more. If you buy either the "dummy" or the "idiot" book, put a brown paper wrapper around its cover. You don't want to give your tenants any wrong ideas about your intelligence.

Kelley, Edward. *Practical Apartment Management.* 430 No. Michigan Ave., Chicago, IL 60611-4090 (irem.org): Institute of Real Estate Management. 1994.

This is a somewhat pedantic, but competent, treatment of the subject, written primarily for the managers of large apartment complexes who aren't owners themselves but need to learn to think like owners.

Lowry, Albert. *How to Manage Real Estate Successfully in Your Spare Time.* New York: Simon & Schuster. 1980.

This book's strong suit is sales, finding warm bodies and getting them to rent empty apartments. It should be particularly helpful to anyone who's trying to fill a new apartment building in an area where others are trying to do the same.

Perry, Greg. *Managing Rental Properties for Maximum Profit.* 3000 Lava Ridge Ct., Roseville,

CA 95661 (primalifestyles.com): Prima Publishing. 2000.

This book has ideas all its own. They're not ones I readily agree with. For example, I don't agree that landlords should omit their telephone numbers from classified ads and rely strictly on open houses. I don't agree that landlords should bother to record tenants' lease agreements at the county courthouse. I don't agree that widely separated rental properties ought to have their locks keyed alike for the landlord's benefit. I do agree that landlords ought to open escrow accounts for deposits. I could go on. Let's just say that this book has a unique personality, one you might want to acquaint yourself with.

Reed, John. *How to Manage Residential Property for Maximum Cash Flow and Resale Value.* 342 Bryan Dr., Alamo, CA 94507 (johntreed.com): Reed Publishing; published on demand.

Should you suspect that you're becoming soft in the heart, read this book. It's written by someone who's hard-hearted, hard-headed, and hard-nosed about rental properties. He's the kind whose heart is eagerly sought after for transplants. It's been so little used. Contrary to what you might think, the book does not come with a black cape, glue-on handlebar mustache, and braided cowhide whip. They're extras.

Robinson, Leigh. *What's a Landlord to Do?* Box 1639, El Cerrito, CA 94530 (landlording.com): ExPress, 2001.

The title of this book is a question because the book itself consists of questions, questions, and more questions. They are questions submitted by many landlords and a few tenants through the landlording.com website. My answers follow every question. Many of the questions I never could have imagined myself, such as the one about coping with the strong odors of East Indian cooking at a duplex. Even though I couldn't have imagined the questions, I could imagine the answers. They're here for you to read.

Books—Tax

Bernstein, Peter W. (ed.). *The Ernst & Young Tax Guide.* New York: John Wiley & Sons; published annually.

There is a book within this book. It's the official IRS tax guide called *Your Income Tax*, and it's reproduced here in its entirety. Arthur Young's (one of the country's top accounting firms) experts expand upon the official IRS information with clear examples, explanations, and tips, all of which are printed on a light blue background so they're easily distinguishable from what the IRS has to say on each subject. The book includes some sample returns, the blank forms you're most likely to need, a glossary of tax and financial terms, and even a special table of contents for the real estate investor.

Reed, John. *Aggressive Tax Avoidance for Real Estate Investors.* 342 Bryan Dr., Alamo, CA 94507 (johntreed.com): Reed Publishing; published on demand.

This "English-language translation" of income tax laws affecting real estate investors minces no words. With mathematical proof, it explains why you should be aggressive in those many gray areas of tax law, and then it shows you how to be aggressive. The book's rules for understanding income taxes may surprise you, but unless you follow them, you're paying more taxes than the law requires. It explains depreciation and exchanging clearly and also tells how to find a good, aggressive tax adviser. It's revised annually to reflect changes in the tax laws themselves and in their interpretation.

Catalogs from Various Suppliers

Catalog shopping has become more and more popular since the first big gas crisis. It is still growing in popularity, and no wonder. It's fun. It's convenient. It saves time. It saves fuel. It offers wide variety. It offers value, and it allows for easy comparison shopping.

Each of the companies listed here publishes a catalog and maintains a website which you may use no matter where you or your rental properties happen to be; some of them also have various locations scattered about the country. Except as noted, the offices listed here are main offices. Contact that office to learn whether there is a location near you.

American Blinds and Draperies. 1168 San Luis Obispo Avenue, Hayward, CA 94544. (americandrapery.com) 800.972.0660; in northern California, call 510.487.3500.

American has become one of the largest apartment drapery, mini-blind, and vertical blind manufacturers in the country by offering landlords long-lasting window coverings at factory-direct wholesale prices. They maintain a large inventory, so they can and will ship most standard sizes the same day they get your order, provided you call before 10:30 a.m. Contact them before you need window coverings in a hurry, and ask them to send you a free information kit with samples, prices, and a credit application. Mention this book when you call to order and ask for a special discount.

Grainger. 5959 W. Howard St., Chicago, IL 60648. (grainger.com) 800.473.3473.

This thick (almost 4,000 pages; more than five pounds), informative catalog lists thousands upon thousands of products, including almost every known electric motor for both general and specialized applications. It also lists compressors, pumps, light fixtures, carpet steam cleaners, electric drain augers, hand tools, testing devices, and so on and so on. The listings include ample information and descriptions to help you select the right item for your application. In addition, it has many pages of technical data and terminology, including a decimal equivalent chart and the codes and standards for plumbing products. Grainger's many branch locations stock lots of catalog items and offer same-day pickup. Call the toll-free number above and ask them to send you one of their catalogs. It doubles as a dumbbell.

Maintenance Warehouse. P.O. Box 85838, San Diego, CA 92186. (mwh.com) 800.431.3000.

This company, now owned by Home Depot, specializes in providing most of the tools, equipment, materials, and supplies we landlords use in our maintenance rounds. In fact, Maintenance Warehouse sells only to the owners and managers of rental housing. Were you to make a list of the many things you use most often and replace most often around your rental property, chances are good that you'd find them all in this catalog. It has faucet parts, stove parts, locksmithing supplies, ganged mailboxes, paint, appliance dollies, cleaning supplies, stove top fire extinguishers, and more, lots more. Need only a toilet tank lid to replace the one a tenant broke with a karate chop? They've got 'em. Need a "shoe" for a toilet? They've got 'em. What's a toilet shoe? It's something designed to hide the ruined or unsightly floor covering surrounding a toilet base. Who else but landlords would ever need a toilet shoe? To guarantee speedy shipment, they direct orders automatically to the warehouse nearest you. Shipping is included on orders totaling more than $50, that is, except for some heavy or bulky items, and orders reach 90% of the U.S. population the day after they're placed. Get one of their wonderful catalogs. Maintenance Warehouse offers a truly unique service, one-call shopping for landlording necessities. Their 1732-page catalog is a must, and it's free for the asking.

Peachtree. P.O. Box 13290, Atlanta, GA 30324. (pbp1.com) 800.241.4623.

Peachtree carries a full line of rental property management forms and other related products, including stationery, parking control supplies, and rent payment systems. They offer free imprinting and free shipping, too.

Recreonics, Inc. 4200 Schmitt Ave., Louisville, KY 40213. (recreonics.com) 800.428.3254.

Looking for something which goes in, on, under, over, or near a swimming pool? You'll find it in this company's extensive catalog listing everything remotely connected with swimming pools, both big and small.

Safe-Hit Corporation. 23785 Cabot Blvd. #322, Hayward, CA 94545. (safe-hit.com) 800.537.8958.

This company makes all kinds of parking and traffic-control signs, as well as traffic guideposts. What's unique about the signs is their flexibility. Bad drivers can run into them and damage neither the signs nor their own cars.

Sears, Roebuck and Co. Contract Sales. 800.359.2000.

Sears, Roebuck and Company is an American institution, but the Sears of today is a very different company from the Sears of yesteryear. It no longer dominates retailing, and it no longer publishes the famous Sears catalog. Nonetheless, it is still very much in business. One of its divisions, which you may not have encountered before and which you as a landlord ought to know something about, is Sears Contract Sales. It publishes a catalog listing items such as refrigerators, stoves, and coin-operated laundry machines, and it sells them for less than Sears in-store prices. Call the 800 number above and ask for a catalog.

Seton Name Plate Corporation. P.O. Box 819, Branford, CT 06405-0819. (seton.com) 800.338.5810.

In this catalog you'll find in-stock and custom signs, stickers, labels, markers, tags, name plates, badges, and decals of all kinds. Need a fire extinguisher sign, an OSHA sign, or a "NO PARKING ANY TIME" sign? Seton has 'em. It also has spray-can graffiti remover and changeable-letter boards which make fine tenant directories for apartment houses.

USA Bluebook, a division of Utility Supply of America. P.O. Box 9004, Gurnee, IL 60031. (usabluebook.com) 800.548.1234.

Have your own well or wastewater treatment system (a septic tank qualifies)? Then you need a copy of USA Bluebook. It lists all kinds of equipment and supplies used in water and wastewater systems, such as pumps of every variety, water meters, safety equipment, and handbooks, plus testing and troubleshooting equipment like underground leak detectors, plastic pipe locators, and sewer pipe videocameras.

Wilmar Industries. 303 Harper Drive, Moorestown, NJ. (wilmar.com) 800.523.7120.

This company bought out the long-established Pier-Angelli Company. It continues in the Pier-Angelli mold as one of the best sources for hard-to-find plumbing parts and hardware. Their large catalog has lots of technical illustrations which make the positive identification of parts as easy as it can be. They ship most orders free of charge from warehouses scattered throughout the country.

Computer Software

These software selections offer good value for money. Yet all of them are quite capable and deliver on their promises. As noted, all of them run on computers using either the Windows or the Macintosh operating systems or both.

AppleWorks® (Macintosh only). Apple Computer, 2420 Ridgepoint Dr., Austin, TX 78754. (apple.com) 800.692.7753.

This integrated software program, preloaded on every new Macintosh, has everything most landlords need to do their word and number processing. It also includes a database component which works much like a stripped-down version of FileMaker. AppleWorks can import and export files in a variety of formats, and it can mix capabilities within documents. In other words, you can put a little spreadsheet directly into a letter you're writing and use both word processor and spreadsheet functions on the same page. It works so smoothly that you'd swear you were driving a computer with an automatic transmission.

Eviction Forms Creator™ (California only) (Windows & Macintosh). ExPress, P.O. Box 1639, El Cerrito, CA 94530. (landlording.com) 800.307.0789.

"Tedious" is the word for the task of filling out all the forms required to evict a tenant through California courts. They require a lot of very repetitive typing. I wrote this program to make the task much easier and much less time-consuming. Enter the name and address of the tenant you're evicting, yourself, and the court, and the program puts those particulars on all the forms in just the right places. Then it prints the forms for you, including the state-mandated Judicial Council forms and many of the locally mandated forms as well, all on plain paper.

FileMaker® (Windows & Macintosh). FileMaker, 5201 Patrick Henry Drive, Santa Clara, CA 95054. (filemaker.com) 800.325.2747.

Anyone who has ever attempted to learn how to use a computerized database management system such as dBASE® will recognize with even a cursory glance just how well-designed FileMaker is. It's especially easy for a non-programmer to learn, set up, and use, and it stores and sorts graphic images as well as alphanumeric data. You could use it for keeping track of your bookkeeping, your buildings (including pictures), your various types of units (including floor plans), your vacancy statistics, your tenants, your loan schedules, your paint cans, your rental furniture, your competition, your ships as they come in, or your cows as they come home. I used FileMaker myself to write both Pushbutton Landlording and Eviction Forms Creator. It's an awesome program. It's the biggest selling database for the Macintosh and the biggest selling database for Windows, that is, when purchased as simply a database and not as part of a larger collection of programs.

Landlording® on Disk (The Forms) (Windows & Macintosh). ExPress, P.O. Box 1639, El Cerrito, CA 94530. (landlording.com) 800.307.0789.

There's nothing awesome here, but you could go a long way toward automating your entire landlording empire with a word processing program, a spreadsheet program, a checkwriting program, and what's on this disk. I have. The disk consists of three major components—all the wordy forms from the *Landlording* book, more than thirty in all, those which can be "word processed" sensibly; more than a dozen spreadsheet templates, including the one shown in chapter 20, and others which calculate loan payments, create loan tables, figure depreciation, and keep track of income; plus a Quicken "jump-start kit," which contains categories (a chart of accounts) specifically designed for landlording and tailor-made spreadsheet templates designed for massaging the data captured by Quicken. Do keep in mind that the word processing forms have to be used with a program capable of reading word processing files, the templates have to be used with a program capable of reading spreadsheet files, and the jump-start kit has to be used with Quicken (see description which follows). They cannot be used by themselves. This is not a "stand-alone program." You could enter everything which comes on this disk into your computer yourself if you were so inclined, but you'd have to spend many hours doing so. This disk is an inexpensive alternative.

Microsoft® Works (Windows only). Microsoft, One Microsoft Way, Redmond, WA 98052. (microsoft.com).

Preloaded on many Windows machines, Microsoft Works is a powerhouse. Like AppleWorks, it may be all the software you need for handling documents and numbers. Its various components will enable you to create documents, spreadsheets, and databases plus keep a personal calendar and an address book and handle your email. Give it a chance before you lay out the bucks for Microsoft Office.

Pushbutton Landlording® (Windows & Macintosh). ExPress, P.O. Box 1639, El Cerrito, CA 94530. (landlording.com) 800.307.0789.

Like the book you are holding in your hands, this program is my own creation. It does virtually everything a computer can do to help the landlord run a landlording business except write checks. It doesn't write checks because Quicken (see below) handles that task better than any single component of a landlording software package ever could. Pushbutton Landlording handles the income and tenant side of the business. You enter information about yourself, your rental property, and your tenants, and it will produce rental agreements, condition and inventory checksheets, rent receipts, monthly statements, maintenance work orders, notices to pay rent or

quit, tenant lists, tenant mailing labels, and a variety of reports. It all works with pushbuttons, hence the name. You push a few buttons, and it will tell you whose rent is one day or more late. You push another button, and it will create late-rent notices for those late tenants. It's a marvel, even if I do have to say so myself.

QuickBooks® (Windows only). Intuit, P.O. Box 28815, Tucson, AZ 85726-8815. (intuit.com) 800.446.8848.

Do not be deceived by this remarkable program. It's inexpensive, readily available, and widely used, and it seems simple enough at first glance, but it will either work wonders for you or cause you grief. Don't start using it right out of the box without first taking the time to learn how to use it right either by studying the user guide, by watching instructive videotapes, by hiring a tutor who knows the program intimately, or by taking a class at your local adult school. It's much more than it seems. It's not just a checkwriting program. It's an accounting program, a double-entry accounting program at that, and you must know at least the rudiments of accounting to take advantage of its many capabilities and benefits. It writes checks. It lists payables. It tracks expenses. It handles payroll. It produces balance sheets. It doesn't sing or dance, but it does reward the knowledgeable user many times over with useful reports and graphs. We use it in our operations. We know it. We love it.

Quicken® (Windows & Macintosh). Intuit, P.O. Box 28815, Tucson, AZ 85726-8815. (intuit.com) 800.446.8848.

Writing checks and reconciling your bank statement were never easier. This program handles your bookkeeping through your checkbook. Write a check and the amount is automatically deducted from your checking account register at the same time the expenditure is posted to the proper category. It stores information for recurring transactions like the loan payments you make every month. It prints checks with the payee's address so they can be inserted into window envelopes, and it produces any number of reports. It can also export data easily into a spreadsheet program. I recommend Quicken highly.

TurboTax® and *MacInTax®* (Windows & Macintosh). Intuit, P.O. Box 28815, Tucson, AZ 85726-8815. (intuit.com) 800.446.8848.

Seeing either of these programs for the first

time is like seeing color TV after a lifetime of viewing black-and-white. Right on the computer's screen are facsimiles of the familiar IRS forms themselves. You enter the appropriate figures once in the same boxes you'd be using if you were filling out the forms manually, and the programs do all the calculations for you. All of the forms are linked, too; complete Schedule E, and the appropriate figures are posted automatically to your 1040. Change something on Schedule E, and everything which is related to it throughout your return will be changed as well. Do "what if" calculations on any part of your return and you'll know instantly how they affect the results. In addition, the entire IRS instruction booklet is "on-line," that is, it's part of the program and available for retrieval on command. Want information about a particular item on an IRS form? Point to that line and click. Presto, the IRS helps appear. No IRS agent could possibly be any faster! Want to print out your return? Well, how do you want it? On blank paper or on the actual IRS pre-printed forms? You make the choice. The IRS will accept either one. If the IRS were sending U.S. taxpayers a manual version and a computer version of its 1040 tax reporting package, these would be the computer versions. I can't imagine better ones. They reduce the onerous tax-preparation chore from days to hours, and they're totally accurate. What's more, they're inexpensive, and you needn't spend a week studying a New-York-City-telephone-directory-sized manual trying to learn how to run the darn things. They use standard commands, so if you know how to run other programs in a window environment, you already know how to run these. For the more populous states there are add-ons for doing state returns using information from your IRS return. The latest versions become available every January. Every year they add improvements.

Computer Software Suppliers

The following computer software suppliers offer speedy delivery, good service, good selection, good prices, toll-free numbers for ordering, and software for both Windows and Macintosh operating systems.

Micro(Mac)Warehouse. 1720 Oak St., Lakewood, NJ 08701. (warehouse.com) 800.367.6808 for Windows software; 800.622.6222 for Macintosh software.

Multiple Zones. 707 South Grady Way, Renton, WA 98055. (zones.com) 800.419.9663 for Windows software; 800.248.0800 for Macintosh software.

PC(Mac)Connection. 730 Milford Rd., Merrimack, NH 03054. (pcconnection.com; macconnection.com) 800.800.5555 for Windows software; 800.800.2222 for Macintosh software.

Z-Law Software. P.O. Box 40602, Providence, RI 02940. (z-law.com) 800.526.5588.

This supplier specializes in real estate software. Its offerings appear in both its printed catalog and on its website.

Forms

Professional Publishing. 365 Bel Marin Keys Blvd., Suite 100, Novato, CA 94949 (profpub.com). 800.288.2006.

Professional Publishing sells real estate forms of all kinds. They're some of the best in the business. A sample book of all the forms is available at a nominal price.

Periodicals

Most of these periodicals carry no advertising and hence have no biases except those of their writers, editors, and publishers, which may in themselves be considerable. Some make sample copies available. Ask.

Consumer Reports. Consumer Reports, Box 51166, Boulder, CO 80323. (consumerreports.org) 12 issues a year, plus an annual buyer's guide, no advertising.

This trustworthy magazine publishes the results of the tests and studies conducted in its own fiercely independent laboratories. Although it is obviously pro-consumer, supposing that *Consumer Reports* is therefore anti-business would be a true non-sequitur. Expect it to publish articles written from a tenant's perspective (they're the "consumers" in our business, remember) from time to time, but also remember that you in your role as landlord are a consumer of various goods and services, too. Look to it for forthright evaluations of fire extinguishers, smoke alarms, ladders, paints, cleaning agents, carpets, computers, appliances, locks, telephones, and tools. You'll even find informative articles on mortgages, wills, banks, and insurance companies. The annual buyer's guide, published in December, summarizes earlier articles and runs to 360 pages. It's available separately at newsstands and bookstores.

Creative Investment Advisor. CIA, P.O. Box 495, Glen Ellyn, IL 60138. 630.858.4663. 12 issues a year, no advertising.

Written by a former professor of business administration, this newsletter is anything but boring. It started out as the house organ for the Chicago Creative Investors Association and has since gone "national." It provides "real estate strategy and tactics for the small investor." In its pages you'll find hard-hitting book reviews, articles debunking popular myths such as those about fifteen-year mortgages and bi-weekly mortgages, tidbits to get you thinking, real estate news, and analyses of the news, all fascinating reading.

Fair Housing Coach. Brownstone Publishers, 149 Fifth Ave., New York, NY 10010. (brownstone.com) 888.456.1696. 12 issues a year, no advertising.

Nobody in the landlording business can afford to ignore the federal fair housing laws. This monthly newsletter in the form of self-study lessons educates its readers in the intricacies of treating all people fairly as applicants and as tenants. Each lesson includes guidelines, examples, case studies, legal interpretations, and pitfalls. The lessons create an on-going awareness of the laws and are especially useful for training employees. Their ignorance of fair housing laws, their flouting of the laws, can cost you big-time in punitive damages and fines and damage your reputation as a landlord who strives to be fair.

John T. Reed's Real Estate Investor's Monthly. Reed Publishing, 342 Bryan Dr., Alamo, CA 94507. (johntreed.com) 925.820.6292. 12 issues a year, no advertising.

Well ahead of the real estate investing herd, this eight-page newsletter, written by the prolific John Reed, divulges real estate investment ideas which make sense and make money. It's newsy, it's current, it's practical, it's lively, it's analytical, and what's more, it's bottom-line oriented, just as you'd expect from a Harvard Business School M.B.A. who's spent almost a lifetime inhaling and exhaling real estate.

Mr. Landlord. Home Rental Publishing Company, P.O. Box 64442, Virginia Beach, VA 23467. (mrlandlord.com) 800.950.2250. 12 issues a year, some advertising.

The expression "down-to-earth" best characterizes this eight-page newsletter which bills itself as "the survival newsletter for landlords and landladies." That it is. It's written by landlords who scramble around in the trenches for landlords who scramble around in the trenches. You can't help but pick up at least one practical idea from each issue. Maybe you'll even see something of yourself in the landlord interview feature; it profiles a different landlord from around the country every month.

Professional Apartment Management. Brownstone Publishers, 149 Fifth Ave., New York, NY 10010. (brownstone.com) 800.643.8095. 12 issues a year, no advertising.

Easily the most expensive of the periodicals mentioned here, it's well worth the money if you want to read about techniques and tactics which the true professionals in the landlording business, that is, those who do nothing else but look after apartment buildings, are sharing with one another. Articles vary from those about crime and security concerns to those about maintenance and legal matters.

The Robert Bruss Real Estate Newsletter. Robert J. Bruss, 251 Park Rd., Burlingame, CA 94010. (bobbruss.com) 800.736.1736. 12 issues a year, no advertising.

In his popular Q&A newspaper column, Mr. Bruss limits himself to answering readers' questions, and each newspaper's real estate editor limits the column to whatever space is available after all the advertising has been set in place; sometimes there's no space for Bruss at all. This monthly newsletter might be called Bruss Unbound or Bruss Unlimited because he chooses the real estate subjects himself, and he has eight full pages for developing them, without ever being squeezed out by advertising layouts and press releases. The subjects are topical and what he says about them is useful and well researched. Subjects he has covered so far include negotiation strategies, equity sharing, tax-deferred exchanges, distress property acquisition, due-on-sale clauses, lease options, and tax law changes. Back issues are available. Californians may keep up with real estate litigation in their state by reading *The Robert Bruss California Real Estate Law Newsletter,* in which he explains selected court decisions in lay terms, adds comments of his own, and then tells why particular decisions are important.

Websites

google.com—Speedy, unadorned, and comprehensive, the Google search engine yields useful lists of websites and web pages related to your search words. Advertising on the site is minimal and nonobtrusive.

inman.com—Updated daily by a staff who take pride in being accurate and being first, it has the very latest in real estate news and information.

johntreed.com—Besides listing all of Mr. Reed's materials, this site includes choice morsels of his writings, such as his "Real Estate B.S. Artist Detection Checklist." He doesn't mince his words here or in his materials.

landlording.com—This is my own website where you will find current information about my books and software. You will also find a page called "What's New?" where I comment on subjects of current interest to landlords and a Q&A page where I answer questions submitted via email. The last page is a list of links to other websites which may be of interest to landlords.

loopnet.com—Buyers and sellers of commercial, industrial, and multi-family residential properties will find listings here organized by location, type, and price. Check the listings in your price range of exactly the type of property you're looking to buy or sell in your area. Then broaden or narrow your criteria to come up with a more useful list. Whether you're in the market to find an exchange property to identify by tomorrow or just browsing to get an idea what your property might be worth were you to put it on the market today, Loopnet will save you hours and hours of trying to locate properties which meet your criteria.

nolo.com—Nolo has long been a publisher of legal books and software oriented toward the layperson. Reinvented as a dot-com company when they were all the rage, it maintains an excellent website with all kinds of information about its products, including sample chapters, plus legal humor and the latest on the struggle between those who want to keep the laity ignorant of our legal system and those who want to give everybody access.

rentals.com—Check out this website and its counterparts, "apartments.com," "rentnet.com," "vacancylist.net," "vacancynet.com," etc., to see how they work and whether they would work well for you and for the tenants you hope to attract to your rentals. Evaluate them the same way you'd evaluate any other kind of advertising, by the cost per suitable prospect they produce.

rhol.org—Rental Housing On Line is a cornucopia of landlording "stuff." The site is stuffed full of information, forms, forums, association listings, laws, a vacancy listing service called "vacancylist.net," and more. Nonmembers may access hundreds of its web pages. Members may access everything. They get credit reports, including credit scoring, for a nominal $9. They get expanded reports, which show tenants' move-in and move-out dates, evictions, lease skips, and items on public record, for $5 (charged only if the search yields useful information). Membership is $39.95 for the first year and $29.95 annually thereafter. Quite simply, it's a deal!

yahoo.com—One of the first of the Internet search engines and still one of the best, Yahoo has become much more than a search engine. It is a comprehensive one-stop site, a portal where you may, among other things, send and receive email, participate in auctions, use classified advertising for buying or selling or renting, pinpoint map locations, secure instructions for driving from point A to point B, search telephone directories, check stock holdings, make travel arrangements, and check the weather, all without ever leaving your computer. Its rental vacancy listings keep growing in number, and searching through them keeps getting easier and easier for tenants.

X-Classification

ApplianceSmart. 7350 Excelsior Blvd., Minneapolis, MN 55426. (appliancesmart.com) 952.930.1740.

ApplianceSmart buys truckloads of new appliances directly from manufacturers. These major household appliances may be closeouts or factory overruns, or they may have slight imperfections. As such, they fall outside the normal distribution channels and can be sold at rock-bottom prices, even with a one-year guarantee. Currently, ApplianceSmart has eight outlets in Minnesota, Ohio, and southern California. Check their website for new locations. Their parent company, Appliance Recycling Centers of America (800.722.9340), will help you find a discarded appliance recycler wherever you happen to be. Call and give them your zipcode.

Index

Order Forms

ExPRESS, P.O. BOX 1639, EL CERRITO, CA 94530-4639

Dear ExPress:

    I'm a scrupulous property owner, and I'd like copies of your materials for my very own. Hurry up with my order. I need all the help I can get right now.

    Please send me:

_____ copies of *Landlording*	@ $27.95	$_____
_____ copies of *What's a Landlord to Do?*	@ $21.95	$_____
_____ copies of *The Eviction Book for California*	@ $24.95	$_____
_____ copies of *Landlording® on Disk (The Forms)*	@ $39.95	$_____
_____ copies of *Eviction Forms Creator™*	@ $79.95	$_____
_____ copies of *Pushbutton Landlording®*	@ $149.95	$_____
> > > > SALES TAX FOR CALIFORNIA RESIDENTS > > > >		$_____
	Shipping and handling	$ 4.00

My computer disk format is Windows___, Macintosh___   TOTAL $_____

PLEASE SEND TO

_____

_____

_____

ExPRESS, P.O. BOX 1639, EL CERRITO, CA 94530-4639

Dear ExPress:

    I'm an unscrupulous property owner who's merciless, lowdown, and greedy, and I'll pay double the usual price for your stuff just to lay my hands on all that great information. It may even reform me. Who knows?

    Please send me:

_____ copies of *Landlording*	@ $55.90	$_____
_____ copies of *What's a Landlord to Do?*	@ $43.90	$_____
_____ copies of *The Eviction Book for California*	@ $49.90	$_____
_____ copies of *Landlording® on Disk (The Forms)*	@ $79.90	$_____
_____ copies of *Eviction Forms Creator™*	@ $159.90	$_____
_____ copies of *Pushbutton Landlording®*	@ $299.90	$_____
> > > > SALES TAX FOR CALIFORNIA RESIDENTS > > > >		$_____
	Shipping and handling	$ 8.00

My computer disk format is Windows___, Macintosh___   TOTAL $_____

PLEASE SEND TO

_____

_____

_____

ExPRESS, P.O. BOX 1639, EL CERRITO, CA 94530-4639

Dear ExPress:

    I'm not a property owner yet, but I think I'd like to be one some day, and I'd certainly like to know what I'm doing. Show me.

    Please send me:

_____ copies of *Landlording*	@ $27.95	$_____
_____ copies of *What's a Landlord to Do?*	@ $21.95	$_____
_____ copies of *The Eviction Book for California*	@ $24.95	$_____
_____ copies of *Landlording® on Disk (The Forms)*	@ $39.95	$_____
_____ copies of *Eviction Forms Creator™*	@ $79.95	$_____
_____ copies of *Pushbutton Landlording®*	@ $149.95	$_____
> > > > SALES TAX FOR CALIFORNIA RESIDENTS > > > >		$_____
	Shipping and handling	$ 4.00

My computer disk format is Windows___, Macintosh___   TOTAL $_____

PLEASE SEND TO

_____

_____

_____

Use one of these forms and mail it to us with your check or money order, OR call ExPRESS at 800.307.0789 and charge to your MasterCard or Visa. Visit our Web site at http://www.landlording.com

wasn't a furry critter either crawling over them or wedging themselves between them. And despite the fact she loved seeing Bella's and the puppies' daily progress, she really needed some one-on-one time with their somewhat cantankerous caretaker.

Her fingers itched to make the long-awaited booty call the second she stepped outside.

Harper stuck her head into the break room just as she'd slid into her coat. "Oh, good. You haven't left yet."

Rose groaned. Damn it. She should've moved faster . . . *freakin' heel blisters.* "Gage changed his mind about me leaving?"

"What? Oh, honey, no. A sexy-as-hell demon is up front asking for you. Whatever he asks of you, do it. He's dripping lust pheromones as if he high-dived into an Olympic swimming pool filled with the stuff. If you don't make an appearance soon, I'm gonna have myself a midshift snack." Harper winked and disappeared back to the main room.

A wave of excitement washed over her as she thought about Damian. Guess she wasn't the only one who'd thought about making that FB call. He'd just decided to do his in person.

She hightailed it out to the front bar, a grin already on her face, but he wasn't the demon waiting for her.

Julius Kontos leaned against the edge of the counter, a woman at each side in heavy flirt mode. Unlike other times she'd seen him, he didn't seem invested. He stood politely and listened to what they said, occasionally giving them a nod or a smile, but the smile didn't reach his eyes.

On anyone else, it might have been cause for alarm.

On Julius, who almost always seemed to find amusement in everything, it was cause for panic.

His gaze met hers, and after saying something to his admirers, he met her by the front door.

"Hey, Julius. Is everything okay?" Rose asked, concerned.